R$33.15

WIE GEHT'S?

DEM LEBENDIGEN GEIST

THIRD EDITION

WIE GEHT'S?

An Introductory German Course

Dieter Sevin
VANDERBILT UNIVERSITY
Ingrid Sevin
Katrin T. Bean

HOLT, RINEHART AND WINSTON, INC.
New York
Philadelphia
London
Chicago
Montreal
Sydney
San Francisco
Toronto
Tokyo

Publisher Vincent Duggan
Acquisitions Editor Laura McKenna
Developmental Editor Clifford Browder
Project Editor Isolde C. Sauer McCarthy
Production Manager Priscilla Taguer
Design Supervisor Renée Davis
Text Design and Layout Gayle Jaeger
Drawings Tom O'Sullivan
Photo Research Rona Tuccillo

Photographic credits appear on page xv.

Library of Congress Cataloging-in-Publication Data

Sevin, Dieter.
  Wie geht's?

  Includes index.
  1. German language—Grammar—1950–   . 2. German
language—Textbooks for foreign speakers—English.
I. Sevin, Ingrid. II. Bean, Katrin T. III. Title.
PF3112.S4 1988   438.2'421   87–11934
ISBN 0–03–008632–9 (Student ed.)
ISBN 0–03–008633–7 (Instructor's ed.)

ISBN 0-03-008632-9

Printed in the United States of America.

8 9 0 1 2 032 9 8 7 6 5 4 3 2 1

Holt, Rinehart and Winston, Inc.
The Dryden Press
Saunders College Publishing

CONTENTS

The enthusiastic response to the first two editions of *Wie geht's?* confirmed the soundness of the basic concept of our introductory text. In this third edition we have made revisions, many of them suggested by colleagues, in all of the course materials without abandoning our original purpose—to create an introductory German text that is flexible, practical, and appealing in format and presentation, focusing on the essential elements of effective communication. The result is a text that lends itself readily to various teaching styles and student backgrounds.

The four skills (listening comprehension, speaking, reading, and writing) are practiced as the student is introduced to various cultural aspects of the German-speaking countries. The double meaning of the title *Wie geht's?* reflects the double goal of the book, which is to show the language at work and how the language works. We believe that explaining how the language works is not an end in itself but only a means of achieving communicative competence in natural, modern German.

Changes in the New Edition

- There are now two editions of this text—the student's edition and the instructor's annotated edition, which replaces the separate instructor's manual.
- All aspects of the book have been carefully evaluated and revised where improvements seemed desirable.
- The basic organization of the "Schritte" and "Kapitel" has been simplified.
- All "Gespräche" have been revised and many replaced.
- "Zum Thema" now contains the former "Mündliche Übungen," which have been shortened considerably and phased out after the first half of the text. The number of questions has been reduced, and guided dialogues and other materials suitable for small-group work have been added.
- Some grammar topics have been placed in a different sequence: subordinate clauses and the present perfect are now presented in Chapter 4; the subjunctive, in Chapter 13; and relative clauses, in Chapter 14. For those who want to introduce indirect speech and the special subjunctive (subjunctive I), these topics have been moved from the Appendix into Chapters 14 and 15.
- Cultural notes in English have been expanded.
- There are fewer purely mechanical exercises in the "Übungen" and many more that have a common context and foster language proficiency.
- The reading texts have been further shortened and updated. Those in Chapters 4, 9, 10, and 13 are considerably revised; those in Chapters 8, 14, and 15 are entirely new.

- The exercises after the reading texts ("Fragen" and "Noch einmal") have been combined into one section: "Zum Text." Questions and mechanical drills have been reduced and/or eliminated. There is now a much greater variety of exercises to check comprehension, review the chapter grammar in new contexts, and provide work with a partner and written practice.

Organization of the Text

Wie geht's? is divided into six pre-units (*Schritte*), fifteen chapters (*Kapitel*), and five review sections (*Rückblicke*). In addition to the student text and instructor's edition, there is a set of tapes and a laboratory manual/workbook.

A. Pre-units

The purpose of these pre-units is to guide students through their first steps in German with intensive aural/oral practice of easily assimilated words, common phrases, and idioms. Grammatical concepts are avoided until the first review section, which follows the sixth pre-unit. By that time, students will be able to communicate with one another on an elementary level. The resulting feeling of accomplishment will let them proceed with confidence to the main chapters.

B. Chapters

1. Gespräche—Wortschatz 1—Zum Thema   One or two short dialogues, written in conversational German, introduce each chapter topic. Grammar constructions that have not yet been presented are generally avoided. Students are not expected to memorize these dialogues but rather to use them as models for conversation. Cultural notes and English translations follow the dialogues.

The active vocabulary pertaining to the chapter topic is presented as *Wortschatz 1*. This list is limited to about forty-five words per chapter. The focus, especially in the earlier chapters, is on practical topics such as foods, shopping, eating out, traveling, and so on. For easier mastery, the vocabulary is arranged by subtopics, and nouns are listed in alphabetical order according to gender. Usefulness in everyday speech was the criterion for vocabulary selection. All active vocabulary has been carefully controlled and repeated throughout the book.

The section *Zum Thema* is meant for practice of the new vocabulary and idioms and to encourage communication. It consists of various drills and vocabulary and communication exercises, such as topical and personalized questions, suggestions for guided dialogues and student interviews, as well as other supplementary materials and exercises. *Zum Thema* ends with a brief pronunciation review.

2. Struktur—Übungen   Each chapter introduces two or three major points of grammar. Essential elements of German grammar are emphasized throughout the text with clear and concise explanations. Wherever appropriate, comparisons are made with English grammar. Charts, tables, and abundant examples illustrate all grammatical concepts. Little class time should be required for additional explanations; most of the time in class can be devoted to practice.

A variety of exercises (*Übungen*) follows each major grammar point to provide ample practice of the principles presented. Active vocabulary is repeated systematically. The exercises under *Zusammenfassung* are designed as a comprehensive review of the entire chapter grammar. They can be done orally or in writing.

3. Einblicke—Wortschatz 2—Zum Text   Each chapter ends with a reading passage (*Einblicke*) that features a relevant, up-to-date view of one or more cultural aspects pertaining to the chapter topic. The reading text provides additional examples of the new grammar and a review of the chapter vocabulary. A variety of styles, both written and spoken, is presented: essays, letters, conversations, and commentaries. Cognates and other easily recognizable words precede the reading in a short section called *Was ist das?* Other words needed for recognition are glossed in the margin.

Wortschatz 2, limited to about fifteen words, precedes the reading text and provides basic common vocabulary related to it. This short list, intended for active use, presents words and phrases that recur in subsequent chapters.

The exercises *Zum Text* follow the reading selection. Some provide additional grammar practice or writing drills, while others check student comprehension of the reading text and encourage communication among students.

C. Review chapters

Grammatical summaries appear after the six pre-units and chapters 3, 7, 11, and 15. They are designed to review structures and vocabulary and to help students understand the grammar in a larger context.

D. Appendixes

The appendixes consist of:

- A brief section on predicting the gender of some nouns, which should help eliminate unnecessary memorizing by students.
- A summary of grammar in chart form, including a table of all basic verb forms in the various tenses; two tables of irregular verbs, one an alphabetical listing and the other arranged by stem changes
- A translation of the proverbs used in Chapter 15.
- A complete pronunciation guide with brief explanations of correct sound production, and corresponding pronunciation exercises that are available on a separate tape in the tape program. (Pronunciation is introduced and practiced in the *Schritte* and systematically reviewed in the chapters and the tape program.)
- A complete German-English end vocabulary, encompassing all words appearing in the text and indicating the first occurrence of all active words. An English-German end vocabulary that lists all active vocabulary is added as a convenience to the students.
- A complete grammar index for quick access to specific grammar points

The Tape Program and Laboratory Manual/Workbook

The tape program and its corresponding laboratory manual provide additional opportunity for students to practice listening, speaking, and writing skills. A complete tape script is available from the publisher by contacting:
Foreign Language Marketing Department
College Division, 5th floor
Holt, Rinehart and Winston, Inc.
111 Fifth Avenue
New York, NY 10003

A. The tapes

The tapes include the dialogues of the chapters, supplementary grammar exercises for each of the points introduced, listening-comprehension exercises, pronunciation practice, and thematic dictations. Most grammar exercises are four-phased: after the task has been set and the student has given an answer, the correct response is provided and repeated by the student.

B. The laboratory manual/workbook

This supplement (*Im Sprachlabor und zu Hause*) is made up of two sections:

1. *Im Sprachlabor* is a guide to the tape program that provides instructions and examples for all of the grammar and pronunciation exercises. For each pre-unit and chapter, a worksheet is available on which students can write answers to questions, complete exercises, or write dictations. The worksheet may be used to monitor progress in the language lab.

2. *Zu Hause* is a workbook focusing on vocabulary building, structure, and cultural enrichment. At least one exercise for each chapter is based on visual stimuli, requiring students to identify objects, interpret what they see, and use the vocabulary actively. Answers to the workbook exercises appear at the end of the manual so that students may use this section for self-directed study.

The Instructor's Edition

The instructor's edition provides detailed suggestions, warm-ups, and supplementary drills and exercises. Scheduling, based on both the quarter system and the semester system, is outlined for classes meeting three, four, or five times a week. It also includes sample lesson plans, the correct responses for the *Übungsblätter*, suggestions for testing and grading, and a reference table of all active vocabulary grouped by chapters to aid in the preparation of exams.

Summary of Special Features

- Six pre-units providing a unique introduction to German
- Topical organization and thorough thematic integration within each chapter

- Dialogues in lively and colloquial German
- Vocabulary arranged thematically and alphabetically by gender, divided into active and passive words, and carefully controlled and reviewed throughout the text
- Concise grammar presentation focusing on communication, using many charts and sample sentences
- Numerous exercises for all four skills
- Translation exercises
- Five grammar review and reference chapters
- Cultural notes
- Tape program and laboratory manual/workbook providing additional exercises for all material presented in the main text
- Instructor's edition with detailed teaching suggestions, supplementary drills and exercises, and a chapter-by-chapter summary of active vocabulary
- Test bank available from publisher

ACKNOWLEDGMENTS

We would like to thank the following colleagues who reviewed the manuscript during its various stages of development: Lida Daves Baldwin, Rutgers University; Clifford A. Barraclough, University of California, Santa Barbara; Sigrun Johanna Braverman; Gudrun Clay, Metropolitan State College; Jerry L. Cox, Furman University; Ronald L. Crawford, Kent State University; Maria Dobozy, University of Illinois, Chicago; Ingeborg Henderson, University of California, Davis; John Irving, California State University, Northridge; George Koenig, State University of New York at Oswego; William F. Lowe, Jr., University of North Carolina, Wilmington; Robert P. Newton, North Carolina University, Greensboro; Craig Nickisch, United States Military Academy; Michael T. O'Pecko, Towson State University; Beverly R. Pfanner, University of New Hampshire; Yvonne Poser, Howard University; James L. Sherman, University of New Hampshire; Suzanne Toliver, University of Cincinnati; Franz-Joseph Wehage, Appalachian State University; Larry D. Wells, State University of New York at Binghamton; Christopher J. Wickham, University of Illinois, Chicago.

We wish to extend special thanks to Joe Rea Phillips of the Blair School of Music at Vanderbilt University for his musical interludes in the tape program. Finally, we are grateful to the following of Holt, Rinehart and Winston: our Publisher, Vincent Duggan; our Developmental Editor, Clifford Browder, who helped refine the manuscript; and our Project Editor, Isolde C. Sauer McCarthy, who diligently oversaw the many stages of production.

D.S.
I.S.
K.T.B.

Learning another language is more like learning a musical instrument or a sport than studying philosophy or history. Just as you can't learn to play the piano or swim by reading about it, you can't learn a foreign language by thinking or reading about it. You must practice. Listen to your instructor, to tapes, to the answers of your fellow students. Speak German every chance you get. Whenever possible, read the language aloud and also write it.

Learning a foreign language does *not* require a special talent or superior intelligence. Millions of small children speak German; if they can, so can you—and much faster because you have already learned a language: your own. Remember also that you are still improving your English, so don't expect perfection in another language. You made mistakes while learning English; when learning a foreign language, mistakes are also inevitable.

Don't let the idea of "grammar" scare you. It's a shortcut to learning, providing you with the patterns native speakers follow when they use the language. The fact that German and English are closely related will be both a help and a hindrance: note well the instances when German functions differently from English.

Make full use of the time spent in the classroom—get fifty minutes of practice out of it. Listen, imitate, memorize. Use the language lab. Divide assignments into small units. It's almost impossible to cram in a foreign language, so don't fall behind, and review regularly. When reading, finish a paragraph or a sentence before looking up unfamiliar words, and don't scribble English translations between the lines. Enjoy your growing skills, and keep in mind that many students have been able to study abroad after only two years of foreign-language study!

Cover: The Stock Market/© Paul Barton 1986.
ii, Beryl Goldberg.   1, Beryl Goldberg.   11, Photo Researchers Inc./Visum/
André Gelpke.   15, Beryl Goldberg.   21, Monkmeyer Press/Renata Hiller.
22, German Information Center.   26, Photo Researchers Inc./Jim Cartier.
37, 38, Photo Researchers Inc./Christa Armstrong.   43, Photo Researchers
Inc./Tom McHugh.   53, Peter Menzel.   57, 58, Monkmeyer Press/Renata
Hiller.   59, Photo Researchers Inc./Yan Lukas.   73, Peter Menzel.
74, Beryl Goldberg.   77, Uta Hoffmann.   79 (top), Peter Menzel.   79 (bottom), Dieter Nübler.   80, German Information Center.   81, 82, Photo
Researchers Inc./Jan Lukas.   96, Austrian Tourist Office.   97, Monkmeyer
Press/Renata Hiller.   98, Peter Menzel.   99, Katrin T. Bean.   100, Photo
Researchers Inc./Margot Granitsas.   101, Swiss Tourist Office.   107, Ger-
man Information Center.   126, German Information Center.
128–132, German Information Center.   134, German Information Center.
135, 136, Photo Researchers Inc./Rapho/Louis Goldman.   137, Austrian
Tourist Office.   139, Katrin T. Bean.   150, 154, Photo Researchers Inc./
Judy Poe.   156, Austrian Tourist Office.   159, 160, German Information
Center.   163, German Information Center.   164, German Information
Center.   177, German Information Center.   178, Beryl Goldberg.
181, Katrin T. Bean.   183, German Information Center.   185, 186, Peter
Menzel.   201, Photo Researchers Inc./Fritz Henle.   202, Photo Researchers Inc./Rapho/Christa Armstrong.   204, German Information Center.
206, Photo Researchers Inc./Christa Armstrong.   216, Center Press.
219, German Information Center.   221, 222, Peter Menzel.   227, Peter
Menzel.   231, Mantel.   232, Ingrid Sevin.   242 (top), Monkmeyer Press.
243, Monkmeyer Press/Silberstein.   244, Swiss Tourist Office.   246, Katrin
T. Bean.   247, Photo Researchers Inc./Christa Armstrong.   251, 252, German Information Center.   255, German Information Center.   256, Austrian Tourist Office.   257, German Information Center.   258, German
Information Center.   270, Eastfoto.   271, Margaret Bean.   272, Eastfoto.
274, Gesamtdeutsches Institut, Bundesanstalt für Gesamtdeutsche Aufga-
ben.   276, Eastfoto.   278, Peter Menzel.   279 (top), Katrin T. Bean.
279 (bottom), German Information Center.   280, Katrin T. Bean.
283, German Information Center.   295, German Information Center.
297, Photo Researchers Inc./Ulrike Welsch.   303, 304, Leo de Wys/H.
Koelbl.   320, German Information Center.   321, German Information
Center.   322, Lufthansa Photo.   335, Monkmeyer Press.   339, Austrian
Tourist Office.   341, 342, Monkmeyer Press/Renata Hiller.   344, 345, (top),
Katrin T. Bean.   346 (top), Beryl Goldberg.   346 (bottom), German Information Center.   357, Photo Researchers Inc./Visum/Rudi Meisel.
363, 364, Stock Boston/Peter Menzel.   365, Katrin T. Bean.   379, German

Information Center. 381 (both), Beryl Goldberg. 387, 388, German Information Center. 389, German Information Center. 403, German Information Center. 405, German Information Center. 407 (top), German Information Center. 407 (bottom), Beryl Goldberg. 411, 412, Photo Researchers Inc./Visum/Wolfgang Steche. 417, German Information Center. 418, German Information Center. 425, German Information Center. 427, Katrin T. Bean. 438, German Information Center. Dieter Sevin, 2, 27, 62, 76, 84, 95, 144, 147, 157, 174 (bottom), 179, 233, 249, 259, 345 (bottom), 419. Ingrid Sevin, 76, 84, 174, 187, 188, 223, 397.

Special thanks to Margaret Bean.

Read the following dialogues out loud until you can do so fluently with good pronunciation and intonation. You are not expected to memorize entire dialogues, but be prepared to answer questions about them and to write them as part of a dictation.

Wie geht's?

HERR SANDERS	Guten Tag!
FRÄULEIN LEHMANN	Guten Tag!
HERR SANDERS	Ich heiße Sanders, Willi Sanders. Und Sie, wie heißen Sie?
FRÄULEIN LEHMANN	Mein Name ist Erika Lehmann.
HERR SANDERS	Freut mich.

HERR MEIER	Guten Morgen, Frau Fiedler! Wie geht es Ihnen?
FRAU FIEDLER	Danke, gut. Und Ihnen?
HERR MEIER	Danke, es geht mir auch gut.

HEIDI	Guten Abend, Ute. Wie geht's?
UTE	Ach, ich bin müde.
HEIDI	Ich auch. Auf Wiedersehen!
UTE	Tschüß!

Guten Tag! Wie geht's?

How Are You?

MR. SANDERS	Hello.
MISS LEHMANN	Hello.
MR. SANDERS	My name is Sanders, Willi Sanders. And what's your name?
MISS LEHMANN	My name is Erika Lehmann.
MR. SANDERS	I'm glad to meet you.

MR. MEIER	Good morning, Mrs. Fiedler. How are you?
MRS. FIEDLER	Fine, thank you. And how are you?
MR. MEIER	I'm fine too, thank you.

HEIDI	Good evening, Ute. How are you?
UTE	Oh, I'm tired.
HEIDI	Me too. Goodbye.
UTE	Bye.

Wie geht's?

You are responsible for all the vocabulary in this section, including the headings. Know it actively—also the gender and plural forms of nouns—both orally and in writing. Words and phrases listed under "Passives Vokabular" are intended for comprehension only; you will not be asked to know them actively.

- *In German, all nouns are capitalized.*
- *The pronoun* **ich (I)** *is never capitalized in German unless it stands at the beginning of a sentence.*

der Herr, die Herren *(pl.)*	*Mr.; gentleman*
das Fräulein, die Fräulein *(pl.)*[1]	*Miss, Ms.; young lady*
die Frau, die Frauen *(pl.)*	*Mrs., Ms.; woman; wife*
Guten Morgen! / Guten Abend!	*Good morning. / Good evening.*
Guten Tag!	*Hello.*
Wie heißen Sie?	*What's your name?*
Mein Name ist . . .	*My name is . . .*

heißen	*to be called*
ich heiße	*my name is . . .*
Sie heißen	*your name is . . .*

Freut mich.	*I'm glad to meet you.*
Wie geht es Ihnen?	*How are you? (formal)*
Wie geht's?	*How are you? (informal)*
wie?	*how?*
Es geht mir . . .	*I'm (feeling) . . .*
danke / bitte	*thank you / please*
auch	*also, too*
gut / schlecht	*good, fine / bad(ly)*
wunderbar	*wonderful(ly)*
Ich bin müde.	*I'm tired.*
ja / nein	*yes / no*
nicht	*not*
und	*and*
Auf Wiedersehen!	*Goodbye.*

Ich bin müde!

1 The title **Fräulein** is used less and less. It is being replaced by **Frau,** regardless of a woman's age or marital status.

PASSIVES VOKABULAR ach *(oh);* ich auch *(me too);* Tschüß! *(colloquial: goodbye, bye)*

AUSSPRACHEÜBUNG

(PRONUNCIATION EXERCISE):
a, e, er, i, o, u

*The words listed below are either familiar words, cognates (words related to English), or proper names (**Erika, Amerika**). In brackets you will find indications of pronunciation in a simplified phonetic spelling. The colon (:) following a vowel means that the vowel is long. See also the section on pronunciation in the Appendix and work with the tape accompanying it.*

Hören Sie gut zu und wiederholen Sie! *(Listen carefully and repeat.)*

[a:]   Adam, Abend, Klara, David, Tag, Banane, Name, ja
[a]   Anna, Albert, Hans, was, das, danke, Hand
[e:]   Erika Lehmann, Eduard, Peter, Amerika, geht, Tee, See
[e]   Ellen, Hermann, es, schlecht
[ə]   (*unstressed* e) Ute, danke, heiße, guten, Morgen, Ihnen
[ʌ]   (*final* -er) Dieter Fiedler, Rainer Meier, Werner Schneider
[i:]   Ihnen, Maria, Sabine, mir, Wiedersehen, wie, Sie
[i]   Ingrid, Linda, ich bin, bitte, nicht, Willi, Schritt
[o:]   Robert, Monika, Rose, Hose, Boot, so, wo, Zoo
[o]   Olga, Oskar, Oliver, oft, Morgen, Sommer, kosten
[u:]   Ute, Uwe, Gudrun, Hugo, gut, Nudel, Schuh
[u]   Ursula, Gustav, und, wunderbar, Gesundheit, Hunger, Butter

▪ *As you may have noticed, double vowels (**Tee**), vowels followed by **h** (**geht**), and the combination **ie** (**wie**) are long. Vowels followed by double consonants (two identical consonants as in **Willi**) are short.*
▪ *Pay particular attention to word stress as you hear it from your instructor or the tape. For a while, you may want to mark words for stress.*

MÜNDLICHE ÜBUNGEN

(ORAL EXERCISES)

A. Mustersätze *(Patterns and cues)*

These drills give you a chance to practice phrases from the dialogues and the vocabulary of each "Schritt." Listen carefully to patterns and cues, and repeat the sentences until you can say them fluently.

1. Willi Sanders: **Ich heiße** Willi Sanders.
   Hugo Schmidt, Helmut Rose, Gudrun Kleese, Anna Peters
2. Erika Lehmann: **Heißen Sie** Erika Lehmann?
   Monika Schulz, Brigitte Fischer, Wolfgang Friedrich, Hermann Schneider
3. Hugo Schmidt: **Ja, ich heiße** Hugo Schmidt.
   Helmut Rose, Hans Holbein, Brigitte Fischer, Gudrun Kleese

4. Oskar Meier: **Nein, ich heiße nicht** Oskar Meier.
   Gustav Mahler, Clara Schumann, Paul Klee, Wolfgang Amadeus
   Mozart
5. Frau Fiedler: **Wie geht es Ihnen,** Frau Fiedler?
   Fräulein Lehmann, Herr Sanders, Frau Bauer, Herr Meier
6. gut: **Es geht mir** gut.
   auch gut, nicht gut, schlecht, nicht schlecht, wunderbar

B. Das Alphabet (The alphabet)

1. Lesen Sie laut! (Read aloud.)

    a b c   d e f g   h i j   k l m   n o p
ah beh tseh deh eh eff geh hah ih jot kah ell emm enn oh peh

    q   r   s   t   u   v   w   x   y   z
kuh err ess teh uh fau weh iks üppsilon tsett

         ä   ö   ü   ß[1]
äh (a-umlaut) öh (o-umlaut) üh (u-umlaut) ess-tsett

1 For further explanation see III A.6 in the pronunciation section of the Appendix.

■ *For capital letters say **Großes A (B, C . . .).***

2. Buchstabieren Sie auf deutsch! (Spell in German.)

ja, gut, müde, danke, schlecht, heißen, Fräulein, Name, Morgen,
wunderbar

AUFGABE (ASSIGNMENT)

Prepare all assignments so that you can answer fluently in class.

A. Buchstabieren Sie Ihren Namen auf deutsch! (Spell your name in German.)

B. Was sagen Sie? (What do you say? Be ready to read the cue lines and prepare appropriate responses.)

x Guten Tag!
y _____ .
x Ich heiße _____ . Und Sie, wie heißen Sie?
y Ich heiße _____ .
x Freut mich.
y Wie geht es Ihnen?
x _____ . Und Ihnen?
y _____ .
x Auf Wiedersehen!
y _____ .

Beispiel geben
Bei Rot stehen
Bei Grün gehen

DEUTSCHPROFESSOR	Hören Sie jetzt gut zu, und antworten Sie auf deutsch! Was ist das?
JIM MILLER	Das ist der Bleistift.
DEUTSCHPROFESSOR	Welche Farbe hat der Bleistift?
SUSAN SMITH	Gelb.
DEUTSCHPROFESSOR	Bilden Sie einen Satz, bitte!
SUSAN SMITH	Der Bleistift ist gelb.
DEUTSCHPROFESSOR	Ist das Heft auch gelb?
DAVID JENKINS	Nein, das Heft ist nicht gelb. Das Heft ist blau.
DEUTSCHPROFESSOR	Richtig! Für morgen lesen Sie bitte das Gespräch noch einmal, und lernen Sie die Wörter! Das ist alles.

Was ist das?

What's That?

GERMAN PROFESSOR	Now listen carefully and answer in German. What is that?
JIM MILLER	That's the pencil.
GERMAN PROFESSOR	What color is the pencil?
SUSAN SMITH	Yellow.
GERMAN PROFESSOR	A complete sentence, please.
SUSAN SMITH	The pencil is yellow.
GERMAN PROFESSOR	Is the notebook yellow too?
DAVID JENKINS	No, the notebook isn't yellow. The notebook is blue.
GERMAN PROFESSOR	Correct. For tomorrow please read the dialogue again and learn the words. That's all.

■ *In English the* DEFINITE ARTICLE *has just one form:* **the**. *The German singular definite article has three forms:* **der, das, die**. *Some nouns take* **der** *and are called* MASCULINE; *some take* **das** *and are called* NEUTER; *and some take* **die** *and are called* FEMININE. *This is a grammatical distinction and has little to do with biological sex, although it is true that most nouns referring to females are feminine and most referring to males are masculine:*

der Herr, **die** Frau, BUT **das** Fräulein.

Inanimate objects such as table, blackboard, *and* book *can be of any gender:*

der Tisch, **die** Tafel, **das** Buch.

Because the gender of many nouns is unpredictable, the article must always be learned with the noun.

■ *In German the plurals of nouns are formed in various ways that are often unpredictable. You must therefore learn the plural together with the article and the noun. Plurals are given in an abbreviated form following the singular forms of nouns. These are the most common plural forms and their abbreviations:*

Type	Signal	Listing	Plural Form
1	-	das Fenster, -	die Fenster
	¨	der Mantel, ¨	die Mäntel
2	-e	der Tisch, **-e**	die Tische
	¨e	der Stuhl, **¨e**	die Stühle
3	-er	das Bild, **-er**	die Bilder
	¨er	das Buch, **¨er**	die Bücher
4	-en	die Frau, **-en**	die Frauen
	-n	die Farbe, **-n**	die Farben
5	-s	der Kuli, **-s**	die Kulis

■ *Plurals do not show gender differences; their article is* **die**. *In this book, when the noun is not followed by one of the plural endings, it either does not have a plural or the plural is rarely used.*

The vocabulary in this section is organized by topic, with the nouns listed alphabetically by gender.

DIE FARBE, **-N** *color*

blau	*blue*	grün	*green*	rot	*red*
braun	*brown*	orange	*orange*	schwarz	*black*
gelb	*yellow*	rosa	*pink*	weiß	*white*
grau	*gray*				

DAS ZIMMER, - *room*

der	Bleistift, -e	*pencil*	*die*	Kreide	*chalk*
	Kuli, -s	*pen*		Tafel, -n	*blackboard*
	Stuhl, ̈e	*chair*		Tür, -en	*door*
	Tisch, -e	*table*		Wand, ̈e	*wall*
das	Bild, -er	*picture*			
	Buch, ̈er	*book*			
	Fenster, -	*window*			
	Heft, -e	*notebook*			
	Papier, -e	*paper*			

WEITERES *(Additional words and phrases)*

auf deutsch / auf englisch	*in German / in English*
für morgen	*for tomorrow*
hier / da	*here / there*
noch einmal	*again, once more*
richtig / falsch	*correct, right / wrong, false*
Was ist das?	*What is that?*
Das ist (nicht) . . .	*That is (not) . . .*
Welche Farbe hat . . .?	*What color is . . .?*
Wo ist . . .?	*Where is . . .?*
antworten	*to answer*
fragen	*to ask*
hören	*to hear*
lernen	*to learn*
lesen	*to read*
wiederholen	*to repeat*

sein	*to be*
ich bin	*I am*
es ist	*it is*
sie sind	*they are*
Sie sind	*you (formal) are*

PASSIVES VOKABULAR der Artikel, - (von); der Plural, - (von); das Beispiel, -e *(example)*; das Gespräch, -e *(dialogue)*; das Wort, ̈er *(word)*; alle zusammen *(all together)*; Bilden Sie einen Satz! *(Make a sentence.)*; Das ist alles. *(That's all.)*; Hören Sie gut zu! *(Listen carefully.)*; jetzt *(now)*; zum Beispiel = z.B. *(for example = e.g.)*

AUSSPRACHEÜBUNG:
ä, ö, ü, eu, äu, au, ei, ie

Hören Sie gut zu und wiederholen Sie!

[e:]   Erika, Käthe, g**e**ht, l**e**sen, Gespräch, Bär

[e]   Ellen Keller, Bäcker, Wände, Hände, hängen

[ö:]   Öl, hören, Löwenbräu, G**oe**the, Österreich

[ö]   Ötker, Pöppel, öffnen, Wörter

[ü:]   Übung, Tür, St**üh**le, Bücher, für, müde, grün, typisch

[ü]   Jürgen Müller, Günter Hütter, müssen, küssen, Tsch**üß**

[oi]   d**eu**tsch, fr**eu**t, **Eu**ropa, Fr**äu**lein, Löwenbr**äu**

[au]   Fr**au** P**au**la B**au**er, Klaus Braun, **au**f, **au**ch, bl**au**grau

[ai]   R**ai**ner, H**ei**nz, H**ei**di, Kr**ei**de, w**ei**ß, h**ei**ßen, n**ei**n

■ *Pay special attention to the pronunciation of* **ei** *and* **ie** *(as in Eisenhower's niece):*

[ai]   **ei**ns, h**ei**ßen, H**ei**di, H**ei**nz M**ei**er

[i:]   S**ie**, w**ie**, W**ie**dersehen, D**ie**ter F**ie**dler

[ai/i:]   H**ei**nz F**ie**dler, B**ei**spiel, H**ei**di Th**ie**lemann

MÜNDLICHE ÜBUNGEN

A.   *Mustersätze*

1. der Tisch: **Das ist** der Tisch.
   das Zimmer, die Tür, das Fenster, die Tafel, die Wand, das Bild, der Stuhl, das Papier, der Kuli, der Bleistift, die Kreide

2. das Papier: **Wo ist** das Papier? **Da ist** das Papier.
   der Kuli, die Kreide, die Tür, der Bleistift, das Buch, der Tisch, die Tafel, das Fenster, das Bild

3. das Buch: **Ist das** das Buch? **Ja, das ist** das Buch.
   der Bleistift, das Fenster, die Tür, der Kuli, die Kreide

4. die Tafel: **Ist das** die Tafel? **Nein, das ist nicht** die Tafel.
   der Tisch, das Papier, der Bleistift, der Kuli, der Stuhl

5. schwarz: **Das ist** schwarz.
   rot, gelb, grün, braun, orange, grau, rosa, blau, weiß

6. der Bleistift: **Welche Farbe hat** der Bleistift?
   der Kuli, das Papier, das Buch, die Tafel, die Kreide

7. lesen: Lesen **Sie bitte**!
   antworten, hören, fragen, lernen, wiederholen

B.   *Fragen und Antworten* (Questions and answers)

1. Ist das Papier weiß? **Ja, das Papier ist weiß**.
   Ist das Buch gelb? die Tafel grün? die Kreide weiß? der Kuli rot?

2. Ist die Kreide grün? **Nein, die Kreide ist nicht grün**.
   Ist die Tafel rot? der Bleistift weiß? das Buch rosa? das Papier braun?

3. Die Kreide ist weiß. *Ist das richtig?* **Ja, das ist richtig.**
   Die Tafel ist schwarz. **Nein, das ist nicht richtig.**

   Das Papier ist weiß. Die Tür ist orange. Der Kuli ist blau. Das Buch ist rosa. Der Tisch ist braun.

C. *Wiederholung* *(Review)*

1. *Kettenreaktion. Antworten Sie, und fragen Sie weiter! (Chain reaction. Answer and ask your neighbor.)*
   a. Wie heißen Sie? **Ich heiße _____ .**
   b. Heißen Sie _____ ? **Ja, ich heiße _____ . / Nein, ich heiße nicht _____ .**
   c. Geht es Ihnen gut? **Ja, es geht mir gut. / Nein es geht mir nicht gut.**

2. *Antworten Sie auf deutsch! (Answer in German.)*
   a. Heißen Sie Fiedler?
   b. Wie heißen Sie?
   c. Wie geht es Ihnen?
   d. Ich sage *(say)* „Guten Tag!" Was sagen Sie?
   e. Ich sage „Auf Wiedersehen!" Was sagen Sie?
   f. Ich sage „Mein Name ist Schmidt." Was sagen Sie?

3. *Buchstabieren Sie auf deutsch!*

   Elefant, Maus, Tiger, Löwe, Katze, Hund, Giraffe, Orang-Utan, Ratte

AUFGABE

A. *Fragen und Antworten*

1. Was ist der Artikel von Tür? **Der Artikel von Tür ist *die*.**
   Zimmer, Bleistift, Bild, Kreide, Kuli, Stuhl, Tafel, Buch, Tisch, Fenster, Farbe, Papier, Wand, Heft, Wort, Herr, Frau, Fräulein
2. Was ist der Plural von Kuli? **Der Plural von Kuli ist *Kulis*.**
   Tür, Bild, Bleistift, Buch, Heft, Tisch, Fenster, Tafel, Stuhl, Wort, Farbe, Zimmer
3. Welche Farben hat das Deutschbuch?
4. Welche Farbe lieben *(love)* Sie? **Ich liebe _____ .**

B. *Was sagen Sie?* *(Ask your neighbor while you point at a familiar object in the room, using the left column as guideline.)*

X Ist das die Tafel?	X Ist das _____ ?
Y Nein, das ist nicht die Tafel. Das ist die Wand.	Y Nein, das ist nicht _____. Das ist _____ .
X Wo ist die Tafel?	X Wo ist _____ ?
Y Da ist die Tafel.	Y _____ .
X Welche Farbe hat die Tafel?	X Welche Farbe hat _____ ?
Y Die Tafel ist grün.	Y _____ ist _____ .
X Was ist auch grün?	X Was ist auch _____ ?
Y Das Buch ist auch grün.	Y _____ ist auch _____ .

Im Kleidungs-geschäft

VERKÄUFER Na, wie ist die Hose?
HERR SEIDL Zu groß und zu lang.
VERKÄUFER Und die Krawatte?
HERR SEIDL Zu teuer.
FRAU SEIDL Aber die Farbe ist wunderbar.
          Schade!

HERR SEIDL Mensch, wo ist meine Jacke?
FRAU SEIDL Ich weiß nicht.
VERKÄUFER Welche Farbe hat die Jacke?
HERR SEIDL Blau!
VERKÄUFER Ist das die Jacke?
FRAU SEIDL Ja, danke!

In the Clothing Store

SALESCLERK Well, how are the pants?
MR. SEIDL Too big and too long.
SALESCLERK And the tie?
MR. SEIDL Too expensive.
MRS. SEIDL But the color is beautiful. Too bad!

MR. SEIDL Hey, where's my jacket?
MRS. SEIDL I don't know.
SALESCLERK What color is the jacket?
MR. SEIDL Blue.
SALESCLERK Is that the jacket?
MRS. SEIDL Yes, thank you.

Kleidung und Gegenteile

DIE KLEIDUNG *clothing*

der Mantel, ¨	*coat*
Pullover, -	*pullover, sweater*
Rock, ¨e	*skirt*
Schuh, -e	*shoe*
das Hemd, -en	*shirt*
Kleid, -er	*dress*
die Bluse, -n	*blouse*
Hose,[1] -n	*slacks, pants*
Jacke, -n	*jacket, cardigan*

DAS GEGENTEIL, -E *opposite*

dick / dünn	*thick, fat / thin, skinny*
groß / klein	*big, large / small, little*
lang / kurz	*long / short*
langsam / schnell	*slow(ly) / fast, quick(ly)*
neu / alt	*new / old*
sauber / schmutzig	*clean, neat / dirty*

WEITERES

aber	*but, however*
oder	*or*
zu	*too (+ adj. or adv.)*
gehen	*to go*
sagen	*to say, tell*
schreiben	*to write*
sprechen	*to speak*
verstehen	*to understand*
Gehen Sie an die Tafel!	*Go to the board.*
Ich weiß nicht.	*I don't know.*
Passen Sie auf!	*Pay attention.*
Sprechen Sie laut!	*Speak up.*
Wie bitte?	*What did you say, please?*

1 Note that **die Hose** is singular in German.

PASSIVES VOKABULAR der Verkäufer, - *(salesclerk)*; das Geschäft, -e *(store)*; die Krawatte, -n *(tie)*; Mensch! *(Man! Boy! Hey!)*; schade *(too bad)*

AUSSPRACHEÜBUNG:
l, s, st, sp, sch, x

Hören Sie gut zu und wiederholen Sie!

[l] lernen, lesen, langsam, alle, Pullover, Kuli, klein, blau, alt, Stuhl, Tafel, Mantel, Beispiel, schnell

[z] so, sagen, sauber, sie sind, lesen, Bluse, Hose

[s]	Professor, passen, heißen, was, groß, weiß
[st]	ist, kosten, Fenster
[št]	Stephan, Stuhl, Stein, Bleistift, verstehen
[šp]	sprechen, Sport, Beispiel, Gespräch, Aussprache
[š]	schlecht, schnell, schmutzig, schwarz, schreiben, falsch, deutsch
[ks]	Axel, Max, Felix, Beatrix

MÜNDLICHE ÜBUNGEN

A. Mustersätze

1. der Schuh: **Das ist** der Schuh.
   die Jacke, das Hemd, der Mantel, das Kleid, die Bluse, der Pullover, der Rock, die Hose

2. alt / neu: **Das Gegenteil von** alt **ist** neu.
   groß / klein; lang / kurz; dick / dünn; langsam / schnell; sauber / schmutzig; richtig / falsch; ja / nein; hier / da

3. der Mantel / alt: **Ist** der Mantel alt? **Nein**, der Mantel **ist nicht** alt.
   die Jacke / dick; das Kleid / lang; der Pullover / dünn; das Hemd / sauber

4. Jacken / klein: **Sind die** Jacken **zu** klein? **Ja**, die Jacken **sind zu** klein.
   Hosen / lang; Röcke / kurz; Blusen / dünn; Pullover / dick; Kleider / groß; Schuhe / schmutzig

5. schreiben: Schreiben **Sie bitte schnell!**
   lesen, sprechen, gehen, wiederholen, antworten

6. verstehen: Verstehen **Sie das? Ja, ich** verstehe **das.**
   sagen, hören, wiederholen, lernen, lesen

B. Fragen und Antworten

1. Ist der Rock rot? **Ja, der Rock ist rot.**
   Ist die Bluse rosa? die Jacke braun? der Kuli neu? das Papier dünn? der Bleistift kurz?

2. Ist der Rock blau? **Nein, der Rock ist nicht blau.**
   Ist das Buch dick? das Wort kurz? das Fenster klein? der Pullover neu? Sind die Schuhe weiß? die Fenster groß? die Bücher neu?

C. Wiederholung

1. Fragen

   a. Wie geht es Ihnen?
   b. Geht es Ihnen schlecht?
   c. Sind Sie müde?
   d. Was ist rot? braun? blau? weiß? gelb? orange? rosa? schwarz? grau?
   e. Ist der Tisch orange? die Tafel grün? das Buch rot? der Bleistift schwarz?

13

2. Wie fragen Sie? *(What questions would elicit the following answers?)*

Ja, ich bin müde.   **Sind Sie müde?**

a. Danke, gut.

b. Nein, ich heiße nicht Heinz Fiedler.

c. Das Buch ist blau.

d. Da ist die Tür.

e. Das ist das Bild.

f. Mein Name ist Schneider.

g. Ja, das ist richtig.

h. Ich antworte auf deutsch.

3. Buchstabieren Sie auf deutsch!

Thomas Mann, Arthur Schnitzler, Christa Wolf, Ilse Aichinger, Friedrich Nietzsche, Heinrich Böll, Günter Grass

AUFGABE

A. *Fragen*

1. Was ist der Artikel von Kleidung? Mantel? Pullover? Bluse? Hemd? Rock? Hose? Kleid? Jacke? Schuh?

2. Was ist der Plural von Schuh? Jacke? Rock? Kleid? Hose? Hemd? Bluse? Pullover? Mantel?

3. Sprechen Sie langsam oder schnell? Hören Sie gut oder schlecht? Sind Sie groß oder klein?

4. Was ist das Gegenteil von lang? dick? sauber? da? richtig? alt? schlecht? schnell? schmutzig? nein? danke?

5. Welche Farbe hat das Buch? das Papier? die Hose? der Rock? die Bluse? . . .

B. *Beschreiben Sie bitte!* *(Describe the clothes of one or two of your fellow students, or describe one or two items you have with you.)*

BEISPIELE: **Die Hose ist blau. Die Schuhe sind . . .**

VERKÄUFER Guten Tag, Frau Ziegler! Was brauchen Sie heute?

Was kostet das?

FRAU ZIEGLER Ich brauche ein paar Bleistifte, zwei Kulis und Papier. Was kosten die Bleistifte?

VERKÄUFER Fünfundsiebzig Pfennig (0,75 DM).

FRAU ZIEGLER Und der Kuli?

VERKÄUFER Eine Mark fünfundneunzig (1,95 DM[1]).

FRAU ZIEGLER Und was kostet das Papier da?

VERKÄUFER Nur vier Mark zwanzig (4,20 DM[1]).

FRAU ZIEGLER Gut. Ich nehme sechs Bleistifte, zwei Kulis und das Papier.

VERKÄUFER Ist das alles?

FRAU ZIEGLER Ja. Danke.

VERKÄUFER Zwölf Mark sechzig (12,60 DM), bitte!

1 Note the difference between English and German: *$1.95* BUT **1,95 DM;** *$1,600.00* BUT **1 600,00 DM** (or **1.600,00 DM**).

How Much Is It?

SALESCLERK Hello, Mrs. Ziegler. What do you need today?

MRS. ZIEGLER I need some pencils, two pens and paper. How much are the pencils?

SALESCLERK Seventy-five pfennig.

MRS. ZIEGLER And the pen?

SALESCLERK One mark ninety-five.

MRS. ZIEGLER And how much is the paper over there?

SALESCLERK Only four marks twenty.

MRS. ZIEGLER Fine. I'll take six pencils, two pens and the paper.

SALESCLERK Is that all?

MRS. ZIEGLER Yes, thank you.

SALESCLERK Twelve marks sixty, please.

Zahlen und Preise

WORTSCHATZ

- To help you remember, note these similarities between English and German: *teen* = *zehn (fourteen*, vierzehn); *-ty* = *-zig (forty*, vierzig).
- *21–29, 31–39, etc. to 91–99 follow the pattern of "four-and-twenty blackbirds baked in a pie": four-and-twenty* = **vierundzwanzig.**
- *Any number up to 1 million is written in one word, no matter how long it is:*

> BEISPIEL: **zweihundertvierunddreißigtausendfünfhundertsiebenundsechzig** *(234 567)*

DIE ZAHL, -EN *number*

1 eins	11 elf	21	einundzwanzig
2 zwei	12 zwölf	22	zweiundzwanzig
3 drei	13 dreizehn	30	dreißig
4 vier	14 vierzehn	40	vierzig
5 fünf	15 fünfzehn	50	fünfzig
6 sechs	16 sechzehn	60	sechzig
7 sieben	17 siebzehn	70	siebzig
8 acht	18 achtzehn	80	achtzig
9 neun	19 neunzehn	90	neunzig
10 zehn	20 zwanzig	100	hundert

0	null
10	zehn
100	hundert
200	zweihundert
1 000	tausend
10 000	zehntausend
100 000	hunderttausend
1 000 000	eine Million

WEITERES

ein Pfennig (zehn Pfennig . . .)   *one pfennig (ten pfennigs . . .)*

eine Mark (zwei Mark . . .)[1]   *one mark (two marks . . .)*

1 **eins** BUT **eine Mark!**

auf Seite 2	on page 2, to page 2
heute / morgen	today / tomorrow
nur	only
von . . . bis . . .	from . . . to . . .
Was kostet / kosten . . .?	How much is / are . . .?
Das kostet . . .	That comes to . . .
wie viele?	how many?
brauchen	to need
kosten	to cost, come to (a certain amount)
nehmen	to take
öffnen	to open
zählen	to count
ich zähle	I count
wir	we count
sie ⎱ zählen	they count
Sie	you (formal) count

Sie finden im

2.OG   **Für Ihn:**
      Anzüge,Mäntel
      Trachten

1.OG   **Für Ihn:**
      Lederjacken,Blousons
      Sportsaccos,Hosen
      mod.Trachten

EG   **Für Ihn:**
      Herren-Strick,Hemden
      Krawatten,Gürtel
      Socken,Jeans
      Nacht-u.Unterwäsche

      Für Sie:
      Damen-Strick
      Blusen,Hosen,Jacken
      Jeans,Röcke

PASSIVES VOKABULAR die Verkäuferin, -nen *(salesclerk, fem.)*; ein paar *(a couple of)*; plus / minus; und so weiter = usw. *(and so on = etc.)*

AUSSPRACHEÜBUNG:
z, w, v, f, pf, qu

Hören Sie gut zu und wiederholen Sie!

[ts]   Fritz, Götz, **Z**immer, **Z**ahl, **z**u, **z**usammen, **z**ählen, **z**wei, **z**ehn, **z**wölf, **z**wanzig, **z**weiund**z**wanzig, **z**weihundert**z**weiund**z**wanzig, je**tz**t

[z/ts]   sech**s**, sech**z**ehn, sech**z**ig, sech**s**und**s**ech**z**ig, sech**s**hundert**s**ech**s**und**s**ech**z**ig, **s**ieben, **s**ieb**z**ig,, **s**iebenund**s**ieb**z**ig, **s**iebenhundert**s**iebenund**s**ieb**z**ig, Sa**tz**

[v]   **W**illi, **W**olfgang, **W**and, **W**ort, **w**ie, **w**as, **w**o, **w**elche, **w**eiß, **w**iederholen, **V**olvo, **V**ase

[f]   **v**ier, **v**ierzehn, **v**ierzig, **v**ierundvierzig, **v**ierhundert**v**ierundvierzig, **v**iele, **v**erstehen, **V**olkswagen

[f]   **f**ün**f**, **f**ün**f**zehn, **f**ün**f**zig, **f**ün**f**und**f**ün**f**zig, **f**ün**f**hundert**f**ün**f**und**f**ün**f**zig, **f**ür, **F**enster, öf**f**nen, Ta**f**el, au**f**, el**f**, zwöl**f**

[pf]   **Pf**ennig, **Pf**effer, **Pf**efferminz, Dummko**pf**, **pf**ui

[kv]   **Qu**alität, **Qu**antität, **Qu**artal, **Qu**artett, **Qu**intett, Ä**qu**ator, Ä**qu**ivalent

MÜNDLICHE ÜBUNGEN

A. Hören Sie gut zu und wiederholen Sie!

1. Wir zählen von eins bis zehn: eins, zwei, drei, vier, fünf, sechs, sieben, acht, neun, zehn.
2. Wir zählen von zehn bis zwanzig: zehn, elf, zwölf, dreizehn, vierzehn, fünfzehn, sechzehn, siebzehn, achtzehn, neunzehn, zwanzig.
3. Wir zählen von zwanzig bis dreißig: zwanzig, einundzwanzig, zweiundzwanzig, dreiundzwanzig, vierundzwanzig, fünfundzwanzig, sechsundzwanzig, siebenundzwanzig, achtundzwanzig, neunundzwanzig, dreißig.
4. Wir zählen von zehn bis hundert: zehn, zwanzig, dreißig, vierzig, fünfzig, sechzig, siebzig, achtzig, neunzig, hundert.
5. Wir zählen von hundert bis tausend: hundert, zweihundert, dreihundert, vierhundert, fünfhundert, sechshundert, siebenhundert, achthundert, neunhundert, tausend.

B. Lesen Sie laut auf deutsch!

1. Seitenzahlen

Seite 1, 5, 7, 8, 9, 11, 12, 14, 17, 19, 22, 25, 31, 36, 42, 57, 66, 89, 92, 101

2. Plus und minus

BEISPIELE: $4 + 4 = 8$: **Vier plus vier ist acht.**
$8 - 4 = 4$: **Acht minus vier ist vier.**

$3 + 2 = 5$	$8 + 1 = 9$	$8 - 2 = 6$
$7 + 3 = 10$	$10 - 2 = 8$	$7 - 6 = 1$
$1 + 1 = 2$	$9 - 4 = 5$	$5 - 5 = 0$

3. Preise (Prices)
   a. 0,10 DM   **zehn Pfennig**
      0,25 DM / 0,31 DM / 0,44 DM / 0,67 DM / 0,72 DM / 0,88 DM / 0,93 DM
   b. 1,20 DM   **eine Mark zwanzig**
      2,50 DM / 4,75 DM / 8,90 DM / 5,60 DM / 10,40 DM / 3,25 DM / 6,30 DM

4. Telefonnummern (Telephone numbers)

BEISPIEL: 7 55 23   **sieben fünfundfünfzig dreiundzwanzig**

9 16 78 / 85 47 72 / 8 43 92 / 60 16 78

C. Mustersätze

1. das Papier: **Was kostet** das Papier?
   die Kreide, die Hose, der Mantel, die Jacke, der Pullover

2. Bleistifte: **Was kosten** die Bleistifte?
   Kulis, Bücher, Schuhe, Hemden, Bilder
3. brauchen: **Was** brauchen **Sie?**
   sagen, hören, schreiben, lesen, zählen, nehmen
4. brauchen: Brauchen **Sie das? Nein, ich** brauche **das nicht.**
   hören, sagen, verstehen, zählen, wiederholen, öffnen
5. brauchen: **Wir** brauchen **das.**
   lesen, nehmen, zählen, verstehen, wiederholen, öffnen

D. Wiederholung

1. *Fragen*
   a. Wie geht's?
   b. Heißen Sie Meier?
   c. Wie heißen Sie? Wie heiße ich?
   d. Was ist das? *(Point to items in the classroom.)*
   e. Ist das Buch dick oder dünn? der Bleistift lang oder kurz? das Zimmer groß oder klein? die Tafel schwarz oder grün?
   f. Welche Farbe hat das Buch? der Kuli? die Bluse? die Hose? die Jacke?

2. *Antworten Sie mit* ja! *(Answer with* **yes.***)*

   BEISPIEL: Wiederholen Sie das?   **Ja, ich wiederhole das.**

   a. Sprechen Sie langsam?
   b. Verstehen Sie die Frage?
   c. Nehmen Sie die Kreide?
   d. Öffnen Sie das Fenster?
   e. Lesen Sie das noch einmal?
   f. Gehen Sie an die Tafel?
   g. Lernen Sie das für morgen?

3. *Antworten Sie mit* nein! *(Answer with* **no.***)*

   BEISPIEL: Sind die Schuhe neu?   **Nein, die Schuhe sind nicht neu.**

   a. Sind die Fenster klein?
   b. Sind die Bücher alt?
   c. Sind die Kulis rot?
   d. Sind die Bleistifte dick?
   e. Sind die Tische grün?

4. *Geben Sie Befehle! (State as requests.)*

   BEISPIEL: antworten   **Antworten Sie bitte!**

   fragen, wiederholen, gehen, lesen, schreiben, lernen

5. *Buchstabieren Sie auf deutsch!*

   Blume *(flower)*, Rose, Tulpe, Narzisse, Gladiole, Nelke *(carnation)*, Sonnenblume, Dahlie, Iris

A. *Wieviel ist das?* (How much is that?)

$$15 + 9 = ? \qquad 20 - 1 = ? \qquad 72 + 8 = ?$$
$$28 + 4 = ? \qquad 12 + 48 = ? \qquad 114 - 16 = ?$$
$$22 - 8 = ? \qquad 60 - 5 = ? \qquad 1\,000 - 25 = ?$$

B. *Wie geht's weiter?* (How does it continue?)

$$100 - 10 = 90 \,/\, 90 - 10 = 80 \,/\, 80 - 10 = ?$$
$$70 - 7 = 63 \,/\, 63 - 7 = 56 \,/\, 56 - 7 = ?$$

C. *Was kostet das zusammen?*

1. Sechs Bleistifte kosten 2,40 DM, der Kuli kostet 1,60 DM, das Buch 24,55 DM und das Papier 3,— DM. Das kostet zusammen _____ .
2. Die Jacke kostet 75,— DM, die Bluse 48,— DM, und die Schuhe kosten 84,— DM. Das kostet zusammen _____ .
3. Das Buch kostet 5,50 DM. Was kosten drei Bücher?
4. Das Hemd kostet 28,50 DM und die Hose 125,— DM. Das kostet zusammen _____ .

D. *Was sagen Sie?*

VERKÄUFERIN Guten Tag, Herr (Frau, Fräulein) _____ . Wie geht es Ihnen?

     x _____ .

VERKÄUFERIN Was brauchen Sie heute?

     x _____ ein paar _____ und ein paar _____ .
     Was kosten / kostet _____ ?

VERKÄUFERIN _____ DM.

     x Und was kostet _____ ?

VERKÄUFERIN _____ DM.

     x Ich nehme zwei (drei . . .) _____ .

VERKÄUFERIN Ist das alles?

     x _____

VERKÄUFERIN _____ DM, bitte!

NORBERT Es ist schön heute, nicht wahr?
JULIA Ja, wirklich. Die Sonne scheint
wieder!
RUDI Aber der Wind ist kühl.
JULIA Ach, das macht nichts.
NORBERT Ich finde es prima.

DOROTHEA Das Wetter ist furchtbar, nicht wahr?
MATTHIAS Das finde ich auch. Es regnet und regnet!
SONJA Und es ist wieder kalt.
MATTHIAS Ja, typisch April.

Das Wetter im April

The Weather in April

NORBERT It's nice today, isn't it?
JULIA Yes indeed. The sun is shining again.
RUDI But the wind is cool.
JULIA Oh, that doesn't matter.
NORBERT I think it's great.

DOROTHEA The weather is awful, isn't it?
MATTHIAS I think so, too. It's raining and raining.
SONJA And it's cold again.
MATTHIAS Yes, typical April.

Das Jahr und das Wetter

DAS JAHR, -E *year*

der Frühling	*spring*
Sommer	*summer*
Herbst	*fall, autumn*
Winter	*winter*

DER TAG, -E *day*

DIE WOCHE, -N *week*

der Montag	*Monday*
Dienstag	*Tuesday*
Mittwoch	*Wednesday*
Donnerstag	*Thursday*
Freitag	*Friday*
Samstag	*Saturday*
Sonntag	*Sunday*

DER MONAT, -E *month*

der Januar	*January*
Februar	*February*
März	*March*
April	*April*
Mai	*May*
Juni	*June*
Juli	*July*
August	*August*
September	*September*
Oktober	*October*
November	*November*
Dezember	*December*

DAS WETTER *weather*

Es ist . . .	*It's . . .*	heiß / kalt	*hot / cold*
Es regnet.	*It's raining.*	furchtbar	*awful, terrible*
Es schneit.	*It's snowing.*	prima	*great, wonderful*
Die Sonne scheint.	*The sun is shining.*	schön	*nice, beautiful, fine*
		warm / kühl	*warm / cool*

Es ist Winter. Es ist kalt und es schneit.

WEITERES

Die Woche hat . . .	*The week has . . .*
nicht wahr?	*isn't it?*
sehr	*very*
wieder	*again*
wirklich	*really, indeed*
Wann sind Sie geboren?	*When were you born?*
Ich bin im Mai[1] geboren.	*I was born in May.*
finden	*to find*
Ich finde es . . .	*I think it's . . .*

1 **Im** is used with the names of months and seasons: **im Mai, im Winter.**

PASSIVES VOKABULAR der Wind; die Jahreszeit, -en *(season)*; Das macht nichts. *(That doesn't matter.)*; typisch

AUSSPRACHEÜBUNG: r; p, t, k; final b, d, g; j, h

Hören Sie gut zu und wiederholen Sie!

[r] **r**ichtig, **r**egnet, **r**ot, **r**osa, **R**ock, b**r**aun, g**r**ün, d**r**ei, f**r**agen, F**r**au, F**r**eitag, P**r**eis, Ma**r**k, le**r**nen, hö**r**en, gebo**r**en, o**r**ange

[ʌ] wi**r**, vie**r**, ode**r**, abe**r**, nu**r**, seh**r**, fü**r**, wiede**r**, Fenste**r**, Papie**r**, Wette**r**, Somme**r**, Winte**r**, Oktobe**r**, Dezembe**r**
  BUT [ʌ/r] Tü**r** / Tü**r**en; Jah**r** / Jah**r**e; Uh**r** / Uh**r**en

[p] **P**eter **P**öppel, **P**apier, **P**ullover, **P**lural, **p**lus, ka**p**utt
  AND [p] Her**b**st, Jako**b**, gel**b**, hal**b**
  BUT [p/b] gel**b** / gel**b**e; hal**b** / hal**b**e

[t] **Th**eo, **T**ür, **T**isch, Doro**th**ea, Mat**th**ias, bi**tt**e
  AND [t] un**d**, tausen**d**, Bil**d**, Klei**d**, Hem**d**, Wan**d**
  BUT [t/d] Bil**d** / Bil**d**er; Klei**d** / Klei**d**er; Hem**d** / Hem**d**en; Wan**d** / Wän**d**e

[k] **k**lein, **k**ühl, **k**urz, **K**uli, **K**leidung, dan**k**e, di**ck**
  AND [k] sa**g**t, fra**g**t, Ta**g**
  BUT [k/g] sa**g**t / sa**g**en; fra**g**t / fra**g**en; Ta**g** / Ta**g**e

[j] **J**akob, **J**osef, **J**ulia, **j**a, **J**anuar, **J**uni, **J**uli

[h] **H**err, **H**erbst, **H**emd, **H**ose, **h**ören, **h**eiß, **h**at, **h**undert

[:] zä**h**len, ne**h**men, ge**h**en, verste**h**en, I**h**nen, Stu**h**l, Schu**h**

MÜNDLICHE ÜBUNGEN

A. *Hören Sie gut zu und wiederholen Sie!*

1. Das Jahr hat vier Jahreszeiten *(seasons)*. Die Jahreszeiten heißen Frühling, Sommer, Herbst und Winter.
2. Das Jahr hat zwölf Monate. Die Monate heißen Januar, Februar, März, April, Mai, Juni, Juli, August, September, Oktober, November und Dezember.
3. Die Woche hat sieben Tage. Die Tage heißen Montag, Dienstag, Mittwoch, Donnerstag, Freitag, Samstag und Sonntag.

B. *Mustersätze*

1. schön: **Es ist heute** schön.
   wunderbar, furchtbar, kalt, heiß, warm, kühl
2. sehr kalt: **Es ist** sehr kalt.
   sehr heiß, sehr schön, schön warm, furchtbar heiß, furchtbar kalt
3. prima: **Ich finde es** prima.
   schön, gut, wunderbar, schlecht, furchtbar
4. Juli: **Ich bin im** Juli **geboren**.
   Januar, März, Mai, Juni, August, Sommer, Winter
5. 19: **Ich bin** neunzehn.
   20, 21, 26, 27, 31

C. Wiederholung

1. Antworten Sie mit ja!

BEISPIEL: Verstehen Sie das?　　Ja, wir verstehen das.

a. Zählen Sie schnell?　　　　e. Lesen Sie auf Seite dreißig?
b. Fragen Sie auf deutsch?　　f. Passen Sie auf?
c. Hören Sie gut zu?　　　　　g. Sprechen Sie laut?
d. Lernen Sie die Wörter?

2. Wie geht's weiter? (How does the sentence go on?)

BEISPIEL: Wo ist _____ ?　　Wo ist das Fräulein?

a. Ich heiße _____ .　　　e. Der Artikel von _____ .
b. Ich bin _____ .　　　　f. Der Pullover _____ .
c. Es geht mir _____ .　　g. Das kostet _____ .
d. Das Gegenteil von _____ .

3. Zahlen, Preise, Telefonnummern und Temperaturen (temperatures)

a. Wieviel ist das?

$3 + 6 = ?$	$65 + 15 = ?$	$50 - 20 = ?$
$9 + 9 = ?$	$75 + 25 = ?$	$33 - 11 = ?$
$23 + 10 = ?$	$100 - 60 = ?$	$16 - 6 = ?$
$40 + 50 = ?$	$80 - 15 = ?$	$12 - 11 = ?$

b. Zählen Sie die geraden (even) / ungeraden (odd) Zahlen von eins bis zwanzig!

c. Lesen Sie laut auf deutsch!

101 / 315 / 463 / 555 / 1 110 / 20 000 / 88 888 / 267 315 / 987 654 / 1 000 000

100,10 DM / 212,25 DM / 667,75 DM / 1 920,— DM / 99 999,99 DM

d. Was sage ich? (What am I saying? Say any number in German and ask your neighbor to write it down. Then alternate.)

BEISPIEL: eintausendzweihundertzwölf　　**1 212**

e. Was ist Ihre Telefonnummer? (What's your telephone number? Ask your neighbor for his/her phone number and write down what he/she tells you. Have your neighbor check the number for accuracy. Then alternate.)

BEISPIEL: Was ist Ihre Telefonnummer?
Meine Telefonnummer ist sechs sechsundvierzig neunzehn fünfundneunzig.
646–1995. Ist das richtig?
Ja, das ist richtig. / Nein, das ist falsch.

f. Öffnen Sie das Buch auf Seite _____ und lesen Sie! (Read the first line on whatever page in the book your instructor indicates.)

g. Temperaturen[1]

1 European thermometers use the centigrade scale. On that scale water freezes at **0°C** and boils at **100°C.** Normal body temperature is about **37°C,** and fever starts at about **37.6°C.** To convert Fahrenheit into Centigrade, subtract 32, multiply by 5, divide by 9. To convert Centigrade into Fahrenheit, multiply by 9, divide by 5, add 32.

Wieviel Grad Celsius sind das? (How many degrees Celsius? Look at the thermometer in order to find the answer.)

BEISPIEL: **32°F = 0°C (Zweiunddreißig Grad Fahrenheit sind null Grad Celsius.)**

100°F, 96°F, 84°F, 68°F, 41°F, 23°F, −4°F, −13°F

h. Wie ist das Wetter?
(What's the weather like?)

BEISPIEL: 12°C (zwölf Grad Celsius) **Es ist kühl.**

21°C, 0°C, 30°C, 38°C, −10°C, −25°C

TEMPERATUREN

GRAD

	Celsius	Fahrenheit
	38	100
Körpertemperatur	► 37	98,6
	36	96
	35	95
	34	94
	32	90
	30	86
	29	84
	28	82
	26	79
	25	77
	22	72
	21	70
	20	68
	18	64
	15	59
	12	53
	10	50
	8	46
	5	41
	3	37
Gefrierpunkt	► 0	32
	− 2	28
	− 5	23
	−10	14
	−15	5
	−20	− 4
	−25	− 13

AUFGABE

A. *Fragen*

1. Welcher Tag ist heute? morgen?
2. Wie viele Tage hat die Woche? Wie heißen die Tage?
3. Wie viele Tage hat der September? der Oktober? der Februar?
4. Wie viele Monate hat das Jahr? Wie heißen die Monate?
5. Wie viele Wochen hat das Jahr?
6. Wie viele Jahreszeiten *(seasons)* hat das Jahr? Wie heißen die Jahreszeiten?
7. Wie heißen die Wintermonate? die Sommermonate? die Herbstmonate?
8. Wie ist das Wetter heute? Scheint die Sonne, oder regnet es?
9. Wie ist das Wetter hier im Winter? im Sommer? im Frühling? im Herbst?
10. Wie geht es Ihnen?
11. Wann sind Sie geboren? Wie alt sind Sie?
12. Was ist das Gegenteil von kalt? kühl? prima? heute?
13. Was ist der Artikel von Montag? September? Donnerstag? Herbst? Juni? Monat? Jahr? Woche?

B. *Was sagen Sie?*

X Wie ist das Wetter heute?
Y ——————— .
X Wie finden Sie das Wetter?
Y ——————— .
X Typisch ——————— , nicht wahr?
Y ——————— .

RITA Axel, wie spät ist es?
AXEL Es ist zehn vor acht.
RITA Mensch, in zehn Minuten
habe ich Philosophie.
Danke schön!
AXEL Bitte schön!

Wie spät
ist es?

MAX HUBER Hallo, Fräulein Lange! Wieviel Uhr ist es?
MARIA LANGE Es ist halb zwölf.
MAX HUBER Gehen Sie jetzt essen?
MARIA LANGE Ja, die Vorlesung beginnt erst um Viertel nach eins.

ROLF RICHTER Wann sind Sie heute fertig?
HORST HEROLD Um zwei. Warum?
ROLF RICHTER Spielen wir heute Tennis?
HORST HEROLD Ja, prima! Es ist jetzt halb eins. Um Viertel vor drei dann?
ROLF RICHTER Gut! Bis später!

How Late Is It?

RITA Axel, what time is it?
AXEL It's ten minutes to eight.
RITA Boy, in ten minutes I have philosophy. Thanks a lot.
AXEL You're welcome.

MAX HUBER Hi, Miss Lange. What time is it?
MARIA LANGE It's eleven thirty.
MAX HUBER Are you going to lunch now?
MARIA LANGE Yes, the lecture doesn't start till a quarter past one.

ROLF RICHTER When are you finished today?
HORST HEROLD At two. Why?
ROLF RICHTER Shall we play tennis today?
HORST HEROLD Yes, great. It's twelve thirty now. At a quarter to three, then?
ROLF RICHTER Fine. See you later.

Die Uhrzeit

• *German has a formal (official) and informal way of telling time. We will deal with the formal time later (see Chapter 7). The informal system is used in everyday speech and varies somewhat from region to region. The system below is a compromise, but certain to be understood everywhere.*

WIE SPÄT IST ES? *How late is it?*
WIEVIEL UHR IST ES? *What time is it?*

die Minute, -n	minute	morgens	in the morning
Sekunde, -n	second	mittags	at noon
Stunde,[1] -n	hour	nachmittags	in the afternoon
Uhr, -en	watch, clock	abends	in the evening
Zeit, -en	time	(um) eins[2]	(at) one o'clock
		(um) Viertel nach eins	(at) a quarter past one
		(um) halb zwei, 1.30[3]	(at) half past one, 1:30
		(um) Viertel vor zwei	(at) a quarter to two, 1:45

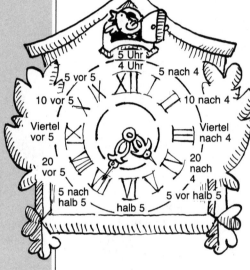

WEITERES

die Vorlesung, -en	lecture, class (university)
Es ist ein Uhr (zwei Uhr).[2]	It's one o'clock (two o'clock).
Es ist eins (zwei).	It's one (two).
fertig	finished, done
jetzt	now
Danke schön!	Thank you very much. Thanks a lot.
Bitte schön!	You're welcome.
beginnen	to begin
essen	to eat
Tennis spielen	to play tennis

1 **Stunde** refers to duration or a particular class: Eine Stunde hat 60 Minuten. Die Deutschstunde ist von acht bis Viertel vor neun. **Uhr** refers to clock time: Wieviel Uhr ist es? Es ist fünf Uhr.

2 **um ein Uhr** BUT **um eins.**

3 Note the difference in punctuation between English and German: *1:30* BUT **1.30.**

haben	to have
ich habe	I have
es hat	it has
wir ⎫	we have
sie ⎬ haben	they have
Sie ⎭	you (formal) have
Ich habe keine Zeit.	I don't have any time.

PASSIVES VOKABULAR die Uhrzeit, -en *(time of day)*; Bis später! *(See you later.)*; dann *(then)*; erst *(only, not before)*; Hallo! *(Hi! Hello!)*; Ich habe eine Frage. *(I have a question.)*; warum? *(why?)*

AUSSPRACHEÜBUNG: ch, ig, ck, ng, gn, kn, ps

Hören Sie gut zu und wiederholen Sie!

[x] a**ch**, a**ch**t, a**ch**thundertachtundachzig, Joa**ch**im, ma**ch**t, au**ch**, brau**ch**en, Wo**ch**e, Mittwo**ch**, Bu**ch**

[ç] i**ch**, mi**ch**, ni**ch**t, wirkli**ch**, Ri**ch**ard, Mi**ch**ael, wel**ch**e, schle**ch**t, spre**ch**en, Gesprä**ch**e, Bü**ch**er

[iç] richt**ig**, fert**ig**, sech**zig**, fünf**zig**, vier**zig**, dreiß**ig**, zwan**zig**, Pfenn**ig**

[ks] se**chs**, se**chs**undse**chz**ig, se**chs**hundertse**chs**undse**chz**ig, Da**chs**hund

[k] **Ch**ristian, **Ch**ristine, **Ch**rista, **Ch**aos

[k] Ja**ck**e, Ro**ck**, di**ck**, Pi**ckn**ick

[ŋ] I**ng**e La**ng**e, Wolfga**ng** E**ng**el, e**ng**lisch, si**ng**en, Fi**ng**er, Hu**ng**er, Frühli**ng**

[gn] **Gn**om, re**gn**et, resi**gn**ieren, Si**gn**al

[kn] **Kn**irps, **Kn**ie, **Kn**oten

[ps] **Ps**ychologie, **Ps**ychiater, **Ps**ychoanalyse, **Ps**eudonym

MÜNDLICHE ÜBUNGEN

A. Wie spät ist es? Wieviel Uhr ist es?

1. 1.00: **Es ist** ein **Uhr.**
   3.00, 5.00, 7.00, 9.00, 11.00

2. 1.05: **Es ist** fünf **nach** eins.
   3.05, 5.05, 7.05, 9.10, 11.10, 1.10, 4.20, 6.20, 8.20

3. 1.15: **Es ist Viertel nach** eins.
   2.15, 4.15, 6.15, 8.15, 10.15

4. 1.30: **Es ist halb** zwei.
   2.30, 4.30, 6.30, 8.30, 10.30

5. 1.40: **Es ist** zwanzig **vor** zwei.
    3.40, 5.40, 7.40, 9.50, 11.50, 1.50, 12.55, 2.55, 4.55

6. 1.45: **Es ist Viertel vor** zwei.
    3.45, 5.45, 7.45, 9.45, 11.45, 12.45

B. Wann ist die Vorlesung? *(When is the lecture?)*

1. 9.00: **Die Vorlesung ist um** neun.
    3.00, 11.00, 1.00, 9.15, 12.15, 9.45, 12.45, 1.30, 3.30

2. 5: **Die Vorlesung beginnt in** fünf **Minuten**.
    2, 10, 12, 15, 20

3. morgens: **Die Vorlesung ist** morgens.
    nachmittags, abends, um acht, um Viertel nach acht, um
    halb neun, um Viertel vor neun

C. Mustersätze

1. essen: Essen **Sie jetzt? Ja, ich** esse **jetzt.**
    gehen, fragen, schreiben, lernen, antworten, beginnen

2. heute: **Ich spiele** heute **Tennis.**
    jetzt, morgens, nachmittags, abends, wieder

3. Sie: **Wann** sind Sie **heute fertig?**
    wir, Horst, ich, Rolf und Maria

4. ich: Ich habe **keine Zeit.**
    wir, Maria, Maria und Rita

D. Wiederholung

1. Wie fragen Sie? (Formulate the questions for these answers.)

BEISPIEL: Das ist die Tafel.   **Was ist das?**

a. Da sind die Schuhe.
b. Der Bleistift ist gelb.
c. Nein, das Heft ist nicht neu.
d. Nein, ich verstehe das nicht.
e. Das Papier kostet 1,50 DM.
f. Ich brauche Zeit.
g. Nein, heute scheint die
    Sonne nicht.
h. Heute ist es furchtbar heiß.
i. Ich finde das nicht schön.

j. Fünf plus fünftausend-
    fünfhundertfünfzig ist
    fünftausendfünfhundert-
    fünfundfünfzig.
k. Der Januar hat einunddreißig
    Tage.
l. Heute ist Dienstag.
m. Nein, ich lese langsam.
n. Nein, das ist falsch.
o. Ja, das ist alles.

2. Und Sie? (And you? Answer, then ask someone else.)
    a. Wie alt sind Sie? (**Ich bin** _____ . **Und Sie?)**
    b. Wann sind Sie geboren? (**Ich bin im** _____ **geboren. Und Sie?)**

*3. Was tun Sie wann? (What do you do when? Match months or seasons
    with the activities below.)*

BEISPIEL: Was tun Sie im Sommer?   **Im Sommer gehe ich Tennis spielen.**

angeln gehen *(go fishing)*, campen gehen, joggen, picknicken gehen, reiten gehen *(go horseback riding)*, schwimmen gehen, segeln gehen *(go sailing)*, Ski laufen gehen, tanzen gehen, wandern *(go hiking)*, Golf / Tennis / Fußball / Volleyball spielen

AUFGABE

A. *Fragen*

1. Wie viele Stunden hat der Tag? Wie viele Minuten hat die Stunde? Wie viele Sekunden hat die Minute?
2. Wie spät ist es (8.45, 9.30, 10.15, 11.30, 1.05, 2.20, 2.45, 6.59)?
3. Wie spät ist es jetzt?
4. Was studieren Sie *(What do you study? Check the list below.)*

   Biologie, Chemie, Deutsch, Englisch, Französisch *(French)*, Geographie, Geologie, Geschichte *(history)*, Informatik *(computer science)*, Kunst *(art)*, Latein, Mathematik, Musik, Philosophie, Physik, Politik, Psychologie, Soziologie, Spanisch, Sport

5. Welche Vorlesungen haben sie heute? wann? **(Ich habe Deutsch um _____ und Englisch um _____ .)**
6. Welche Vorlesungen haben Sie morgen? wann?
7. Wie heißt der Deutschprofessor (Englischprofessor . . .)?
8. Wann sind Sie heute fertig? **(Ich bin heute um _____ fertig.)**
9. Wann essen Sie morgens? mittags? abends?
10. Wie geht es Ihnen?
11. Sind Sie müde?
12. Sie lernen viel Deutsch, nicht wahr?

B. *Was sagen Sie?*

x Wie spät ist es?
Y _____ .
x Danke schön!
Y _____ .
x Gehen Sie jetzt essen?
Y _____ .
x Wann sind Sie heute fertig?
Y _____ . Und Sie?
x _____ .
Y Bis später!
x _____ !

(REVIEW): Schritte

By now you have learned quite a few German words and a number of idiomatic expressions; you have learned how to pronounce German and to say a few things about yourself. Without being fully conscious of it, you also have learned a good deal about the structure of the German language. What you have learned will help you considerably in the following chapters.

I. *Nouns*

1. German has three genders: MASCULINE, NEUTER, and FEMININE. Nouns are distinguished by **der**, **das**, and **die** in the singular. In the plural there are no gender distinctions; the article is **die** for all plural nouns:

der Herr, **der** Bleistift		Herren, Bleistifte
das Fräulein, **das** Bild	**die**	Fräulein, Bilder
die Frau, **die** Tafel		Frauen, Tafeln

2. German nouns have a great variety of plural forms. You have learned how to interpret the most common plural abbreviations found in dictionaries and vocabulary lists:

das Fenster, -		Fenster
der Mantel, ⸚		Mäntel
der Tag, **-e**		Tage
der Stuhl, ⸚**e**		Stühle
das Kleid, **-er**	die	Kleider
das Buch, ⸚**er**		Bücher
die Uhr, **-en**		Uhren
die Sekunde, **-n**		Sekunden
der Kuli, **-s**		Kulis

3. Its gender and plural forms must be learned with each noun.

4. All nouns are capitalized.

Ich brauche **Bleistifte**, **Kulis** und **Papier**.

II. *Pronouns*

You have used the following pronouns:

ich	*I*	Ich heiße Sanders.
es	*it*	Es regnet.
wir	*we*	Wir zählen von eins bis zehn.
sie	*they*	Sind sie neu?
Sie	*you (formal)*	Wann sind Sie heute fertig?

▪ *The pronoun* **ich** *is not capitalized unless it stands at the beginning of a sentence.*

   Ja, **ich** finde das Wetter schön.

▪ *The pronoun* **Sie** (***you***), *which is always capitalized, is used in all formal relationships, and always when others are addressed with such titles as* **Herr**, **Frau**, *and* **Fräulein**. *It is used to address one or more persons.*

Fräulein Thielemann, verstehen Sie das?
Fräulein Thielemann und Herr Fiedler, verstehen Sie das?

III. *Verbs*

1. You have realized that German verbs have different endings—that is, they are INFLECTED, or CONJUGATED. You have used the following verb endings:

ich	-e	Ich brauche Papier.
wir	-en	Wir brauchen Papier.
sie, Sie	-en	Sie brauchen Papier.

2. **Sein** and **haben** are two important verbs. They are frequently used as AUXILIARY, or helping, verbs. As in English, their forms are not regular. You have learned these forms:

ich	bin	Ich bin groß.	ich	habe	Ich habe Zeit.
es	ist	Es ist groß.	es	hat	Es hat Zeit.
sie, Sie	sind	Sie sind groß.	sie, Sie	haben	Sie haben Zeit.

IV. *Sentence Structure*

You have encountered three basic sentence types: STATEMENTS, QUESTIONS, and IMPERATIVES. In all of them, verb position plays a significant role.

1. Statements

One of the most important observations you will make is that the verb is always the second element in a statement. (As you see from the examples, a SENTENCE ELEMENT can consist of more than one word.)

Sie **schreiben** schön.
Mein Name **ist** Dieter Schneider.
Gerda und Dorothea **sind** fertig.
Der Rock und die Bluse **kosten** 150,— DM.

2. Questions

You have practiced two types of questions: INFORMATION QUESTIONS and YES/NO QUESTIONS.

a. Information questions begin with a question word or phrase and ask for specific information: *what, where,* and *how* something is. In information questions, too, the verb is the second element. You have learned the following question words and phrases:

Wann **haben** Sie Deutsch?
Was **kostet** das?
Wo **ist** der Stuhl?
Wie **geht** es Ihnen?
Welche Farbe **hat** das Buch?
Wieviel Uhr **ist** es?
Wie viele Tage **hat** die Woche?

Note that all question words begin with **w**!

b. Yes/no questions, on the other hand, begin with the verb.

Haben Sie Zeit?
Regnet es morgen?
Spielen wir heute Tennis?
Ist das richtig?

3. Imperatives

Imperatives (commands, requests, suggestions) also begin with the verb.

Antworten Sie bitte!
Nehmen Sie die Kreide!
Öffnen Sie das Buch!
Sagen Sie das noch einmal!
Zählen Sie von zwanzig bis dreißig!

WIEDERHOLUNG

A. *Was ist . . .?*

1. der Artikel von
Tisch, Mantel, Hemd, Pfennig, Mark, Tag, Woche, Jahr, Fräulein, Tafel

Herren-Hemd
½ Arm, Baumwolle/Jersey,
in mod. Ringel-Dessins,
Größen: S - XL

17,95

Kinder-Jeans
3-Teiler
besteh. aus: Jeans, Weste und
Hemd, 100% Baumwolle,
Größen: 98–122

29,95

Damen-Caddy-Hose
100% Baumwolle,
Farben: weiß, marine, schilf, kitt
Größen: S - M - L

29,95

Da.-T-Shirt-Kleider
Polyester, Baumwolle,
Block- u. Ringelstreifen,
Größen: 36–46

39,-

2. der Plural von
    Tür, Schuh, Buch, Fräulein, Kuli, Mantel, Pullover, Minute, Bild, Wand
3. das Gegenteil von
    bitte, dick, falsch, gut, heiß, heute, hier, klein, kühl, lang, nein, neu,
    schön, sauber

B. Zahlen und Zeiten

1. Zählen Sie von 1 bis 10; 11 bis 20; 61 bis 70; 121 bis 130!
2. Plus oder minus. Wie geht's weiter? (*Add to or subtract from the previous sum. Continue from one person to another.*)

    BEISPIEL: $7 + 5 = 12 + 9 = 21 - ? = ? \ldots$

3. Was kostet das? Lesen Sie laut! (*Someone writes prices on the board and others read them out loud.*)
4. Was ist die Telefonnummer? (*Tell each other telephone numbers in German and write down what you hear. Check for accuracy.*)
5. Wie spät ist es? Lesen Sie laut! (*Someone writes times of day on the board and others read them out loud.*)

C. Buchstabieren Sie bitte!

   Mozart, Wagner, Haydn, Händel, Schubert, Brahms, Bach

D. Fragen

1. Wie geht's?
2. Welche Farben lieben Sie? Was ist blau? rot? grün? gelb? orange?
    braun? rosa? schwarz? weiß? grau?

3. Was ist groß? klein? schön? lang? neu? alt? schmutzig? prima? furchtbar?
4. Wie heißen die Jahreszeiten? die Monate? die Tage der Woche?
5. Wie ist das Wetter heute? im Winter? im Sommer?
6. Wie heißen Sie? Wann sind Sie geboren? Wie alt sind Sie?
7. Welche Vorlesungen lieben Sie?
8. Wann essen Sie morgens? mittags? abends?
9. Wieviel Uhr ist es jetzt?

E. Sagen Sie das auf deutsch!

1. Good morning. 2. Please open the book to page ten. 3. Do you understand that? 4. Yes, but please read slowly. 5. What's the weather like? 6. It's raining, isn't it? 7. No, the sun is shining. 8. Really? I think that's wonderful. 9. How late is it? 10. It's a quarter to twelve. 11. Thank you very much. 12. You're welcome. 13. When do you eat? 14. At half past twelve. 15. Goodbye.

F. Was paßt? *(What fits? Match each classroom expression on the left with the English equivalent on the right. Although not all of these are active vocabulary, you should be able to understand them.)*

___ 1. Alle zusammen!		a. Make a sentence.
___ 2. Antworten Sie bitte!		b. Listen well.
___ 3. Auf deutsch, bitte!		c. Please learn that.
___ 4. Bilden Sie einen Satz!		d. Again, please.
___ 5. Gehen Sie an die Tafel bitte!		e. I don't understand that.
		f. Please repeat.
___ 6. Hören Sie gut zu!		g. In German, please.
___ 7. Ich habe eine Frage!		h. Speak up.
___ 8. Ich verstehe das nicht.		i. All together.
___ 9. Ich weiß nicht.		j. Please write.
___ 10. Lernen Sie das bitte!		k. I have a question.
___ 11. Lesen Sie laut!		l. Please answer.
___ 12. Noch einmal, bitte!		m. What did you say, please?
___ 13. Passen Sie auf!		n. Please go to the board.
___ 14. Schreiben Sie bitte!		o. I don't know.
___ 15. Sprechen Sie laut!		p. Pay attention.
___ 16. Sprechen Sie langsam!		q. Read aloud.
___ 17. Wie bitte?		r. Speak slowly.
___ 18. Wiederholen Sie bitte!		

KAPITEL

1

GESPRÄCHE

These dialogues are models for everyday speech. They set the scene for the chapter's topic. All subsequent activities focus on this theme. Although the dialogues as a whole need not be memorized, you should become so familiar with them that you will remember individual sentences.

Deutsch für Ausländer

MARIA Roberto, woher kommst du[1]?
ROBERTO Ich bin aus Rom. Und du?
MARIA Meine Familie wohnt in Seattle.
ROBERTO Wie groß ist deine Familie?
MARIA Wir sind fünf—mein Vater, meine Mutter, mein Bruder, meine Schwester und ich.
ROBERTO Ich habe nur eine Schwester. Sie heißt auch Maria, genauso wie du.
MARIA Wirklich?

Später

ROBERTO Maria, wann ist die Prüfung?
MARIA In zehn Minuten. Du, wie heißen ein paar Flüsse in Deutschland?
ROBERTO Im Norden ist die Elbe, im Osten die Oder, im Süden . . .
MARIA Die Donau?
ROBERTO Und im Westen der Rhein. Wo liegt Vaduz?
MARIA In Liechtenstein. Liechtenstein liegt westlich von Österreich.
ROBERTO In Liechtenstein sprechen die Leute Französisch, nicht wahr?
MARIA Nein, Deutsch.
ROBERTO Na, viel Glück!

ÜBRIGENS *(BY THE WAY)*

1. There is no equivalent form of address in English for **du**. Although it has become customary for university students to address each other with the **du**-form, all adults must be addressed with **Sie** unless they are relatives (see also p. 44).

German for Foreigners

MARIA Roberto, where are you from?

ROBERTO I'm from Rome. And you?

MARIA My family lives in Seattle.

ROBERTO How big is your family?

MARIA There are five of us—my father, my mother, my brother, my sister, and I.

ROBERTO I only have a sister. Her name is Maria, too, just like yours.

MARIA Really?

Later

ROBERTO Maria, when is the exam?

MARIA In ten minutes. What are the names of some rivers in Germany?

ROBERTO In the north is the Elbe, in the east the Oder, in the south . . .

MARIA The Danube?

ROBERTO And in the west the Rhine. Where's Vaduz?

MARIA In Liechtenstein. Liechtenstein is west of Austria.

ROBERTO In Liechtenstein people speak French, don't they?

MARIA No, German.

ROBERTO Well, good luck!

Familie, Länder, Sprachen   **WORTSCHATZ I**

We have already emphasized that nouns must be memorized with their articles because their genders are not readily predictable. However, the gender of some nouns can be predicted. (For helpful hints, see Appendix p. 441).

DIE FAMILIE, -N *family*

der Bruder, ⸚	brother	*die* Mutter, ⸚	mother
Junge, -n	boy	Großmutter, ⸚	grandmother
Onkel, -	uncle	Schwester, -n	sister
Sohn, ⸚e	son	Tante, -n	aunt
Vater, ⸚	father	Tochter, ⸚	daughter
Großvater, ⸚	grandfather	Eltern *(pl.)*	parents
das Kind, -er	child	Großeltern *(pl.)*	grandparents
Mädchen, -	girl		

DAS LAND, ⸚ER *country, state*
DIE SPRACHE, -N *language*

der Berg, -e	mountain
Fluß, Flüsse	river
See, -n	lake
die Landkarte, -n	map
Stadt, ⸚e	city
Hauptstadt, ⸚e (von)	capital (of)
Leute *(pl.)*	people

die Schweiz	Switzerland	der Schweizer, -[1]	
(das) Deutschland[3]	Germany	Deutsche, -n	} Deutsch[2]
Österreich	Austria	Österreicher, -	
Frankreich	France	Franzose, -n	Französisch
Spanien	Spain	Spanier, -	Spanisch
Italien	Italy	Italiener, -	Italienisch
England	England	Engländer, -	
Amerika	America	Amerikaner, -	} Englisch
Kanada	Canada	Kanadier, -	

WEITERES

der Satz, ⁻e	sentence
die Frage, -n	question
kommen	to come
liegen	to lie (be located)
wohnen	to live, reside
woher?	from where?
Ich bin aus . . .	I'm from . . . (a native of)
im Norden (Süden, Osten, Westen)[4]	in the north (south, east, west)
nördlich (südlich, östlich, westlich) von	north (south, east, west) of
mein(e) / Ihr(e)[5]	my / your (formal)

1 Many feminine nouns can be derived from masculine ones by adding **-in**: **die Schweizerin, die Amerikanerin, die Französin.** Their plurals end in **-nen**: die Schweizerin**nen**, die Amerikanerin**nen**, die Französin**nen**. BUT: **der Deutsche, -n / die Deutsche, -n** (see also p. 355).

2 Antworten Sie **auf deutsch** (in German)! BUT: Ich spreche **Deutsch** (the German language).

3 All countries and cities are neuter unless indicated otherwise (e.g. **die Schweiz**).

4 im is used with months, seasons, and points of the compass: **im** Mai, **im** Winter, **im** Norden; **in** is used with the names of cities, countries, and continents: **in** Berlin, **in** Deutschland, **in** Europa.

5 Before masculine and neuter nouns, **mein** and **Ihr** have no ending. Before feminine and plural nouns, they end in **-e** (see p. 48):

mein Bruder, **mein** Kind / **meine** Schwester, **meine** Eltern
Ihr Bruder, **Ihr** Kind / **Ihre** Schwester, **Ihre** Eltern

PASSIVES VOKABULAR der Ausländer, - *(foreigner)*; die Prüfung, -en *(test, exam)*; dein(e) *(your, familiar)*; genauso wie *(just like)*; Viel Glück! *(Good luck!)*

ZUM THEMA

A. Mustersätze

1. Ihre Familie: **Woher kommt** Ihre Familie?
   Ihr Vater, Ihre Mutter, Ihr Onkel, Ihre Tante
2. Rom: **Ich bin aus** Rom.
   Frankfurt, Österreich, Amerika, Berlin
3. Hamburg / Norden: Hamburg **liegt im** Norden.
   Berlin / Osten; München / Süden; Bonn / Westen; Wien / Osten

4. Liechtenstein / westlich: Liechtenstein **liegt** westlich **von Österreich.**
die Schweiz / westlich; Deutschland / nördlich; Italien / südlich

5. Liechtenstein / Deutsch: **In** Liechtenstein **sprechen die Leute** Deutsch.
Frankreich / Französisch; England / Englisch; Österreich / Deutsch; Spanien / Spanisch

B. *Was sind sie?*

1. BEISPIEL: Monika und Uwe sind aus Frankfurt.
Uwe ist Frankfurter. Monika ist Frankfurterin.

    a. Evi und Robert sind aus Berlin.

    b. Klaus und Inge sind aus Hamburg.

    c. Rolf und Katrin sind aus Wien.

    d. Johanna und Ulrich sind aus Zürich.

2. BEISPIEL: Juan ist Spanier. Und Juanita?
Juanita ist Spanierin.

    a. Antonio ist Italiener. Und Luisa?

    b. Hugo ist Österreicher. Und Lieselotte?

    c. Walter ist Schweizer. Und Helga?

    d. Pierre ist Franzose. Und Monique?

C. *Was sagen Sie?* *(Ask each other, then report to the class. Alternate roles.)*

1. *Interview*

    X *(name of student)*, woher kommst du?
    Y Ich bin aus _____ .
    X Wie findest du es hier?
    Y Ich finde es _____ .
    X Wo wohnt deine Familie?
    Y Meine Familie wohnt in _____ .
    X Wie groß ist deine Familie?
    Y Wir sind _____ : mein(e) _____ und ich.
    X Wie heißt dein _____ (Vater / Bruder), und wie heißt deine _____ (Mutter / Schwester)?
    Y Mein _____ heißt, und meine _____ heißt _____ .

2. *Bericht (Report to the class)*

    ~~Mike~~ _____ *(name of student)* kommt aus _____ und findet es hier _____ . Die Familie wohnt in _____ . Sie sind _____ *(how many?)*: _____ und _____ *(name of student)*. Der _____ *(father or brother)* heißt _____ und die _____ *(mother or sister)* heißt _____ .

D. *Fragen*

1. Woher kommen Sie? Ihre Eltern? Ihre Großeltern?

2. Wo wohnt Ihre Familie?

   BEISPIEL: **Meine Familie wohnt in Santa Barbara.**

3. Wo liegt ――――― (name of city)?

   BEISPIEL: **Santa Barbara liegt in Kalifornien.**

4. Wo liegt ――――― (name of state or province)?

   BEISPIEL: **Kalifornien liegt südlich von Oregon.**

5. Wie heißt die Hauptstadt von ――――― (name of state)?

   BEISPIEL: **Die Hauptstadt von Kalifornien heißt Sacramento.**

6. Welche Stadt liegt im Norden und im Süden von ――――― (name of your city)?

   BEISPIEL: **Im Norden von Santa Barbara liegt San Francisco und im Süden Los Angeles.**

7. Ist ――――― (name of your city) groß oder klein? Wie viele Leute wohnen da?

8. Ist da ein Fluß, ein See oder der Ozean (ocean)? Wenn ja (if so), wie heißt der Fluß, der See oder der Ozean? Ist der Fluß (der See, der Ozean) schön? sauber?

9. Sind da Berge? Wenn ja, wie heißen sie? Wenn nein, wo sind Berge?

10. Wie ist das Wetter da im Frühling? im Sommer? im Herbst? im Winter?

E. *Viele Millionen Leute sprechen andere Sprachen:*

Chinesisch (Mandarin)	771 Millionen	Bengalisch	165 Millionen
		Portugiesisch	161 Millionen
Englisch	415 Millionen	Malayisch	125 Millionen
Hindi	287 Millionen	Japanisch	121 Millionen
Spanisch	285 Millionen	Deutsch	118 Millionen
Russisch	280 Millionen	Französisch	112 Millionen
Arabisch	171 Millionen	Italienisch	63 Millionen

1. Was sprechen die Österreicher? Franzosen? Spanier? Italiener? Amerikaner? Kanadier? Chinesen? Russen? Japaner? Inder? Ägypter? Portugiesen? Australier?

2. Wie viele Menschen sprechen Englisch? Spanisch? Französisch? Italienisch? Deutsch? Russisch? Chinesisch? Japanisch?

3. Woher kommen viele Leute in New York und San Francisco? Welche Sprachen sprechen sie?

4. Welche Sprache oder Sprachen sprechen Sie? Ihre Eltern? Ihre Großeltern?

5. Welche Sprachen finden Sie wichtig (important)? Welche Sprachen finden Sie nicht so wichtig?

F. Was paßt? *(For each question or statement on the left, select one or several appropriate responses from the right column, or give your own.)*

___ 1. Wir haben heute eine Prüfung, nicht wahr?

___ 2. In Liechtenstein sprechen die Leute Französisch, nicht wahr?

___ 3. Wie heißt die Hauptstadt von Westdeutschland?

___ 4. Liegt Hamburg im Süden?

___ 5. Ich habe zwei Brüder und eine Schwester.

___ 6. Was sprechen Ihre Eltern?

___ 7. Auf Wiedersehen!

a. Nein, im Norden.
b. Ich weiß nicht.
c. Wirklich?
d. Tschüß!
e. Ja, in Deutsch.
f. Wie bitte?
g. Bonn.
h. Schade!
i. Nein, aber morgen.
j. Ich auch.
k. Französisch.
l. Nein, Deutsch.

G. Aussprache *(See also II. 1, 3–4, 11–13, 17, 19–20 in the pronunciation section of the Appendix.)*

1. [iː] **Ih**nen, l**ie**gen, w**ie**der, W**ie**n, Berl**i**n

2. [i] **i**ch b**i**n, b**i**tte, K**i**nd, r**i**chtig

3. [aː] Fr**a**ge, Spr**a**che, Amerik**a**ner, Sp**a**nier, V**a**ter

4. [a] St**a**dt, L**a**ndkarte, K**a**nada, S**a**tz, T**a**nte

5. [uː] g**u**t, Br**u**der, K**u**li, Min**u**te, d**u**

6. [u] **u**nd, St**u**nde, J**u**nge, M**u**tter, Fl**u**ß

7. Wortpaare

   a. still / Stil   *c.* Kamm / komm   *e.* Rum / Ruhm

   b. Stadt / Staat   *d.* Schiff / schief   *f.* Ratte / rate

STRUKTUR

I. *The Present Tense*

1. You are already familiar with some of the PERSONAL PRONOUNS; there are four others; **du**, **er**, **sie**, and **ihr**.

	singular	plural	singular/plural
1st person	ich	wir	
2nd person	**du**	**ihr**	Sie
3rd person	**er**, es, **sie**	sie	

I   *we*
you (familiar)   *you (familiar)*   *you (formal)*
he, it, she   *they*

- **du** *and* **ihr** *are intimate forms of address used with family members, close friends, children up to the age of fourteen, and animals.*
- **Sie**, *which is always capitalized, is used in all formal relationships and always when others are addressed with titles such as* **Herr, Frau, and Fräulein**. *It is used to address one or more persons.* **Sie** *(**you**) and* **sie** *(not capitalized) can be distinguished in conversation only through context:*

> BEISPIEL: Herr Schmidt, wo wohnen **Sie**? Und Ihre Eltern, wo wohnen **sie**?
> *Mr. Schmidt, where do you live? And your parents, where do they live?*

- *The pronouns* **sie** *(**she, it**) and* **sie** *(**they**) can be distinguished through the personal endings of the verb:*

> BEISPIEL: **Sie** kommt im Mai, und **sie** kommen im Juni.
> *She comes in May, and they come in June.*

2. Almost every German INFINITIVE ends in **-en: lernen, antworten**. The stem of the verb is the part that precedes the infinitive ending **-en**. Thus the stem of **lernen** is **lern-**, and that of **antworten** is **antwort-**.

English verbs have at most only one personal ending in the present tense, **-s**: *I (you, we, they) learn*, BUT *he (it, she) learns*. In German, endings are added to the verb stem for all persons.

> stem + personal ending = present tense verb form

German verb endings vary, depending on whether the subject is in the FIRST, SECOND or THIRD PERSON, and in the SINGULAR or PLURAL. The verb must agree with the subject. You have already learned the endings used for some persons. Here is the complete list:

	singular	plural	formal (sg./pl.)
1st person	ich lerne	wir lernen	
2nd person	du lernst	ihr lernt	Sie lernen
3rd person	er, es, sie lernt	sie lernen	

Note: Formal *you* (**Sie**) and the plural *they* (**sie**) are followed by identical verb forms. For that reason we won't repeat **Sie** in future chapters.

These familiar verbs follow the model of **lernen**. Be sure to review them carefully.

beginnen	*to begin*	sagen	*to say, tell*
brauchen	*to need*	schreiben	*to write*
fragen	*to ask*	spielen	*to play*
gehen	*to go*	verstehen	*to understand*
hören	*to hear*	wiederholen	*to repeat, review*
kommen	*to come*	wohnen	*to live, reside*
liegen	*to be (located)*	zählen	*to count*

3. When a verb stem ends in **-d** or **-t** (**antwort-**), or in certain consonant combinations (**öffn-, regn-**), an **-e** is inserted between the stem and the **-st** and **-t** endings to make these endings clearly audible:

	singular	plural	formal (sg./pl.)
1st person	ich antworte	wir antworten	
2nd person	du antwortest	ihr antwortet	Sie antworten
3rd person	er, es, sie antwortet	sie antworten	

These familiar verbs follow the model of **antworten**:

finden	*to find*
kosten	*to cost*
öffnen	*to open*

4. The **du**-form of verbs with a stem ending in any **s**-sound (**-s, -ss, -ß, -tz, -z**) adds only a **-t** instead of **-st**: **ich heiße, du heißt**. Thus, the **du**-form is identical with the **er**-form of these verbs: **du heißt, er heißt**.

5. German has only one verb form to express what English says with several forms:

er kommt { *he comes*
he is coming
he does come

6. Both languages frequently use present tense verb forms to express future time, particularly when a time expression clearly points to the future.

In dreißig Minuten **gehe** ich in die Stadt.	*I'm going downtown in thirty minutes.*
Er **kommt** im Sommer.	*He's coming in the summer.*

ÜBUNGEN *(EXERCISES)*

A. *Ersetzen Sie das Subjekt!* (Replace the subject. Use the words in parentheses. Be sure that the verb form agrees with the new subject.)

> BEISPIEL: Ich sage das noch einmal. (wir, Maria)
> **Wir sagen das noch einmal.**
> **Maria sagt das noch einmal.**

1. Wir antworten auf deutsch. (Roberto, du, ich, die Mutter)
2. Ich wiederhole die Frage. (er, wir, ihr, Sie)
3. Ihr lernt die Wörter. (ich, du, die Kinder, wir)
4. Du öffnest das Buch auf Seite 3. (der Franzose, ich, ihr, sie/*sg.*)
5. Heidi Bauer geht an die Tafel. (ihr, sie/*pl.*, ich, du)
6. Brauchst du Papier und Bleistifte? (wir, ich, Sie, ihr)
7. Wie finden Sie das? (ihr, du, Ihre Familie, die Leute)

B. *Kombinieren Sie!* (Create sentences by combining items from each column.)

> BEISPIEL: **Er kommt aus Kanada.**

1	2	3
ich	beginnen	auf deutsch
du	hören	auf englisch
er	kommen	aus . . .
es	kosten	(das) nicht
sie	regnen	heute
das	schreiben	in . . .
die Deutschvorlesung	spielen	jetzt
das Mädchen	wohnen	morgen
wir	zählen	(nicht) gut
ihr		Tennis
Sie		um . . .
sie		vier Mark
		von zehn bis zwanzig

C. *Was fehlt?* (What's missing? Fill in the missing forms of the verbs.)

> JENS Inge und Heidi, woher _____ ihr? (kommen)
> HEIDI Ich _____ aus Heidelberg. (kommen)
> INGE Und ich _____ aus Berlin. (sein)

JENS Wirklich? Meine Großmutter _____ auch aus Berlin. (kommen) Aber sie _____ jetzt in Hamburg. (wohnen) Wie _____ ihr es hier? (finden)

HEIDI Wir _____ es hier prima. (finden)

INGE Ich _____ die Berge wunderbar. (finden)

JENS Ich auch!

D. Auf deutsch, bitte!

1. We're learning German.
2. I'm counting slowly.
3. Where do you (pl. fam.) come from?
4. They come from Canada.
5. I'm from America.
6. Are you (sg. fam.) answering in English?
7. No, I'll speak German.
8. She's opening the book.
9. I do need the book.
10. What does she say?
11. Do you (sg. fam.) understand that (**das**)?
12. Is she repeating that (**das**)?

II. *The Nominative Case*

The nominative case has two functions: it is the case of the subject and of the predicate noun. (The latter is discussed in Section III. 2, p. 50.)

In the English sentence *The boy asks the father*, the SUBJECT of the sentence is *the boy*; he does the asking. We know that *the boy* is the subject from its position because in English the subject usually precedes the verb. This is not always true in German, where one frequently knows the function of a word or phrase from its form rather than from its position. In the sentence **Der Junge fragt den Vater**, the phrase **der Junge** tells us we are dealing with the subject, whereas **den Vater** tells us we are dealing with a direct object (more about this in Chapter 2). In dictionaries and vocabulary lists, nouns are given in the nominative. The nominative answers the questions *who?* for persons or *what?* for objects and ideas.

Der Junge fragt den Vater.	*The boy asks the father.*
Der See ist schön.	*The lake is beautiful.*

1. The nominative forms of the INTERROGATIVE PRONOUNS are **wer** *(who)* and **was** *(what)*:

	persons	things and ideas
nom.	wer?	was?

Wer fragt den Vater? **Der Junge.**	*Who is asking the father? The boy.*
Was ist schön? **Der See.**	*What is beautiful? The lake.*

2. The nominative forms of the DEFINITE ARTICLE *(the)* and the INDEFINITE ARTICLE *(a, an)* are already familiar. Note that the indefinite article does not distinguish between masculine and neuter nouns because it has no ending. It also has no plural *(I have a pencil,* BUT *I have pencils).*

		singular		plural	
	masc.	neut.	fem.		
nom.	der	das	die	die	*the*
	ein	ein	eine	—	*a, an*
	kein	kein	keine	keine	*no, not a*

The possessive adjectives **mein** *(my)* and **Ihr** *(your)* follow the pattern of **ein** and **kein**.

Der Vater, das Kind und die Mutter wohnen in Amerika. Die Großeltern wohnen in Deutschland. Ein Vater, ein Kind und eine Mutter sind da, aber keine Großeltern. Mein Vater und meine Mutter sprechen Deutsch. Sprechen Ihre Eltern auch Deutsch?

3. Nouns can be replaced by PERSONAL PRONOUNS. In English we replace persons with *he, she,* or *they,* and objects and ideas with *it* or *they.* In German the pronoun used depends on the gender of the noun. You already know the nominative forms of the third-person pronouns. Note how similar they are to the forms of the articles: **der** → **er; das** → **es; die** → **sie.**

der Vater =	**er**	*(he)*
das Kind =	**es**	*(it)*
die Mutter =	**sie**	*(she)*
die Eltern =	**sie**	*(they)*
der Stuhl =	**er**	*(it)*
das Buch =	**es**	*(it)*
die Tafel =	**sie**	*(it)*
die Kulis =	**sie**	*(they)*

Da ist **der Stuhl. Er** ist neu.	*There is the chair. It's new.*
Das Buch liegt hier. **Es** ist dick.	*The book is here. It's thick.*
Das Kind heißt Elke. **Es** ist fünf.	*The child's name is Elke. She's five.*
Wo ist **die Tafel?** Da ist **sie.**	*Where is the board? There it is.*
Die Kulis kosten 2,00 DM. **Sie** sind blau.	*The pens cost 2 marks. They're blue.*
Da sind **die Eltern. Sie** sind aus Zürich.	*There are the parents. They're from Zurich.*

Note that German uses three pronouns (**er, es, sie**) when dealing with objects where English uses only one *(it).*

ÜBUNGEN

E. Ersetzen Sie die Wörter mit Pronomen! *(Replace the nouns with pronouns.)*

BEISPIELE: Fritz   **er**
           die Landkarte   **sie**

der Vater, der Berg, das Land, die Großmutter, der Junge, die Stadt, der Bleistift, der Pullover, Österreich, der Österreicher, die Schweiz, die Schweizerin, Deutschland, das Kind

F. Antworten Sie!

1. Was ist das? *(Form a sentence using the appropriate form of* **ein***.)*

BEISPIEL: Frankfurt / Stadt   **Frankfurt ist eine Stadt.**

Österreich / Land; die Donau / Fluß; Italienisch / Sprache; Berlin / Stadt; der Main / Fluß; das Matterhorn / Berg; Französisch / Sprache; Kanada / Land; der Bodensee / See; Bremen / Stadt

2. Ist das richtig? *(Answer with* **no***, using the appropriate form of* **kein***. Then supply the answer.)*

BEISPIEL: Ist die Donau ein Land?   **Nein, die Donau ist kein Land.**
                                   Die Donau ist ein Fluß.

Ist Frankfurt ein Fluß? Frankreich eine Sprache? Heidelberg ein Berg? der Rhein eine Stadt? die Schweiz ein See? Spanien eine Sprache? Vaduz ein Land?

3. Woher kommen sie? *(Use the appropriate form of* **mein** *in your answer.)*

BEISPIEL: Woher kommt Ihr Vater?   **Mein Vater kommt aus Salzburg.**

Woher kommt Ihr Vater oder Ihr Stiefvater *(stepfather)*? Ihre Mutter oder Ihre Stiefmutter *(stepmother)*? Ihr Großvater? Ihre Großmutter? Ihr Urgroßvater *(great-grandfather)* oder Ihre Urgroßmutter *(great-grandmother)*?

G. Ersetzen Sie das Subjekt! *(Replace the subject with a pronoun.)*

1. Antworten Sie mit ja!

BEISPIEL: Die Eltern fragen auf deutsch, nicht wahr?
           Ja, sie fragen auf deutsch.

a. Der Sohn antwortet auf englisch, nicht wahr?
b. Die Tochter versteht Deutsch, nicht wahr?
c. Das Kind ist fünf Jahre alt, nicht wahr?
d. Ihre Familie kommt aus Dresden, nicht wahr?
e. Ihr Großvater wohnt da, nicht wahr?
f. Dresden liegt an der *(on the)* Elbe, nicht wahr?
g. Die Elbe ist lang, nicht wahr?
h. Das Land ist schön, nicht wahr?

2. *Antworten Sie bitte! (Answer appropriately to your situation using pro-nouns.)*

BEISPIEL: Wann beginnt Ihr Tag?   **Er beginnt morgens um sechs.**

a. Wann beginnt die Deutsch-vorlesung?
b. Ist das Vorlesungszimmer groß?
c. Wie heißt Ihr Deutschbuch?
d. Ist Ihr Kuli schwarz?
e. Welche Farbe hat Ihr Heft?
f. Welche Farbe hat Ihre Jacke?
g. Wo sind Ihre Schuhe?
h. Wo ist das Fenster?
i. Wie ist das Fenster?
j. Wie viele Monate hat das Jahr?
k. Wie viele Wochen hat der Monat?
l. Wie viele Tage hat die Woche?
m. Wie viele Stunden hat der Tag?
n. Wie viele Minuten hat die Stunde?

III. *Sentence Structure*

You have already learned a good deal about German sentence structure, especially the position of the verb (see "Rückblick: Schritte"). To this topic we will return regularly. Here are two more points to remember.

1. There are two points of contrast between German and English usage of which you must be aware. In English the subject usually precedes the verb, and more than one element may do so.

They *speak Italian.*
There **they** *speak Italian.*

In the second sentence, both *there* and *they* are sentence elements.

In German, however, only one sentence element may precede the verb, and this element is not necessarily the subject. If another element precedes the verb, the subject then follows the verb.

Sie sprechen Italienisch.
Da sprechen **sie** Italienisch.

2. The verbs **sein** *(to be)* and **heißen** *(to be called)* are LINKING VERBS. They normally link two words referring to the same person or thing, both of which are in the nominative: the first is the subject, the other a PREDICATE NOUN.

subject   predicate noun

Der Herr **ist**   Schweizer.
    Er **heißt** Stefan Wolf.

The verb **sein** can be complemented not only by a predicate noun, but also by a PREDICATE ADJECTIVE. Both are considered part of the verb phrase (i.e., the complete verb). This is the first example of a typical and important feature of German sentence structure: when the verb consists of more than one part, the inflected part (V1) is the second element in the sentence, and the uninflected part (V2) stands at the very end of the sentence.

$$\begin{array}{cc} \text{V1} & \text{V2} \end{array}$$

Stefan Wolf **ist** auch   **Ausländer.**

Er **ist** heute sehr **müde.**

▶ *REMEMBER: In German no indefinite article is used before nationalities:* **Er ist Österreicher** *(an Austrian).*

ÜBUNGEN

H. Sagen Sie es anders! *(Say it differently. Begin the sentence with the boldface sentence element.)*

BEISPIEL: Mein Bruder kommt **morgen.**   *Morgen kommt mein Bruder.*

1. Es geht **mir** gut.
2. Ich bin nicht **müde.**
3. Der Bleistift ist **da.**
4. Wir lesen **für morgen** das Gespräch.
5. Die Hose ist auch **zu groß.**
6. Das kostet **zusammen** 12,60 DM.
7. Es ist **heute** 27°C.
8. Es ist **schön** heute!
9. Die Sonne scheint **jetzt** wieder.
10. Es regnet oft **im April.**
11. Es schneit aber **im Winter** nicht.
12. Sie finden die Wörter **auf Seite 50.**
13. Ich habe **morgen** keine Zeit.
14. Rita hat **in zehn Minuten** Philosophie.
15. Wir spielen **um halb drei** Tennis.
16. Die Leute sprechen **hier** nur Deutsch.

I. Was sind sie?

BEISPIEL: Pierre kommt aus Frankreich.   **Er ist Franzose.**

1. Mitzi kommt aus Österreich.
2. Roberto kommt aus Italien.
3. Sam kommt aus Amerika.
4. Carla kommt aus Spanien.
5. James kommt aus England.
6. Helen kommt aus Kanada.
7. Maria und Caroline kommen aus Amerika.
8. Marie und Simone kommen aus Frankreich.
9. Eva und Franz kommen aus Österreich.

IV. *Compound Nouns*

German typically uses many compound nouns that consist of two or more nouns, a verb and a noun, or an adjective and a noun. The last component determines the gender and the plural form:

das Land + **die** Karte = **die** Landkarte, -n
der Winter + **der** Mantel = **der** Wintermantel, ⸚
der Arm + das Band + **die** Uhr = **die** Armbanduhr, -en

schreiben + **der** Tisch = **der** Schreibtisch, -e
wohnen + **das** Zimmer = **das** Wohnzimmer, -

groß + **die** Mutter = **die** Großmutter, ⸚
klein + **die** Stadt = **die** Kleinstadt, ⸚e

ÜBUNG

J. *Was bedeuten die Wörter? Was sind die Artikel?* *(What is the meaning of these words? What must their gender be?)*

BEISPIEL: Kleinkind   **little child, toddler; das**

Wochentag, Abendkleid, Morgenmantel, Altstadt, Großstadtkind, Neujahr, Lesebuch, Sprechübung, Bergsee, Familienvater, Sommerbluse, Zimmertür, Jungenname, Frühlingswetter, Wanduhr, Deutschstunde, Uhrzeit

ZUSAMMENFASSUNG

These sentences include what you have learned in this chapter and in the "Schritte." Watch particularly for points of contrast between English and German patterns.

K. *Auf deutsch, bitte!*

1. Tomorrow my parents will come. *2.* My father is (a) French(man), and my mother is (an) Austrian. *3.* In France they (the people) speak French, and in Austria they speak German. *4.* France is west of Germany, and Austria is south of Germany. *5.* I do understand French and German, but I answer in English. *6.* Where are you *(fam.)* from? *7.* I'm from Texas. *8.* There's Thomas. Thomas is (an) American. *9.* He's learning Spanish. *10.* I think it's beautiful here. *11.* But I am very tired.

The division of Germany and Europe into East and West is the result of World War II and the ensuing cold war. As the confrontation between the United States and Russia intensified, the chances for a reunited Germany diminished. Two states emerged, integrated politically, economically, and militarily into opposite power blocks. As West Germany (the FRG) does not consider East Germany (the GDR) a foreign country, goods from the GDR enter the FRG duty-free. This, ironically,

gives the GDR de facto access to the increasingly important market of the European Economic Community (**Europäische Wirtschaftsgemeinschaft = EWG**). Efforts to go beyond an economic union of Europe continue. A European Parliament, albeit with limited powers, already meets regularly in Strasbourg.

EINBLICKE

(INSIGHTS)

This reading text expands on the chapter topic. All vocabulary that is to become active is listed under "Wortschatz 2." Learn these words well; they will recur in grammar exercises of future chapters.

der Mensch, -en	*human being, person (pl. people)*
Nachbar, -n	*neighbor*
Teil, -e	*part*
die Bundesrepublik (BRD)	*Federal Republic of Germany (FRG)*
Deutsche Demokratische Republik (DDR)	*German Democratic Republic (GDR)*
ungefähr	*about, approximately*
so . . . wie . . .	*as . . . as . . .*
wichtig	*important*

Each reading selection is introduced by a short set of cognates and compounds that you should be able to recognize but do not have to master actively. This section can increase your recognition skills and passive vocabulary considerably.

WAS IST DAS? der Europäer; (das) Europa, Mitteleuropa; Dänisch, Finnisch, Griechisch, Holländisch, Norwegisch, Polnisch, Portugiesisch, Russisch, Tschechisch, Schwedisch

Oregon	Ohio	Maine	Maine
die BRD	die DDR	die Schweiz	Österreich

Die BRD ist ungefähr so groß wie Oregon.

Die DDR ist ungefähr so groß wie Ohio.

Die Schweiz ist ungefähr halb so groß wie Maine.

Österreich ist fast so groß wie Maine.

Sprachen sind wichtig.

Deutschland liegt in Mitteleuropa. Es hat zwei Teile: Westdeutschland (die Bundesrepublik oder die BRD) und Ostdeutschland (die Deutsche Demokratische Republik oder die DDR). Die Bundesrepublik ist ungefähr so groß wie Oregon. 5
Da wohnen 60 Millionen Menschen, aber in Oregon nur 2,4 (zwei Komma vier) Millionen. Die Deutsche Demokratische Republik ist ungefähr so groß wie Ohio. Da wohnen 17 Millionen Menschen, aber in Ohio nur 11 Millionen. Die Hauptstadt von Westdeutschland heißt Bonn. Bonn liegt am°
Rhein. Die Hauptstadt von Ostdeutschland heißt (Ost-)Berlin. 10

on the

Österreich, mit° etwa° 7,5 Millionen Menschen, ist fast° so groß wie Maine. Die Schweiz, mit ungefähr 6 Millionen Menschen, ist ungefähr halb so groß wie Maine. Aber in Maine wohnen nur etwa 1 Million Menschen. Liechtenstein ist nur ungefähr so groß wie Washington, D.C. Es ist sehr klein. In Liechtenstein wohnen etwa 24,000 Menschen, aber in Washington, 15 D.C., 27 mal so viel°. Die Schweiz, Liechtenstein und Österreich liegen südlich von Deutschland. Die Hauptstädte von Österreich und von der° Schweiz sind Wien und Bern. Die Hauptstadt von Liechtenstein heißt Vaduz.

In Deutschland, Österreich, Liechtenstein und in einem Teil der° 20 Schweiz sprechen die Leute Deutsch. Aber° in Europa gibt es° viele Länder und viele Sprachen. Im Norden sprechen die Leute Dänisch, Schwedisch, Norwegisch und Finnisch, im Osten Polnisch, Tschechisch und Russisch, im Westen Holländisch, Französisch und Englisch, und im Süden Griechisch, Italienisch, Spanisch und Portugiesisch. Viele Europäer 25 sprechen zwei oder drei Sprachen. Sprachen sind wichtig in Europa. Europa braucht sie für eine gute Nachbarschaft°. Gute Nachbarn sind wichtig.

times as many
of (the)

of (the)
but/ there are

neighborly relations

ZUM TEXT

A. Richtig oder falsch?

___ 1. Deutschland liegt in Osteuropa.
___ 2. Deutschland hat zwei Teile: die BRD und die DDR.
___ 3. Die Hauptstadt von Ostdeutschland heißt Bonn.
___ 4. Die Schweiz ist ungefähr halb so groß wie Maine.
___ 5. Die Hauptstadt von Österreich heißt Bern.
___ 6. Nur in Deutschland sprechen die Menschen Deutsch.
___ 7. Viele Europäer sprechen zwei oder drei Sprachen.

B. Was fehlt? *(Fill in each blank with the proper form of one of the verbs given. Each verb is used at least once.)*

finden, haben, heißen, lernen, liegen, sein, sprechen, wohnen

1. Deutschland _____ zwei Teile. *2.* Die Länder _____ zwei verschiedene *(different)* Namen. *3.* Die Bundesrepublik _____ auch die BRD. *4.* Da _____ viele Menschen. *5.* Die DDR _____ im Osten. *6.* Sie _____ ungefähr so groß wie Ohio. *7.* Viele Europäer _____ zwei oder drei Sprachen. *8.* _____ Sprachen hier auch wichtig? *9.* _____ wir hier viele Sprachen? *10.* Welche Sprache _____ ihr? *11.* Wir _____ Deutsch. *12.* Ich _____ Deutsch schön.

C. Wie viele Menschen wohnen wo?

___	1. Schweiz	a.	7,5 Millionen
___	2. Bundesrepublik	b.	1 Million
___	3. Liechtenstein	c.	60 Millionen
___	4. Österreich	d.	11 Millionen
___	5. Deutsche Demokratische Republik	e.	648,000
___	6. Oregon	f.	6 Millionen
___	7. Ohio	g.	2,4 Millionen
___	8. Maine	h.	24,000
___	9. Washington, D.C.	i.	17 Millionen

D. Sehen Sie auf die Landkarte von Europa! *(See back of book. With a partner, work out the answers to the questions below. Take turns.)*

1. Wie viele Nachbarn hat Deutschland? Wie heißen sie?
2. Wo liegt Dänemark? Belgien? Spanien? Frankreich? Italien? die Tschechoslowakei? Schweden?
3. Wie heißt die Hauptstadt von Dänemark? Belgien? Frankreich? Spanien? Italien? Jugoslawien? Finnland? Norwegen? Schweden? England? Polen?
4. Welche Sprache sprechen die Leute wo?

BEISPIEL: **In Frankreich sprechen die Leute Französisch.**

E. Sehen Sie auf die Landkarten von Deutschland, Österreich und von der Schweiz, und antworten Sie! *(See front of book.)*

1. Welche Städte haben wir in Österreich? in der Schweiz? in der DDR?
2. Welche Städte liegen im Norden (im Westen, im Süden, im Osten) von Westdeutschland?
3. Welche Flüsse (Seen und Berge) gibt es in Westdeutschland? in Ostdeutschland? in Österreich? in der Schweiz?
4. Wo liegt die Nordsee? die Ostsee? der Bodensee? der Genfer See?

F. Was sind sie? *(Match the people with the country according to the pattern. Nationalities marked with an asterisk drop the -e before adding the feminine ending -in: Pole, Polin.)*

BEISPIEL: Herr und Frau Watzlik sind aus Warschau.
   Er ist Warschauer, sie ist Warschauerin.
   Er ist Pole, sie ist Polin.

1. Joan und Mike sind aus London.	Däne*
2. Ivan und Tatjana sind aus Moskau.	Engländer
3. Oskar und Irene sind aus Salzburg.	Grieche*
4. Zorba und Sophia sind aus Athen.	Österreicher
5. Sven und Ingrid sind aus Stockholm.	Russe*
6. Peter und Anneli sind aus Zürich.	Schwede*
7. Tile und Ulla sind aus Kopenhagen.	Schweizer

GESPRÄCHE

Im
Lebensmittel-
geschäft[1]

VERKÄUFER Guten Tag! Was darf's sein?
HERR SCHÄFER Ich brauche etwas Obst. Haben Sie keine Bananen?
VERKÄUFER Doch, hier!
HERR SCHÄFER Was kosten sie?
VERKÄUFER 1,80 DM das Pfund.
HERR SCHÄFER Und die Orangen?
VERKÄUFER 60 Pfennig das Stück.
HERR SCHÄFER Gut, dann nehme ich zwei Pfund Bananen und sechs Orangen.
VERKÄUFER Sonst noch etwas?
HERR SCHÄFER Ja, zwei Kilo[2] Äpfel.
VERKÄUFER 14,20 DM bitte! Danke schön! Auf Wiedersehen!

In der
Bäckerei

VERKÄUFERIN Guten Morgen! Was darf's sein?
FRAU MEYER Ich möchte sechs Brötchen. Ist der Apfelstrudel frisch?
VERKÄUFERIN Natürlich.
FRAU MEYER Gut, dann nehme ich vier Stück.
VERKÄUFERIN Es gibt heute auch Schwarzbrot[3] im Sonderangebot.
FRAU MEYER Nein, danke. Aber was für Plätzchen haben Sie?
VERKÄUFERIN Butterplätzchen, Schokoladenplätzchen . . .
FRAU MEYER Ach, ich nehme 300 Gramm[2] Schokoladenplätzchen.
VERKÄUFERIN Sonst noch etwas?
FRAU MEYER Nein, danke. Das ist alles.
VERKÄUFERIN 13,50 DM bitte!

ÜBRIGENS

1. In Germany, Switzerland, and Austria small specialty shops are still very common. Many housewives, particularly in small towns, shop almost daily, going from the butcher to the bakery, then to the grocery store and the fish market.

2. Everywhere in Europe the metric system is used to measure distances and weights. A shopper may ask for various weights: **100 Gramm Leberwurst, ein Pfund Kaffee,** or **ein Kilo (2 Pfund) Äpfel.**

German:
    1 g = 1 **Gramm**
    125 g = 1 **Viertelpfund**
    250 g = 1 **halbes Pfund**
    500 g = 1 **Pfund**
    1000 g = 1 **Kilo(gramm)**

U.S.: 1 oz. = 28.3 g
1 lb. = 454 g

3. When Germans think of **Brot**, they probably think first of a firm, heavy loaf of rye bread, and not of the soft white bread so common in America. White loaves and rolls are prized for their crisp crust. There are over two hundred varieties of bread available in Central Europe. For Germans, bread is the most important food—on the average, they eat four slices of bread and one roll a day. There are approximately 40,000 bakeries in the Federal Republic, and they supply about 80 percent of the baked goods consumed.

At the Grocery Store

CLERK Good morning. May I help you?
MR. SCHÄFER I'd like some fruit. Don't you have any bananas?
CLERK Certainly. Here they are.
MR. SCHÄFER How much are they?
CLERK 1 mark 80 a pound.
MR. SCHÄFER And the oranges?
CLERK 60 pfennig each.
MR. SCHÄFER Fine, then I'll take two pounds of bananas and six oranges.
CLERK Anything else?
MR. SCHÄFER Yes, 2 kilos of apples.
CLERK 14 marks 20, please. Thank you very much. Goodbye.

In the Bakery

CLERK Good morning. May I help you?
MRS. MEYER I'd like six rolls. Is the apple strudel fresh?
CLERK Of course.
MRS. MEYER Fine. Then I'll take four pieces.
CLERK Today there's also a special on rye bread.
MRS. MEYER No, thank you. But what kind of cookies do you have?
CLERK Butter cookies, chocolate cookies . . .
MRS. MEYER Oh, I'll take 300 grams of chocolate cookies.
CLERK Anything else?
MRS. MEYER No, thank you. That's all.
CLERK 13 marks 50, please.

Lebensmittel und Geschäfte   WORTSCHATZ I

DIE LEBENSMITTEL *(pl.) groceries*

der Apfel, ¨	apple	*die* Banane, -n	banana
Fisch, -e	fish	Bohne, -n	bean
Kaffee	coffee	Butter	butter
Käse	cheese	Cola	coke
Kuchen, -	cake	Erbse, -n	pea
Saft, ¨e	juice	Erdbeere, -n	strawberry
Salat, -e	lettuce, salad	Gurke, -n	cucumber
Tee	tea	Karotte, -n	carrot
Wein, -e	wine	Limonade, -n	soft drink,
das Bier	beer		lemonade
Brot, -e	bread	Marmelade, -n	marmalade,
Brötchen, -	roll		jam
Ei, -er	egg	Milch	milk
Fleisch	meat	Orange, -n	orange
Gemüse, -	vegetable(s)	Tomate, -n	tomato
Obst	fruit	Wurst, ¨e	sausage
Plätzchen, -	cookie	Zitrone, -n	lemon
Wasser	water		

WEITERES

der (Super)markt, ¨e	(super)market
das Geschäft, -e	store
Kaufhaus, ¨er	department store
die Bäckerei, -en	bakery
das Pfund; vier Pfund[1] . . .	pound; four pounds of . . .
das Stück, -e; vier Stück[1] . . .	piece; four pieces of . . .
doch	yes, sure, certainly, of course (see p. 70)
es gibt[2]	there is, there are

1 One says **ein Pfund Fleisch, zwei Pfund Fleisch; ein Stück Kuchen, zwei Stück Kuchen.** Remember also **eine Mark, zwei Mark.**
2 See Struktur II, 1 d.

etwas . . .	*a little, some . . . (used with sg.* *collective nouns)*
frisch	*fresh*
gern	*gladly*
Ich esse (trinke) gern . . .	*I like to eat (drink) . . .*
Ich möchte . . .	*I would like (to have) . . .*
kaufen / verkaufen	*to buy / sell*
machen	*to make, do*
natürlich	*of course*
was für (ein)?[3]	*what kind of (a)?*

3 Treat this phrase as you would treat **ein** by itself: **Das ist ein Kuchen. Was für ein Kuchen? Das ist eine Wurst. Was für eine Wurst?** There's no **ein** in the plural: **Das sind Plätzchen. Was für Plätzchen?**

PASSIVES VOKABULAR   der Apfelstrudel, -; sonst noch etwas? *(anything else?)*; das Kilo / vier Kilo; Was darf's sein? *(May I help you?)*; im Sonderangebot *(on sale, special)*

ZUM THEMA

A. Mustersätze

1. Bananen: **Ich esse gern** Bananen.
   Äpfel, Erdbeeren, Orangen, Gurken, Plätzchen
2. Fisch: **Die Kinder essen nicht gern** Fisch.
   Salat, Tomaten, Karotten, Gemüse, Eier
3. Cola: **Wir trinken gern** Cola.
   Limonade, Kaffee, Tee, Bier, Wein
4. Obst: **Ich brauche etwas** Obst.
   Brot, Fleisch, Marmelade, Käse, Wurst
5. Bananen: **Haben Sie keine** Bananen?
   Erdbeeren, Bohnen, Erbsen, Zitronen, Brötchen

B. Was paßt nicht? *(What doesn't fit?)*

1. die Butter—der Käse—die Wurst—die Bohne
2. das Brötchen—die Zitrone—das Plätzchen—der Kuchen
3. der Saft—das Bier—die Milch—das Wasser
4. die Limonade—die Cola—das Wasser—der Kaffee
5. die Tomate—die Erdbeere—die Gurke—der Salat
6. das Gemüse—der Apfel—die Orange—die Banane
7. das Obst—das Gemüse—der Salat—der Tee
8. der Wein—das Bier—die Zitrone—die Milch
9. das Geschäft—die Lebensmittel—die Bäckerei—das Kaufhaus
10. essen—trinken—gern—kaufen

C. Was bedeuten (mean) die Wörter, und was sind die Artikel?

Bohnensalat, Buttermilch, Delikatessengeschäft, Erdbeermarmelade, Fischbrötchen, Kaffeemilch, Käsestück, Milchkaffee, Obstsalat, Orangenlimonade, Schreibwarengeschäft, Teewasser, Weißwein, Wurstbrot, Zitronensaft

D. Und Sie? *(Write six to eight sentences about your food likes and dislikes and eating habits. Use the questions as a guide.)*

1. Was für Obst essen Sie (nicht) gern?
2. Was für Gemüse essen Sie (nicht) gern?
3. Was für Kuchen, Plätzchen, Salat essen Sie gern?
4. Was trinken Sie (nicht) gern?
5. Was essen Sie morgens, mittags, abends?

E. Im Lebensmittelgeschäft. Was sagen Sie?

X Guten Tag! Was darf's sein?

Y Ich brauche _____ und _____ . Was kosten/kostet _____ ?

X _____ .

Y Und was kosten/kostet _____ ?

X _____ .

Y Gut, dann nehme ich _____ und _____ .

X Sonst noch etwas?

Y _____ .

X _____ DM, bitte!

F. Was paßt?

____ 1. Der Fisch ist nicht frisch.

____ 2. Möchten Sie etwas Obst?

____ 3. Die Bäckerei verkauft Wurst, nicht wahr?

____ 4. Wir kaufen auch Kuchen.

____ 5. Ich trinke morgens gern Cola.

a. Wirklich?
b. Wie bitte?
c. Ich nicht.
d. Ja, gern.
e. Ja, bitte.
f. Natürlich nicht.
g. Prima!
h. Wir auch.
i. Richtig.
j. Nein, danke.
k. Doch.

G. *Aussprache* (See also II. 2, 5, 14–16, 18, and 21 in the pronunciation section of the Appendix.)

1. [e:] **geh**en, **Kä**se, **Mä**dchen, Apoth**e**ke, Am**e**rika, **neh**men, **Tee**, **See**
2. [ə] **es**, **et**was, spr**e**chen, M**e**nsch, Gesch**ä**ft, **e**ssen, **He**md
3. [o:] **oh**ne, **o**der, **O**bst, w**oh**nen, Br**o**t, **Boh**ne, M**o**ntag, s**o**
4. [o] **O**sten, k**o**mmen, N**o**rden, Kar**o**tte, d**o**ch, S**o**nne
5. Wortpaare
   a. *gate* / geht
   b. den / denn
   c. zähle / Zelle
   d. *shown* / schon
   e. Ofen / offen
   f. Bonn / Bann

STRUKTUR

I. *The Present Tense of* sein *(to be)* and haben *(to have)*

You are already familiar with some of the forms of these two IRREGULAR VERBS. They are both very important, since they are often used as auxiliary or helping verbs. Be sure to memorize the forms.

	sein		haben	
1st person	ich bin	wir sind	ich habe	wir haben
2nd person	du bist	ihr seid	du hast	ihr habt
3rd person	er ist	sie sind	er hat	sie haben

ÜBUNGEN

A. Ersetzen Sie das Subjekt!

BEISPIEL: Haben Sie Zeit? (du, ihr) **Hast du Zeit?**
Habt ihr Zeit?

1. Ich bin fertig. (er, wir, sie/*sg.*)
2. Sind Sie müde? (du, ihr, sie/*pl.*)
3. Sie hat die Landkarte. (ich, er, wir)
4. Haben Sie Papier? (sie/*sg.*, ihr, du)
5. Wir sind Amerikaner. (er, sie/*pl.*, ich)
6. Er hat eine Frage. (ich, wir, Sie)
7. Seid ihr aus Wien? (Sie, du, sie/*sg.*)
8. Er hat Bier. (sie/*pl.*, ich, ihr)

II. *The Accusative Case*

The accusative case has two major functions: it is the case of the direct object and it follows certain prepositions.

1. In the English sentence *The boy asks the father,* the DIRECT OBJECT of the sentence is *the father.* He is being asked; he is the target of the verb's action. One determines what the direct object is by asking *who* or *what* is directly affected by the verb's action. In other words, the person you see, hear, or ask, or the thing you have, buy, or eat is the direct object.

Der Junge fragt **den Vater.**   *The boy asks the father.*
   Ich kaufe **den Kuchen.**   *I buy the cake.*

a. The accusative forms of the INTERROGATIVE PRONOUN are **wen** *(whom)* and **was** *(what).* You now know two cases for this pronoun.

	persons	things and ideas
nom.	wer?	was?
acc.	wen?	was?

Wen fragt der Junge? **Den Vater.**   *Whom does the boy ask? The father.*
Was kaufe ich? **Den Kuchen.**   *What do I buy? The cake.*

b. Only the ARTICLES for masculine nouns have special forms for the accusative. In the other genders the nominative and accusative are identical in form.

	singular			plural
	masc.	neut.	fem.	
nom.	der	das	die	die
	ein	ein	eine	—
	kein	kein	keine	keine
acc.	den	das	die	die
	einen	ein	eine	—
	keinen	kein	keine	keine

   PETER Der Käse, das Obst, die Wurst und die Brötchen sind frisch.
   PETRA Dann kaufe ich den Käse, das Obst, die Wurst und die Brötchen.
   PETER Aber wir brauchen keinen Käse, kein Obst, keine Wurst und keine Brötchen.

The POSSESSIVE ADJECTIVES **mein** and **Ihr** follow the pattern of **ein** and **kein:**

Brauchen Sie meinen Bleistift? Nein danke, ich brauche Ihren Bleistift nicht.

c. German has a few masculine nouns that have an **-n** or **-en** ending in all cases (singular and plural) except in the nominative singular. They are called N-NOUNS. Note how they are listed in vocabularies and dictionaries: the first ending refers to the singular for cases other than the nominative, the second one to the plural. You are already familiar with four such nouns and the fifth one will be used in the reading text of this chapter.

der **Herr, -n, -en**	*gentleman*
Junge, -n, -n	*boy*
Mensch, -en, -en	*human being, person*
Nachbar, -n, -n	*neighbor*
Student, -en, -en	*student*

	singular	plural
nom.	der Student	die Studenten
acc.	den Studenten	die Studenten

Der Herr heißt Müller. Fragen Sie Herr**n** Müller!
Da kommt ein Student. Fragen Sie den Student**en**!

d. Verbs that can take accusative objects are called TRANSITIVE. (Not all verbs can take direct objects: for example **gehen**, *to go*). Here are some familiar transitive verbs. Be sure to review them.

brauchen	*to need*	machen	*to make, do*
es gibt	*there is,*	möcht-	*would like*
	there are,	nehmen	*to take*
essen	*to eat*	öffnen	*to open*
finden	*to find*	sagen	*to say*
fragen	*to ask*	schreiben	*to write*
haben	*to have*	sprechen	*to speak, talk*
hören	*to hear*	trinken	*to drink*
kaufen	*to buy*	verkaufen	*to sell*
lernen	*to learn*	verstehen	*to understand*
lesen	*to read*		

Sie kauft den Rock und die Bluse.
Schreiben Sie den Satz!
Ich esse einen Apfel und eine Banane.
Wir haben einen Supermarkt und ein Kaufhaus.
Das Geschäft verkauft keinen Wein und kein Bier.

▪ **es gibt** *is an idiom that is always followed by the accusative case (***sg.*** or* ***pl.****).*

Es gibt hier einen Markt.   *There's a market here.*
Es gibt auch Lebensmittelgeschäfte.   *There are also grocery stores.*

es *is the subject of the sentence, and what there is, is in the accusative.*
es gibt *implies a general, unspecified existence, unlike* **Hier** (**da**) **ist**, *which points to a specific item.*

Gibt es hier einen Markt?   *Is there a market here (in town)?*
Ja, **es gibt** einen Markt.   *Yes, there's a market.*

Wo ist ein Markt?   *Where is a market?*
Da ist ein Markt.   *There's a market. (There it is.)*

▪ **möcht-** *is a special verb form that will be explained later. For the time being, we will use only* **ich möchte** *and* **Sie möchten.**

Möchten Sie keinen Kaffee?   *Wouldn't you like (to have) some coffee?*
Nein, ich möchte Tee.   *No, I'd like (to have) some tea.*

2. ACCUSATIVE PREPOSITIONS are always followed by the accusative case:

durch	*through*
für	*for*
gegen	*against*
ohne	*without*
um	*around (the circumference)*

☞ *CAUTION:*

▶ **Sie geht um den Tisch** (*around the table*), BUT **um zwölf** (*at twelve o'clock*). In this time expression, **um** *does not mean* ***around!***

Sie geht durch das Kaufhaus. Für den Vater möchte sie einen Pullover, für das Kind ein Bilderbuch, für die Mutter eine Jacke und für die Großmutter Saft.

▪ *Some prepositions may be contracted with the definite article. These forms are especially common in everyday speech.*

durch + das = **durchs** / für + das = **fürs** / um + das = **ums**

Sie geht durchs Lebensmittelgeschäft.

▪ *Note that a sentence can contain two accusatives, one the direct object and the other the object of a preposition:* **Sie kauft Tomaten für den Salat.**

ÜBUNGEN

B. *Wiederholen Sie die Sätze noch einmal mit* **ein** *und* **kein!**

> BEISPIEL: Er kauft den Bleistift, das Buch und die Landkarte.
> **Er kauft einen Bleistift, ein Buch und eine Landkarte.**
> **Er kauft keinen Bleistift, kein Buch und keine Landkarte.**

1. Sie möchte den Rock, das Kleid und die Bluse.
2. Du brauchst das Hemd, die Hose und den Pullover.
3. Ich esse das Brötchen, die Orange und den Apfel.

C. Ersetzen Sie das Akkusativobjekt!

BEISPIEL: Wir kaufen den Saft. (Salat, Kuchen)
Wir kaufen den Salat.
Wir kaufen den Kuchen.

1. Hast du den Tee? (Saft, Wein, Käse)
2. Ich nehme das Fleisch. (Gemüse, Obst, Schwarzbrot)
3. Die Wurst essen wir. (Marmelade, Tomate, Gurke)
4. Gibt es hier eine Bäckerei? (Markt, Delikatessengeschäft, Kaufhäuser)
5. Fragen Sie den Herrn! (Junge, Mensch, Nachbar, Student, Studenten/pl.)
6. Sie findet keinen Salat. (Fleisch, Fisch, Erbsen)
7. Ich trinke kein Wasser. (Kaffee, Bier, Limonade)
8. Meinen Vater verstehe ich nicht. (Großmutter, Bruder, Nachbar)

D. Präpositionen und Objekte *(Combine each preposition in group 1 with a noun from group 2.)*

BEISPIEL: durch / Zimmer   **durch das Zimmer**

1: durch, für, gegen, ohne, um
2: Bild, Bleistift, Buch, Fenster, Satz, Tafel, Tisch, Tür, Wand, Zimmer, Berge, Fluß, Land, See, Stadt, Wetter, Bruder, Fräulein, Großmutter, Herr, Herren, Junge, Student

E. Sagen Sie es noch einmal! *(Replace the noun following the preposition with another noun.)*

BEISPIEL: Ich möchte etwas für meinen Vater. (Mutter, Kind)
Ich möchte etwas für meine Mutter.
Ich möchte etwas für mein Kind.

1. Wir gehen durch die Geschäfte. (Supermarkt, Kaufhaus, Bäckerei)
2. Er kommt ohne das Bier. (Wein, Cola, Kaffee, Käsebrot, Salat)
3. Was haben Sie gegen den Herrn? (Frau, Mädchen, Junge, Nachbarin, Kinder)
4. Wiederholen Sie das für Ihren Großvater! (Bruder, Schwester, Nachbar, Eltern)

F. Kombinieren Sie! *(Form questions by combining items from each column. Add to the list in column 2.)*

BEISPIEL: **Was für einen Pullover kauft sie?**

1	2	3	4
was für ein	Rock	kaufen	du
	Hemd	brauchen	sie
	Jacke	möchten	ihr
	Schuhe		Sie
	...?...		

G. Was kaufen Sie? *(Answer each question with four to six items, drawing on all the vocabulary you have had so far. Use articles whenever possible.)*

BEISPIEL: Sie sind im Supermarkt. Was kaufen Sie?
Ich kaufe einen Kuchen, eine Cola, ein Pfund Butter, ein Stück Käse, etwas Obst . . .

1. Sie sind in der Bäckerei. Was kaufen Sie?
2. Sie sind im Lebensmittelgeschäft. Was kaufen Sie?
3. Sie sind im Kaufhaus. Was kaufen Sie?
4. Sie sind im Schreibwarengeschäft. Was kaufen Sie?

H. *Stellen Sie Fragen mit* **wer, wen** *oder* **was!** *(Ask about the subject and object of each sentence. Then answer.)*

BEISPIELE: Das Mädchen fragt den Herrn.
Wer fragt den Herrn? Das Mädchen.
Wen fragt das Mädchen? Den Herrn.

Die Studenten spielen Tennis.
Wer spielt Tennis? Die Studenten.
Was spielen die Studenten? Tennis.

1. Der Vater hört den Nachbarn.
2. Der Junge fragt den Großvater.
3. Die Mutter kauft Obst.
4. Die Kinder möchten einen Apfel.
5. Die Leute verstehen die Engländer nicht.
6. Wir lernen Deutsch.

I. *Im Kaufhaus. Sagen Sie es auf deutsch!*

X Hello! May I help you?
Y Hello! I need a sweater for my son.
X The sweater here is from England. Would you like a sweater in blue (**in Blau**)?
Y No. Don't you have any sweater in red?
X Of course we do—here.
Y Fine. I think the color is very beautiful. (**finden**)
X Do you also need a shirt or (a pair of) slacks (*sg.!*)?
Y No, he doesn't need any shirt or (any) slacks. (He needs no shirt and no slacks.)

III. *Sentence Structure*

1. Objects and Verbs as Verb Complements (V2)

As you know from Chapter 1, predicate nouns and predicate adjectives are VERB COMPLEMENTS (V2). Sometimes objects or another verb also become part of the verb phrase, i.e., verb complements, and in that combination complete the meaning of the main verb (V1).

Sie **sprechen Deutsch.**		Wir **spielen Tennis.**	
Sie **sprechen** gut **Deutsch.**		Wir **spielen** gern **Tennis.**	
Sie **sprechen** wirklich gut **Deutsch.**		Wir **spielen** morgens gern **Tennis.**	
V1	V2	V1	V2

Er **geht essen.**
Er **geht** hier **essen.**
Er **geht** mittags hier **essen.**
   V1   V2

2. Negation

Negation is a rather complex subject. By following the guidelines below, you can deal with most situations.

a. **kein** must be used to negate a sentence containing either a predicate noun or an object that is preceded by **ein** (**ein Apfelkuchen**) or unpreceded (**Zitronen**).

> **kein** + noun = *no, not a(n), not any*

Ist das **ein** Apfelkuchen?	*Is that an apple cake?*
Nein, das ist **kein** Apfelkuchen.	*No, that's no (not an) apple cake.*
Ist er Kanadier?	*Is he a Canadian?*
Nein, er ist **kein** Kanadier.	*No, he isn't a Canadian.*
Kaufen sie **einen** Mantel?	*Are you buying a coat?*
Nein, ich kaufe **keinen** Mantel.	*No, I'm not buying a coat.*
Haben Sie Zitronen?	*Do you have (any) lemons?*
Nein, wir haben **keine** Zitronen.	*No, we have no (don't have any) lemons.*

b. **nicht** is used under all other circumstances. Its position is determined as follows:

> S V1 0   time expression ↑ other adverbs or adverbial phrases V2.
>   **nicht**

▪ **nicht** *usually comes after the subject and verb, after all objects, and after time expressions. Therefore it stands at the end of many sentences.*

> Der Junge fragt **nicht.**
> Der Junge fragt den Vater **nicht.**
> Der Junge fragt den Vater heute **nicht.**

▪ **nicht** *usually comes before adverbs of manner (**how?**) or place (**where?**), before adverbial phrases with prepositions, and before verb complements (V2).*

Ich kaufe das **nicht** gern.	*I don't like to buy that.*
Ich kaufe das **nicht** hier.	*I don't buy that here.*
Ich kaufe das **nicht** für Ute.	*I don't buy that for Ute.*
Das Buch ist **nicht** neu.	*The book isn't new.*
Das ist **nicht** mein Buch.	*That's not my book.*

Sie sprechen **nicht** Deutsch.	*They don't speak German.*
Wir spielen **nicht** Tennis.	*We don't play tennis.*
Ich gehe heute **nicht** essen.	*I'm not going out to eat today.*

c. kein vs. nicht

Compare: Ich kaufe **ein** Brot.   Ich kaufe **kein** Brot.
Ich kaufe Brot.   Ich kaufe **kein** Brot.
Ich kaufe das Brot.   Ich kaufe das Brot **nicht**.

d. ja, nein, doch

Compare: Hast du das Buch?   **Ja!** *Yes.*
Nein! *No.*
Hast du das Buch **nicht**?   **Doch!** *Of course I do.*

doch is an affirmative response to a negative question.

Wohnt Erika Schwarz **nicht** in Salzburg?—**Doch!**
Haben Sie **keine** Wintermäntel?—**Doch**, hier sind sie.

3. Joining Sentences

Two independent clauses can be joined into one sentence by means of
COORDINATING CONJUNCTIONS. Each of the two clauses keeps the original word
order.

aber	*but*
denn	*because, for*
oder	*or*
und	*and*

Ich kaufe Erdbeeren.   Er kauft Äpfel.
Ich kaufe Erdbeeren, **und** er kauft Äpfel.

Ich kaufe Erdbeeren.   Sie sind frisch.
Ich kaufe Erdbeeren, **denn** sie sind frisch.

Wir essen Fisch.   Sie essen Fleisch.
Wir essen Fisch, **aber** sie essen Fleisch.

Nehmen Sie Käsekuchen?   Möchten Sie Apfelstrudel?
Nehmen Sie Käsekuchen, **oder** möchten Sie Apfelstrudel?

ÜBUNGEN

J. *Verneinen Sie* (negate) *die Sätze mit* kein!

BEISPIEL: Sie braucht ein Kleid.   **Sie braucht kein Kleid.**

1. Das ist ein Kaufhaus.
2. Sabine hat einen Bruder.
3. Haben Sie Erdbeeren?
4. Kaufst du Käsekuchen?
5. Ich nehme Fisch.
6. Möchten Sie Äpfel?
7. Trinkt ihr Bier?
8. Ist das ein Lebensmittelgeschäft?
9. Haben sie Kinder?
10. Ich möchte eine Cola.

K. *Verneinen Sie die Sätze mit* nicht!

BEISPIEL: Das Gemüse ist frisch.   **Das Gemüse ist nicht frisch.**

1. Ich heiße Dieter Fiedler.
2. Es geht mir gut.
3. Das ist richtig.
4. Verstehen Sie das?
5. Heute ist das Wetter schön.
6. Hamburg liegt im Süden.
7. Wir kommen morgen.
8. Die Familie wohnt in Österreich.
9. Ich esse gern Sauerkraut.
10. Der Kaffee ist heiß.
11. Ich kaufe den Mantel.
12. Er findet die Bäckerei.
13. Hier sprechen die Leute Deutsch.
14. Herr Niemöller verkauft das Geschäft.

L. *Verneinen Sie die Sätze mit* kein *oder* nicht. *(Decide first whether* kein *or* nicht *must be used.)*

1. Haben Sie Weißbrot?
2. Ich brauche Eier.
3. Heute scheint die Sonne.
4. Die Tage sind sehr lang.
5. Haben Sie Fragen?
6. Ist der Wein kalt?
7. Sie hat heute Zeit.
8. Mein Großvater ist alt.
9. Wir brauchen den Salat heute.
10. Wir brauchen heute Salat.
11. Er braucht eine Landkarte.
12. Er braucht Ihre Landkarte.

Frischeinudeln **3.99**
Orig. ital.   1000 g
Spaghetti   **1.79**
lang, weiß   500 g

M. *Antworten Sie mit* **ja, nein** *oder* **doch!**

BEISPIELE: Ist der Rhein im Westen von Deutschland?   **Ja!**
Ist der Rhein im Osten von Deutschland?   **Nein!**
Ist der Rhein nicht im Westen von Deutschland?   **Doch!**

1. Sprechen die Österreicher nicht Deutsch?
2. Hat Deutschland viele Nachbarn?
3. Ist Bonn die Hauptstadt von Ostdeutschland?
4. Ist Wien nicht die Hauptstadt von Österreich?
5. Hamburg liegt in Norddeutschland, nicht wahr?
6. Gibt es in Deutschland keine Supermärkte?
7. Ist der Artikel von Stadt **die**?
8. Sind 500 Gramm ein Pfund?
9. Ein Viertelpfund ist nicht 125 Gramm, oder?
10. Ein Kilogramm ist ein halbes Pfund, nicht wahr?

N. *Verbinden Sie die Sätze!* (Join the two sentences with the conjunctions indicated).

BEISPIEL: Wir haben keine Erbsen. Wir haben Karotten. *(but)*
Wir haben keine Erbsen, aber wir haben Karotten.

1. Er trinkt keinen Kaffee. Ich trinke keinen Tee. *(and)*
2. Die Kinder essen nicht gern Fisch. Sie essen gern Fleisch. *(but)*
3. Ich kaufe Brot. Sie haben keine Brötchen. *(because)*
4. Trinken Sie gern Wein? Möchten Sie Bier? *(or)*
5. Meine Eltern wohnen in Europa. Ich wohne in Amerika. *(and)*
6. Ich schreibe nicht. Ich habe keine Zeit. *(because)*

ZUSAMMENFASSUNG

O. *Auf deutsch, bitte!*

1. What would you like? *2.* What kind of vegetables do you have today? *3.* I'll take two pounds of beans. *4.* The eggs are fresh, aren't they?—Of course. *5.* We don't need (any) eggs. *6.* But we need some fish and lettuce. *7.* I'm not buying any wine. *8.* Don't you like (to drink) wine?—Of course I do. *9.* Do you have (any) beer? *10.* Oh, students don't like (to drink) beer. *11.* She's buying a coke and some juice. *12.* That's it?—No, I'd also like two pieces of strawberry cake.

Most Central European cities have developed traffic-free areas called **Fußgänger-zonen**, usually in the center of town where streets are crooked and narrow. No motor vehicles or streetcars are allowed. The result is a street or whole area free of traffic noise and exhaust fumes where the pedestrian is king. In warm weather people sit on benches or have refreshments in sidewalk cafés. Although merchants initially feared a decrease in business from closing streets to traffic, there has been an increase instead. Establishing these areas provided an incentive for property owners to refurbish and restore older buildings, which typically combine apartments in the upper stories and retail businesses on the first and second floors.

EINBLICKE

Die Apotheke verkauft Medizin.

der Durst / *der* Hunger	*thirst / hunger*
die Apotheke, -n	*pharmacy*
Blume, -n	*flower*
Drogerie, -n	*drugstore (see "Übrigens," p. 80)*
Studentin, -nen	*student (fem.)*
Tasse, -n; eine Tasse[1] . . .	*cup; a cup of . . .*
das Glas, ̈er; ein Glas[1] . . .	*glass; a glass of . . .*
alles	*everything*
billig / teuer	*inexpensive, cheap / expensive*
ein paar[2]	*a few, some (used with plural nouns)*
montags (dienstags usw.)	*on Mondays (Tuesdays, etc.)*
offen / zu	*open / closed*
oft	*often*
warum?	*why?*
Ich gehe . . . einkaufen.	*I go shopping . . .*
Ich habe Hunger / Durst.	*I'm hungry / thirsty.*

1 Möchten Sie **ein Glas Milch** *(a glass of milk)* oder **eine Tasse Kaffee** *(a cup of coffee)?*

2 **ein paar** Tomaten, **ein paar** Äpfel *(pl.),* BUT **etwas** Kaffee, **etwas** Butter *(sg., collective noun)*

WAS IST DAS? das Auto, Café, Sauerkraut, Spezialgeschäft; die Boutique, Medizin; romantisch, studieren

---

dorm kitchen

just now/ breakfast

Carolyn ist Studentin. Sie studiert ein Jahr in Regensburg[1]. In der Studentenheimküche° findet sie zwei Regensburger Studenten, Ursula und Peter.

Sonntags sind die Geschäfte zu.

5

CAROLYN Guten Morgen! Mein Name ist Carolyn.

URSULA Freut mich. Das ist Peter, und ich heiße Ursula.

PETER Guten Morgen, Carolyn! Woher kommst du?

CAROLYN Ich komme aus Colorado.

PETER Du, wir essen gerade° Frühstück°. Möchtest du eine Tasse Kaffee? 10

CAROLYN Ja, gern. Ich habe wirklich Hunger.

URSULA Hier hast du ein Stück Brot, etwas Butter und Marmelade.

CAROLYN Danke schön!

PETER Etwas Milch für den Kaffee?

CAROLYN Ja, bitte. 15

PETER Auch ein Ei?

1 These superscript numbers, as well as all others in the reading texts, refer to additional cultural information in the "Übrigens" section at the end of most chapters.

	CAROLYN Nein, danke.—Mm, das Brot ist gut!—Wo gibt es hier Geschäfte?
corner/ butcher shop	URSULA Um die Ecke° gibt es ein Lebensmittelgeschäft, eine Metzgerei° und eine Drogerie².
	CAROLYN Prima! Ich brauche auch etwas Medizin. 20
	URSULA Da findest du auch eine Apotheke.
	CAROLYN Ist das Lebensmittelgeschäft sehr teuer?
	PETER Billig ist es nicht. Wir gehen oft in die Stadt, denn da findest du alles. Da gibt es Spezialgeschäfte, Supermärkte und auch Kaufhäuser. 25
cathedral	URSULA Regensburg ist wirklich sehr schön. Es ist alt und romantisch, und um den Dom° gibt es viele Boutiquen.
pedestrian area *watch*	PETER Ich finde die Fußgängerzone° prima, denn da gibt es keine Autos, nur Fußgänger. Da beobachte° ich gern die Leute.
mean	URSULA Du meinst° die Mädchen. 30
So what!	PETER Na und°!
	URSULA Da gehen wir auch oft in ein Café³ und essen ein Stück Kuchen.
to the	PETER Oder wir gehen an die Donau zur° „Wurstküche", essen ein paar Würstchen und trinken ein Glas Bier.
farmers	URSULA Samstags ist Markt. Da verkaufen die Bauern° Obst, Gemüse, Eier 35 und Blumen⁴. Alles ist sehr frisch.
	CAROLYN Und wann sind die Geschäfte offen?
out here	URSULA Die Kaufhäuser sind von morgens um neun bis abends um halb sieben offen, aber hier draußen° ist mittags von halb eins bis zwei alles zu. 40
	CAROLYN Gut, dann gehe ich heute nachmittag einkaufen.
that won't work	PETER Das geht nicht°.
	CAROLYN Warum nicht?
	PETER Heute ist Samstag. Samstags sind die Geschäfte nur bis zwei offen, und sonntags ist alles zu. 45
	CAROLYN Aber nicht die Kaufhäuser, oder?
once a month	URSULA Doch! Nur einmal im Monat° sind sie samstags bis fünf offen.
	CAROLYN Gut. Dann gehe ich jetzt schnell einkaufen. Danke fürs Frühstück!
	PETER Bitte schön! 50

ZUM TEXT

A. Was paßt wo? *(What fits where? Find the correct places for the listed words.)*

Apotheke, einkaufen, Hunger, Kaffee, Kuchen, Kaufhäuser, Lebensmittelgeschäft, samstags, Studenten, Studentin

1. Carolyn ist _____ . 2. Peter und Ursula sind auch _____ .
3. Carolyn hat wirklich _____ . 4. Um die Ecke gibt es ein _____
und eine _____ . 5. Die Leute im Café essen _____ und trinken
_____ . 6. Von Montag bis Freitag sind die _____ von morgens
bis abends um halb sieben offen. 7. _____ sind die Geschäfte nur
bis zwei offen. 8. Carolyn geht schnell noch *(still)* _____ .

B. Antworten Sie mit ja, nein oder doch!

1. Essen Peter und Ursula zum Frühstück Wurst und Käse?
2. Gibt es um die Ecke eine Apotheke?
3. Regensburg ist nicht sehr alt, nicht wahr?
4. Ist samstags Markt?
5. Verkaufen die Bauern da Kuchen und Kaffee?
6. Sind die Geschäfte samstags nicht offen?

C. Fragen und Antworten *(Find the appropriate question for every answer.)*

___ 1. Sie ist aus Colorado.
___ 2. Ja, gern.
___ 3. Um die Ecke gibt es eine Metzgerei und eine Apotheke.
___ 4. Billig ist es nicht.
___ 5. Da gibt es keine Autos.
___ 6. Von morgens um neun bis abends um halb sieben.
___ 7. Sie verkaufen Obst, Gemüse, Eier und Blumen.

a. Wo gibt es hier Geschäfte?
b. Ist das Lebensmittelgeschäft sehr teuer?
c. Wann sind die Geschäfte offen?
d. Möchtest du eine Tasse Kaffee?
e. Was verkaufen die Bauern?
f. Woher kommt Carolyn?
g. Warum findet Peter die Fußgängerzone prima?

Fußgängerzone

Anliegerfahrzeuge
Zufahrt 18-10h frei

Schrittempo
Fußgänger haben Vorrang

D. Verneinen Sie die Sätze! *(Negate the sentences.)*

1. Sie möchte ein Ei.
2. Sie möchte Milch für den Kaffee.
3. Die Kaufhäuser sind samstags zu.
4. Verkauft die Drogerie Medizin?
5. Das Lebensmittelgeschäft ist billig.
6. Gibt es da Autos?
7. Die Blumen sind frisch.
8. Mittags sind die Geschäfte offen.

E. Carolyns Einkaufsliste. *(In answering the questions below, consult Carolyn's shopping list where she has checked what she needs.)*

1. Was hat sie, und was braucht sie nicht?
   a. Carolyn hat noch *(still)* etwas _____ , ein paar _____ und ein Stück _____ .
   b. Sie braucht kein(e/en) _____ .
2. Was hat sie nicht, und was kauft sie?
   a. Carolyn hat kein(e/en) _____ .
   b. Sie kauft ein paar _____ , ein Pfund _____ und etwas _____ .

F. Fragen *(Take turns with a partner, or write eight to ten sentences in answer to these questions.)*

1. Gehen Sie gern einkaufen? Was kaufen Sie oft? Kaufen Sie oft Blumen?
2. Welche Geschäfte sind billig? Welche Geschäfte sind teuer?
3. Gibt es hier eine Fußgängerzone? Wo?

4. Haben wir hier ein Café? Was gibt es da?
5. Gibt es hier einen Markt oder einen Flohmarkt *(flea market)*? Was kaufen die Leute da?
6. Wann sind die Geschäfte hier offen? Sind hier sonntags auch alle Geschäfte zu?

Hier kaufen die Leute Obst und Gemüse.

Hier gibt es Würstchen und Sauerkraut.

ÜBRIGENS

1. What has been called the city of **Regensburg** since the Middle Ages actually dates back to Roman times. This city is one of the few in Germany that was not seriously damaged during World War II, so a varied architecture spanning the centuries has survived. A tour through the old section of town reveals Romanesque, Gothic, and Baroque buildings, of which many are undergoing expert restoration.

Regensburg liegt an der Donau. Es ist ungefähr 1800 Jahre alt.

2. The German **Drogerie** is nothing like an American drugstore. It sells neither prescription drugs (available only in the **Apotheke**) nor toys, books, records, school supplies, or snacks. It does offer soaps and other toiletries, cosmetics, over-the-counter drugs, herb teas, etc.

3. **Cafés** and **Konditoreien** are favorite places for conversation or for breaks in shopping excursions. Coffee, tea, or hot chocolate is served, along with a great variety of delicious cakes and pastries, which are part of the Central European tradition.

4. Germans are very fond of having fresh flowers in their homes. It is customary for coffee or dinner guests to bring their hosts a little gift, usually flowers. A mixed flower bouquet is always nice. Red roses are a token of love.

GESPRÄCHE

Im Restaurant[1]

AXEL Herr Ober, die Speisekarte bitte!
OBER Hier bitte!
AXEL Was empfehlen Sie heute?
OBER Die Menüs sind sehr gut.
AXEL Gabi, was nimmst du?
GABI Ich weiß nicht. Was nimmst du?
AXEL Ich nehme Menü eins: Schnitzel und Kartoffelsalat.
GABI Und ich nehme Menü zwei: Rindsrouladen mit Kartoffelklößen.
OBER Und was möchten Sie trinken?
GABI Ein Glas Apfelsaft. Und du, Axel?
AXEL Mineralwasser.

Im Café

FRAU MOLLIG Ach, jetzt eine Tasse Kaffee!
FRAU ARENDT Ich esse ein Eis[2]!
FRAU MOLLIG Fräulein!
FRÄULEIN Guten Tag! Was darf's sein?
FRAU MOLLIG Zwei Tassen Kaffee, ein Stück Erdbeertorte mit Schlagsahne und ein Schokoladeneis.
FRÄULEIN Wir haben heute leider keine Erdbeertorte.
FRAU MOLLIG Na, dann bringen Sie ein Stück Käsekuchen!—(Das Fräulein kommt mit dem Essen.)—Guten Appetit[3]!
FRAU ARENDT Danke, gleichfalls. Ach, das schmeckt gut.
FRAU MOLLIG Der Kuchen auch.—Gehen Sie jetzt nach Hause?
FRAU ARENDT Nein, ich gehe noch einkaufen. Und Sie?
FRAU MOLLIG Ich auch.—Fräulein, wir möchten bezahlen!

ÜBRIGENS

1. Many Europeans still eat the main meal at noon. It often consists of soup, meat or fish, vegetables, and a dessert. Salads are not eaten before the meal, but with the main course. Europeans do not usually drink water with the meal, but rather (if anything) mineral water, beer, or wine. Coffee is never served with a meal, but afterward.

2. Eis means both *ice* and *ice cream*. If you ask for **Eis** in a restaurant, you will get ice cream. Ice water is not served in German-speaking countries.

3. It shows good manners to wish others a pleasant meal (**Guten Appetit!**) before they begin to eat.

In the Restaurant

AXEL Waiter, the menu, please.

WAITER Here you are.

AXEL What do you recommend today?

WAITER The complete dinners are very good.

AXEL Gabi, what are you having?

GABI I don't know. What are you going to have?

AXEL I'll take dinner number one: veal cutlet and potato salad.

GABI And I'll take dinner number two: stuffed beef rolls with potato dumplings.

WAITER And what would you like to drink?

GABI A glass of apple juice. And you, Axel?

AXEL Mineral water.

In the Café

MRS. MOLLIG Ah, now for a cup of coffee.

MRS. ARENDT I'll have ice cream.

MRS. MOLLIG Miss!

WAITRESS Hello. May I help you?

MRS. MOLLIG Two cups of coffee, one piece of strawberry cake with whipped cream, and one chocolate ice cream.

WAITRESS I'm sorry, but we don't have any strawberry cake today.

MRS. MOLLIG Well, then bring a piece of cheesecake.—(The waitress returns with the food.)—Enjoy your food.

MRS. ARENDT Thanks, the same to you. Oh, that tastes good.

MRS. MOLLIG The cake, too.—Are you going home now?

MRS. ARENDT No, I'm still going shopping. And you?

MRS. MOLLIG So am I.—Miss, we'd like to pay.

Im Restaurant

WORTSCHATZ 1

DAS **RESTAURANT,** -s *restaurant*

CAFÉ, -s *café*

DIE MENSA *student cafeteria*

der			*das*		
	Löffel, -	*spoon*		**Eis**	*ice cream*
	Nachtisch	*dessert*		**Essen**	*food, meal*
	Pfeffer	*pepper*		**Frühstück**	*breakfast*
	Pudding, -s	*pudding*		**Mittagessen**	*lunch*
	Reis	*rice*		**Abendessen**	*supper*
	Teller, -	*plate*		**Messer,** -	*knife*
	Zucker	*sugar*		**Salz**	*salt*

die	Gabel, -n	*fork*
	Kartoffel, -n	*potato*
	Nudel, -n	*noodle*
	Rechnung, -en	*check; bill*
	Speisekarte, -n	*menu*
	Suppe, -n	*soup*

WEITERES

der	Ober, -; Herr Ober!	*waiter; Waiter!*
das	Fräulein, -; Fräulein!	*young lady; Waitress! Miss!*

Das schmeckt gut.	*That tastes good.*
Guten Appetit!	*Enjoy your meal.*
Danke, gleichfalls!	*Thanks, the same to you.*
etwas	*something*
nichts	*nothing*
noch ein(e)	*another*
viel(e)[1]	*much, many*
wieviel? / wie viele?[1]	*how much? / how many?*
zu Hause / nach Hause[2]	*at home / (toward) home*
zum Frühstück (Mittagessen usw.)	*for breakfast (lunch, etc.)*
bestellen	*to order*
bezahlen	*to pay (for)*
bringen	*to bring*
empfehlen	*to recommend*

1 **viel Obst** *(sg., collective noun)* BUT **viele Äpfel** *(pl.)*
 wieviel Obst? BUT **wie viele Äpfel?**
2 Ich bin **zu Hause.** BUT Ich gehe **nach Hause.** (See Struktur II.3)

PASSIVES VOKABULAR der Braten, - *(roast)*; der Kartoffelsalat, -e; der Kloß, ¨e *(dumpling)*; das Menü, -s *(dinner, daily special)*; das Mineralwasser; das Schnitzel, - *(veal cutlet)*; die Rindsroulade, -n *(stuffed beef roll)*; die Torte, -n *(fancy cake)*; Hier bitte! *(Here you are.)*; leider *(unfortunately)*; noch *(still)*

Abends ißt man gern kalt.

ZUM THEMA

A. Mustersätze

1. die Speisekarte: **Herr Ober,** die Speisekarte **bitte!**
   ein Glas Bier, eine Tasse Kaffee, ein Stück Kuchen, ein Eis, die Rechnung
2. eine Tasse: **Fräulein, ich brauche** eine Tasse.
   einen Teller, einen Löffel, ein Messer, eine Gabel
3. eine Tasse Tee: **Ich möchte noch** eine Tasse Tee.
   eine Tasse Kaffee, ein Glas Limonade, ein Glas Mineralwasser, einen Teller Suppe
4. gut: **Der Kuchen schmeckt** gut.
   auch gut, wunderbar, nicht schlecht, furchtbar
5. ein Eis: **Zum Nachtisch nehme ich** ein Eis.
   Schokoladenpudding, etwas Käse, ein Stück Apfelkuchen, ein paar Erdbeeren

B. Was paßt nicht?

1. der Teller—das Messer—die Speisekarte—die Gabel
2. das Frühstück—der Nachtisch—das Mittagessen—das Abendessen
3. das Salz—der Zucker—der Pfeffer—der Pudding
4. die Rechnung—die Kartoffeln—die Nudeln—der Reis
5. das Café—der Appetit—das Restaurant—die Mensa
6. bestellen—empfehlen—sein—bezahlen

C. Was paßt?

___ 1. Die Suppe ist eiskalt.	a. Danke schön!
___ 2. Der Kartoffelsalat schmeckt prima.	b. Wirklich?
___ 3. Möchten Sie etwas zum Nachtisch?	c. Freut mich.
___ 4. Guten Appetit!	d. Das finde ich auch.
___ 5. Möchtest du nichts trinken?	e. Ja, bitte.
	f. Ja, wirklich.
	g. Doch!
	h. Nein, danke.
	i. Ja, sie schmeckt furchtbar.
	j. Ja, gern.
	k. Natürlich.
	l. Danke, gleichfalls.

D. Was noch? (What else? See how many items you can find for each word or phrase.)

BEISPIEL: ein Stück . . .   **Ich möchte ein Stück Brot.**

1. ein Stück . . .
2. ein Glas . . .
3. eine Tasse . . .
4. ein paar . . .
5. etwas . . .
6. ein Pfund . . .
7. viel . . .
8. viele . . .

Tageskarte

Tagesmenü: I Nudelsuppe, Schnitzel und Kartoffelsalat, Eis			13,80
II Gemüsesuppe, Rindsrouladen mit			
Kartoffelklößen, Eis			16,50

Tagesspezialitäten:

Bratwurst und Sauerkraut	8,60
Omelett mit Schinken°, Salat	10,00
Kalbsleber°, Erbsen und Karotten, Pommes frites	12,25
Sauerbraten°, Kartoffelbrei°, Salat	14,00
Schweinebraten°, Kartoffelbrei, Salat	14,75
Hühnchen° mit Weinsoße°, Reis, Salat	17,00
Gemischte Fischplatte, Kartoffeln, Salat	18,40

Suppen:

Tomatensuppe, Erbsensuppe, Bohnensuppe, Kartoffelsuppe	3,20

Salate:

Grüner Salat, Tomatensalat, Gurkensalat°, Bohnensalat	3,20

Getränke°:

Apfelsaft	2,50	Bier (0,2 1)[1]	2,20
Limonade	2,50	Wein (0,2 1)	2,85
Tee	2,80		
Kaffee	3,20		

Zum Nachtisch:

Schokoladenpudding	2,20	Käsekuchen	3,10
Vanilleeis	2,30	Apfelstrudel	3,10
Frische Erdbeeren	2,80	Erdbeerkuchen	3,25
Schlagsahne	-,60	Kirschtorte°	3,65

[1]A liter is a little more than a quart. 0,2 1 therefore is approximately three-fourths of a cup.

ham

calves' liver

marinated pot roast / mashed ...

pork ...

chicken ... sauce

cucumber ...

beverages

cherry cake

E. Fragen

1. Was hat Menü eins? Menü zwei? Was haben die Menüs zum Nachtisch?
2. Was für Suppen gibt es im Gasthof Post? was für Salate? was für Getränke?
3. Was kostet eine Tasse Kaffee? ein Glas Apfelsaft? ein Teller Suppe? ein Salat?
4. Wer bringt das Essen?
5. Sie haben keine Speisekarte, kein Messer, keinen Löffel, kein Salz. Was sagen Sie?
6. Sie möchten bezahlen. Was sagen Sie?

F. **Was bestellen Sie?** *(Form groups of three to five students; one is the waiter/waitress and takes orders from the others. Then report to the kitchen, i.e., the entire class, what to prepare.)*

G. **Was kostet das?** *(Order two to three items from the menu; let the others tell you how much it costs.)*

> BEISPIEL: Ich bestelle Bratwurst, Sauerkraut und ein Bier. Was kostet das?
> **Das kostet 11,40 DM.**

H. *Persönliche Fragen*

1. Wie viele Tassen Kaffee trinken Sie morgens? Trinken Sie Ihren Kaffee schwarz oder mit *(with)* Milch?
2. Essen Sie mittags oder abends warm?
3. Was essen Sie gern zum Nachtisch?
4. Trinken Sie mittags Bier? wenn ja, wieviel Bier?
5. Was trinken Sie gern abends?

I. *Aussprache (See also II. 22–28 in the pronunciation section of the Appendix.)*

1. [ü:] über, Tür, für, Frühling, Prüfung, Gemüse, südlich, grün, natürlich, müde
2. [ü] Flüsse, Würste, Stück, Müller, München, fünf, fünfundfünfzig, dünn
3. Wortpaare
   a. vier / für
   b. missen / müssen
   c. Stuhle / Stühle
   d. Mutter / Mütter
   e. fühle / fülle
   f. Goethe / Güte

STRUKTUR

I. *Verbs with Vowel Changes*

Some very common verbs have a STEM-VOWEL CHANGE in the SECOND and THIRD PERSON SINGULAR. These changes will be clearly noted in all vocabularies.

	e > i **sprechen** *to speak*	e > ie **sehen** *to see*	a > ä **fahren** *to drive*	au > äu **laufen** *to walk, run*
ich	spreche	sehe	fahre	laufe
du	**sprichst**	**siehst**	**fährst**	**läufst**
er	**spricht**	**sieht**	**fährt**	**läuft**
wir	sprechen	sehen	fahren	laufen
ihr	sprecht	seht	fahrt	lauft
sie	sprechen	sehen	fahren	laufen

A few verbs in this group have additional changes:

	nehmen *to take*	essen *to eat*	werden *to become, get*
ich	nehme	esse	werde
du	**nimmst**	**ißt**	**wirst**
er	**nimmt**	**ißt**	**wird**

■ *As you know, the* **du**-*form of verbs with a stem ending in any* **s**-*sound* (**-s, -ß, -tz, -z**) *adds only* **-t** *instead of* **-st**: **essen, du ißt**. *Thus, the* **du**-*form is identical with the* **er**-*form of these verbs:* **du ißt, er ißt; du liest, er liest**. *You need to know the following common verbs with stem-vowel changes, many of which are already familiar:*

essen (**ißt**)	*to eat*	lesen (**liest**)	*to read*
empfehlen	*to recommend*	nehmen	*to take, have*
(empfiehlt)		**(nimmt)**	*(food)*
fahren (fährt)	*to drive*	**sehen (sieht)**	*to see*
geben (gibt)	*to give*	sprechen	*to speak*
gefallen (gefällt)	*to please*	**(spricht)**	
helfen (hilft)	*to help*	**tragen (trägt)**	*to carry; wear*
laufen (läuft)	*to run, walk*	**werden (wird)**	*to become, get*

Throughout this book you will find lists like this. Only the boldface words are new; the other words are being reviewed in connection with the grammar topic.

ÜBUNGEN

A. Ersetzen Sie das Subjekt!

BEISPIEL: Der Ober trägt die Teller. (ich, ihr)   **Ich trage die Teller.**
Ihr tragt die Teller.

1. Fahren Sie zum Kaufhaus? (wir, er, ihr, du)
2. Wir nehmen Nudelsuppe. (er, ich, sie/*pl.*, du)
3. Ich werde müde. (das Kind, wir, sie/*sg.*, sie/*pl.*)
4. Sie empfehlen das Schnitzel. (der Ober, ich, du, das Fräulein)
5. Sehen Sie die Apotheke nicht? (du, ihr, er, die Leute)
6. Ich esse Käsekuchen. (wir, sie/*pl.*, er, du)
7. Sprechen Sie Deutsch? (er, du, sie/*pl.*)
8. Hilfst du heute nicht? (ihr, Sie, sie/*sg.*)
9. Lesen Sie gern Bücher? (du, ihr, er, sie/*pl.*)

B. Was tun sie? *(Answer logically, telling what others do. Make use of pronouns and irregular verbs.)*

    BEISPIEL: Ich esse schnell. Und Ihr Großvater?   **Er ißt sehr langsam.**

1. Ich spreche Englisch. Und Ihre Großmutter?
2. Ich helfe gern. Und Ihr Nachbar?
3. Ich nehme Apfelstrudel. Und Frau Mollig?
4. Ich empfehle den Schweinebraten. Und der Ober?
5. Ich laufe langsam. Und Ihr Bruder oder Ihre Schwester?
6. Ich lese gern? Und Ihre Mutter?
7. Ich fahre im Sommer nach Deutschland. Und Ihre Familie?
8. Ich sehe alles. Und Ihre Nachbarin?
9. Ich trage gern blau. Und Ihr Bruder oder Ihre Schwester?
10. Ich gebe gern Hausaufgaben. Und Ihr Englischprofessor?

II. *The Dative Case*

In this chapter the focus is on the dative case. The dative case has three major functions: it is the case of the INDIRECT OBJECT, it follows certain verbs, and it follows certain prepositions.

1. In English the INDIRECT OBJECT is indicated in two ways:

- *with a preposition:* The boy gives the plate **to the father.**
- *through word order:* The boy gives **the father** the plate.

In German this function is expressed through case form and word order. One finds the indirect object by asking for whom or in reference to whom (or occasionally what) the action of the verb is taking place.

Der Junge gibt **dem Vater** den   *The boy gives the father the plate.*
  Teller.

a. The dative form of the INTERROGATIVE PRONOUN is **wem** *(to whom).*

	persons	things and ideas
nom.	wer?	
acc.	wen?	was?
dat.	wem?	—

Wem gibt der Junge den Teller?   *To whom does the boy give the*
  Dem Vater.   *plate? To the father.*

b. The dative forms of the DEFINITE and INDEFINITE ARTICLE are as follows:

	singular			plural
	masc.	**neut.**	**fem.**	
nom.	der ein kein	das ein kein	die eine keine	die — keine
acc.	den einen keinen			
dat.	dem einem keinem	dem einem keinem	der einer keiner	den — keinen

Der Ober empfiehlt dem Vater, der Mutter und den Kindern das Schnitzel. Er bringt dem Kind einen Löffel, aber er gibt einem Kind kein Messer und keine Gabel.

- *The POSSESSIVE ADJECTIVES* **mein** *and* **Ihr** *follow the pattern of* **ein** *and* **kein:**

Was empfiehlt er Ihr**em** Vater und Ihr**er** Mutter?
Er empfiehlt mein**em** Vater und mein**er** Mutter den Fisch.

- *In the dative plural all nouns add an* **-n** *ending, unless the plural form already ends in* **-n** *or* **-s.**

die Väter / den Väter**n**   BUT: die Eltern / den Eltern
die Kinder / den Kinder**n**   die Mädchen / den Mädchen
die Äpfel / den Äpfel**n**   die Kulis / den Kuli**s**

N-nouns also have an **-n** *or* **-en** *ending in the dative singular, as they do in the accusative singular:* **dem Studenten.**

c. Here are familiar verbs that can have both accusative and dative objects. You will notice that the direct object is usually a thing and the indirect object a person.

bringen	*to bring*	öffnen	*to open*
empfehlen	*to recommend*	sagen	*to say*
geben	*to give*	schreiben	*to write*
kaufen	*to buy*	verkaufen	*to sell*

Der Ober bringt den Leuten das Bier.

The waiter brings the people the beer.

Er empfiehlt dem Fräulein den Fisch.

He recommends the fish to the young lady.

Ich gebe dem Kind ein paar Erdbeeren.	*I give the child some strawberries.*
Die Mutter kauft der Großmutter eine Jacke.	*The mother buys a jacket for the grandmother.*

d. In sentences with two objects, the direct object, if it is a noun, generally follows the indirect object.

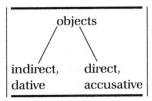

Das Fräulein bringt den Herren den Wein.

2. Dative Verbs

Some German verbs take only dative objects. At this point you need to know:

antworten	*to answer*	**gehören**	*to belong to*
danken	*to thank*	helfen	*to help*
gefallen	*to please*		

Der Bruder antwortet der Schwester.	*The brother answers (gives an answer to) the sister.*
Frau Mollig dankt dem Fräulein.	*Mrs. Mollig thanks (gives thanks to) the waitress.*
Die Mensa gefällt den Amerikanern.	*The cafeteria pleases the Americans. (The Americans like the cafeteria.)*
Der Mantel gehört dem Mädchen.	*The coat belongs to the girl.*
Ich helfe dem Nachbarn.	*I'm helping (giving help to) the neighbor.*

3. Dative Prepositions

These prepositions are always followed by the dative case:

aus	*out of, from (a place of origin)*
außer	*besides, except for*
bei	*at, near, at the home of*
mit	*with, together with*
nach	*after (time); to (cities, countries, continents)*
seit	*since, for (time)—NOT because!*
von	*of, from, by*
zu	*to, in the direction of, at, for (purpose)*

- *Some of these prepositions may be contracted with the definite article. This is especially typical of everyday speech.*

bei + dem = **beim** / von + dem = **vom** / zu + dem = **zum** / zu + der = **zur**

aus:	Sie kommt aus dem Geschäft.	*She's coming out of the store.*
	Er kommt aus Berlin.	*He comes from (is a native of) Berlin.*
außer:	Außer dem Café ist alles zu.	*Except for the café, everything is closed.*
bei:	Sie arbeitet bei VW.	*She's working for VW.*
	Die Drogerie ist beim Café.	*The drugstore is near(by) the café.*
	Er wohnt bei Frau Müller.	*He's living at Mrs. Müller's.*

☞ *CAUTION:*

▶ *Don't use **mit**! This would give the wrong impression of their relationship!*

mit:	Ich schreibe mit einem Kuli.	*I'm writing with a pen.*
nach:	Kommst du nach dem Mittagessen?	*Are you coming after lunch?*
	Fahrt ihr nach Deutschland?	*Are you going to Germany?*
	Gehen Sie nach Hause!	*Go home.*
seit:	Sie wohnen seit Mai in Bonn.	*They've been living in Bonn since May.*
	Sie wohnen seit drei Tagen da.	*They've been living there for three days.*

*NOTE: **seit** translates as* for *in English when it expresses duration of time* (three minutes, two weeks, one year) *that began in the past and still continues in the present.*

von:	Kommst du von der Mensa?	*Are you coming from the cafeteria?*
	Wir fahren von Berlin nach Wien.	*We're going from Berlin to Vienna.*
zu:	Sie fährt zum Supermarkt.	*She's driving to the supermarket.*
	Was gibt es zum Nachtisch?	*What's for dessert?*
	Sie sind nicht zu Hause.	*They aren't at home.*

- *Pay particular attention to the contrasting use of these pairs of prepositions:*

Sie fährt **zum** *(to the)* Supermarkt.	BUT Fahrt ihr **nach** *(to)* Deutschland?
Wir fahren **von** *(from)* Berlin nach Wien.	Er kommt **aus** *(from)* Berlin.
Gehen Sie **nach Hause** *(home)*!	Sie sind nicht **zu Hause** *(at home)*.

*NOTE: **nach Hause** and **zu Hause** are idioms, not typical patterns. **Nach Hause** does not follow the rule that "**nach** is used for cities, countries, continents."*

ÜBUNGEN

C. *Sagen Sie die Sätze im Plural!* (Restate the boldface phrases in the plural.)

BEISPIEL: Wir sprechen mit **dem Kanadier**.　　**Wir sprechen mit *den Kanadiern*.**

1. Das Fräulein kommt mit **dem Messer**.
2. Er lernt seit **einem Jahr** Deutsch. **(drei)**
3. Das Restaurant gehört **dem Schweizer**.
4. Sie kommen aus **dem Geschäft**.
5. Der Bleistift liegt bei **dem Buch**.
6. Nach **einem Monat** bezahlt er die Rechnung. **(zwei)**
7. Ich gehe nur mit **dem Kind**.
8. Die Stadt gefällt **dem Amerikaner**.
9. Sie gibt **dem Engländer** eine Landkarte.
10. Die Löffel liegen bei **dem Teller**.

D. *Ersetzen Sie das Dativobjekt!*

BEISPIEL: Der Ober bringt dem Kind ein Eis. (Großvater)
Der Ober bringt dem Großvater ein Eis.

1. Das Fräulein empfiehlt dem Vater den Braten. (Bruder, Spanier, Schweizer)
2. Der Junge gibt der Mutter ein Bild. (Schwester, Studentin, Frau)
3. Der Ober bringt den Eltern das Essen. (Leute, Amerikaner/*pl.*, Studenten/*pl.*)
4. Die Drogerie gehört meiner Großmutter. (Großvater, Eltern, Familie)
5. Axel dankt dem Bruder. (Schwester, Vater, Leute)
6. Meine Großmutter hilft meinem Vater. (Mutter, Schwestern, Brüder)

E. *Sagen Sie es noch einmal!* (Replace the nouns following the prepositions with the words suggested.)

BEISPIEL: Eva geht zum Lebensmittelgeschäft. (Apotheke, Supermarkt)
Eva geht zur Apotheke.
Eva geht zum Supermarkt.

1. Paula kommt aus dem Kaufhaus. (Drogerie, Café, Mensa)
2. Seit Sonntag ist er wieder hier. (zwei Tage, eine Stunde, ein Monat)
3. Wir gehen mit dem Großvater. (Frau, Fräulein, Großeltern)
4. Ich wohne bei meinen Eltern. (Bruder, Schwester, Familie)
5. Er möchte etwas Salat zu den Rouladen. (Schnitzel, Suppe, Würstchen/*pl.*, Fleisch)
6. Das Café ist bei der Apotheke. (Kaufhaus, Lebensmittelgeschäft, Drogerie)
7. Nach dem Mittagessen spielen sie Tennis. (Frühstück, Kaffee, Deutschstunde)
8. Außer meinem Bruder sind alle hier. (Vater, Mutter, Nachbar, Studentin)

F. Stellen Sie Fragen mit wer, wen, wem oder was! *(Ask about the subject and each object, using the appropriate form of the interrogative pronoun.)*

BEISPIELE: Das Fräulein bringt den Leuten die Speisekarte.
Wer bringt den Leuten die Speisekarte? Das Fräulein.
Wem bringt das Fräulein die Speisekarte? Den Leuten.
Was bringt das Fräulein den Leuten? Die Speisekarte.

1. Frau Schmidt kauft den Kindern ein paar Bananen.
2. Der Ober empfiehlt der Studentin die Rouladen.
3. Der Nachbar gibt dem Kind einen Apfel.
4. Die Großeltern verkaufen den Leuten die Apotheke.

G. Bilden Sie Sätze!

1	2	3
das Kleid	gehört	Herr Huber
die Blusen	gehören	Fräulein
das Bild		mein Bruder
der Pullover		meine Eltern
die Uhr		meine Familie
die Berge		die Leute
der See		die Nachbarin
das Restaurant		die Kinder
die Blumen		
die Bilderbücher		

H. Was gefällt wem? Auf deutsch, bitte!

1. Miss Meyer likes the country.
2. My father likes the city.
3. My mother likes the South.
4. My sister likes the lakes.
5. My brothers like the mountains.
6. My grandparents like the people.
7. The people like the language.
8. And what do you *(formal)* like?

I. Was kaufen Sie wem? *(Answer by starting each sentence with* **Ich kaufe . . .** *For each sentence choose an indirect object from group 1 and a direct object from group 2.)*

BEISPIEL: **Ich kaufe meiner Freundin Blumen.**

1: Bruder, Schwester, Mutter, Vater, Großeltern, Onkel, Tante, Freund(in)
2: Blumen, Buch, Bild, Kuli, Hemd, Pullover, Bluse, Uhr, Kuchen, Wein, Plätzchen

J. nach Hause _oder_ zu Hause?

BEISPIEL: Die Kinder laufen schnell _____ .
Die Kinder laufen schnell nach Hause.

1. Heute essen wir _____ .
2. Ich habe die Bilder _____ .
3. Jürgen kommt oft spät _____ .
4. Ich lese das Buch _____ .
5. Bringst du die Großeltern _____ ?
6. Geht ihr um sechs _____ ?
7. Er ist jetzt nicht _____ .

ZUSAMMENFASSUNG

K. *Bilden Sie Sätze!*

    BEISPIEL: das / sein / für / Onkel   **Das ist für den Onkel.**

1. Ober / kommen / mit / Speisekarte
2. Mutter / kaufen / Kind / Apfelsaft
3. Fräulein / empfehlen / Studentin / Apfelkuchen
4. er / sehen / Großvater / nicht
5. kommen / du / von / Mensa?
6. Familie / fahren / nicht / nach Berlin

L. *Was fehlt?*

1. Zu_____ Essen braucht man ein_____ Messer und ein_____ Gabel.
2. Suppe ißt man mit ein_____ Eßlöffel *(tablespoon)*, und für d_____ Kaffee braucht man ein_____ Kaffeelöffel. 3. Wir haben kein_____ Messer, kein_____ Gabel und keinen Löffel *(sg.)*. 4. Gibt es hier kein— Salz und keinen Pfeffer? 5. Doch, das Salz steht bei dem Pfeffer. 6. Jetzt habe ich alles außer einer Speisekarte. 7. Der Ober empfiehlt der Studentin den Schweinebraten *(m.)*. 8. Nach d_____ Essen bringt er ein_____ Eis und ein_____ Kaffee. 9. D_____ Restaurant gefällt d_____ Studenten *(pl.)*. 10. Aber sie haben etwas gegen d_____ Preise *(prices)*. 11. Wir sprechen von d_____ Professor und von d_____ Prüfung *(f.)*. 12. Ich bestelle noch ein_____ Cola. 13. Hier trinke ich d_____ Cola aus ein_____ Glas, aber zu Hause aus ein_____ Flasche *(f., bottle)*. 14. Da kommt der Ober mit d_____ Rechnung. 15. Ohne d_____ Rechnung geht's nicht. 16. Danke für d_____ Mittagessen!

M. *Auf deutsch, bitte!*

1. We're going through the cafeteria with the students. *2.* They're from Hamburg. They're Hamburgers. *3.* Paul lives with *(at the home of)* a family, and Helga lives at home. *4.* Helga, what are you having? *5.* I'll take the roast (**der Braten**), peas and carrots, and a glass of juice. *6.* Would you *(formal)* like a piece of cake for dessert? *7.* No, I'm not eating any cake because it's fattening (**dick machen**). *8.* I have no knife, no fork, and no spoon. *9.* Paul brings the student *(f.)* a knife, a fork, a spoon, and (some) ice cream. *10.* Who's ice cream is that? (To whom does the ice cream belong?) *11.* Would you *(fam.)* like some ice cream with a cookie? *12.* She thanks the student. *13.* Who's paying for the lunch?

Usually there's a difference between a German **Restaurant** and a **Gasthof** (or **Gaststätte**). The **Gasthof** is less formal, less expensive, and the menu is more geared to local tastes and specialties. In both places the tip is already included in the price, but it's customary to add a small amount to round out the total. Thus for **11.26 DM** one would give **12.00 DM**.

der Freund, -e	(boy)friend
die Freundin, -nen	(girl)friend
Flasche, -n; eine Flasche . . .	bottle; a bottle of . . .
Hand, ⸚e	hand
besonders	especially
dann	then
gewöhnlich	usual(ly)
man	one (they, people)
manchmal	sometimes
nicht nur . . . sondern auch	not only . . . but also
überall	everywhere
vielleicht	perhaps
schlafen (schläft)	to sleep

WAS IST DAS? der Kaffeeklatsch, Teenager; das Büro, Joghurt; die Hausfrau, Pause, Mittagspause, Kaffeepause, Schule; die Geschäftsleute, Kartoffelchips, Spezialitäten; interessant, lokal, relativ, typisch, voll; dick machen

Die Deutschen beginnen den Tag gewöhnlich mit einem guten Frühstück. Zum Frühstück gibt es Brot oder Brötchen, Butter, Marmelade, vielleicht auch ein Ei,

Man ist, was man ißt.

with it

etwas Wurst oder Käse und manchmal etwas Joghurt. Dazu° trinkt man 5 Kaffee, Milch oder Tee.

Mittags ißt man warm. Um die Zeit sind die Schulen aus[1], und die Geschäfte und Büros machen oft eine Mittagspause. Viele essen mittags zu Hause. Andere° gehen nicht nach Hause, sondern° in die Kantine° oder in ein Restaurant. 10

Im Restaurant gibt es gewöhnlich ein Tagesmenü. Das ist besonders gut oder billig. Außer Bratwurst, Omelett oder Hühnchen° findet man natürlich auch lokale Spezialitäten[2]. So finden Sie auf der Speisekarte im Rheinland Sauerbraten, in Schwaben° Spätzle° und in Bayern° Schweinshax'n° oder Knödel°. Zum Mittagessen trinkt man gern Saft, Mineralwasser, 15 Bier oder Wein, aber kein Wasser. Ob° im Norden oder Süden, im Osten oder Westen, überall findet man etwas Besonderes°. Wenn° Sie in Deutschland sind, bestellen Sie auch einmal° etwas anderes°! Nehmen Sie das Messer in die rechte° Hand und die Gabel in die linke° Hand, und dann Guten Appetit! Noch etwas: Manchmal sitzen° auch andere Leute bei Ihnen am° 20 Tisch. So° gibt es hier und da interessante Gespräche.

Fürs Mittagessen braucht man gewöhnlich Zeit. Leute mit wenig° Zeit gehen gern zu einer Imbißstube°. Da gibt es Bratwurst, Fischbrötchen oder Schaschlik°. In Großstädten finden Sie gewöhnlich auch McDonald's. Schnell essen ist manchmal besser als° nichts, aber ein Mittagessen ist das 25 für die meisten° Deutschen nicht.

Nachmittags sieht man viele Menschen in Cafés. Das sind nicht nur Großmütter und Hausfrauen, sondern auch Teenager und Geschäftsleute. Sie sitzen gemütlich° bei einer Tasse Kaffee und reden°. Auch zu Hause hat man gern einen Kaffeeklatsch. Besonders sonntags kommt man oft mit 30 Freunden zusammen zu einer Tasse Kaffee und einem Stück Kuchen.

stomach

pickles
Careful!/ stronger than

pretzel sticks

more . . . than
artificial colors/ preserva-
tives/ know

Abends ißt man gewöhnlich kalt und nicht so viel. Man sagt: Mit einem vollen Bauch° schläft man schlecht. Was man abends ißt, macht dick. So gibt es nur etwas Brot mit Käse, Wurst oder Fisch, ein paar Tomaten oder saure Gurken°. Dazu gibt es vielleicht eine Tasse Tee oder ein Bier. Vor- 35
sicht°, das Bier ist stärker als° in Amerika! Man trinkt aber nicht nur Bier, sondern auch Wein[3]. Abends öffnet man auch gern eine Flasche Wein für Freunde. Dazu gibt es Salzstangen° oder Kartoffelchips.

Den meisten Deutschen ist wichtig, was sie essen. Sie essen relativ viel Obst und Gemüse. Qualität ist gewöhnlich wichtiger als° Quantität. Sie ha- 40
ben etwas gegen Farbstoffe° und Konservierungsmittel°. Sie wissen°: „Man ißt, was man ißt."

Die Grünen (eine
politische Partei)
haben etwas gegen
Chemie in
Lebensmitteln.

Auch in Hamburg gibt es Burger King.

ZUM TEXT

A. Welche Antwort paßt? *(Indicate the correct answer.)*

1. Zum Frühstück gibt es . . .
   - *a.* Sauerbraten
   - *b.* Kuchen und Plätzchen
   - *c.* viel Obst und Gemüse
   - *d.* Brot, Butter und Marmelade
2. Mittags essen die Schulkinder . . .
   - *a.* in der Schule
   - *b.* zu Hause
   - *c.* im Restaurant
   - *d.* etwas Besonderes
3. Zum Mittagessen trinkt man gern . . .
   - *a.* Kaffee, Milch oder Tee
   - *b.* Eiswasser
   - *c.* Mineralwasser, Bier oder Wein
   - *d.* Cola
4. In den Cafés sind . . .
   - *a.* nur Großmütter und Hausfrauen
   - *b.* auch Teenager und Geschäftsleute
   - *c.* viele Schulkinder
   - *d.* keine Geschäftsleute
5. Zum Abendessen ißt man gewöhnlich . . .
   - *a.* Kaffee und Kuchen
   - *b.* Brot, Wurst, Käse und Fisch
   - *c.* Suppe, Fleisch und Gemüse
   - *d.* Salzstangen und Kartoffelchips

B. Was fehlt?

1. Ich beginne den Tag gewöhnlich mit ein_____ guten Frühstück: mit ein_____ Brötchen, ein_____ Ei und ein_____ Tasse Tee. *2.* Gehst du mittags _____ Hause? *3.* Ja, _____ Hause ist es nicht so teuer. *4.* Bei d_____ Preisen *(pl.)* esse ich gern _____ Hause. *5.* Warum gehst du nicht zu_____ Mensa? *6.* D_____ Essen schmeckt nicht. *7.* Manchmal gehe ich zu ein_____ Imbißstube *(f.)*. *8.* Dann esse ich nichts außer ein_____ Bratwurst, und die Cola trinke ich schnell aus d_____ Flasche. *9.* Oft habe ich kein_____ Hunger. *10.* Dann esse ich nur ein_____ Apfel oder ein_____ Banane. *11.* Möchtest du etwas Brot mit ein_____ Stück Käse? *12.* Es ist von d_____ Reformhaus *(n., health-food store)* und hat kein_____ Konservierungsmittel!

C. Vergleichen Sie! *(Compare. With a partner make two lists that compare German and North American food and drink preferences.)*

	In Deutschland	in Nordamerika
zum Frühstück ißt man trinkt man		
zum Mittagessen ißt man trinkt man		
zum Abendessen ißt man trinkt man		

D. Schreiben Sie! *(Write eight to ten answers based on these questions.)*

1. Um wieviel Uhr essen Sie Frühstück?
2. Was essen Sie morgens? mittags? abends? Was trinken Sie zum Frühstück? zum Mittagessen? zum Abendessen?
3. Trinken Sie viel Wasser? Schmeckt Ihr Wasser gut?
4. Was essen Sie nicht gern?
5. Wo essen Sie Frühstück: zu Hause, in der Mensa oder im Restaurant?
6. Essen Sie oft in Imbißstuben? Wo sind Hamburger und Pommes frites *(French fries)* besonders billig? besonders gut?

E. Käsefondue für vier bis sechs Personen

1 lb (4 cups)/ grated
garlic
2 cups/ light
potato starch
cherry brandy
nutmeg
bite-size pieces of French bread

500 g° geriebener° Gruyere- und Emmentalerkäse
etwas Knoblauch°
½ l° leichter° Weißwein
2 Teelöffel Kartoffelmehl°
2 Teelöffel Kirsch°
etwas Salz, Pfeffer und Muskat°
Weißbrotwürfel°

Ein Schweizer Fondue schmeckt wunderbar.

Den Fonduetopf° innen° mit Knoblauch aus-
reiben°. Den Wein hineingeben° und langsam
erwärmen°. Den Käse dazugeben°, und unter
Rühren° schmelzen lassen° und zum Kochen°
bringen (ungefähr 5 Minuten). Das Kartoffel-
mehl mit dem Kirsch kombiniert darunter-
mischen°. Das Fondue ist jetzt cremig° dick.
Mit Salz, Pfeffer und Muskat würzen°. Das
Fondue zusammen mit den Brotwürfeln ser-
vieren. Beim Essen Würfel mit der Gabel in
das Fondue tauchen°. Guten Appetit!

ÜBRIGENS

1. In Germany and Austria schools generally let out between 12 noon and 1:30 pm; children usually eat their main meal at home after school. The afternoons are for homework and play. In Switzerland children attend school from 8 to 12 and from 2 to 4, but Wednesday and Saturday afternoons are free.

2. Swiss cooking has borrowed from the French, German, and Italian cuisines, but has developed many specialties of its own, such as **Röschti** *(fried potatoes)* and **Geschnetzeltes** *(minced veal in a cream sauce)*. The most famous Swiss dish is probably the cheese fondue, a reminder that Switzerland still produces a great variety of excellent cheeses.—Most famous among Austrian dishes is the **Wiener Schnitzel**, but desserts such as **Palatschinken** *(dessert crêpes)*, **Salzburger Nockerl** *(soufflé)* and magnificent **Torten** delight visitors even more. Austrian coffee houses serve coffee in many different ways, the best-known among them being **Kaffee mit Schlag** *(with whipped cream)*.

3. German wines are produced mainly in western and southwestern Germany. The Rhine and Moselle (**Mosel**) rivers have given their names to two great wines famous throughout the world.—The Swiss, too, love wine, which is for them what beer is to a Bavarian. Out of 23 cantons 18 grow wine.—In Austria there are excellent vineyards along the Danube around Vienna.—Wines are classified as **Tafelwein** *(table* or *ordinary wine)*, **Qualitätswein** *(quality wine)*, and **Qualitätswein mit Prädikat** *(superior wine)*. A wine's classification and vintage year determine its quality.

Nein danke, ich fahre.

This section gives you a periodic summary of what has been introduced in the preceding chapters. It is intended for reference and as a preparation for quizzes, tests, and finals. The first part sums up points of structure, and the second part practices familiar structures and vocabulary. If there is no time for discussing the "Aufgabe" in class, ask your instructor for a copy of the answers.

I. *Verbs*

1. Forms: PRESENT TENSE

a. Most verbs inflect like **danken**:

singular	plural
ich dank**e**	wir dank**en**
du dank**st**	ihr dank**t**
er dank**t**	sie dank**en**

b. Verbs whose stem ends in **-d**, **-t**, or certain consonant combinations inflect like **antworten**:

singular	plural
ich antwort**e**	wir antwort**en**
du antwort**est**	ihr antwort**et**
er antwort**et**	sie antwort**en**

c. Some verbs have vowel changes in the second and third person singular:

	a > ä **fahren**	au > äu **laufen**	e > i **sprechen**	e > ie **sehen**
ich	fahre	laufe	spreche	sehe
du	**fährst**	**läufst**	**sprichst**	**siehst**
er	**fährt**	**läuft**	**spricht**	**sieht**

d. Some verbs are irregular in form:

	haben	sein	werden	essen	nehmen
ich	habe	**bin**	werde	esse	nehme
du	**hast**	**bist**	**wirst**	**ißt**	**nimmst**
er	**hat**	**ist**	**wird**	**ißt**	**nimmt**
wir	haben	**sind**	werden	essen	nehmen
ihr	habt	**seid**	**werdet**	**eßt**	nehmt
sie	haben	**sind**	werden	essen	nehmen

2. Usage

a. German has only one verb form to express what English says with several forms:

Er antwortet meinem Vater.
$\begin{cases} \textit{He answers my father.} \\ \textit{He's answering my father.} \\ \textit{He does answer my father.} \end{cases}$

b. The present tense occasionally expresses future time:

Im Mai fährt sie nach Heidelberg.   *She's going to Heidelberg in May.*

II. *Nouns and Pronouns*

1. You have learned three of the four German cases:

a. NOMINATIVE

This is the case of the SUBJECT:

Da kommt **der Ober. Er** bringt das Essen.

It is also used for PREDICATE NOUNS following the linking verbs **heißen** and **sein**:

Der Herr **heißt** Oskar Meyer.
    Er **ist**   Wiener.

b. ACCUSATIVE

This is the case of the DIRECT OBJECT:

Wir fragen **den Freund.**

It follows these prepositions: | durch, für, gegen, ohne, um |

Sie laufen **um den See.**

C. DATIVE

This is the case of the INDIRECT OBJECT:

Rotkäppchen bringt **der Großmutter** den Wein.

It follows these prepositions: | aus, außer, bei, mit, nach, seit, von, zu |

Ich wohne **bei meinen Eltern.**

It also follows these verbs: antworten, danken, gefallen, gehören, helfen.

Das Buch **gehört meiner Freundin.**

Nouns in the dative plural have an **-n** ending unless the plural form ends in **-s**:

die Freunde / den Freunde**n**   BUT: die Kulis / den Kulis

d. N-NOUNS

Some masculine nouns have an **-n** or **-en** ending in all cases (singular and plural) except in the nominative singular:

der Herr, **-n**, -en
der Junge, **-n**, -n
der Mensch, **-en**, -en
der Nachbar, **-n**, -n
der Student, **-en**, -en

Der Junge fragt den Nachbarn. Der Nachbar antwortet dem Jungen.

2. The case forms of the DEFINITE and INDEFINITE ARTICLES:

	singular			plural
	masc.	neut.	fem.	
nom.	der ein kein	das ein kein	die eine keine	die — keine
acc.	den einen keinen			
dat.	dem einem keinem	dem einem keinem	der einer keiner	den — keinen

Mein and **Ihr** follow the pattern of **ein** and **kein.**

3. The case forms of the INTERROGATIVE PRONOUN:

	persons	things and ideas
nom.	wer?	was?
acc.	wen?	
dat.	wem?	—

III. *Sentence Structure*

1. Verb position

a. In a German statement the verb must be the second grammatical ELE-MENT, but the element before the verb is not necessarily the subject.

> Ich **sehe** meinen Vater morgen.
> Morgen **sehe** ich meinen Vater.
> Meinen Vater **sehe** ich morgen.

b. A verb phrase consists of an INFLECTED VERB and a COMPLEMENT that completes its meaning. Such complements include predicate nouns, predicate adjectives, some accusatives, and other verbs. When the verb consists of more than one part, the inflected part (V1) is the second element in a statement, and the other part (V2) stands at the very end of the sentence.

Das	**ist**		meine Schwester.
Du	**bist**		prima.
Er	**spielt**	sehr gut	Tennis.
Jetzt	**gehen**	wir schnell	essen.
V1			V2

2. Negation

a. | nicht + (ein)___ = kein___ |

Möchten Sie **ein** Eis?   Nein, ich möchte **kein** Eis.
Möchten Sie Erdbeeren?   Nein, ich möchte **keine** Erdbeeren.

b. | S V1 0 time expression ↑ other adverbs or adverbial phrases V2. |
| **nicht** |

Wir spielen heute **nicht** mit den Kindern Tennis.

3. Clauses

Coordinate clauses are introduced by COORDINATING CONJUNCTIONS:

| aber, denn, oder, und |

Coordinating conjunctions do not affect the original word order of the two sentences.

Ich bezahle den Kaffee.   Du bezahlst das Eis.
Ich bezahle den Kaffee, **und** du bezahlst das Eis.

WORTSCHATZWIEDERHOLUNG

A. *Welches Wort kommt Ihnen in den Sinn? (What word comes to mind?)*

BEISPIEL: Winter   **kalt**

Sprache, Fluß, Gemüse, Glas, Bäckerei, Frühstück, Suppe, Rechnung, trinken, Restaurant, Geschäft, schlafen, Sommer, Tasse, Schokoladen-kuchen, Mensa, Messer, Nachtisch

So ein Butterbrot mit Ei schmeckt gut.

B. Geben Sie das Gegenteil!

kaufen, fragen, kommen, nördlich, im Westen, offen, alles, bitte, eiskalt

C. Was ist das? Geben Sie den Artikel!

Buttermilch, Bananeneis, Buttermesser, Frühstückstisch, Gurkensalat, Kaffeetasse, Kartoffelsalat, Obstkuchen, Lebensmittelrechnung, Marmeladenbrot, Salatkartoffel, Suppenteller, Teelöffel, Weinglas, Zitronenpudding

D. Was fehlt? *(What's missing?)*

1. Vater, Mutter und Kinder sind zusammen eine _____ .
2. In Deutschland ißt man Brot mit Wurst, Käse oder Fisch zum _____ .
3. Für Suppe, Pudding oder Eis braucht man einen _____ .
4. Orangen, Bananen, Erdbeeren und Äpfel sind _____ .
5. Karotten, Erbsen und Bohnen sind _____ .
6. Der Vater von meiner Mutter ist mein _____ , aber der Bruder von meiner Mutter ist mein _____ .
7. Zum Schreiben braucht man einen _____ oder einen _____ und ein Stück _____ .
8. Im Winter braucht man einen _____ oder eine _____ .
9. Hier essen die Studenten: _____ .
10. Hier essen die Leute Kuchen, und sie trinken Kaffee oder Tee: _____ .
11. Hier kauft man Röcke und Blusen, Jacken und Hosen, auch Schuhe: _____ .

STRUKTURWIEDERHOLUNG

E. Verben. Variieren Sie die Sätze! *(Vary the German base sentence as suggested.)*

1. **Ich trinke Wein.**
   We drink wine. Do you drink wine? *(3 ×)* She doesn't drink wine.
2. **Sie antwortet den Leuten.**
   I'm answering the people. They answer the people. Does she answer the people? Answer the people. Don't answer the people. Why aren't you answering the people? *(3 ×)*
3. **Er fährt nach Berlin.**
   They're driving to Berlin. Why is she driving to Berlin? I'm not going to drive to Berlin. Are you driving to Berlin? *(3 ×)* Drive to Berlin. Don't drive to Berlin.
4. **Wir essen Fisch.**
   Who's eating fish? Are you eating fish? *(3 ×)* They don't eat fish. Eat fish.

5. **Sie werden müde.**

I'm getting tired. She's not getting tired. Don't get tired. Who's getting tired? We're getting tired, too.

6. **Er hat Hunger.**

I'm hungry. Are you hungry? *(3 ×)* Who's hungry? They're hungry. They're not hungry. We're hungry.

7. **Sie ist sehr groß.**

You're very tall. *(3 ×)* They're not very tall. I'm very tall. Isn't he tall?

F. *Nominativ, Akkusativ und Dativ. Variieren Sie die Sätze!*

1. **Herr Díaz ist Spanier.**

Mr. Schmidt is (an) Austrian. No, he's from Switzerland. Is Miss Bayer an Austrian? She's not an Austrian either. (She's also not an Austrian.) They say Miss Klein is an American. Joe is an American, too.

2. **Hier gibt es einen Supermarkt.**

There's a river here. (a restaurant, no cafeteria, no lake, a department store)

There are mountains here. (bakeries, lakes, no stores, no cafés)

3. **Das Geschäft gehört den Großeltern.**

Who does the store belong to? (To whom does the store belong?) What belongs to the grandfather? She says it doesn't belong to the brother. It doesn't belong to the aunt.

4. **Der Herr bringt dem Fräulein Blumen.**

What is he bringing to the young lady? Who's he bringing flowers to? (To whom is he bringing flowers?) Who's bringing the flowers? Why is he bringing flowers? Isn't he bringing flowers to the young lady? They're bringing the children some cookies. Is she bringing the friends a bottle of wine? He's bringing the neighbors apples. I'm bringing the sisters some books.

G. *Präpositionen* (Prepositions). **Kombinieren Sie** (combine) **die Präpositionen mit den Wörtern!**

BEISPIEL: durch: Land, Berge   **durch das / durchs Land**
                                    durch die Berge

DURCH: Stadt, Zimmer/*pl.*, Kaufhaus, Supermarkt
   FÜR: Kuchen, Vater, Junge, Eltern, Familie
GEGEN: Leute, Restaurant, Kinder, Ober, Mensch
 OHNE: Essen, Speisekarte, Pudding, Herr, Freunde
    UM: Geschäft, Markt, Mensa, Tisch

   AUS: Flasche, Gläser, Supermarkt, Bäckerei, Café
AUßER: Bruder, Eltern, Schwester, Leute, Student
   BEI: Supermarkt, Familie Schmidt, Apotheke, Nachbar
   MIT: Herr, Freundin, Leute, Messer, Gabel
  NACH: Frühstück, Mittagessen, Vorlesung, Kaffee
   SEIT: Abendessen, Frühling, Zeit
   VON: Ober, Fräulein, Kinder, Mutter, Studentin
    ZU: Restaurant, Mensa, Markt, Apotheke

H. *Verneinen Sie die Sätze mit* **kein** *oder* **nicht!**

1. Heute gibt es Schokoladenpudding.
2. Der Junge hilft dem Vater.
3. Sehen Sie den Ober?
4. Ich habe ein Messer.
5. Wir brauchen heute Milch.
6. Geht ihr nach Hause?
7. Haben Sie Rindsrouladen?
8. Er trinkt Kaffee.
9. Sie ißt gern Eis.
10. Joachim ist mein Freund.
11. Hast du Durst?
12. Heute ist es sehr kalt.

AUFGABE

I. *Was fehlt?*

1. Heute geht Frau Müller _____ Drogerie _____ Bäckerei und _____ Supermarkt. *(from the, to the/2 ×)*
2. Dann geht sie _____ Markt. *(to the)*
3. Da kauft sie Blumen _____ Großmutter, denn sie hat Geburtstag *(birthday)*. *(for the)*
4. Frau Müller braucht auch ein paar Flaschen Wein, denn Freunde kommen _____ Wien. *(from)*
5. Dann geht sie wieder _____ Hause und macht das Mittagessen _____ Familie: _____ Vater und _____ Kinder. *(—, for the/3 ×)*
6. _____ eins sind alle _____ Hause. *(at/2 ×)*
7. _____ Mittagessen gibt es heute Schnitzel, Kartoffelsalat und Bohnen. *(for)*
8. _____ Mittagessen machen die Kinder die Hausaufgaben. *(after)*
9. _____ halb fünf geht Frau Müller _____ Kindern _____ Großmutter. *(at, with the, to the)*
10. _____ Großeltern feiern *(celebrate)* sie _____ Kaffee und Kuchen. *(at the, with)*
11. _____ Kaffee gehen Müllers _____ Stadt _____ Hause. *(after the, through the, —)*
12. Die Kinder essen abends _____ Eltern, denn sie gehen früh *(early)* schlafen. *(without the)*
13. Die Eltern lesen und sprechen noch etwas _____ Abendessen, aber nicht lange, denn sie sind schon *(already)* _____ halb sieben auf. *(after, since)*
14. _____ zehn gehen sie auch schlafen. *(at)*

J. *Auf deutsch, bitte!*

1. John is an Englishman, but he's studying German. 2. In Europe languages are important. 3. Where is (there) a pharmacy and a supermarket? 4. Carolyn needs not only bread, butter, and jam, but also some cheese, a bottle of juice, two pounds of apples, and some bananas. 5. The stores are closed on Sundays. 6. Mr. and Mrs. Schmidt are coming for dinner. 7. Axel and I are helping at home. 8. He's carrying the plates and I'm carrying the forks and knives. 9. What's for dessert, pudding or ice cream? 10. I have no pudding and no ice cream. 11. They don't like (to eat) dessert. 12. What kind of people are they?

365 Tage
Gesundheit
und Glück

♥ 52 Wochen
Lebensfreude
und Liebe

12 Monate
reichlich Geld
und Erfolg

Zum Geburtstag
herzliche Glückwünsche

GESPRÄCHE

Am Telefon

CHRISTA Hallo, Michael!

MICHAEL Hallo, Christa! Was gibt's?

CHRISTA Was machst du am Wochenende?

MICHAEL Nichts Besonderes. Warum?

CHRISTA Klaus hat übermorgen Geburtstag, und wir geben eine Party.

MICHAEL Bist du sicher? Klaus hat doch vor einem Monat Geburtstag gehabt!

CHRISTA Quatsch! Klaus hat am dritten Mai (3.5.) Geburtstag. Und Samstag ist der dritte.

MICHAEL Na gut! Wann und wo ist die Party?

CHRISTA Samstag um sieben bei mir. Aber nichts sagen! Es ist eine Überraschung.

MICHAEL Ach so! Also, bis dann!

CHRISTA Tschüß! Mach's gut!

Klaus klingelt bei Christa

CHRISTA Tag, Klaus! Herzlichen Glückwunsch zum Geburtstag!

KLAUS Grüß dich! Danke!

MICHAEL Alles Gute zum Geburtstag!

KLAUS Tag, Michael . . . Gerda, Kurt, Sabine. Was macht ihr denn hier?

ALLE Wir gratulieren zum Geburtstag!

KLAUS Danke! Was für eine Überraschung!

On the Telephone

CHRISTA Hi, Michael!

MICHAEL Hi, Christa! What's up?

CHRISTA What are you doing on the weekend?

MICHAEL Nothing special. Why?

CHRISTA Klaus has a birthday the day after tomorrow, and we're giving a party.

MICHAEL Are you sure? Klaus had his birthday a month ago.

CHRISTA Nonsense. Klaus's birthday is on the third of May (5/3). And Saturday is the third.

MICHAEL All right. When and where is the party?

CHRISTA Saturday at seven at my place. But don't say anything. It's a surprise.

MICHAEL Oh, I see. All right, see you then.

CHRISTA Goodbye. Take care!

Klaus Rings Christa's Doorbell

CHRISTA Hello, Klaus! Happy birthday!

KLAUS Hi! Thanks!

MICHAEL All the best on your birthday!

KLAUS Hi, Michael . . . Gerda, Kurt, Sabine. What are you doing here?

ALL Congratulations!

KLAUS Thanks! What a surprise!

Feste und Daten

DAS FEST, -E *celebration, festival*

der Feiertag, -e[1]	*holiday*	*die* Ferien[1] *(pl.)*	*vacation*
Geburtstag, -e	*birthday*	Party, Parties	*party*
Sekt	*champagne*	Überraschung, -en	*surprise*
das Geschenk, -e	*present*		

bekommen	*to get, receive*	schenken	*to give (a present)*
dauern	*to last (duration)*		
denken	*to think*	singen	*to sing*
feiern	*to celebrate*	tanzen	*to dance*
gratulieren (+ *dat.*)	*to congratulate*	tun	*to do; put*
		überraschen	*to surprise*

DAS DATUM, DIE DATEN *date (calendar)*

Der wievielte ist heute? — *What's the date today?*

Heute ist der erste Mai (1.5.)[2]. — *Today is the first of May (5/1).*

Ich habe am ersten Mai (1.5.[2]) Geburtstag. — *My birthday is on the first of May (5/1).*

Die Ferien sind vom zweiten Juli (2.7.) bis zum zehnten September (10.9.). — *The vacation is from July 2 (7/2) until September 10 (9/10).*

1. **erste**[3]	7. **siebte**	13. dreizehnte
2. zweite	8. **achte**	19. neunzehnte
3. **dritte**	9. neunte	20. zwanzigste
4. vierte	10. zehnte	21. einundzwanzigste
5. fünfte	11. elfte	22. zweiundzwanzigste
6. sechste	12. zwölfte	30. dreißigste

1 Note the difference between **Feiertag** and **Ferien**. **Feiertag** refers to a *special day, a holiday,* and can be in either the singular or the plural, whereas **Ferien** refers to *school* or *university vacation time,* a plural word in German.

2 In writing dates Americans give the month and then the day: *5/1 (May 1), 1/5 (January 5),* whereas in German one usually gives the day and then the month. In German an ordinal number is followed by a period: **1.5. (1. Mai), 5.1. (5. Januar),** So **1.5** reads **der erste Mai,** and **5.1.** reads **der fünfte Januar.** Note the **-en** ending after **am, vom,** and **zum: am ersten Mai, vom zweiten Juli bis zum zehnten September.**

3 From 1 to 19, the ordinal numbers show a **-te(n)** ending. Starting with 20, they end in **-ste(n).** Note the irregularities within the numbers.

am Wochenende	*on the weekend*
gerade	*just, right now*
noch	*still; else*
sicher	*sure, certain*
vor einer Woche[4]	*a week ago*
vorgestern	*the day before yesterday*
gestern / morgen	*yesterday / tomorrow*
übermorgen	*the day after tomorrow*
wie lange?	*how long?*
Bis später!	*See you later. So long.*
Tschüß!	*Goodbye. So long.*
zum Geburtstag	*on the/for the birthday*
(zu) Ostern	*(at/for) Easter*
(zu) Weihnachten	*(at/for) Christmas*
(zu) Silvester	*(on/for) New Year's Eve*

4 vor meaning *ago* is PREpositional rather than POSTpositional as it is in English: **vor einem Monat** *(a month ago)*, **vor zwei Tagen** *(two days ago)*.

PASSIVES VOKABULAR Ach so! *(Oh, I see.)*; Alles Gute! *(All the best!)*; Grüß Gott! *(Hi! Hello!)*; Herzlichen Glückwunsch zum Geburtstag! *(Happy birthday!)*; klingeln *(to ring)*; Mach's gut! *(Take care.)*; na gut *(all right)*; Quatsch! *(Nonsense!)*; Was gibt's? *(What's up?)*; nichts Besonderes *(nothing special)*

ZUM THEMA

A. *Lesen Sie!*

1. BEISPIEL: 1.5.   **Heute ist der erste Mai.**

31.12. / 4.10. / 14.5. / 28.8. / 1.4. / 4.1. / 30.9. / 9.3. / 7.6. / 10.11. / 31.1.

2. BEISPIEL: 3.5.   **Er hat am dritten Mai Geburtstag.**

1.11. / 2.12. / 3.1. / 4.2. / 5.3. / 15.4. / 19.5. / 20.6. / 21.7. / 31.8.

B. *Kettenreaktion (Start with any date, then follow through.)*

1. Heute ist der . . . . Was ist morgen und übermorgen?

BEISPIELE: Heute ist der zweite Juli.   **Morgen ist der dritte Juli.**
Übermorgen ist der vierte Juli.

2. Die Party ist am Tag nach dem Geburtstag. Wann ist die Party?

BEISPIEL: 1.2.   Der Geburtstag ist am ersten Februar.
Die Party ist am zweiten Februar.

4.5. / 2.6. / 7.7. / 10.8. / 12.9. / 17.10. / 19.11. / 20.12. / 2.1.

C. *Wann hast du Geburtstag? (Ask each other your birthday and find out what sign of the zodiac you are.)*

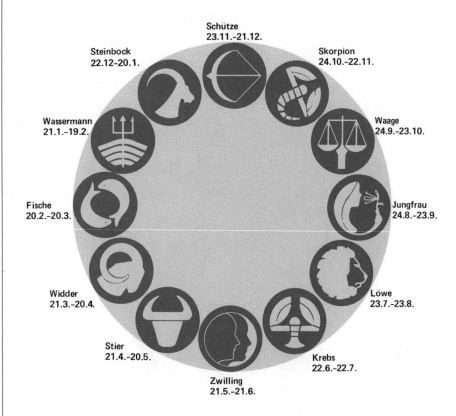

Schütze
23.11.–21.12.

Steinbock
22.12–20.1.

Skorpion
24.10.–22.11.

Wassermann
21.1.–19.2.

Waage
24.9.–23.10.

Fische
20.2.–20.3.

Jungfrau
24.8.–23.9.

Widder
21.3.–20.4.

Löwe
23.7.–23.8.

Stier
21.4.–20.5.

Krebs
22.6.–22.7.

Zwilling
21.5.–21.6.

BEISPIELE: Wann hast du Geburtstag?   **Ich habe am 21. November Geburtstag.**

Was bist du?   **Ich bin ein Skorpion.**

D. Fragen

1. Wie alt sind Sie?
2. Bekommen Sie Geschenke zum Geburtstag? Was für Geschenke bekommen Sie gern?
3. Welche Feiertage und Feste feiern wir? Wann sind sie? Welcher Feiertag gefällt Ihnen besonders gut? Welcher Feiertag ist bald *(soon)*?
4. Was für Geschenke schenkt man zum Muttertag? zum Vatertag?

E. Wir planen eine Party. *(With one or several partners, work out a plan for a party. Be prepared to outline your ideas.)*

Sagen Sie, . . .!
a. wann und wo die Party ist
b. wie lange sie dauert
c. wer kommt
d. was Sie trinken und essen
e. was Sie noch brauchen

F. Ferienkalender für deutsche Schulen

The German vacation schedule is staggered in order to relieve overcrowding on the freeways during holidays and vacations. Every **Land** *(state) except Bavaria changes its vacation schedule from year to year so that no* **Land** *will always have a very late or very early summer vacation.*

Die BRD hat 11 Länder: 1. Schleswig-Holstein 2. West-Berlin 3. Hamburg 4. Bremen 5. Niedersachsen 6. Nordrhein-Westfalen 7. Hessen 8. Rheinland-Pfalz 9. Bayern 10. Baden-Württemberg 11. Saarland.

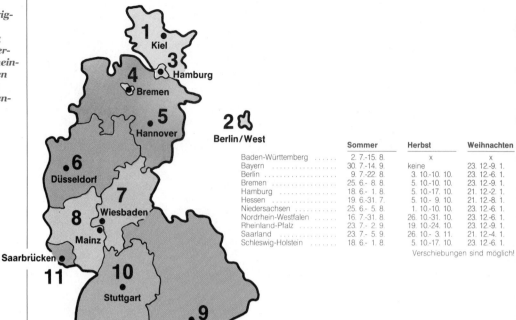

	Sommer	Herbst	Weihnachten
Baden-Württemberg	2. 7.-15. 8.	x	x
Bayern	30. 7.-14. 9.	keine	23. 12.-9. 1.
Berlin	9. 7.-22. 8.	3. 10.-10. 10.	23. 12.-6. 1.
Bremen	25. 6.- 8. 8.	5. 10.-10. 10.	23. 12.-9. 1.
Hamburg	18. 6.- 1. 8.	5. 10.-17. 10.	21. 12.-2. 1.
Hessen	19. 6.-31. 7.	5. 10.- 9. 10.	21. 12.-8. 1.
Niedersachsen	25. 6.- 5. 8.	1. 10.-10. 10.	23. 12.-6. 1.
Nordrhein-Westfalen	16. 7.-31. 8.	26. 10.-31. 10.	23. 12.-6. 1.
Rheinland-Pfalz	23. 7.- 2. 9.	19. 10.-24. 10.	23. 12.-9. 1.
Saarland	23. 7.- 5. 9.	26. 10.- 3. 11.	21. 12.-4. 1.
Schleswig-Holstein	18. 6.- 1. 8.	5. 10.-17. 10.	23. 12.-6. 1.

Verschiebungen sind möglich!

1. Wie viele Länder gibt es in der Bundesrepublik? Wie heißen sie? Wie heißen die Hauptstädte von den Ländern?
2. Was für Ferien gibt es? Wie lange sind sie ungefähr?
3. Wo gibt es keine Herbstferien?
4. Von wann bis wann sind die Osterferien? Sommerferien? Weihnachtsferien?
5. Was für Ferien gibt es hier? Wann sind sie? Wie lange dauern sie?
6. Wann beginnen die nächsten (*next*) Ferien? Wann enden sie? Was tun Sie dann?

G. Aussprache (*See also III.13–15 in the pronunciation section of the Appendix.*)

1. [ç]   i**ch**, di**ch**, ni**ch**t, ni**ch**ts, si**ch**er, fur**ch**tbar, vollei**ch**t, man**ch**mal, mö**ch**ten, spre**ch**en, Re**ch**nung, Mäd**ch**en, Mil**ch**, dur**ch**, gewöhnli**ch**, ri**ch**tig, wi**ch**tig, se**ch**zig

2. [x]   a**ch**, a**ch**t, ma**ch**en, na**ch**, Weihna**ch**ten, Spra**ch**e, au**ch**, brau**ch**en, Wo**ch**e, no**ch**, do**ch**, Bu**ch**, Ku**ch**en

3. [ks]   se**chs**, se**chs**te

4. [k]   di**ck**, **Z**u**ck**er, Bä**ck**er, Ro**ck**, Ja**ck**e, Frühstü**ck**, Glü**ck**wunsch, schme**ck**en

5. Wortpaare
   a. mich / misch
   c. nickt / nicht
   e. Nacht / nackt
   b. Kirche / Kirsche
   d. lochen / locken
   f. möchte / mochte

STRUKTUR

I. *The Present Perfect with* haben

1. The PRESENT PERFECT corresponds closely in form to the English present perfect. In both languages it consists of an inflected auxiliary verb and an unchanging past participle.

*You **have learned** that well.*	Du **hast** das gut **gelernt.**
*She **has brought** the books.*	Sie **hat** die Bücher **gebracht.**
*We **haven't spoken** any English.*	Wir **haben** kein Englisch **gesprochen.**

2. In the USE of this tense, however, there is a considerable difference between German and English. In everyday conversation English makes much use of the simple past, whereas German uses the present perfect.

Du **hast** das gut **gelernt.**	*You **learned** that well.*
Sie **hat** die Bücher **gebracht.**	*She **brought** the books.*
Wir **haben** kein Englisch **gesprochen.**	*We **didn't speak** any English.*

In fact, the German present perfect corresponds to four past-tense forms in English.

Wir haben gelernt.
$\begin{cases} \textit{We have learned.} \\ \textit{We learned.} \\ \textit{We did learn.} \\ \textit{We were learning.} \end{cases}$

3. Most German verbs FORM the present perfect by using the present tense of **haben** (V1) with the past participle (V2).

ich **habe** . . . gelernt	wir **haben** . . . gelernt
du **hast** . . . gelernt	ihr **habt** . . . gelernt
er **hat** . . . gelernt	sie **haben** . . . gelernt

4. German has two groups of verbs that form their past participles in different ways: t-verbs (also called "weak verbs") with the participle ending in **-t** (**gelernt**), and n-verbs (also called "strong verbs") with the participle ending in **-en** (**gesprochen**). Any verb not specifically identified as an irregular t-verb or as an n-verb can be assumed to be a regular t-verb.

a. The majority of German verbs are regular T-VERBS. They form their past participles with the prefix **ge-** and the ending **-t**. They correspond to such English verbs as *learn, learned,* and *ask, asked.*

| ge + stem + t | lernen → | ge | lern | t |

Verbs that follow this pattern include: brauchen, danken, dauern, feiern, fragen, hören, kaufen, machen, sagen, schenken, spielen, tanzen, wohnen, zählen.

■ *Verbs with stems ending in* -d, -t, *or certain consonant combinations make the final* -t *audible by inserting an* -e-.

ge + stem + et		kosten →	ge	kost	et

Other verbs that follow this pattern include: antworten, öffnen, regnen.

■ *A few t-verbs are irregular* (MIXED VERBS), *i.e., they change their stem. They can be compared to such English verbs as* bring, brought, *and* think, thought.

ge + stem (change) + t		bringen →	ge	brach	t

Here are the participles of familiar irregular t-verbs:

bringen	**gebracht**
denken	**gedacht**
haben	**gehabt**

b. A smaller but extremely important group of verbs, the N-VERBS, form their past participles with the prefix **ge-** and the ending **-en.** They correspond to such English verbs as *write, written,* and *speak, spoken.* The n-verbs frequently have a stem change in the past participle; their forms are not predictable. (Many of them also have a stem change in the second and third person singular of the present tense: **sprechen, du sprichst, er spricht.** Note: those that do have this change are always n-verbs.)

ge + stem (change) + en	geben →	ge	geb	en
	finden →	ge	fund	en

You will need to learn the past participles of these n-verbs before doing the following exercises (for a complete alphabetical listing, see p. 448.):

essen	**gegessen**	schlafen	**geschlafen**
finden	**gefunden**	schreiben	**geschrieben**
geben	**gegeben**	sehen	**gesehen**
heißen	**geheißen**	singen	**gesungen**
helfen	**geholfen**	sprechen	**gesprochen**
lesen	**gelesen**	tragen	**getragen**
liegen	**gelegen**	trinken	**getrunken**
nehmen	**genommen**	tun	**getan**
scheinen	**geschienen**		

5 Two groups of verbs have no **ge-prefix.**

a. INSEPARABLE-PREFIX verbs—verbs with the unstressed prefixes **be, emp-, ent-, er-, ge-, ver-,** and **zer-:**

bestellen →	be	stell	t
verstehen →	ver	stand	en

Familiar t-verbs that also follow this pattern include: **bezahlen, gehören, verkaufen; überraschen** and **wiederholen** also belong to this group, although **über-** and **wieder-** are not always inseparable prefixes.

You will need to learn the past participles of these familiar n-verbs:

beginnen	**begonnen**
bekommen	**bekommen**
empfehlen	**empfohlen**
gefallen	**gefallen**
verstehen	**verstanden**

b. Verbs ending in **-ieren** (all of which are t-verbs): **gratulieren, gratuliert; studieren, studiert.**

ÜBUNGEN

A. Geben Sie das Partizip (participle)!

BEISPIEL: fragen   **gefragt**

1. dauern, feiern, kaufen, danken, wohnen, tanzen, schneien, antworten, kosten, öffnen, regnen, verkaufen, bezahlen, wiederholen, gehören, gratulieren, denken, bringen, studieren
2. essen, finden, tun, helfen, lesen, heißen, trinken, schlafen, scheinen, singen, bekommen, empfehlen, beginnen, gefallen, verstehen

B. Ersetzen Sie das Subjekt!

BEISPIEL: Ich habe eine Flasche Sekt gekauft. (er, sie/*pl.*)
Er hat eine Flasche Sekt gekauft.
Sie haben eine Flasche Sekt gekauft.

1. Du hast nichts gesagt. (ihr, man, ich)
2. Ich habe auf englisch geantwortet. (wir, du, er)
3. Er hat Klaus Geschenke gebracht. (ihr, sie/*pl.*, ich)
4. Sie haben nur Deutsch gesprochen. (du, ihr, Robert und Silvia)

C. Ersetzen Sie das Partizip!

BEISPIEL: Ich habe das Buch geschenkt. (bestellen, lesen)
Ich habe das Buch bestellt.
Ich habe das Buch gelesen.

1. Wir haben viel gefeiert. (tanzen, spielen, singen, bekommen)
2. Sie haben Bananen gekauft. (brauchen, verkaufen, nehmen, essen)
3. Hast du ihr geantwortet? (helfen, gratulieren, schreiben)
4. Wann habt ihr es gesehen? (bekommen, bringen, finden, tun)
5. Er hat alles wiederholt. (hören, sehen, verstehen, öffnen)
6. Joachim hat nichts gefragt. (verstehen, antworten, hören)
7. Das habe ich nicht gezählt. (bringen, denken, haben, empfehlen)

D. Auf deutsch, bitte!

1. She was still sleeping.
2. They helped, too.
3. Have you (3 ×) just eaten?
4. Did you (formal) find it?
5. I didn't understand that.
6. Have you (sg. fam.) read the book?
7. I repeated the question.
8. Who took it?

II. Present Perfect with sein

Whereas most German verbs use **haben** as the auxiliary in the perfect tenses, a few very common verbs use **sein**. You will probably find it easiest to memorize **sein** together with the past participles of those verbs requiring it. But you can also determine which verbs take **sein** by remembering that they must fulfill two conditions:

- *They are* INTRANSITIVE, *i.e., they do not take an object, like* **gehen, kommen, laufen** *and* **fahren.**
- *They express a* CHANGE OF PLACE OR CONDITION (sein *and* bleiben—"Wortschatz 2"—**are exceptions to this rule**).

Wir **sind** nach Hause **gegangen.**   *We went home.*
Er **ist** müde **geworden.**   *He got tired.*

☞ *CAUTION:*

▶ *A change in prefix may cause a change in auxiliary because the meaning of the verb changes.*

Ich **bin** nach Hause **gekommen.**   *I came home.*
Ich **habe** ein Geschenk **bekommen.**   *I received a present.*

The present perfect of such verbs is formed with the present tense of **sein** (V1) and the past participle (V2).

ich **bin** . . . gekommen	wir **sind** . . . gekommen
du **bist** . . . gekommen	ihr **seid** . . . gekommen
er **ist** . . . gekommen	sie **sind** . . . gekommen

You will need to learn these past participles of n-verbs:

sein	ist gewesen	kommen	ist gekommen
gehen	ist gegangen	laufen	ist gelaufen
fahren[1]	ist gefahren	werden	ist geworden

1 Occasionally **fahren** takes an object. In that case the auxiliary **haben** is used:
Sie **sind** nach Hause **gefahren**.   *They drove home.*
Sie **haben** mein Auto nach Hause **gefahren**.   *They drove my car home.*

Of course, there are also t-verbs requiring **sein** as the auxiliary, but you have not learned any yet.

ÜBUNGEN

E. Sein *oder* **haben?** *Geben Sie das Partizip!*

BEISPIELE: empfehlen   **hat empfohlen**
                    fahren   **ist gefahren**

essen, bringen, werden, sein, gefallen, liegen, kommen, sprechen, gehen, laufen, helfen

F. *Ersetzen Sie das Subjekt!*

BEISPIEL: Sie ist gerade gegangen. (sie/*pl.*)   **Sie sind gerade gegangen.**

1. Wir sind spät nach Hause gekommen. (er, ich, Sie, du)
2. Sie sind müde gewesen. (ihr, sie/*sg.*, du, ich)
3. Sie sind zum Supermarkt gefahren. (er, wir, ihr)

G. *Auf deutsch, bitte!*

1. She drove slowly.
2. Have you (*pl. fam.*) been in Munich?
3. It has gotten cold.
4. I went to the bakery.
5. Did they come?
6. My shoes got dirty.

H. *Sagen Sie die Sätze im Perfekt!* *(Present perfect: in each case decide whether to use the auxiliary* **haben** *or* **sein**.*)

BEISPIEL: Was machst du zu   **Was hast du zu Weihnachten gemacht?**
                    Weihnachten?

1. In den Ferien fahre ich nach Zell.
2. Ich nehme zwei Wochen frei.
3. Ich wohne bei Familie Huber.
4. Das Haus liegt direkt am See.
5. Zell gefällt mir gut.
6. Nachmittags laufe ich in die Stadt.
7. Manchmal gehen wir auch ins Café.
8. Das Café gehört Familie Huber.
9. Mittwochs hilft Renate da.
10. Renate bringt mir (*me*) oft Kuchen.
11. Ich bekomme alles frei.
12. Sie empfiehlt die Sahnetorte.
13. Die schmeckt wirklich gut.
14. Den Apfelstrudel finde ich besonders gut.
15. Renate ist in den Sommerferien bei uns.
16. Wir werden gute Freunde.
17. Leider regnet es viel.
18. Wir lesen viel und hören Musik.

I. ***Stellen Sie Fragen!*** *(Working with a partner, prepare to tell the class what you learned from him/her.)*

1. Wann bist du gestern ins Bett gegangen? Wie hast du geschlafen? Wie lange hast du geschlafen?
2. Was hast du heute zum Frühstück gegessen und getrunken?
3. Wie bist du zur Uni(versität) gekommen, bist du gelaufen oder gefahren?
4. Was hast du heute zur Deutschstunde mitgebracht? Wann hat die Deutschstunde begonnen?
5. Wie viele Vorlesungen hast du heute schon gehabt?

III. *Subordinate Clauses*

You already know how to join sentences with a coordinating conjunction. Clauses can also be joined with SUBORDINATING CONJUNCTIONS. Subordinating conjunctions introduce a subordinate or dependent clause, i.e., a statement with a subject and a verb that cannot stand alone as a complete sentence:

because it's his birthday
that they have left already

While coordinating conjunctions don't affect word order, subordinating conjunctions do. German subordinate clauses are always set off by a COMMA and the inflected verb (V1) stands at the very end.

1. Six common subordinating conjunctions are:

bevor	*before*
daß	*that*
ob	*if, whether*
obwohl	*although*
weil	*because*
wenn	*if, when(ever)*

☞ *CAUTION:*

▶ *When it is possible to replace* if *with* whether, *use* **ob**; *otherwise use* **wenn**.

Ich kaufe ein Geschenk.	Ich frage Helga, **bevor** ich ein Geschenk **kaufe.**
Klaus hat Geburtstag.	Sie sagt, **daß** Klaus Geburtstag **hat.**
Ist sie sicher?	Ich frage, **ob** sie sicher **ist.**
Sie hat nicht viel Zeit.	Sie kommt zur Party, **obwohl** sie nicht viel Zeit **hat.**

Er trinkt gern Sekt.	Wir bringen eine Flasche Sekt, **weil** er gern Sekt **trinkt.**
Ich habe Zeit.	Ich komme auch, **wenn** ich Zeit **habe.**

I'll ask Helga before I buy a present.
She says that Klaus has a birthday.
I ask if she is sure.
She's coming to the party although she doesn't have much time.
We bring a bottle of champagne because he loves to drink champagne.
I'll come, too, if I have time.

2. Information questions can become subordinate clauses by using the question word as a conjunction and putting the verb last.

Wie schmeckt der Kartoffelsalat?	Sie fragt, **wie** der Kartoffelsalat **schmeckt.**
Wo sind sind die Brötchen?	Sie fragt, **wo** die Brötchen **sind.**

She asks how the potato salad tastes.
She asks where the rolls are.

Note the similarity with English:

Where are the rolls?	*She asks where the rolls **are.***

3. *Yes/no* questions require **ob** as a conjunction.

Schmeckt der Salat gut?	Sie fragt, **ob** der Salat gut **schmeckt.**
Sind die Würstchen heiß?	Sie fragt, **ob** die Würstchen heiß **sind.**

She asks whether the salad tastes good.
She asks if the franks are hot.

4. Subordinate Clauses as the First Sentence Element

Basically, a subordinate clause is a sentence element like other elements, such as objects, adverbs, etc. If the subordinate clause is the first sentence element, then the inflected verb of the main clause—the second element—comes right after the comma.

Ich **komme,** wenn ich Zeit habe.
Wenn ich Zeit habe, **komme** ich.

When listening or reading, pay special attention to the end of the sentence, which often contains crucial sentence elements. Don't make up your mind about the meaning of a sentence until you have heard the last word. As Mark Twain said in *A Connecticut Yankee in King Arthur's Court*, "Whenever the literary German dives into a sentence, that is the last we are going to see of him till he emerges on the other side of his Atlantic with his verb in his mouth."

5. The Present Perfect in Subordinate Clauses

a. In subordinate (or dependent) clauses, sentences in the present perfect follow the same rules as mentioned above: the inflected verb **haben** or **sein** (V1) stands at the end of the sentence.

Er hat ein Radio bekommen.
Er sagt, **daß** er ein Radio bekommen **hat.**

Er ist überrascht gewesen.
Er sagt, **daß** er überrascht gewesen **ist.**

ÜBUNGEN

J. Verbinden Sie die Sätze!

BEISPIEL: Frau Loth geht zur Bäckerei. Sie braucht noch etwas Brot. *(because)*
Frau Loth geht zur Bäckerei, weil sie noch etwas Brot braucht.

1. Der Herr fragt die Studentin. Kommt sie aus Amerika? *(whether)*
2. Die Stadt gefällt den Amerikanern. Sie ist alt und romantisch. *(because)*
3. Eine Tasse Kaffee tut gut. Man ist müde. *(when)*
4. Zählen Sie alles! Sie bezahlen die Rechnung! *(before)*
5. Wir spielen nicht Tennis. Das Wetter ist schlecht. *(if)*
6. Sie hat geschrieben. Sie ist in Österreich gewesen. *(that)*
7. Ich habe Hunger. Ich habe gerade ein Eis gegessen. *(although)*
8. Wiederholen Sie das bitte! Ich habe es nicht verstanden. *(because)*

K. Sagen Sie die Sätze noch einmal!

1. Beginnen Sie mit **Sie sagt, daß . . .!**

BEISPIELE: Es ist heute wunderbar.   **Sie sagt, daß es heute wunderbar ist.**

Es ist wieder schön geworden.   **Sie sagt, daß es wieder schön geworden ist.**

   a. Die Ferien beginnen am 2. Juli.
   b. Familie Bäcker fährt nach Italien.
   c. In Deutschland regnet es zuviel.
   d. In Italien scheint die Sonne.
   e. Sie haben gerade gegessen.
   f. Zum Nachtisch hat es Erdbeeren gegeben.
   g. Sie haben gut geschmeckt.
   h. Sie sind schön frisch gewesen.

2. Beginnen Sie mit **Er fragt, . . .!**

BEISPIELE: Wer hat Geburtstag?   **Er fragt, wer Geburtstag hat.**
        Wie alt ist sie geworden?   **Er fragt, wie alt sie geworden ist.**

a. Wann hat sie Geburtstag?
b. Wo feiert ihr?
c. Warum kommt Alfred nicht?
d. Was für ein Geschenk bringst du?
e. Mit wem hast du getanzt?
f. Was habt ihr getrunken?
g. Wie lange hat die Party gedauert?
h. Wie bist du nach Hause gekommen?

3. Beginnen Sie mit **Er fragt, ob . . .!**

BEISPIEL: Ißt du gern Butter mit Marmelade?
Er fragt, ob du gern Butter mit Marmelade ißt.

a. Trinkst du Kaffee mit oder ohne Milch?
b. Sind mittags die Geschäfte zu?
c. Ißt du zu Hause oder in der Mensa?
d. Hast du Durst?
e. Möchtest du etwas trinken?
f. Hat das Mittagessen lange gedauert?
g. Bist du noch einkaufen gegangen?
h. Hast du etwas Obst gekauft?

L. *Beginnen Sie mit dem Nebensatz!* (Begin with the subordinate clause.)

BEISPIEL: Ich trinke Wasser, wenn ich
Durst habe.   **Wenn ich Durst habe, trinke
ich Wasser.**

1. Ich habe ein Stück Käse gegessen, weil ich Hunger gehabt habe.
2. Ich verstehe nicht, warum die Lebensmittel Farbstoffe brauchen.
3. Ihr habt eine Party gegeben, weil ich 21 geworden bin.
4. Ich finde (es) prima, daß ihr nichts gesagt habt.
5. Ich bin nicht müde, obwohl wir bis morgens um sechs gefeiert haben.
6. Ich schlafe etwas, bevor der Tag beginnt.

ZUSAMMENFASSUNG

M. *Was haben Sie gestern gemacht? Schreiben Sie acht Sätze im Perfekt!*

BEISPIEL: **Ich habe bis 10 Uhr geschlafen. Dann . . .**

N. *Wiederholen Sie die Texte im Perfekt!*

1. Wir fahren durch Deutschland. Es gefällt mir gut. Wir sehen viel. Man fährt nicht weit, und wieder kommt eine Grenze. Wir hören viele Sprachen. Viele Europäer verstehen Englisch. In Deutschland gibt es viele Gastarbeiter. Sie arbeiten in den Großstädten. Auch sie lernen oft Deutsch. Aber ich verstehe sie nicht.

2. Gerade um die Ecke gibt es ein Lebensmittelgeschäft. Aber es ist nicht billig. Oft gehen wir in die Stadt, denn da findet man alles. Ich finde die Fußgängerzone prima, weil da keine Autos fahren. Manchmal gehen wir zur Wurstküche, essen ein paar Würstchen und trinken ein Glas Bier.

O. *Auf deutsch, bitte!*

1. The day before yesterday I gave a birthday party. *2.* Did Volker and Bettina come? *3.* Yes, they came, too. *4.* All *(alle)* brought presents. *5.* My father opened a bottle of champagne. *6.* How long did you *(pl. fam.)* celebrate? *7.* Until three o'clock. We danced, ate well, and drank a lot of Coke. *8.* The neighbors said that the music was too loud *(laut)*. *9.* Did you *(sg. fam.)* hear that? *10.* Yesterday one neighbor came and spoke with my parents. *11.* I liked the party.

You might easily think the Germans had suddenly gone crazy if you passed through Mainz or Cologne (**Köln**) on Rose Monday (**Rosenmontag**) without being fore-warned. Everywhere you would see people laughing, singing, or dancing in fantastic costumes and masks. The days before Ash Wednesday (**Aschermittwoch**), usually in February, are the climax of the carnival season, which is celebrated with great enthusiasm in those parts of the FRG where there is a Catholic majority, particularly in the south (where the carnival is called **Fasching**) and along the Rhine (where it is called **Karneval**). The custom goes back to pre-Christian times and is rooted in superstition and fear at the change of the seasons, when evil spirits had to be scared away with noise and light. Eventually the church reinterpreted this crazy time as a healthy outlet of joy before settling down for a sober Lent. Although the carnival starts officially on November 11 at 11:11 P.M. with the crowning of its prince and princess, the masquerade balls and parties don't start until the middle of January. Three days of public celebrations and parades climax the season. Cologne, Mainz, and Munich are the three major carnival cities of Germany, each celebrating in its own style.—Going back to the same tradition, but beginning the Monday *after* Ash Wednesday, is the **Basler Fasnacht**. The holiday starts early in the morning, at 4 A.M. with the **Morgestraich**, when drums and piccolos are heard in the streets and **Ladärnen** (lanterns) are the only source of light. In the afternoon costumed groups (**die Cliquen**) walk through town, often throwing **Räppli** (**Rappen**, i.e., small coins) into the crowds. At night there is dancing and fun as **Schnitzelbänglers** (comedians) make fun of politicians and current events.

EINBLICKE

WORTSCHATZ 2

das Lied, -er	*song*
die Kerze, -n	*candle*
dort	*there*
eigentlich	*actual(ly)*
ein bißchen	*some, a little bit*
immer	*always*
laut	*loud, noisy*
lustig	*funny*
(noch) nie	*never, not ever*
verrückt	*crazy*
arbeiten	*to work*
bleiben, ist geblieben	*to remain, stay*
fallen (fällt), ist gefallen	*to fall*
Spaß machen	*to be fun*
studieren[1]	*to study a particular field, be a student at a university*

1 Ich **studiere** in Heidelberg. Ich **studiere** Philosophie. BUT: Ich muß **lernen.** *(I have to study.)*

WAS IST DAS? der Prinz, Studentenball; das Kostüm, Musikinstrument, Weihnachtslied; die Adventszeit, Altstadt, Brezel, Form, Kontaktlinse, Konversationsstunde, Prinzessin, Weihnachtsdekoration, Weihnachtszeit; Ende Juli, ins Bett; dekorieren; authentisch, erst, exakt, historisch, Hunderte von, kommerziell, steif, wunderschön

(Carolyn berichtet° für die Konversations-stunde.)

Wenn sie feiern, feiern sie richtig.

5

Wie ihr gehört habt, habe ich gerade ein Jahr in Deutschland studiert. Ich bin erst° vor einem Monat wieder nach Hause gekommen, weil ich dort mit der Uni erst Ende Juli fertig geworden bin. Es ist wunderschön gewesen. Ich habe viel gesehen und viel gelernt. Heute habe ich ein paar Bilder gebracht.

Im Herbst feiert man Winzerfeste am Rhein und an der Mosel.

vintage festival

them

...tent

*Das Münchner
Oktoberfest beginnt
im September, weil es
im Oktober oft schon
kalt ist.*

Hier ist ein Bild vom Winzerfest° in Rüdesheim am Rhein. Da bin ich
im September mit Freunden gewesen. Wir haben Wein getrunken, gesungen 10
und getanzt. Ich habe immer gedacht, daß die Deutschen etwas steif sind.
Aber nicht, wenn sie feiern! So lustig und verrückt habe ich sie° noch nie
gesehen. Das ist ein Bild vom Oktoberfest in München. In dem Bierzelt°

haben wir Brezeln gegessen und natürlich Bier getrunken. Die Musik ist
sehr laut gewesen, aber es hat Spaß gemacht.   15

Halloween gibt es in Deutschland nicht, aber dafür° gibt es im Februar
den Fasching. Das ist so etwas wie° Mardi Gras in New Orleans, mit
Umzügen° und Kostümen. Ich bin als Zigeunerin° zu einem Studentenball
gegangen. Wir haben lange gefeiert, und morgens bin ich dann todmüde°
ins Bett gefallen.   20

Außer diesen° Festen gibt es natürlich noch viele Feiertage. Die Weihnachtszeit hat mir besonders gut gefallen. In einer Altstadt wie Regensburg
wirken° die Weihnachtsdekorationen nicht so kommerziell. Ich bin auch

instead

something like

parades/ gypsy

dead-tired

these

appear

Viele Menschen kommen zum Christkindlmarkt nach Nürnberg.

booths/ gingerbread/
mulled wine
. . . angel

. . . wreath/ . . . tree

zum Christkindlmarkt[1] nach Nürnberg gefahren. Da gibt es Hunderte von
Buden° mit Weihnachtsdekorationen, Lebkuchen° und Glühwein°. Den 25
Weihnachtsengel° habe ich dort gekauft. Schön, nicht wahr? In der Ad-
ventszeit hat man nur einen Adventskranz°. Den Weihnachtsbaum° sehen

their

real/ dangerous/ festive

goose/ red cabbage

alcoholic punch/ at midnight
cheers to the New Year

Die Landshuter Fürstenhochzeit ist sehr authentisch.

forget
medieval/ knights
tournaments
glasses
Middle Ages
was lucky/ every

hard

die Kinder erst am 24. Dezember, am Heiligabend² , aber dann bleibt er bis zum 6. Januar im Zimmer. Zu Weihnachten bin ich bei Familie Fuchs gewesen. Das hier ist ihr° Weihnachtsbaum. Ist er nicht schön dekoriert? Die 30 Kerzen sind übrigens echt° . Ein bißchen gefährlich° , aber festlich° ! Bevor das Christkind² die Geschenke gebracht hat, haben wir Weihnachtslieder gesungen. Am 25. und 26. Dezember sind alle Geschäfte zu. Die zwei Feiertage sind nur für Familie und Freunde. Das finde ich eigentlich gut. Hier ist ein Bild vom Weihnachtsessen: Gans° mit Rotkraut° und Knödeln. Außer 35 den Knödeln hat alles gut geschmeckt, besonders der Stollen² und die Plätzchen.

Silvester habe ich mit Freunden gefeiert. Wir haben Würstchen und Kartoffelsalat gegessen und Bowle° getrunken. Um Mitternacht° haben wir dann mit Sekt und „Prost Neujahr° !" das neue Jahr begonnen. 40

Das Bild hier ist von der Fürstenhochzeit³ in Landshut. Da bin ich im Juni gewesen. Das vergesse° ich nie. Viele Landshuter haben mittelalterliche° Kleidung getragen, und alles ist sehr authentisch gewesen: die Ritter° , Prinzen und Prinzessinnen, die Musikinstrumente und Tourniere° . Man ist historisch so exakt, daß Leute mit Brillen° Kontaktlinsen tragen, weil es im 45 Mittelalter° noch keine Brillen gegeben hat. Übrigens habe ich Glück gehabt° , denn das Fest feiert man nur alle° drei Jahre.

Ich habe immer gedacht, daß die Deutschen viel arbeiten. Aber das ist eigentlich nur halb richtig: Wenn sie arbeiten, arbeiten sie schwer° . Aber sie feiern auch viel. Und wenn sie feiern, feiern sie richtig. 50

ZUM TEXT

A. *Welche Satzteile passen zusammen?*

___ **1.** Wie ihr gehört habt,

___ **2.** Ich bin erst vor einem
Monat wieder nach Hause
gekommen,

___ **3.** Ich habe immer gedacht,

___ **4.** Bevor das Christkind die
Geschenke gebracht hat,

___ **5.** Man ist historisch so
exakt,

___ **6.** Wenn die Deutschen
arbeiten,

___ **7.** Wenn sie feiern,

a. haben wir Weihnachtslieder
gesungen.

b. arbeiten sie schwer.

c. weil ich dort mit der Uni erst
Ende Juli fertig geworden bin.

d. daß Leute mit Brillen
Kontaklinsen tragen.

e. habe ich gerade ein Jahr in
Deutschland studiert.

f. daß die Deutschen etwas steif
sind.

g. feiern sie richtig.

B. *Was fehlt? (Fill in the missing verb forms with an appropriate verb from the list below. Use present perfect.)*

bringen, fahren, feiern, gefallen, gehen, kaufen, kommen, sein, studieren

1. Carolyn _____ vor einem Monat nach Hause _____ . 2. Sie _____ ein Jahr in Deutschland _____ . 3. Es _____ wunderbar _____ . 4. Sie _____ ein paar Bilder in die Deutschstunde _____ . 5. Im September _____ sie mit Freunden zum Winzerfest nach Rüdesheim _____ . 6. Im Fasching _____ sie als Zigeunerin zu einem Studentenball _____ . 7. Die Weihnachtszeit _____ Carolyn besonders gut _____ . 8. In Nürnberg _____ sie einen Weihnachtsengel _____ . 9. Sie _____ Weihnachten bei der Familie Fuchs _____ .

C. Persönliche Fragen

1. Welches Fest hier ist so wie der Fasching? Sind Sie einmal dort gewesen, oder haben Sie es im Fernsehen (on TV) gesehen? Wie finden Sie es?

2. Wie feiern Sie Weihnachten (oder Hanukkah)? Sind Ihre Kerzen echt oder elektrisch (electric)? Warum? Schreiben Sie zu Weihnachten viele Karten? Warum? Warum nicht?

3. Wie feiern Sie gewöhnlich Silvester? Was essen und trinken Sie dann? Wie lange feiern Sie gewöhnlich? Haben Sie auch Feuerwerk (fireworks) oder Kracher (firecrackers)?

D. Schriftliche Übung (Written exercise. Jot down some key words about two of the holidays Carolyn mentions, then write three to five sentences about each.)

BEISPIEL: **Winzerfest—Rüdesheim am Rhein, September, Wein, singen, tanzen, lustig**

> Carolyn ist zum Winzerfest nach Rüdesheim am Rhein gefahren. Das Winzerfest ist im September. Die Leute haben viel Wein getrunken, gesungen und getanzt. Es ist sehr lustig gewesen.

E. Plätzchen für die Feiertage: Spritzgebäck

¾ *cup*
½ *cup*

2 *cups/ flour*

175 g° Butter oder Margarine
100 g° Zucker
1 Teelöffel Vanille
1 Eigelb
300 g° Mehl°
¼ Teelöffel Salz

350°F/ preheat/ cream until fluffy add/ sift

mix/ dough/ cookie press/ put different/ greased/ cookie sheet/ press

Ofen auf 175–190 Grad° vorwärmen°. Butter schaumig rühren°; Zucker, Vanille und Eigelb dazu geben°. Mehl und Salz sieben° und in die Masse geben, gut mischen°. Den Teig° in eine Teigspritze° füllen° und verschiedene° Formen auf ein gefettetes° Backblech° spritzen°. Acht bis zehn Minuten backen, oder bis die Plätzchen braun werden.

Guten Appetit!

> **Jetzt sagen Sie bitte Ihrer Nachbarin/Ihrem Nachbarn, wie Sie die Plätzchen gemacht haben!** (Except for **backen / gebacken**, all new verbs in this recipe are t-verbs.)

BEISPIEL: **Ich habe den Ofen auf 175 Grad vorgewärmt. Dann habe ich . . .**

ÜBRIGENS

1. **Nürnberg**'s outdoor **Christkindlmarkt** is the largest German Christmas market. Over two million people visit it during the four weeks before Christmas. Booths offer Christmas decorations, candy, toys, etc. The smell of hot punch, burnt almonds, and roasted chestnuts is in the air, and there are performances by choirs

and instrumentalists. **Nürnberg** is also the source of the delicious **Nürnberger Lebkuchen**, a fancy kind of gingerbread.

2. In the German-speaking countries, Christmas includes a late afternoon or midnight church service on Christmas Eve (**Heiligabend**). Presents, usually not wrapped but displayed on tables, are exchanged on the evening of the 24th. Then follow not one, but two holidays, December 25 and 26. In southern Germany the **Christbaum** and gifts are brought by the **Christkind**, in northern Germany by the **Weihnachtsmann**. No Christmas would be complete without the traditional **Weihnachtsplätzchen** and especially **Stollen**, a fragrant buttery yeast bread filled with almonds, currants, raisins, and candied citrus peel.

3. In 1475 Duke Ludwig the Rich of **Landshut** ordered a lavish feast prepared for his son's wedding to a Polish princess. Its splendor became part of folk legend. Today the **Fürstenhochzeit** is reenacted every three years with authentic costumes, instruments, games, parades, and other observances.

GESPRÄCHE

TOURIST Entschuldigen Sie! Können Sie mir sagen, wo das Hotel Sacher[1] ist?

WIENER Erste Straße links hinter der Staatsoper[2].

TOURIST Und wie komme ich von da zum Stephansdom[3]?

WIENER Geradeaus, die Kärntnerstraße entlang.

TOURIST Wie weit ist es zum Dom?

WIENER Nicht weit. Sie können zu Fuß gehen!

TOURIST Danke schön!

WIENER Bitte schön!

Da drüben

TOURIST Entschuldigen Sie bitte! Wo ist das Burgtheater[4]?

HERR Es tut mir leid. Ich bin nicht aus Wien.

TOURIST Entschuldigen Sie! Ist das das Burgtheater?

DAME Nein, das ist nicht das Burgtheater, sondern die Staatsoper. Fahren Sie mit der Straßenbahn zum Rathaus! Gegenüber vom Rathaus ist das Burgtheater.

TOURIST Und wo hält die Straßenbahn?

DAME Da drüben links!

TOURIST Vielen Dank!

DAME Bitte schön!

ÜBRIGENS

1. The **Hotel Sacher** is probably the best-known hotel in Vienna. One of the reasons for its popularity is its famous café, for which a rich, delicious cake (**Sacher Torte**) has been named.

2. The **Staatsoper**, completed in 1869, is one of the foremost European opera houses. Like most European theaters, it is supported through public funds.

3. The **Stephansdom** is a masterpiece of Gothic architecture dating from the twelfth century. Its roof of colored tile and its spire (137 meters—about 450 feet—high) make it the landmark of Vienna.

4. The **Burgtheater** (1776) is one of the great theaters of the German-speaking world.

Excuse Me! Where Is . . .?

TOURIST Excuse me! Can you tell me where the Sacher Hotel is?
VIENNESE First street to the left behind the opera.
TOURIST And how do I get from there to St. Stephen's Cathedral?
VIENNESE Straight ahead along Kärtnerstraße.
TOURIST How far is it to the cathedral?
VIENNESE Not far. You can walk there.
TOURIST Thank you very much.
VIENNESE You're welcome.

Over There

TOURIST Excuse me. Where is the Burgtheater?
GENTLEMAN I'm sorry. I'm not from Vienna.
TOURIST Excuse me. Is that the Burgtheater?
LADY No, that's not the Burgtheater but the opera house. Take the streetcar to city hall. The Burgtheater is across from city hall.
TOURIST And where does the streetcar stop?
LADY Over there to the left.
TOURIST Thank you very much.
LADY You're welcome.

In der Stadt

DER STADTPLAN, ̈E *city map*

der Bahnhof, ̈e	*train station*	*die* Bank, -en	*bank*
Bus, -se	*bus*	Bibliothek, -en	*library*
Dom, -e	*cathedral*	Brücke, -n	*bridge*
Park, -s	*park*	Haltestelle, -n	*(bus etc.) stop*
Platz, ̈e	*place; square*	Kirche, -n	*church*
Weg, -e	*way; trail*	Post	*post office*
das Auto, -s	*car*	Schule, -n	*school*
Hotel, -s	*hotel*	Straße, -n	*street*
Kino, -s	*movie theater*	Straßenbahn, -en	*streetcar*
Museum, Museen	*museum*	U-Bahn	*subway*
Rathaus, ̈er	*city hall*	Universität, -en	*university*
Schloß, ̈sser	*palace*		
Taxi, -s	*taxi*		
Theater, -	*theater*		

WEITERES

der Mann, ̈er[1]	*man; husband*
Tourist, -en, -en	*tourist*
die Dame, -en	*lady*
da drüben	*over there*
Entschuldigen Sie!	*Excuse me!*
Es tut mir leid.	*I'm sorry.*
Fahren Sie mit dem Bus!	*Go by bus.*
gegenüber von *(+ dat.)*	*across from*
(immer) geradeaus	*(always) straight ahead*
in der Nähe von *(+ dat.)*	*near the . . . (in the vicinity of . . .)*
links / rechts	*on the left / on the right*
nah / weit	*near / far*
schade	*too bad*
sondern[2]	*but (on the contrary)*
Vielen Dank!	*Thank you very much.*
halten (hält), gehalten[3]	*to stop*
zeigen	*to show*
zu Fuß gehen, ist zu Fuß gegangen	*to walk*

1 Don't confuse the indefinite pronoun **man** with the noun **der Mann:**

Hier spricht **man** Deutsch.　　BUT **Der Mann** spricht Deutsch.
Here one *speaks (they/people*　　*The* man *speaks German.*
　speak) German.

2 For the difference between **aber** and **sondern,** see p. 149.
3 **halten** here refers to a vehicle coming to a stop: **Der Bus hält.** You might tell a taxi driver: **Halten Sie da drüben!** To stop doing something (e.g., *Stop bothering me.*) cannot be expressed by this verb.

PASSIVES VOKABULAR die Oper, -n *(opera house)*; hinter *(behind)*

ZUM THEMA

A. Mustersätze

1. das Theater / die Oper: **Das ist nicht** das Theater, **sondern** die Oper.
   das Rathaus / die Universität; das Museum / die Bibliothek; die Bank /
   die Post; die Bushaltestelle / die Straßenbahnhaltestelle

2. zur Universität: **Können Sie mir sagen, wie ich** zur Universität
   komme?
   zum Rathaus, zur Bibliothek, zum Museum, zur Schulstraße

3. erste / links: **Die** erste **Straße** links.
   zweite / rechts; dritte / links; vierte / rechts

4. Straßenbahn: **Fahren Sie mit** der Straßenbahn!
   dem Bus, dem Auto, der U-Bahn, dem Taxi

5. da drüben: **Die Straßenbahn hält** da drüben.
   da drüben rechts, beim Bahnhof, in der Nähe vom Park, gegenüber
   vom Theater

B. Was bedeuten die Wörter, und was sind die Artikel?

Domplatz, Fußgängerweg, Schloßhotel, Postbus, Touristenstadt, Kir-
chenfest, Schulferien, Studentenkino, Bahnhofsdrogerie, Universitätsparkplatz, Parkuhr

C. Wo ist . . .? (Ask for various places in your town or on your campus.)

x Entschuldigen Sie! Ist das _____ ?
y Nein, das ist nicht _____ , sondern _____ .
x Wo ist _____ ?
y _____ ist in der Nähe von _____ .
x Und wie komme ich von hier zu _____ ?
y _____ .
x Wie weit ist es zu _____ ?
y _____ .
x Vielen Dank!
y _____ !

139

D. Fragen zum Stadtplan

Sehen Sie auf den Stadtplan! Sie sind am Bahnhof. Fragen Sie, . . .!

1. wo _____ ist
2. wie Sie zum/zur _____ kommen
3. ob es weit oder nah ist
4. ob Sie zu Fuß gehen können (usw.)

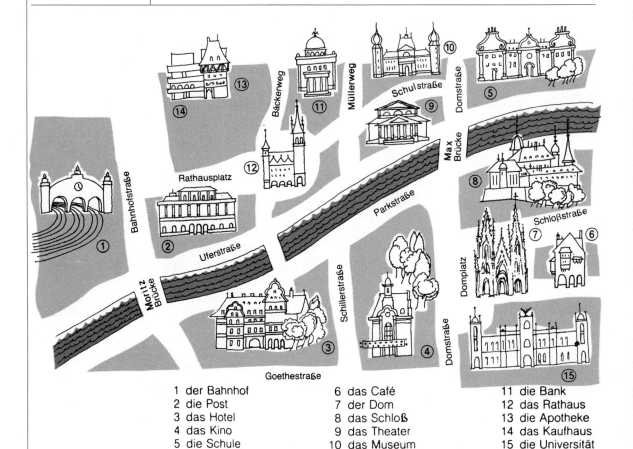

1 der Bahnhof
2 die Post
3 das Hotel
4 das Kino
5 die Schule

6 das Café
7 der Dom
8 das Schloß
9 das Theater
10 das Museum

11 die Bank
12 das Rathaus
13 die Apotheke
14 das Kaufhaus
15 die Universität

E. Aussprache (See also II.29–36 in the pronunciation section of the Appendix.)

1. [ö:] Österreich, Brötchen, Bahnhöfe, Klöße, Goethe, schön, gewöhnlich, französisch, hören

2. [ö] öffnen, östlich, können, Löffel, zwölf, nördlich, möchten, Wörter, Röcke

3. Wortpaare
   a. kennen / können
   b. Sehne / Söhne
   c. große / Größe
   d. schon / schön
   e. Sühne / Söhne
   f. Höhle / Hölle

Jederzeit

STRUKTUR

I. *Personal Pronouns*

1. In English the PERSONAL PRONOUNS are *I, me, you, he, him, she, her, it, we, us, they,* and *them.* Some of these pronouns are used as subjects, others as direct or indirect objects, or objects of prepositions.

SUBJECT: *He is coming.*
DIRECT OBJECT: *I see him.*
INDIRECT OBJECT: *I give him the book.*
OBJECT OF A PREPOSITION: *We'll go without him.*

The German personal pronouns are likewise used as subjects, direct or indirect objects, or objects of prepositions. Like the definite and indefinite articles, personal pronouns have special forms in the various cases. You already know the nominative case of these pronouns. Here now are the nominative, accusative, and dative cases together:

	singular					plural			sg./pl.
nom.	ich	du	er	es	sie	wir	ihr	sie	Sie
acc.	mich	dich	ihn	es	sie	uns	euch	sie	Sie
dat.	mir	dir	ihm	ihm	ihr	uns	euch	ihnen	Ihnen

SUBJECT: **Er** kommt.
DIRECT OBJECT: Ich sehe **ihn.**
INDIRECT OBJECT: Ich gebe **ihm** das Buch.
OBJECT OF A PREPOSITION: Wir gehen **ohne ihn.**

▪ *Note the similarities between the definite article of the noun and the pronoun that replaces it.*

	masc.	neut.	fem.	pl.
nom.	der Mann = **er**	das Kind = **es**	die Frau = **sie**	die Leute = **sie**
acc.	den Mann = **ihn**	das Kind = **es**	die Frau = **sie**	die Leute = **sie**
dat.	dem Mann = **ihm**	dem Kind = **ihm**	der Frau = **ihr**	den Leuten = **ihnen**

2. As in English, the dative object usually precedes the accusative object unless the accusative object is a pronoun.

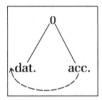

Ich gebe **dem Studenten** den Kuli.   *I'll give the student the pen.*
Ich gebe **ihm** den Kuli.   *I'll give him the pen.*
Ich gebe ihn **dem Studenten.**   *I'll give it to the student.*
Ich gebe ihn **ihm.**   *I'll give it to him.*

ÜBUNGEN

A. ***Ersetzen Sie die Hauptwörter durch Pronomen!*** *(Replace the nouns with pronouns in the appropriate cases.)*

BEISPIELE: den Bruder   **ihn**
der Schwester   **ihr**

1. der Vater, dem Mann, den Großvater, dem Freund, den Ober, der Herr
2. die Freundin, der Großmutter, der Dame, die Frau, der Familie, die Schwester
3. die Eltern, den Jungen, den Frauen, die Freundinnen, den Schweizern, die Touristen, den Männern, den Deutschen
4. für die Mutter, ohne die Kinder, mit den Freunden, gegen die Studenten, außer dem Großvater, ohne den Ober, von den Eltern, für die Mädchen, zu dem Fräulein, bei der Großmutter

B. Kombinieren Sie mit den Präpositionen! Was sind die Akkusativ- und Dativformen?

BEISPIELE: ich (ohne, mit) **ohne mich**
mit mir

1. er (für, mit)
2. wir (durch, von)
3. Sie (gegen, zu)
4. du (ohne, bei)
5. ihr (für, außer)
6. sie/*sg.* (um, nach)
7. sie/*pl.* (für, aus)
8. es (ohne, außer)

C. Antworten Sie! Ersetzen Sie die Hauptwörter durch Hauptwörter und Pronomen!

BEISPIELE: Wo ist das Hotel? / Es ist da drüben (Bank, Bus)
Und die Bank?   Sie ist da drüben.
Und der Bus?   Er ist da drüben.

1. Wo ist die Post? / Da ist sie. (Dom, Rathaus, Apotheke)
2. Ist das Museum weit von hier? / Nein es nicht weit von hier. (Kirche, Lebensmittelgeschäft, Marktplatz)
3. Zeigen Sie der Dame den Weg? / Ja, ich zeige ihr den Weg. (Mann, Leute, Touristin)
4. Helfen Sie dem Herrn? Ja, ich helfe ihm. (Kind, Damen, Tourist)
5. Haben Sie die Straßenbahn genommen? / Ja, ich habe sie genommen. (Bus, U-Bahn, Taxi)
6. Wie hat dir die Stadt gefallen? / Sie hat mir gut gefallen. (Hotel, Universität, Park)

D. Was fehlt? (*Complete the sentences with the appropriate German case forms of the suggested pronouns.*)

BEISPIELE: Sie kauft _____ das Buch. (*me, you/formal*)
Sie kauft mir das Buch.
Sie kauft Ihnen das Buch.

1. Siehst du _____ ? (*them, him, her, me, us*)
2. Geben Sie es _____ ! (*him, me, her, us, them*)
3. Sie braucht _____ . (*you/sg., you/pl., you/formal, me, him, them, us*)
4. Wie geht es _____ ? (*How is/are . . . he, they, you/formal, she, you/sg., you/pl.*)
5. Das Fräulein hat _____ das Eis gebracht. (*you/sg., you/pl., us, him, her, me, you/formal*)
6. Hat die Party _____ überrascht? (*you/formal, me, you/sg., us, her, him, you/pl.*)

E. Auf deutsch, bitte!

1. Did you (*sg. fam.*) thank him?
2. We congratulated her.
3. I surprised them.
4. We'll show you (*pl. fam.*) the palace.
5. Did they answer you (*pl. fam.*)?
6. I was writing (to) you (*sg. fam.*).
7. Are you (*sg. fam.*) going to give him the present?

F. Variieren Sie die Sätze!

1. Es tut mir leid.
   - a. He's sorry.
   - b. She's sorry.
   - c. They're sorry.
   - d. Are you (3 ×) sorry?
   - e. We aren't sorry.
   - f. Why are you (*sg. fam.*) sorry?
   - g. I was sorry.
   - h. We weren't sorry.
   - i. Who was sorry?

2. Wien gefällt mir.
   - a. They like Vienna.
   - b. Do you (3 ×) like Vienna?
   - c. He doesn't like Vienna.
   - d. We like Vienna.
   - e. I liked Vienna.
   - f. How did you (*sg. fam.*) like Vienna?
   - g. Who didn't like Vienna?
   - h. She didn't like Vienna.

G. Ersetzen Sie die Hauptwörter durch Pronomen! *(Restate the sentences three times, each time replacing one more noun.)*

BEISPIEL: Der Herr zeigt der Dame den Weg. **Er zeigt der Dame den Weg.**
Er zeigt ihr den Weg.
Er zeigt ihn ihr.

1. Die Frau zeigt dem Mann die Haltestelle.
2. Der Junge zeigt den Touristen den Bahnhof.
3. Das Fräulein zeigt dem Kind das Museum.
4. Die Studentin hat den Freunden die Universität gezeigt.

Viele Städte in Europa haben noch Straßenbahnen.

II. *Modal Auxiliary Verbs*

1. Both English and German have a small group of MODAL AUXILIARY VERBS that in some way modify the meaning of an ordinary verb. Modal verbs express such ideas as the permission, ability, necessity, obligation, or desire to do something.

dürfen	*to be allowed to, may*		sollen	*to be supposed to*
können	*to be able to, can*		wollen	*to want to*
müssen	*to have to, must*		mögen	*to like*

- *The German modals are irregular in the singular of the present tense:*

	dürfen	können	müssen	sollen	wollen	mögen	
ich	**darf**	**kann**	**muß**	**soll**	**will**	**mag**	**möchte**
du	**darfst**	**kannst**	**mußt**	**sollst**	**willst**	**magst**	**möchtest**
er	**darf**	**kann**	**muß**	**soll**	**will**	**mag**	**möchte**
wir	dürfen	können	müssen	sollen	wollen	mögen	möchten
ihr	dürft	könnt	müßt	sollt	wollt	mögt	möchtet
sie	dürfen	können	müssen	sollen	wollen	mögen	möchten

- *The **möchte**-forms of **mögen** occur more frequently than the **mag**-forms. You already know that they mean* would like (to have); ***mögen** is usually used in a negative sentence. In the exercises you will find only the **möchte**-forms.*

Ich **möchte** ein Bier.	*I would like (to have) a beer.*
Ich **mag** Bier nicht.	*I don't like beer.*

2. Modals are another example of the two-part verb phrase. In statements and information questions, the modal is the inflected second element of the sentence (V1). The modified verb (V2) appears at the very end of the sentence in its infinitive form.

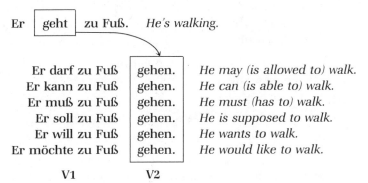

| Er | geht | zu Fuß. | *He's walking.* |

Er darf zu Fuß	gehen.	*He may (is allowed to) walk.*
Er kann zu Fuß	gehen.	*He can (is able to) walk.*
Er muß zu Fuß	gehen.	*He must (has to) walk.*
Er soll zu Fuß	gehen.	*He is supposed to walk.*
Er will zu Fuß	gehen.	*He wants to walk.*
Er möchte zu Fuß	gehen.	*He would like to walk.*

V1   V2

☞ *CAUTION:*

▶ *The English set of modals is incomplete and frequently is supplemented by such forms as* is allowed to, is able to, has to, is supposed to. *The German modals, however, do not use such supplements. They follow the pattern of* may, can, *and* must: **Ich muß gehen.** *(I must go.)*

3. Modals can be used without an infinitive, provided the modified verb is clearly understood. This happens particularly often with verbs of motion:

Mußt du jetzt nach Hause?—Ja, ich **muß.**
Willst du zum Supermarkt?—Ja, ich **will**, aber ich **kann** nicht.

4. Watch these important differences in meaning:

a. gern vs. **mögen**

Ich **esse gern** Kuchen.　BUT　Ich **möchte** ein Stück Kuchen (**haben**).

The first sentence says that *I am generally fond of cake (I like to eat cake. I enjoy eating it.)* The second sentence, on the other hand, implies a desire for a piece of cake at this particular moment (*I'd like a piece of cake*).

b. wollen vs. **mögen**

Notice the difference in tone and politeness between these two sentences:

Ich **will** Kuchen.　BUT　Ich **möchte** Kuchen.

The first might be said by a spoiled child (*I want cake*), the second by a polite adult (*I would like cake.*)

NOTE: Because modals use two different forms in the present perfect, we have avoided sentences with modals in that tense. The simple past of the modals will be discussed in Chapter 11.

5. Modals in Subordinate Clauses

a. Remember that the inflected verb stands at the very end of clauses introduced by subordinate conjunctions such as **bevor, daß, ob, obwohl, wenn,** and **weil:**

Sie sagt, **daß** du zu Fuß gehen **kannst.**
Du kannst zu Fuß gehen, **wenn** du **möchtest.**

b. If the sentence starts with the subordinate clause, then the inflected verb of the main sentence (the modal) follows right after the comma.

　　　　　　Du **kannst** zu Fuß gehen, wenn du möchtest.
Wenn du möchtest, **kannst** du zu Fuß gehen.

ÜBUNGEN

H. Ersetzen Sie das Subjekt!

BEISPIELE: Wir sollen zum Markt fahren.   **Ich soll zum Markt fahren.**
(ich, du)   **Du sollst zum Markt fahren.**

1. Wir wollen zu Hause bleiben. (er, sie/*pl.*, du, ich)
2. Sie müssen noch die Rechnung bezahlen. (ich, ihr, du, Vater)
3. Du darfst zum Bahnhof kommen. (er, ihr, die Kinder, ich)
4. Möchtet ihr ein Eis haben? (sie, du, er, das Fräulein)
5. Können Sie mir sagen, wo das ist? (du, ihr, er, die Damen)

I. Sagen Sie die Sätze noch einmal mit den Modalverben!

BEISPIEL: Ich finde das Rathaus nicht. (können)
Ich kann das Rathaus nicht finden.

1. Ich empfehle die Schule. (können)
2. Der Vater hilft dem Nachbarn. (müssen)
3. Der Tourist dankt der Wienerin. (möchten)
4. Die Studenten bleiben in Wien. (wollen)
5. Man versteht nicht alles. (können)
6. Sprecht ihr Deutsch? (wollen)
7. Das Fräulein bringt dem Mädchen einen Löffel. (sollen)
8. Ißt das Kind ein Eis? (dürfen)
9. Die Kinder fragen die Großeltern. (sollen)
10. Paul fährt mit dem Freund nach Österreich. (dürfen)
11. Ich gehe zur Post. (müssen)
12. Wir fahren mit dem Auto zum See. (möchten)

J. Sagen Sie die Sätze noch einmal!

1. Beginnen Sie mit **Heike fragt, ob . . .**!
   a. Können Sie ihr helfen?
   b. Kannst du ihr den Stadtplan geben?
   c. Willst du mit ihr einkaufen gehen?
   d. Sollen wir zur Apotheke gehen?
   e. Möchtet ihr hier bleiben?
   f. Müssen Sie wieder nach Hause?
   g. Können wir zu Fuß zum Dom gehen?

2. Beginnen Sie mit **Sabine fragt, . . .**!
   a. Wo kann man Blumen bekommen?
   b. Wer will eine Tasse Kaffee?
   c. Was soll sie ihm zum Geburtstag schenken?
   d. Wie lange soll die Party dauern?
   e. Wo wollen wir die Party halten?
   f. Warum kann er heute nicht arbeiten?

K. Auf deutsch, bitte!

1. He wants to see the cathedral.
2. They have to go to the post office.
3. I can't read that.
4. You (*pl. fam.*) are supposed to speak German.
5. You (*sg. fam.*) may order a piece of cake.
6. She's supposed to study (**lernen**).
7. We have to find the way.
8. Do you (*sg. fam.*) want to surprise him?
9. Can't you (3 ×) help me?
10. We'd like to drive to Vienna.
11. Are we allowed to see the palace?
12. She would like to show us the city.

L. Welches Modalverb fehlt? (Complete with a partner or in a small group. Compare your answers with those in other groups and see how meaning is affected by your choice of modal.)

UWE Till, _____ du mit mir gehen? Ich _____ einen Stadtplan kaufen.

TILL Wo _____ wir einen Stadtplan bekommen?

UWE Das Büchergeschäft _____ Stadtpläne haben.

TILL Gut. Ich _____ zwei Bücher für meinen Bruder kaufen. Ich gehe mit dir.

UWE _____ wir zu Fuß gehen, oder _____ wir mit dem Fahrrad (*bicycle*) fahren?

TILL Ich _____ mit dem Fahrrad fahren. Dann _____ wir noch zur Bank, bevor sie zu ist. Die Bücher sind bestimmt nicht billig. _____ du nicht auch zur Bank?

UWE Ja, richtig. Ich _____ diese Rechnung bezahlen.

III. sondern *vs.* aber

German has two coordinating conjunctions corresponding to the English *but*.

but
- **aber** → *but, however*
- **sondern** → *but on the contrary, but rather*

- **sondern** *must be used when the first clause is negated* AND *the meaning* ***but on the contrary*** *is implied (frequently with opposites,* **Gegenteile***).*

sondern or aber?
↓
Is the first clause negated? → NO → **aber**: Das Restaurant ist teuer, **aber** gut.

↓
YES
↓

Is there a contrast implied? → NO → **aber**: Das Restaurant ist nicht teuer, **aber** gut.

↓
YES
↓

sondern: Das Restaurant ist nicht teuer, **sondern** billig.

- **nicht nur . . . sondern auch . . .**

Das Restaurant ist **nicht nur** billig, **sondern auch** gut.
The restaurant is not only inexpensive, but also good.

ÜBUNGEN

M. **sondern** *oder* aber?

BEISPIEL: Er geht nicht zu Fuß, _____ er fährt mit dem Bus.
Er geht nicht zu Fuß, sondern er fährt mit dem Bus.

1. Wien ist sehr schön, _____ Salzburg gefällt mir besser (*better*).
2. Die Straßenbahn hält nicht hier, _____ gegenüber von der Post.
3. Gehen Sie beim Theater nicht rechts, _____ geradeaus!
4. Die Kirche ist nicht alt, _____ neu.
5. Er ist nicht besonders intelligent, _____ sexy.
6. Das ist kein Museum, _____ eine Bibliothek.
7. Mein Großvater ist nicht alt, _____ es geht ihm nicht gut.

ZUSAMMENFASSUNG

N. ***Bilden Sie Sätze!*** *(Double slashes separate one clause from the other.)*

BEISPIEL: können / Sie / sagen / mir // wo / sein / Universität?
Können Sie mir sagen, wo die Universität ist?

1. können / du / sagen / ihm // wie / heißen / Straße?
2. können / er / sagen / uns // wie / weit / es / sein / zu / Bahnhof?
3. können / sie (*pl.*) / sagen / euch // ob / es / geben / hier / Straßenbahn oder Bus?
4. können / Sie / sagen / ihr // wo / Bus / hält?
5. können / ihr / sagen / mir // wie lange / Geschäfte / sein / offen?

O. ***Auf deutsch, bitte!*** *(In this exercise use the formal address with* **Sie.**)

1. What's the matter? *2.* I like the café, but I've got to go to the bank.
3. Excuse (*formal*) me, can you tell me where there's a bank? *4.* I'm sorry,
but I'm not from Vienna. *5.* Whom can I ask? *6.* Who can help me?
7. May I help you? *8.* I'd like to find a bank. *9.* Near the cathedral (there)
is a bank. *10.* Can you tell me whether that's far from here? *11.* You can
walk (there), but the banks close (are closed) in twenty minutes. *12.* Take
the subway or a taxi!

Wien (Vienna) is the capital of Austria and with 1.6 million inhabitants also its largest city. The heart of the city is the **Innenstadt** (Inner City), which dates from medieval times. The Romanesque-Gothic **Stephansdom**, built between the thirteenth and sixteenth centuries, is its symbol. Also notable are the magnificent eighteenth-century baroque buildings. The medieval city walls (**Stadtmauer**) were replaced in 1858 by the modern **Ringstraße.** Vienna reached its zenith of power and wealth as the capital of the Austro-Hungarian Empire during the reign of Emperor Franz Joseph (1848–1916), when it developed into one of Central Europe's most important cultural centers. Today Vienna is associated especially with music. Composers such as Haydn, Mozart, Beethoven, Brahms, Johann and Richard Strauß, Mahler and Schönberg, all lived and worked there for at least part of their lives and left a lasting imprint on the cultural life of the city.

EINBLICKE

bekannt	*well-known*
Das macht nichts.	*That doesn't matter.*
einmal	*once, (at) one time*
gemütlich	*pleasant, cozy*
genug	*enough*
interessant	*interesting*
leider	*unfortunately*
lieb[1]	*dear*
schon	*already*
stundenlang	*for hours*
toll	*great, super*
bummeln, ist gebummelt	*to stroll*

1 lieb**e** Eltern, lieb**er** Michael, lieb**e** Elisabeth

NOTE: In the following letter Michael capitalizes **Du, Ihr,** *and* **Euer** *(your) when he addresses his parents. This is proper in letters.*

WAS IST DAS? der Garten, Kilometer, Ring, Sport, Walzer; die Großstadt, Rock-Musik, Romantik, Winterresidenz; die Kronen, Juwelen; elegant, zentral

HOTEL WOLF

greetings

on the go/ by far not

reach

Grüße° aus
Wien

Liebe Eltern!

Jetzt sind wir schon drei Tage in Wien. Obwohl wir von morgens bis abends unterwegs° sind, haben wir noch lange nicht° alles gesehen. Wien ist groß und sehr interessant. Unser Hotel liegt übrigens 5 sehr zentral, in der Nähe von der Staatsoper, und wir können fast alles zu Fuß erreichen°. So viel bin ich noch nie gelaufen!

Seht° einmal auf den Stadtplan, dann könnt Ihr mir besser° folgen°! Bei der Staatsoper seht Ihr den Ring und die Kärtnerstraße. Der Ring führt° um die Altstadt. Er ist vier Kilometer[1] lang und läuft an der früheren° Stadt- 10 mauer° entlang. Am Ring liegen die Hofburg, das Burgtheater, die Universität, das Rathaus, Museen und Parks.

MUSEUM FÜR VÖLKERKUNDE

A-1014 WIEN, NEUE HOFBURG
TELEFON (0222) 93 45 41

Von der Staatsoper kann man zu Fuß durch den Burggarten zur Hofburg gehen. Die Hofburg ist einmal die Winterresidenz der° Habsburger

Die Hofburg ist einmal die Winterresidenz der Habsburger Kaiser gewesen.

Kaiser° gewesen. Sie ist nicht nur bekannt für die Schatzkammer° mit Kro- 15
nen und Juwelen, sondern auch für die Spanische Reitschule°. Dort ist das
Reiten° kein Sport, sondern Kunst°. Von überall kommen die Menschen
und wollen die weißen Pferde° (sie heißen Lippizaner) tanzen sehen°. Sonntags singen hier auch die Wiener Sängerknaben°. Die Hofburg ist wirklich
interessant. Von der Hofburg kann man durch den Volksgarten zum Burg- 20
theater laufen. Das Burgtheater hat mir besonders gut gefallen, weil es so
elegant ist.

Wien ist wirklich schön! Überall findet man bekannte Namen: das
Goethe²-Denkmal°, Mozart-Denkmal, Beethoven-Denkmal, Johann Strauß-
Denkmal und so weiter. Ihr dürft aber nicht denken, daß man hier nur 25
Walzer hört. Hier kann man genauso° viel Rock-Musik hören, wie° bei uns!
Aber zurück° zum Stadtplan, zur Kärntnerstraße. Die Kärntnerstraße ist

eine Fußgängerzone, wo man stundenlang gemütlich bummeln kann. Hier
gibt es auch viele Geschäfte, aber alles ist sehr teuer. Die Kärntnerstraße
bringt Euch zum Stephansdom. Ich bin mit dem Aufzug° im Turm° hin- 30

ST.-STEPHANS-DOM

TURM

Eintrittskarte für Studenten

INKLUSIVE 8% MEHRWERTSTEUER

S 8.—   № 43524

aufgefahren° und habe von dort oben° Bilder gemacht°. Hoffentlich° sind sie etwas geworden°! Übrigens kann man auch mit einer Kutsche° durch die Altstadt fahren. Etwas Romantik aus der guten alten Zeit°!

Gestern sind wir mit der Straßenbahn und mit dem Bus durch den Wiener Wald° zum Kahlenberg³ gefahren, wo die Europäer vor ungefähr 35 vierhundert Jahren gegen die Türken gekämpft° haben. In der Nähe° steht heute noch ein Kloster°. Vom Kahlenberg kann man Wien auch wunderbar sehen.

In Grinzing kann man gemütlich Wein trinken und tanzen.

Bevor wir wieder nach Hause fahren, wollen wir noch nach Grinzing. Dort soll es viele Weinstuben° geben, wo man gemütlich essen, Wein 40 trinken und tanzen kann. Bestimmt° gibt es da auch viele Touristen. Aber das macht nichts. Man muß alles einmal sehen.

Wie Ihr seht, geht es mir gut. Ihr sollt aber nicht denken, daß Wien nur romantisch ist. Es ist auch eine Großstadt mit vielen Menschen und viel Verkehr°. Es gefällt mir hier so gut, daß ich gern länger° bleiben möchte. 45 Leider geht das nicht. Schade!

Viele Grüße!

Euer Michael

PS. Ich schreibe auf deutsch, weil ich Euch zeigen möchte, daß ich auch etwas gelernt habe. Mein Freund Rainer hat mir natürlich etwas geholfen, 50 aber es geht schon viel besser.

ZUM TEXT

A. **_Wo oder wer ist das?_** *(Match the descriptions with the places or people in the list below.)*

Beethoven, Burgtheater, Goethe, Grinzing, Hofburg, Kahlenberg, Kärntner-straße, Spanische Reitschule, Ring, Staatsoper, Stephansdom, Strauß

1. Dort liegen die Hofburg, das Burgtheater, die Universität, das Rathaus, Museen und Parks.
2. Dort kann man sonntags die Wiener Sängerknaben hören.
3. Von dort kann man Bilder machen und ganz Wien sehen.
4. Hier gibt es viele Geschäfte, aber alles ist sehr teuer.
5. Dort haben die Europäer vor vielen Jahren gegen die Türken gekämpft.
6. Dort kann man gemütlich essen, Wein trinken und tanzen.
7. Michaels Hotel ist nicht weit von dort.
8. Dort kann man die Lippizaner „tanzen" sehen.
9. Es gefällt Michael gut, denn es ist sehr elegant.
10. Er ist Komponist gewesen und hat klassische Musik geschrieben.
11. Er ist auch Komponist gewesen, aber er hat Walzer komponiert.
12. Auch für ihn gibt es ein Denkmal in Wien. Er ist aus Frankfurt gewesen und hat in Weimar gelebt.

Johann Strauß, der Walzerkönig (. . . king).

B. sondern *oder* aber?

1. Mein Hotel ist nicht billig, _____ es liegt zentral.
2. Die Hofburg ist nicht nur bekannt für die Schatzkammer, _____ auch für die Spanische Reitschule.
3. Dort ist das Reiten kein Sport, _____ Kunst.
4. Zeit habe ich genug, _____ nicht genug Geld.
5. Man muß viel laufen, _____ es gefällt mir.
6. Ich schreibe nicht auf englisch, _____ auf deutsch.

C. *Sagen Sie die Sätze noch einmal mit den Modalverben!*

BEISPIEL: Überall findet man bekannte Namen. (können)
Überall kann man bekannte Namen finden.

1. Von der Staatsoper geht man zu Fuß zum Stephansdom. (können)
2. Wir fahren mit dem Aufzug im Turm hinauf. (wollen)
3. Von dort hat man einen wunderbaren Blick (*view*). (sollen)
4. Ich fahre gern mit der Kutsche durch die Altstadt. (möchten)
5. Das ist sicher romantisch. (müssen)
6. Ihr denkt aber nicht, daß hier alles romantisch ist. (dürfen)
7. Ich sehe aber alles. (wollen)

D. *Persönliche Fragen*

1. Wer von Ihnen ist schon einmal in Wien gewesen? Was möchten Sie sehen, wenn Sie einmal nach Wien fahren? Warum?
2. Wohnen wir hier in einer Großstadt oder Kleinstadt? Haben wir auch eine Altstadt? Wenn ja, ist sie schön? Wenn nein, warum nicht?
3. Gibt es hier auch eine Straßenbahn, eine U-Bahn oder Busse? Was für Sehenswürdigkeiten (*attractions*) gibt es hier? Was gefällt Ihnen hier besonders und was nicht?
4. Sind Sie schon einmal in einem Schloß gewesen? Wenn ja, wo? Wenn nein, welches Schloß möchten Sie einmal sehen?
5. Was für Denkmäler und Straßen mit bekannten Namen gibt es hier? Geben Sie Beispiele!

Unterwegs sein macht Appetit.

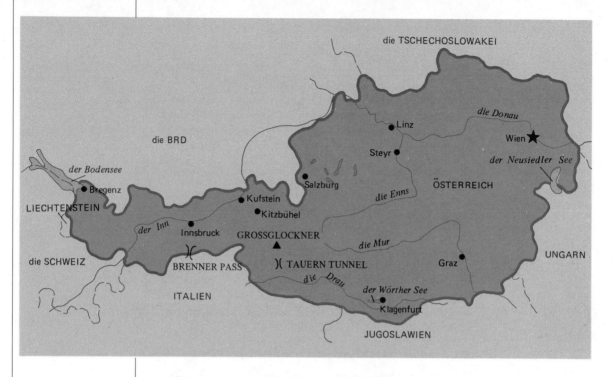

*E. **Österreich. Sehen Sie auf die Landkarte, und beantworten Sie die Fragen!*** *(Work with a partner to answer the questions orally, or write eight to ten sentences about Austria, using the questions as guidelines.)*

1. Wie viele Nachbarn hat Österreich? Wie heißen sie, und wo liegen sie?
2. Wie heißt die Hauptstadt von Österreich? Wie heißen ein paar Städte in Österreich?
3. Welcher Fluß fließt *(flows)* durch Wien? Innsbruck? Linz? Graz?
4. Welcher See liegt nicht nur in Österreich, sondern auch in Deutschland und in der Schweiz? Welcher See teilt Österreich von Ungarn? Wie heißt der See, wo Klagenfurt (Bregenz) liegt?
5. Was ist der Großglockner? der Brenner?

ÜBRIGENS

1. Everywhere in Europe distances are measured in kilometers (1 mile = 1.61 km; 1 km = 0.62 miles).

2. The poet, dramatist, novelist, scientist, and statesman **Johann Wolfgang von Goethe** (1749–1832) was born in **Frankfurt** and spent most of his life in the duchy of **Weimar** (now in the GDR). He was one of the most influential intellectuals in German history.

3. For about two centuries the Turks tried to conquer Europe, which culminated in two major sieges of Vienna (1529 and 1683). In the last siege the Turks might have succeeded had it not been for a relief army attacking from the **Kahlenberg**, which defeated the Turkish forces and ended the threat to Europe.

GESPRÄCHE

Wohnung zu vermieten

INGE Hallo, Sie haben eine Zwei-
Zimmer-Wohnung[1] zu vermieten, nicht wahr?

VERMIETER Ja, in der Nähe vom Dom.

INGE Wie alt ist die Wohnung?

VERMIETER Ziemlich alt, aber sie ist renoviert[2] und schön groß und hell. Sie
hat sogar einen Balkon.

INGE Im welchem Stock liegt sie?

VERMIETER Im dritten Stock[3].

INGE Ist sie möbliert oder unmöbliert?

VERMIETER Unmöbliert[4].

INGE Und was kostet die Wohnung?

VERMIETER 600 Mark.

INGE O, das ist ein bißchen zu teuer. Vielen Dank! Auf Wiederhören!

VERMIETER Auf Wiederhören!

In der Wohngemeinschaft[5]

INGE Euer Haus gefällt mir!

HORST Wir haben noch Platz für dich!
Komm, ich zeige es dir! . . . Hier
links ist die Küche. Unsere
Küche ist klein, aber praktisch.

INGE Wer kocht?

HORST Wir alle: Jens, Gisela, Renate und ich.

INGE Und das ist das Wohnzimmer?

HORST Ja. Es ist ein bißchen dunkel, aber es geht.

INGE Eure Sessel gefallen mir.

HORST Sie sind alt, aber sehr bequem. Oben sind dann vier Schlafzimmer und das Bad.

INGE Nur ein Bad?

HORST Ja, leider! Aber hier unten ist noch eine Toilette.

INGE Was bezahlt ihr im Monat?

HORST 200 DM pro Nase.

INGE Nicht schlecht! Und wie kommst du zur Uni?

HORST Zu Fuß natürlich! Es ist ja nur ein Katzensprung!

INGE Das klingt gut!

1. The size of apartments is determined by the number of rooms: If you want one bedroom and a living room, look for a **Zwei-Zimmer-Wohnung**. Bathroom, toilet, and kitchen are not included in the room count.

2. Although in the fifties and sixties many new apartments were built in the Federal Republic to alleviate the postwar housing shortage, more recently people rediscovered the beauty of older buildings, many of which are being renovated and modernized with the help of generous subsidies and tax incentives.

3. In Germany the first floor, or ground floor, is called **Parterre**. Only the floors above the **Parterre** are numbered. Where we say *on the second floor*, Germans say **im ersten Stock**.—German homes and apartments usually have an entrance foyer, or hallway (**Flur**), with doors opening into the various rooms. Because Germans cherish privacy, these doors are usually kept closed. Germans feel uncomfortably exposed when doors are open, quite unlike Americans, who prefer to see and be seen.

4. Furnished apartments are relatively rare. Unfurnished is usually to be taken literally: no light fixtures, built-in cabinets, closets, kitchen cupboards, appliances—just bare walls. The tenant is responsible for the regular maintenance of the apartment, especially interior painting and decorating and, in some places, for cleaning the stairs between the floors.

5. **Wohngemeinschaften**, where several students share an apartment or a house, are quite common because suitable rooms in dormitories are still scarce and have long waiting lists. This also provides a way to experiment with alternative, communal, ways of living.

Apartment for Rent

INGE Hello, you have a two-room apartment for rent, don't you?
LANDLORD Yes, near the cathedral.
INGE How old is the apartment?
LANDLORD Quite old, but it's renovated and quite big and bright. It even has a balcony.
INGE What floor is it on?
LANDLORD On the fourth floor.
INGE Is it furnished or unfurnished?
LANDLORD Unfurnished.
INGE And how much is the rent?
LANDLORD 600 marks.
INGE Oh, that's a little too expensive. Thank you very much. Goodbye!
LANDLORD Goodbye!

With a Group Sharing a House

INGE I like your house.
HORST We still have room for you. Come, I'll show it to you ... Here to the left is the kitchen. Our kitchen is small but practical.
INGE Who cooks?

HORST We all (do): Jens, Gisela, Renate, and I.

INGE And that's the living room?

HORST Yes. It's a bit dark, but that's all right.

INGE I like your chairs.

HORST They're old but very comfortable. Upstairs are four bedrooms and the bathroom.

INGE Only one bathroom?

HORST Yes, unfortunately. But down here is another toilet.

INGE How much do you pay per month?

HORST 200 marks per person.

INGE Not bad. And how do you get to the university?

HORST I walk, of course. It's only a stone's throw from here.

INGE That sounds good.

Das Haus und die Möbel

DAS HAUS, ¨ER *house*
   STUDENTENHEIM, -E *dorm*
DIE WOHNUNG, -EN *apartment*

der			die		
der Balkon, -s	*balcony*		die Ecke, -n	*corner*	
Baum, ¨e	*tree*		Garage, -n	*garage*	
Flur	*hallway, foyer*		Küche, -n	*kitchen*	
Garten, ¨	*garden*		Toilette, -n	*toilet*	
das Bad, ¨er	*bathroom*				
Schlafzimmer, -	*bedroom*				
Wohnzimmer, -	*living room*				

DIE MÖBEL (*pl.*) *furniture*

der Fernseher, -	*TV set*		das Bett, -en	*bed*
Kühlschrank, ¨e	*refrigerator*		Radio, -s	*radio*
Schrank, ¨e	*closet, cupboard*		Regal, -e	*shelf*
Schreibtisch, -e	*desk*		Sofa, -s	*sofa*
Sessel, -	*armchair*		Telefon, -e	*telephone*
Teppich, -e	*carpet*		die Kommode, -n	*dresser*
Vorhang, ¨e	*curtain*		Lampe, -n	*lamp*

WEITERES

hell / dunkel	*bright / dark*
im Parterre	*on the first floor (ground level)*
im ersten Stock	*on the second floor*
im Monat	*per month*
oben / unten	*upstairs / downstairs*
praktisch	*practical(ly)*
sogar	*even*
(un)bequem	*(un)comfortable; (in)convenient*
ziemlich	*quite, rather*
baden	*to take a bath; swim*
duschen	*to take a shower*
kochen	*to cook*
mieten / vermieten	*to rent / rent out*

PASSIVES VOKABULAR die Wohngemeinschaft, -en *(group sharing a place)*; Auf Wiederhören! *(Goodbye!/on phone)*; Das klingt gut. *(That sounds good)*; ein Katzensprung zu *(a stone's throw from, lit. a cat's jump away)*; Es geht. *(That's all right.)*; pro Nase *(per person, lit. per nose)*; renoviert *(renovated)*; unmöbliert *(unfurnished)*

ZUM THEMA

A. Mustersätze

1. das Haus: Das Haus **gefällt mir**.
   das Wohnzimmer, die Küche, das Bad, der Garten
2. der Sessel: **Wie gefällt dir** der Sessel?
   das Sofa, der Teppich, das Regal, das Radio
3. die Möbel: Die Möbel **gefallen mir**.
   Sessel, Stühle, Vorhänge, Schränke
4. sehr praktisch: **Die Wohnung ist** sehr praktisch.
   schön hell, ziemlich dunkel, zu klein, sehr gemütlich, wirklich bequem
5. unten: **Die Wohnung ist** unten.
   oben, im Parterre, im ersten Stock, im zweiten Stock, im dritten Stock

So eine Eckbank **(corner bench)** *ist doch sehr gemütlich.*

Weil der Winter so
lang ist und es so oft
regnet, sind die
Deutschen gern im
Garten, wenn die
Sonne scheint.

B. Was bedeutet das, und was ist der Plural?

Balkontür, Bücherregal, Duschvorhang, Elternschlafzimmer, Eßzimmer, Farbfernseher, Garagentür, Gartenmöbel, Kinderzimmer, Küchen- fenster, Kleiderschrank, Kochecke, Nachttisch, Schreibtischlampe, Sitzecke, Waschecke, Wohnzimmerteppich

C. Beschreiben Sie das Haus auf Seite 165!

Words you may need:

der Gefrierschrank, ¨e *(freezer),* Herd, -e *(range),* Keller, - *(basement),*
    Mikrowellenherd, -e *(microwave oven),* Müllschlucker, - *(disposal),*
    Ofen, ¨, Pool, -s, Spiegel, - *(mirror),* Trockner, - *(dryer)*
das Dach, ¨er *(roof),* Waschbecken, - *(washbasin, sink)*
die Badewanne, -n *(bathtub),* Dusche, -n *(shower),* Heizung *(heating),*
    Klimaanlage *(air-conditioning),* Spülmaschine, -n *(dishwasher),*
    Stereoanlage, -n *(stereo set),* Terrasse, -n *(terrace),* Treppe, -n
    (stairway), Waschmaschine, -n.

1. Wie viele Zimmer hat das Haus? Wie viele Bäder?
2. Wo kann man hier essen?
3. Was für Möbel gibt es im Wohnzimmer? im Elternschlafzimmer? im
    Kinderschlafzimmer? Was hat eine Küche gewöhnlich?
4. Was hat das Haus noch?
5. Ist das Haus groß oder klein?
6. Wie gefällt Ihnen das Haus? Warum?

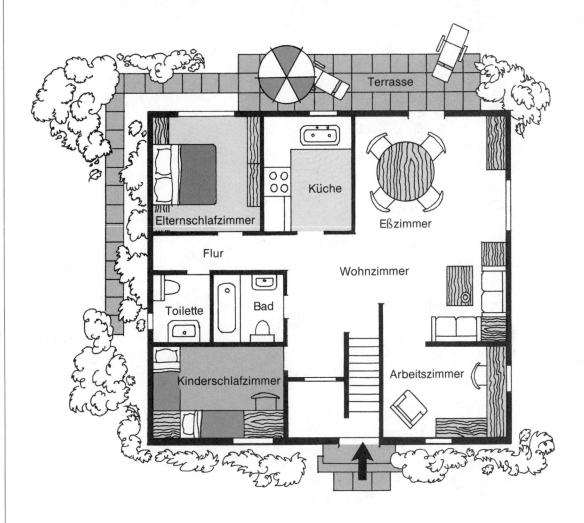

Terrasse

Elternschlafzimmer

Küche

Eßzimmer

Flur

Wohnzimmer

Toilette

Bad

Kinderschlafzimmer

Arbeitszimmer

D. Interview

From now on you will have to make direct questions from the indirect ones given. Use the **du***-form with your fellow students.*

1. Fragen Sie Ihren Partner/Ihre Partnerin, . . .!

    a. wo er/sie wohnt

    b. was für Möbel er/sie im Zimmer hat

    c. was man vom Zimmerfenster sehen kann

    d. Wie lange er/sie schon da wohnt

    BEISPIEL: **Wo wohnst du?**

2. Sagen Sie uns, was Sie erfahren haben! *(Report what you found out.)*

    BEISPIELE: **Sie sagt, daß sie im Studentenheim (zu Hause, in einer Wohngemeinschaft) wohnt.**
                    Sie sagt, daß sie eine Wohnung hat.

E. Eine Wohnung zu vermieten. Was sagen Sie?

    x Ich habe gelesen, daß Sie ein Haus zu vermieten haben. Wo ist das Haus?

    Y _____ .

    x Können Sie mir das Haus etwas beschreiben *(describe)*?

    Y Ja, gern. Es hat _____ .

    x Gibt es auch _____ (eine Terrasse, einen Balkon, einen Pool . . .)?

    Y _____ .

    x Wie weit ist es zu _____ ?

    Y _____ .

    x Und was kostet das Haus?

    Y _____ .

    x _____ *(Make a final comment.)*

F. Aussprache *(See also II.37–39 in the pronunciation section of the Appendix.)*

  1. [ai]   **Ei,** H**ei**zung, w**ei**t, w**ei**l, l**ei**der, **ei**gentlich, **ei**nmal, z**ei**gen, f**ei**ern, bl**ei**ben

  2. [au]   **auf, au**ch, br**au**n, bl**au**grau, K**au**fhaus, B**au**m, br**au**chen, l**au**fen, d**au**ern

  3. [oi]   **eu**ch, n**eu**, h**eu**te, t**eu**er, d**eu**tsch, L**eu**te, Fr**eu**nde, H**äu**ser, B**äu**me, Fr**äu**lein

  4. Wortpaare

    a. *by* / bei

    b. *Troy* / treu

    c. *mouse* / Maus

    d. Haus / Häuser

    e. aus / Eis

    f. euer / Eier

STRUKTUR

I. *Two-Way Prepositions*

You have learned some prepositions that are always followed by the dative and some that are always followed by the accusative. You will now learn a set of prepositions that sometimes take the dative and sometimes the accusative.

1. The basic meanings of the nine TWO-WAY PREPOSITIONS are:

an	to, at (the side of), on (vertical surface)
auf	on (top of, horizontal surface)
hinter	behind
in	in, into, inside of
neben	beside, next to
über	over, above
unter	under, below
vor	before, in front of
zwischen	between

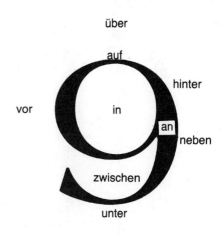

Most of these prepositions may be contracted with articles. The most common contractions are:

an das = **ans**   auf das = **aufs**   in das = **ins**
an dem = **am**   in dem = **im**

In colloquial speech you will also find: hinter**s**, hinter**m**, über**s**, über**m**, unter**s**, unter**m**, vor**s**, vor**m**.

☞ *CAUTION:*

▶ *Don't confuse the preposition* **vor** *with the coordinating conjunction* **bevor***! The preposition* **vor** *precedes a noun:* **vor dem Haus***. The conjunction* **bevor** *stands at the beginning of a clause:* **Bevor du das Haus mietest,** ...

2. Wo? Wohin?

a. German has two words for the English *where:* **wo?** *(in what place?)* and **wohin?** *(to what place?)*. **Wo** asks about location, where something is, or an activity within a place. **Wohin** asks about destination or a change of place.

LOCATION: **Wo** ist Horst?   *Where's Horst? (in what place)*
DESTINATION: **Wohin** geht Horst?   *Where's Horst going? (to what place)*

b. The difference between location and destination also plays a role in determining the case following two-way prepositions. If the question is **wo?**, the dative is used. If the question is **wohin?**, the accusative is used.

Wo ist Horst? **In der Bibliothek.**   *Where's Horst? In the library.*
Wohin geht Horst? **In die Bibliothek.**   *Where's Horst going? To the library.*

wo?   location   → DATIVE
wohin? destination → ACCUSATIVE

3. The difference lies entirely in the verb!

- *Some verbs denoting location or activity within a place (→ DATIVE) are:*

baden	*to bathe, swim*	schlafen	*to sleep*
bleiben	*to stay, remain*	schreiben	*to write*
essen	*to eat*	sein	*to be*
finden	*find*	**sitzen**	*to sit, be sitting*
hängen	*to hang, be hanging*	spielen	*to play*
kaufen	*to buy*	**stehen**	*to stand, be standing*
kochen	*to cook*	trinken	*to drink*
lesen	*to read*	wohnen	*to live, reside*
liegen	*to lie, be lying (flat)*		

NOTE: **hängen, liegen, sitzen,** *and* **stehen** *are new n-verbs. Learn their participles:* **gehangen, gelegen, gesessen, gestanden**

- *Typical verbs implying change of place (→ ACCUSATIVE) are:*

bringen	*to bring*	hängen	*to hang (up)*	**legen**	*to put (flat), lay*
fahren	*to drive*	kommen	*to come*	**stellen**	*to put (upright)*
gehen	*to go*	laufen	*to walk*	tragen	*to carry*

NOTE: **legen** *and* **stellen** *are new t-verbs.*

WOHIN?	WO?
Der Junge hängt den Teppich **über das** Balkongeländer.	Der Teppich hängt **über dem** Balkongeländer.
Die Mutter stellt die Leiter *(ladder)* **an die** Wand.	Die Leiter steht **an der** Wand.
Das Kind legt den Teddy **auf die** Bank (bench).	Der Teddy liegt **auf der** Bank.
Das Auto fährt **neben das** Haus.	Das Auto steht **neben dem** Haus.
Das Kind läuft **hinter die** Mutter.	Das Kind steht **hinter der** Mutter.
Der Hund läuft **vor das** Auto.	Der Hund steht **vor dem** Auto.
Der Großvater nimmt die Pfeife *(pipe)* **in den** Mund *(mouth)*.	Der Großvater hat die Pfeife **in dem** Mund.
Das Huhn *(chicken)* läuft **unter die** Bank **zwischen die** Bankbeine *(... legs)*.	Das Huhn sitzt **unter der** Bank **zwischen den** Bankbeinen.

Note particularly these sets of verbs:

to put (upright)	Sie stellt die Leiter an die Wand.
to be standing	Die Leiter steht an der Wand.
to put (flat), lay	Das Kind legt den Teddy auf die Bank.
to be lying (flat)	Der Teddy liegt auf der Bank.

*Note also these uses of **an**, **auf** and **in**; you are already familiar with most of them:*

an: Die Stadt liegt **am Rhein (an der Donau).**

The city is on the Rhine (on the Danube).

auf: Sie spielen **auf der Straße.**

They're playing in the street.

in: Sie wohnen **in Eisenach.**
Das ist **in Deutschland (in der DDR).**
Sie wohnen **im Osten.**
Sie wohnen **im Parterre (im ersten Stock).**

They live in Eisenach.
That's in Germany (in the GDR).
They live in the East.
They live on the first (second) floor.

▪ *With feminine names of countries, like **die Schweiz, die Bundesrepublik, die DDR, in** is used rather than **nach** to express* to.

Wir fahren **in** die Schweiz (BUT **nach** Deutschland, **nach** Berlin.)

We are going to Switzerland (to Germany, to Berlin).

▪ *If you plan to see a film or play, or to attend a church service, **in** must be used; **zu** implies going in the direction of, up to, BUT NOT into a place:*

Wir gehen **ins** Kino (**ins** Theater, **in die** Kirche).

We are going to the movies (to the theater, to church).

ÜBUNGEN

A. ***Sagen Sie es noch einmal!*** *(Replace the nouns following the prepositions with the words suggested. Don't forget that dative plural nouns must end in **-n**.)*

BEISPIEL: Der Bleistift liegt unter dem Papier. (Jacke)
Der Bleistift liegt unter der Jacke.

1. Die Post ist neben der Bank. (Bahnhof, Kino, Apotheke)
2. Ursula kommt in die Wohnung. (Küche, Eßzimmer, Garten)
3. Die Mäntel liegen auf dem Bett. (Sofa, Kommode, Stühle)
4. Mein Schlafzimmer ist über der Küche. (Wohnzimmer, Garage, Bad)
5. Willi legt den Pullover auf die Kommode. (Bett, Schreibtisch, Sessel)

6. Renate fährt vor das Haus. (Garage, Studentenheim, Drogerie)
7. Frau Loth kauft etwas in der Bäckerei. (Supermarkt, Fleischerei, Geschäfte)
8. Der Park ist hinter der Kirche. (Dom, Bibliothek, Häuser)
9. Wir wollen heute ins Kino. (Stadt, Theater, Museen)
10. Gehst du in die Küche? (Garten, Garage, Bett, Kinderzimmer/*pl.*)

B. Stellen Sie Fragen mit wo oder wohin!

BEISPIEL: Horst schläft im Wohnzimmer.   **Wo schläft Horst?**

1. Sie hat die Milch in den Kühlschrank gestellt.
2. Das Fleisch ist auf dem Teller.
3. Er hat die Blumen auf dem Markt gekauft.
4. Sie muß das Kind ins Bett bringen.
5. Die Nachbarin liest auf dem Balkon.
6. Wir wollen morgen ins Kino.
7. Sie hängen das Bild zwischen die Fenster.
8. Schmidts wohnen jetzt in der Schweiz.

C. Antworten Sie! (Use the cues provided.)

BEISPIEL: Wo essen wir heute? (in / Garten)   **Wir essen heute im Garten.**

1. Wo ist Marianne? (in / Bad; auf / Balkon; in / Küche)
2. Wo spielen die Kinder? (unter / Baum; vor / Haus; in / Ecke; hinter / Vorhänge)
3. Wo gibt es Obst? (auf / Markt; in / Mensa; in / Kühlschrank)
4. Wo liegt die Stadt? (an / Rhein; an / Donau; an / See; in / Berge; in / Schweiz)
5. Wohin möchten Sie gehen? (in / Park; in / Studentenheim; an / Fluß)
6. Wo ist das Restaurant? (an / Domplatz; neben / Bank; hinter / Theater)
7. Wohin gehen sie jetzt? (in / Kirche; in / Kino; auf / Straße)
8. Wohin fahrt ihr im Sommer? (in / Schweiz; an / Rhein; in / Bundesrepublik)

D. Was fehlt? Heike und Sabine kommen heute abend. Was müssen wir tun?

1. Die Gläser sind in _____ Küche. 2. Ich muß die Gläser in _____ Wohnzimmer bringen und sie auf _____ Tisch stellen. 3. Der Wein ist noch in _____ Kühlschrank. 4. Wir müssen die Teller neben _____ Gläser stellen. 5. Ich muß in _____ Küche gehen und die Wurst und den Käse auf _____ Teller legen. 6. Haben wir Blumen in _____ Garten? 7. Wir stellen die Blumen auf _____ Tischchen vor _____ Sofa. 8. Sind die Kerzen in _____ Schrank? 9. Nein, sie sind in _____ Kommode auf _____ Flur.

E. Im Wohnzimmer

1. *Wohin sollen wir das stellen? (Tell where the movers are supposed to put things.)*

BEISPIEL: Kommode / an / Wand **Stellen Sie die Kommode an die Wand!**

a. Regal / auf / Kommode
b. Radio / in / Regal
c. Fernseher / neben / Radio
d. kleine Regal / unter / Fenster
e. Blumen / an / Fenster
f. Glasschrank / zwischen / Kommoden
g. Bücher / auf / Kommode
h. Tischen / vor / Sessel
i. Bild / in / Regal

2. *Was ist wo? (As you check the picture below, make ten statements telling where things are standing, lying, or hanging.)*

BEISPIEL: **Das Glas steht auf dem Fernseher.**

3. *Was ist wo in Ihrem Zimmer? (Write eight to ten sentences about your room. Use a two-way preposition in each sentence.)*

II. The Imperative

You are already familiar with the FORMAL IMPERATIVE, which addresses one individual or several people. You know that the verb is followed by the pronoun **Sie**:

Schreiben Sie bitte!

1. The FAMILIAR IMPERATIVE has two forms: one for the plural and one for the singular.

a. The plural is the **ihr**-form of the verb WITHOUT the pronoun **ihr**:

ihr schreibt   ihr antwortet   ihr nehmt   ihr lest   ihr eßt

Schreibt!	Antwortet!	Nehmt!	Lest!	Eßt!

b. The singular usually is the **du**-form of the verb WITHOUT the pronoun **du** and WITHOUT the **-st** ending:

du schreibst   du antwortest   du nimmst   du liest   du ißt

Schreib!	Antworte!	Nimm!	**Lies!**	Iß!

NOTE: **lesen** *and* **essen** *retain the s of the verb stem:* **Lies! Iß!**

■ *There is an* OPTIONAL *-e ending in the* **du***-form (***Schreibe** *mir!). However, the more informal the situation, the less likely its use.*

■ *Note that verbs ending in -d, -t, and certain other consonant combinations (plus -n or -m)* USUALLY *have an -e ending in the* **du***-form:* **Antworte** ihm! **Öffne** die Tür! **Entschuldige** bitte!

■ *Verbs with vowel changes from* **e** > **i(e)** *in the present singular* NEVER *have an -e ending in the* **du***-form.*

Sprich! Sieh!

■ *Verbs with vowel changes from* **a** > **ä** *in the present singular do* NOT *make this change in the imperative.*

Fahren Sie langsam!   Halten Sie bitte!
Fahrt langsam!   Haltet bitte!
Fahr(e) langsam!   **Halte** bitte!

2. Here now are the imperatives of several verbs. Note that the three different forms of the German imperative all correspond to one form in English *(Write (to) me. Answer us. Take the Bus.)* and that the German imperative is always followed by an EXCLAMATION MARK!

Frau Schmidt, **schreiben Sie** mir!
Kinder, **schreibt** mir!
Helga, **schreib(e)** mir!

Herr Schmidt, **antworten Sie** uns!
Kinder, **antwortet** uns!
Fritz, **antworte** uns!

Herr und Frau Schmidt, **nehmen Sie** den Bus!
Helga und Fritz, **nehmt** den Bus!
Helga, **nimm** den Bus!

3. English imperatives beginning with *Let's . . .* are expressed in German as follows:

Sprechen wir Deutsch!   *Let's talk German.*
Gehen wir nach Hause!   *Let's go home.*

ÜBUNGEN

F. Geben Sie den Imperativ! *(First form the plural familiar and then the singular familiar.)*

BEISPIELE: Bleiben Sie bitte!   **Bleibt bitte!**
                                       Bleib bitte!

1. Sagen Sie nichts!
2. Antworten Sie mir!
3. Wiederholen Sie das bitte!
4. Fragen Sie ihn!
5. Kommen Sie später!
6. Zählen Sie noch einmal!
7. Helfen Sie uns!
8. Lesen Sie langsam!
9. Nehmen Sie es!
10. Essen Sie schnell!
11. Fahren Sie geradeaus!
12. Schlafen Sie gut!
13. Halten Sie hier!
14. Öffnen Sie das!

Schreib mal wieder...

Absender

_____

_____

Ein Brief muß nicht immer lang sein.

G. Geben Sie den Imperativ! *(Form formal and familiar imperatives, using the phrases below.)*

BEISPIELE: zur Post gehen   **Gehen Sie zur Post!**
                                       Geht zur Post!
                                       Geh zur Post!

1. noch einmal beginnen
2. auf deutsch lesen
3. laut sprechen
4. das nicht tun
5. bitte entschuldigen
6. ihr den Stadtplan geben
7. ihm danken
8. ihnen den Weg zeigen
9. nicht fallen
10. zu Fuß gehen
11. schön feiern
12. nicht zuviel essen

Bitte langsam fahren!

Kinder!

H. Bilden Sie den Imperativ mit wir!

BEISPIEL: ins Kino gehen   **Gehen wir ins Kino!**

1. durch die Stadt bummeln
2. ein paar Erdbeeren kaufen
3. im Garten sitzen
4. den Mann fragen
5. mit der U-Bahn fahren

I. ***Geben Sie Befehle an . . .!*** *(Address three commands to each.)*

1. einen Freund oder eine Freundin
2. einen Touristen oder einen Angestellten *(employee at work)*
3. zwei kleine Kinder

III. wissen *vs.* kennen

In German two verbs correspond to the English *to know*:

to know
- **kennen, gekannt** → *to be acquainted with a person or thing*
- **wissen, gewußt** → *to know a fact (the fact is often expressed in a subordinate clause)*

Whereas **kennen** is regular in the present tense, the forms of **wissen** are very similar to the forms of the modals.

„. . . und ich weiß, daß du weißt, daß ich weiß, daß das nicht wahr ist!"

ich weiß
du weißt
er weiß
wir wissen
ihr wißt
sie wissen

Ich **kenne** das Buch.   BUT Ich **weiß, daß** es gut ist.
Ich **kenne** den Lehrer. BUT Ich **weiß, daß** er aus Wien ist.

ÜBUNGEN

J. ***Wie schnell können Sie diesen Zungenbrecher*** *(tongue twister)* **sagen?**

Wenn ich weiß, was du weißt, und du weißt, was ich weiß,
dann weißt du, was ich weiß, und ich weiß, was du weißt.

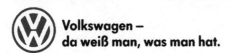

**Volkswagen —
da weiß man, was man hat.**

K. kennen *oder* wissen? *(Fill in the appropriate forms.)*

1. Entschuldigen Sie! _____ Sie, wo die Bushaltestelle ist?
2. _____ du, wieviel Uhr es ist?
3. _____ Sie Wien? Nein, ich _____ nur, daß es sehr schön ist.
4. Ich _____ Professor Müller nicht.
5. _____ ihr, wann sie Geburtstag hat?
6. Woher _____ du die Dame?
7. Wer _____ , wann das Kino beginnt?
8. Man _____ Dieter überall.
9. Ich möchte _____ , wo man gemütlich sitzen kann.
10. Wo ist mein Pullover? Ich _____ nicht.

L. Auf deutsch, bitte!

1. Do you *(formal)* know where the dormitories are?
2. She doesn't know him.
3. Who knows when the party is?
4. I am not familiar with the song.
5. Do you *(pl. fam.)* know the café?
6. Don't you *(sg. fam.)* know how old he is?

ZUSAMMENFASSUNG

M. Bilden Sie Sätze! *(Add suitable subjects and verbs.)*

BEISPIEL: über dem Tisch   **Die Lampe hängt über dem Tisch.**

1. in den Schrank
2. unter dem Bett
3. über dem Sofa
4. hinter der Staatsoper
5. in die Bank
6. vor das Haus
7. neben dem Telefon
8. zwischen der Schulstraße und dem Domplatz
9. auf den Schreibtisch
10. unter dem Baum
11. ins Regal
12. ans Fenster

N. Auf deutsch, bitte!

1. Hello, Hans! Where have you been? 2. I'm coming from the dorm. 3. Where are you going?—To the library. 4. I'd like to live in a dorm, too. 5. Where do you live now? 6. In an apartment. Unfortunately it's over a disco (die Disko) and next to a restaurant. 7. I hear that the rooms in the dorm are nice. 8. I like my room, but I don't like the furniture. 9. Which floor do you live on?—On the third floor. 10. Do you know how much it costs?—270 marks a month. 11. There's Reinhart. 12. Who's that? Where am I supposed to know him from? 13. I didn't know that you don't know him. 14. Let's say hello.

During the sixties, modern high-rise communities were built around many old German cities; the new buildings often contrasted sharply with the traditional architecture. Today, such **Wohnsilos** (high-rise apartment clusters) are no longer built in the FRG because it has been recognized that they are sterile and not conducive to social interaction. New housing developments try hard to make the architecture fit into the landscape and conform to local building styles. Also, to prevent loss of open space and agricultural land, the necessity of controlling urban sprawl has resulted in strict zoning laws. In the GDR, however, where most building is done by the government, the development of modern satellite cities continues, as in the Berlin suburb **Marzahn.** Yet in smaller GDR towns the old appearance has been preserved, since little building was done before the seventies. Thus, the visitor to the GDR gets more of a feel of the old Germany than in most towns of the FRG.

EINBLICKE

der Wald, ̈er	*forest, woods*
das Fahrrad, ̈er	*bicycle*

am Abend	*in the evening*
am Tag	*during the day*
aufs Land	*in(to) the country(side)*
auf dem Land	*in the country*
ausgezeichnet	*excellent*
außerdem	*besides (adverb)*
mitten in	*in the middle of*
noch nicht	*not yet*
trotzdem	*nevertheless, in spite of that*
bauen	*to build*
leben	*to live*
lieben	*to love*
sparen	*to save (money)*

WAS IST DAS? der Clown, Dialekt, Fahrradweg, Münchner, Musiker, Spielplatz, Stadtpark, Wanderweg; das Feld, Leben, Konsulat, Zentrum; die Arbeit, Energie, Innenstadt, Wirklichkeit; frei, idyllisch, jung, relativ; Ball spielen, eine Pause machen, formulieren, picknicken

Schaffen°, sparen, Häuschen° bauen.

5

Dieser Spruch° aus Schwaben (im Dialekt[1] heißt es „Schaffe, spare, Häusle baue") ist nicht nur typisch für die Schwaben, sondern für die meisten° Deutschen, Österreicher und Schweizer.

In den drei Ländern leben viele Menschen, aber es gibt wenig° Land. Die meisten wohnen in Wohnungen und träumen von° einem Haus mit Garten. Für viele bleibt das aber nur ein Traum°, denn in den Städten ist Bauland° sehr teuer. Es gibt auch nicht genug Bauland, weil man nicht überall bauen 10 darf.

Margin glosses:
work hard/ little house
this saying
most
little
dream of
dream/ building lots

Das Leben zwischen Wäldern und Feldern ist oft idyllisch, aber nicht immer sehr bequem.

edge of . . . / move

out(side)/ back and forth/
commute
money/ easily

necessarily

sidewalks

*In vielen
europäischen Städten
gibt es Wege, wo nur
Fahrräder fahren
dürfen.*

Oft muß man an den Stadtrand° oder aufs Land ziehen°, wo es mehr Platz gibt und wo Land noch nicht so teuer ist. Aber nicht alle möchten so weit draußen° wohnen und stundenlang hin und her° pendeln°. Das kostet Energie, Zeit und Geld°. Abends kommt man auch nicht leicht° ins Kino 15 oder ins Theater. Das Leben zwischen Wäldern und Feldern ist oft idyllisch, aber nicht immer sehr bequem.

In der Stadt kann man eigentlich sehr gut leben. Die Wohnungen sind oft groß und schön. Man braucht nicht unbedingt° ein Auto, weil alles in der Nähe liegt. Überall gibt es Bürgersteige° und Fahrradwege, und die 20

public transportation

on time

commuter train/ with
them
all across

display . . .

entertainment/ . . . artists

going on

öffentlichen Verkehrsmittel°² sind ausgezeichnet. Die Busse kommen relativ oft und pünktlich°. In Großstädten gibt es auch Straßenbahnen, eine U-Bahn und eine S-Bahn°. Damit° können Sie nicht nur aus der Stadt oder quer durch° die Stadt, sondern auch mitten ins Zentrum, in die Fußgängerzonen fahren, wo die Leute am Tag einkaufen und am Abend gern bummeln gehen. Man sieht ein bißchen in die Schaufenster° und geht vielleicht 25 in ein Restaurant und trinkt ein Glas Wein. Oft bekommt man auch freie Unterhaltung° durch Straßenkünstler°, Musiker und Clowns. In der Innenstadt ist eigentlich immer etwas los°.

any time

out into nature

dependent

almost

whole/ appear

bigger than

Wenn man in der Stadt wohnt, kann man aber auch jederzeit° leicht 30
ins Grüne° fahren. Viele tun das gern und oft. Wenn man nicht jeden Tag
vom Auto abhängig° ist, fährt man am Wochenende gern einmal an den
Ozean, aufs Land oder in die Berge. Überall in Wäldern und Feldern findet
man Wanderwege³ und oft auch Fahrradwege³. Fast° alle Wege sind öffentlich. So ist das ganze° Land dem Menschen offen, und die Länder scheinen° 35
größer als° sie sind. Unterwegs findet man oft auch ein Café, wo man gemütlich Pause machen kann.

Man muß aber nicht unbedingt aufs Land fahren, wenn man ins Grüne
will. Fast alle Städte, ob groß oder klein, haben Stadtparks. Die Münchner
z.B. lieben ihren Englischen Garten (in der Nähe vom amerikanischen Kon- 40
sulat). Dort gibt es nicht nur Wanderwege, sondern auch Spielplätze und

benches

rowboats

Bänke°, Platz zum Picknicken und zum Ball spielen und Seen mit Ruder-
booten°. Hier sieht man jung und alt, und das nicht nur am Wochenende.

So eine Bierkellnerin (. . .waitress) kann in jeder (each) Hand fünf bis sechs volle Maßkrüge (beer steins) tragen.

even if

condominium

Die meisten leben eigentlich gern in der Stadt, selbst wenn° sie dort
nur eine Eigentumswohnung° haben können oder vielleicht eine Wohnung 45
mieten. In der Stadt gibt es viel zu sehen und zu tun. Alles ist ziemlich
nah, nicht nur der Arbeitsplatz, die Geschäfte und die Schulen, sondern
auch die Theater, Kinos, Museen und Parks. Natürlich träumen viele trotzdem von einem Haus mit Garten, einem Häuschen im Grünen. Sie wissen,

hard

daß sie schwer° arbeiten und sparen⁴ müssen, wenn der Traum Wirklich- 50
keit werden soll. Und das tun auch viele.

A. Richtig oder falsch? Wenn falsch, warum?

___ 1. In Deutschland, in Österreich und in der Schweiz gibt es nicht viel Bauland, besonders nicht in den Städten.

___ 2. Die meisten Leute dort wohnen in einem Haus mit Garten.

___ 3. Auf dem Land ist Bauland nicht so teuer wie in der Stadt.

___ 4. Das Leben zwischen Wäldern und Feldern ist sehr bequem.

___ 5. In allen Städten gibt es Straßenbahnen, eine U-Bahn und eine S-Bahn.

___ 6. Mit öffentlichen Verkehrsmitteln kann man quer durch die Stadt fahren.

___ 7. Überall in Wäldern und Feldern gibt es Fahrradwege und Fußgängerzonen.

___ 8. In der Fußgängerzone kann man am Tag einkaufen, am Abend bummeln und manchmal Musik hören.

___ 9. Im amerikanischen Konsulat in München kann man picknicken.

___ 10. Wenn man ein Haus kaufen oder bauen möchte, muß man schwer arbeiten und sparen.

In der Innenstadt ist immer etwas los. Hier machen junge Leute ein bißchen Musik.

B. Was fehlt?

1. Die meisten wohnen in ein_____ Wohnung. *2.* In d_____ Städten ist Bauland sehr teuer. *3.* Der Traum von Häuschen mit Garten hat viele an d_____ Stradtrand *(m.)* oder auf d_____ Land gebracht. *4.* Zwischen d_____ Wäldern und auf d_____ Feldern stehen Reihenhäuser *(town houses).* *5.* Die Reihenhäuser stehen manchmal direkt an d_____ Straße. *6.* Morgens fahren viele in d_____ Stadt. *7.* Das Leben auf d_____ Land kann unbequem sein. *8.* Viele bleiben in d_____ Stadt, weil dort alles in d_____ Nähe liegt. *9.* Nach d_____ Arbeit fahren viele noch einmal in _____ Innenstadt. *10.* Mitten in d_____ Zentrum *(n.)* ist immer etwas los.

C. Stellen Sie Fragen mit wo oder wohin!

BEISPIEL: In Großstädten gibt es eine U-Bahn. **Wo gibt es eine U-Bahn?**

1. Mit der U-Bahn kann man mitten in die Fußgängerzone fahren.
2. Dort kann man immer schön bummeln.
3. Abends kann man ins Kino gehen.
4. Man geht in den Park, wenn man ins Grüne will.
5. Dort gibt es überall Wege und Bänke.

D. wissen oder kennen?

1. _____ du, daß wir auf dem Land wohnen?
2. _____ du Gaibach?
3. Nein, das _____ ich nicht. Ist das in der Nähe von Volkach?
4. Ja. Wenn du Volkach _____ , dann _____ du auch, wo Gaibach liegt.
5. _____ du, daß ich morgens eine Stunde zur Arbeit pendele?
6. _____ ihr München?
7. Nein, aber ich _____ , daß es dort interessant ist.

E. Fragen

1. Leben die meisten Leute hier in Wohnungen oder in Häusern mit Garten?
2. Wo ist Bauland teuer? Wo ist es billiger?
3. Was für öffentliche Verkehrsmittel gibt es hier?
4. Wie kommen die meisten Leute zur Arbeit? Wie kommen Sie zur Universität? Braucht man hier unbedingt ein Auto?
5. Gibt es hier Schlafstädte *(bedroom communities),* von wo die Leute morgens in die Stadt pendeln? Geben Sie Beispiele!
6. Wohin gehen oder fahren die Leute hier, wenn sie ins Grüne wollen?

F. Wo möchten Sie wohnen? Warum? *(Write three to four sentences about where you would like to live and why. Include one phrase or word from each group below. After you have completed the exercise, poll the entire class and see what choices others have made.)*

in einer Wohngemeinschaft   mitten in . . .
in einer Wohnung   in der Nähe von . . .
in einer Eigentumswohnung   am Stradtrand von . . .
in einem Reihenhaus   auf dem Land . . .
in einem Haus mit Garten

In der Fußgängerzone kann man einkaufen, bummeln oder auch in einem Café sitzen und etwas trinken.

BEISPIEL: **Ich möchte in einem Reihenhaus mitten in San Francisco, in der Nähe vom Golden Gate Park, wohnen. Da komme ich schnell zur Arbeit und zum Ozean. Man braucht nicht unbedingt ein Auto.**

ÜBRIGENS

1. German belongs to the Germanic branch of the Indo-European language family and is closely related to Dutch, English, and the Scandinavian languages. For various political, literary, and linguistic reasons we speak of Germans and the German language as dating from around the year 800. At that time at least six major dialects and numerous variations of them were spoken. Not until the twelfth and thirteenth centuries was an effort made to write a standardized form of German; the period from 1170 to 1254 was one of great literary achievement. But afterwards this literary language declined and, with few exceptions, Latin was used in writing. (It remained the sole language of instruction at German universities until the 1700s!) Luther's translation of the Bible in the sixteenth century was a major influence on the development of a common written German language. However, because of the political fragmentation of Germany, a standard language was slow to develop. As late as the beginning of this century, most people spoke only in dialect. First newspapers and magazines, and later radio and television, have together fostered the use of standard German, but regional accents are still very common, even among the highly educated.

2. Germany has an excellent public transportation system that makes it relatively easy to get along without a car and helps reduce congestion in the cities. Many of the major cities have a system of suburban **Schnellbahnen (S-Bahn)** and inner-city **U-Bahnen** that are connected under the **Fußgängerzone**. During peak hours, a suburban train comes punctually every few minutes. Streetcars and buses are used for less-traveled routes. Many riders have passes (especially schoolchildren, students, and senior citizens); those who don't are expected to purchase and cancel their own tickets despite infrequent inspections. Fines are high, of course, for those caught without a ticket.

3. **Wanderwege** *(public trails)* are found all over Germany, Austria, and Switzerland. **Fahrradwege** are becoming more and more common, particularly in non-mountainous areas. People enjoy bike-riding because it's fun, healthy, and inexpensive and doesn't pollute. There are practically no private roads, which means that almost all forests and fields are open for hiking and bicycling. Forest rangers (**Förster**) keep the woods clear of dead trees, and in Switzerland and Austria the corps of engineers helps maintain hiking trails. Although Germany, Switzerland, and Austria are densely populated, it is relatively easy to "get back to nature." Unfortunately, however, forests in the higher elevations of Europe are slowly dying from the impact of acid rain. Efforts are being made to neutralize the acidity by spraying large amounts of lime in the forests, and more and more people use lead-free gasoline to reduce the impact of driving on the ecology.

4. Germans, Swiss, and Austrians are known for their hard work and thrift. Their per capita rate of bank savings is unusually high. Generous tax incentives encourage people to save in special savings institutions for the building of private homes and condominiums. Thrift is also reflected in the relatively low consumption of energy. In the FRG per capita consumption of energy is only about half that of North America, yet the standard of living and the industrial output are just as high.

Hotel Regina

GESPRÄCHE

Auf der Bank

TOURISTIN Guten Tag! Können Sie mir sagen, wo ich Geld umwechseln kann?

ANGESTELLTER Am Schalter 2.

TOURISTIN Vielen Dank! (Sie geht zum Schalter 2). Guten Tag! Ich möchte Dollar in Franken[1] umwechseln. Hier sind meine Reise-schecks.

ANGESTELLTE Darf ich bitte Ihren Paß sehen?

TOURISTIN Bitte schön!

ANGESTELLTE Unterschreiben Sie hier!—Gehen Sie dort zur Kasse! Hier ist Ihre Nummer.

TOURISTIN Danke! (Sie geht zur Kasse.)

KASSIERER 224 Franken 63 (Fr. 224,63): einhundert—zweihundert—zehn—zwanzig—vierundzwanzig Franken und dreiund-sechzig Rappen. Bitte schön!

TOURISTIN Danke schön! Auf Wiedersehen!

An der Rezeption im Hotel

EMPFANGSDAME Guten Abend!

GAST Guten Abend! Haben Sie ein Einzelzimmer frei?

EMPFANGSDAME Für wie lange?

GAST Für zwei oder drei Nächte. Wenn möglich ruhig und mit Bad.

EMPFANGSDAME Leider haben wir nur noch ein Doppelzimmer, und das nur für eine Nacht. Wollen Sie es sehen?

GAST Ja, gern.

EMPFANGSDAME Zimmer Nummer 12, im ersten Stock rechts. Hier ist der Schlüssel.

GAST Sagen Sie, wo kann ich mein Auto lassen?

EMPFANGSDAME In der Garage hinterm Hotel.

GAST Und wann machen Sie abends zu?

EMPFANGSDAME Um 24 Uhr. Wenn Sie später kommen, müssen Sie klingeln.

Österreichisches Geld: Ein Schilling hat 100 Groschen.

ÜBRIGENS

1. The basic Swiss monetary unit is the Swiss franc (**der Schweizer Franken**): **1 Franken (Fr.) = 100 Rappen.** One sFr. is worth about 10 to 20 percent more than 1 DM. The basic Austrian monetary unit is the **Schilling: 1 Schilling (S) = 100 Groschen.** One DM is worth about 7 öS. The basic monetary unit of the GDR is the **Mark: 1 Mark (M) = 100 Pfennig.** According to the official exchange rate of the GDR, 1 East German **Mark (M)** equals 1 West German **Deutsche-Mark (DM).**

In the Bank

TOURIST Hello. Can you tell me where I can exchange money?

TELLER At counter 2.

TOURIST Thank you very much. (She goes to counter 2.) Hello. I'd like to change some dollars into francs. Here are my traveler's checks.

TELLER May I please see your passport?

TOURIST Here you are.

TELLER Sign here.—Go to the cashier over there. Here's your number.

TOURIST Thank you. (She goes to the cashier.)

CASHIER 224 francs 63: one hundred—two hundred—ten—twenty—twenty-four francs and sixty-three rappen. Here you are.

TOURIST Thank you. Goodbye.

At the Hotel Reception Desk

RECEPTIONIST Good evening.

GUEST Good evening. Do you have a single room available?

RECEPTIONIST For how long?

GUEST For two or three nights. If possible, quiet and with a bath.

RECEPTIONIST Unfortunately we have only one double room, and that for only one night. Do you want to see it?

GUEST Yes, I'd like to.

RECEPTIONIST Room number 12, on the second floor to the right. Here's your key.

GUEST Say, where can I leave my car?

RECEPTIONIST In the garage behind the hotel.

GUEST And when do you close at night?

RECEPTIONIST At midnight. If you come in later, you'll have to ring the bell.

Auf der Bank und im Hotel

WORTSCHATZ I

DIE UHRZEIT *time (of the day)*

▪ *The formal (official) time system is like the one used by the military. The hours are counted from 0 to 24, with 0 to 11 referring to A.M. and 12 to 24 referring to P.M. The system is commonly used in timetables for trains, buses, planes, etc., on radio and TV, and to state business hours of stores and banks.*

16.05 Uhr = sechzehn Uhr fünf	*4:05* P.M.
16.15 Uhr = sechzehn Uhr fünfzehn	*4:15* P.M.
16.30 Uhr = sechzehn Uhr dreißig	*4:30* P.M.
16.45 Uhr = sechzehn Uhr fünfundvierzig	*4:45* P.M.
17.00 Uhr = siebzehn Uhr	*5:00* P.M.

DIE BANK, -EN *bank*

der Ausweis, -e	*ID*	*das* Geld	*money*
Dollar, -	*dollar*	Bargeld	*cash*
Paß, Pässe	*passport*	Kleingeld	*change*
Schalter, -	*counter, ticket window*	*die* Kasse, -n	*cashier's window (lit. cash register)*
Scheck, -s	*check*		
Reisescheck, -s	*traveler's check*		

HYPO BANK

Bayerische Hypotheken- und Wechsel-Bank
Aktiengesellschaft

DAS HOTEL, -s *hotel*

der Ausgang, ⸚e	*exit*	*das*	Einzelzimmer, -	*single room*
Eingang, ⸚e	*entrance*		Doppelzimmer, -	*double room*
Gast, ⸚e	*guest*		Gepäck	*baggage, luggage*
Koffer, -	*suitcase*	*die*	Nacht, ⸚e	*night*
Schlüssel, -	*key*		Nummer, -n	*number*
			Tasche, -n	*bag; pocket*

WEITERES

frei	*free, available*
geöffnet / geschlossen	*open / closed*
möglich	*possible*
ruhig	*quiet(ly)*
Wann machen Sie auf/zu?	*When do you open/close?*
Wie steht . . . ?	*What's the exchange rate of . . . ?*
einen Scheck einlösen	*to cash a check*
Geld wechseln	*to make (get) change (DM > Pfennige)*
Geld umwechseln	*to (ex)change money (e.g., $ > DM)*
lassen (läßt), gelassen	*to leave (behind)*
unterschreiben, unterschrieben	*to sign*

PASSIVES VOKABULAR die Empfangsdame, -n *(receptionist)*; die Kredit-karte, -n; klingeln *(to ring a bell)*

ZUM THEMA

A. Mustersätze

1. Geld wechseln: **Wo kann ich hier** Geld wechseln?
   Dollar umwechseln, einen Scheck einlösen, Reiseschecks einlösen
2. Paß: **Darf ich bitte Ihren** Paß **sehen**?
   Scheck, Reisecheck, Ausweis
3. Dollar: **Können Sie mir das in** Dollar **geben**?
   D-Mark, Franken, Schilling, Kleingeld, Bargeld
4. mein Auto: **Wo kann ich** mein Auto **lassen**?
   meinen Schlüssel, mein Gepäck, meinen Koffer, meine Tasche
5. 24 Uhr: **Wir machen um** 24 Uhr **zu**.
   22 Uhr, 22.15 Uhr, 22.30 Uhr, 22.45 Uhr, 23 Uhr

Wer spart, kann große Sprünge machen.

BfG: Die Bank für Gemeinwirtschaft.

B. Was sagen Sie?

1. Kein Kleingeld

X Ich habe kein Kleingeld. Kannst du mir _____ Mark wechseln?

Y Nein, _____

X Schade!

Y Aber du kannst _____ .

X Wo ist _____ ?

Y _____ .

X Danke schön!

Y _____ !

2. Im Hotel

X Guten _____ ! Haben Sie ein _____ mit _____ frei?

Y Wie lange wollen Sie bleiben?

X _____ .

Y Ja, wir haben ein Zimmer im _____ Stock.

X Was kostet es?

Y _____ .

X Kann ich es sehen?

Y _____ . Hier ist der Schlüssel. Zimmer Nummer _____ .

X Sagen Sie, wo kann ich _____ lassen?

Y _____ .

X Und wann machen Sie abends zu?

Y _____ .

DER HOTELEINGANG
IST AB 24⁰⁰ GESCHLOSSEN

Hausschlüssel MITNEHMEN.

Abreisen BITTEN WIR BIS 10⁰⁰ UHR anzukündigen

U. DAS ZIMMER BIS 12⁰⁰ FREIZUGEBEN,
ANDERNFALLS MUSS EINE WEITERE
NACHT BERECHNET WERDEN.

Frühstückszeiten

MONTAG u. SAMSTAG VON 7⁰⁰ – 10⁰⁰

DIENSTAG, MITTWOCH, DONNERSTAG
UND FREITAG   VON 6³⁰ – 10⁰⁰

C. Wie spät ist es? Sehen Sie auf die Karte!

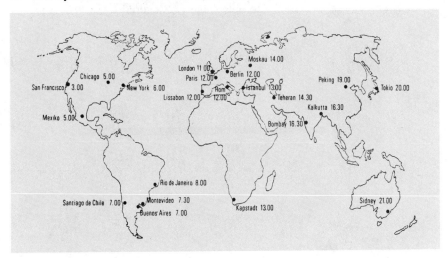

1. Wenn es in Berlin zwölf Uhr ist, wie spät ist es dann in Mexiko? New York? Kapstadt? Kalkutta? Tokio? Sidney?
2. Wo ist es so spät wie in Berlin?
3. Wie viele Stunden später ist es in Istanbul? Moskau? Peking?
4. Wie viele Stunden früher *(earlier)* ist es in Chicago? San Francisco? Rio de Janeiro? Santiago de Chile?

D. Fragen

1. Wo bekommt man Bargeld? Kleingeld?
2. Wie bezahlen Sie, wenn Sie einkaufen: bar, mit einem Scheck oder mit einer Kreditkarte? Wie bezahlen Sie unterwegs, wenn Sie reisen *(travel)*?
3. Wo können Sie hier D-Mark, Schillinge oder Franken bekommen?
4. Wissen Sie, wie viele Mark man für einen Dollar bekommt? wie viele Schillinge? wie viele Franken? Wo können Sie das herausfinden *(find out)*?
5. Wissen Sie, ob ein Amerikaner (ein Kanadier) in Europa mit einem persönlichen *(personal)* Scheck bezahlen kann? Was braucht man, wenn man durch Europa als Tourist fährt?
6. Was tun Sie, wenn Sie kein Geld mehr haben?

E. Was bedeuten die Wörter, und was ist der Artikel?

Ausgangstür, Gästeausweis, Geldwechsel, Gepäckstück, Handtasche, Hoteleingang, Kofferschlüssel, Nachtapotheke, Nachthemd, Nachtmensch, Paßnummer, Scheckbuch, Sparbuch, Postsparbuch, Taschengeld, Taschenlampe, Theaterkasse

F. Aussprache *(See also II.37, 40–41 in the pronunciation section of the Appendix.)*

1. [ei] weil, weit, seit, sein, weißt, bleibst, leider, bei, frei
2. [ie] wie, wieviel, nie, lieben, liegen, mieten, liest, siehst, Dienstag

3. **Beispiel, vielleicht, Wien / Wein; Beine / Biene; bleiben / blieben; Lieder / leider; zeigen / Ziegen; hießen / heißen**

4. Wortpaare
   - *a.* See / Sie
   - *b.* beten / bieten
   - *c.* biete / bitte
   - *d.* Miete / Mitte
   - *e.* leider / Lieder
   - *f.* Mais / mies

STRUKTUR

I. der- *and* ein-*Words*

1. der-Words

This small but important group of limiting words is called DER-WORDS because their case endings are the same as those of the definite article **der**:

der, das, die	*the, that (when stressed)*
dieser, -es, -e	*this, these*
jeder, -es, -e	*each, every (sg. only, pl. alle)*
mancher, -es, -e	*many a (sg.); several, some (usually pl.)*
solcher, -es, -e	*such (usually pl.)*
welcher, -es, -e	*which?*

☞ *CAUTION:*

▶ *The singular of* **solcher** *usually is* **so ein**, *which is not a* **der**-*word:* **so ein Hotel** (such a hotel) BUT **solche Hotels** (such hotels).

Compare:

	masc.	neut.	fem.	pl.
nom.	der dieser welcher	das dieses welches	die diese welche	die diese welche
acc.	den diesen welchen			
dat.	dem diesem welchem	dem diesem welchem	der dieser welcher	den diesen welchen

nom.	Wo ist **der** Schlüssel?—**Welcher** Schlüssel? **Dieser** Schlüssel?	
acc.	Hast du **den** Kofferschlüssel gesehen?—Wie soll ich **jeden** Schlüssel kennen?	
dat.	Kannst du ihn mit **dem** Schlüssel öffnen?—Mit **welchem** Schlüssel?	
pl.	Gib mir **die** Schlüssel!—Hier sind **alle** Schlüssel. **Manche** Schlüssel sind vom Haus, **solche** Schlüssel zum Beispiel.	

BUT: **Der** Kofferschlüssel ist **so ein** Schlüssel!

2. ein-Words

The POSSESSIVES are called **ein**-words because their case endings are the same as those of the indefinite article **ein** and the negative **kein**.

mein	*my*
dein	*your (sg. fam.)*
sein	*his*
sein	*its*
ihr	*her*
unser	*our*
euer	*your (pl. fam.)*
ihr	*their*
Ihr	*your (sg./pl. formal)*

Compare:

	masc.	neut.	fem.	pl.
nom.	ein mein unser	ein mein unser	eine meine unsere	keine meine unsere
acc.	einen meinen unseren	ein mein unser	eine meine unsere	keine meine unsere
dat.	einem meinem unserem	einem meinem unserem	einer meiner unserer	keinen meinen unseren

NOTE: ▪ *The* **-er** *of* **unser** *and* **euer** *is not an ending!*
▪ *The shaded area in the chart above shows where the* **der**-*words have endings but the* **ein**-*words do not.*

nom.	Hier ist **ein** Paß. Ist das **mein** Paß oder **dein** Paß?
acc.	Braucht er **keine** Kreditkarte?—Wo ist **seine** Kreditkarte?
	Hat sie **einen** Ausweis?—Natürlich hat sie **ihren** Ausweis. Haben Sie **Ihren** Ausweis?
dat.	In **welcher** Tasche sind die Schlüssel?—Sie sind in **meiner** Tasche.
	Oder sind die Schlüssel in **einem** Koffer?—Sie sind in **Ihrem** Koffer.
pl.	Wo sind **die** Schecks?—Hier sind **unsere** Schecks, und da sind **euere** Schecks.

ÜBUNGEN

A. *Ersetzen Sie die Artikel!* (Use **der**-words or **so ein**, as suggested.)

> BEISPIEL: die Tasche (this, such a)   **diese Tasche**
> **so eine Tasche**

1. das Zimmer (every, which, this, such a)
2. der Student (this, every, such a, which)
3. die Freundin (which, such a, every, this)
4. die Nummern (some, such, these, which)
5. in dem Hotel (this, which, each, such a)
6. auf den Schreibtisch (this, every, such a, which)
7. mit den Gästen (these, all, some, such)

B. *Ersetzen Sie die Artikel!* (Use **ein**-words, as suggested.)

> BEISPIEL: die Eltern (my, his)   **meine Eltern**
> **seine Eltern**

1. der Paß (her, your/3×, his, no)
2. das Gepäck (their, her, our, his)
3. die Wohnung (her, my, no, your/3×, our)
4. neben den Koffer (your/3×, her, their, our)
5. in dem Studentenheim (our, your/3×, my, no)
6. auf den Reiseschecks (your/3×, his, my, their)

C. *Ersetzen Sie die Artikel!* (Replace the boldface articles.)

> BEISPIEL: **Das** Bad ist klein. (this, our)   *Dieses* Bad ist klein.
> *Unser* Bad ist klein.

1. **Das** Zimmer hat einen Fernseher. (each, my, his, our)
2. Bitte bringen Sie **den** Koffer zum Auto! (this, her, our, my)
3. Ich kann **die** Schlüssel nicht finden. (your/3×, our, some, my)
4. Darf ich **das** Gepäck hier lassen? (her, his, this, our)
5. Der Ober kennt **den** Gast. (each, our, this, your/3×)
6. **Die** Taschen sind schon vor dem Ausgang. (our, all, some, my)
7. **Den** Leuten gefällt das Hotel nicht. (these, some, such)
8. Du kannst **den** Scheck auf der Bank einlösen. (this, my, every, such a, your/sg. fam.)

D. Bilden Sie Sätze auf deutsch!

BEISPIEL: except for our bag   *Wir* haben alles außer unserer Tasche.

1. for his guest
2. after every meal
3. around their hotel
4. to your (pl. fam.) apartment
5. without my money
6. since that day

7. out of our suitcase
8. through this exit
9. from some people
10. into which restaurant
11. near this bridge
12. with your (sg. fam.) ID.

II. Separable-Prefix Verbs

1. English has a number of two-part verbs that consist of a verb and a preposition or an adverb.

Watch out! Get up! Buzz off!

In German such verbs are called SEPARABLE-PREFIX VERBS. You are already somewhat familiar with two of them:

Passen Sie auf! Hören Sie zu!

Their infinitives are **aufpassen** and **zuhören**. The prefixes **auf** and **zu** carry the main stress: **auf'passen, zu'hören.** From now on we will identify such separable-prefix verbs by placing a raised dot (·) between the prefix and the verb in vocabulary lists: **auf·passen, zu·hören.**

■ *These verbs are* SEPARATED *from the prefixes when the inflected part of the verb is the first or second sentence element: in imperatives, questions, and statements:*

Hören Sie bitte **zu!**
Hören Sie jetzt **zu?**
Warum **hören** Sie nicht **zu?**
Wir **hören** immer gut **zu.**
V1   V2

■ *These verbs are* NOT SEPARATED *from the prefixes when the verb stands at the end of a sentence or clause: with modals, in the present perfect, and in subordinate clauses. However, in the present perfect the* **-ge-** *of the past participle is inserted* BETWEEN *the stressed prefix and the participle.*

Ich soll immer gut **zuhören.**
Ich habe immer gut **zugehört.**

Ich weiß, daß ich immer gut **zuhöre.**
Ich weiß, daß ich immer gut **zuhören** soll.
Ich weiß, daß ich immer gut **zugehört** habe.

2. Knowing the basic meaning of some of the most frequent separable prefixes will help you derive the meanings of some of the separable-prefix verbs.

ab-	*away, off*
an-	*to, up to*
auf-	*up, open*
aus-	*out, out of*
ein-	*into*
her-	*toward (the speaker)*
hin-	*away from (the speaker)*

mit-	*together with, along with*
nach-	*after, behind*
vor-	*ahead, before*
vorbei-	*past, by*
zu-	*closed*
zurück-	*back*

BEISPIEL:

an·kommen	*to arrive (come to)*
her·kommen	*to come (toward the speaker)*
hin·kommen	*to get there (away from the point of reference)*
mit·kommen	*to come along*
nach·kommen	*to follow (come after)*
vorbei·kommen	*to come by*
zurück·kommen	*to come back*

▪ *Here are some common separable-prefix verbs. You will need to learn them before doing the exercises.*

an·rufen	*to call, phone*
auf·machen	*to open*
auf·passen, aufgepaßt	*to pay attention, watch out*
auf·schreiben, aufgeschrieben	*to write down*
auf·stehen, ist aufgestanden	*to get up*
aus·gehen, ist ausgegangen	*to go out*
ein·kaufen	*to shop*
ein·lösen	*to cash (in)*
mit·bringen, mitgebracht	*to bring along*
mit·gehen, ist mitgegangen	*to go along*
mit·kommen, ist mitgekommen	*to come along*
mit·nehmen, mitgenommen	*to take along*
um·wechseln	*to exchange*
vorbei·gehen (an, bei), ist vorbeigegangen[1]	*to pass by*
zu·hören (+ *dat.*)	*to listen*
zu·machen	*to close*
zurück·kommen, ist zurückgekommen	*to come back*

☞ *CAUTION:*

▶ *Not all verbs with prefixes are separable—for example* **unterschreiben** *and* **wiederholen**. *Here the main stress is on the verb, not on the prefix:* **unterschrei'ben, wiederho'len.**

ÜBUNGEN

E. Was bedeuten diese Verben? *(Knowing the meanings of the basic verbs and the prefixes, can you tell what these separable-prefix verbs mean?)*

abgeben, abnehmen
ansprechen
aufbauen, aufgeben, aufstehen, aufstellen
ausarbeiten, aushelfen, aus(be)zahlen
hingehen, hinfahren
mitgehen, mitfahren, mitfeiern, mitsingen, mitspielen
nachkommen, nachlaufen
vorbeibringen, vorbeifahren, vorbeikommen
zuhalten
zurückbekommen, zurückbleiben, zurückbringen, zurückgeben, zu-
   rücknehmen, zurücksehen

F. Sagen Sie die Sätze noch einmal ohne Modalverb!

BEISPIEL: Sie soll ihm zuhören. **Sie hört ihm zu.**

1. Wir dürfen am Wochenende ausgehen.
2. Wann mußt du morgens aufstehen?
3. Wollt ihr mit mir einkaufen?
4. Ich soll Wein mitbringen.
5. Er will morgen zurückkommen.
6. Ich möchte dich gern mitnehmen.
7. Du kannst das Geld umwechseln.
8. Er will an der Universität vorbeigehen.
9. Können Sie bitte die Fenster aufmachen!
10. Ihr sollt gut aufpassen.

G. Machen Sie jede indirekte Aussage *(statement)* **und Frage direkt!**

BEISPIEL: Sie sagt, daß er am Abend zurückkommt.
Er kommt am Abend zurück.

1. Er sagt, daß sie um neun ausgehen.
2. Sie fragen, ob ihr die Kinder mitbringt.
3. Sie fragt, wann Sie am Samstag aufstehen.
4. Er fragt, wieviel Geld sie umwechselt.
5. Sie sagen, daß sie morgen vorbeikommen.
6. Sie fragt, ob seine Freunde mitgehen.

H. Sagen Sie die Sätze im Präsens *(present time)*!

BEISPIEL: Wann seid ihr angekommen?   **Wann kommt ihr an?**

1. Du hast wieder nicht aufgepaßt.
2. Peter ist immer noch nicht aufgestanden.
3. Erika ist oft ausgegangen.
4. Uwe hat auf dem Markt eingekauft.
5. Haben Sie meine Bücher mitgebracht?
6. Doris ist nicht mitgegangen.
7. Sie haben das Geschäft schon zugemacht.
8. Wir sind noch schnell bei der Bäckerei vorbeigegangen.

I. Sagen Sie die Sätze im Perfekt!

BEISPIEL: Löst du die Schecks ein? **Hast du die Schecks eingelöst?**

1. Bringst du die Karten mit?
2. Wir gehen am Montag nicht aus.
3. Sie macht den Kühlschrank auf.
4. Wir kaufen oft in der Stadt ein.
5. Er nimmt nur eine Tasche mit.
6. Macht ihr die Vorhänge zu?
7. Kommt Hans auch mit?
8. Ich gehe an der Post vorbei.
9. Bringt ihr das Gepäck mit?
10. Wann kommen Sie zurück?

J. Auf deutsch, bitte!

1. You (sg., fam.) didn't close your book.
2. Listen! (formal).
3. They came back on the weekend.
4. Are you (pl., fam.) going out?
5. I don't know if he's coming along.
6. Do you (sg., fam.) know when she went out?
7. I exchanged our money.
8. Whom did you (formal) bring along?

K. Geben Sie alle drei Imperative!

BEISPIEL: die Tür aufmachen **Machen Sie die Tür auf!**
Macht die Tür auf!
Mach die Tür auf!

1. jetzt aufstehen
2. in der Stadt einkaufen
3. den Scheck noch nicht einlösen
4. genug Bargeld mitbringen
5. das Gepäck mitnehmen
6. mit uns mitkommen
7. bei der Bank vorbeigehen
8. trotzdem zuhören
9. wieder zurückkommen

L. Antworten Sie bitte in ganzen Sätzen!

1. Was kann man aufmachen? (z.B. **einen Schrank**)
2. Wo muß man aufpassen? (z.B. **auf der Straße**)
3. Wann sind Sie heute aufgestanden? Wann stehen Sie gewöhnlich am Wochenende auf?
4. Wohin gehen Sie, wenn Sie ausgehen?
5. Wo kaufen Sie ein?
6. Wo kann man Schecks einlösen?
7. Was haben Sie heute mitgebracht? (drei Beispiele bitte!)

III. *Gesture Words*

Germans frequently use GESTURE WORDS in their everyday speech. These words intensify emotionally what is said; they express what gestures and intonation do when we speak English, but can't be translated literally. There are many of them; we will introduce only four at this point. It's much more important that you recognize gesture words for what they are than that you use them yourself.

aber	*expresses admiration*
denn	*expresses curiosity, interest*
doch	*expresses concern, impatience, assurance*
ja	*adds emphasis*

Euer Haus gefällt mir **aber**!	*I do like your house.*
Du bist **aber** heute hübsch!	*Don't you look pretty today!*
Das kann **doch** nicht richtig sein.	*That can't be right.*
Paß **doch** auf!	*Watch out!*
Sie haben **doch** eine Wohnung zu vermieten?	*You do have an apartment for rent, don't you?*
Was ist **denn** das?	*What (on earth) is that?*
Wieviel Geld brauchst du **denn**?	*How much money do you need?*
Euer Garten ist **ja** phantastisch!	*(Wow,) your garden is fantastic!*
Morgen hast du **ja** Geburtstag!	*(Hey,) tomorrow is your birthday!*

ÜBUNGEN

M. *Was bedeutet das auf englisch?* (Give the English equivalent.)

> BEISPIEL: Hier ist ja mein Schlüssel!   **Oh, here's my key!**

1. Ihr seid doch gestern im Theater gewesen?
2. Haben Sie denn kein Einzelzimmer mehr frei?
3. Euer Wohnzimmer ist aber gemütlich!
4. Hast du denn keinen Durst?
5. Du bist ja schon fertig!
6. Das Hotel ist ja nicht weit von hier.
7. Hilf mir doch!
8. Ihre Blumen sind ja wunderbar!
9. Das ist doch das Rathaus!
10. Das ist aber kein Hausschlüssel!
11. Laß den Koffer doch hier!
12. Du arbeitest ja immer.

ZUSAMMENFASSUNG

N. *Bilden Sie Sätze!* (*Use the tenses suggested.*)

BEISPIEL: Eva / gestern / ausgehen / mit Willi (*present perfect*)
Eva ist gestern mit Willi ausgegangen.

1. man / umwechseln / Geld / auf / eine Bank (*present tense*)
2. welch- / Koffer (*sg.*) / du / mitnehmen? (*present tense*)
3. einkaufen / ihr / gern / in / euer / Supermarkt? (*present tense*)
4. unser / Nachbarn (*pl.*) / zurückkommen / vor einer Woche (*present perfect*)
5. wann / ihr / aufstehen / am Sonntag? (*present perfect*)
6. ich / mitbringen / dir / mein / Stadtplan (*present perfect*)
7. vorbeigehen / noch / schnell / bei / Apotheke! (*imperative/sg. fam.*)
8. zumachen / Schalter / um 17.30 Uhr! (*imperative/formal*)
9. umwechseln / alles / in Schilling! (*imperative/pl. fam.*)

O. *Auf deutsch, bitte!*

1. All (the) hotels are full (**voll**). *2.* Look (*sg. fam.*), there's another hotel. *3.* Let's ask once more. *4.* Do you (*formal*) still have a room available? *5.* Yes, one room without (a) bath on the first floor and one room with shower (**Dusche**) on the second floor. *6.* Excellent! Which room would you (*sg. fam.*) like? *7.* Give (*formal*) us the room on the second floor. *8.* Where can I leave these suitcases? *9.* Over there. But don't go yet. *10.* May I see your ID, please? *11.* Gladly. Do you cash traveler's checks?—Of course. *12.* Did you see our restaurant?—Which restaurant? *13.* This restaurant. From each table you can see the mountains. *14.* A restaurant like this (*such a restaurant*) you don't find everywhere.

Names of small hotels (**Gasthöfe** or **Gasthäuser**) which first sprang up around monasteries toward the end of the Middle Ages, often referred to the Bible: **Gasthof Engel** (angel), **Gasthof Drei Könige** (the Kings were symbols of travel), **Gasthof Rose** or **Lilie** (both flowers representing the Virgin Mary), and **Gasthof Lamm** (the Lamb of God). In the 1400s when a postal system was developing, names like **Gasthof Goldenes Posthorn, Alte Post, Neue Post,** and **Zur Post** appeared.

EINBLICKE

der Gasthof, -̈e	*small hotel*
Name, -n	*name*
die Jugendherberge, -n	*youth hostel*
Pension, -en	*boarding house; hotel*
Reise, -n	*trip*
einfach	*simple, simply*
fast	*almost*
meistens	*mostly*
an·kommen, ist angekommen	*to arrive*
bedeuten	*to mean, signify*
kennen·lernen[1]	*to get to know, meet*
Glück (Pech) haben	*to be (un)lucky*
packen	*to pack*
reisen, ist gereist	*to travel*
reservieren	*to reserve*
übernachten	*to spend the night*

1 The verb **kennen** functions as a separable prefix in this combination: **Er hat sie hier kennengelernt.** *(He met her here.)*

Übernachtungsmöglichkeiten

Wo kann man gut übernachten? Nun,° das kommt darauf an,° ob das Hotel elegant oder einfach, international oder typisch deutsch sein soll, ob es zentral liegen muß, oder ob es weiter draußen° sein darf. 5

In Amerika gibt es viele Hotels mit gleichen° Namen, weil sie zu einer Hotelkette° gehören, z.B. „Holiday Inn" oder „Hilton". Bei diesen Hotels wissen Sie immer, wie es innen° ist. In Deutschland gibt es auch Hotels mit gleichen Namen, z.B. „Hotel zur Sonne" oder „Gasthof Post". Aber das bedeutet nicht, daß solche Hotels innen gleich sind. Im Gegenteil°, sie sind 10 meistens sehr verschieden°, weil sie privat sind. Ihre Namen gehen oft bis ins Mittelalter° zurück. Oft sagen sie etwas über° ihre Lage°, z.B. Berghotel, Pension Waldsee. Andere° Namen, wie z.B. Gasthof zum Löwen°, zum Adler°, zum Bären° oder zum Stier° sind aus der Bibel genommen. Sie sind Symbole für die vier Evangelisten. 15

Manche Hotels sind sehr luxuriös und teuer, andere sind einfach und billig. Sprechen wir von einem normalen Hotel, einem Gasthof oder Gasthaus. Wenn Sie ankommen, gehen Sie zur Rezeption! Dort müssen Sie ein Formular° ausfüllen[1] und bekommen dann Ihr Zimmer: ein Einzelzimmer oder Doppelzimmer, ein Zimmer mit oder ohne Bad. Für Zimmer ohne Bad 20 gibt es auf dem Flur eine Toilette und meistens auch eine Dusche.[2] Das Frühstück ist gewöhnlich im Preis einbegriffen°. Der Herr oder die Dame an der Rezeption kann Ihnen auch Geschäfte und Sehenswürdigkeiten° empfehlen, manchmal auch Geld umwechseln. Aber Vorsicht°! Auf der Bank ist der Wechselkurs° fast immer besser°. 25

Das Übernachten in einem Gasthof kann sehr bequem sein. Aber passen Sie auf, daß er nicht gerade an einer Hauptstraße° liegt oder der Hauptgasthof im Städtchen ist, weil es dort oft viel Lärm° gibt: Lärm von der Straße, Lärm vom Tanzen° und vom Feiern°. Übrigens hat jeder Gasthof seinen Ruhetag°. Dann ist das Restaurant geschlossen, und man nimmt 30 keine neuen Gäste an°.

Wenn Sie nicht vorher reservieren können, dann finden Sie auch Übernachtungsmöglichkeiten durch die Touristeninformation am Bahnhof.[3] Hier gibt es Adressen von Privatfamilien und Pensionen. So eine Übernachtung ist gewöhnlich nicht sehr teuer, aber doch sauber und gut. 35

Margin glosses:
well
that depends

farther out
same
. . .chain
inside

on the contrary
different
Middle Ages/ about/ location
other/ lion
eagle/ bear/ bull

form

included
attractions
careful
exchange rate/ better

main street
noise
dancing/ celebrating
day off
accept

Haben Sie schon einmal in einer Jugendherberge[4] oder einem Jugendgästehaus (in der DDR heißt es Jugendtouristenhotel) übernachtet? Wenn
nicht, tun Sie es einmal! Aber was Sie dann brauchen, ist ein Jugendher-
bergsausweis. So einen Ausweis können Sie aber schon vorher° in Amerika

in advance

**Wenn man in einer
Jugendherberge
übernachten will,
braucht man einen
Jugendherbergs-
ausweis.**

Jugendherberge
»15. August«
5300 Weimar
Humboldtstraße 17
Telefon 4021

Gästeausweis

Aushändigung des Zimmerschlüssels nur gegen Vorlage dieses Ausweises.

Zimmernummer: *14*

Name: *Bean* Vorname: *Margaret*

Anschrift:

Paß/PA-Nr.:

Reiseroute:

Anreisetag: Abreisetag:

---

oder Kanada bekommen. Fast jede Stadt hat eine Jugendherberge, manch- 40
mal in einem modernen Gebäude°, manchmal in einer Burg° oder in einem
Schloß. Jugendherbergen und Jugendgästehäuser sind in den Ferien meistens schnell voll, denn alle Gruppen reservieren schon vorher. Das Übernachten in einer Jugenherberge kann ein Erlebnis° sein, weil man immer
wieder interessante Leute kennenlernt. Abends sitzt man gern gemütlich 45
zusammen und diskutiert, macht ein bißchen Musik oder spielt Karten.
Jugendherbergen haben nur einen Nachteil°: Sie machen gewöhnlich
abends um 22 Uhr zu. Wenn Sie später zurückkommen, haben Sie Pech
gehabt. In fast allen Großstädten gibt es Jugendgästehäuser. Wenn Sie
schon vorher wissen, daß Sie fast jeden Abend ausgehen und spät nach 50
Hause kommen, dann übernachten Sie lieber° in so einem Jugendgästehaus, denn diese machen erst° um 23 oder 24 Uhr zu, und in manchen
Gästehäusern kann man sogar einen Hausschlüssel bekommen.

Man kann natürlich auch anders° übernachten, z.B. auf dem Campingplatz, aber da braucht man ein Zelt° oder einen Wohnwagen°. Campen 55
gefällt nicht jedem°. Ob im Hotel oder auf dem Campingplatz, in einer
Pension oder Jugendherberge, überall brauchen Sie etwas Glück. Und das
wünschen° wir Ihnen auf Ihrer Reise durch Europa.

building/ castle

experience

disadvantage

rather
only

differently
tent/ camper
everybody

wish

ZUM TEXT

A. Was paßt? *(Indicate the correct answer.)*

1. Deutsche Hotels mit gleichen Namen sind . . .
   - *a.* immer alle gleich
   - *b.* innen meistens nicht gleich
   - *c.* alle aus dem Mittelalter
   - *d.* Symbole

2. Wenn Sie in einem Gasthof ankommen, gehen Sie erst . . .
   - *a.* ins Bad
   - *b.* ins Restaurant
   - *c.* zur Rezeption
   - *d.* in Ihr Zimmer

Wenn man in einem Hotel übernachtet, bekommt man meistens auch ein Frühstück.

3. Im Hotel kann man Geld umwechseln, aber ...
   a. nur an der Rezeption
   b. nicht an der Rezeption
   c. der Wechselkurs ist meistens nicht sehr gut
   d. der Wechselkurs ist oft eine Sehenswürdigkeit

4. Das Übernachten in einem Gasthof kann sehr bequem sein, wenn ...
   a. der Gasthof an der Hauptstraße liegt
   b. Ruhetag ist
   c. es viel Lärm gibt
   d. der Gasthof nicht der Hauptgasthof im Städtchen ist

5. Wenn Sie jung sind, können Sie auch in ... übernachten.
   a. einem Luxushotel billig
   b. einer Jugendherberge oder einem Jugendgästehaus
   c. der DDR
   d. einem Schloß

6. Das Übernachten in einer Jugendherberge kann sehr interessant sein, weil ...
   a. Jugendherbergen in den Ferien schnell voll sind
   b. sie gewöhnlich abends um 22 Uhr zumachen
   c. man oft interessante Leute kennenlernt
   d. sie immer auf einer Burg sind

7. Übernachten Sie in einem Jugendgästehaus, wenn Sie ...!
   a. spät nach Hause kommen wollen
   b. Pech gehabt haben
   c. es gern primitiv haben wollen
   d. Karten spielen wollen

8. Auf dem Campingplatz ...
   a. gibt es eine Toilette auf dem Flur
   b. ist das Frühstück im Preis einbegriffen
   c. gibt es viele Zelte und Wohnwagen
   d. darf man nicht früh ankommen

B. *Was fehlt?*

1. In _____ Hotel kann man gut übernachten, aber das kann man nicht von _____ Hotel sagen. *(this, every)*
2. Bei _____ Hotel wissen Sie immer, wie es innen aussieht. *(such a)*
3. _____ Hotels sind sehr luxuriös und teuer, _____ Hotel zum Beispiel. *(some, this)*
4. _____ Hotel ist sehr schön gewesen. *(our)*
5. Hast du schon einmal von _____ Pension gehört? *(this)*
6. Wie gefällt es euch in _____ Jugendherberge? *(your)*
7. _____ Jugendherberge ist in einer Burg. *(our)*
8. In _____ Jugendherberge gibt es noch Platz. *(this)*
9. Wollen wir auf _____ Campingplatz übernachten? *(this)*
10. _____ Campingplatz meinst du *(do you mean)*? *(which)*

C. Sagen Sie die Sätze noch einmal ohne Modalverb, (a) im Präsens und (b) im Perfekt!

BEISPIEL: Ihre Namen sollen bis ins Mittelalter zurückgehen.
Ihre Namen gehen bis ins Mittelalter zurück.
Ihre Namen sind bis ins Mittelalter zurückgegangen.

1. An der Rezeption können wir Geld umwechseln.
2. Sie müssen ein Formular ausfüllen.
3. Wollt ihr spät ausgehen?
4. Wann möchten Sie ankommen?
5. Die Studenten wollen billig in Jugendherbergen übernachten.
6. Da können sie Leute kennenlernen.
7. Wenn Sie zu spät zurückkommen, können Sie Pech haben.

D. Von welcher Übernachtungsmöglichkeit ist hier die Rede? *(To which type of accommodation does each paragraph refer?)*

Campingplatz, Gasthof, Jugendgästehaus, Jugendherberge,
Luxushotel, Pension

1. Diese Übernachtungsmöglichkeit ist meistens nicht teuer, aber doch gut. Man kann sie z.B. durch die Touristeninformation am Bahnhof finden.
2. Hier ist es besonders billig, aber wenn es regnet, kann es hier sehr ungemütlich sein. Man ist in der Natur, aber es ist nicht für alle Leute.
3. Wenn man viel Geld hat, ist es hier natürlich wunderbar: die Betten sind ausgezeichnet, vielleicht hat man nicht nur ein Schlafzimmer, sondern auch ein Wohnzimmer, das Bad ist groß und elegant, und im Kühlschrank findet man Wein und Sekt.
4. Diese Möglichkeit ist für junge Leute. Sie ist nicht teuer, und man kann abends spät zurückkommen oder einen Schlüssel bekommen.
5. Das Übernachten kann hier sehr bequem und gemütlich sein; das Frühstück kostet nichts extra. Man muß aber aufpassen, denn manchmal ist es dort sehr laut. Auch kann man am Ruhetag dort nicht essen.
6. Hier können Leute mit Ausweis billig übernachten, manchmal sogar auf einer Burg. Man kann hier interessante Leute kennenlernen, aber man darf abends nicht nach zehn zurückkommen.

E. Was packen Sie in den Koffer, wenn Sie einen Monat nach Europa fahren? Machen Sie eine Liste!

Falls *(in case)* Sie es brauchen:
der Anorak, -s *(parka)*, Badeanzug, ⸚e *(swimsuit)*, Bikini, -s, BH, -s *(bra)*, Handschuh, -e *(glove)*, Hut, ⸚e *(hat)*, Regenschirm, -e *(umbrella)*, Strumpf, ⸚e *(stockings)*, das Handtuch, ⸚er *(towel)*, Wörterbuch, ⸚er *(dictionary)*
die Badehose, -n *(swimming trunks)*, Creme, -n, Kamera, -s, Sandalen *(pl.)*, Seife, -n *(soap)*, Socken *(pl.)*, Sonnenbrille, -n *(sunglasses)*, Unterwäsche *(underwear)*

F. ***Wohin fahren Sie, oder wo sind Sie gewesen?*** *(Write four sentences for each of the questions.)*

1. Wohin geht Ihre nächste *(next)* Reise? Wann? Wo übernachten Sie dann, und warum dort?
2. Wo sind Sie das letzte Mal *(the last time)* gewesen? Wann? Wo haben Sie übernachtet, und wie ist das gewesen?

ÜBRIGENS

1. Most Americans traveling in Europe for the first time are a bit annoyed at having to fill out official forms when registering in a hotel (home address, date of birth, nationality, etc.). These forms must be filled out by all guests, German or foreign. They are required by law in the interest of public safety.

2. If you intend to stay in a moderately priced hotel, bring your own soap and washcloths along. All hotels supply towels, but only the more expensive ones supply soap.

3. The Tourist Information Office has a room-referral service (**Zimmernachweis**). It usually charges a small fee for locating a room in the price range you indicate. **Pensionen**, by the way, usually have no rooms with bath. **Fremdenzimmer** are rooms in private homes.

4. **Jugendherbergen** can be found in almost every German city and many small towns. Only people under twenty-nine may stay in these low-priced, plain "hotels." They are particularly popular with students, who can stretch their travel budgets over many miles because of the low rates and large numbers of these hostels.

I. *Verbs*

1. wissen

wissen, like the modals below, is irregular in the singular of the present tense.

singular	plural
ich weiß	wir wissen
du weißt	ihr wißt
er weiß	sie wissen

2. Modals

	dürfen	können	müssen	sollen	wollen	mögen
ich	darf	kann	muß	soll	will	möchte
du	darfst	kannst	mußt	sollst	willst	möchtest
er	darf	kann	muß	soll	will	möchte
wir	dürfen	können	müssen	sollen	wollen	möchten
ihr	dürft	könnt	müßt	sollt	wollt	möchtet
sie	dürfen	können	müssen	sollen	wollen	möchten

The modal is the second sentence element (V1); the infinitive of the main verb (V2) stands at the end of the sentence:

Sie **sollen** ihr den Kaffee **bringen**. *You're supposed to bring her the*
    V1   V2   *coffee.*

3. The Imperative

The forms of the familiar imperative have no pronouns; the singular familiar imperative has no **-st** ending.

Schreiben Sie!	Schreibt!	Schreib(e)	Schreiben wir . . .!
Antworten Sie!	Antwortet!	Antworte!	Antworten wir . . .!
Fahren Sie!	Fahrt!	**Fahr(e)!**	Fahren wir . . .!
Nehmen Sie!	Nehmt!	**Nimm!**	Nehmen wir . . .!

4. The Present Perfect

a. Past Participles

t-verbs (weak and mixed verbs)	n-verbs (strong verbs)
(ge) + stem (change) + (e)t	(ge) + stem (change) + en
gekauft gearbeitet gebracht	geschrieben
eingekauft verkauft reserviert	mitgeschrieben unterschrieben

b. Most verbs use **haben** as the auxiliary. Those that use **sein** are intransitive (take no object) and imply a change of place or condition. (**Bleiben** and **sein** are exceptions to the rule.)

Wir haben Wien gesehen.
Wir sind viel gelaufen.
Abends sind wir müde gewesen.

5. Verbs with Inseparable and Separable Prefixes

a. Inseparable-prefix verbs (verbs with the unstressed prefixes **be-, emp-, ent-, er-, ge-, ver-** and **zer-**) are never separated.

Was bedeutet das?
Das verstehe ich nicht.

über-, unter-, and **wieder-** can be used as separable or inseparable prefixes.

Übernachtet ihr in der Jugendherberge?
Unterschreiben Sie bitte hier!

b. Separable-prefix verbs (verbs where the prefix is stressed) are separated in statements, questions, and imperatives.

Du **bringst** deine Schwester **mit.**
Bringst du deine Schwester **mit?**
Bring doch deine Schwester **mit!**

They are not separated when used with modals, in the present perfect, or in dependent clauses.

Du sollst deine Schwester **mitbringen**.
Hast du deine Schwester **mitgebracht**?
Sie will wissen, ob du deine Schwester **mitbringst**.

II. *Cases*

1. Two-Way Prepositions: Accusative or Dative?

an, auf, hinter, in, neben, über, unter, vor, zwischen

The nine two-way prepositions take either the dative or the **accusative**, depending on the verb.

wo?	LOCATION, *activity within a place* → dative
wohin?	DESTINATION, *motion to a place* → accusative

Remember the difference between these two sets of verbs:

to put (upright)	Er **stellt** den Koffer neben den Ausgang.
to stand	Der Koffer **steht** neben dem Ausgang.
to put (flat), lay	**Legen** Sie den Ausweis auf den Tisch!
to lie (flat)	Der Ausweis **liegt** auf dem Tisch.

2. **der**-Words and **ein**-Words

a. **der**-words have the same endings as the definite article **der** (see pp. 105 and 192).

dieser	solcher (so ein)
jeder	welcher
mancher	alle

b. **ein**-words (or possessives) have the same endings as **ein** and **kein** (see charts on pp. 105 and 193).

mein	unser
dein	euer
sein, sein, ihr	ihr, Ihr

3. Pronouns

a. Personal Pronouns

	singular					plural			sg./pl.
nom.	ich	du	er	es	sie	wir	ihr	sie	Sie
acc.	mich	dich	ihn	es	sie	uns	euch	sie	Sie
dat.	mir	dir	ihm	ihm	ihr	uns	euch	ihnen	Ihnen

Don't confuse these pronouns with the **ein**-words (or **possessives**), which are always followed by a noun:

mein dein sein sein ihr unser euer ihr Ihr

b. Interrogative Pronouns

nom.	wer?	was?
acc.	wen?	was?
dat.	wem?	—

4. Summary of the Three Cases

	use	follows ...	masc.	neut.	fem.	pl.
nom.	Subject, Predicate noun	**heißen, sein, werden**	der dieser ein mein	das dieses ein mein	die diese eine meine	die diese keine meine
acc.	Direct object	**durch, für, gegen, ohne, um**	den diesen einen meinen			
		an, auf, hinter, in, neben, über, unter, vor, zwischen				
dat.	Indirect object	**aus, außer, bei, mit, nach, seit, von, zu** **antworten, danken, gefallen, gehören, helfen, zuhören**	dem diesem einem meinem	dem diesem einem meinem	der dieser einer meiner	den diesen keinen meinen

III. *Sentence Structure*

1. Verb Position

a. V1—V2

In declarative sentences, yes/no questions, and imperatives, two-part verb phrases are split: The inflected part (V1) is the first or second sentence element, the other part (V2) appears at the end of the clause.

Er **ist** hier an der Uni **Student.**
Er **ist** wirklich sehr **interessant.**
    Hast du ihn schon **kennengelernt?**
Ich **kann** jetzt nicht lange **sprechen.**
    Komm doch später bei uns **vorbei!**
    V1   V2

b. Subordinate Clauses

- *Subordinate clauses are introduced by subordinating conjunctions or interrogatives:*

> bevor, daß, ob, obwohl, weil, wenn

> wer? wen? wem? was? was für ein(e)? wohin? woher? wo? wann? warum? wie? wie lange? wieviel? wie viele?

- *In subordinate clauses the subject usually comes right after the conjunction and the inflected verb (V1) is at the end of the clause.*

Sie sagt, **daß** sie das Einzelzimmer **nimmt.**
Er sagt, **daß** er den Zimmerschlüssel **mitbringt.**

- *Two-part verb phrases appear in the order V2 V1.*

Sie sagt, **daß** er den Koffer **mitbringen soll.**

- *If a subordinate clause is the first sentence element, then the inflected part of the verb in the main clause comes right after the comma.*

Ich habe den Schlüssel mitgenommen, **weil** das Hotel um 24 Uhr zumacht.
Weil das Hotel um 24 Uhr zumacht, **habe ich** den Schlüssel mitgenommen.

2. Sequence of Objects

The indirect object usually precedes the direct object unless the direct object is a pronoun.

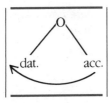

Sie gibt dem Herrn den Reisescheck.
Sie gibt ihm den Reisescheck.
Sie gibt ihn **dem Herrn**.
Sie gibt ihn **ihm**.

3. sondern vs. **aber**

sondern must be used when the first clause is negated AND the meaning *but on the contrary* is implied.

Er wohnt hier, **aber** er ist gerade nicht zu Hause.
Heinz ist nicht hier, **aber** er kommt in zehn Minuten zurück.
Heinz ist nicht hier, **sondern** bei Freunden.

WORTSCHATZWIEDERHOLUNG

A. Geben Sie das Gegenteil von . . .!

Ausgang, Tag, antworten, fahren, Glück haben, mieten, zumachen, bequem, furchtbar, geöffnet, hier, immer, links, ruhig, unten, weit

B. Was ist der Artikel und der Plural?

Ausweis, Bank, Bibliothek, Fest, Garten, Gast, Gasthof, Haus, Hotel, Jugendherberge, Koffer, Lied, Mann, Nacht, Radio, Regal, Reise, Schlüssel, Sessel, Tasche, Taxi, Universität, Wald, Weg

C. Welche Wörter kommen Ihnen in den Sinn?

BEISPIEL: aufmachen   **die Tür, das Fenster, der Schlüssel**

baden, bekommen, bummeln, einkaufen, feiern, Geld einlösen, halten, kochen, packen, singen, sitzen, sparen, Spaß machen, übernachten

D. Was für Wortkombinationen gibt es?

BEISPIEL: Telefon   **Telefonnummer, Telefonbuch**

1. Ausweis
2. Eingang
3. Ferien
4. Flasche
5. Gast
6. Geld
7. Haltestelle
8. Scheck
9. Schrank

E. ***Worttreppe.*** *(Stairway with words. Create new words with the last letter of each preceding word. How far can you get in two minutes?)*

BEISPIEL: Post
    Theater
      Radio

F. ***Wie viele Sätze können Sie bilden?***

BEISPIELE: Das Rathaus ist . . .
    Das Rathaus ist gegenüber von der Bank.

    Fahren Sie mit . . .!
    Fahren Sie mit dem Fahrrad!

G. ***Was paßt?***

___ 1. Können Sie mir sagen, wo das Hotel ist?

___ 2. Wie komme ich dorthin *(to it)*?

___ 3. Wie lange dauert das?

___ 4. Wo kann ich das Gepäck lassen?

___ 5. Einen Moment! Das gehört mir!

___ 6. Wann machen Sie zu?

___ 7. Wo ist das Zimmer?

___ 8. Haben Sie kein Zimmer mit Bad?

___ 9. Das Zimmer ist zu klein.

a. An der Rezeption.
b. Da drüben.
c. Das macht nichts.
d. Das tut mir leid.
e. Doch!
f. Ein paar Minuten.
g. Entschuldigen Sie!
h. Fahren Sie immer geradeaus!
i. Ich weiß nicht.
j. Im Parterre.
k. In ein paar Minuten.
l. Ja, gern.
m. Leider nicht.
n. Mit dem Bus.
o. Neben dem Rathaus.
p. Sind Sie sicher?
q. Um 23.00 Uhr.
r. Wirklich?
s. Zu Fuß!

STRUKTURWIEDERHOLUNG

H. *Verben*

1. wissen *oder* kennen?

    a. Ich möchte _____ , für wen das Geschenk ist.

    b. _____ du einen Herrn Mayerhofer?

    c. _____ ihr eure Nachbarn nicht?

    d. Nein, ich _____ sie nicht, aber ich _____ , daß sie aus Österreich sind.

    e. _____ du, wann sie zurückkommen sollen?

2. *Geben Sie alle Imperative!*

BEISPIEL: Überraschen wir ihn!   **Überraschen Sie ihn!**
                                       Überrascht ihn!
                                       Überrasch ihn!

    a. Tun wir die Milch in den Kühlschrank!

    b. Stellen wir die Teller auf den Tisch!

    c. Gehen wir ins Wohnzimmer!

    d. Sprechen wir ein bißchen!

    e. Lassen wir alles liegen und stehen!

    f. Nehmen wir ein paar Gläser mit!

    g. Essen wir ein paar Kartoffelchips!

    h. Bleiben wir noch ein Stündchen!

    i. Fahren wir später!

3. *Sagen Sie es im Perfekt!*

    a. Wohin geht ihr?—Wir fahren zum Museum.

    b. Was machst du heute?—Ich packe meinen Koffer.

    c. Wie feiert ihr seinen Geburtstag?—Wir überraschen ihn mit einer Party.

    d. Wie gefällt Ihnen die Landshuter Fürstenhochzeit?—Sie macht mir viel Spaß.

    e. Vermieten Sie die Wohnung?—Ja, eine Studentin nimmt sie.

    f. Weißt du, wo der Scheck ist?—Ja, er liegt auf dem Schreibtisch.

    g. Wie lange dauert die Party?—Sie ist um 12.00 Uhr vorbei.

    h. Wo sind Paula und Robert?—Sie kaufen ein.

4. *Variieren Sie die deutschen Sätze!*

Ihr dürft das Geschenk aufmachen.

    a. May we open the present?

    b. We want to open it.

    c. I can't open it.

    d. He has to open it.

    e. Why am I not supposed to open it?

    f. You *(3×)* have to open it.

    g. Wouldn't you *(3×)* like to open it?

Wir kommen morgen an.

a. I arrived yesterday.
b. She's arriving today.
c. When are they arriving?
d. When did he arrive?
e. Is he arriving, too?

f. I know that they're not arriving tomorrow.
g. They're supposed to arrive the day after tomorrow.
h. Has she arrived yet (**schon**)?

I.   *Personalpronomen* (Personal Pronouns). *Variieren Sie die Sätze!*

1. **Ich frage sie.**

a. He's asking you (*formal*).
b. She's asking him.
c. Are they asking us?
d. Yes, they are asking you (*sg. fam.*).
e. We're asking you (*pl. fam.*).

f. Don't ask them!
g. Did you (*sg. fam.*) ask them?
h. Weren't they asking you (*sg. fam.*)?
i. Have you asked me?

2. **Dieses Museum gefällt mir.**

a. He likes our museum.
b. Do you (*formal*) like this museum?
c. They don't like their museum.
d. Which museum do you (*sg. fam.*) like?

e. I like such a museum.
f. Don't you (*pl. fam.*) like any museum? (Do you like no museum)?
g. I don't like museums.
h. I never liked such museums.
i. He likes each museum.

3. **Das tut mir leid.**

a. She's sorry.
b. Are you (3×) sorry?
c. He isn't sorry.

d. I was sorry.
e. They were sorry.

J.   *Präpositionen. Bilden Sie Sätze wie in den Beispielen!* (Ask about various things.)

1. BEISPIELE: **Wo ist der Koffer? Der Koffer steht an der Tür.**
   Wohin soll ich den Koffer stellen? Stellen Sie ihn an die Tür!

   vor / Haus; in / Gästezimmer; neben / Sofa; hinter / Sessel; unter / Tisch; zwischen / Stuhl / und / Bett

2. BEISPIELE: **Wohin soll ich das Messer legen? Legen Sie es auf den Tisch!**
   Wo liegt das Messer? Es liegt auf dem Tisch.

   neben / Gabel; auf / Teller; zwischen / Butter / und / Käse; in / Küche; in / Eßzimmer

K.   *Konjunktionen* (Conjunctions)

1. *Verbinden Sie die Sätze!* (Note that both coordinating and subordinating conjunctions are used.)

a. Ich lerne Deutsch. Meine Großeltern wohnen in der DDR. *(because)*
b. Sie möchte wissen. Bist du schon einmal in der DDR gewesen? *(whether)*
c. Ich sage ihr. Ich bin im Sommer dort gewesen. *(that)*
d. Braucht man ein Visum *(visa)*? Man fährt in die DDR. *(when)*
e. *(before)* Du reist in die DDR. Du brauchst natürlich ein Visum.
f. *(although)* Meine Großeltern wohnen dort. Es hat lange gedauert, bis ich das Visum bekommen habe.
g. Man muß alles gut planen. Man möchte in die DDR. *(if)*

2. sondern *oder* aber?

a. Momentan habe ich kein Kleingeld, _____ später gehe ich zur Bank.
b. Die Bank ist um diese Zeit geschlossen, _____ sie macht in einer Stunde wieder auf.
c. Wir möchten nicht in die Stadt gehen, _____ hier bleiben.
d. In der Stadt kann man viel sehen, _____ wir haben schon alles gesehen!
e. Das bedeutet nicht, daß die Stadt mir nicht gefällt, _____ es bedeutet nur, daß ich müde bin.

AUFGABE

L. Was fehlt?

1. _____ Wochenende fahren Monika und Reinhold _____ Auto _____ Land. Dort wollen sie ein Picknick machen. *(on the, by, to the)*

2. Sie halten _____ Städtchen und gehen dann zu Fuß _____ Feldweg _____ Wald. *(in a, on a, into the)*

3. Sie bummeln gemütlich _____ Wald und kommen dann _____ See. *(through the, to a)*

4. Reinhold stellt das Essen _____ Baum, weil er und Monika _____ See baden wollen. *(under a, in the)*

5. Aber was sehen sie, als *(when)* sie wieder _____ Wasser kommen? Ameisen *(ants)*, viele Ameisen! *(out of the)*

6. Sie sind überall: _____ Brötchen *(pl.)*, _____ Käse, _____ Butter, _____ Kuchen und sogar _____ Limonade. *(between the, under the, on the, behind the, in the)*

7. Aber nicht nur das! Jetzt krabbeln *(crawl)* sie auch noch _____ Kleidung, _____ Bluse, _____ Hosenbeine *(pl.)* und _____ Rock! *(into the, onto the, between the, under the)*

8. Einfach furchtbar! Da läuft Monika _____ Kleidung zurück _____ See und schüttelt *(shakes)* die Ameisen _____ Wasser. *(with the, to the, into the)*

9. Weg *(away)* _____ Ameisen! *(with the)*

10. Und Reinhold fischt die Ameisen _____ Brötchen *(pl.)*, _____ Butter, _____ Kuchen und _____ Limonade. Guten Appetit! *(out of the, the/3 ×)*

M. Auf deutsch, bitte! *(Unless special instructions are given, use pl. fam. forms in this exercise.)*

1. How do you like your rooms? *2.* I like my room. *3.* One can see not only the city, but also the lake. *4.* Do you know that my room has even a TV? *5.* Which room do you *(sg. fam.)* have? *6.* Look over there, the room next to the entrance. *7.* What are we doing now? *8.* Nothing. I have to talk with your father. *9.* And you must go to *(ins)* bed, because we'll have to get up early *(früh)* tomorrow. *10.* We only sit in the car and aren't allowed to do anything. *11.* Where do you want to go? *12.* I know a hotel near the lake where one can dance. *13.* When are you coming back? *14.* When are we supposed to come back? *15.* Where are the car keys? *16.* Please give *(sg. fam.)* them to me. *17.* Did you *(sg., fam.)* see my keys? *18.* Who had them last *(zuletzt)*? *19.* I didn't take them. *20.* Where were you *(sg., fam.)* last?—I don't know.

GESPRÄCHE

ANNEMARIE Ich möchte dieses Paket nach Amerika schicken.

POSTBEAMTER Normal oder mit Luftpost?

ANNEMARIE Mit Luftpost. Wie lange dauert das denn?

POSTBEAMTER Ungefähr zehn Tage. Füllen Sie bitte diese Paketkarte aus!— Moment! Hier fehlt noch Ihr Absender!

ANNEMARIE Ach ja!—Noch etwas. Ich muß telefonieren.

POSTBEAMTER Wohin?

ANNEMARIE Nach Basel. Hier ist die Telefonnummer.

POSTBEAMTER Gehen Sie da drüben in Zelle vier![1]

ANNEMARIE Danke!

ANNEMARIE Wann fährt der nächste Zug nach Basel?

BEAMTIN In einer Viertelstunde. Abfahrt 14.55, Gleis zwei.

ANNEMARIE Und wann kommt er dort an?

BEAMTIN Ankunft in Basel 19.40 Uhr.

ANNEMARIE Muß ich umsteigen?

BEAMTIN Ja, in Mannheim. Aber Sie haben Anschluß zum TEE[2] mit nur fünf Minuten Aufenthalt.

ANNEMARIE Prima. Dann geben Sie mir bitte eine Rückfahrkarte nach Basel!

BEAMTIN Erster oder zweiter Klasse?

ANNEMARIE Zweiter Klasse.

BEAMTIN 220 Mark, bitte!

Das Postpaket

Schnell und sicher

ÜBRIGENS

1. The telephone system in the Federal Republic, as in many European countries, is a state monopoly and is administered by the postal service. In German post offices there are several phone booths from which long-distance calls can be made and then paid for at the counter. This is useful if you don't have small change for coin phones or if you stay in a hotel, since many hotels impose considerable surcharges on long-distance and overseas calls. Collect calls can be made to foreign countries, but not within West Germany. The **Bundespost** also offers banking services, which makes it easy to transfer money to other parts of the country and allows travelers access to their funds at any post office.

2. Train travel in Europe can be a pleasant experience. A tight net of rail lines serves commuters as well as long-distance travelers, and trains are comfortable, clean, punctual, and fast. The **IC** (intercity) and **TEE** (Trans-Europe-Express) trains connect all major European cities. The **ICE**, a luxury train, will soon allow quiet, comfortable traveling twice as fast as by car and "half as fast as by jet." Non-European travelers can buy a Eurail-Pass that permits unlimited train and some bus and boat travel in the FRG and twelve other Western European countries.

At the Post Office in the Train Station

ANNEMARIE I'd like to send this package to the United States.

CLERK By surface mail or by airmail?

ANNEMARIE By airmail. How long will it take?

CLERK About ten days. Please fill out this parcel form.—Just a minute. Your return address is missing.

ANNEMARIE Oh yes.—One more thing. I have to make a phone call.

CLERK Where to?

ANNEMARIE To Basel. Here's the phone number.

CLERK Go over there to booth four.

ANNEMARIE Thank you.

At the Ticket Counter

ANNEMARIE When does the next train leave for Basel?

CLERK In a quarter of an hour. Departure at 14:55, track two.

ANNEMARIE And when will it arrive there?

CLERK Arrival in Basel at 19:40.

ANNEMARIE Do I have to change trains?

CLERK Yes, in Mannheim. But you have a connection to the Trans-Europe-Express with only a five-minute stopover.

ANNEMARIE Great. Then give me a round-trip ticket to Basel, please.

CLERK First or second class?

ANNEMARIE Second class.

CLERK 220 marks, please.

		1.		
Köln Hbf .... ab	14.55			16.00 ...
Bonn-Beuel .... ab				
Bonn Hbf .... ab	15.14			16.19 ...
Bonn-Bad Godesberg				
Remagen				
Andernach				
Trier Hbf .... ab				14.25
Koblenz Hbf .... an				15.46
Koblenz Hbf .... ab		15.49		16.54 16.25
Boppard....................				
Bingerbrück...............				
Bingen (Rhein)............				
Rüdesheim (Rhein).........				17.12
Wiesbaden Hbf				17.43
Mainz Hbf		16.41		17.46 17.57
Worms Hbf				18.25
Ludwigshafen (Rh) Hbf		ab		18.43
Mannheim Hbf		17.23	17.28	18.27 18.47
Heidelberg Hbf .... an				18.39
Bruchsal .... an				
Karlsruhe Hbf .... an			17.56	19.23
Karlsruhe Hbf .... ab				20.09
Pforzheim Hbf .... an				20.49
Rastatt .... an	E 3151			
Rastatt .... ab	◄3)			
Freudenstadt Hbf....... an				
Baden-Oos.............. an	17.50	18.11		19.45
Baden-Oos .... ab		18.41		20.11
Baden-Baden .... an	E 3815	18.52	#3)	20.20
Appenweier .... an	18.24			
Offenburg .... an	18.35			20.07
Offenburg .... ab	17.17	18.40		20.11
Hausach .... an	17.42			
Triberg .... an	18.05			
St Georgen (Schwarzw) ..... an	18.20			
Villingen (Schwarzw) .... an	18.31			
Donaueschingen .... an	18.50	von Heidelberg	nach Zürich (E 6)	
Immendingen............. an	19.05			
Singen (Hohentwiel) .... an	19.33			
Radolfzell .... an	19.43			
Konstanz .... an	19.59			
Lahr (Schwarzw) .... an	18.53			
Freiburg (Brsg) Hbf .... an	19.28	18.57		20.43
Freiburg (Brsg) Hbf.......ab		h 19.14		
Neustadt (Schwarzw) .....an		h 20.09		
Müllheim (Baden) .... an	h 20.02			21.02
Basel Bad Bf .... an	h 20.35	19.34		21.29
Basel Bad Bf .... ab		19.35		21.54
Basel SBB .... an		19.40		22.00

Post und Reisen

DIE POST *post office, mail*

der Absender, -	*return address*
Brief, -e	*letter*
Briefkasten, ¨	*mailbox*
das Paket, -e	*package, parcel*
die Adresse, -n	*address*
Briefmarke, -n	*stamp*
(Post)karte, -n	*(post)card*

DIE REISE, -N *trip*

der Aufenthalt	*stopover*
Bahnsteig, -e	*platform*
Fahrplan, ¨e	*schedule*
Flug, ¨e	*flight*
Flughafen, ¨	*airport*
Wagen, -	*car; railroad car*
Zug, ¨e	*train*
das Flugzeug, -e	*plane*
Gleis, -e	*track*
die Abfahrt, -en	*departure*
Ankunft, ¨e	*arrival*
Bahn, -en	*railway, train*
Fahrt, -en	*trip, drive*
Fahrkarte, -n	*ticket*
Rückfahrkarte, -n	*round-trip ticket*

DB	Erster Geltungstag	Zur Hinfahrt	Zur Rückfahrt gültig bis einschließlich	Ausgabe-Nr
	22.04.86	21.06.86	21.06.86	420700

Klasse	Tarif		halber Preis
2	HIN- UND RUECKFAHRT***		JUNPASS

von FRANKFURT (MAIN)

nach BONN
über KO

Verkaufsstelle	Z A	km	DM
	XX	0189	***36,00

FRANKFURT
(MAIN) HBF   11070070   ***
Bitte Rückseite beachten

WEITERES

in einer Viertelstunde	*in a quarter of an hour*
in einer halben Stunde	*in half an hour*
in einer Dreiviertelstunde	*in three quarters of an hour*
ab·fahren (fährt ab), ist abgefahren (von)	*to leave (from)*
ab·fliegen, ist abgeflogen (von)	*to take off, fly (from)*
aus·steigen, ist ausgestiegen	*to get off*
ein·steigen, ist eingestiegen	*to get on (in)*
um·steigen, ist umgestiegen	*to change (trains etc.)*
aus·füllen	*to fill out*
besuchen	*to visit*
fliegen, ist geflogen	*to fly, go by plane*
landen, ist gelandet	*to land*
schicken	*to send*
telefonieren	*to call up, phone*
mit dem Zug (der Bahn) fahren	*to go by train*

PASSIVES VOKABULAR der Anschluß, ¨-sse *(connection)*; der nächste Zug nach *(the next train to)*; die Klasse, -n; die Paketkarte, -n *(parcel form)*; die Telefonzelle, -n *(phone booth)*; Einen Moment! *(One moment! Just a minute!)*; mit Luftpost *(by airmail)*; noch etwas *(one more thing, something else)*

ZUM THEMA

A. Was paßt nicht?

1. der Absender—der Briefkasten—die Adresse—die Briefmarke
2. der Bahnhof—der Bahnsteig—das Gleis—der Flugkartenschalter
3. die Luftpost—die Ankunft—die Abfahrt—der Fahrplan
4. fliegen—fahren—schicken—fehlen
5. abfahren—abfliegen—ausfüllen—ankommen
6. hinaufsteigen—aussteigen—einsteigen—umsteigen

B. Was bedeutet das, und was muß der Artikel sein?

Adreßbuch, Abfahrtszeit, Ankunftsfahrplan, Bahnhofseingang, Briefträger, Busbahnhof, Busfahrt, Flugkarte, Flugschalter, Flugsteig, Gepäckkarte, Landung, Zwischenlandung, Mietwagen, Nachtzug, Paketschalter, Rückflugkarte, Speisewagen, Telefonrechnung

VON HAUS ZU HAUS - GEPÄCK VORAUS

Von uns abgeholt – von uns
zugestellt. Fragen Sie nach unserem
Sonderprospekt.

C. Fragen

1. Was kostet es, wenn man einen Brief innerhalb *(inside)* von Amerika schicken will? Wie lange braucht ein Brief innerhalb der Stadt? nach Europa?

2. Was muß man auf alle Briefe, Postkarten und Pakete schreiben? Schreiben Sie oft Briefe? Wem?

3. In Deutschland sind die Briefkästen gelb. Welche Farbe haben die Briefkästen hier?

4. Wo kann man hier telefonieren? Kann man hier auch auf der Post telefonieren?

5. Wie kann man reisen? Wie reisen Sie gern? Warum?

6. Wo sind Sie das letzte Mal *(the last time)* gewesen? Sind Sie geflogen oder mit dem Wagen gefahren?

7. Wie heißt der Platz, wo Züge abfahren und ankommen? wo Flugzeuge abfliegen und landen? wo Busse halten?

8. Was ist das Gegenteil von abfahren? abfliegen? einsteigen? Abfahrt? Abflug?

D. Am Flugschalter. Was sagen Sie?

X Wann gehen Flüge nach _____ ?

Y Zu welcher Tageszeit möchten Sie denn fliegen?

X Ich muß um _____ in _____ sein.

Y Wir haben einen Flug um _____ .

X Hat er eine Zwischenlandung?

Y Ja, in _____ . Dort haben Sie _____ Aufenthalt.

X Muß ich umsteigen?

Y _____ .

X _____ . Dann geben Sie mir eine Rückflugkarte nach _____ !

Y Erster oder zweiter Klasse?

X _____ .

E. *Fragen über den Fahrplan*

1. Wie viele Kilometer sind es von Hannover nach Düsseldorf?
2. Wann fährt der erste Zug morgens? der letzte *(last)* Zug abends?
3. Welche Züge sind (a) D-Züge *(express trains)*, (b) IC-Züge *(intercity trains)*? Geben Sie ein paar Beispiele!
4. Welcher Zug fährt täglich *(daily)*? täglich außer Samstag? nur freitags?
5. Wann ist man in Düsseldorf, wenn man um 7.07 (13.14, . . .) von Hannover abfährt? Ungefähr wie lange dauert die Fahrt?
6. Wie kann man vom Düsseldorfer Hauptbahnhof (Hbf) schnell zum Flughafen kommen? Wie oft fährt die S-Bahn? (**alle . . . Minuten**) Wie lange dauert die Fahrt mit der S-Bahn vom Hauptbahnhof zum Flughafen?

Hannover

km 285 → **Düsseldorf**

ab	Zug	an	
0.34	**D** 14146	4.40	
2.58	**D** 440	6.28	
3.25	**D** 244	6.30	
3.25	**D** 244	6.48	
7.07	*IC* 7	9.30	
8.09	*IC* 513	10.36	
9.09	*IC* 521	11.30	
10.09	*IC* 523	12.30	
10.19	**D** 348	13.52	
11.09	*IC* 515	13.30	
12.09	*IC* 9	14.30	
13.09	*IC* 525	15.30	
13.14	**D** 18.40	16.43	
14.09	*IC* 517	16.30	
14.47	**D** 346	17.59	
15.09	*IC* 527	17.30	④
15.57	**D** 444	19.38	
16.09	*IC* 501	18.30	
16.25	*IC* 1519	19.13	③
16.30	**D** 442	1954	
17.09	*IC* 519	19.30	
18.09	*IC* 619	20.30	④
19.09	*IC* 544	21.30	
19.38	**D** 242	22.59	
20.09	*IC* 542	22.30	④
21.17	**E** 3648	1.21	

Zeichenerklärung
③ = an Freitagen
④ = täglich außer Samstag

Ab Düsseldorf Hbf:

mit Ⓢ-Bahn (alle 20 Minuten) nach Düsseldorf (Flughafen)!
Fahrzeit: alle 13 Minuten

F. Aussprache *(See also II.8–10 in the pronunciation section of the Appendix.)*

1. [ə] Adresse, Briefe, Pakete, Flüge, Züge, Wagen, Ecke, Haltestelle, bekommen, besuchen, eine halbe Stunde
2. [ʌ] aber, sauber, euer, unser, Zimmer, Absender, Koffer, Nummer, Uhr, wir, vier, vor, nur, unter, über, hinter, außer, feiern, wiederholen, verkaufen
3. Wortpaare
   a. Studenten / Studentin
   b. Touristen / Touristin
   c. diese / dieser
   d. arbeiten / Arbeitern
   e. lese / Leser
   f. mieten / Mietern

STRUKTUR

I. *The Genitive Case*

In this chapter the focus is on the genitive case. The genitive case has two major functions: it expresses possession or another close relationship between two nouns, and it follows certain prepositions.

1. The English phrases *the son's letter* and *the date of the letter* correspond to German phrases in the genitive.

Das ist **der Brief des Sohnes.**	*That's the son's letter.*
Was ist **das Datum des Briefes?**	*What's the date of the letter?*

a. The genitive form of the INTERROGATIVE PRONOUN is **wessen** *(whose)*. This chart is now complete.

	persons	things and ideas
nom.	wer?	was?
acc.	wen?	
dat.	wem?	—
gen.	wessen?	—

Wessen Brief ist das? **Der Brief des Sohnes.**
Whose letter is that? The son's letter.

b. The genitive forms of the DEFINITE and INDEFINITE ARTICLE complete this chart:

	singular			plural
	masc.	neut.	fem.	
nom.	der ein kein	das ein kein	die eine keine	die — keine
acc.	den einen keinen			
dat.	dem einem keinem	dem einem keinem	der einer keiner	den — keinen
gen.	des eines keines	des eines keines	der — keiner	der — keiner

c. The genitive case is signaled not only by a special ending on the article but also by an ending on many nouns.

- FEMININE *nouns and* PLURAL *nouns have no special genitive endings.*

die Reise / **der** Reise   *the trip's, of the trip*
die Reisen / **der** Reisen   *the trips', of the trips*

- MASCULINE *and* NEUTER *nouns, however, do have endings in the singular.*

-es: *Most one-syllable nouns and those ending in -s, -ß, -z, -tz, and -zt, add an -es.*

der Zug / des Zug**es**   der Paß / des Pass**es**
das Geld / des Geld**es**   der Platz / des Platz**es**
das Gleis / des Gleis**es**

-s: *Most nouns with more than one syllable and proper names add an -s.*

der Flughafen / des Flughafens   *the airport's, of the airport*
Wien, Flughafen / Wiens Flughafen   *Vienna's airport*
Annemarie, Flug / Annemaries Flug   *Annemarie's flight*
Frl. Strobel, Fahrt / Frl. Strobels Fahrt   *Miss Strobel's trip*

Note that German uses no apostrophe (') for the genitive!

Die Züge sind bequem, sauber, pünktlich (on time) und schnell.

☞ *CAUTION:*

▶ *N-nouns are an exception to this rule. They have an **-n** or **-en** ending in* ALL *cases except in the nominative singular. (Very rarely is there a genitive* **-s**: der Name / des Namen**s**.*) Note how they are listed in vocabularies and dictionaries: the first ending refers to the accusative, dative, and genitive singular; the second one, to the plural.*

der Herr, -n, -en	des Herrn	*der* Name, -ns, -n	des Namens
Junge, -n, -n	des Jungen	Student, -en, -en	des Studenten
Mensch, -en, -en	des Menschen	Tourist, -en, -en	des Touristen
Nachbar, -n, -n	des Nachbarn		

d. Nouns in the genitive NORMALLY FOLLOW the nouns they modify.

Er trägt den Koffer **der Dame**.   *He's carrying the lady's suitcase.*

Proper names COME BEFORE the noun they modify.

Er liest **Annemaries Brief**.   *He's reading Annemarie's letter.*
Er liest **Frl. Strobels Brief**.   *He's reading Miss Strobel's letter.*

☞ *CAUTION:*

▶ *Don't confuse the use of the possessive adjectives* **mein, dein,** *etc., with that of the genitive case.*

Da ist mein Onkel.   *There's my uncle. (possessive adj.)*
Da ist der Koffer **meines Onkels**.   *There's my uncle's suitcase (the suitcase of my uncle). (genitive)*

2. Prepositions with the Genitive

These prepositions are followed by the genitive case:

statt	*instead of*
trotz	*in spite of*
während	*during*
wegen	*because of*

Ich nehme meistens den Bus statt der Straßenbahn oder eines Taxis. Trotz des Wetters bummele ich gern durch die Stadt. Während der Mittagspause gehe ich manchmal in den Park. Aber heute bleibe ich wegen des Regens *(rain)* und des Windes hier.

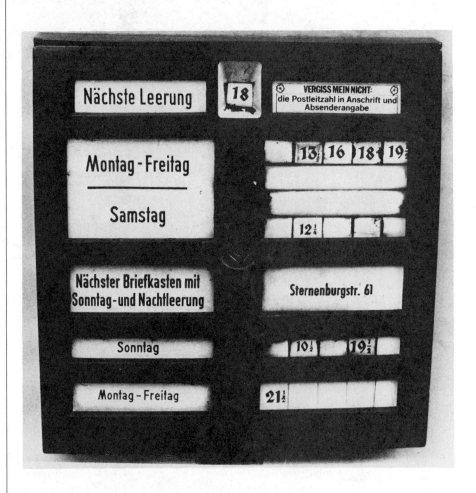

ÜBUNGEN

A. Wissen Sie, wer das ist?

BEISPIEL: Wer ist der Vater Ihrer Mutter?   Das ist mein Großvater.

1. Wer ist der Sohn Ihres Vaters?
2. Wer ist die Mutter Ihrer Mutter?
3. Wer ist die Tochter Ihrer Mutter?
4. Wer ist der Großvater Ihrer Mutter?
5. Wer ist die Schwester Ihrer Mutter?
6. Wer ist der Mann Ihrer Tante?
7. Wer ist die Tochter Ihres Großvaters?
8. Wer ist der Sohn Ihres Urgroßvaters?

B. Ersetzen Sie den Genitiv!

1. BEISPIEL: Was ist die Farbe der Tafel?   (Buch, Bleistifte)
    Und des Buches?
    Und der Bleistifte?

a. Was ist die Größe *(size)* der Jacke? (Rock, Hemd, Bluse, Schuhe)
b. Wo ist die Adresse des Freundes? (Freundin, Onkel, Eltern, Tochter, Herr)
c. Wo ist die Fahrkarte dieser Dame? (Kind, Gast, Mädchen, Student, Studentin)
d. Wann ist die Ankunft unseres Busses? (Zug, Flugzeug, Großeltern, Gäste)
e. Wie ist das Ende *(end)* jeder Reise? (Fahrt, Flug, Buch, Bahnsteig)
f. Was ist der Name des Vaters? (Herr, Herren, Junge, Nachbar, Nachbarin)

2. BEISPIEL: Ich schreibe während des Tages. (Ferien)
Ich schreibe während der Ferien.

  a. Die Stadt gefällt mir wegen des Sees. (Universität, Theater, Dom, Berge)
  b. Wir kommen trotz des Wetters. (der Feiertag, das Fest, die Prüfung)
  c. Ich komme statt meines Vaters. (Schwester, Nachbarn, Bruder, Mutter)

C. Wem gehört das?

BEISPIEL: Gehört die Jacke Ihrem Freund?
Nein, das ist nicht die Jacke meines Freundes. Das ist meine Jacke.

Gehört das Hemd Ihrem Bruder? die Uhr Ihrer Mutter? das Buch Ihrem Professor? die Tasche Ihrer Freundin? das Papier Ihrem Nachbarn? der Kuli Fräulein _____ (name a student)? das Heft Herrn _____ (name a student)? der Platz Peter (add another name)?

D. Bilden Sie Sätze mit dem Genitiv!

1	2	3	4	5
die Farbe	des	Hose	ist	_____
der Name	der	Auto	gefällt	
die Adresse	dieses	Freund		
die Nummer	dieser	Großmutter		
die Abfahrt	meines	Haus		
das Gepäck	meiner	Herr		
usw.	usw.	Gleis		
		usw.		

E. Auf deutsch, bitte! (Eva is going on a trip and friends accompany her to the train. Use the sg. fam. for **you**.)

  1. Is that Eva's train? 2. Do you know the number of the platform? 3. No. Where's the train schedule (schedule of the trains)? 4. The departure of her train is in a few minutes (her train leaves in a few minutes). 5. Take along Kurt's package. 6. Kurt is a student and a friend of my friend (f.). 7. Eva, do you have the address of the student? 8. No, but I know the name of the dorm. 9. I'll take it to him during the holidays. 10. Because of the exams (**die Prüfungen**) I don't have time now. 11. I'll send you a postcard instead of a letter.

Den Fahrer während der Fahrt nicht ansprechen
Do not speak to the driver
Ne pas parler au conducteur durant la conduite

II. *Time Expressions*

1. Adverbs of Time

a. To refer to SPECIFIC TIMES, such as *yesterday evening* or *Monday morning*, combine one word from group A with one from group B:

vorgestern	*the day before yesterday*
gestern	*yesterday*
heute	*today*
morgen	*tomorrow*
übermorgen	*the day after tomorrow*
Montag	

Dienstag	**früh**[1]**, morgen**	*early, morning*
Mittwoch	**vormittag**	*midmorning (9 to 12 a.m.)*[2]
Donnerstag	**mittag**	*noon (12 to 2 p.m.)*
Freitag	**nachmittag**	*afternoon (2 to 6 p.m.)*
Samstag	**abend**	*evening (6 to 10 p.m.)*
Sonntag	**nacht**	*night (after 10 p.m.)*

A   B

1 *Tomorrow morning* is always **morgen früh**.
gestern + abend   = gestern abend
Montag + morgen   = Montag morgen
Sonntag + nachmittag = Sonntag nachmittag
2 This varies somewhat, but these times are reasonable guidelines.

☞ *CAUTION:*

▶ *The words in group A can be used alone; those in group B must be used in combination:*

Heute fliege ich von New York ab. Dann bin ich morgen früh in Frankfurt. Übermorgen fahre ich nach Bonn und Montag nachmittag nach Düsseldorf. Montag abend besuche ich Krauses. Dann fahre ich Dienstag mit dem Zug nach Frankfurt zurück.

b. Such familiar adverbs as **montags** and **morgens** don't refer to specific time (a specific Monday or morning), but rather imply that events occur USUALLY (more or less regularly) for example, *on Mondays* or *in the morning, most mornings.*

montags, dienstags, mittwochs, donnerstags, freitags, samstags, sonntags; morgens, vormittags, mittags, nachmittags, abends, nachts

Sonntags tue ich nichts, aber montags arbeite ich schwer. Morgens und nachmittags gehe ich zur Universität, und mittags spiele ich eine halbe Stunde Tennis.

2. Other Time Expressions

a. The Accusative of Time

To refer to a DEFINITE point in time (**wann?**) or length of time (**wie lange?**), German often uses time phrases in the accusative, without any prepositions. Here are some of the most common expressions:

wann?			**wie lange?**	
jeden Tag	*every day*		zwei Wochen	*for two weeks*
diese Woche	*this week*		einen Monat	*for one month*

Haben Sie diese Woche Zeit?　　*Do you have time this week?*
Ich bin zwei Tage in Frankfurt.　*I'll be in Frankfurt for two days.*

b. The Genitive of Time

To refer to an INDEFINITE point of time (in the past or future), German uses the genitive:

eines Tages	*one day*

Eines Tages ist ein Brief gekommen.　*One day a letter came.*
Eines Tages fahre ich in die Schweiz.　*One day I'll go to Switzerland.*

c. Prepositional Time Phrases

You are already familiar with the phrases below:

an¹: am Abend, am Wochenende, am Montag, am 1. April
bis: bis morgen, bis 2.30 Uhr, bis (zum) Freitag, bis (zum) Januar
für: für morgen, für Freitag, für eine Nacht
in¹: im Juli, im Sommer, im Monat; in zehn Minuten, in einer Viertelstunde, in einer Woche, in einem Jahr
nach: nach dem Essen, nach einer Stunde
seit²: seit einem Jahr, seit September
um: um fünf (Uhr)
von . . . bis: vom 1. Juni bis (zum) 25. August; von Juli bis August
vor: vor einem Monat, vor ein paar Tagen
während: während des Sommers, während des Tages

---

1. *Two-way prepositions usually use the dative in time expressions: Wir fahren* **in einer Woche** *in die Berge.* **Am Freitag** *fahren wir ab.*
2. *German uses the present tense with* **seit** *where English uses the past progressive to express the same thing:* **Er wohnt seit zwei Jahren hier.** *(He has been living here for two years.)*

ÜBUNGEN

F. *Was fehlt?*

1. Erich ist _____ angekommen. *(one week ago)*
2. Wir sind _____ abgefahren. *(Thursday evening at 7 o'clock)*
3. Er ist _____ geflogen. *(for nine hours)*
4. Ich habe ihn schon _____ nicht mehr gesehen. *(for one year)*
5. Er schläft _____ gewöhnlich nicht lange. *(in the morning)*
6. Aber er hat _____ geschlafen. *(Friday morning until 11 a.m.)*
7. Er bleibt noch ungefähr _____ bei uns. *(for one week)*
8. _____ sind wir bei meiner Tante gewesen. *(the day before yesterday)*
9. _____ gehen wir ins Kino. *(this evening)*
10. _____ kommen Erika und Uwe vorbei. *(tomorrow midmorning)*
11. _____ gehen wir alle essen. *(tomorrow noon)*
12. _____ bummeln wir etwas durch die Stadt. *(in the afternoon)*
13. Was wir _____ tun, weiß ich noch nicht. *(the day after tomorrow)*
14. _____ machen wir etwas Besonderes. *(every day)*
15. _____ wollen wir an den See fahren. *(on the weekend)*
16. Was machst du _____ ? *(this weekend)*
17. Komm doch _____ mit! *(Friday afternoon)*
18. Du tust doch _____ und _____ nichts. *(on Saturdays/Sundays)*
19. _____ fahren wir ab. *(on Saturday morning)*
20. Wir bleiben _____ dort. *(for two days)*
21. _____ ist der See wunderbar. *(in the summer)*
22. Schade, daß Erich _____ schon wieder zu Hause sein muß. *(in one week)*

G. *Was hat er/sie gemacht? (You've been asked to escort a visiting German politician/musician/professor, who will lecture on your campus. The dean asks you to report, indicating what he/she did.)*

BEISPIEL: **Morgens um acht ist er/sie am Flughafen angekommen. Wir sind erst zum Hotel gefahren, und dann . . .**

III. *Sentence Structure*

1. Types of Adverbs

You have already encountered various adverbs and adverbial phrases. They are usually divided into three major groups.

a. ADVERBS OF TIME, answering the questions **wann? wie lange?**

am Abend, am 1. April, eines Tages, heute, im Juni, immer, jetzt, manchmal, meistens, montags, morgens, nie, oft, um zwölf, vor einer Woche, während des Winters, bis Mai, eine Woche, stundenlang, ein paar Minuten, usw.

b. ADVERBS OF MANNER, answering the question **wie?**

gemütlich, langsam, laut, mit der Bahn, ohne Geld, schnell, zu Fuß, zusammen, usw.

c. ADVERBS OF PLACE, answering the questions **wo? wohin? woher?**

auf der Post, bei uns, da, dort, hier, im Norden, zu Hause, mitten in der Stadt, überall, nach Berlin, nach Hause, auf die Post, zur Uni, aus Kanada, von Amerika, aus dem Flugzeug, usw.

2. Sequence of Adverbs

If two or more adverbs or adverbial phrases occur in one sentence, they usually follow the sequence TIME, MANNER, PLACE.

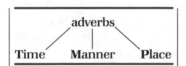

Er kann das Paket **morgen mit dem Auto zur Post** bringen.
                               T   M   P

Like other sentence elements, adverbs and adverbial phrases may precede the verb.

      Morgen kann er das Paket mit dem Auto zur Post bringen.
Mit dem Auto kann er das Paket morgen zur Post bringen.
      Zur Post kann er das Paket morgen mit dem Auto bringen.

3. Position of **nicht**

As you already know, **nicht** usually comes after adverbs of time but before adverbs of manner.

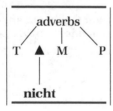

Er bringt das Paket ▲.
Er bringt das Paket ▲ mit.
 Er kann das Paket ▲ mitbringen.

 Er kann das Paket **morgen** ▲ mitbringen.
 Er kann das Paket **morgen** ▲ **mit dem Auto** mitbringen.
 Er kann das Paket **morgen** ▲ **mit dem Auto zur Post** bringen.

ÜBUNGEN

H. Sagen Sie es noch einmal! *(Use the adverbial expressions in proper order.)*

BEISPIEL: Ich kaufe die Briefmarken. (auf der Post, morgen)
Ich kaufe die Briefmarken morgen auf der Post.

1. Er kommt an. (heute abend, in Wien, mit dem Bus)
2. Sie reist. (nach Westdeutschland, ohne ihre Familie)
3. Dein Pullover liegt auf dem Sofa. (seit drei Tagen)
4. Wir fahren. (zu meiner Tante, am Sonntag, mit der Bahn)
5. Gehst du? (zu Fuß, in die Stadt, heute nachmittag)
6. Ich kaufe die Eier. (samstags, auf dem Markt, billig)
7. Wir wollen ins Kino gehen. (zusammen, morgen abend)
8. Ihr müßt umsteigen. (in einer Viertelstunde, in den Zug nach Nürnberg)
9. Sie läßt die Kinder in Salzburg. (bei den Großeltern, ein paar Tage)

I. Beginnen Sie den Satz anders! Was bedeutet der neue Satz auf englisch? *(Start each sentence with the boldface sentence element.)*

BEISPIEL: Wir bleiben **während der Ferien** gewöhnlich zu Hause.
***Während der Ferien* bleiben wir gewöhnlich zu Hause.**
During the vacation we usually stay home.

1. Wir geben nicht viel Geld **für Reisen** aus.
2. Manfred hat **gerade** mit seiner Schwester in Holland gesprochen.
3. Sie ist **seit einer Woche** bei ihrem Bruder in Florida.
4. Wir wollen sie alle **am Wochenende** besuchen *(visit)*.
5. Das finde ich **schön**.

J. Verneinen Sie die Sätze mit nicht!

GISELA Ich möchte diesen Winter in die Berge fahren.
  OTTO Gefallen dir die Berge?
GISELA Das habe ich gesagt. Warum fliegen wir diesen Winter nach Spanien? 179.—DM ist sehr teuer.

1 Woche Sonnenland
Spanien
Costa Brava

Termin: 20.–26. 2.
Fahrpreis mit ÜF
in **Lloret de Mar**
Alle Zimmer Du/WC
in gutem Hotel
in zentraler Lage

nur **179.-**

OTTO Ich weiß.

GISELA Im Flugzeug wird man so müde.

OTTO Ich fliege gern.

GISELA Ich möchte mit dem Auto fahren.

OTTO Mittags kannst du lange in der Sonne liegen.

GISELA Morgens und nachmittags ist die Sonne so heiß.

OTTO In den Bergen ist es so langweilig.

GISELA Gut. Wenn wir nach Spanien fliegen, komme ich mit.

ZUSAMMENFASSUNG

K. ***Was machen Sie wann?*** *(Write eight to ten sentences telling what your typical week looks like, i.e., when you get up; when you eat; when you leave for class; what classes you have when; what you do in the evening and on the weekend. Use as many time expressions as possible.)*

> BEISPIEL: **Ich bin fast jeden Tag an der Uni. Morgens stehe ich um sechs auf . . .**

L. *Bilden Sie Sätze!*

> BEISPIEL: Hauptstadt / Schweiz / sein / Bern
> **Die Hauptstadt der Schweiz ist Bern.**

1. Tante / unsere Freunde / leben / hier in Bern
2. leider / ich / nicht / wissen / die / Adresse / diese Tante
3. Name / Dame / sein / Köchli
4. wegen / dieser Name / ich / nicht / können / finden / Frau Köchli
5. statt / ein Köchli *(m.)* / da / sein / viele Köchlis
6. du / nicht / wissen / Telefonnummer / euere Freunde?
7. Nummer / stehen / in / Adreßbuch / mein Frau
8. ich / nicht / können / finden / Inge / Adreßbuch
9. ein Tag / Inge / es / sicher / wieder / finden
10. können / ihr / mir / empfehlen / Name / ein Hotel?
11. trotz / Preise *(pl.)* / wir / brauchen / Hotelzimmer
12. während / Feiertage / du / haben / Probleme *(pl.)* / wegen / Touristen

---

Switzerland, a country less than half the size of Indiana, is a confederation of twenty-six cantons (**Kantone**). The capital is Berne. In a population of approximately 6.4 million, 70 percent speak German (**Schweizerdeutsch**, or **Schwyzertütsch**, the spoken dialect, as well as standard German), 20 percent speak French, and 9 percent Italian. These are the official languages of the country. A small minority (1 percent) speaks Romansch (**Rätoromanisch**), a variant of Latin. Most Swiss people understand two if not all three of the official languages, by which goods are labeled and currency is designated.—Although women won the right to vote in federal elections in 1971, one canton (**Appenzell**) still withholds the vote from women in its local elections. Women are, however, beginning to gain important positions in government.—Geneva (**Genf**) is the European headquarters for the United Nations and the home of the International Committee of the Red Cross.

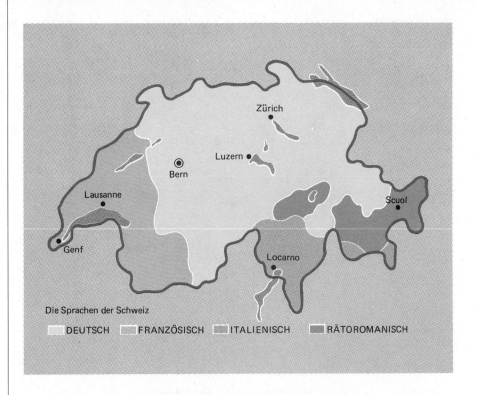

Die Sprachen der Schweiz

□ DEUTSCH □ FRANZÖSISCH □ ITALIENISCH ■ RÄTOROMANISCH

EINBLICKE

WORTSCHATZ 2

das Dorf, -̈er	*village*
die Gegend, -en	*area, region*
Geschichte, -n	*history; story*
sofort	*immediately, right away*
Geld aus·geben (gibt aus), ausgegeben	*to spend money*
erzählen	*to tell*
hinauf·fahren (fährt hinauf), ist hinaufgefahren	*to go or drive up (to)*
weiter·fahren (fährt weiter), ist weitergefahren	*to drive on, keep on driving*
1291[1] (zwölfhunderteinundneunzig)	*in 1291*

1 Unlike English, in which we use *in* with years (**in 1291**), German does not use a preposition:
Er hat uns 1986 (neunzehnhundertsechsundachtzig) besucht.

WAS IST DAS? der Film, Hollywoodstar, Kanton, Kurzkommentar, Meter, Sessellift, Wintersport; das Ferienhaus, Schiff, Uhrengeschäft; die Alpenblume, Arkade, Armee, Bergbahn, Konferenz, Nation, Rückreise; faszinieren, filmen, interessieren, mobilisieren, wandern, Ski laufen; autofrei, nämlich, natürlich, phantastisch

(Kurz-Interviews mit Touristen in der Schweiz)

Felix: Ich finde die Gegend hier um den Vierwaldstätter See so interessant wegen ihrer Geschichte—das ist nämlich mein

Die Schweiz ist eine Reise wert.°

worth

wooden . . .
Swiss Confederation

confederacy

Hobby. Gestern bin ich in Luzern gewesen und über die alte Holzbrücke° gegangen, wo man in Bildern die Geschichte der Eidgenossenschaft° sehen kann. Heute früh bin ich mit dem Schiff von Luzern zum Rütli[1] gefahren, wo 1291 die drei Kantone Uri, Schwyz und Unterwalden ihren Bund° gemacht haben und die Schweiz als eine Nation begonnen hat. Dann bin ich weitergefahren nach Altdorf. Hier in Altdorf steht ja Wilhelm Tells Denk-

5

10

*Das Wilhelm Tell Denkmal (**monument**) in Altdorf*

monument/ outdoor per-
  formances
national holiday/ parades

fireworks

mal°². Heute abend gehe ich zu den Wilhelm Tell Freilichtspielen°. Dieses Wochenende ist außerdem noch Bundesfeier° mit Umzügen° und Feuer-werk°. Das möchte ich einmal sehen.

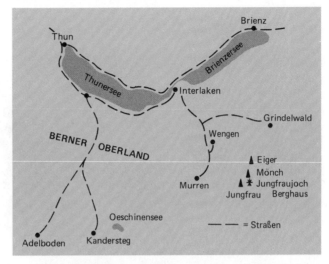

narrow streets/ fountains

Middle Ages

Yvonne: Bern³, die Hauptstadt der Schweiz, gefällt mir besonders gut 15 wegen seiner alten Gassen°, Arkaden und Brunnen°, viele noch aus dem Mittelalter°. Meine Eltern und ich fahren fast jedes Jahr zum Wintersport in die Schweiz. Auf unserer Fahrt kommen wir gewöhnlich durch Bern und

**Bern, die Hauptstadt
der Schweiz**

bleiben dort einen Tag. Letztes° Jahr sind wir ins Berner Oberland gefahren, und zwar° nach Wengen. Wir sind auch mit der Bergbahn zum Jungfrau- 20 joch[4] hinaufgefahren. Der Blick auf° die Berge ist phantastisch. Haben Sie

snow scenes

as an aside
world

übrigens gewußt, daß man fast alle Schneeszenen° der James Bond Filme im Berner Oberland gefilmt hat und daß viele Hollywoodstars im Berner Oberland Ferienhäuser haben? Aber das nur nebenbei°. Was mich faszi-niert, ist die Welt° der Berge. Trotz der vielen Touristen ist alles relativ 25 natürlich geblieben. Eines Tages möchte ich die Gegend um Kandersteg und Adelboden besser kennenlernen.

**Ab Winter 1984/85 mit der höchsten Standseilbahn der Welt
ins Reich der ewigen Gletscher.**

Bergsteigerfest
in Saas-Fee

glaciers/ all around

*go mountain climbing/
  altitude*
*mountain goats/
  directions/ cable cars*
*Alpine metro/ under-
  ground*
altitude

Hansruedi: Ich fahre gern nach Saas-Fee, weil das Dorf autofrei ist und man auf den Bergen und Gletschern° ringsum° schön wandern und berg-steigen° kann. Wegen der Höhenlage° gibt es hier viele Alpenblumen und Gemsen°. In allen Richtungen° gehen Sessellifte und Seilbahnen°. Und wenn ich im Juli Ski laufen möchte, fahre ich mit der Metro Alpin° unterirdisch° bis auf eine Höhe° von 3500 Metern. Dort oben auf den Gletschern kann man auch während des Sommers wunderbar Ski laufen. 30

Frau Weber: Mein Mann hat oft in Zürich[5] und Basel[6] mit den Schweizer Banken zu tun. Zürich ist eine schöne Stadt am Zürichsee, mit einer Bank neben der anderen. Viele Ausländer haben hier Nummernkon-ten°. Während der Konferenzen meines Mannes bummele ich gern durch die Bahnhofstraße mit ihren eleganten Uhrengeschäften[7] und Boutiquen. Hier kann man leicht° viel Geld ausgeben. Auf der Rückreise bleiben wir dieses Mal° vielleicht ein paar Tage länger in Basel wegen der Basler Fasnacht°. 35

numbered bank accounts

easily

this time

carnival

militia

Sepp: Als Österreicher interessiert mich hier die Miliz°, denn in 48 Stun-den kann die Schweiz eine Armee von 625 000 Mann mobilisieren und alle Straßen und Pässe sofort zumachen[8]. 45

ZUM TEXT

A. Richtig oder falsch? Wenn falsch, sagen Sie warum!

___ 1. Felix findet die Gegend um den Bodensee so interessant wegen ihrer Geschichte.

___ 2. Die Schweiz hat 1691 als Nation begonnen.

___ 3. Felix ist wegen des Wilhelm Tell Denkmals und der Freilichtspiele in Altdorf.

___ 4. Yvonne und ihre Eltern fahren jeden Sommer zum Sport in die Schweiz.

___ 5. Während ihrer Reise bleiben sie gewöhnlich einen Tag in Bern, weil ihnen die Stadt so gut gefällt.

___ 6. Hansruedi besucht Saas-Fee so gern, weil er sein Auto mitbringen kann.

___ 7. Oben auf den Gletschern kann man auch während des Sommers Ski laufen.

___ 8. Frau Webers Mann muß oft nach Zürich oder Basel, weil er viel mit Schweizer Banken zu tun hat.

___ 9. Zürich ist eine schöne Stadt am Genfer See.

___ 10. Sepp geht zur Armee.

B. Wann ist das gewesen? Lesen Sie laut!

1. 1291 machten Uri, Schwyz und Unterwalden am Rütli einen Bund.
2. Luzern ist 1332 dazu *(to it)* gekommen und Zürich 1351.
3. 1513 hat es dreizehn Kantone gegeben.
4. Heute, 19__ *(add present year)*, sind es sechsundzwanzig Kantone.
5. 1848 ist die Schweiz ein Bundesstaat geworden.
6. Im 1. Weltkrieg (1914–1918) und im 2. Weltkrieg (1939–1945) ist die Schweiz neutral geblieben.

C. Wohin gehört das im Satz? *(Where do these adverbs or adverbial phrases belong? Incorporate them into the sentences. There may be more than one appropriate place for them.)*

> BEISPIEL: Viele Touristen fahren in die Schweiz. (jedes Jahr)
> **Viele Touristen fahren jedes Jahr in die Schweiz.**
> **Jedes Jahr fahren viele Touristen in die Schweiz.**

1. Felix findet die Gegend um den Vierwaldstätter See interessant. (wegen ihrer Geschichte)
2. Man kann die Geschichte der Eidgenossenschaft in Bildern auf einer alten Holzbrücke in Luzern sehen. (noch heute)
3. Felix ist mit einem Schiff zum Rütli gefahren. (von Luzern)
4. Wilhelm Tell ist aus Altdorf gewesen. (wie Sie wissen)
5. Viele Touristen wollen Wilhelm Tells Denkmal sehen. (natürlich)
6. In der Schweiz feiert man die Bundesfeier. (jedes Jahr am 1. August)
7. Felix ist noch einen Tag geblieben. (wegen dieses Festes)

D. Ersetzen Sie den Genitiv!

1. Kennst du die Geschichte der Schweiz? (Land, Eidgenossenschaft)
2. Das ist die Welt meiner Großeltern. (unser Nachbar, euere Freunde)
3. Trotz der Touristen gefällt es mir dort. (Wetter, Sprache)
4. Ich finde unser Dorf interessant wegen seiner Lage *(f.)*. (Berge, See)

Solche Häuser kann man nicht nur in der Schweiz, sondern auch in Bayern und in Österreich finden.

E. ***Welche Frage gehört zu welcher Antwort?*** *(Find the correct question for each of the responses below.)*

1. Geschichte ist mein Hobby.
2. Hier haben die drei Kantone Uri, Schwyz und Unterwalden ihren Bund gemacht, das heißt, hier hat die Schweiz als Nation begonnen.
3. Die Stadt gefällt uns so gut wegen ihrer alten Gassen, Arkaden und Brunnen.
4. Es ist trotzdem alles noch relativ natürlich geblieben.
5. Man kann hier wunderbar wandern, bergsteigen und Ski laufen.
6. Dort oben auf den Gletschern gibt es auch während des Sommers Schnee *(snow)*.
7. Hier gibt es Nummernkonten.
8. Mir gefallen die Uhrengeschäfte und Boutiquen.

a. Warum bleiben Sie immer einen Tag in Bern?
b. Warum haben so viele Ausländer ein Bankkonto in der Schweiz?
c. Warum kommen Sie so gern nach Saas-Fee?
d. Warum finden Sie die Gegend um den Vierwaldstätter See so interessant?
e. Finden Sie die vielen Touristen nicht furchtbar?
f. Warum bummeln Sie gern auf der Bahnhofstraße in Zürich?
g. Warum haben Sie jetzt, im Juli, Skier *(skis)* mitgebracht?
h. Warum ist er mit dem Schiff zum Rütli gefahren?

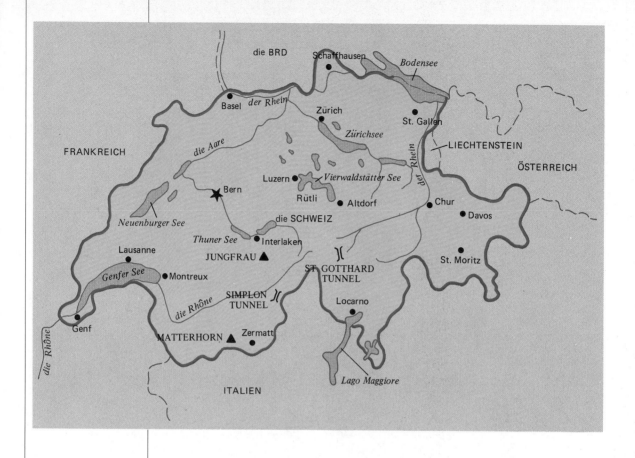

F. **Die Schweiz. Sehen Sie auf die Landkarte, und beantworten Sie die Fragen!** *(Answer the questions about Switzerland below. Then write eight to ten sentences about Switzerland, using some of the questions as guidelines.)*

1. Wie heißen die Nachbarn der Schweiz? Wo liegen sie?
2. Wie heißt die Hauptstadt der Schweiz?
3. Nennen Sie ein paar Schweizer Flüsse, Seen und Berge! Welcher Fluß fließt weiter *(flows on)* nach Deutschland? nach Frankreich? Welcher See liegt zwischen der Schweiz und (a) Deutschland? (b) Italien? (c) Frankreich?
4. Wo liegt Bern? Basel? Zürich? Luzern? Genf? Zermatt? Locarno? St. Moritz? Davos?
5. Wie heißen zwei der Tunnel durch die Alpen?
6. Wo spricht man Deutsch? Französisch? Italienisch? Romansch? (Sehen Sie auf die Karte auf Seite 241!)

ÜBRIGENS

1. In 1291 a meeting of representatives of the cantons of **Uri**, **Schwyz** and **Unterwalden** took place at the famous **Rütli** meadow, at the southern tip of Lake Lucerne (**Vierwaldstätter See**). Their pact marks the birth of modern Switzerland. Each year on August 1, the Swiss National Holiday (**Bundesfeier**) commemorates that event with bonfires, parades and fireworks.

2. According to legend, the tyrannical Austrian bailiff Geßler forced the Swiss folk hero **Wilhelm Tell** to shoot an arrow through an apple on his son's head. Tell did, but later took revenge by killing Geßler, which was the beginning of a general uprising of the Swiss against Austria. This story inspired Friedrich Schiller's drama *Wilhelm Tell* (1804) and Rossini's opera *Guillaume Tell* (1829).

3. **Bern,** a small medieval city (only half the size of Zurich), is the capital of Switzerland. It is characterized by the arcades that cover the sidewalks of many streets and by its fountains surrounded by flowers.

4. Besides the **Matterhorn** (4505 meters above sea level), the most famous Swiss mountain peaks are the **Jungfrau, Mönch,** and **Eiger** (all around 4000 meters high). A tunnel, seven kilometers long, leads steeply up to the **Jungfraujoch** terminus (3454 meters). Its observation terrace offers a superb view of the surrounding mountains and the lakes of central Switzerland, and sometimes even of the Black Forest in Germany.

5. **Zürich,** the industrial heart and largest city (720,000 inhabitants) of Switzerland, is built around the northern tip of Lake Zurich and is characterized by its many bridges over the Limmat River. Zurich has been the home of many famous people, among them the writers Thomas Mann (1875–1955) and Hermann Hesse (1877–1962), both recipients of the Nobel Prize in literature.

6. **Basel,** Switzerland's northern gateway to the Rhine, is above all a center of international banking and insurance. Elements of quaint medievalism and bustling modernism are unexpectedly mingled. Although banking is an old tradition in Switzerland, it expanded enormously after World War II. Unlike most of Europe, Switzerland had not been much disturbed by the war. It had a stable government and a sound, freely convertible currency. These circumstances, along with a bank-secrecy law that allows numbered accounts without names (**Nummernkonten**), continue to attract capital from all over the world.

7 Forty percent of the world's watches are still produced in Switzerland. The Swiss are very time-conscious. Every day at 12:30 pm, every radio station reports the exact time and most Swiss check their watches. Trains leave punctually on the second.

8. Switzerland has a militia (**Milizarmee**), in which all able-bodied men between the ages of 20 to 50 must serve three weeks a year. If for some reason (such as a job abroad) someone cannot serve, he has to pay a fee instead. Refusal to comply is punished with a prison term. Switzerland has undertaken many national-security precautions: mountains shelter underground military installations; freeways can easily be converted into landing strips and blocked at strategic points; caves hold underground hospitals and shelters in case of an NBC (nuclear, biological, or chemical) emergency; all new houses must have shelters built and stocked with food according to specifications. Plans call for NBC protection for the entire population by the year 2000.

GESPRÄCHE

Am Telefon

FRAU SCHMIDT Hier Frau Schmidt[1].

BÄRBEL Guten Tag, Frau Schmidt! Ich bin's, Bärbel. Ist Karl-Heinz da?

FRAU SCHMIDT Nein, er ist gerade zur Post gegangen.

BÄRBEL Bitte sagen Sie ihm, daß ich heute abend nicht mit ihm ausgehen kann!

FRAU SCHMIDT Ach, was ist denn los?

BÄRBEL Ich bin krank. Mir tut der Hals weh, und ich habe Kopfschmerzen.

FRAU SCHMIDT Das tut mir aber leid. Gute Besserung!

BÄRBEL Danke. Auf Wiederhören!

FRAU SCHMIDT Auf Wiederhören!

Eine gute Idee!

YVONNE Hier bei Mayer.

DANIELA Hallo, Yvonne! Ich bin's, Daniela.

YVONNE Tag, Daniela! Was gibt's Neues?

DANIELA Nichts Besonderes. Hast du Lust, Tennis zu spielen oder zum Trimm-dich-Pfad[2] zu gehen?

YVONNE Zum Trimm-dich-Pfad? Nein, danke. Ich habe noch Muskelkater von vorgestern. Mir tun alle Knochen weh.

DANIELA Lahme Ente![3] Wollen wir dann Schach spielen?

YVONNE Ja, das ist eine gute Idee! Komm 'rüber!

1. If Mrs. Schmidt answers her own phone, she says **Hier Frau Schmidt**. If someone else answers, he/she would say **Hier bei Schmidt** *(Schmidt residence, see Yvonne)*. It's considered common courtesy to identify yourself on the phone and not just answer with "Hello!"

2. The need for exercise to promote better health has been widely recognized and led to the development of so-called exercise trails (**Trimm-dich-Pfade**) in attractive surroundings near many towns and cities. Early in the morning before work, in the evening, and on weekends, many Germans jog and do a wide variety of prescribed exercises along these trails.

Schwein kann man nicht genug haben.

3. As in the case of **lahme Ente** (lit. *lame duck*), names of animals are frequently used in everyday speech to characterize people, usually in a derogatory way: **Du Kamel! Du Schaf! Du Esel!** *(camel, sheep, donkey)* for someone who has made a mistake or behaves stupidly; **Du hast einen Vogel! Bei dir piept's!** *(You're cuckoo.)* for someone crazy; **Dumme Gans! Dumme Kuh!** *(stupid goose, cow)* for a girl or woman one dislikes; **Fauler Hund!** *(dog)* for someone lazy; **Brummbär!** *(bear)* for someone grumpy; **Alter Fuchs!** *(fox)* for someone very sly; **Falsche Katze! Du Schlange!** *(cat, snake)* for a woman one can't trust; **Kalter Fisch!** for someone coldhearted; **Du Schwein!** *(pig)* for someone messy or for a scoundrel. **Schwein haben**, however, has quite a different meaning: *to be lucky.*—In addition, names of food are used in special expressions: **Das ist Käse!** *(That's nonsense.)* or **(Das) ist doch Wurst!** *(It doesn't matter.)*

On the Telephone

MRS. SCHMIDT This is Mrs. Schmidt.

BÄRBEL Hello, Mrs. Schmidt. It's me, Bärbel. Is Karl-Heinz there?

MRS. SCHMIDT No, he just went to the post office.

BÄRBEL Please tell him that I can't go out with him tonight.

MRS. SCHMIDT Oh, what's the matter?

BÄRBEL I'm sick. My throat hurts and I have a headache.

MRS. SCHMIDT I'm sorry. Hope you get better.

BÄRBEL Thank you. Goodbye.

MRS. SCHMIDT Goodbye.

A Good Idea

YVONNE Mayer residence.

DANIELA Hello, Yvonne! It's me, Daniela.

YVONNE Hi, Daniela! What's up?

DANIELA Nothing special. Do you feel like playing tennis or going to the exercise trail?

YVONNE The exercise trail? No thanks. I'm still sore from the day before yesterday. All my bones ache.

DANIELA Poor baby! Shall we play some chess then?

YVONNE Yes, that's a good idea! Come on over.

Hobbys und der Körper

WORTSCHATZ 1

DAS HOBBY, HOBBYS *hobby*

der Fußball	*soccer*	*die* Gitarre, -n	*guitar*
das Klavier, -e	*piano*	Karte, -n	*card*
Spiel, -e	*game*	Kassette, -n	*cassette*
		(Schall)platte, -n	*record*

fern·sehen (sieht fern), ferngesehen	*to watch TV*
photographieren	*to take pictures*
sammeln[1]	*to collect*
schwimmen, geschwommen	*to swim*
schwimmen gehen, ist schwimmen gegangen[2]	*to go swimming*
Ski laufen gehen, ist Ski laufen gegangen[2]	*to go skiing*
spazieren·gehen, ist spazierengegangen	*to go for a walk*
(Schach) spielen[2]	*to play (chess)*
wandern, ist gewandert	*to hike*
wünschen	*to wish*

DER KÖRPER, - *body*

der Arm, -e	*arm*	*das* Auge, -n	*eye*
Bauch, ¨e	*stomach, belly*	Bein, -e	*leg*
Finger, -	*finger*	Gesicht, -er	*face*
Fuß, ¨e	*foot*	Haar, -e	*hair*
Hals, ¨e	*neck; throat*	Knie, -	*knee*
Kopf, ¨e	*head*	Ohr, -en	*ear*
Mund, ¨er	*mouth*	*die* Hand, ¨e	*hand*
Zahn, ¨e	*tooth*	Nase, -n	*nose*

der Kopf, :-e
das Haar, -e
das Auge, -n
die Hand, :-e   der Arm, -e
das Ohr, -en
die Nase, -n
das Gesicht, -er
der Hals, :-e
der Zahn, :-e   der Mund, :-er
der Bauch, :-e
der Finger, -
das Bein, -e
das Knie, -
der Fuß, :-e

WEITERES

die Freizeit	*leisure time*
Idee, -n	*idea*
gesund / krank	*healthy / sick, ill*
phantastisch	*fantastic, great, super*
Ich habe (Kopf)schmerzen.	*I have a (head)ache.*
Ich habe (keine) Lust, Tennis zu spielen.	*I (don't) feel like playing tennis.*
Mir tut (der Hals) weh.	*My (throat) hurts.*
Was gibt's Neues?[3]	*What's new?*
nichts Besonderes[3]	*nothing special*
Was ist los?	*What's the matter?*

1 Like **bummeln: ich samm(e)le, du sammelst, er sammelt, wir sammeln, ihr sammelt, sie sammeln.**

2 In each of these combinations, **gehen** and **spielen** function as V1, while the other word, the verb complement, functions as V2: **Ich gehe heute schwimmen** (Ski laufen, wandern . . .). **Sie spielen Schach** (Karten, Klavier, Platten, Tennis . . .).

3 SIMILARLY etwas Besonderes, etwas Interessantes, etwas Schönes AND nichts Neues, nichts Gutes, nichts Schlechtes

PASSIVES VOKABULAR der Knochen, - *(bone)*; der Muskelkater *(sore muscles, charley horse)*; der Trimm-dich-Pfad, -e *(exercise trail)*; Gute Besserung! *(Get well soon.)*; Hallo!; Hier bei . . . *(. . . residence)*; Ich bin's. *(It's me.)*; Komm 'rüber! *(Come on over.)*

ZUM THEMA

A. Mustersätze

1. Hals: **Mir tut** der Hals **weh.**
   Kopf, Zahn, Bauch, Fuß, Knie, Hand
2. Hände: **Mir tun die** Hände **weh.**
   Füße, Finger, Ohren, Beine, Augen
3. Kopf: **Ich habe** Kopf**schmerzen.**
   Hals, Zahn, Bauch, Ohren
4. Tennis: **Hast du Lust,** Tennis **zu spielen?**
   Fußball, Klavier, Schallplatten, Karten

B. Was kann man in der Freizeit tun?

1. Verstehen Sie diese Hobbys?

backen, laufen, lesen, Kanu fahren, Fahrrad fahren, in der Sonne liegen
. . . **gehen:** bergsteigen, campen, wandern, Ski laufen, Wasserski laufen
. . . **spielen:** Basketball, Fußball, Volleyball, Golf, Hockey, Tennis, Tischtennis, Monopoly

Passives Vokabular:
kochen, malen *(to paint)*, nähen *(to sew)*, turnen *(to do gymnastics)*
. . . **gehen:** angeln, reiten *(horseback riding)*, Rollschuh laufen *(roller-
skating)*, Schlittschuh laufen *(ice-skating)*, segeln *(sailing)*
. . . **spielen:** Federball *(badminton)*, Cello, Geige *(violin)*, Flöte *(recorder)*,
Querflöte *(flute)*, Trommel, Trompete

2. Was tust du gern in deiner Freizeit? *(Chain reaction.)*

BEISPIEL: Ich lese gern, und du?   **Ich spiele gern Flöte, und du?**

Es macht Spaß, mit dem Rad aufs Land zu fahren.

C. Interview. Fragen Sie Ihren Nachbarn/Ihre Nachbarin, . . .!

1. ob er/sie als Kind ein Instrument gelernt hat, und wenn ja, welches Instrument; seit wann er/sie spielt und ob er/sie das heute noch spielt
2. ob er/sie gern singt, und wenn ja, was und wo (in der Dusche oder Badewanne [*bathtub*], im Auto, im Chor . . .)
3. was für Musik er/sie schön findet (klassische Musik, moderne Musik, Jazz, Rockmusik, Popmusik . . .)
4. ob er/sie viel fernsieht, und wenn ja, wie lange pro Tag; was er/sie gestern abend gesehen hat
5. ob er/sie oft lange am Telefon spricht, und wenn ja, mit wem

D. Was paßt? (*Finish the sentence either with one of the responses supplied or with one of your own.*)

1. Wenn ich Kopfschmerzen habe . . .
2. Wenn mir die Füße weh tun . . .
3. Wenn mir der Bauch weh tut . . .
4. Wenn ich Halsschmerzen habe . . .
5. Wenn ich Augenschmerzen habe . . .
6. Wenn ich krank bin . . .

mache ich die Augen zu.
gurgele (*gargle*) ich.
sehe ich nicht fern.
nehme ich Aspirin.
trinke ich einen Schnaps (*brandy*).
esse ich nichts.
rufe ich Doktor Schmidt an.
gehe ich ins Bett.
gehe ich nicht spazieren.
trinke ich Tee.

In den Sommerferien fahren viele gern an die Nordsee.

E. Was sagen Sie?

X Hallo, _____ ! Hast du Lust _____ ?

Y Nein, ich kann nicht mit dir _____ .

X Warum? Was ist los?

Y Ich bin krank. Mir tut/tun _____ weh.

X _____ . Wie lange hast du schon _____ schmerzen?

Y Seit _____ .

X _____ . Ich wünsche dir gute Besserung.

Y _____ .

X Hast du Lust _____ ?

Y _____ .

F. Aussprache *(See also III. 8–10 in the pronunciation section of the Appendix.)*

1. [l] laut, lustig, leben, liegen, leider, Lampe, Luft, Hals, Geld, Platte, malen, spielen, fliegen, stellen, schnell, Schlüssel, Teil, Ball, hell

2. [ts] zählen, zeigen, zwischen, ziemlich, zurück, Zug, Zahn, Schmerzen, Kerzen, Einzelzimmer, bezahlen, erzählen, tanzen, ausgezeichnet, jetzt, schmutzig, trotz, kurz, schwarz, Salz, Schweiz, Sitzplatz

3. Wortpaare

   a. felt / Feld   *c. plots* / Platz   *e.* seit / Zeit

   b. hotel / Hotel   *d.* Schweiß / Schweiz   *f.* so / Zoo

In den Bergen kann man wunderbar wandern.

STRUKTUR

I. *Endings of Preceded Adjectives*

PREDICATE ADJECTIVES and ADVERBS do not have endings.

Willi fährt schnell.	*Willi drives fast.*
Er ist schnell.	*He is fast.*

However, ADJECTIVES MODIFYING A NOUN do have an ending that varies with the noun's case, gender, and number, and the preceding article. As in English, an adjective always precedes the noun it modifies.

Er ist ein schnell**er** Fahrer *(masc.)*.	*He's a fast driver.*
Er hat ein schnell**es** Auto *(neut.)*.	*He has a fast car.*

Fortunately, there isn't a different ending for each gender, number, and case. If you compare the two tables below, you will readily see that there are only four different endings: **-en, -e, -er, -es.**

▪ *The ending* **-en** *predominates and is used in all plural cases and in the dative and genitive singular.*
▪ *The cases that require special attention are the nominative and accusative singular. As you can see from the table on the left, adjectives preceded by the definite article or any* **der**-*word have either an* **-e** *or* **-en** *ending. The table on the right shows that adjectives preceded by the indefinite article or any* **ein**-*word have two different adjective endings* WHERE **ein** HAS NO ENDING: **-er** *for masculine nouns and* **-es** *for neuter nouns.*

after der-words	masc.	neut.	fem.	pl.
nom.	-e	-e	-e	
acc.	-e	-e	-e	
dat.	-en	-en	-en	-en
gen.	-en	-en	-en	-en

after ein-words	masc.	neut.	fem.	pl.
nom.	-er	-es	-e	
acc.		-es	-e	
dat.	-en	-en	-en	-en
gen.	-en	-en	-en	-en

der neu**e** Wagen, das neu**e** Auto, die neu**e** Nummer
ein neu**er** Wagen, ein neu**es** Auto, eine neu**e** Nummer

BUT: den neu**en** Wagen, mit dem neu**en** Auto, wegen der neu**en** Nummer, die schön**en** Farben, einen neu**en** Wagen, mit deinem neu**en** Auto, wegen seiner neu**en** Nummer, keine schön**en** Farben

Or, to put it another way, the endings are

a. *in the* NOMINATIVE *and* ACCUSATIVE *singular:*
- *after* **der, das, die,** *and* **eine** ⟶ **-e**
- *after* **ein**
  - with masc. nouns ⟶ **-er**
  - with neut. nouns ⟶ **-es**

b. *in* ALL OTHER *cases* ⟶ **-en**
   (masc. accusative sg., all datives, genitives and plurals)

Der schwarz**e** Wagen ist prima, aber das rot**e** Auto ist auch nicht schlecht. Die rot**e** Farbe gefällt mir und es hat auch eine schön**e** Form. Das ist ein gut**er** Preis *(price)* und ein schön**es** Auto. Solche klein**en** Autos sind sehr bequem. Was ist der Preis dieses klein**en** Wagens?

If a noun is modified by more than one adjective, all the adjectives have the same ending.

Das ist ein klein**es**, schnell**es**, aber teuer**es** Auto.
Haben Sie keinen ander**en**, gut**en**, aber nicht so teuer**en** Wagen?

ÜBUNGEN

A. *Sagen Sie die Sätze noch einmal mit den Adjektiven!*

BEISPIEL: Ich lese ein Buch. (neu, bekannt)   **Ich lese ein neues Buch.**
Ich lese ein bekanntes Buch.

1. Wo ist mein Kuli? (schwarz, blau)
2. Er liegt auf dem Teppich. (grün, rot)
3. Müllers haben ein Klavier. (alt, ausgezeichnet)
4. Wem gehört das Paket? (groß, dick)
5. Das Geschenk gefällt mir. (klein, praktisch)
6. Renate liest solche Bücher auch gern. (verrückt, gut)
7. Ich kann den Brief nicht finden. (lang, geöffnet)
8. Uwe hat uns eine Postkarte geschickt. (lustig, interessant)
9. Sie sind mit einem Schiff gefahren. (wunderbar, englisch)
10. Er reist mit seiner Freundin. (neu, spanisch)

B. *Lesen Sie den Dialog mit den Adjektiven!*

BEISPIEL: Ist der Schrank neu? (groß)   **Ist der große Schrank neu?**

X Ist dieser Sessel bequem? (braun)
Y Ja, und das Sofa auch. (lang)
X Die Lampe gefällt mir. (klein)
   Woher hast du diesen Teppich? (phantastisch)
   Und wo hast du dieses Bild gefunden? (supermodern)
Y In einem Geschäft. (alt)
   Wenn du willst, kann ich dir das Geschäft mal zeigen. (interessant)
X Ist es in der Müllergasse (f.)? (klein)
Y Ja, auf der Seite. (link-)
X Während der Woche habe ich keine Zeit. (nächst-)
Y Sind diese Möbel teuer gewesen? (schön)
X Natürlich nicht. Für solche Möbel gebe ich nicht viel Geld aus. (alt)

261

C. *Inge zeigt Jens ihr neues Zimmer. Jens stellt Fragen und macht Kommentare* (comments). *Bilden Sie aus zwei Sätzen einen Satz!*

> BEISPIEL: Woher kommt dieses Schachspiel? Es ist interessant.
> **Woher kommt dieses interessante Schachspiel?**

1. Weißt du, was so ein Schachspiel kostet? Es ist chinesisch (*Chinese*).
2. Bist du eine Schachspielerin? Bist du gut?
3. Ich bin kein Schachspieler (*m.*). Ich bin nicht gut.
4. Woher hast du diese Briefmarkensammlung? Sie ist alt.
5. Mein Vater hat auch eine Sammlung. Sie ist groß.
6. Sammelst du solche Briefmarken auch? Sie sind normal (*regular*).
7. Was machst du mit so einer Briefmarke? Sie ist doppelt (*double*).
8. Darf ich diese Briefmarke haben? Sie ist ja doppelt!
9. Hast du diese Bilder photographiert? Sie sind groß.
10. Wer ist der Junge? Er ist klein.
11. Ich habe nicht gewußt, daß du einen Bruder hast. Er ist noch so klein!
12. Was für ein Gesicht! Es ist phantastisch!
13. Die Augen gefallen mir! Sie sind dunkel.
14. Mit meiner Kamera (*f.*) ist das nicht möglich. Sie ist billig.
15. Und das hier ist ein Tennisspieler, nicht wahr? Er ist bekannt und kommt aus Deutschland.
16. Weißt du, daß wir gestern trotz des Wetters Fußball gespielt haben? Das Wetter ist schlecht gewesen.
17. Leider kann ich wegen meines Knies nicht mehr mitspielen. Das Knie ist kaputt.

D. *Antworten und Fragen.* (Show agreement and ask according to the pattern.)

1. BEISPIEL: Ist der Pullover nicht warm?   **Ja, das ist ein warmer Pullover. Woher hast du den warmen Pullover?**

   a. Ist das Hemd nicht elegant?
   b. Ist die Uhr nicht phantastisch?
   c. Ist der Hut (*hat*) nicht verrückt?

2. BEISPIEL: Ist das Hotel nicht gut?   **Ja, das ist ein gutes Hotel. Wie bist du zu diesem guten Hotel gekommen?**

   a. Ist die Pension nicht wunderbar?
   b. Ist der Gasthof nicht billig?
   c. Ist das Restaurant nicht gemütlich?

3. BEISPIEL: Ist das alte Schloß nicht schön?   **Ja, das ist ein altes, schönes Schloß. Ich gehe gern in solche alten, schönen Schlösser.**

   a. Ist der neue Supermarkt nicht modern?
   b. Ist das kleine Café nicht gemütlich?
   c. Sind die alten Kirchen nicht interessant?

E. *Beschreibung* (description) *einer Wohnung*

1. *Petras Wohnung* (Read about her apartment and fill in the missing adjective endings.)

Petra wohnt in einem alt_____ Haus im neu_____ Teil unserer schön_____ Stadt. Ihre klein_____ Wohnung liegt im neunt_____ Stock eines modern_____ Hochhauses *(high-rise)*. Sie hat eine praktisch_____ Küche und ein gemütlich_____ Wohnzimmer. Von dem groß_____ Wohnzimmerfenster kann sie unsere ganz_____ Stadt und die viel_____ Brücken über den breit_____ *(wide)* Fluß sehen. Petra liebt ihre Wohnung wegen des schön_____ Blickes *(view, m.)* und der billig_____ Miete. In ihrem hell_____ Schlafzimmer steht ein einfach_____ Bett und ein klein_____ Nachttisch mit einer klein_____ Nachttischlampe. An der Wand steht ein braun_____ Schreibtisch, und über dem braun_____ Schreibtisch hängt ein groß_____ Regal mit ihren viel_____ Büchern. Petra findet ihr Zimmer schön_____ .

2. *Ihre Wohnung* (Write eight to ten sentences about your own place. Use at least one adjective with an ending in each sentence.)

II. *Reflexive Verbs*

1. If the subject and one of the objects of a sentence are the same person or thing, a reflexive pronoun must be used for the object. In the English sentence, *I see myself in the picture,* the reflexive pronoun *myself* is the accusative object. *(Whom do I see?—Myself.)* In the sentence, *I am buying myself a record,* the pronoun *myself* is the dative object. *(For whom am I buying the record?—For myself.)*

2. In German only the third-person singular and plural have a special reflexive pronoun: **sich.** The other persons use the accusative and dative forms of the personal pronouns, which you already know.

Compare: Ich sehe meinen Bruder auf dem Bild.
               Ich sehe **mich** auf dem Bild.

            Ich kaufe meinem Bruder eine Platte.
            Ich kaufe **mir** eine Platte.

	singular					plural			sg./pl.
nom.	ich	du	er	es	sie	wir	ihr	sie	Sie
acc.	mich	dich		**sich**		uns	euch	sich	**sich**
dat.	mir	dir							

a. Many familiar verbs CAN BE USED REFLEXIVELY. (Note that the English equivalent may not include a reflexive pronoun.)

- *The reflexive pronoun used as the direct object* (ACCUSATIVE):

sich fragen *(to wonder)*, sich legen *(to lie down)*, sich sehen *(to see oneself)* usw.

Ich frage **mich**, ob das richtig ist.	*I wonder (ask myself) whether that's right.*
Ich lege **mich** aufs Sofa.	*I lie down on the sofa.*
Ich sehe **mich** im Spiegel.	*I see myself in the mirror.*

- *The reflexive pronoun used as the indirect object* (DATIVE):

sich bestellen, sich kaufen, sich kochen, sich nehmen, sich wünschen *(to wish)* usw.

Ich bestelle **mir** ein Eis.	*I order an ice cream (for myself).*
Ich koche **mir** ein Ei.	*I'm cooking an egg (for myself).*
Ich wünsche **mir** ein Auto.	*I'm wishing for a car (for myself).*

b. Some verbs are ALWAYS REFLEXIVE, or are reflexive when they express a certain meaning. (Their English counterparts are usually not reflexive.) Here are some of those verbs that you must learn before doing the exercises.

sich an·hören	*to listen to*
sich an·sehen, angesehen	*to look at*
sich an·ziehen, angezogen	*to put on (clothing), get dressed*
sich aus·ziehen, ausgezogen	*to take off (clothing), get undressed*
sich beeilen	*to hurry*
sich duschen	*to take a shower*
sich erkälten	*to catch a cold*
sich (wohl) fühlen	*to feel (well)*
sich (hin·)legen	*to lie down*
sich kämmen	*to comb (one's hair)*
sich (die Zähne) putzen	*to brush, clean (one's teeth)*
sich rasieren	*to shave*
sich (hin·)setzen	*to sit down*
sich waschen (wäscht), gewaschen	*to wash oneself*

Warum beeilt ihr **euch** so?	*Why are you in such a hurry?*
Setz **dich** aufs Bett!	*Sit on the bed.*
Ich habe **mich** erkältet.	*I caught a cold.*
Sie hat **sich** nicht wohl gefühlt.	*She didn't feel well.*

- *With some of these verbs, the reflexive pronoun may be* EITHER THE ACCUSATIVE OR THE DATIVE OBJECT. *If there are two objects, then the person (the reflexive pronoun) is in the dative and the thing in the accusative.*

Ich habe **mich** gewaschen.	*I washed myself.*
Ich habe **mir die Hände** gewaschen.	*I washed my hands.*

Zieh **dich** an! Get dressed.
Zieh **dir eine Jacke** an! Put on a jacket.

3. In English we use possessive adjectives when referring to parts of the body: *I'm washing my hands.* In German frequently the definite article is used together with the reflexive pronoun in the dative.

Ich wasche **mir die** Hände. *I wash my hands.*
Sie kämmt **sich die** Haare. *She's combing her hair.*
Putz **dir die** Zähne! *Brush your teeth.*

> *Du kannst dir auch mal wieder die Ohren waschen.*

☞ *CAUTION:*

▶ *Remember, when there are two object pronouns, the accusative precedes the dative.*

Ich wasche **mir die Hände.** BUT Ich wasche **sie mir.**
Du putzt **dir die Zähne.** Du putzt **sie dir.**

ÜBUNGEN

F. *Was wünschst du dir zum Geburtstag? (Chain reaction)*

BEISPIEL: Ich wünsche mir ein Klavier, **Ich wünsche mir eine Uhr,**
und du? **und du?**

G. *Antworten Sie mit ja!*

1. *Singular (formal and familiar)*

BEISPIEL: Soll ich mir die Hände **Ja, waschen Sie sich die Hände!**
waschen? **Ja, wasch dir die Hände!**

a. Soll ich mich warm anziehen? d. Soll ich mich jetzt setzen?
b. Soll ich mir die Haare kämmen? e. Soll ich mir die Bilder
c. Soll ich mir ein Auto kaufen? ansehen?

2. *Plural (formal and familiar)*

BEISPIEL: Sollen wir uns die Hände **Ja, waschen Sie sich die Hände!**
waschen? **Ja, wascht euch die Hände!**

a. Sollen wir uns ein Zimmer d. Sollen wir uns die Kassetten
mieten? anhören?
b. Sollen wir uns ein Haus e. Sollen wir uns die
bauen? Briefmarken ansehen?
c. Sollen wir uns in den Garten
setzen?

265

Antworten Sie mit **ja!**

BEISPIEL: Fühlen Sie sich wohl?   **Ja, ich fühle mich wohl.**

1. Legen Sie sich aufs Sofa?
2. Möchten Sie sich die Jacke ausziehen?
3. Haben Sie sich wieder erkältet?
4. Haben Sie sich zu elegant angezogen?
5. Haben Sie sich die Bilder angesehen?
6. Haben Sie sich auf dem Bild gefunden?

I. *Was fehlt?*

1. Kinder, zieht _____ schnell an!
2. Ich muß _____ noch die Haare kämmen.
3. Wir haben _____ ein Klavier gekauft.
4. Setzen Sie _____ bitte, Herr Engel!
5. Putz _____ die Nase, Peter!
6. Kinder, erkältet _____ nicht!
7. Karin hat _____ ein Fahrrad gewünscht.
8. Ich will _____ etwas im Radio anhören.
9. Fühlst du _____ nicht wohl, Dieter?
10. Möchten Sie _____ die Hände waschen?

J. *Antworten Sie auf deutsch!*

1. Mit welcher Zahnpasta *(toothpaste)* haben Sie sich die Zähne geputzt? Mit welchem Shampoo haben Sie sich die Haare gewaschen? Duschen Sie sich gern heiß oder kalt?
2. Wie fühlen Sie sich heute? Wie haben Sie sich gestern gefühlt?
3. Kochen Sie sich gern etwas? Was? Bestellen Sie sich manchmal eine Pizza? Wenn ja, wo? (**bei . . .**)
4. Haben Sie sich vor kurzem *(recently)* etwas Besonderes gekauft? Wenn ja, was? Was möchten Sie sich gern kaufen?
5. Was für Zeitschriften *(magazines)* sehen Sie sich gern an? Was für Musik hören Sie sich gern an?
6. Haben Sie sich heute leicht oder warm angezogen? Was haben Sie sich angezogen?

K. *Auf deutsch, bitte!* (*Mrs. Brockmann is a health nut. She's determined to get her whole family up early and out on the exercise trail, but they aren't too eager.*)

1. Otto, get dressed. 2. Christian, hurry. 3. Lotte and Ulle, are you putting on sweaters? 4. We still have to brush our teeth. 5. Peter, comb your hair. 6. I don't feel well. 7. Then lie down. 8. Otto, have you shaved? 9. Yes, but I've caught a cold. 10. Nonsense (**Quatsch**)! Today we're all going to the exercise trail (**der Trimm-dich-Pfad**).

III. *The Infinitive with* zu

English and German use infinitives in much the same way.

Es ist interessant **zu** reisen. *It's interesting to travel.*
Ich habe keine Zeit gehabt **zu** essen. *I didn't have time to eat.*

1. If the infinitive is combined with other sentence elements, a COMMA separates the infinitive phrase from the main clause.

Haben Sie Zeit, eine Reise **zu** machen? *Do you have time to take a trip?*

Note that in German the infinitive comes at the end of the phrase.

2. If a separable-prefix verb is used, the **-zu-** is inserted between the prefix and the verb.

| prefix + **zu** + verb |

Es ist Zeit ab**zu**fahren. *It's time to leave.*

☛ *CAUTION:*

▶ *No* **zu** *after modals! Wir müssen jetzt abfahren.* We have to leave now.

„Die Menschen
haben gelernt,
  zu schwimmen wie die Fische
und zu fliegen wie die Vögel,
  aber wie Brüder
    zusammenzuleben
haben sie nicht
    gelernt".
M. L. King

L. Wie geht's weiter? *(Complete the sentences with infinitives with* **zu**.*)*

> **BEISPIEL:** Hast du Lust . . .? (tanzen, dir Kassetten anhören)
> **Hast du Lust zu tanzen?**
> **Hast du Lust, dir Kassetten anzuhören?**

1. Dort gibt es viel . . . (sehen, tun, photographieren, zeigen, essen)
2. Habt ihr Zeit . . .? (vorbeikommen, die Nachbarn kennenlernen, ein Glas Wein trinken, euch ein paar Bilder ansehen)
3. Es ist wichtig . . . (aufpassen, Sprachen lernen, einmal etwas anderes tun, Freunde haben)
4. Es ist interessant . . . (ihm zuhören, Briefmarken sammeln, mit der Bahn fahren, mit dem Flugzeug fliegen)
5. Es hat Spaß gemacht . . . (reisen, wandern, singen, spazierengehen, ins Grüne fahren, Freunde anrufen)

M. Bilden Sie Sätze!

1. heute / wir / haben / nicht viel / tun
2. es / machen / ihm Spaß // Fußball spielen
3. sie *(sg.)* / müssen / einlösen / Scheck
4. ich / haben / nicht / Zeit // Geschichte / fertig / erzählen *(pres. perf.)*
5. du / haben / keine / Lust // auf den Stefansdom / hinauffahren? *(pres. perf.)*
6. möchten / du / fernsehen / bei uns?
7. wir / wollen / kaufen / neu / Auto
8. es / sein / sehr bequem // hier / sitzen
9. ich / sein / zu müde // Tennis spielen
10. du / sollen / anrufen / dein- / Mutter

N. Wie geht's weiter?

1. Ich habe keine Lust . . .
2. Ich habe nie Zeit . . .
3. Mir macht es Spaß . . .
4. Ich finde es wichtig . . .
5. Ich finde es langweilig . . .
6. Als *(as)* Kind hat es mir Spaß gemacht . . .

„Hatschi!"–Gesundheit!

O. **_Was machen Sie morgens, bevor Sie aus dem Haus gehen?_** (Write six to eight sentences using reflexive verbs.)

P. **_Was fehlt?_**

1. Es hat einmal ein_____ gut_____ Mutter mit ihr_____ klein_____ Mädchen in ein_____ ruhig_____ Dorf gewohnt. *2.* Sie hat zu ihr_____ klein_____ Tochter gesagt: „Geh zu dein_____ alt_____ Großmutter, und bring ihr dies_____ gut_____ Flasche Wein und dies_____ frisch_____ Kuchen! *3.* Aber du mußt in d_____ dunkl_____ Wald aufpassen, weil dort d_____ bös_____ (bad) Wolf (m.) wohnt." *4.* D_____ klein_____ Mädchen ist mit sein_____ groß_____ Tasche in d_____ grün_____ Wald gegangen. *5.* Auf d_____ dunkl_____ Weg ist d_____ bös_____ Wolf gekommen und hat d_____ klein_____ Mädchen gefragt, wo sein_____ alt_____ Großmutter lebt. *6.* Er hat d_____ gut_____ Kind auch d_____ wunderbar_____ Blumen am Weg gezeigt. *7.* Dann hat d_____ furchtbar_____ Wolf d_____ arm_____ (poor) Großmutter gefressen (swallowed) und hat sich in d_____ bequem_____ Bett d_____ alt_____ Frau gelegt. *8.* D_____ müd_____ Rotkäppchen (n.) ist in d_____ klein_____ Haus gekommen und hat gefragt: „Großmutter, warum hast du solch_____ groß_____ Ohren? Warum hast du solch_____ groß_____ Augen? Warum hast du so ein_____ groß_____ Mund?" *9.* Da hat d_____ bös_____ Wolf geantwortet: „Daß ich dich besser fressen (eat) kann!" *10.* Nun (well), Sie kennen ja das Ende dies_____ bekannt_____ Geschichte (story, f.)! *11.* D_____ Jäger (hunter) hat d_____ dick_____ Wolf getötet (killed) und d_____ klein_____ Mädchen und sein_____ alt_____ Großmutter aus d_____ Bauch d_____ tot_____ (dead) Wolfes geholfen.

Q. **_Auf deutsch, bitte!_**

1. Hello Max! What have you been doing today? *2.* Oh, nothing special. I listened to my old records. *3.* Do you feel like going swimming? *4.* No, thanks. I don't feel well. I have a headache and my throat hurts. Call Stephan. *5.* Hello, Stephan! Do you have time to go swimming? *6.* No, I have to buy (myself) a new pair of pants and a warm coat. Do you feel like coming along? *7.* No, I already went shopping this morning. I bought (myself) a blue sweater and a white shirt. *8.* Too bad. I've got to hurry. I want to put on my trunks (**die Badehose**) and go swimming. Bye!

Approximately the size of Ohio, the GDR has a population of about 17 million. It has become highly industrialized and is now the most prosperous state in the Soviet block. Although the standard of living is considerably lower than that of the FRG, GDR citizens are provided with a high degree of economic security through free medical care, subsidized rent and food, and guaranteed employment. Travel restrictions, as symbolized by the wall dividing Berlin, are probably the greatest cause of dissatisfaction among the citizens of the GDR. The GDR has a flourishing cultural life. Government-subsidized theaters, operas, and orchestras offer numerous performances that attract a large percentage of the population. GDR writers such as Christa Wolf, Volker Braun, and Christoph Hein have produced works of high merit and are recognized internationally. A few, such as the poet Sarah Kirsch and the author Günter Kunert, have received permission to leave the GDR and now live in the FRG.

der Bürger, -	*citizen*
Sport	*sport(s)*
Staat, -en	*state*
die Kunst, ⁻e	*art*
Musik	*music*
Prüfung, -en	*exam, test*
(genauso) wie . . .	*(just) like . . .*
verschieden	*different(ly)*
sich fit halten (hält), gehalten	*to keep in shape*
gewinnen, gewonnen	*to win*
mit·machen	*to participate, get involved*

mach mit . . .

WAS IST DAS? der Ferienplatz, ⁻e, Kontakt, Malclub, Schachclub; das Gefühl, Sportfest, System, Talent; die Eingangsprüfung, Medaille, Möglichkeit, Musikschule, Privatwelt, Schulung, Spezialschule, Sportschule, Tanzschule, Theatergruppe, Zusammengehörigkeit; die Hobbyzentren, Olympischen Spiele, Reisemöglichkeiten; kein Wunder; trainieren, vortrainieren, akademisch, aktiv, intensiv, international, jung, körperlich, persönlich, politisch, positiv, sechsjährig, sozialistisch, sportlich, staatlich, talentiert, zehnjährig, zweiseitig, zweitägig, zwölfmonatig

focus/ opinion

amazing

contests

Pro: Manfreds Meinung°

Es ist immer erstaunlich°, wie viele Medaillen ein kleines Land wie die DDR bei den Olympischen Spielen oder anderen sportlichen Wettbewerben° gewinnt. Und

Blickpunkt°
**DDR: Mach
mit! Bleib fit!**

5

Alles mit dem Volk,
alles durch das Volk,
alles für das Volk.

JAZZ

271

again

athletic clubs

mentally

promotion/ in general/ it
doesn't matter

requirements

sewing...

develop

dann wiederum° ist es kein Wunder, wenn man sieht, wieviel Geld der Staat
für Sport ausgibt. Überall gibt es Schwimmbäder und Turnvereine°. Immer
wieder gibt es Sportfeste, wo jung und alt mitmacht. „Mach mit—bleib fit"
ist populär. Wer mitmacht, hält sich geistig° und körperlich fit.

Genauso wie mit dem Sport ist es mit der Musik, der Kunst und der 10
Förderung° von Talenten und von Hobbys im allgemeinen°. Es ist egal°,
welches Hobby oder Talent man hat, in der DDR findet man überall Möglichkeiten mitzumachen. Musik und Kunst sind nicht nur Pflichtfächer° in
den Schulen, sondern auch sehr populär in Hobbyzentren und Abend-
schulen. Jede kleine Stadt hat einen Schachclub, Malclub, Nähclub°, eine 15
Theatergruppe, ein Orchester und einen Chor. Wer besonders talentiert ist,
hat die Möglichkeit, in einer Spezialschule—z.B. der Staatlichen Musik- und
Tanzschule in Dresden[1]—sein Talent zu entwickeln°. Die Lehrer dieser

*Junge Tänzerinnen
an einer staatlichen
Tanzschule*

look for
probation
students/ education

subjects

future/ secured
tie together/ within

a kind of Olympics

Schule reisen durch die ganze DDR und suchen° Kinder mit Talent. Nach
einer zweitägigen Eingangsprüfung und einer zwölfmonatigen Probezeit° 20
beginnen die zehnjährigen Schüler° eine sechsjährige Ausbildung°. Neben
ihrem besonderen Programm, z.B. in Musik oder Tanz, ist es eine normale
Schule mit allen akademischen Fächern°. Talent ist aber nicht genug, denn
die Schüler müssen auch schwer arbeiten. Doch wissen sie alle, daß am
Ende dieser freien Ausbildung ihre persönliche Zukunft° gesichert° ist. 25

Sport, Musik und Kunst verbinden° nicht nur innerhalb° einer Stadt
oder der DDR, sondern auch international, z.B. bei der bekannten Massen-
spartakiade°[2] und beim internationalen Bach[3]-Wettbewerb in Leipzig[4] oder
beim Liszt[5]-Wettbewerb in Weimar[6]. Dieses Gefühl der Zusammengehörigkeit, auch mit anderen Ländern, ist den Menschen in der DDR wichtig. 30

Contra: Giselas Meinung

Der Sport in der DDR ist nicht nur positiv zu sehen. Auf der einen Seite ist
es natürlich phantastisch, daß der Staat so viel für den Sport tut. Auf der
anderen Seite will die DDR bei den Olympischen Spielen zeigen, daß das
sozialistische System besser° ist. Der Sport macht es dem Staat möglich, 35
die Bürger der DDR zu beeinflussen°. Für die Schüler der verschiedenen
staatlichen Sportschulen ist alles frei: Wohnung und Essen, Turnschuhe°,
Badehosen° usw. Sie bekommen aber nicht nur eine gute akademische und
sportliche Ausbildung, sondern auch eine intensive politische Schulung.
Sie dürfen keine Kontakte mit Menschen im Westen haben, z.B. mit Ver- 40
wandten° in der Bundesrepublik. „Mitmachen" bedeutet also° auch, politisch das zu tun, was der Staat will. Außerdem: Wer sportlich aktiv ist, ist
auch für die Armee vortrainiert.

better
influence
gym shoes
swim wear

relatives/ therefore

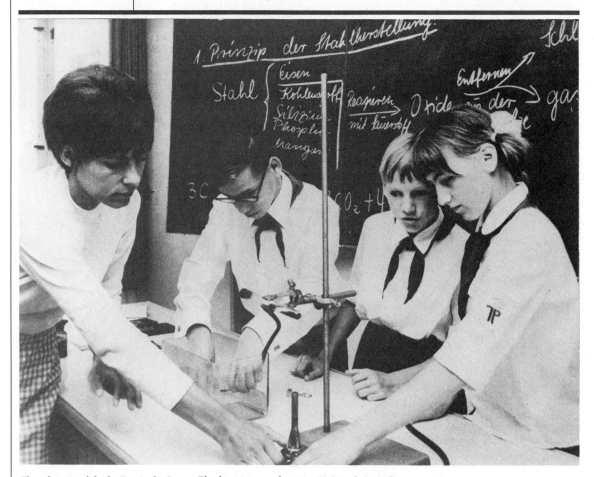

Chemieunterricht in Rostock. Junge Pioniere tragen ein rotes Halstuch (scarf).

loner

lure

most/ normally

seldom

get canceled

    In einem Staat wie der DDR darf man kein Einzelgänger° sein. Alle sollen „mitmachen". Wenn der Staat einen Bürger nicht mit Sport aus seiner 45 Privatwelt locken° kann, dann kann er es vielleicht mit Musik, Kunst oder Hobbys. Mitmachen bringt auch oft Reisemöglichkeiten. das ist für die meisten° Bürger sehr interessant, weil es normalerweise° nicht so einfach ist zu reisen. Es gibt nicht genug Ferienplätze, und die jungen Menschen dürfen nur selten° in andere Länder, besonders in den Westen. Natürlich 50 hat man, wenn man zu einer besonderen Schule wie in Erfurt oder Dresden gegangen ist, meistens eine gesicherte Zukunft. Ich sage meistens, denn wenn man statt in der FDJ[8] in der Kirche aktiv wird, sieht man viele Zukunftspläne ins Wasser fallen°.

A. Was paßt? *(Match choices a. to m. with the blanks in 1 to 13.)*

Pro: 1. Es ist immer erstaunlich, wie viele Medaillen _____ . **2.** Es ist aber kein Wunder, wenn man sieht, _____ . **3.** _____ ist populär. **4.** In der DDR findet man überall _____ . **5.** Jede kleine Stadt hat _____ . **6.** Wer besonders talentiert ist, kann _____ . **7.** Talent ist aber nicht genug, die Schüler _____ .

Contra: 8. _____ macht es dem Staat möglich, die Bürger zu beeinflussen. **9.** Sie sollen keine Kontakte _____ . **10.** „Mitmachen" bedeutet das zu tun, was _____ . **11.** Mitmachen bringt auch oft _____ . **12.** Normalerweise ist es nicht so einfach _____ . **13.** Wenn man statt in der FDJ _____ aktiv wird, ist die Zukunft nicht so sicher.

a. Möglichkeiten mitzumachen
b. der Staat will
c. dieses kleine Land nach Hause bringt
d. müssen schwer arbeiten
e. eine Theatergruppe, ein Orchester und einen Chor
f. Reisemöglichkeiten
g. zu reisen
h. wieviel Geld der Staat für Sport ausgibt
i. in der Kirche
j. Der Sport
k. mit Menschen im Westen haben
l. in eine Spezialschule gehen
m. Mach mit—bleib fit!

B. Wie geht's weiter?

1. Du hast viele Möglichkeiten . . . (mitmachen, dich fit halten, dein Talent entwickeln, Geld ausgeben)
2. Aber es ist nicht einfach . . . (in den Westen reisen, Ferienplätze bekommen, Verwandte in der Bundesrepublik haben, zur Kirche gehören)
3. Hast du Lust . . .? (zur Spartakiade gehen, eine Sportschule besuchen, nach Weimar weiterreisen, ein paar Leute von der FDJ kennenlernen)

C. Was fehlt?

1. D___ zehnjährig___ Ulli geht auf ein___ staatlich___ Sportschule. 2. Nach ein___ zweitägig___ Eingangsprüfung hat er ein___ zwölfmonatig___ Probezeit gehabt. 3. Neben sein___ besonder___ Sportprogramm hat er all___ ander___ akademisch___ Fächer *(pl.)* wie an ein___ normal___ Schule. 4. Er darf aber kein___ schlecht___ Noten *(grades)* haben, und auch bei d___ politisch___ Unterricht *(lesson, m.)* darf er nicht fehlen *(be missing)*. 5. Er muß ein___ ausgezeichnet___ Schüler sein. 6. Am Ende dies___ frei___ Ausbildung *(f.)* hat er ein___ sicher___ Zukunft *(f.)*. 7. Ulli macht bei jed___ Sport mit. 8. Jed___ sportlich___ Wettbewerb *(m.)* ist ein___ gut___ Training *(n.)* nicht nur für die Olympiade, sondern auch für die ostdeutsch___ Armee. 9. Ulli hat schon bei viel___ international___ Sportfesten mitgemacht.

10. Manchmal darf er auch ein＿＿＿ lang＿＿＿ Reise machen. **11.** Er fühlt sich wohl in sein＿＿＿ klein＿＿＿ Land, denn es ist ein＿＿＿ schön＿＿＿ Land.

D. Interviews *(Form groups of two to four students; decide who plays what role in the interview, then ask the suggested questions and respond to them. Afterward report some of the answers to the entire class.)*

1. *mit einem Lehrer der Staatlichen Musik- und Tanzschule in Dresden* (Ask (a) who can go there; (b) if there is an exam and what kind; (c) about the age of the students; (d) why this school is so special.)

2. *mit ein paar Sportlern* (athletes) *aus der DDR* (Ask (a) about their age; (b) what sports they like and why; (c) if they've ever won any medals; (d) what their plans are for the future.)

3. *zwischen einem DDR-Sportler und Ihnen* (You're asked (a) whether your state spends a lot of money on sports, arts, and music, and what you think of that; (b) what hobbies you have and if you're in any club; (c) whether you can travel freely and where you've been; (d) whether there's a problem if people are active in church.)

E. Die DDR *(Working with a partner, answer the questions. Then write eight to ten sentences about the geography of the GDR, using some of the questions as guidelines.)*

1. Wie heißen die Nachbarn der DDR? Wo liegen sie? Wie heißt die Hauptstadt der DDR?

2. Wo ist die Ostsee? Welche Städte liegen an der Ostsee? Wie heißt die große Insel im Norden der DDR? Wo gibt es viele Seen?

3. Nennen Sie ein paar Flüsse in der DDR! Welcher Fluß fließt weiter *(flows on)* nach Polen? Welcher Fluß kommt aus der Tschechoslowakei und fließt weiter nach Westdeutschland?
4. Wo ist der Harz? der Thüringer Wald? das Erzgebirge?
5. Wo liegt Berlin? Potsdam? Frankfurt? Dresden? Meißen? Leipzig? Weimar? Wie heißt Chemnitz heute?

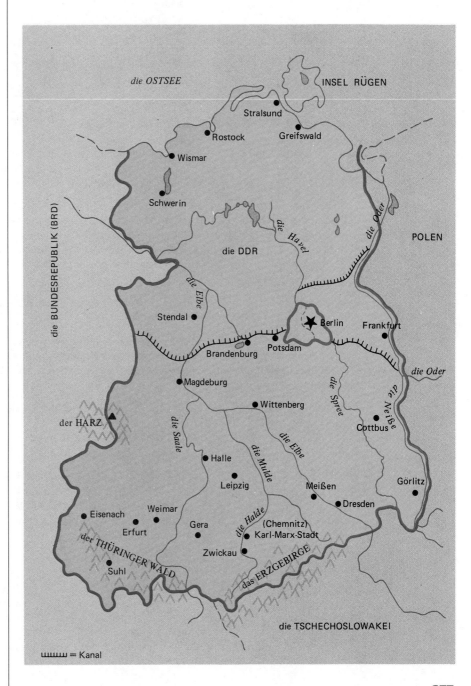

1. **Dresden**, after East Berlin and Leipzig the third-largest city in the GDR, is known for its beautiful setting on the Elbe River and its magnificent baroque buildings erected by the dukes of Saxony. Most of those buildings were destroyed during World War II, but some have been rebuilt in the old style.

Dresden, eine schöne alte Stadt an der Elbe

2. The climax and goal of all sports activities is the athletic "talent show" of youth at the **Spartakiade** (named after Spartacus, the leader of the Roman slave revolt in 71 B.C.). It combines sports with a solemn pledge to socialism, a parade of flags, and the presentation of foreign visitors.

3. **Johann Sebastian Bach** (1685–1750) was one of two composers whose work was the culmination of the baroque era (the other was **Georg Friedrich Händel**, 1685–1759). From 1723 until his death, Bach was music director of the Church of St. Thomas in Leipzig. Most of his immense output of choral music was written during this period.

4. **Leipzig**, an industrial city of over half a million people, is famous for its annual industrial fair (**Leipziger Messe**).

5. **Franz Liszt** (1811–1886), a Hungarian virtuoso pianist, was one of the late romantic composers whose work led to musical innovations of the twentieth century. He spent most of his productive life in Weimar, where his house can still be visited today.

6. **Weimar** was the home of two of Germany's greatest poets, **Goethe** and **Schiller**. After World War I, the Weimar Republic was founded here with the intent of symbolically instilling the spirit of the classical humanistic German tradition into the new German parliamentary democracy.

7. Travel to the West is one of the rewards for party-loyal athletes, musicians, and artists. Other than public officials, only retired people can easily obtain permits to visit the West. The GDR government is still afraid that the West's higher living standards and more open society might induce citizens to leave the country if it opened its fortified borders. As of now, younger people may visit relatives in the West only for special occasions (such as weddings and funerals) and only if other members of the immediate family stay behind.

8. The **FDJ** (**Freie Deutsche Jugend**), an organization for young people between the ages of 14 and 25, has more than 90,000 youth groups. It is strongly political and organizes most youth activities. Members up to age 13 are called **Junge Pioniere**. Only the church has a nongovernmental youth organization (**Junge Gemeinde**), but members often encounter educational and economic disadvantages.

GESPRÄCHE

Blick in die Zeitung

SONJA Sag mal, Stephan, was gibt's denn heute abend im Fernsehen?

STEPHAN Keine Ahnung! Bestimmt nichts Besonderes.

SONJA Laß mich mal sehen!—*Familie Feuerstein*, einen Dokumentarfilm und einen alten Krimi.

STEPHAN So ein Quatsch!

SONJA Vielleicht gibt's 'was im Kino?

STEPHAN Ja, *Die Ehre der Prizzis* und *Männer*.

SONJA Interessiert mich nicht.

STEPHAN Im Theater[1] gibt's *Mutter Courage*[2].

SONJA Toll! Hast du Lust?

STEPHAN Ja, das klingt gut. Gehen wir!

An der Theaterkasse

STEPHAN Haben Sie noch Karten für heute abend?

FRÄULEIN Ja, erste Reihe erster Rang rechts und Parkett Mitte.

STEPHAN Zwei Plätze im ersten Rang! Hier sind unsere Studentenausweise.

FRÄULEIN 14 DM, bitte!

SONJA Wann fängt die Vorstellung an?

FRÄULEIN Um 20.15 Uhr.

Während der Pause

STEPHAN Möchtest du eine Cola?

SONJA Ja, gern. Aber laß mich bezahlen! Du hast schon die Programme gekauft.

STEPHAN Na gut. Wie hat dir der erste Akt gefallen?

SONJA Prima! Ich habe *Mutter Courage* mal in der Schule gelesen, aber noch nie auf der Bühne gesehen.

STEPHAN Du, wir müssen zurück auf unsere Plätze.

1. The FRG has nearly 300 theaters, the majority of them heavily subsidized by public funds. Most are repertory theaters with resident actors who present a number of different plays each season. Most municipal theaters in medium-sized cities also present ballets, musicals, and operas as part of their regular repertoire. Audiences are still primarily from the middle and upper classes of society. The GDR with over 130 theaters has an even larger number of theaters per capita, and a special effort is made to entice the working class to theaters, concert halls, and museums.—In German-speaking countries senior citizens and students with valid ID's usually are able to purchase tickets at a considerable discount (**Ermäßigung**). This is true also for museums and galleries, so be sure to take your student ID along when you go to Europe.

2. **Bertolt Brecht** (1898–1956) is one of the most important German playwrights of the twentieth century *(Die Dreigroschenoper, Mutter Courage und ihre Kinder, Der kaukasische Kreidekreis)*. His theory of "epic theater" has had a considerable impact on German as well as non-German drama.

A Glance at the Newspaper

SONJA Say, Stephan, what's on TV tonight?
STEPHAN I have no idea. Nothing special for sure.
SONJA Let me check.—*The Flintstones*, a documentary, and an old detective story.
STEPHAN Such junk.
SONJA Maybe there's something at the movies.
STEPHAN Yes, *Prizzi's Honor* and *Men*.
SONJA Not interested.
STEPHAN *Mother Courage* is playing in the theater.
SONJA Great! Do you feel like going?
STEPHAN Yes, that sounds good. Let's go.

At the Ticket Window

STEPHAN Do you have any tickets for tonight?
YOUNG LADY Yes, in the first row of the first balcony on the right and in the middle of the orchestra.
STEPHAN Two seats on the first balcony. Here are our student ID's.
YOUNG LADY Fourteen marks, please.
SONJA When does the performance start?
YOUNG LADY At 8:15 P.M.

During the Intermission

STEPHAN Would you like a coke?
SONJA: Yes, I'd love one. But let me pay. You've already bought the programs.
STEPHAN OK. How did you like the first act?
SONJA Great. I once read *Mother Courage* at school, but I've never seen it on stage.
STEPHAN We have to get back to our seats.

Unterhaltung

DIE UNTERHALTUNG *entertainment*

der Anfang, ⸚e	*beginning, start*
Autor, -en	*author*
Chor, ⸚e	*choir*
Film, -e	*film*
Komponist, -en, -en	*composer*
Krimi, -s	*detective story*
Plattenspieler, -	*record player*
Roman, -e	*novel*
Schauspieler, -	*actor*
das Ende	*end*
Konzert, -e	*concert*
Orchester, -	*orchestra*
Programm, -e	*program; channel*
Stück, -e	*play*
die Oper, -n	*opera*
Pause, -n	*intermission, break*
Reklame, -n	*advertisement*
Vorstellung, -en	*performance*
Zeitschrift, -en	*magazine*
Zeitung, -en	*newspaper*
dumm	*stupid, silly*
komisch	*funny (strange, comical)*
langweilig	*boring*
spannend	*exciting, suspenseful*
traurig	*sad*
an·fangen (fängt an), angefangen	*to start, begin*
an·machen / aus·machen	*to turn on / to turn off*
klatschen	*to clap, applaud*
lachen / weinen	*to laugh / to cry*

WEITERES

am Anfang / am Ende	*in the beginning / at the end*
ander-	*other*
ganz	*whole, entire(ly)*
letzt-	*last*
Was gibt's im Fernsehen?	*What's (playing) on TV?*

PASSIVES VOKABULAR der Akt, -e; der Blick *(view)*; das Feuer, - *(fire)*; die Reihe, -n *(row)*; bestimmt *(certainly)*; Das klingt gut. *(That sounds good.)*; Keine Ahnung! *(I've no idea.)*; im Parkett *(in the orchestra)*; im Rang *(on the balcony)*

A. Was sagen Sie?

1. x Was gibt's heute abend im Kino?
   y _____ .
   x Hast du Lust, ins Kino zu gehen?
   y Ja/nein, _____ .
   x Hast du schon _____ *(name of a movie)* gesehen?
   y Ja/nein, _____ , aber _____ .
   x Das ist ein _____ Film!
   y Wieso?
   x _____ .
   y Wo läuft dieser Film?
   x _____ .

B. Interview. Fragen Sie Ihren Partner/Ihre Partnerin, . . .! *(First ask each other, then report what you found out.)*

1. ob er/sie viel fernsieht
2. welche Sendungen *(programs)* ihm/ihr gefallen
3. ob er/sie ein Bücherwurm *(bookworm)* ist
4. welche Zeitschrift oder Zeitung er/sie interessant findet

Der Bücherwurm *von Carl* **Spitzweg, gemalt** (painted) *um* **1845.**

C. Fragen

1. Was kann man hier zur *(for)* Unterhaltung tun? Gehen Sie gern tanzen? Wo kann man hier tanzen?

2. Gehen Sie oft ins Kino? Was für Filme sehen Sie gern, z.B. Geschichtsfilme, Krimis, Zeichentrickfilme *(cartoons)*, Zukunftsfilme *(science fiction)*, Horrorfilme, Liebesfilme *(love stories)*?

3. Wo kann man hier Theaterstücke sehen? Haben Sie dieses Jahr ein interessantes Stück gesehen? Welches? Wie heißen ein paar Autoren von guten Theaterstücken?

4. Gehen Sie oft ins Konzert? Wohin? Welche Komponisten hören Sie gern?

5. Kann man hier Opern sehen? hören? Welche Opern haben Sie schon gesehen?

6. Wer von Ihnen singt gern? Wer singt im Chor? Wer spielt im Orchester? Wer hat schon einmal eine Rolle *(role)* in einem Theaterstück gespielt? Was für eine Rolle?

7. Wie heißen ein paar gute amerikanische Zeitungen? Nennen *(name)* Sie ein paar interessante Zeitschriften!

8. Wer kann einen guten Roman empfehlen? Wie dick ist er (wie viele Seiten hat er)? Wie oft haben Sie das Buch schon gelesen? Welche Autoren finden Sie besonders gut?

D. Wie geht's weiter?

1. Auf diesem Bild gehört zu einem guten Frühstück die _____
Zeitung. *2.* Das ist natürlich _____ für diese Zeitung. *3.* Ich kenne
diese Zeitung _____ . *4.* Auf dem Frühstückstisch stehen _____ .
5. Ich esse morgens gern _____ und trinke _____ . *6.* Wenn ich
Zeit habe, lese ich _____ . *7.* Diese Woche liest man in den
Zeitungen viel über *(about)* _____ . *8.* Ich interessiere mich
besonders für *(am interested in)* _____ . *9.* Am _____ ist die
Zeitung immer sehr dick.

E. Aussprache *(See also II. 9 and III. 11 in the pronunciation section of the
Appendix.)*

1. [r]   **r**ot, **r**osa, **r**uhig, **r**echts, **R**adio, **R**egal, **R**eklame, **R**oman,
P**r**ogramm, A**r**m, Ame**r**ika, Do**r**f, Konze**r**t, Fah**r**t, Gita**rr**e,
t**r**au**r**ig, k**r**ank, wäh**r**end, mo**r**gens, He**rr**

2. [ʌ]   Absend**er**, Fing**er**, Koff**er**, Orchest**er**, Tocht**er**, Theat**er**,
Mess**er**, Tell**er**, v**er**rückt, ab**er**, hint**er**, unt**er**, üb**er**, wied**er**,
weit**er**

3. [ʌ/r]   Uh**r** / Uh**r**en; Oh**r** / Oh**r**en; Tü**r** / Tü**r**en; Cho**r** / Chö**r**e; Auto**r** /
Auto**r**en; Klavi**er** / Klavi**er**e; saub**er** / saub**er**e

4. Wortpaare

a. ring / Ring	*c. fry* / frei	*e. tear* / Tier
b. Rhine / Rhein	*d. brown* / braun	*f. tour* / Tour

285

STRUKTUR

I. *Verbs with Prepositional Objects*

In both English and German a number of verbs are used together with certain prepositions. These combinations have special idiomatic meanings. Since the German combinations differ from English, they must be memorized.

I'm thinking of my vacation. I'm waiting for my flight.

denken an *(+ acc.)*	*to think of*
schreiben an *(+ acc.)*	*to write to*
sprechen über *(+ acc.)*	*to talk about*
warten auf *(+ acc.)*	*to wait for*
sich ärgern über *(+ acc.)*	*to get annoyed (upset) about*
sich freuen auf *(+ acc.)*	*to look forward to*
sich interessieren für *(+ acc.)*	*to be interested in*
erzählen von *(+ dat.)*	*to tell about*
halten von *(+ dat.)*	*to think of, be of an opinion*

NOTE: In these idiomatic combinations, two-way prepositions most frequently take the accusative.

Er denkt an seine Reise.	*He's thinking of his trip.*
Sie schreibt an ihre Eltern.	*She's writing to her parents.*
Wir haben über unsere Hobbys gesprochen.	*We talked about our hobbies.*
Ich habe auf ein Telefongespräch gewartet.	*I was waiting for a call.*
Ich ärgere mich über den Brief.	*I'm upset about the letter.*
Freut ihr euch aufs Wochenende?	*Are you looking forward to the weekend?*
Interessierst du dich für Sport?	*Are you interested in sports?*
Erzählt von euerem Flug!	*Tell about your flight.*
Was hältst du von dem Film?	*What do you think of the movie?*

☞ *CAUTION:*

▶ *In these idiomatic combinations, **an, auf, über,** etc., are not separable prefixes, but prepositions followed by nouns or pronouns in the appropriate cases:*

Ich rufe dich morgen **an**.   BUT Ich denke **an dich**.
I'll call you tomorrow.   *I'm thinking of you.*

*Note also these two different uses of **auf:***

Ich warte **auf dem** Bahnsteig.   BUT Ich warte **auf den** Zug.
*Where? **On the** platform.*   *For what? **For the** train.*

A. Sagen Sie es noch einmal! *(Replace the nouns following the prepositions with the words suggested.)*

BEISPIEL: Sie warten auf den Zug. (Brief, Telefongespräch)
Sie warten auf den Brief.
Sie warten auf das Telefongespräch.

1. Wir interessieren uns für Kunst. (Sport, Musik)
2. Er spricht über seine Ferien. (Bruder, Hobbys)
3. Sie erzählt von ihrem Flug. (Familie, Geburtstag)
4. Ich denke an seinen Brief. (Postkarte, Name)
5. Wartest du auf deine Familie? (Gäste, Freundin)
6. Freut ihr euch auf das Volksfest? (Vorstellung, Konzert)
7. Ich habe mich über das Wetter geärgert. (Junge, Kinder)
8. Haben Sie an Ihre Freunde geschrieben? (Frau, Vater)
9. Was haltet ihr von der Idee? (Krimi, Leute)

B. Was fehlt?

1. Meine Tante hat _____ mein____ Vater geschrieben. 2. Sie will uns _____ ihr____ Reise durch Afrika erzählen. 3. Wir freuen uns _____ ihr____ Besuch *(m.)*. 4. Meine Tante interessiert sich sehr _____ Afrika. 5. Sie spricht hier im Museum _____ ihr____ Fahrten. 6. Sie denkt nie _____ ihr____ Gesundheit *(f.)*. 7. Wir können kaum *(hardly)* _____ _____ warten.

C. Was tun Sie?

1. Ich denke oft _____ 2. Ich warte _____ 3. Ich schreibe gern _____ 4. Ich interessiere mich _____ 5. Ich freue mich _____ 6. Ich ärgere mich manchmal _____ 7. Ich spreche gern _____ 8. Ich halte nicht viel _____ .

D. Auf deutsch, bitte!

1. Don't wait for me *(3 ×)*.
2. I'm writing to the newspaper.
3. He didn't think of the family.
4. Why do you *(3 ×)* always get upset about every performance?
5. I'm looking forward to the concert.
6. He isn't interested in such music.
7. We don't think much of his letter.

287

II. da- and wo-Compounds

1. da-Compounds

In English, pronouns following prepositions can refer to people, things, and ideas:

I'm coming with him.
I'm coming with it.

In German, this is not the case; pronouns following prepositions refer only to people:

Ich komme **mit ihm.** < Ich komme **mit meinem Freund.**

If you wish to refer to a thing or an idea, you must use a **da-**COMPOUND.

Ich komme **damit.** < Ich komme **mit unserem Auto.**

Most accusative and dative prepositions (except **außer, ohne** and **seit**) can be made into **da-**compounds. If the preposition begins with a vowel (**an, auf, in,** etc.), it is used with **dar-**:

darauf	*on it (them)*
dafür	*for it (them)*
dagegen	*against it (them)*
damit	*with it (them)*
danach	*after it (them)*
darüber	*about it (them)*
usw.	

„Können Sie mir sagen, wo ein Briefkasten ist?"—„Ja, sehen Sie die Kirche dort? **Daneben** ist eine Apotheke, **dahinter** ist die Post, und **davor** ist ein Briefkasten."

2. wo-Compounds

The interrogative pronouns **wer, wen,** and **wem** refer to people.

An wen denkst du?	*Of whom are you thinking? (Who are you thinking of))*
Auf wen wartet ihr?	*For whom are you waiting? (Who are you waiting for?)*

When asking about things or ideas, **was** is used. But if a preposition is involved, you must use a **wo-**COMPOUND.

Woran denkst du?	*Of what are you thinking? (What are you thinking of))*
Worauf wartet ihr?	*For what are you waiting? (What are you waiting for?)*

Again, if the preposition begins with a vowel, it is combined with **wor-**:

worauf?	*on what? for what?*
worin?	*in what?*
wofür?	*for what?*
womit?	*with what?*
wodurch?	*through what?*
usw.	

Wofür interessiert er sich? Für Religion und Philosophie.
Womit kann man Pech haben? Mit Filmen und Theaterstücken.

DEUTSCHES THEATER

DER ZIGEUNERBARON
PREMIERE

Deutsches Theater München · Betriebs - GmbH · Schwanthalerstraße 13 · 8000 München

PARKETT RECHTS	Reihe 17	Platz 2	Preis DM 27,00

009   DONNERSTAG
9 . AUG . 84
20 . 00 UHR

Kein Anspruch auf Rückzahlung des Eintrittspreises.

009301702027

... und abends ins Deutsche Theater ...

Oper Großes Haus	LEIPZIGER THEATER **OPER GROSSES HAUS**	
Rang 5 - 13 8,–	Reihe **5**	Rang RECHTS 8,–	Sitz Nr. **13**
11. 4. 86	Freitag 11. April	III/10/135

ÜBUNGEN

E.

1. *Kombinieren Sie mit* da- *und* wo-!

BEISPIEL: für   **dafür / wofür?**

durch, gegen, um, an, auf, hinter, in, neben, über, unter, vor, zwischen,
aus, bei, mit, nach, von, zu

2. *Wo liegen die Zeitungen?* (Repeat each sentence with a **da**-compound.)

BEISPIEL: auf dem Sofa   **Sie liegen darauf.**

unter dem Stuhl, hinter den Büchern, auf den Platten, zwischen dem
Radio und dem Fernseher, neben dem Bett, im Wohnzimmer, vor der Tür

F. Sagen sie es noch einmal! *(Replace the boldface phrases with a preposition and a pronoun, or with a **da**-compound. Always consider whether the sentence deals with a person or with an object or idea.)*

BEISPIELE: Hans steht **neben Christa**.　　　**Hans steht neben ihr.**
　　　　　　Die Lampe steht **neben dem Klavier.**　　**Die Lampe steht danebeп.**

1. Was machst du **nach den Ferien?**
2. Bist du auch **mit dem Bus** gefahren?
3. Er hat die Gitarre **für seine Freundin** gekauft.
4. Was hast du **gegen Ski laufen?**
5. Das Paket ist **von meinen Eltern** gewesen.
6. Die Karten liegen **auf dem Tisch.**
7. Die Kinder haben **hinter der Garage** gespielt.
8. Anja hat **zwischen Herrn Fiedler und seiner Frau** gesessen.
9. Was sagen Sie **zu dem Haus?**
10. Ist die Nummer **im Telefonbuch?**
11. Er hat sich furchtbar **über diese Idee** geärgert.
12. Wir denken oft **an unseren kranken Freund.**
13. Freust du dich auch so **auf unsere Fahrt?**
14. Der Koffer ist **auf dem Schrank.**
15. Ich habe diese Theaterkarten **für meine Großeltern** gekauft.

G. Stellen Sie Fragen! *(Ask about the boldface phrase with a preposition and **wen** or **wem**, or with a **wo**-compound.)*

BEISPIELE: Horst interessiert sich **für Sport.**　　　**Wofür interessiert sich Horst**
　　　　　　Horst interessiert sich **für das Fräulein.**　　**Für wen interessiert sich Ho**

1. Barbara wartet **auf die Straßenbahn.**
2. Jutta erzählt von **ihrem Onkel.**
3. Die Berliner Studenten interessieren sich besonders **für Politik.**
4. Sie sprechen **über ihre Hobbys.**
5. Herr Gnom denkt nie **an den Geburtstag seiner Frau.**
6. Dieter ist mit Wolf **auf dem Trimm-dich-Pfad** gelaufen.
7. Sie hat **an ihre Eltern** geschrieben.
8. Klaus hat sich oft **über seinen Bruder** geärgert.
9. Daniel trinkt Limonade **aus der Flasche.**
10. Caroline spricht **von ihrem alten Großvater.**
11. Die Kinder sitzen **auf dem Teppich.**
12. Sie ärgern sich **über solche Fragen.**
13. Gerd freut sich **auf die Schiffahrt.**
14. Brigitte fährt **mit ihrer Schwester.**

H. *Auf deutsch, bitte!*

1. a. She's sitting next to them (i.e., their friends).
   b. They have two presents, one (**eins**) for her and one for him.
   c. Do you see the chair? The presents are lying on it.
   d. What's in them?
   e. Who are they for?
   f. Is this for me?
   g. What does one do with it?
   h. Don't *(sg. fam.)* sit down on it.

2. a. With whom is he coming?
   b. What are they talking about?
   c. What are you *(sg. fam.)* thinking of?
   d. For whom is he waiting?
   e. What are you *(pl. fam.)* annoyed about?
   f. What is she interested in?
   g. To whom are you *(formal)* writing?
   h. For whom is this present?
   i. What do you *(sg. fam.)* think of it?

III. *Endings of Unpreceded Adjectives*

You already know how to deal with adjectives preceded by either **der-** or **ein-**words. But occasionally adjectives are preceded by neither; these are called UNPRECEDED ADJECTIVES. The equivalent in English would be adjectives preceded by neither *the* nor *a(n)*:

We bought fresh fish and fresh eggs.

1. Unpreceded adjectives have the endings that the definite article would have if it were used.

der frische Fisch   das frische Obst   die frischen Eier
    frisch**er** Fisch   frisch**es** Obst   frisch**e** Eier

	masc.	neut.	fem.	pl.
nom.	frischer Fisch	frisches Obst	frische Wurst	frische Eier
acc.	frischen Fisch	frisches Obst	frische Wurst	frische Eier
dat.	frischem Fisch	frischem Obst	frischer Wurst	frischen Eiern
gen.	—	—	—	frischer Eier

Heute abend gibt es frischen Salat, kaltes Fleisch, schöne Wurst und gekochte Eier.

NOTE:
- *The genitive singular forms are irregular and relatively rare.*
- *If there are several unpreceded adjectives, all have the same ending.*
Er hat interessante, aber auch verrückte Ideen.

2. Several important words are often used as unpreceded adjectives:

einig-	*some, a few (pl. only)*
mehrer-	*several (pl. only)*
viel	*much, many*
wenig	*little (not much), few*

Wir haben uns mehrer**e** neu**e** Filme angesehen.
Einig**en** jung**en** Leuten haben sie gefallen, aber mir nicht.

Usually neither **viel** nor **wenig** has an ending in the singular. But the words are often used as unpreceded adjectives in the plural.

Er hat viel Geld, aber wenig Zeit.   BUT Wenig**e** Städte haben so einen großen Park. Am Wochenende gehen dort viel**e** Leute spazieren.

- *Numerals and **ein paar** have no endings:*

Wir haben **drei** wunderbare Tage bei meinem Onkel verbracht *(spent)*.
Vielleicht bleiben wir noch **ein paar** Tage.

ÜBUNGEN

I. Ersetzen Sie die Adjektive!

BEISPIEL: Das sind nette Leute. (verrückt)   **Das sind verrückte Leute.**

1. Geben Sie mir eine Tasse schwarzen Kaffee. (heiß, frisch)
2. Sie braucht ein Paket dünnes Papier. (billig, weiß)
3. Er schreibt tolle Bücher. (spannend, lustig)
4. Heute haben wir wunderbares Wetter. (ausgezeichnet, furchtbar)
5. Dort gibt es gutes Essen. (einfach, gesund)
6. Hier bekommen wir frischen Fisch. (wunderbar, gebacken)
7. Er hat oft verrückte Ideen. (dumm, phantastisch)

Bade nicht mit vollem Bauch!

J. Sagen Sie es noch einmal! *(Omit the **der-** or **ein-**word preceding the adjective.)*

BEISPIEL: Der holländische Käse ist ausgezeichnet.
Holländischer Käse ist ausgezeichnet.

1. Die deutschen Zeitungen haben auch viel Reklame.
2. Der Mann will mit dem falschen Geld bezahlen.
3. Sie hat das frische Brot gekauft.
4. Er hat den schwarzen Kaffee getrunken.
5. Wir haben die braunen Eier genommen.
6. Er ist mit seinen alten Tennisschuhen auf die Party gegangen.
7. Sie trinken gern das dunkle Bier.
8. Auf der Party haben sie diese laute Musik gespielt.
9. Er erzählt gern solche traurigen Geschichten.
10. Sie hat Bilder der bekannten Schauspieler.

K. Was fehlt?

1. Geben Sie mir bitte ein par_____ rot_____ Äpfel!
2. Wir haben einig_____ bekannt_____ Autoren kennengelernt.
3. Ich habe nur wenig_____ amerikanisch_____ Geld.
4. Viel_____ neu_____ Studenten sind heute gekommen.
5. Trinkst du gern warm_____ Milch?
6. Wir wünschen Ihnen schön_____ und interessant_____ Ferien.
7. Sie haben mit mehrer_____ ander_____ Ausländern an einem Tisch gesessen.
8. Regensburg und Landshut sind zwei hübsch_____ alt_____ Städte.
9. In der Prüfung habe ich ein paar_____ dumm_____ Fehler *(mistake, m.)* gemacht.
10. Trink nicht so viel_____ kalt_____ Bier!
11. Lieb_____ Bettina, lieb_____ Hans, lieb_____ Freunde!
12. Lieb_____ Onkel Max, lieb_____ Tante Elisabeth!

L. Wie geht's weiter? *(Include an unpreceded adjective.)*

BEISPIEL: Ich singe . . .   **Ich singe alte Lieder.**

1. Ich esse gern . . .
2. Ich trinke meistens . . .
3. Ich sammle . . .
4. Ich lese gern . . .
5. Ich trage . . .
6. Ich sehe gern . . .
7. Ich finde . . . prima.
8. Ich möchte . . .

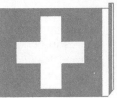

Schweiz für Kenner –
Ferien
par excellence:

Schweizer Qualität,
französischer Charme
bei deutscher
Sprache…

ZUSAMMENFASSUNG

M. *Bilden Sie ganze Sätze!*

1. wie lange / du / warten /—/ ich? *(pres. perf.)*
2. ich / sich freuen /—/ Reise nach Spanien *(pres.)*
3. er / sich ärgern /—/ Film *(pres. perf.)*
4. wo- / ihr / sich interessieren? *(pres.)*
5. wollen / sich kaufen / du / einig- / deutsch / Zeitschriften? *(pres.)*
6. in London / wir / sehen / mehrer- / interessant / Stücke *(pres. perf.)*
7. während / Pause / wir / trinken / billig / Sekt *(pres. perf.)*
8. Renate / schon / lesen / ein paar / spannend / Krimi *(pres. perf.)*
9. am Ende / viel / modern / Stücke / Leute / nicht / klatschen / lange *(pres.)*

N. *Auf deutsch, bitte!*

1. Two weeks ago an old friend of my father's visited us. *2.* He is the author of several plays. *3.* I'm very interested in the theater. *4.* He knows many interesting people, also several well-known actors. *5.* He spoke about them. *6.* He also told us some exciting stories. *7.* He has just been to (in) Vienna. *8.* He saw several performances of his new play. *9.* He's coming back in the summer. *10.* We all look forward to that.

Although Germany produced many outstanding films in the 1920s and 1930s, it was long after World War II before German filmmaking again reached its prewar level of excellence. During the early 1970s, many German films won praise from critics and prizes at film festivals, but most of them were considered difficult or obscure and lacked popular appeal. During the late seventies and the eighties, however, many excellent films have reached the domestic and international markets. Television has helped by making money available to beginning and experienced directors for experimentation in the film medium. Some directors and representative films now known internationally are: Doris Dörrie, *Männer*; Rainer Werner Fassbinder, *Die Ehe der Maria Braun*; Hans W. Geissendörfer, *Der Zauberberg (The Magic Mountain)*; Werner Herzog, *Fitzcarraldo*; Alexander Kluge, *Krieg und Frieden*; Wolfgang Peterson, *Das Boot* and *Die unendliche Geschichte (The Never-Ending Story)*; Margarethe von Trotta, *Rosa Luxemburg*; Volker Schlöndorff, *Die Blechtrommel (The Tin Drum)*.

der Zuschauer, -	*viewer, spectator*
das Fernsehen	*television (the medium)*
die Nachricht[1], -en	*news (usually pl. in radio and TV)*
Sendung[1], -en	*program*
amerikanisch	*American*
leicht / schwer	*light, easy / heavy, difficult*
monatlich (täglich, wöchentlich)	*monthly (daily, weekly)*
vor allem	*mainly*
weder . . . noch	*neither . . . nor*

1 Note the difference between **das Programm** and **die Sendung** as they refer to television. **Das Programm** generally refers to a *channel*: **Es gibt *drei Programme.*** **Die Sendung** refers to a *particular program*: **Ich sehe mir gern diese *Sportsendung* an.**

WAS IST DAS? der Haushalt, Kritiker; das Kabelfernsehen, Nachbarland, Satellitenprogramm; die Diskussion, Droge, Information, Kolonialisierung, Kreativität, Kultursendung, Serie, Sportsendung; die Kosten, Massenmedien, Statistik, Walkmänner; kritisieren, registrieren, eine Rolle spielen, warnen; finanziell, informativ, international, kontrolliert, kulturell, negativ, passiv, manipuliert, privat, staatlich

---

Die Kolonialisierung der Köpfe

Wie überall spielt das Fernsehen auch in der Bundesrepublik eine wichtige Rolle. Ungefähr fünf Stunden jeden Tag nutzen° die Westdeutschen im Durchschnitt° Fernsehen, Radio, Zeitungen und Zeitschriften. Fast jeder Haushalt hat heute einen Fernseher. Die Auswahl° an Sendungen ist groß und wird jedes Jahr größer°. In der Bundesrepublik gibt es drei Hauptprogramme°[1], aber dazu kommen Programme aus den Nachbarländern—so kann man im Norden Sendungen aus Holland, Belgien und Luxemburg sehen und im Süden aus Österreich und der Schweiz. Im Nordosten der BRD und im Westen der DDR kann man auch Fernsehsendungen der anderen Seite empfangen°, so daß das Fernsehen ein Fenster im Eisernen Vorhang° ist[2]. In der BRD kommt jetzt noch das Kabelfernsehen dazu mit Satellitenprogrammen, einige davon auf englisch und französisch[3].

In der DDR ist das Fernsehen staatlich kontrolliert; in der Bundesrepublik ist es weder staatlich noch privat, sondern unabhängig°, sowohl politisch wie auch° finanziell. Alle Bundesbürger° müssen ihre Fernseher und Radios bei der Post registrieren und monatliche Gebühren° bezahlen[4].

Marginal glosses:

use

on the average

selection

bigger

main channels

receive

Iron Curtain

independent

as well as/ citizens of the FRG

fees

5

10

15

cable TV/ grow

fear/ more important

is deteriorating

by it

up-to-date/ . . . reports

mixture

cleverly

therefore

just/ valuable

violence

influence

let themselves be show-ered

constant showering

at work

. . . association/ against it

Reklame gibt es im westdeutschen Fernsehen auch, aber nie während einer Sendung, sondern nur davor oder danach. Mit der Verkabelung° wachsen° 20 aber Kosten, und manche Leute fürchten°, daß Reklame wichtiger° wird und daß sich die Qualität verschlechtert°.

Was aber ist Qualität? Manche Leute verstehen darunter° kulturelle Sendungen wie Theaterstücke oder Konzerte, andere denken dabei an ak-tuelle° Sportsendungen, informative Reiseberichte°, spannende Filme oder 25 leichte Unterhaltung. Das westdeutsche Fernsehen hat eigentlich eine gute Mischung° davon. Die Nachrichten⁵ sind ziemlich international. Bei poli-tischen Programmen (z.B. beim Schwarzen Kanal in der DDR und beim ZDF-Magazin in der BRD) muß man aufpassen, denn manche Information ist darin oft geschickt° manipuliert. Manche Kritiker ärgern sich darüber, 30 daß im westdeutschen Fernsehen so viele amerikanische Filme und Serien laufen, aber die Statistiken zeigen, daß sich ein großer Teil der Zuschauer sehr dafür interessiert. Man zeigt also°, was die Zuschauer sehen wollen, und das sind eben° nicht nur wertvolle° und informative Kultursendungen, sondern auch viel Sex und Gewalt°⁶. Aber nicht nur darin sehen die Kritiker 35 einen negativen Einfluß° des Fernsehens, sondern auch in der passiven Rolle der Zuschauer. Manche Menschen, und vor allem die Kinder, lassen sich täglich stundenlang vom Fernsehen „berieseln°." Sie werden dadurch passiv und verlieren an Kreativität.

Viele kritisieren nicht nur die Dauerberieselung° durchs Fernsehen, 40 sondern auch die Musik. Ob zu Hause oder bei der Arbeit°, beim Autofahren oder Laufen, viele Menschen können gar nicht mehr ohne Musik sein. So hat der deutsche Skiverband° davor° gewarnt, mit Walkmännern auf den

Viele Menschen lassen sich den ganzen Tag von Musik „berieseln".

acid rain/ damaged

visible

dangerous

Ohren Ski zu laufen. Zeitungen und Zeitschriften warnen heute vor der Kolonialisierung der Köpfe durch die Massenmedien, und man spricht von 45 der Musik als Droge: „Was der saure Regen° in den Wäldern angerichtet° hat, ist sichtbar° geworden. Was die Massenmedien in unseren Köpfen anrichten, ist aber nicht sichtbar, und trotzdem nicht weniger gefährlich°."

ZUM TEXT

A. Richtig oder falsch?

___ 1. In der Bundesrepublik spielt das Fernsehen keine wichtige Rolle.

___ 2. Die Menschen dort sehen sich ungefähr fünf Stunden am Tag Fernsehen an.

___ 3. In der Bundesrepublik gibt es drei Hauptprogramme.

___ 4. Im Süden der Bundesrepublik kann man Programme aus Belgien und Holland sehen.

___ 5. Das Fernsehen in der DDR ist staatlich kontrolliert.

___ 6. In der Bundesrepublik muß man alle Radios und Fernseher bei der Post registrieren und monatliche Gebühren zahlen.

___ 7. Es gibt relativ wenig Reklame im westdeutschen Fernsehen.

___ 8. Reklame läuft gewöhnlich während einer Sendung.

___ 9. Manche Kritiker finden, daß man im westdeutschen Fernsehen nicht genug amerikanische Filme und Serien sieht.

___ 10. Wenn die Zeitungen über die Kolonialisierung der Köpfe sprechen, denken sie vor allem an die Nachrichten.

B. Was fehlt? Geben Sie die Präpositionen!

1. Der Artikel spricht _____ deutschen Fernsehen. 2. Viele denken bei Qualitätssendungen _____ internationale Nachrichten. 3. Manche Kritiker ärgern sich _____ die vielen amerikanischen Filme. 4. Sie interessieren sich nicht _____ amerikanische Serien. 5. Andere warten jede Woche _____ diese Serien. 6. Sie freuen sich schon _____ die nächste Woche. 7. Die Kritiker sprechen _____ einer Kolonialisierung der Köpfe durch die Massenmedien. 8. Wenn Sie das Quatsch finden, schreiben Sie bitte _____ die Frankfurter Rundschau!

C. Wiederholen Sie die Sätze mit einem da-Wort oder einer Präposition plus Pronomen, und fragen Sie dann danach!

BEISPIEL: Das deutsche Fernsehen ist unabhängig von der Reklame.
Das deutsche Fernsehen ist unabhängig davon.—Wovon?

1. Für Kabelempfänger gibt es mehr Programme.
2. Mit der Verkabelung wachsen natürlich die Kosten.
3. Manche Zuschauer lassen sich täglich stundenlang vom Fernsehen oder von moderner Musik berieseln.
4. Durch diese Berieselung verlieren sie an Kreativität.

D. Was fehlt? Geben Sie die Adjektivendungen, wo nötig (where necessary)!

1. In der Bundesrepublik gibt es drei_____ Programme. *2.* Außerdem bekommt man auch manch_____ gut_____ Sender *(pl.)* aus der DDR und aus ander_____ Nachbarländern. *3.* Dazu kommen noch verschied_____ Satellitenprogramme. *4.* Die BRD finanziert das Fernsehen durch monatlich_____ Gebühren. *5.* Eigentlich hat das westdeutsch_____ Fernsehen eine gut_____ Mischung von kulturell_____ Sendungen und leicht_____ Unterhaltung. *6.* Bei politisch_____ Diskussionen muß man aufpassen, weil man darin oft wichtig_____ Information manipuliert.

E. Was halten Sie davon? (Poll class members on their opinion to the following statements. Use the board.)

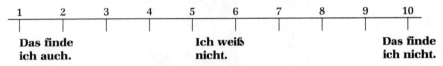

1	2	3	4	5	6	7	8	9	10

Das finde ich auch.   **Ich weiß nicht.**   **Das finde ich nicht.**

1. Wir sitzen alle zu viel vor dem Fernseher.
2. Fernsehen macht dumm.
3. Reklame im Fernsehen ist Quatsch.
4. Kauf dir keinen Fernseher, denn es gibt sowieso *(anyhow)* nichts Gutes darin!
5. Die Nachrichten im Fernsehen sind gewöhnlich geschickt manipuliert.
6. Sex und Gewalt im Fernsehen beeinflussen *(influence)* uns negativ.
7. Die Nachrichten in Zeitungen und Zeitschriften beeinflussen uns auch negativ.
8. Bei der Arbeit und beim Autofahren soll man nicht Musik hören.
9. Walkmänner sind gefährlich *(dangerous)*.
10. Musik ist wie eine Droge.

1. PROGRAMM

10.00–13.30 ARD/ZDF-Vormittagsprogramm (siehe ZDF)

14.30 ●● Videotext für alle – live

14.50 Die Goldenen Schuhe
(5) (SDR) Fernseh-Serie in fünf Teilen nach dem gleichnamigen Roman von Vicki Baum – Fernsehbearbeitung: Helmut Pigge

Katja Milenkaja. . .	Claudine Auger
Kati Milenz	Nicole Kunz
Dr. Ted Marshall	Klaus Barner
Grischa Kuprin . . .	Jacques Breuer
Mirko Bagoryan . . .	Klaus Löwitsch
Sandy Lazar	Ernst Stankovski
Phil Daniels . .	Karl-Heinz Vosgerau
Olivia Beauchamps . .	Susi Nicoletti
Henry Elkan	Walter Riss
Enrico Mattoni	Paolo Gozlino
Joyce Lyman	Petra Constanza
Gabrilowa	Blanche Aubry
Masuroff	Wilfried Baasner

u. a. – Musik: Gerhard Wimberger Kamera: Josef Vilsmeier – Choreographie: Dieter Gackstetter
Regie: Dietrich Haugk
Wh. vom 9. 1. 1984 – Sehbtlg.: 19%

15.50 Tagesschau

16.00 Michael, der Indianerjunge
(Three warriors)
Amerikanischer Spielfilm von 1977

Michael. . .	McKee „Kiko" Redwing
Seine Mutter. . .	Lois Red Elk
Sein Großvater. .	Charles White Eagle

101 Min
u. a. – Regie: Keith Merrill
Wiederholung vom 1. 11. 1983
„Der ambitionierte Jugendfilm vermittelt ein eindrucksvolles Bild indianischer Denkweisen" (ARD).

17.45 Tagesschau

Regionalprogramm BR:

17.55 Bayernstudio

18.05 Familie Feuerstein
Heute: **Das Hausboot**
Deutsche Sprecher:

Fred. . . .	Eduard Wandrey († 1974)
Barney	Gerd Duwner
Wilma	Inge Landgut
Betty	Inge Wellmann

Dt. Bearbeitung (Buch und Dialogregie): Alexander Welbat († 1977)
Erstsendung am 8. 2. 1971 – 1. Wh. am 14. 3. 1974 – 2. Wh. am 13. 11. 1982

18.35 Tagesthema

18.50 Ein schönes Wochenende.

Anschl.: **Stichworte**
Diskussion zu einem akt. Thema

19.50 Bayernstudio mit Wetter

3. Bayern

16.05 Black Beauty (19)
TV-Serie für Kinder (26 Folgen)
Heute: **Beauty soll in den Krieg**

---

2. PROGRAMM

Gräfin Mariza Mit viel Schwung verfilmt
Beliebte Operette mit Evergreens wie „Komm, Zigan", „Auch ich war einst ein feiner Csárdáskavalier" und „Brüderlein . . ."

Mariza und der verarmte Tassilo: Liebe
Fürst Populescu (r.) und Tschekko (K. Grosskurth)

Freizeit
Italien-Reise für 2 Personen zu gewinnen
Entdecken Sie das Hinterland der Adria (mit Quiz) / Urlaub auf dem Bauernhof in der Toscana.

Rauchende Colts
Wiedersehen mit Lee J. Cobb

Der alte Colonel Johnson ist froh, daß er Carl in dessen Laden ein paar Tage vertreten soll. Doch dann geschieht durch die Unachtsamkeit des Ex-Offiziers ein Unglück: Carls Geschäft gerät in Brand. Damit nicht genug . . .

Was kann Dillon tun?
Der Colonel (Lee J. Cobb, r.) fragt Festus um Rat

ARD/ZDF-Vormittagsprogramm

10.00 Tagesschau
Anschl.: **Tagesthemen**

10.23 100 Karat (8/9)
ZDF-Wh. vom Dienstag und Mittwoch

12.10 Kinder Kinder
ZDF-Wiederholung vom Vorabend

12.55 Presseschau

13.00 Tagesschau

13.15–13.30 ●● Videotext für alle

14.40 ZDF – Ihr Programm

14.45 ●● Gräfin Mariza
Operette von Emmerich Kálmán. Libretto: Julius Brammer und Alfred Grünwald. TV-Bearbeitung: Rolf und Alexandra Becker und Eugen York

Gräfin Mariza	Erszebeth Házy
Graf Tassilo.	René Kollo
Lisa	Dagmar Koller
Koloman Zsupán. . . .	Kurt Huemer
Fürst Populescu . . .	Benno Kusche
Fürstin Bozena	Ljuba Welitsch
Tschekko. .	Kurt Grosskurth († 1975)
Mamutschka	Irma Patkos

u. a. – Es spielen die Wiener Symphoniker unter Wolfgang Ebert
Regie: Eugen York
Erstsdg.: 2. 2. 1974 – Sehbetlg.: 45% – 1. Wh.: 25. 4. 1976 – Sehbetlg.: 9% – 2. Wh.: 18. 4. 1982 – Sehbtlg.: 11%

„Der ‚Gräfin Mariza' setzte der strahlende Tenor brillante Glanzpunkte auf" (Frankfurter Rundschau).
Der Musikfilm wurde an ungarischen Originalschauplätzen gedreht.
Anschl.: Heute-Schlagzeilen

16.30 Freizeit
Moderation: Gerd Mausbach
Quizadresse: ZDF, Freizeit-Redaktion, Kennwort „Italien", 6500 Mainz 500

17.00 Heute
Anschl.: Aus den Ländern

17.15 Tele-Illustrierte
Vorauss. im Studio: Nina Corti mit ihrer Flamenco-Gruppe

17.45 Rauchende Colts
Heute: **Ein alter Soldat (1)**

Matt Dillon	James Arness
Doc Adams. .	Milburn Stone († 1980)
Festus Haggen	Ken Curtis
Newly	Buck Taylor
Colonel Johnson .	L. J. Cobb († 1976)
Anne	Julie Cobb
Bill Higgins	Richard Ely
Carl.	Dan Travanty

u. a. – Regie: Bernard McEveety
Wiederholung vom 25. 5. 1983
Anschl.: Heute-Schlagzeilen

18.20 Rauchende Colts
Ein alter Soldat (2)

18.56 ZDF – Ihr Programm

19.00 Heute

19.30 Auslandsjournal

Belgien

NIEDERLÄNDISCH
15.15 Kochen ist Kunst. – 15.30 Jugendfilm. – 16.55 De vorstinnen van Brugge (3) Serie. – 17.55 Nachr. – 18.00 Tik Tak. – 18.05 Tom und Tina. – 18.10 Liegebeest (25) Waar ist het liegebeest? – 18.25 The Tripods Jugendserie. – 18.55 Unbekannte Welt (13. und letzte Folge). – 19.40 Tagesschau

FRANZÖSISCH
16.45 Mémoire du rail. – 17.30 Ça c'est l'opéra. – 18.00 Les Schtroumpfs. – 18.30 Sport. – 19.30 Tagesschau

Luxemburg

16.00 La mémoire des siècles Serie. – 16.30 Un shérif à New York: Le crépuscule du bout du monde. – 18.00 Reilly (10). – 19.00 Nachr. – 19.25 Bip Bip. – 20.00 Blood and sand Film

---

„DDR" 1

9.10 Vorschau. – 9.15 Medizin nach Noten. – 9.25 Aktuelle Kamera. – 10.00 ☐ Brand im Ozean Deutscher Spielfilm (1939). Mit Hans Söhnker, René Deltgen, Winnie Markus (Wh.). – 11.25 Der schwarze Kanal (Wh.). – 11.45 ☐ Die Spur führt in den 7. Himmel 4. Teil: Siebter Himmel (Wh.). – 12.35 Du und dein Garten (Wh.). – 13.00 Nachrichten (bis 13.10 Uhr). – 13.45 Mobil (bis 15.40 Uhr). – 16.20 Ur- – 16.15 Vorschau. – 16.20 Urkungen und Wirsachen (Kinderfernsehen). – 16.50 Medizin nach Noten. – 17.00 Nachrichten. – 17.15 Wie wär's – Ferientour Für Kinder. – 17.45 Dominic 3. Teil: Ein Kinderfreund. – 18.15 Alles Trick. – 18.50 Sandmännchen

19.00 Hobbys, Tips – so wird's gemacht

19.30 Aktuelle Kamera

„DDR" 2

14.25 Siehste

14.30 Kreisläufe

15.00 König Drosselbart

15.30 Für Freunde der russischen Sprache:
(Mit deutschen Untertiteln)
Jeder Zehnte
Sowjetischer Spielfilm (1984)

16.40 Jagdflieger
Sowjet. Dokumentarfilm

16.55 Sternchen Für Kinder

17.40 Siehste

17.45 Nachrichten

17.50 Sandmännchen

18.00 Die silberne Säge
3. Teil: Das neue Heim

18.52 Siehste

18.55 Nachrichten

19.00 Sport

F. Was gibt's im Fernsehen? Sehen Sie aufs Programm, und beantworten Sie die Fragen darüber!

1. Wann beginnen die Vormittagssendungen?
2. Wann ist *die Tagesschau* (Nachrichten) im 1. Programm? Wann läuft *Heute* (Nachrichten) im 2. Programm? Wie lange sind diese Nachrichten?
3. Welche TV-Serie läuft im 3. Programm? Für wen ist sie?
4. Welchen amerikanischen Film gibt's im 1. Programm? Welche amerikanische Serie läuft im 2. Programm?
5. Wann läuft *Familie Feuerstein*? Warum heißt es „deutsche Sprecher"?
6. Welche Operette läuft im 2. Programm?
7. Was gibt's danach? Was kann man dabei gewinnen?
8. Wie viele Programme hat die DDR?
9. Was für Filme gibt's im DDR 1 und DDR 2? Wie alt sind diese Filme?
10. In welchem der zwei DDR Programme gibt's die politische Sendung *Der schwarze Kanal*? Wann?
11. In welchen Sprachen senden *(broadcast)* das belgische und luxemburgische Fernsehen?
12. Womit endet das Tagesprogramm des Kabelprogramms RTL-plus?

G. Das Fernsehen dort und hier. Was ist gleich *(alike)*, **und was ist verschieden?** *(Compare the system in the FRG and here by writing brief statements of two to four sentences for each of the points below. Use the reading text and the TV program as references.)*

1. Popularität
2. Anzahl der *(number of)* Programme
3. Art der *(type of)* Programme
4. Kabelfernsehen
5. Reklame und Fernsehgebühren
6. Qualität der Sendungen
7. Politik im Fernsehen
8. Lieblingsprogramme *(favorite . . .)*

ÜBRIGENS

1. The FRG has two major TV networks and nine regional broadcasting corporations—one in each of the **Länder** (states). Whereas the programming on **ARD (1. Programm)** and **ZDF (2. Programm)** is the same throughout all of the FRG, each of the regional broadcasting companies decides what is shown locally on Channel 3 (**3. Programm**).

2. Because of technical differences, GDR television can be seen only in black and white in the FRG, and vice versa. Even so, many viewers watch programs from the other Germany and thus get exposed to the other side's political opinion. For East Germans it often accentuates their frustration about not being able to travel to the West.

3. The FRG offers a number of cable channels, e.g., **Sat 1** and **RTL-plus** (done in cooperation with German newspapers and magazine publishers), **3-Sat** (with programs from the FRG, Austria, and Switzerland), **Sky Channel** and **Music Box** (in English), **Satellimages** and **TV-5** (in French). Recently the FRG and the GDR have begun to offer each other's entire TV program on cable. Plans are under way to add cable channels that will be available in most of Switzerland, Austria, and the FRG.

4. Financing is provided mainly by monthly viewer and listener fees. Advertising on TV is limited to a total of twenty minutes between 6:00 and 8:00 P.M. FRG television and radio are supervised by boards made up of representatives of the public and private sectors, whose purpose it is to keep the broadcast media free from interference by the government or by economic interests.

5. News reports are quite frequent throughout the day. The ARD calls them **Tagesschau**, and the ZDF calls them **Heute**. They are generally much shorter and have much less on-the-spot reporting than in the US.

6. Some time ago, an American group studied the TV fare in the FRG and reported that the two German networks showed on the average 1.6 violent scenes per hour. This compared favorably with the main networks and cable film channels in the United States, which showed on the average 6.4 and 22 violent scenes per hour respectively.

GESPRÄCHE

Gesucht wird

HOLGER Na, Lothar, woran denkst du?
Oder soll ich fragen an wen?

LOTHAR Ach, an Sabine.

HOLGER Sabine, Sabine. Du denkst den ganzen Tag an Sabine.

LOTHAR Ich weiß. Sie aber nicht an mich. Sie will diesen Sommer auch nicht mit mir segeln.

HOLGER Vergiß sie! Setz doch mal eine Anzeige in die Zeitung[1]! Vielleicht lernst du auf diese Weise ein anderes Mädchen kennen.

LOTHAR Da hast du recht. Man kann's ja mal versuchen.

HOLGER Komm, ich helfe dir! Also, du bist sympathisch, sportlich, naturverbunden, frei und segelst gern. Und wie muß sie sein?

LOTHAR Einfach nett, attraktiv und unternehmungslustig.

UTE Du, hör mal! „Sympathischer, sportlicher Typ, 29/170^2, naturverbunden, frei, segelt gern im Mittelmeer. Sucht nette, attraktive, unternehmungslustige Partnerin. Wenn's paßt, für mehr als einen Sommer." Wollen wir da mal schreiben?

ANNELIE Das klingt nicht schlecht.

UTE Aber?

ANNELIE Wer weiß, was das für ein Typ ist.

UTE Versuch's doch mal! Was kannst du schon verlieren?

ANNELIE Nein, ich habe keine Lust. Tu du's doch!

UTE Ja, warum nicht?

ÜBRIGENS

1. Advertising for marriage partners is generally accepted and not at all unusual in the German-speaking countries. Many newspapers and magazines carry such ads (see "Zum Thema").

2. In Europe the metric system is standard. Is someone who has a height of 180 cm short or tall? Figure it out yourself. Since 1 inch = 2.54 cm, divide the height by 2.54 to get the number of inches. How tall are you in metric terms? Multiply your height in inches by 2.54.

Wanted

HOLGER Well, Lothar, what are you thinking about? Or shall I ask about whom?

LOTHAR Oh, about Sabine.

HOLGER Sabine, Sabine. You think of Sabine all day long.

LOTHAR I know. But she doesn't think of me. Nor does she want to go sailing with me this summer.

HOLGER Forget her. Why don't you put a personal ad in the paper. That way you might get to know another girl.

LOTHAR You're right. It's worth a try.

HOLGER Come on, I'll help you. You're congenial, athletic, nature loving, single, and you love sailing. And what does she have to be like?

LOTHAR Simply nice, attractive, and enterprising.

A Glance at the Paper

UTE Hey, listen! "Congenial, athletic fellow, 29 years old, 1 meter 70, nature loving, single, loves sailing on the Mediterranean. Looking for nice, attractive, enterprising partner. If things work out, for more than one summer." Shall we write?

ANNELIE That sounds good.

UTE But?

ANNELIE Who knows what he's like.

UTE　Try it. What have you got to lose?
ANNELIE　No, I don't feel like it. You do it.
UTE　OK, why not?

Liebe und Eigenschaften

DIE LIEBE *love*

der Partner, -	*partner*
Wunsch, ⸚e	*wish*
die Hochzeit, -en	*wedding*
verliebt *(in + acc.)*	*in love (with)*
verlobt (mit)	*engaged (to)*
(un)verheiratet	*(un)married*

DIE EIGENSCHAFT, -EN *characteristic*

attraktiv	*attractive*
charmant	*charming*
fleißig / faul	*industrious / lazy*
gebildet	*well educated*
hübsch / häßlich	*pretty / ugly*
intelligent	*intelligent*
jung	*young*
nett	*nice*
reich / arm	*rich / poor*
schick	*chic, neat*
schlank	*slim, slender*
temperamentvoll	*dynamic*
(un)freundlich	*(un)friendly*

(un)glücklich	*(un)happy*
(un)musikalisch	*(un)musical*
(un)sportlich	*(un)athletic*
(un)sympathisch	*(un)congenial, (un)likable*
(un)talentiert	*(un)talented*
unternehmungslustig	*enterprising*
verständnisvoll	*understanding*

WEITERES

auf diese Weise	*this way*
beid-	*both*
bestimmt	*surely, for sure, certain(ly)*
Du hast recht / unrecht.	*You're right / wrong.*
jemand	*someone, somebody*
ein·laden (lädt ein), eingeladen	*to invite*
heiraten	*to marry, get married to*
setzen[1]	*to put, place*
suchen	*to look for*
träumen (von)	*to dream (of)*
vergessen (vergißt), vergessen	*to forget*
verlieren, verloren	*to lose*
versuchen	*to try*

---

1 Compare **Ich setze das Paket auf den Stuhl.** AND **Ich setze mich auf den Stuhl.**
Also remember that **sich setzen** means *to sit down* and **sitzen** means *to be sitting.*
Don't confuse **setzen** with **sitzen.**

ZUM THEMA

A. Was ist das Adjektiv dazu?

der Charme, Freund, Reichtum, Sport, Verstand; das Glück, Temperament, Unternehmen; die Bildung, Intelligenz, Musik, Sympathie; heiraten, sich verlieben, sich verloben

Kinder – nein danke!

B. Partner-Wunsch. Machen Sie mit, und beantworten Sie die Fragen!

1. Wie soll Ihr Partner sein?
   Alter *(age)*: von _____ bis _____ Jahre
   Größe *(height)*: von _____ bis _____ cm
   Haar: ☐ schwarz ☐ blond ☐ braun ☐ grau ☐ rötlich
   Staatsangehörigkeit *(nationality)*: _____

2. Eigenschaften des Partners: *(circle five)*

☐ zärtlich	☐ ruhig	☐ temperamentvoll
☐ häuslich	☐ tolerant	☐ verständnisvoll
☐ treu	☐ sportlich	☐ unternehmungslustig
☐ natürlich	☐ musikalisch	☐ kinderlieb
☐ reich	☐ lustig	☐ tierlieb

3. Das macht mir besonders Spaß: *(Circle five)*

Autos	Film und Theater	Photographieren
Basteln *(crafts)*	Handarbeiten *(needlework)*	Politik
Blumen	Kochen, Essen	Reisen
Computer	Literatur	Tiere *(animals)*
Diskutieren	Musik, Kunst	Wissenschaft

4. So bin ich:

ja	nein	manchmal	nie	
☐	☐	☐	☐	Sprechen Sie gern über Probleme?
☐	☐	☐	☐	Können Sie über sich lachen?
☐	☐	☐	☐	Können Sie anderen lange zuhören?
☐	☐	☐	☐	Ärgern Sie sich manchmal?
☐	☐	☐	☐	Machen Sie viele Pläne für Ihre Zukunft *(future)*?
☐	☐	☐	☐	Finden Sie, daß Sex etwas Wichtiges ist?
☐	☐	☐	☐	Sind Sie spontan und flexibel?

Name: _____

Adresse: _____

_____

Telefon: _____

Geburtstag: _____ Größe (cm): _____ Haarfarbe: _____

Familienstand: *(Circle one)*

unverheiratet, getrennt *(separated)*, geschieden *(divorced)*, verwitwet

(widowed)

Nationalität: _____   Zahl der Kinder _____

Muttersprache _____   Fremdsprachen _____

Beruf *(profession)* _____

Unterschrift *(signature)* _____

C. *Lesen Sie, und beantworten Sie die Fragen!*

Es gibt, was ich suche! Aber wie finden? Akademikerin°, Mitte 20/153°, schlank, musikalisch, sportlich, sucht charmanten, gebildeten ADAM.

Die 22jährige Edith, eine hübsche Verkäuferin, möchte gern ihr Herz° verschenken°. Wo ist der junge Mann, den° sie mit Liebe verwöhnen° kann?

Millionär bin ich nicht! Will mir ja auch kein Glück kaufen, sondern verdienen°. Ich, 28/170°, suche keine Modepuppe° oder Disco-Queen, sondern ein nettes, natürliches Mädchen, das° auch hübsch sein darf.

Gesucht wird: attraktive, lustige, zärtliche EVA. Belohnung°: gutaussehender, generöser Junggeselle°, Ende 40, mit allen männlichen° Schwächen°.

Es ist ganz einfach . . .

. . . mit einer Anzeige in der
FRANKFURTER RUNDSCHAU

1. Wie soll der Partner/die Partnerin sein? *(Make a list of the qualities wanted.)*
2. Wie sehen die Leute sich? *(Make a list of what these people stress about themselves.)*
3. Was sagen sie nicht?
4. Schreiben Sie Ihre eigene *(own)* Anzeige!

Margin notes:

woman with university degree/ mid-20s/ 1 meter 53 (5 feet)

heart

give away

whom/ spoil

earn/ 1 meter 70 (5 feet 7)/ fashion doll/ who

reward

bachelor/ male

weaknesses

D. Fragen

1. Was machen Sie und Ihre Freunde in der Freizeit? Worüber sprechen Sie?
2. Was für Eigenschaften finden Sie bei Freunden wichtig? Wie dürfen sie nicht sein?
3. Waren Sie schon einmal in einen Schauspieler/eine Schauspielerin verliebt? In wen?
4. Was halten Sie vom Zusammenleben mit einem Freund/einer Freundin vor dem Heiraten?
5. Was halten Sie vom Heiraten? Wie alt sollen Leute wenigstens *(at least)* sein, wenn sie heiraten? Finden Sie eine lange Verlobung wichtig? Warum? Warum nicht?

E. Schreiben Sie eine Charakterisierung *(characterization)* von acht bis zehn Sätzen!

1. So bin ich.
2. Ein Freund/eine Freundin von mir *(or anybody else you would like to write about).*

F. Aussprache *(See also III. 1, 4, and 5 in the pronunciation section of the Appendix.)*

1. [f]   für, fast, frei, früh, fertig, fit, fühlen, fehlen, freundlich, Film, Fernsehen, öffnen, Brief, elf, auf
2. [f]   verliebt, verlobt, verheiratet, verständnisvoll, vergessen, verlieren, versuchen, verschieden, vorbei, vielleicht, phantastisch, photographieren, Geographie, wieviel
3. [v]   Vanille, Vision, Video, Klavier, reservieren, Silvester, Pullover, Universität
4. [v]   wer, wen, wem, wessen, warum, werden, wünschen, Waldweg, schwimmen, schwarz, schwer, Schwester, zwischen
5. Wortpaare
   a. *wine* / Wein   c. *oven* / Ofen   e. Vetter / Wetter
   b. *when* / wenn   d. *veal* / viel   f. vier / wir

STRUKTUR

I. The Simple Past (Imperfect, Narrative Past)

The past tense is often referred to as the SIMPLE PAST because it is a single verb form in contrast to the perfect tenses (also called "compound past tenses"), which consist of two parts, an auxiliary and a past participle.

We spoke German.   Wir **sprachen** Deutsch.

In spoken German the present perfect is the preferred tense, especially in Southern Germany, Austria, and Switzerland. Only the simple past of **haben**, **sein**, and the modals are common everywhere.

The simple past is primarily used in continuous narratives such as novels, short stories, newspaper reports, and letters relating a sequence of events. Therefore, it is often also called the "narrative past."

Again, one German verb form corresponds to several in English.

Wir sprachen. $\begin{cases} \textit{We spoke.} \\ \textit{We were speaking.} \\ \textit{We did speak.} \\ \textit{We used to speak.} \end{cases}$

1. t-Verbs (weak verbs)

t-Verbs can be compared to such English verbs as *learn, learned* and *work, worked*. To form the simple past, add **-t** to the stem of the verb (**lern +** t), then add the endings **-e, -est, -e, -en, -et, -en.**

ich lernte	wir lernten
du lerntest	ihr lerntet
er lernte	sie lernten

Verbs that follow this pattern include:

fragen, freuen, hören, interessieren, lachen, machen, sagen, sammeln, setzen, spielen, suchen, träumen, wandern, weinen, wohnen

a. Verbs with stems ending in **-d, -t,** or certain consonant combinations make the simple-past signal **-t** audible by inserting an **-e-.**

ich arbeitete	wir arbeiteten
du arbeitetest	ihr arbeitetet
er arbeitete	sie arbeiteten

Verbs that follow this pattern include:

antworten, baden, bedeuten, erkälten, heiraten, kosten, landen, mieten, öffnen, übernachten, warten

b. The irregular t-verbs also have a stem change. Compare the English *bring, brought* and the German **bringen, brachte.**

ich brachte	wir brachten
du brachtest	ihr brachtet
er brachte	sie brachten

Below is a list of the PRINCIPAL PARTS of all the irregular t-verbs (mixed verbs) that you have used up to now. Irregular present-tense forms are specially noted. You already know all the forms except the simple past. Verbs with prefixes have the same forms as the corresponding simple verbs (**brachte mit**). If you know the principal parts of a verb, you can derive all the verb forms you need!

infinitive	present	simple past	past participle
bringen		**brachte**	gebracht
denken		**dachte**	gedacht
haben	hat	**hatte**	gehabt
kennen		**kannte**	gekannt
wissen	weiß	**wußte**	gewußt

The modals also belong to this group. (Their past participles are rarely used.)

dürfen	darf	**durfte**	(gedurft)
können	kann	**konnte**	(gekonnt)
müssen	muß	**mußte**	(gemußt)
sollen	soll	**sollte**	(gesollt)
wollen	will	**wollte**	(gewollt)

NOTE: The simple past of the irregular t-verbs has the same stem change as the past participle.

2. n-Verbs (strong verbs)

n-Verbs correspond to such English verbs as *write, wrote* and *speak, spoke*. They usually have a stem change in the simple past, which is not predictable and must be memorized. (Overall they fall into a number of groups with the same changes. For a listing by group, see p. 449 in the Appendix.) n-verbs follow this pattern: To the (irregular) stem of the verb add the endings -, **st**, -, **-en, -t, -en.**

ich sprach	wir sprachen
du sprachst	ihr spracht
er sprach	sie sprachen

Below is a list of the PRINCIPAL PARTS of n-verbs that you have used up to now. Irregular present-tense forms and the auxiliary **sein** are specially noted. You already know all the forms except the simple past.

infinitive	present	simple past	past participle
an·fangen	fängt an	**fing an**	angefangen
an·ziehen		**zog an**	angezogen
beginnen		**begann**	begonnen
bleiben		**blieb**	ist geblieben
ein·laden	lädt ein	**lud ein**	eingeladen
empfehlen	empfiehlt	**empfahl**	empfohlen
essen	ißt	**aß**	gegessen
fahren	fährt	**fuhr**	ist gefahren
fallen	fällt	**fiel**	ist gefallen
finden		**fand**	gefunden
fliegen		**flog**	ist geflogen
geben	gibt	**gab**	gegeben
gefallen	gefällt	**gefiel**	gefallen
gehen		**ging**	ist gegangen
gewinnen		**gewann**	gewonnen
halten	hält	**hielt**	gehalten
heißen		**hieß**	geheißen
helfen	hilft	**half**	geholfen
kommen		**kam**	ist gekommen
lassen	läßt	**ließ**	gelassen
laufen	läuft	**lief**	ist gelaufen
lesen	liest	**las**	gelesen
liegen		**lag**	gelegen
nehmen	nimmt	**nahm**	genommen
rufen		**rief**	gerufen
schlafen	schläft	**schlief**	geschlafen
schreiben		**schrieb**	geschrieben
schwimmen		**schwamm**	geschwommen
sehen	sieht	**sah**	gesehen
sein	ist	**war**	ist gewesen
singen		**sang**	gesungen

sitzen		**saß**	gesessen
sprechen	spricht	**sprach**	gesprochen
stehen		**stand**	gestanden
steigen		**stieg**	ist gestiegen
tragen	trägt	**trug**	getragen
trinken		**trank**	getrunken
tun	tut	**tat**	getan
vergessen	vergißt	**vergaß**	vergessen
verlieren		**verlor**	verloren
waschen	wäscht	**wusch**	gewaschen
werden	wird	**wurde**	ist geworden

3. Sentences in the simple past follow familiar word-order patterns.

Der Zug **kam** um acht.
Der Zug **kam** um acht **an**.
Der Zug **sollte** um acht **ankommen**.
V1   V2

Er wußte, daß der Zug um acht **kam**.
Er wußte, daß der Zug um acht **ankam**.
Er wußte, daß der Zug um acht **ankommen sollte**.
V2   V1

313

ÜBUNGEN

A. Geben Sie das Imperfekt (simple past)!

BEISPIEL: feiern   **feierte**

1. fragen, fehlen, erzählen, klatschen, lachen, legen, bummeln, wechseln, photographieren, schicken, putzen, sich kämmen, sich rasieren, sich setzen, versuchen
2. arbeiten, baden, bedeuten, kosten, antworten, übernachten, öffnen
3. haben, müssen, denken, wissen, können, kennen
4. geben, nehmen, essen, sehen, lesen, finden, singen, sitzen, liegen, kommen, tun, sein, schreiben, heißen, einsteigen, schlafen, fallen, lassen, fahren, tragen, waschen, werden, einladen

B. Ersetzen Sie die Verben!

BEISPIEL: Sie schickte das Paket. (mitbringen, aufmachen)
       Sie brachte das Paket mit.
       Sie machte das Paket auf.

1. Sie schickten ein Taxi. (suchen, bestellen, mieten, warten auf)
2. Das hatte ich nicht. (wissen, kennen, denken, mitbringen)
3. Wann solltet ihr zurückkommen? (müssen, wollen, dürfen, können)
4. Wir fanden es dort. (sehen, lassen, verlieren, vergessen)
5. Ich dankte seiner Mutter. (antworten, zuhören, helfen, schreiben)
6. Du empfahlst den Sauerbraten. (nehmen, wollen, bringen)

C. Wiederholen Sie die Texte im Imperfekt!

1. **Weißt du noch, wie das bei uns war?** (A brother and sister reminisce. Repeat in the simple past.)

   BEISPIEL: Großvater erzählt stundenlang von seinen jungen Jahren.
          Großvater erzählte stundenlang von seinen jungen Jahren.

   Ich setze mich aufs Sofa und höre ihm zu. Seine Geschichten interessieren mich. Vater arbeitet im Garten. Du telefonierst oder besuchst die Nachbarn. Und Karin wechselt dreimal am Tag die Kleidung. Mutter kauft ein oder bezahlt Rechnungen. Großmutter legt sich nachmittags ein Stündchen hin und freut sich später auf ihre Tasse Kaffee. Das wiederholt sich oft am Wochenende. Richtig?

2. **Hast du das nicht gewußt?** (Two neighbors gossip about Lothar and Ute.)

   BEISPIEL: Hat Ute ihren Mann schon lange gekannt?
          Kannte Ute ihren Mann schon lange?

   Wie hat sie ihn kennengelernt? Der Postbote (*mailman*) hat ihr einen Brief von einem jungen Herrn gebracht. Hast du nichts von ihrer Anzeige gewußt? Sie hat Lothar durch die Zeitung kennengelernt. Gestern haben sie Hochzeit gehabt. Sie hat Glück gehabt. Das habe ich mir auch gedacht.

3. Schade! *(Bärbel talks to her friend about plans that didn't materialize.)*

    BEISPIEL: Was willst du denn machen?
             Was wolltest du denn machen?

Ich will mit Karl-Heinz ins Kino gehen, aber ich kann nicht.—Warum, darfst du nicht?—Doch, aber meine Kopfschmerzen wollen einfach nicht weggehen.—Mußt du im Bett bleiben?—Nein, aber ich darf nicht schon wieder krank werden. Leider kann ich nicht mit Karl-Heinz sprechen. Aber seine Mutter will es ihm sagen. Er soll mich anrufen.

4. Wo wart ihr? *(Caroline tells about a short trip to Switzerland.)*

    BEISPIEL: Wir sind eine Woche in Saas-Fee gewesen.
             Wir waren eine Woche in Saas-Fee.

Von unserem Zimmer haben wir einen Blick auf *(view of)* die Alpen gehabt. Die Pension hat natürlich „Alpenblick" geheißen. Morgens haben wir lange geschlafen, dann haben wir gemütlich Frühstück gegessen. Später bin ich mit dem Sessellift auf die Berge gefahren und bin den ganzen Nachmittag Ski laufen gegangen. Wolfgang ist unten geblieben, hat Bücher gelesen und Briefe geschrieben.

D. Jetzt erzählen Sie! *(Write eight to ten sentences on one of the topics below. Write in the simple past, not using any verb more than once.)*

1. Als ich sechzehn war *(Tell where you lived, went to school, how and why you liked or didn't like it, etc. You may also pick any other age.)*

2. Eine interessante Party *(Tell where the party was, who was there, what was so special about it, etc.)*

3. Eine schöne Reise *(Tell where you went, who you traveled with, what you saw, etc.)*

II. *The Conjunctions* als, wann, wenn

Care must be taken to distinguish between **als**, **wann**, and **wenn**, all of which correspond to the English *when*. **Als** refers to a SINGLE EVENT IN THE PAST *(When I came home at 6 P.M., he wasn't back yet)*. **Wann** introduces direct or indirect questions REFERRING TO TIME *(I wonder when he'll return)*. **Wenn** covers all other situations, including repeated events in the past *(When he came, he always brought flowers. We'll call you, when he comes in)*.

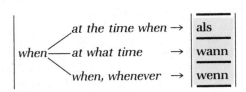

Als ich nach Hause kam, war er noch nicht zurück.
Ich frage mich, **wann** er nach Hause kommt.
Wenn er kam, brachte er immer Blumen.
Wir rufen dich an, **wenn** er zurückkommt.

☞ *CAUTION:*

▶ **Wenn** *also means* **if**! **Wenn** *es nicht regnet, gehen wir spazieren.*

ÜBUNGEN

E. Was fehlt: als, wann oder wenn?

1. _____ ihr kommt, zeigen wir euch die Bilder von unserer Reise.
2. Können Sie mir sagen, _____ der Zug aus Köln ankommt?
3. _____ wir letzte Woche im Theater waren, sahen wir Stephan und Sonja.
4. Sie freute sich immer sehr, _____ wir sie besuchten.
5. Sie bekommen diese Möbel, _____ sie heiraten. Wer weiß, _____ sie heiraten!
6. _____ ich ein Kind war, habe ich nur Deutsch gesprochen.

F. Bilden Sie aus zwei Sätzen einen Satz! Verbinden Sie (link) **sie mit als, wann oder wenn!** *(If when stands at the beginning, make the first sentence the dependent clause. Watch the position of the verb.)*

BEISPIELE: Sie riefen an. Ich duschte mich. (when)
Sie riefen an, als ich mich duschte.

(when) Ich duschte mich. Sie riefen an.
Als ich mich duschte, riefen sie an.

1. Wir sahen Frau Loth heute früh. Wir gingen einkaufen. *(when)*
2. *(when)* Sie spricht von Liebe. Er hört nicht zu.
3. Sie möchte (es) wissen. Die Weihnachtsferien fangen an. *(when)*
4. *(when)* Ich stand gestern auf. Es regnete.
5. *(when)* Das Wetter war schön. Die Kinder spielten immer im Park.
6. Er hat mir nicht geschrieben. Er kommt. *(when)*

III. *The Past Perfect*

1. Like the present perfect, the PAST PERFECT in both English and German is a compound form consisting of an auxiliary and a past participle. However, the AUXILIARY IS IN THE SIMPLE PAST.

Ich **hatte** das gut **gelernt.** *I had learned that well.*
Er **war** um zehn Uhr nach Hause   *He had come home at ten o'clock.*
  gekommen.

ich	hatte	. . . gelernt	war	. . . gekommen
du	hattest	. . . gelernt	warst	. . . gekommen
er	hatte	. . . gelernt	war	. . . gekommen
wir	hatten	. . . gelernt	waren	. . . gekommen
ihr	hattet	. . . gelernt	wart	. . . gekommen
sie	hatten	. . . gelernt	waren	. . . gekommen

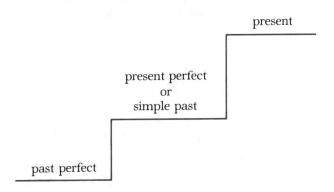

2. The past perfect is used to refer to events preceding other events in the past.

Er hat mich gestern angerufen.	*He called me yesterday.*
Ich **hatte** gerade einen Brief an ihn **geschrieben**.	*I had just written him a letter.*

Wir kamen zu spät am Bahnhof an.	*We arrived too late at the station.*
Der Zug **war** schon **abgefahren**.	*The train had already left.*

The conjunction **nachdem** *(after)* is usually followed by the past perfect in the subordinate clause, whereas the main clause is in the present perfect or simple past.

Nachdem er mich **angerufen hatte**, schickte ich den Brief nicht mehr ab.
Nachdem der Zug **abgefahren war**, mußte ich eine Stunde auf den nächsten Zug warten.

ÜBUNGEN

G. Ersetzen Sie das Subjekt!

BEISPIEL: Sie hatten uns besucht. (er, du)   **Er hatte uns besucht.**
                                                                       Du hattest uns besucht.

1. Du hattest den Schlüssel gesucht. (ihr, Sie, sie/*sg.*)
2. Sie hatten das nicht gewußt. (wir, ihr, sie/*sg.*)
3. Ich war nach Dresden gereist. (sie/*pl.*, du, wir)
4. Sie waren auch in der Dresdener Oper gewesen. (er, du, ich)

H. Auf englisch, bitte! *(Last night Stephan and Sonja looked at the video* Männer, *but they tell about when it first appeared as a movie.)*

BEISPIEL: Ich hatte den Film schon einmal gesehen.
                    I had already seen the movie once before.

1. Er war eine Sensation gewesen.
2. Man hatte den Film zur gleichen Zeit in sieben Kinos gezeigt.
3. Ich hatte Glück gehabt.
4. Durch Walter hatte ich noch Karten für die Premiere bekommen.
5. Die Regisseurin Doris Dörrie war sogar da gewesen.
6. Ich hatte schon lange nicht mehr so gelacht!

I. Auf deutsch, bitte!

1. We got to the airport after the plane had landed. *2.* When I arrived, they had already picked up (**holen**) their luggage. *3.* After I had found them, we drove home. *4.* My mother had been looking forward to this day. *5.* When she had shown them the house, we sat down in the living room and talked about the family.

J. Und dann?

1. Zu Hause (Mrs. Schneider recounts a typical day at home. Find out what happened next by asking **Und dann?** *Note how she'll switch from the present perfect to the past perfect.)*

BEISPIEL: **Ich bin aufgestanden.** Und dann?
                    Nachdem ich aufgestanden war, habe ich mir die Zähne geputzt.

a. Ich bin aufgestanden.
b. Ich habe mir die Zähne geputzt.
c. Ich habe mich angezogen.
d. Ich habe Frühstück gemacht.
e. Alle haben sich an den Tisch gesetzt.
f. Das Telefon hat geklingelt *(rang)*.
g. Ich bin aufgestanden.
h. Helmut hat die Zeitung gelesen.
i. Er ist zur Arbeit gegangen.
j. Ich habe die Betten gemacht.

2. *Was haben Sie am Wochenende gemacht?* (Write five sentences in the simple past, then follow the pattern in exercise 1, **Nachdem ich ...** Don't use any of the above verbs.)

ZUSAMMENFASSUNG

K. *Wiederholen Sie die Sätze im Imperfekt!*

Verliebt...
...Verlobt...
...Verheiratet

Lothar Müller
Ute Müller
geb. Kaiser

Vahrenwalder Str. 93
Hannover 1

Kirchliche Trauung am 24. Mai 1986, 15⁰⁰ Uhr in der Ev.-luth.
Vahrenwalder Kirche

1. Lothar denkt an Sabine. Er will segeln gehen. Aber sie hat keine Lust dazu. Er spricht mit Holger. Die beiden setzen eine Anzeige in die Zeitung. Ute liest die Anzeige und antwortet darauf. Durch die Anzeige finden sie sich. Jetzt hat Holger für Sabine keine Zeit mehr. Er träumt nur noch von Ute. Am 24. Mai heiraten die beiden. Sie laden Holger zur Hochzeit ein. Die Trauung *(wedding)* ist in der lutherischen Kirche. Ute heißt vorher *(before)* Kaiser. Jetzt wird sie Ute Müller.

2. Weil es im Fernsehen nichts Besonderes gibt, gehen Sonja und Stephan ins Theater. Sie haben keine Lust, einen Krimi zu sehen. Aber *Mutter Courage* gefällt ihnen gut. Sonja kennt das Stück schon, aber sie sieht es gern noch einmal. Während der Pause lädt Stephan sie zu einer Cola ein. Leider haben sie nur ein paar Minuten, weil die Pause kurz ist.

L. *Auf deutsch, bitte!* (Use the simple past unless another tense is clearly called for.)

1. Arthur had been thinking of his daughter's wedding. *2.* When we saw her in December, she was in love with a charming, well-to-do man. *3.* They were supposed to get married in April. *4.* I had already bought a beautiful present. *5.* Two weeks ago she got engaged to (**sich verloben mit**) another man. *6.* He's a poor student at (**an**) her university. *7.* They didn't say when they wanted to get married. *8.* On the weekend she called her parents. *9.* She and the student had just gotten married. *10.* They hadn't invited their parents to (**zu**) the wedding. *11.* Arthur gets annoyed when he thinks about it.

Jakob Grimm (1785–1863) and **Wilhelm Grimm** (1786–1859) are well remembered for their collection of fairy tales, including "Rapunzel," "Rumpelstilzchen," "Hänsel und Gretel," "Schneewittchen," "Rotkäppchen," and many others. Few realize that they were also scholars of the German language and the older literature. Jakob wrote the first historical grammar of German and a history of the language. In addition, the brothers began the monumental *Deutsches Wörterbuch*, a task completed only recently.

EINBLICKE

WORTSCHATZ 2

der König, -e	*king*
bald	*soon*
böse	*angry, mad*
endlich	*finally*
niemand	*nobody, no one*
plötzlich	*sudden(ly)*
stolz	*proud*
um . . . zu	*in order to*
auf·hören (zu + *inf.*)	*to stop (doing something)*
geschehen (geschieht), geschah, ist geschehen	*to happen*
herein·kommen, kam herein; ist hereingekommen	*to enter, come in*

kaputt·gehen, ging kaputt, ist kaputtgegangen	to get broken, break
sich lustig machen über (+ acc.)	to make fun of
rennen, rannte, ist gerannt	to run
ziehen, zog, gezogen	to pull

WAS IST DAS? der Rest, Ton; das Unglück; die Ware; eine Weile; betrunken, delikat, golden, hart, nobel; aufessen, verdammen, vorbei sein

König Drosselbart

Es war einmal° ein König. Der° hatte eine schöne, aber sehr stolze Tochter. Eines Tages gab er ein großes Fest, wozu er alle heiratslustigen° noblen Männer von nah und fern° einlud. Aber niemand war der Tochter gut genug. Der eine war 5 zu dick, der andere zu dünn, der dritte zu lang, der vierte zu kurz und so weiter. Besonders aber machte sie sich über einen guten König mit einem krummen Kinn° lustig. „O," rief sie und lachte, „er hat ein Kinn wie ein Drosselschnabel°!" Seit dieser Zeit hieß er nur noch Drosselbart°.

Als der König sah, daß seine Tochter sich über alle Leute nur lustig 10 machte, wurde er böse. Jetzt sollte sie den ersten besten Bettler° heiraten. Als ein paar Tage später ein Bettler kam, mußte sie ihn heiraten. Da half kein Betteln° und Weinen. Der Bettler nahm sie bei der Hand, und sie mußte mit ihm zu Fuß das Schloß verlassen°.

once upon a time/ he

eager to marry
far

crooked chin
a thrush's beak/ . . . beard

first beggar who comes along

begging

leave

Darf ich zum Tanz bitten?

Als sie in einen großen Wald kamen, fragte sie: „Wem gehört der schöne 15
Wald?" „Dem König Drosselbart", antwortete er. Bald kamen sie über ein
Feld. Da fragte sie wieder: „Wem gehört das schöne Feld?" „Dem König
Drosselbart", war wieder seine Antwort. Danach kamen sie durch eine große
Stadt, und sie fragte: „Wem gehört diese schöne, große Stadt?" „Dem König
Drosselbart", hörte sie wieder. Endlich kamen sie an ein kleines Häuschen, 20
da sprach sie: „Ach, wem gehört dieses kleine Häuschen?" „Das gehört mir
und dir", antwortete der Bettler. Sie mußte sich bücken°, um durch die Tür
zu kommen. „Und wo sind die Diener°?" fragte die Königstochter. „Was für
Diener? Hier mußt du alles tun. Koch mir jetzt mein Essen, ich bin müde!"

    Die Königstochter konnte aber gar nicht kochen, und der Bettler mußte 25
ihr dabei helfen. Als sie das bißchen° Essen gegessen hatten, gingen sie zu
Bett. Am nächsten Morgen mußte sie schon früh aufstehen und kochen,

stoop

servants

little bit of

waschen und putzen. Nach ein paar Tagen sagte der Mann: „Das geht nicht, daß wir alles aufessen und nichts verdienen°. Du sollst Körbe flechten°." Er ging hinaus und brachte Weiden°. Da machte sie den ganzen Tag Körbe, 30 aber die harten Weiden taten ihren zarten° Händen weh.

„Ich sehe, das geht nicht", sprach der Mann. „Vielleicht kannst du spinnen°." So setzte sie sich hin und spann, aber der harte Faden° tat ihren zarten Fingern weh. „Siehst du", sprach der Mann, „nichts kannst du. Vielleicht kannst du Töpfe° auf dem Markt verkaufen." Ach, dachte sie, wenn 35 mich da die Leute aus dem Reich° meines Vaters sehen, machen sie sich bestimmt über mich lustig. Aber es half alles nichts°. Sie mußte es tun, wenn sie nicht verhungern° wollte.

Das erste Mal° ging es gut. Weil die Frau so schön war, kauften die Leute gern ihre Ware. Manche schenkten ihr sogar Geld. Davon lebten sie 40 eine Weile. Das zweite Mal setzte sie sich an die Ecke des Marktes. Plötzlich kam ein betrunkener Husar° und ritt° mitten durch ihre Töpfe. Alles ging kaputt. Sie weinte sehr, lief nach Hause und erzählte alles ihrem Mann. „Wer setzt sich auch an eine Ecke des Marktes!" sprach der Mann. „Hör auf zu weinen! Ich sehe, du kannst wirklich nichts. Ich bin heute auf dem 45 Schloß unseres Königs gewesen. Dort wollen sie dich als Küchenmagd° nehmen. Dafür bekommst du freies Essen." So wurde die Königstochter Küchenmagd und mußte alle schmutzige Arbeit tun. Sie machte sich in beiden Taschen ein Töpfchen fest°. Darin brachte sie täglich Überreste° nach Hause, wovon sie lebten. 50

Eines Tages war auf dem Schloß ein großes Fest, die Hochzeit des Königssohnes. Da ging die arme Frau hin, stellte sich an die Tür und wollte alles sehen. Als alles so wunderschön war, da dachte sie mit traurigem Herzen° an ihr Leben und verdammte ihren Stolz°, der° ihr soviel Unglück gebracht hatte. Manchmal gaben ihr die Diener Reste von den delikaten 55 Speisen°. Sie tat sie in ihre Töpfchen und wollte sie nach Hause tragen. Plötzlich kam der Königssohn herein. Er trug elegante Kleider und hatte goldene Ketten° um den Hals. Als er die schöne Frau an der Tür stehen sah, nahm er sie bei der Hand und wollte mit ihr tanzen. Aber sie wollte nicht, denn sie sah, daß es König Drosselbart war. Aber es half alles nichts; 60 er zog sie in den Saal°. Plötzlich fielen die Töpfchen auf den Boden°: Suppe, Überreste, alles lag da. Als die Leute das sahen, machten sie sich über sie lustig. Die arme Königstochter rannte, so schnell sie konnte, aber im Flur war ein Mann, und er brachte sie zurück. Als sie ihn ansah, war es wieder König Drosselbart. „Fürchte dich nicht°!" sagte er in freundlichem Ton. „Ich 65 und der Bettler sind eins. Und der Husar, das bin ich auch gewesen. Das alles ist aus Liebe zu dir geschehen, weil du so stolz warst." Da weinte sie sehr und sagte: „Ich habe großes Unrecht° getan und bin nicht wert°, deine Frau zu sein."

Er aber sprach: „Deine schlechten Tage sind vorbei. Jetzt wollen wir 70 unsere Hochzeit feiern." Bald kamen die Kammerfrauen° und zogen ihr

Marginal glosses (left column):

earn/ weave baskets
willow twigs
tender

spin (yarn)/ thread

pots
kingdom
she had no choice
starve
time

cavalryman/ rode

...maid

fastened/ leftovers

heart/ pride/ which

delicious foods

chains

ballroom/ floor

don't be afraid

wrong/ worthy

ladies in waiting

wunderschöne Kleider an. Und ihr Vater, der ganze Hof°, alle wünschten ihr Glück mit König Drosselbart. Und wenn sie nicht gestorben° sind, dann leben sie noch heute.

Märchen° der Brüder Grimm (nacherzählt°) ⁷⁵

ZUM TEXT

A. ***Erzählen Sie die Geschichte vom König Drosselbart!*** *(Retell the story in your own words, using the simple past. The key words may help you.)*

König, Tochter, Fest, sich lustig machen, Bettler heiraten, Wald, Feld, Stadt, Häuschen, arbeiten, Körbe flechten, spinnen, Töpfe verkaufen, Husar, Küchenmädchen, Fest, Königssohn, tanzen, Hochzeit

B. ***Ein böses Spielchen*** *(Read what Drosselbart's wife tells her son. Underline the past perfect tense.)*

Bevor wir heirateten, spielten dein Großvater und dein Vater ein böses Spielchen mit mir. Weil ich mich über deinen Vater lustig gemacht hatte, hat Großvater mich mit dem ersten besten Bettler weggeschickt. Er hatte mir natürlich nicht gesagt, daß der Bettler König Drosselbart, dein Vater, war. Nachdem wir eine Weile in einer alten Gartenhütte *(. . . hut)* gelebt hatten, fand ich Arbeit im Schloß. Eines Tages feierte man dort Hochzeit, wozu dein Vater viele noble Gäste eingeladen hatte. Ich hatte mich erst ein paar Minuten an die Tür gestellt, als dein Vater mich zum Tanzen holte. Vor Schreck *(out of shock)* waren mir meine Töpfchen hingefallen. Er und der Bettler waren der gleiche gewesen. Erst hatte ich mich sehr darüber geärgert, aber dann war ich sehr glücklich. Nachdem ich mich umgezogen hatte, feierten wir Hochzeit.

C. **Als, wenn** *oder* **wann?**

1. _____ die Prinzessin das hörte, fing sie an zu weinen.
2. Ich weiß nicht genau, _____ sie geheiratet haben, aber _____ sie nicht gestorben sind, dann leben sie noch heute.
3. _____ ich Märchen *(fairy tales)* lese, suche ich immer nach einer Moral.

D. ***Mischmasch*** *(Below you'll find three familiar fairy tales all mixed together. In each numbered item, select one of the three phrases provided to retell one of these stories in its familiar form or, if you prefer, with a different twist. Or you can create an original fairy tale by supplying your own phrases.)*

1. Es war einmal . . .
   a. ein junger Prinz. Der . . .
   b. ein kleines Mädchen. Das . . .
   c. ein kleiner Junge. Der . . .
   d. _____

2. *a.* hatte eine alte Großmutter.
   b. war nicht besonders attraktiv.
   c. hatte immer Hunger.
   d. _____

3. Eines Tages ...
   a. lud ihn/es der Nachbarkönig zu einem Ball ein.
   b. wurde die Großmutter krank.
   c. war wieder nichts im Kühlschrank.
   d. _____

4. Da ging er/es/sie ...
   a. in den dunklen Wald.
   b. mit einem Kuchen und etwas Wein hin.
   c. natürlich hin.
   d. _____

5. a. um ihr zu helfen.
   b. um die Prinzessin kennenzulernen.
   c. um etwas Essen zu finden.
   d. _____

6. Aber er/es/sie ...
   a. machte sich nur über alle lustig.
   b. verlief sich (got lost) im Wald.
   c. dachte nicht an den bösen Wolf.
   d. _____

7. Plötzlich ...
   a. wurde es dem Vater zuviel, und er sagte ...
   b. sah er/sie ein paar schöne Blumen und sagte ...
   c. war da ein Häuschen aus Kuchen und Plätzchen, und jemand sagte ...
   d. _____

8. a. „Jetzt heiratest du den ersten besten Bettler."
   b. „Wer knuspert (nibbles) an meinem Häuschen?"
   c. „Sie freut sich bestimmt über ein paar Blumen."
   d. _____

9. Da kam ...
   a. der Prinz als Bettler zurück und sagte ...

   b. eine alte Frau und sagte ...
   c. der böse Wolf und fragte ...
   d. _____

10. a. „Bleib bei mir, ...
    b. „Jetzt mußt du mit mir kommen, ...
    c. „Wohin gehst du? ...
    d. _____

11. a. und ich will alles für dich tun."
    b. weil du so stolz warst."
    c. Ich habe Hunger."
    d. _____

12. Später ...
    a. wollte er/sie/es wieder nach Hause und sagte ...
    b. erzählte er/es/sie, wer er/es/sie wirklich war und sagte ...
    c. fragte er/es/sie ...
    d. _____

13. a. „Vergiß alles, und laß uns neu anfangen!"
    b. „Warum hast du so ein großes Maul (mouth)?"
    c. „Ich habe genug und möchte nach Hause."
    d. _____

14. Da ...
    a. warf (threw) sie ihm die Töpfe vor die Füße.
    b. freute er/es/sie sich und war glücklich.
    c. wurde er/es/sie furchtbar böse.
    d. _____

15. Die Moral von der Geschicht':
    a. Spiele mit der Liebe nicht!
    b. Traue (trust) einem Wolf nicht!
    c. Geh zu fremden Leuten (strangers) nicht!
    d. _____

E. Fragen

1. In den Augen von König Drosselbart, wie soll eine Frau (nicht) sein? Was für ein Mann ist der König?
2. Was ist die Moral dieses Märchens? Wie finden Sie dieses Märchen und seine Moral?
3. Lesen Sie gern Märchen? Warum? Warum nicht? Welche anderen Märchen kennen Sie?

   BEISPIELE: „Rapunzel", „Rumpelstilzchen", „Hänsel und Gretel", „Die Bremer Stadtmusikanten", „Rotkäppchen", „Schneewittchen", „Der Froschkönig"

HALTET MIT HUMOR UND CHARME
EURE JUNGE LIEBE WARM!
MIT ALLEN GUTEN WÜNSCHEN

I. *Verbs*

1. Reflexive Verbs

If the subject and object of a sentence are the same person or thing, the object is a reflexive pronoun. The reflexive pronouns are as follows:

	singular					plural			sg./pl.
nom.	ich	du	er	es	sie	wir	ihr	sie	Sie
acc.	mich	dich				uns	euch	sich	**sich**
dat.	mir	dir		**sich**					

a. Many verbs can be used reflexively.

Ich habe (mir) ein Auto gekauft. *I bought (myself) a car.*

b. Other verbs must be used reflexively, even though their English counterparts are often not reflexive.

Ich habe mich erkältet. *I caught a cold.*

c. With parts of the body, German normally uses the definite article together with a reflexive pronoun in the dative.

Ich habe **mir die** Haare gewaschen. *I washed my hair.*

You are familiar with the following:

sich anhören, sich ansehen, sich anziehen, sich ausziehen, sich beeilen, sich duschen, sich erkälten, sich fit halten, sich (wohl) fühlen, sich kämmen, sich (hin)legen, sich (die Nase) putzen, sich rasieren, sich setzen, sich waschen, sich wünschen (see also 2 below)

2. Verbs with Prepositional Objects

Combinations of verbs and prepositions often have a special idiomatic meaning. These patterns cannot be translated literally but must be learned.

Er denkt an seine Reise. *He's thinking of his trip.*

You are familiar with the following:

denken an, erzählen von, halten von, schreiben an, sprechen über, warten auf, sich ärgern über, sich freuen auf, sich interessieren für, sich lustig machen über, träumen von

3. Infinitive with **zu**

The use of the infinitive in German is much like that in English.

Ich habe viel zu tun.	*I have a lot to do.*
Ich habe keine Zeit, eine Reise zu machen.	*I don't have time to take a trip.*

If the infinitive is combined with other sentence elements, a COMMA separates the infinitive phrase from the main clause. If a separable prefix is used, **zu** is inserted between the prefix and the verb.

Hast du Lust, heute nachmittag mitzukommen?

☞ *CAUTION:*

▶ *Don't use* **zu** *with modals! Ich will* **mitkommen.**

4. Summary of Past Tenses

☞ *REMINDER:*

▶ *Learn the principal parts of verbs! If you know that a verb is a regular t-verb, all its forms can be predicted; but the principal parts of irregular t-verbs and n-verbs must be memorized. You must also memorize those verbs that take* **sein** *as the perfect auxiliary.*

a. The Perfect Tense

■ *Past participles:*

t-verbs (weak verbs)	n-verbs (strong verbs)
(ge) + stem (change) + (e)t	(ge) + stem (change) + en
gekauft geheiratet gedacht	gestanden
eingekauft verkauft telefoniert	aufgestanden verstanden

■ *When used as auxiliaries in the* PRESENT PERFECT, **haben** *and* **sein** *are in the present tense. In the* PAST PERFECT, **haben** *and* **sein** *are in the simple past.*

Er **hat** eine Flugkarte gekauft.	Er **ist** nach Kanada geflogen.
Er **hatte** eine Flugkarte gekauft.	Er **war** nach Kanada geflogen.

■ *In conversation, past events are usually reported in the present perfect. (The modals,* **haben,** *and* **sein** *may be used in the simple past.) The past perfect is used to refer to events happening* BEFORE *other past events.*

Nachdem wir den Film gesehen hatten, haben wir eine Tasse Kaffee getrunken.

b. The Simple Past

- *Forms:*

	t-verbs (weak verbs)		n-verbs (strong verbs)	
ich		(e)te		—
du		(e)test		st
er	stem (change) +	(e)te	stem (change) +	—
wir		(e)ten		en
ihr		(e)tet		t
sie		(e)ten		en
	kaufte		stand	
	heiratete			
	dachte			
	kaufte ein		stand auf	
	verkaufte		verstand	
	telefonierte			

- *In writing, the simple past is used to describe past events. (However, in dialogues within narration the present perfect is correct.)*

5. Sentence Structure in the Past Tenses

Er **brachte** einen Freund.
Er **brachte** einen Freund **mit.**
Er **wollte**   einen Freund **mitbringen.**
Er **hat**   einen Freund **mitgebracht.**
Er **hatte**   einen Freund **mitgebracht.**
—   V1 ——————————— V2

. . ., weil er einen Freund **brachte.**
. . ., weil er einen Freund **mitbrachte.**
. . ., weil er einen Freund **mitbringen wollte.**
. . ., weil er einen Freund **mitgebracht hat.**
. . ., weil er einen Freund **mitgebracht hatte.**
——————————————— V2   V1

II. *The Conjunctions* als, wann, wenn

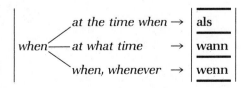

when		
at the time when →	als
at what time →	wann
when, whenever →	wenn

III. *Cases*

1. Genitive

a. Masculine and neuter nouns have endings in the genitive singular.

-es: for one-syllable words and words ending in **-s, -ß, -z, -tz,** and **-zt.**

des Kopfes, Halses, Fußes, Salzes, Platzes, Arztes *(physician's)*

-s: for nouns of more than one syllable and proper nouns.

des Bahnhofs, Lothars, Lothar Müllers

b. n-Nouns usually have no -(e)s ending but rather end in -(e)n. (Der Name, **-ns, -n** is an exception).

des Herr**n**, des Student**en**   BUT des Name**ns**

2. Summary of the Four Cases

a. Interrogative Pronouns

nom.	wer?	was?
acc.	wen?	was?
dat.	wem?	—
gen.	wessen?	—

b. Use of the Four Cases and Forms of **der-** and **ein-**Words

	use	follows . . .	masc.	neut.	fem.	pl.
nom.	Subject, Predicate noun	**heißen, sein, werden**	der dieser ein mein	das dieses ein	die diese eine	die diese keine meine
acc.	Direct object	**durch, für, gegen, ohne, um**	den diesen einen meinen	mein	meine	meine
	____	**an, auf, hinter, in, neben, über, unter, vor, zwischen**				
dat.	Indirect object	**aus, außer, bei, mit, nach, seit, von, zu**	dem diesem einem meinem	dem diesem einem meinem	der dieser einer meiner	den diesen keinen meinen
		antworten, danken, gefallen, gehören, helfen, zuhören				
gen.	Possessive	**statt, trotz, während, wegen**	des dieses eines meines	des dieses eines meines		der dieser keiner meiner

IV. Da- *and* wo-*Compounds*

Pronouns following prepositions refer to people; **da-** and **wo-**compounds refer to objects and ideas. Most accusative and dative prepositions, and all two-way prepositions, can be part of such compounds. Prepositions beginning with a vowel are preceded by **dar-** and **wor-**.

Er wartet auf einen Brief.
Er wartet **dar**auf. **Wor**auf wartet er?

V. *Adjective Endings*

1. Preceded Adjectives

Predicate adjectives and adverbs have no endings. However, adjectives followed by nouns do have endings.

a. In the nominative and accusative singular:

- *preceded by* **der, das, die,** *and* **eine:** **-e**
- *preceded by* **ein**⟨ *with masc. nouns:* **-er**
  with neut. nouns: **-es**

b. In all other cases (sg. masc. acc., all dat., gen., and pl.): **-en**

	masc.	neut.	fem.	pl.
nom.	-e / -er	-e	-e	
acc.		-es		
dat.	-en			
gen.				

Der alte Fernseher und das alte Radio sind kaputt.
Mein alter Fernseher und mein altes Radio sind kaputt.

2. Unpreceded Adjectives

a. Unpreceded adjectives have the endings that the definite article would have if it were used.

Kühler Wein und kaltes Bier schmecken bei heißem Wetter prima.

b. The following words are often used as unpreceded adjectives: **einig-, mehrer-,** and **viel** and **wenig** in the plural. Numerals, **ein paar,** and **viel** and **wenig** in the singular, have no endings.

Er hat einige interessante Geschichten und mehrere spannende Stücke geschrieben. Er hat auch viele langjährige Leser.

BUT Sie hat wirklich ein paar gute Ideen.
Sie hat viel Geld, aber wenig Zeit.

VI. *Sentence Structure*

1. Sequence of Adverbs

If two or more adverbs or adverbial phrases occur in one sentence, they usually follow the sequence time, manner, place. The negative **nicht** usually comes after adverbs of time but before adverbs of manner or place:

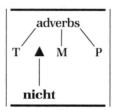

Er fährt morgens gern mit dem Wagen zur Arbeit.
Er fährt morgens **nicht** gern mit dem Wagen zur Arbeit.

2. Summary Chart

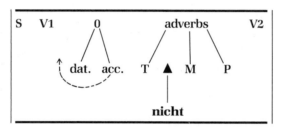

3. Time Expressions

- *Specific time*[1]

To refer to a definite point in time or length of time, German uses the accusative: **jeden Tag, nächstes Jahr, eine Woche, einen Monat.**

Other familiar phrases referring to specific time are:

a. gerade, am Abend, am 1. Mai, im Mai, in einer Viertelstunde, um zwei Uhr, von Juni bis September, vor einer Woche

b. vorgestern, gestern, heute, morgen, übermorgen, Montag, Dienstag, Mittwoch

c. früh (morgen), vormittag, mittag, nachmittag, abend, nacht

1 The words in group b can be combined with those in group c: vorgestern früh, Montag abend, etc.

- *Nonspecific time*

To refer to an indefinite point in time, the genitive is used: **eines Tages.** *Other familiar time expressions referring to nonspecific time are:*

montags, dienstags, mittwochs, morgens, mittags, abends, bald, manchmal, meistens, oft, stundenlang

WORTSCHATZWIEDERHOLUNG

A. Fragen

1. Welches Hauptwort *(noun)* kennen Sie dazu?
   anfangen, fahren, fliegen, schenken, sprechen, amerikanisch, deutsch, freundlich, glücklich, monatlich, musikalisch, sportlich, verliebt

2. Was ist ein Synonym dazu?

   BEISPIEL: **mit der Bahn = mit dem Zug**

   mit dem Auto, in 30 Minuten, in einer Viertelstunde, beginnen, laufen, telefonieren, schön

3. Was ist das Gegenteil davon?
   abfliegen, sich anziehen, aufhören, ausmachen, einsteigen, finden, gewinnen, weinen, böse, dick, dumm, furchtbar, gesund, glücklich, hübsch, jung, leicht, lustig, nett, nie, reich, sympathisch, verheiratet

4. Daten. Antworten Sie mündlich *(orally)*!

   BEISPIELE: Wann sind Sie geboren?   **Ich bin am 25. Mai 1969 geboren.**
   Wann wurde *(was)* Hesse   **Hesse wurde 1877 geboren.**
   geboren? (1877)

   a. Johann Sebastian Bach (1685)   d. Franz Liszt (1811)
   b. Johann Wolfgang von Goethe   e. Thomas Mann (1875)
   (1749)   f. Bertolt Brecht (1898)
   c. Friedrich Schiller (1759)   g. Friedrich Dürrenmatt (1921)

B. Welches Wort paßt nicht?

1. wandern—gewinnen—spazierengehen—laufen
2. häßlich—gemütlich—sympathisch—charmant
3. die Autorin—der Komponist—der Schauspieler—der Plattenspieler
4. die Tochter—der Sohn—der Nachbar—die Tante
5. täglich—wöchentlich—monatlich—gewöhnlich

C. Was kommt Ihnen dabei in den Sinn?

BEISPIEL: Koffer   **packen, Reise, Ferien, . . .**

Wunsch, Hochzeit, Plattenspieler, Zeitung, Fernsehpause, Hobby, Nase, Auge, Bauch

D. Bilden Sie eine Worttreppe. Wie weit kommen Sie in einer Minute?

BEISPIEL: charmant
                    treu
                         ungemütlich

STRUKTURWIEDERHOLUNG

E. *Reflexivverben*

1. Variieren Sie die Sätze!

   a. **Willi hält sich fit.**

   Do you *(formal)* keep fit? They're not keeping fit. How did she keep fit? Keep fit *(3 ×)*. I'd like to keep fit. We must keep fit. We had to keep fit.

   b. **Sie erkälten sich wieder.**

   We'll get a cold again. Don't catch a cold again *(3 ×)*. They've caught a cold again. She doesn't want to get a cold again. We had caught a cold again. Why do you *(sg. fam.)* always get a cold? They always caught a cold.

2. Auf deutsch, bitte!

   a. You've *(sg. fam.)* got to get dressed.
   b. First I want to take a shower and wash my hair.
   c. And you *(sg. fam.)* need to shave.
   d. Why don't you *(pl. fam.)* hurry up?
   e. Listen *(pl. fam.)* to that.
   f. He got annoyed and sat down.

F. *Verben mit Präpositionen. Bilden Sie Sätze!*

BEISPIEL: schreiben   **Ich muß an meine Eltern schreiben.**

denken, erzählen, sich freuen, sich interessieren, sich lustig machen, sprechen, träumen, warten

G. *Infinitiv mit zu. Bilden Sie Sätze!*

1. **Es ist zu spät . . .**
   in die Oper gehen, ein Geschenk kaufen, an ihn schreiben, mit dem Krimi anfangen, alle einladen

2. **Es ist nicht leicht . . .**
   so früh aufstehen, immer aufpassen, Zeit zum Sport finden, moderne Musik verstehen, einen Roman schreiben, eine Sprache lernen

H. *Sagen Sie es . . .!*

1. im Perfekt

   a. Wohin geht ihr?—Wir besuchen Onkel Erich.
   b. Was machst du heute?—Ich gehe schwimmen.
   c. Wie gefällt Ihnen der Film?—Er ist wirklich ausgezeichnet.
   d. Warum beeilt sie sich so?—Die Vorstellung fängt um acht an.
   e. Weißt du, daß er ein sehr guter Schwimmer ist?—Nein, er spricht nicht viel über sich.
   f. Wen ladet ihr ein?—Ein paar Mädchen und ein paar Freunde kommen.

2. im Plusquamperfekt *(past perfect)*

   a. wir / nicht / denken / daran
   b. Daniela und Yvonne / gehen / zum Trimm-dich-Pfad
   c. wir / sich anziehen / warm
   d. er / sich lustig machen / über uns
   e. Auto / kaputtgehen / plötzlich
   f. das / sein / nicht so lustig
   g. aber / das / verdienen / er

3. im Imperfekt

Sonja und Stephan gehen am Samstag abend aus. Zuerst versuchen sie, Opernkarten zu bekommen, aber alle Karten sind schon ausverkauft *(sold out)*. Dann wollen sie mit einem Taxi zum Theater fahren, aber sie können kein Taxi finden. Als sie zum Theater kommen, gibt es auch keine Karten mehr. Aber in der Nähe des Theaters ist ein Kino. Dort läuft ein neuer Film. Der Film gefällt ihnen prima, weil er sehr komisch ist. Die Zuschauer lachen oft so laut, daß man nichts hören kann. Als sie aus dem Kino kommen, sehen sie plötzlich Jürgen und Barbara. In einem kleinen Restaurant essen sie ein paar Würstchen und trinken dazu ein Glas Bier. Dann bummeln sie gemütlich durch die Stadt nach Hause.

Als, wann *oder* wenn?

1. _____ das Stück zu Ende war, klatschten die Leute.
2. Weißt du, _____ die Party anfängt?
3. Könnt ihr mir die Zeitschrift geben, _____ ihr damit fertig seid?
4. _____ ich den Roman vor zwei Jahren las, gefiel er mir nicht so gut.
5. Ich muß immer an euch denken, _____ ich dieses Lied im Radio höre.
6. Er wußte auch nicht, _____ seine Nachbarn zurückkommen sollten.

J. ***Der Genitiv. Verbinden Sie die zwei Wörter wie in den Beispielen!***

> **BEISPIELE:** der Sender / der Brief   **der Sender des Briefes**
> der Brief / Annette   **Annettes Brief**

1. das Ende / der Krimi
2. der Genitiv / der Satz
3. die Farbe / unser Auto
4. der Flughafen / diese Stadt
5. der Sohn / mein Onkel
6. der Eingang / euer Haus
7. der Name / der Komponist
8. der Anfang / der Name
9. der Wunsch / alle Kinder
10. die Taschen / manche Frauen
11. die Musik / Beethoven
12. das Stück / Bertolt Brecht
13. die Geschichten / Herr Keuner

K. **da-*Wörter* und wo-*Wörter***

1. Kombinieren Sie!

> **BEISPIEL:** mit   **damit / womit?**

durch, in, vor, zu, für, von, über, an, auf, bei

2. Was fehlt?

a. _____ denkst du? _____ Reise. *(of what, of my)*
b. _____ spricht Professor Schulz heute? _____ spannenden Roman. *(about what, about a)*
c. _____ macht er sich jetzt lustig? _____ uns. *(of whom, of)*
d. _____ hast du geträumt? _____ Ferien. *(about what, about my)*
e. _____ wartest du? _____ Brief von Paul. Warte nicht _____ ! *(for what, for a, for that)*
f. Trudi erzählt immer gern _____ Partys. _____ hat sie gerade erzählt. *(about her, about that)*
g. Hast du schon _____ Eltern geschrieben? Ja, ich habe am Wochenende _____ geschrieben. *(to your, to them)*
h. Er hat sich furchtbar _____ Brief geärgert, aber _____ ärgert er sich nicht? *(about the, about what)*
i. Interessiert Jürgen sich _____ Sport? Nein, _____ interessiert er sich nicht. *(in, in that)*

L. Was fehlt?

1. Vorgestern haben wir fast den ganz____ Abend vor unserem
neu____ Fernseher gesessen. *2.* Um 18.20 Uhr gab es einen interes-
sant____ Bericht *(report)* über das alt____ Frankfurt mit seinen
viel____ klein____ Gassen *(streets)* und hübsch____ Häusern, so wie
es einmal war, und was man in letzt____ Zeit damit gemacht hat.
3. Nach den kurz____ Nachrichten um 19.00 Uhr sahen wir eine inter-
national____ Show mit gut____ Musikgruppen aus verschieden____
Nachbarländern. *4.* Dazu gehörte auch ein toll____ Orchester und ein
groß____ Chor. *5.* Nach diesem nett____ Unterhaltungsprogramm
haben wir zum dritt____ Programm gewechselt und uns eine
komisch____ Oper von dem italienisch____ Komponisten Rossini
angesehen. *6.* Eine ausgezeichnet____ Vorstellung! *7.* Ein gut____
Fernseher ist etwas Schönes, denn man kann sich manche gut____
Sendung gemütlich____ zu Hause ansehen.

M. Wann *und* wie lange?

1. **Er fährt morgen.**

the day after tomorrow, after supper, Sundays, tomorrow morning, at
4:30, in 15 minutes, Monday morning, on Tuesday, in February, on
the weekend, in the evening, in the fall, most of the time, sometimes,
each year, now, never, one day

2. **Er bleibt zwei Tage.**

from March to May, until Wednesday, until Friday afternoon, until
10:45, for months, one day

HABE HEUTE NACHT
EINEN GANZEN TAG
GEWONNEN.

DB

IM SCHLAFWAGEN.

N. Erweitern Sie die Sätze! *(Expand the sentences by including the phrases in parentheses.)*

BEISPIEL: Renate geht zur Musikschule in Dresden. (seit ein paar Jahren)
Renate geht seit ein paar Jahren zur Musikschule in Dresden.

1. Ihre Eltern leben in der Nähe von Meißen. (schon lange)
2. Aber Renate wohnt in einem Schülerheim in Dresden. (mit vielen Mädchen)
3. Sie kann am Wochenende einfach schnell nach Hause fahren. (nicht)
4. Sie hat keine Zeit, jeden Tag mit der Bahn zu fahren. (stundenlang)
5. Dafür ist sie während der Ferien zu Hause. (gewöhnlich)
6. Ihre Schule soll leicht sein. (nicht)
7. Sie muß jeden Tag arbeiten. (schwer)
8. Sie spielt manchmal stundenlang Klavier. (mit ihrer Freundin)
9. Renate interessiert sich für klassische Musik. (besonders)
10. Wir haben uns letztes Jahr kennengelernt. (bei einem Musikwettbewerb in Weimar)
11. Ich möchte gern Klavier spielen. (mit ihr)
12. Aber junge Menschen wie sie dürfen nicht einfach kommen. (in den Westen)

AUFGABE

O. **Was fehlt?**

1. Gestern abend haben sie in d_____ zweit_____ Programm d_____ deutsch_____ Fernsehens d_____ bekannt_____ Film über d_____ österreichisch_____ Familie Trapp gespielt. *2.* Erst ist es ein_____ deutsch_____ Theaterstück gewesen, und dann ist daraus ein_____ amerikanisch_____ Film geworden. *3.* Eigentlich kannte ich dies_____ interessant_____ Film schon von d_____ amerikanisch_____ Kino. *4.* Aber ich sehe mir gern amerikanisch_____ Stücke in deutsch_____ Sprache an. *5.* D_____ ganz_____ Film spielt rings um d_____ hübsch_____ Stadt Salzburg. *6.* Am Anfang ist Maria in ein_____ alt_____ Kloster *(convent, n.)*, aber sie fühlt sich bei d_____ streng_____ *(strict)* Nonnen *(nuns, pl.)* nicht richtig_____ wohl. *7.* Eines Tages schickt d_____ verständnisvoll_____ Oberin *(mother superior)* sie zu d_____ groß_____ Familie ein_____ reich_____, verwitwet_____ *(widowed)* Kapitäns *(m.)*. *8.* Sein_____ sieben_____ klein_____ Kinder sind anfangs nicht gerade nett_____, aber d_____ temperamentvoll_____ Maria hat viel_____ gut_____ Ideen, womit sie die sieben Kinder unterhalten kann. *9.* Später heiratet d_____ verwitwet_____ Kapitän d_____ jung_____ Fräulein Maria. *10.* Kurz nach ihr_____ phantastisch_____ Hochzeit kommt d_____ deutsch_____ Militär *(n.)* nach Österreich. *11.* Weil d_____ österreich_____ Kapitän

Salzburg ist eine der schönsten Städte Europas. Hoch über der Stadt steht die alte Burg.

nicht zu d_____ deutsch_____ Marine *(f.)* will, verlassen *(leave)* sie nach kurz_____ Zeit ihr_____ schön_____ groß_____ Haus und fliehen *(escape)* über d_____ hoh_____ *(high)* Berge in d_____ neutral_____ Schweiz. **12.** Heute hat d_____ bekannt_____ Trappfamilie ein_____ neu_____, groß_____ Haus in d_____ amerikanisch_____ Staat Vermont. **13.** Wie in viel_____ der sogenannt_____ *(so-called)* wahr_____ *(true)* Geschichten, ist in d_____ amerikanisch_____ Film *The Sound of Music* nicht alles wahr_____ . **14.** Aber es ist ein_____ nett_____ Film mit viel_____ schön_____ Musik.

P. *Auf deutsch, bitte!*

1. Kurt, what are you thinking of?—My vacation. **2.** I'd like to hike in the mountains with Karl. **3.** I've written to him, and now I'm waiting for his letter. **4.** For that you can wait a long time. **5.** And when he says "yes," it doesn't mean much. *6.* Two years ago it was the same (**genauso**), *(pres. perf.).* *7.* When you had bought the tickets, suddenly he got ill. *8.* He had caught a cold again. *9.* If you like, I'll come along. *10.* Do you feel like hiking in the mountains?—I'd love to. *11.* When can we go?—On the first day of the vacation. *12.* How are we going?—By train. *13.* Where will we spend the nights?—In inexpensive youth hostels. *14.* Can you bring along your father's camera (**die Kamera**)? *15.* No, his camera is too expensive; it can break. *16.* Maybe I'll take along Susi's camera. Her camera is good, too.

GESPRÄCHE

Weißt du, was du werden willst?

TRUDI Sag mal Fränzi, weißt du schon, was du werden willst?

FRANZISKA Ja, Tischlerin[1].

TRUDI Ist das nicht sehr anstrengend?

FRANZISKA Ach, daran gewöhnt man sich. Vielleicht mache ich mich eines Tages selbständig.

TRUDI Du hast ja große Pläne!

FRANZISKA Warum nicht? Ich habe keine Lust, immer nur im Büro zu sitzen und für andere Leute zu arbeiten.

TRUDI Glaubst du, du bekommst eine Lehrstelle[2]?

FRANZISKA Ja, meine Tante hat ihre eigene Firma[3]. Sie hat mir schon einen Platz angeboten.

TRUDI Da hast du aber Glück![4]

FRANZISKA Und wie ist es denn mit dir? Weißt du, was du machen willst?

TRUDI Vielleicht werde ich Zahnärztin. Gute Zahnärzte braucht man immer, und außerdem verdient man gut.

FRANZISKA Da mußt du aber lange studieren.

TRUDI Ich weiß, aber ohne das geht's nicht.

ÜBRIGENS

1. **Glaser, Dachdecker** *(roofer),* **Elektriker** *(electrician),* **Maler** *(painter),* **Maurer** *(brick layer),* **Mechaniker, Tischler** *(carpenter):* these are just a few of the many trades. **"Das Handwerk hat goldenen Boden"** *("Trade has a golden foundation")* says an old proverb, and that is still very true today.

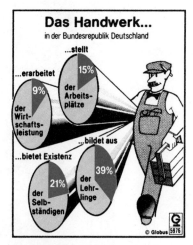

Goldener Boden

2. Training through **Lehrstellen** *(apprenticeships)* is widespread in commerce, trade, and industry, and has a long tradition dating back to the Middle Ages, when apprentices served for three years under one **Meister**, or several, in order to learn a trade. By combining practical training with several days of schooling per week, industry still maintains a well-trained work force and high quality in its products.

3. In the GDR over 90 percent of the women work. It's not only an economic necessity but also their legal right and duty. In the FRG roughly half of the women now work, not only for personal fulfillment but also to supplement the family budget. More and more women are entering professions, politics, and the management positions traditionally dominated by men.

4. In the 1980s, the FRG, Austria, and Switzerland have had their highest unemployment rates since World War II owing to a worldwide recession, rapid technological changes, and too many university graduates in such fields as teaching. The generous social benefits implemented in better times have severely strained government budgets.

Do You Know What You Want to Be?

TRUDI   Say, Fränzi, do you know yet what you want to be?

FRANZISKA   Yes, a carpenter.

TRUDI   Isn't that very strenuous?

FRANZISKA   Oh, you get used to it. Perhaps someday I'll become self-employed.

TRUDI   You have big plans.

FRANZISKA   Why not? I don't feel like always sitting in an office and working for other people.

TRUDI   Do you think you can get an apprenticeship?

FRANZISKA   Yes, my aunt has her own business. She's already offered me a place (as an apprentice).

TRUDI   Boy, are you lucky!

FRANZISKA   And how about you? Do you know what you want to do?

TRUDI   Perhaps I'll be a dentist. Good dentists are always needed and, besides, it pays well.

FRANZISKA   But then you have to study for a long time.

TRUDI   I know, but you can't do it otherwise.

Beruf und Arbeit   WORTSCHATZ I

DER BERUF, -E *profession*

der Arzt, ⸚e	*physician*
Beamte, -n (ein Beamter)[1]	*civil servant*
Geschäftsmann, -leute	*businessman*
Ingenieur, -e[2]	*engineer*
Journalist, -en, -en	*journalist*
Lehrer, -	*teacher*
Polizist, -en, -en	*policeman*

der Rechtsanwalt, ⸚e	lawyer
Verkäufer, -	salesman
Wissenschaftler, -	scientist
Zahnarzt, ⸚e	dentist
die Geschäftsfrau, -en	businesswoman
Hausfrau, -en	housewife
Krankenschwester, -n	nurse
Sekretärin, -nen	secretary

DIE ARBEIT *work*

DIE STELLE, -N *job, position, place*

der Arbeiter, -	(blue-collar) worker	anstrengend	strenuous
Haushalt	household	eigen-	own
Plan, ⸚e	plan	gleich	equal, same
das Büro, -s	office	hoch (hoh-)[4]	high
Einkommen	income	selbständig	self-employed,
Geschäft, -e	business		independent
Leben[3]	life	sicher	safe, secure
die Ausbildung	training, education		
Firma, Firmen	company, business		
Zukunft	future		

WEITERES

sich gewöhnen an (+ acc.)	to get used to
glauben (an + acc.)	to believe (in); think
verdienen	to earn, make money
Ich will . . . werden.	I want to be a(n) . . .
Was willst du werden?	What do you want to be?

1 See "Struktur" III in this chapter, p. 355.
2 In most cases the feminine forms can be derived by adding **-in: der Ingenieur** > **die Ingenieurin.** Some require an umlaut in the feminine form: **der Rechtsanwalt** > **die Rechtsanwältin, der (Zahn)arzt** > **die (Zahn)ärztin.**
3 In German **Leben** is used only in the singular: **ihr Leben** > *their lives.*
4 **hoh-** is the adjective, **hoch** is the predicate adjective and adverb.

PASSIVES VOKABULAR

der Angestellte, -n (ein Angestellter) *(employee, clerk)*; Apotheker, -; Dirigent, -en, -en *(music conductor)*; Elektriker, -; Künstler, - *(artist)*; Landwirt, -e *(farmer)*; Makler, - *(real-estate agent)*; Mechaniker, -; Pfarrer, - *(minister)*; Pilot, -en, -en; Professor, -en; Programmierer, -; Schriftsteller, - *(writer)*; Techniker, -; Tischler, - *(carpenter)*
die Lehrstelle, -n *(apprenticeship)*; anbieten, bot an, angeboten *(to offer)*

ZUM THEMA

A. Was sagen Sie:?

  x Weißt du schon, was du werden willst?
  y Ich werde _____ .
  x Und warum?

Notar

Friedrich Trüe
Rolf Müller-Blom

Rechtsanwälte

Y _____ . Und wie ist es denn mit dir?
Weißt du, was du machen willst?

X _____ .

Y Ist das nicht sehr _____ ?

X _____ .

**Karl-Heinz Lehmann
Rechtsanwalt**

**Elisabeth Landgraf
Rechtsanwältin**

B. *Was bin ich?*

1. In meinem Beruf habe ich es mit vielen jungen Menschen zu tun.
Viele denken, daß mein Beruf leicht ist, weil ich so viele Ferien habe.
Aber mein Beruf ist manchmal sehr anstrengend. Meine Arbeit geht
zu Hause weiter, weil ich viel lesen und korrigieren *(correct)* muß.
Was bin ich?

2. Viele Leute kommen zu mir nur, wenn ihnen etwas weh tut. Meistens
kommen sie nicht gern, weil sie denken, daß ich ihnen noch mehr
weh tue. Aber da haben sie unrecht. Sie kommen mit Schmerzen,
setzen sich in meinen gemütlichen Stuhl, öffnen ihren Mund und
bald sind die Schmerzen weg *(gone)*. Was bin ich?

3. Ich bin viel unterwegs. Wenn es eine Katastrophe oder etwas
Besonderes gibt, bin ich da. Ich spreche mit Politikern,
Wissenschaftlern, Rechtsanwälten, Polizisten, Menschen aus allen
Berufen, mit den Leuten auf der Straße. Ich hoffe *(hope)*, daß Sie
dann meine Artikel in der Zeitung oder in einer Zeitschrift lesen. Was
bin ich?

4. Ich bin Mädchen für alles, Putzfrau, Köchin *(cook)*, Lehrerin,
Beraterin *(counselor)*, Sekretärin und Chauffeur. Meine Arbeit hat kein
Ende, sie fängt immer wieder neu an. Dabei verdiene ich nichts, nur
ab und zu ein *Danke schön*. Was bin ich?

5. Schreiben Sie Ihr eigenes **Was bin ich?,** und lassen Sie die anderen
raten *(guess)*, was Sie sind!

C. *Zu welchem Arzt / welcher Ärztin geht man?*

1. Wenn man Zahnschmerzen hat, geht man zu . . .
2. Wenn man schlechte Augen hat, geht man zu . . .
3. Mit kranken Kindern geht man zu . . .
4. Wenn man Hals-, Nasen- oder Ohrenprobleme hat, geht man zu . . .
5. Frauen gehen zu . . .

1. Was ist die feminine Form von Journalist? Lehrer? Polizist? Arzt? Wissenschaftler? Ingenieur? Rechtsanwalt? Verkäufer? Beamter? Geschäftsmann?
2. Wo arbeitet die Verkäuferin? der Bäcker? der Fleischer (oder auch Metzger)? der Apotheker? die Lehrerin? die Ärztin? die Beamtin? die Krankenschwester? die Stewardeß? der Pfarrer?
3. Was macht eine Journalistin? eine Hausfrau? ein Hausmakler? ein Komponist? ein Autor? ein Schauspieler? ein Ober?

Der Computer kann ein guter Lehrer sein.

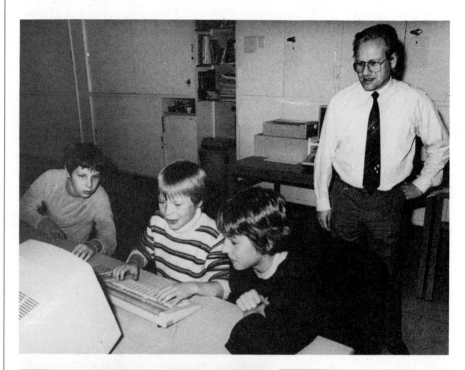

Staatsanwältin (public prosecutor) in Köln. Es gibt schon einige wenige Frauen in höheren Stellen im öffentlichen Dienst (public service).

E. *Was sind das für Berufe? Sagen Sie's auf englisch, und erklären Sie (explain) dann auf deutsch, was diese Leute tun!*

Zahntechniker/in

Uhrmacher (Meister)

Gebrauchtwagenverkäufer Putzfrau

Fernfahrer Koch

Bankangestellter **Chemie-Laboranten(innen)**

Damen- und Herrenfriseur **Telefonistin** Sozialpädagogin

Phonotypistinnen **Arztsekretärin**

Industriekaufmann

Rechtsanwaltsgehilfin

Diplom-Ingenieur Krankengymnast(in)

REISELEITER/-INNEN **Systemberater(in)** **Repräsentanten** Bäcker

Haushälterin Zahnarzthelferin

Kassiererin *Buchhalter/in* PSYCHOLOGE/IN

Fremdsprachenkorrespondentin

F. *Ein interessanter Beruf*

1. *Was ist Ihnen im Beruf wichtig? (Poll each other as to the sequence of importance of the points below; then report to the class.)*

- ☐ interessante Arbeit
- ☐ ruhige Arbeit
- ☐ saubere Arbeit
- ☐ hohes Einkommen
- ☐ viel Prestige
- ☐ viel Reisen
- ☐ viel Freizeit
- ☐ viel Fahrerei *(driving)*
- ☐ viel Papierkrieg *(paper work)*

- ☐ Sicherheit *(security)*
- ☐ Selbständigkeit *(independence)*
- ☐ Verantwortung *(responsibility)*
- ☐ Gleichberechtigung *(equality)*
- ☐ Abwechslung *(variety)*
- ☐ Aufgabe *(challenge)*
- ☐ Risiken *(risks)*
- ☐ nette Kollegen
- ☐ ein Geschäftsauto

2. *In welchen Berufen finden Sie das? (Tell which professions best meet the criteria mentioned above and which would be least attractive to you. Support your statements.)*

G. *Aussprache (See also III. 3 in the pronunciation section of the Appendix.)*

1. [p] A**b**fahrt, A**b**sender, O**b**st, Her**b**st, Er**b**se, hü**b**sch, o**b**, hal**b**, gel**b**
BUT [p / b] verlie**b**t / verlie**b**en; blei**b**t / blei**b**en; ha**b**t / ha**b**en

2. [t] un**d**, gesun**d**, spannen**d**, anstrengen**d**, Gel**d**, Han**d**, währen**d**, sin**d**, sei**d**, aben**d**s
BUT [t / d] Freun**d** / Freun**d**e; Ba**d** / Bä**d**er; Kin**d** / Kin**d**er; wir**d** / wer**d**en

3. [k] mitta**g**s, unterwe**g**s, Ta**g**, Zu**g**, We**g**, Bahnstei**g**, Flu**g**zeug, Ber**g**
BUT [k / g] fra**g**st / fra**g**en; flie**g**st / flie**g**en; trä**g**st / tra**g**en; le**g**st / le**g**en

STRUKTUR

I. *The Comparison of Adjectives and Adverbs*

In English and German adjectives have three forms:

POSITIVE	COMPARATIVE	SUPERLATIVE
cheap	*cheaper*	*cheapest*
expensive	*more expensive*	*most expensive*

Whereas there are two ways to form the comparative and the superlative in English, there is only ONE WAY in German; it corresponds to the forms of *cheap* above.

☛ *CAUTION:*

▶ *In German there is no equivalent to such forms as* more *and* most expensive.

1. In the COMPARATIVE adjectives add **-er**; in the SUPERLATIVE they add **-(e)st**.

billig	billig**er**	billig**st**-

a. Some one-syllable adjectives with the stem vowel **a**, **o**, or **u** have an umlaut in the comparative and superlative.

warm   wärmer   wärmst-
jung   jünger   jüngst-

Other adjectives that take an umlaut include:

alt, arm, kalt, krank, lang, nah, schwarz, groß, rot, dumm, gesund, kurz.

If an adjective has an umlaut in the comparative or superlative, it is shown in the end vocabulary as follows: **warm** (ä), **jung** (ü), **groß** (ö).

b. Most adjectives ending in **-d** or **-t**, in an **s**-sound, or in vowels add **-est** in the superlative.

kalt   kälter   kält**est**-
heiß   heißer   heiß**est**-
neu   neuer   neu**est**-

Adjectives that follow this pattern include:

alt (ä), bekannt, charmant, gesund (ü), intelligent, interessant, laut, leicht, nett, oft (ö), rot (ö), schlecht, talentiert, verrückt; hübsch, weiß, kurz (ü), schwarz (ä), stolz; frei

c. A few adjectives and adverbs have irregular forms in the comparative and / or superlative.

gern	**lieber**	**liebst-**
groß	**größer**	**größt-**
gut	**besser**	**best-**
hoch (hoh-)	**höher**	**höchst-**
nah	**näher**	**nächst-**
viel	**mehr**	**meist-**

2. The comparative of PREDICATE ADJECTIVES (after **sein, werden** and **bleiben**) and of ADVERBS is formed as described above. The superlative is preceded by **am** and ends in **-sten**.

billig	billiger	am billigsten

Die Wurst ist billig.
Der Käse ist **billiger**.
Das Brot ist **am billigsten**.

Ich fahre **gern** mit dem Bus.	*I like to go by bus.*
Ich fahre **lieber** mit dem Fahrrad.	*I prefer to go by bike.*
	I'd rather go by bike.
Ich gehe **am liebsten** zu Fuß.	*I like best to walk.*
	Best of all I like to walk.

☞ *CAUTION:*

Die meisten Leute gehen gern spazieren.	***Most** people love to walk.*
Mein Vater geht **am meisten** spazieren.	*My father walks **the most**.*
Meistens geht er in den Park.	*He goes **mostly** to the park.*

3. Adjectives in the comparative and superlative forms that describe nouns (e.g., *the better wine*) have the same endings as preceded and unpreceded adjectives in the positive forms (see Chapters 9 and 10).

der gut**e** Wein	der besser**e** Wein	der best**e** Wein
Ihr gut**er** Wein	Ihr besser**er** Wein	Ihr best**er** Wein
gut**er** Wein	besser**er** Wein	best**er** Wein

Haben Sie keinen besseren Wein? Doch, aber besserer Wein ist teuerer.

4. There are four special phrases frequently used in comparisons.

■ *When you want to say that one thing is like another, use* (**genau**)**so . . . wie . . .**

Ich bin (**genau**)**so alt wie** du.   *I'm (just) as old as you are.*

■ *If you want to bring out a difference, use the **comparative** + als . . .*

Helga ist **älter als** ich.   *Helga is older than I am.*

■ *If you want to express that something is getting continually more so, use* **immer** + *the comparative.*

Die Tage werden **immer länger**. *The days are getting longer and longer.*

- *If you are dealing with a pair of comparatives, use* **je + comparative + desto + comparative**.

Je länger, **desto** besser.	*The longer the better.*
Je früher du kommst, **desto** besser ist es für uns.[1]	*The earlier you come, the better it is for us.*

1 Note that **je** is followed by dependent word order, while **desto** is a coordinating conjunction.

ÜBUNGEN

A. *Geben Sie den Komparativ und den Superlativ, und dann die Formen des Gegenteils!*

BEISPIELE: **schnell, schneller, am schnellsten**
langsam, langsamer, am langsamsten

billig, sauber, gesund, groß, gut, hübsch, intelligent, jung, kalt, lang, laut, nah, neu, viel

B. *Ersetzen Sie die Adjektive!*

BEISPIEL: Diese Zeitschrift ist so langweilig wie die andere Zeitschrift. (interessant)
Diese Zeitschrift ist so interessant wie die andere Zeitschrift.

1. Axel ist so groß wie Horst. (alt, nett)
2. Hier ist es kühler als bei euch. (kalt, heiß)
3. Fernsehsendungen werden immer langweiliger. (verrückt, dumm)
4. Je länger das Buch ist, desto besser. (spannend, interessant)

C. *Antworten Sie mit* **nein!** *(Use the new adjective or adverb in your response, as shown in the example.)*

BEISPIEL: Ist dein Großvater auch so alt? (jung)   **Nein, er ist jünger.**

1. Waren euere Schuhe auch so schmutzig? (sauber)
2. Verdient Jutta auch so wenig? (viel).
3. Ist seine Wohnung auch so toll? (einfach)
4. Sind die Geschäftsleute dort auch so unfreundlich? (freundlich)
5. Ist es bei Ihnen auch so laut? (ruhig)
6. Ist die Schule auch so weit weg? (nah)
7. Ist Ihre Arbeit auch so angstrengend? (einfach)

D. Wie geht's weiter? *(Complete each sentence, first with a comparative and then with a superlative.)*

BEISPIEL: Inge spricht schnell, aber . . .   **Maria spricht schneller.**
Peter spricht am schnellsten.

1. Willi hat lange geschlafen, aber . . .
2. Brot zum Frühstück schmeckt gut, aber . . .
3. Ich trinke morgens gern Tee, aber . . .
4. Die Montagszeitung ist dick, aber . . .
5. Ich spreche viel am Telefon, aber . . .
6. Deutsch ist schwer, aber . . .
7. Hier ist es schön, aber . . .

E. Ersetzen Sie die Adjektive!

BEISPIEL: Peter ist der sportlichste Junge. (talentiert)
Peter ist der talentierteste Junge.

1. Da drüben ist ein moderneres Geschäft. (gut)
2. Mein jüngster Bruder ist nicht verheiratet. (alt)
3. Das ist die größte Nachricht. (neu)
4. Zieh dir einen wärmeren Pullover an! (dick)
5. Die besten Autos sind sehr teuer. (viel)

F. Wie ist es in anderen Berufen? *(Complete each sentence with a superlative. Add two sentences of your own.)*

BEISPIEL: Professoren haben viel Prestige, aber . . .   **Ärzte haben das meiste Prestige.**

1. Elektriker haben ein hohes Einkommen, aber . . .
2. Beamte haben große Sicherheit, aber . . .
3. Rechtsanwälte haben viel Papierkrieg *(m.)*, aber . . .
4. _____, aber . . .
5. _____, aber . . .

G. Was fehlt?

1. Möchtest du nicht _____ Postbeamter werden? *(rather)*
2. Der Staat bezahlt _____ deine Firma. *(better than)*
3. Da hast du _____ Sicherheit *(f.)*. *(the greatest)*
4. Bei der Post hast du _____ Freizeit _____ bei deiner Firma. *(just as much ... as)*
5. Vielleicht hast du sogar _____ Zeit _____ jetzt. *(more ... than)*
6. Es ist auch nicht _____ anstrengend _____ jetzt. *(as ... as)*
7. _____ Leute arbeiten für den Staat. *(more and more)*
8. _____ Leuten gefällt es. *(most)*
9. Ich finde es bei der Post _____ und _____ . *(the most interesting; the safest)*
10. Eine _____ Stelle gibt es nicht. *(nicer)*
11. _____ du wirst, _____ ist es zu wechseln. *(the older ... the harder)*
12. Wenn du eine _____ Stelle haben willst, dann wechsele bald! _____ früher, _____ besser. *(better; the ... the)*
13. Beamter ist für mich _____ Beruf. *(the most beautiful)*
14. Vielleicht verdienst du etwas _____ . *(less)*
15. Aber dafür hast du _____ _____ Probleme *(pl.)*. *(mostly, few)*

H. Interviews. Fragen Sie Ihren Nachbarn/Ihre Nachbarin, . . .! *(Then report to the class.)*

1. ob er/sie größer als die Eltern oder Großeltern ist
2. ob er/sie jüngere Brüder oder Schwestern hat und wer am jüngsten und ältesten ist
3. was er/sie am liebsten ißt und trinkt und ob er/sie abends meistens warm oder kalt ißt
4. wo er/sie am liebsten essen geht und wo es am billigsten und am teuersten ist
5. welche Fernsehsendung ihm/ihr am besten gefällt und was er/sie am meisten sieht
6. was er/sie am liebsten in der Freizeit macht und was er/sie am nächsten Wochenende tut
7. welche amerikanische Stadt er/sie am schönsten und am häßlichsten findet und warum
8. wo er/sie jetzt am liebsten sein möchte und warum

II. *The Future*

As you know, future events are often referred to in the present tense in both English and German, particularly when a time expression points to the future.

Wir **gehen** heute abend ins Kino. $\begin{cases} \textit{We're going to the movies tonight.} \\ \textit{We will go to the movies tonight.} \\ \textit{We shall go to the movies tonight.} \end{cases}$

In German conversation this is the preferred form. However, German does have a future tense. It is used when there is no time expression and under somewhat formal circumstances.

1. The FUTURE consists of **werden** as the auxiliary plus the infinitive of the verb:

werden . . . + infinitive

ich **werde** . . . **gehen**	wir **werden** . . . gehen
du **wirst** . . . gehen	ihr **werdet** . . . gehen
er **wird** . . . gehen	sie **werden** . . . gehen

Wirst du ins Büro **gehen**? *Will you go to the office?*
Ich **werde** ihn **anrufen**.   *I'll call him.*

2. If the future sentence also contains a modal, the modal appears as an infinitive at the very end.

werden . . . + verb infinitive + modal infinitive

Wirst du ins Büro **gehen müssen**?   *Will you have to go to the office?*
Ich **werde** ihn **anrufen müssen**.   *I will have to call him.*

3. Sentences in the future follow familiar word-order rules.

Er **wird** auch **kommen**.
Er **wird** auch **mitkommen**.
Er **wird** auch **mitkommen wollen**.
— V1 —— V2

Ich weiß, daß er auch **kommen wird**.
Ich weiß, daß er auch **mitkommen wird**.
—————— V2   V1

4. The future form can also express PRESENT PROBABILITY when used with the word **wohl**.

Er wird **wohl** auf dem Weg sein.   *He is probably on the way (now).*
Sie wird **wohl** krank sein.   *She is probably sick (now).*

☞ *CAUTION:*

▶ *Don't confuse the modal* **wollen** *with the future auxiliary* **werden**.

Er **will** auch mitkommen.   *He wants to come along, too.*
                                   He intends to come along, too.
Er **wird** auch mitkommen.   *He will come along, too.*

▪ *Remember that* **werden** *is also a full verb in itself, meaning* to get, to become.

Es wird kalt.   *It's getting cold.*
Er wird Journalist.   *He's going to be a journalist.*

ÜBUNGEN

I. *Sagen Sie die Sätze in der Zukunft!*

    BEISPIEL: Gute Zahnärzte braucht man immer.
                Gute Zahnärzte wird man immer brauchen.

1. Dabei verdiene ich auch gut.
2. Aber du studierst einige Jahre auf der Universität.
3. Ich gehe nicht zur Uni.
4. Meine Tischlerarbeit ist anstrengend.
5. Aber daran gewöhnst du dich.
6. Fängst du bei deiner Tante an?
7. Dieser Beruf hat bestimmt Zukunft.
8. Ihr seht das schon.
9. Eines Tages mache ich mich selbständig.
10. Als Chefin *(boss)* in einem Männerberuf muß ich besonders gut sein.
11. Das darfst du nicht vergessen.
12. Aber ich kann vielen Leuten helfen.
13. Es macht mir Spaß.

J. *Beginnen Sie jeden Satz mit* Wissen Sie, ob . . .?

    BEISPIEL: Er wird bald zurückkommen.
                Wissen Sie, ob er bald zurückkommen wird?

1. Wir werden in Frankfurt umsteigen.
2. Sie wird sich die Sendung ansehen.
3. Zimmermanns werden die Wohnung mieten.
4. Willi und Eva werden bald heiraten.
5. Müllers werden in Zürich bleiben.
6. Wir werden fahren oder fliegen.

Viele Menschen haben Angst vor der Radioaktivität. (Strahlend heißt normalerweise shiny, *hier aber* full of radiation).

strahlende

Zukunft?

K. Was bedeutet das auf englisch?

BEISPIEL: Martina wird Journalistin.   **Martina is going to be a journalist.**

1. Walter will Polizist werden.
2. Die Kinder werden zu laut.
3. Ich werde am Bahnhof auf Sie warten.
4. Petra wird wohl nicht kommen.
5. Wir werden Sie gern mitnehmen.
6. Sie wird Informatik studieren wollen.
7. Oskar wird wohl noch im Büro sein.
8. Wirst du wirklich Lehrer?

L. Auf deutsch, bitte!

1. Children, I want to tell you something. 2. Your mother is going to be a lawyer. 3. I'll have to stay home. 4. I'll (do the) cook(ing). 5. Helga, you will (do the) wash(ing). 6. Karl and Maria, you will (do the) clean(ing). 7. We'll (do the) shop(ping) together. 8. We'll have to work hard. 9. But we'll get used to it. 10. When we get tired, we'll take a break (eine **Pause machen**). 11. Your mother will make a lot of money (earn well). 12. And we will help her.

III. Nouns with Special Features

1. As you already know, German, unlike English, does NOT use the indefinite article before predicate nouns denoting professions, nationalities, religious preference, or political adherence:

Er ist **Amerikaner**.   *He is an American.*
Sie ist **Rechtsanwältin**.   *She's a lawyer.*

However, when an adjective precedes that noun, **ein** is used.

Er ist **ein** typischer Amerikaner.   *He's a typical American.*
Sie ist **eine** gute Rechtsanwältin.   *She's a good lawyer.*

2. German has a few nouns that are derived from adjectives and therefore change their endings with the preceding article and case.

	singular		plural
	masc.	**fem.**	
nom.	der Deutsche ein Deutscher	die Deutsche	die Deutschen
acc.	den Deutschen einen Deutschen	eine Deutsche	keine Deutschen
dat.	dem Deutschen einem Deutschen	der Deutschen einer Deutschen	den Deutschen keinen Deutschen
gen.	des Deutschen eines Deutschen	der Deutschen einer Deutschen	der Deutschen keiner Deutschen

Also: der Beamte (ein Beamter)   BUT die Beamtin (eine Beamtin)

Karl ist Beamter, und seine Frau ist Beamtin.
Ein Beamter hat das gesagt. Wie heißt der Beamte?
Hast du den Beamten da drüben gefragt? Ich sehe keinen Beamten.

ÜBUNGEN

M. Auf deutsch, bitte!

1. He's a composer.
2. Is she a housewife?
3. She's a very good scientist.
4. He's going to be a policeman.
5. He was a bad teacher but a good car salesman.
6. She is Austrian.

N. Was fehlt?

1. Ein Deutsch_____ hat mir das erzählt.
2. Hast du den nett_____ Deutsch_____ kennengelernt?
3. Geben Sie dem Beamt_____ die Papiere!
4. Auch viele Deutsch_____ sind heute ohne Arbeit.
5. Der Deutsch_____ ist Journalist.
6. Zeigen Sie den Deutsch_____ die Büros!
7. Was hat der Beamt_____ Ihnen gesagt?
8. In Deutschland verdient ein Beamt_____ sehr gut.

ZUSAMMENFASSUNG

O. Ich möchte . . . werden. *(Write eight to ten sentences explaining what you want to be and why.)*

P. Auf deutsch, bitte!

1. Did you *(pl. fam.)* know that Volker wants to become a journalist? *2.* He doesn't want to be a teacher. *3.* There are only a few teaching positions (**Lehrerstellen**). *4.* I've gotten used to it. *5.* Trudi is as enterprising as he is. *6.* She was my most talented student (**Schülerin**). *7.* If she wants to become a dentist, she will become a dentist. *8.* She's smarter, more independent, and more likable than her brother. *9.* She says she will work hard. *10.* I know that she'll be self-employed one day. *11.* I'll go to her rather than to another dentist. *12.* The more I think of it, the better I like the idea.

Since 1976, according to the Basic Law of the Federal Republic, women have equal rights with men. The clause that women could work only if it was compatible with their obligations toward marriage and family was eliminated at that time. Today a couple can work out their own arrangement; they can also choose either the husband's or the wife's name, or both, at marriage. Women now have equal access to schools, universities, and other training facilities, and there has been a steady increase in the percentage of women completing university studies or job training. However, men are still better paid, and women tend to work in areas that are undervalued and therefore pay less. Although German women won full voting rights in 1918, the number of women at the upper levels of business, government, and politics is still very small. In recent years there have been clear signs that women as well as men are changing their attitudes about their roles; eventually, full equality may be achieved.

EINBLICKE

die Erde	earth
Erfindung, -en	invention
Gefahr, -en	danger
Welt	world
darum	therefore
breit	broad; wide
früher	earlier; formerly
verantwortungsvoll	responsible
so daß	so that (subord. conj.)
Angst haben (vor + *dat.*)	to be afraid (of)
hoffen	to hope
teilen	to share
sich vor·stellen	to imagine
Ich stelle mir vor, daß . . .	I imagine that . . .
Ich stelle mir das schwer vor.	I imagine that's hard.
wachsen (wächst), wuchs, ist gewachsen	to grow

WAS IST DAS? der Biochemiker, Elektromechaniker, Heimcomputer, Leserbrief, Roboter; das Arsenal, Geschäftsleben; zum Guten; die Arbeitslosigkeit, Flexibilität, Größe, Qualifikation, Sicherheit, Spezialisierung; arbeitslos, computerisiert, halbtags, klar, kreativ, problematisch, proportional, total, zukunftssicher; dominieren, integrieren, lehren

---

(Leserbriefe über das Jahr 2000)

Was wird werden?

Im Jahr 2000 werden die Kinder nur einen Teil des Jahres zur Schule gehen müssen. Sie werden durch Fernseher und Heimcomputer lernen. In der Schule wird es ein Extrafach° geben: „Was mache ich mit meiner Freizeit?" Vielleicht 5 werden die meisten dann auch Brillen° tragen, weil man stundenlang am Computer sitzen wird.

Schüler

Ich stelle mir vor, daß in der Zukunft der Haushalt viel einfacher sein wird. Alles wird praktischer sein. Weniger Frauen werden nur Hausfrau 10 sein, weil mit Mikroofen, anderen Maschinen und mit computerisierter Buchführung° alles viel schneller gehen wird. Damit gewinnt die Hausfrau Zeit fürs Familienleben und Arbeit außerhalb° des Hauses. Ich hoffe nur, daß der Computer die Familie nicht zu sehr dominieren wird. Ich hasse° jetzt schon die Videospiele, wo man zusammen ist und doch nichts von- 15 einander° hat.

Hausfrau

extra subject
glasses

bookkeeping
outside
hate

each other

Ich hoffe, daß die Frauen den Männern im Jahr 2000 nicht nur gesetz-lich° gleich sind, sondern auch im wirklichen Leben; daß Frauen dann an den Universitäten nicht nur studieren, sondern auch lehren werden; daß 20 sie im Geschäftsleben und im öffentlichen Dienst° in höheren Stellen sein werden, und daß sie für gleiche Arbeit gleiches Einkommen bekommen werden. Die Rollen der Männer und Frauen sind heute nicht mehr so klar getrennt° wie früher; aber es wird bestimmt noch Jahre dauern, bis nie-mand es mehr° komisch findet, wenn der Mann zu Hause bleibt und auf 25 die Kinder aufpaßt und die Frau das Geld verdient. Ich hoffe, daß es dann auch leichter sein wird, halbtags zu arbeiten oder eine Stelle zu teilen, so daß Arbeit und Familie für Mann und Frau leichter zu integrieren sind.

Studentin

Ich glaube, daß Computer und Roboter unsere Zukunft total verändern° 30 werden. Es wird nicht mehr ohne sie gehen. Manche glauben, daß das die Menschen arbeitslos und die Arbeitsplätze menschenfeindlich° machen wird. Aber das glaube ich nicht. Im Gegenteil, das wird mehr Flexibilität bringen, mehr Freizeit und mehr Reisen. Wegen der Benzinknappheit° wird man aber neue Energiequellen° finden müssen. Vielleicht werden die Autos 35 eines Tages elektrisch oder mit Wasserstoff° fahren. Vielleicht ist Atomkraft° die Antwort, aber nur, wenn wir eine Möglichkeit finden, den Atommüll° loszuwerden°, sonst° Gute Nacht!

Automechaniker

Ganz klar, die Berufswahl° wird immer problematischer. Sicher werden 40 viele wenigstens° einmal Ihren Beruf wechseln müssen. Darum wird eine breite Ausbildung wichtiger sein als eine Spezialisierung. Neben guten Fach- und Sprachkenntnissen° wird man andere Qualifikationen suchen, z.B. die Fähigkeit°, dazu zu lernen, kreativ zu denken und Verantwortung zu tragen. Auf die Frage nach zukunftssicheren Berufen kann man nur 45 schwer eine Antwort geben. Bestimmt zählen Biochemiker, Programmierer, Elektromechaniker, Ingenieure, Ärzte, Krankenschwestern und Wissen-schaftler dazu. Auch Handwerker° wird man nie genug haben. Im Hotel- und Restaurantgeschäft, in verkaufs- und hauswirtschaftlichen° Berufen wird es immer Arbeitsplätze geben. Eins ist sicher: eine gute Ausbildung 50 ist die beste Sicherheit gegen Arbeitslosigkeit.

Berufsberaterin°

Lieber heute aktiv, als morgen Radioaktiv!

Wenn die Menschen nicht verantwortungsvoller werden, sehe ich die Gefahr, daß sie sich eines Tages selbst vernichten°. Unsere schönsten Pläne für die Zukunft sind sinnlos°, wenn das wahnsinnige° Wettrüsten° in aller 55 Welt nicht aufhört. Die Gefahr, daß man die Arsenale wirklich gebraucht°, wächst proportional mit Größe und Verbreitung°. Je mehr Staaten Atomwaffen° haben, desto weniger Sicherheit wird es auf dieser Erde geben. Wir müssen alles tun, so daß die Technik zum Guten und nicht zur Vernichtung° der Erde führt°. 60

Professor

ZUM TEXT

A. Wie geht's weiter?

1. Im Jahr 2000 werden die Kinder . . .

   a. mehr zur Schule gehen müssen
   b. nicht mehr zur Schule gehen müssen
   c. weniger in der Schule und mehr zu Hause lernen

2. In Zukunft wird der Haushalt . . .

   a. mehr Zeit kosten
   b. die Familie dominieren
   c. weniger Arbeit machen

3. Die Studentin hofft, daß die Frauen im Jahr 2000 . . .

   a. dann auch an den Universitäten studieren können
   b. für gleiche Arbeit gleiche Bezahlung bekommen
   c. das Geld verdienen und die Männer zu Hause bleiben

4. Der Automechaniker glaubt, daß . . .

   a. die Computer und Roboter die Menschen arbeitslos machen werden
   b. die Menschen mehr Freizeit haben und mehr reisen werden
   c. alle Autos in Zukunft mit Atomkraft fahren werden

5. In der Zukunft brauchen die Menschen vor allem (above all) . . .

   a. berufliche Spezialisierung
   b. weniger Sprachkenntnisse
   c. Qualifikationen wie die Fähigkeit, Verantwortung zu tragen

6. Wenn die Menschen nicht verantwortungsvoller werden, ist es
   möglich, daß ...

   a. man Atomwaffen gebraucht
   b. sie die Erde sicherer machen
   c. die Technik zum Guten führt

B. Wiederholen Sie das in der Zukunft!

BEISPIEL: Im Jahr 2000 ist alles anders.
          Im Jahr 2000 wird alles anders sein.

Auf die Frage nach zukunftssicheren Berufen kann ich nur schwer eine
Antwort geben. Krankenschwestern und Wissenschaftler hat man nie
genug. Eine gute Ausbildung ist die beste Sicherheit gegen Arbeitslosigkeit. Wir müssen verantwortungsvoller sein. Sonst vernichten wir
uns selbst.

C. Was fehlt?

1. Vielleicht werden _____ dann Brillen tragen. (*most [of them]*)
2. Der Computer wird nie _____ kreativ sein _____ ein
   Mensch. (*as ... as*)
3. Aber er kann viel _____ denken _____ wir. (*faster ... than*)
4. Die Berufswahl wird _____ problematischer werden. (*more and
   more*)
5. Darum wird eine breite Ausbildung _____ sein _____ eine
   Spezialisierung. (*more important ... than*)
6. _____ Staaten Atomwaffen haben, _____ Sicherheit wird es
   geben. (*the more ... the less*)

Ohne Worte
Dick Lucas, Masters Agency

361

D. **_Wie sehen Sie das Leben im Jahr 2000?_** _(Respond to each question with your own best guess about what the future will hold.)_

Glauben Sie auch, . . .

1. daß die Kinder im Jahr 2000 nur einen Teil des Jahres zur Schule gehen werden? Wie sehen Sie die Schule der Zukunft?
2. daß der Haushalt viel einfacher sein wird? Warum?
3. Daß die Situation der Frauen anders sein wird? Wie?
4. daß Computer unser Leben total verändern werden? Wie?
5. daß wir mehr Freizeit haben werden? Warum?
6. daß eine breite Ausbildung wichtiger sein wird als Spezialisierung? Warum?
7. daß es möglich ist, daß wir das Leben auf der Erde durch Atomwaffen vernichten werden?

E. **_Stellenangebot_** _(job offer)._ **_Was für Fragen haben Sie an Frau Mohib?_** _(Write down a list of five to six questions you would ask when responding to the ad.)_

Das McDonald's Hauptbüro für Europa in Frankfurt sucht zum baldmöglichsten Eintritt eine

Fremdsprachensekretärin

mit sehr gutem bzw. muttersprachlichem Italienisch sowie perfekten Deutsch- und Englischkenntnissen zur Unterstützung unserer Abteilungssekretärin für die Real Estate, Licensing und Legal Departments.

Wenn Sie eine bewegliche und umsichtige Kollegin sind, die Spaß an viel Arbeit in einem jungen Team hat, sollten Sie sich umgehend bei uns melden.

Bewerbungen für diese Position senden Sie bitte an:

McDonald's System of Europe, Inc.
z. Hd. Frau Mohib
Kennedyallee 109
6000 Frankfurt/Main 70

Das etwas andere
Restaurant

F. **_In zehn (zwanzig / dreißig) Jahren._** _(Write a paragraph of eight to ten sentences telling how you picture your life ten, twenty, or thirty years from now.)_

BEISPIEL: In zehn Jahren werde ich dreißig sein. Dann werde ich . . .

GESPRÄCHE

Bei der Immatrikulation

PETRA Tag, David! Wie geht's?
DAVID Danke, gut. Und dir?
PETRA Prima! Was machst du denn da?
DAVID Ich muß diese Antragsformulare hier ausfüllen.
PETRA Soll ich dir helfen?
DAVID Wenn du Zeit hast.
PETRA Hast du deinen Paß dabei?
DAVID Nein, wieso?
PETRA Darin ist deine Aufenthaltserlaubnis[1]. Die brauchen wir.
DAVID Ich kann ihn ja schnell holen.
PETRA Tu das! Ich warte hier auf dich.

Etwas später

DAVID Hier ist mein Paß. Ich muß mich jetzt auch bald entscheiden, was ich belegen soll. Kannst du mir da auch ein bißchen helfen?
PETRA Na klar. Was ist denn dein Hauptfach? Wofür interessierst du dich?
DAVID Mein Hauptfach ist moderne Geschichte. Ich möchte Kurse über deutsche Geschichte und Literatur belegen.
PETRA Hier ist mein Vorlesungsverzeichnis. Sehen wir mal . . .!

ÜBRIGENS

1. Everyone in the FRG has to be registered with the **Einwohnermeldeamt** at his or her place of residence. Non-Germans who wish to reside in Germany longer than two months must get a residence permit (**Aufenthaltserlaubnis**). In addition, any non-German who wants to work in Germany has to apply for a work permit (**Arbeitserlaubnis**), which officials are very reluctant to issue in times of unemployment.

During Registration

PETRA Hi, David. How are you?

DAVID Thanks, alright. And how are you?

PETRA Fine. What are you doing there?

DAVID I've got to fill out these application forms.

PETRA Do you want me to help you?

DAVID If you have time.

PETRA Do you have your passport along?

DAVID No, why?

PETRA In it is your residence permit. We need it.

DAVID I can get it quickly.

PETRA Do that. I'll wait for you here.

A Little Later

DAVID Here is my passport. I'll soon have to decide what to take. Can you help me a little with that, too?

PETRA Sure. What's your major? What are you interested in?

DAVID My major is modern history. I'd like to take some courses in German history and literature.

PETRA Here's my course catalog. Let's see . . .

Das Studium

DAS STUDIUM *(course of) study*

der Hörsaal, -säle	*lecture hall*
Kurs, -e	*course*
Professor, -en	*professor*
Zimmerkollege, -n, -n	*roommate*
das Fach, ¨er	*subject*
Hauptfach, ¨er	*major (field)*
Nebenfach, ¨er	*minor (field)*
Labor, -s	*lab*
das Semester, -	*semester*
Seminar, -e	*seminar*
Stipendium, Stipendien	*scholarship*
Arbeit, -en	*(term) paper*
die Note, -n	*grade*
Wissenschaft, -en	*science, academic discipline*
Zimmerkollegin, -nen	*roommate*
belegen	*to sign up for, take (a course)*
bestehen, bestand, bestanden	*to pass (an exam)*

sich entscheiden, entschied, entschieden	to decide
holen	to get (fetch)
lehren	to teach
eine Prüfung schreiben	to take an exam

WEITERES

fleißig / faul *industrious(ly), hard-working / lazy*
wieso? *why? how come?*

PASSIVES VOKABULAR der Antrag, ̈-e *(application)*; das College, -s; das For-mular, -e, das System, -e; das Quartal, -e *(quarter)*; das Vorlesungsver-zeichnis, -se *(course catalog)*; die Aufenthaltserlaubnis *(residence permit)*; da-bei *(with/on you)*

ZUM THEMA

A. **Mein Studium** *(Either orally with a partner or in writing, tell about your studies. Use the questions below as guidelines.)*

1. Wie lange sind Sie schon an dieser Uni?
2. Wie viele Kurse haben Sie belegt? Welche?
3. Welche Kurse finden Sie besonders gut? Worin haben Sie die besten Noten?
4. Haben Sie ein Laborfach belegt? Welches?
5. Müssen Sie viele Arbeiten schreiben? In welchen Fächern?
6. Lernen Sie noch andere Sprachen außer Deutsch?
7. Was ist Ihr Hauptfach? Ihr Nebenfach?

B. **Füllen Sie den Antrag auf Seite 367 aus!**

1. Was ist Ihr Familienname? Vorname *(first name)*? Haben Sie auch einen Spitznamen *(nickname)*?
2. Wo sind Sie geboren? Wann?
3. Sind Sie ledig (unverheiratet), verheiratet, verwitwet *(widowed)* oder geschieden *(divorced)*? Haben Sie Kinder? Wenn ja, wie viele?
4. Was für eine Staatsangehörigkeit *(citizenship)* haben Sie?
5. Wo ist Ihr ständiger Wohnsitz *(permanent residence)*? Was ist Ihre Semesteranschrift *(address at school)*? Vergessen Sie die Postleitzahl *(zip code)* nicht!

C. **Fragen übers Studium.** *(First read through the various fields of spe-cialization. Then ask your partner the questions that follow. Be prepared to report to the class.)*

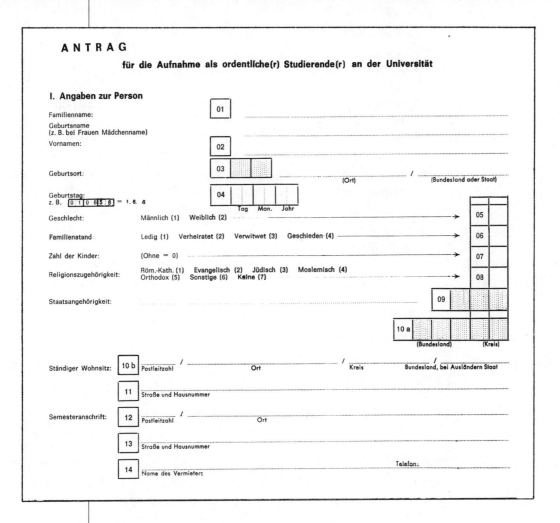

ANTRAG

für die Aufnahme als ordentliche(r) Studierende(r) an der Universität

I. Angaben zur Person

Familienname: | 01 |

Geburtsname
(z. B. bei Frauen Mädchenname)

Vornamen: | 02 |

Geburtsort: | 03 |
(Ort) / (Bundesland oder Staat)

Geburtstag:
z. B. [0|1|0|6|5:6] = 1. 6. 8 | 04 |
Tag Mon. Jahr

Geschlecht: Männlich (1) Weiblich (2) → | 05 |

Familienstand: Ledig (1) Verheiratet (2) Verwitwet (3) Geschieden (4) → | 06 |

Zahl der Kinder: (Ohne = 0) → | 07 |

Religionszugehörigkeit: Röm.-Kath. (1) Evangelisch (2) Jüdisch (3) Moslemisch (4)
Orthodox (5) Sonstige (6) Keine (7) → | 08 |

Staatsangehörigkeit: | 09 |

| 10 a |
(Bundesland) (Kreis)

Ständiger Wohnsitz: | 10 b | Postleitzahl / Ort / Kreis / Bundesland, bei Ausländern Staat

| 11 | Straße und Hausnummer

Semesteranschrift: | 12 | Postleitzahl / Ort

| 13 | Straße und Hausnummer

| 14 | Name des Vermieters Telefon:

Anglistik[1]	Informatik[5]	Pharmazie
Archäologie	Krankenpflege[6]	Philologie
Architektur	Kunstgeschichte	Philosophie
Bergbau[2]	Landwirtschaft[7]	Physik
Betriebswirtschaft[3]	Lebensmittelchemie	Politik(wissenschaft)
Biochemie	Linguistik	Psychologie
Biologie	Maschinenbau[8]	Romanistik[10]
Chemie	Mathematik	Slawistik
Elektrotechnik	Medizin	Soziologie
Forstwirtschaft[4]	Mineralogie	Theologie
Geologie	Musikwissenschaft	Tiefbau[11]
Germanistik	Naturwissenschaften	Volkswirtschaft[12]
Hauswirtschaft	Pädagogik[9]	Zahnmedizin

1 English *2* mining *3* business administration *4* forestry *5* computer science
6 nursing *7* agriculture *8* mechanical engineering *9* education *10* Romance languages *11* civil engineering *12* economics

Fragen Sie Ihren Nachbarn/Ihre Nachbarin, . . .!

1. was er/sie studiert und warum
2. welche andere Fachrichtung (*specialization*) ihn/sie auch interessiert und warum
3. welche Fachrichtung ihn/sie nicht interessiert und wieso nicht
4. wie lange er/sie noch studieren muß
5. was er/sie danach macht
6. wo er/sie gern leben möchte

D. Was sagt Ihnen der Schein? (*What does this certificate tell you about Miriam and her studies? Make five statements in German.*)

Universität Regensburg
Deutsch als Fremdsprache

~~Herrn~~
~~Frau~~/Frl. Miriam Burton ....

aus   den USA ....

wird hiermit bescheinigt, daß ~~er~~/sie an dem DEUTSCHKURS

Landeskunde – Oberstufe I
....

im ~~Sommer~~/Winter Semester 19 87/88...... teilgenommen hat.

~~Er~~/Sie hat die Abschlußprüfung mit sehr gut ....

bestanden.

Regensburg, den 25.2.88 .... *(Dr. Armin Wolff, Akad. Direktor)*

Bewertung: sehr gut (1): gut (2); befriedigend (3): ausreichend (4)

E. Aussprache (*See also III. 6 and 12 in the pronunciation section of the Appendix.*)

1. [z]   **s**o, **s**auber, **s**icher, **S**aal, **S**emester, **S**eminar, Mu**s**ik, Phy**s**ik, Rei**s**e, Pau**s**e, le**s**en
2. [s]   bi**s**, ein**s**, Au**s**wei**s**, Kur**s**, Profe**ss**or, Adre**ss**e, wi**ss**en, la**ss**en, verge**ss**en, intere**ss**ant, au**ß**erdem, flei**ß**ig, hä**ß**lich, Fu**ß**, Flu**ß**, Pa**ß**
3. [št]   **st**att, **st**olz, **St**udium, **St**ipendium, **St**udent, **St**ück, **St**aat, **St**unde, be**st**ehen, **st**udieren, an**st**rengend, be**st**immt
4. [st]   er**st**e, be**st**e, mei**st**ens, de**st**o, Kompon**ist**, Kun**st**, Lu**st**, Pro**st**
5. [šp]   **Sp**iel, **Sp**ort, **Sp**aß, **Sp**eisekarte, **Sp**rache, **sp**ät, **sp**anisch, **sp**ortlich, **sp**annend

STRUKTUR

I. *The Subjunctive Mood*

Until now, almost all sentences in this book have been in the INDICATIVE mood; they were assumed to be based on reality. Sometimes, however, we want to speculate on matters that are unreal, uncertain, or unlikely, or we wish for something that cannot be, or we want to approach other people less directly, more discreetly and politely. These things are done in the SUBJUNCTIVE MOOD. The subjunctive is not an exotic way of expressing yourself but part of everyday speech.

1. Polite Requests or Questions

Would you like a cup of coffee?
Would you pass me the butter?
Could you help me for a moment?

2. Hypothetical Statements and Questions

He should be here any moment.
What would you do?
You should have been there.

3. Wishes

If only I had more time.
I wish you would hurry up.
I wish I had known that.

4. Unreal Conditions

If I had time, I'd go to a movie. (But I don't have time, so I'm not going.)
If the weather were good, we'd go for a walk. (But it's raining, so we won't go.)
If you had told me, I could have helped you. (But you didn't tell me, so I couldn't help you.)

Contrast the sentences above with real conditions:

If I have time, I'll go to a movie.
If the weather is good, we'll go for a walk.

In real conditions the possibility exists that the events will take place. In unreal conditions this possibility does not exist or is highly unlikely.

***NOTE:** The forms of the present-time subjunctive are derived from the simple past:* If I told you (now) . . . *Those of the past-time subjunctive are derived from the past perfect:* If you had told me (yesterday) . . . *Another very common way to express the subjunctive mood is the form* would: I'd go; I would not stay home.

ÜBUNG

A. *Indikativ oder Konjunktiv* (subjunctive)? *(Read these sentences and decide whether they are in the indicative or the subjunctive. Also state whether they refer in meaning to the present, the future, or the past.)*

BEISPIELE: What would you do?   **subjunctive, present-time**
If you don't ask, you won't know. **indicative**

1. If she can, she'll write.
2. If only he'd study more!
3. If only I had known that.
4. They could be here any minute.
5. Will you take the bike along?
6. Would you please hold this?
7. Could they help us for a minute?
8. I had known that all along.
9. We should really be going.
10. I wish you had told me that.
11. I wish I could buy that car.
12. If you were a student, you could fly cheaper.
13. Could you take the children along?
14. You shouldn't go barefoot in this weather.
15. What would she have done if you hadn't come along?
16. If it rains, we won't go.
17. If we had had the money, we'd have bought it.
18. I couldn't come yesterday because I was ill.
19. If she has the money, she'll give it to us.
20. You could have told me.
21. We really shouldn't laugh at them.

II. *The Present-Time General Subjunctive*

German has two subjunctives. The one most commonly used is often referred to in grammar books as the GENERAL SUBJUNCTIVE or SUBJUNCTIVE II. (The SPECIAL SUBJUNCTIVE or SUBJUNCTIVE I, primarily found in written German, is explained in Chapter 15.)

1. Forms

The PRESENT-TIME SUBJUNCTIVE refers to the present *(now)* or the future *(later)*. The forms of the present-time subjunctive are derived from the forms of the simple past. You already know the verb endings from having used the forms of **mögen**, that is, **ich möchte, du möchtest, er möchte,** etc. (which are actually subjunctive forms). All verbs have these endings:

ich -e	wir -en
du -est	ihr -et
er -e	sie -en

a. t-Verbs

The present-time subjunctive forms of the regular t-verbs cannot be distinguished from those of the simple past; their use usually becomes clear from context.

Wenn Sie mir nur glaubten! *If you would only believe me.*
Wenn er mir nur antwortete! *If only he would answer me.*

b. Irregular t-Verbs

Most of the irregular t-verbs, which include the modals, have an umlaut in the present-time subjunctive. Exceptions are **sollen** and **wollen**.

	müssen **mußte**	**sollen** **sollte**	**haben** **hatte**	**wissen** **wußte**
ich	müßte	sollte	hätte	wüßte
du	müßtest	solltest	hättest	wüßtest
er	müßte	sollte	hätte	wüßte
wir	müßten	sollten	hätten	wüßten
ihr	müßtet	solltet	hättet	wüßtet
sie	müßten	sollten	hätten	wüßten

had to, *would have to*	*should,* *ought to*	*had,* *would have*	*knew,* *would know*

Hättest du Zeit? *Would you have time?*
Könntest du kommen? *Could you come?*

c. n-Verbs

The present-time subjunctive forms of n-verbs add the subjunctive endings to the past stem. If the past stem vowel is an **a**, **o**, or **u**, the subjunctive forms have an umlaut.

	gehen **ging**	**kommen** **kam**	**sein** **war**	**werden** **wurde**
ich	ginge	käme	wäre	würde
du	gingest	kämest	wärest	würdest
er	ginge	käme	wäre	würde
wir	gingen	kämen	wären	würden
ihr	ginget	kämet	wäret	würdet
sie	gingen	kämen	wären	würden

went, *would go*	*came,* *would come*	*were,* *would be*	*got, became,* *would get, would become*

Wenn ich du **wäre**, **ginge** ich nicht. *If I were you, I wouldn't go.*

d. würde-Form

In conversation speakers of German commonly use the subjunctive forms of **haben**, **sein**, **werden**, **wissen**, and the modals.

Hättest du Zeit?	*Would you have time?*
Das wäre schön.	*That would be nice.*
Was möchtest du tun?	*What would you like to do?*
Wenn ich das nur wüßte!	*If only I knew that.*
Wir könnten ins Kino gehen.	*We could go to the movies.*

For the subjunctive forms of other verbs, however, they frequently substitute a simpler verb phrase.

würde . . . + infinitive

This phrase closely corresponds to the English *would* + infinitive.

Was **würde** dir Spaß **machen**?	*What would amuse you?*
Ich **würde** lieber tanzen **gehen**.	*I'd rather go dancing.*

2. Uses

You are already familiar with the most common uses of the subjunctive in English. Here are examples of these uses in German.

a. Polite Requests or Questions

Möchtest du eine Tasse Kaffee?	*Would you like a cup of coffee?*
Würdest du mir die Butter geben?	*Would you pass me the butter?*
Könntest du mir einen Moment helfen?	*Could you help me for a minute?*

b. Hypothetical Statements and Questions

Er sollte jeden Moment hier sein.	*He should be here any minute.*
Das wäre schön.	*That would be nice.*
Was würdest du tun?	*What would you do?*
Ich würde spazierengehen.	*I'd go for a walk.*

c. Wishes

Wenn ich nur mehr Zeit hätte!	*If only I had more time.*
Ich wünschte, du würdest dich beeilen!	*I wish you'd hurry up.*

- *Wishes starting with* **Wenn . . .** *usually add* **nur** *after the subject or any pronoun object.*
- *Wishes starting with* **Ich wünschte, . . .** *have* BOTH *clauses in the subjunctive.*

d. Unreal Conditions

Wenn ich Zeit hätte, würde ich ins Kino gehen.	*If I had time, I'd go to a movie.*
Wenn ihr mitkommen wolltet, müßtet ihr euch beeilen.	*If you wanted to come along, you'd have to hurry.*
Wenn wir euch helfen könnten, würden wir das tun.	*If we could help you, we would do it.*

Contrast the preceding sentences with real conditions.

Wenn ich Zeit habe, gehe ich ins Kino.	*If I have time, I'll go to a movie.*
Wenn ihr mitkommen wollt, müßt ihr euch beeilen.	*If you want to come along, you'll have to hurry.*
Wenn wir euch helfen können, tun wir es.	*If we can help you, we'll do it.*

Wenn ich ein Vöglein° wär',	*little bird*
und auch zwei Flügel° hätt',	*wings*
flög' ich zu dir.	
Weil's aber nicht kann sein,	
weil's aber nicht kann sein,	
bleib' ich allhier°.	*right here*
Mein Hut°, der hat drei Ecken.	*hat*
Drei Ecken hat mein Hut.	
Und hätt' er nicht drei Ecken,	
dann wär' es nicht mein Hut.	

ÜBUNGEN

B. Was bedeuten diese Sätze? (*Give the English equivalent.*)

1. Wohin möchtest du gehen?
2. Wir könnten uns einen Film ansehen.
3. Wir sollten in die Zeitung sehen.
4. Ich würde lieber zu Hause bleiben.
5. Ich wünschte, ich wäre nicht so müde.
6. Hättest du morgen abend Zeit?
7. Ich ginge heute lieber früh ins Bett.
8. Morgen könnte ich länger schlafen.

Peter

Wenn ich meinen Eltern alles erzählen würde, na dann gute Nacht!

C. Geben Sie das Imperfekt und die Konjunktivform! (*Give the simple-past indicative and the form of the present-time subjunctive.*)

BEISPIELE: ich hole   **ich holte**   **ich holte**
du bringst   **du brachtest** **du brächtest**
er kommt   **er kam**   **er käme**

1. ich frage, mache, belege, studiere, lehre, versuche
2. du arbeitest, antwortest, wartest, öffnest, heiratest
3. er muß, kann, darf, soll, mag
4. wir bringen, denken, wissen, haben
5. ihr bleibt, fliegt, seid, werdet, seht, gebt, eßt, schlaft, fahrt, singt, sitzt, tut

D. Reisepläne. Was würden sie tun? (*Fill in the blanks, using the* **würde**-*form in exercise 1 and the verb form in the subjunctive in exercise 2.*)

1. Bauers würden nach Wien fahren.

    x Dort _____ wir erst eine Stadtrundfahrt machen.
    y Dann _____ Dieter sich sicher den Stephansdom ansehen.
    Und du _____ dann durch die Kärntnerstraße bummeln.
    Natürlich _____ ihr auch in die Hofburg gehen.
    x Ja, und einen Abend _____ wir in Grinzing feiern.
    y Das _____ euch bestimmt gefallen.

2. Ute führe in die Schweiz.

    a. Ich _____ mit ein paar Freunden in die Schweiz fahren. (können)
    b. Erst _____ wir an den Bodensee. (fahren)
    c. Von dort _____ es weiter nach Zürich und Bern. (gehen)
    d. In Zürich _____ ich mir gern das Thomas-Mann-Archiv (*archives*) _____ . (ansehen)
    e. Ihr _____ auch nach Genf fahren. (sollen)
    f. Dort _____ du Französisch sprechen. (müssen)
    g. Das _____ keine schlechte Idee! (sein)

E. Sagen Sie es höflicher! (*How would you say this more politely?*)

1. BEISPIEL: Können Sie uns die Mensa zeigen?   **Könnten Sie uns die Mensa zeigen?**

    a. Darf ich kurz mit Ihnen sprechen?   *c.* Können wir uns an einen Tisch setzen?
    b. Haben Sie Lust mitzukommen?   *d.* Haben Sie eine Zigarette?

2. BEISPIEL: Rufen Sie mich morgen an!   **Würden Sie mich morgen anrufen?**

    a. Erzählen Sie uns von der Reise!   *c.* Machen Sie mir eine Tasse Kaffee!
    b. Bringen Sie die Bilder mit!   *d.* Geben Sie mir die Milch!

F. Wünsche (wishes)

1. *Beginnen Sie mit* Ich wünschte . . .! *Was bedeutet das auf englisch?*

> BEISPIEL: Der Kurs ist schwer. **Ich wünschte, der Kurs wäre nicht so schwer.**
> *I wish the course weren't so hard.*

  a. Ich muß viel lesen.
  b. Das nimmt viel Zeit.
  c. Ich bin müde.
  d. Ihr seid faul.

2. *Beginnen Sie mit* Wenn nur . . .! *Was bedeutet das auf englisch?*

> BEISPIEL: Ich wünschte, ich könnte schlafen. **Wenn ich nur schlafen könnte!**

  a. Ich wünschte, wir hätten keine Prüfungen.
  b. Ich wünschte, ich könnte das verstehen.
  c. Ich wünschte, du könntest mir helfen.
  d. Ich wünschte, diese Woche wäre schon vorbei.

G. Wechseln Sie vom Indikativ zum Konjunktiv!

> BEISPIEL: Wenn das Wetter schön ist, kann man die Berge sehen.
> **Wenn das Wetter schön wäre, könnte man die Berge sehen.**

1. Wenn es möglich ist, zeige ich euch das Schloß.
2. Wenn du das Schloß sehen willst, mußt du dich beeilen.
3. Wenn ihr zu spät kommt, ärgert ihr euch.
4. Wenn das Schloß zu ist, können wir wenigstens in den Schloßpark gehen.
5. Wenn ihr mehr sehen wollt, müßt ihr länger hier bleiben.

Wenn ich hier der Chef* wäre, dann...

_____

_____

_____

_____

* Bitte sagen Sie uns ehrlich die Meinung. Über die
Speisen, Getränke, Sauberkeit, das Personal, was auch
immer Ihnen einfällt.
Damit wir erfahren, wo wir noch besser werden können.
Vielen Dank. Ihr Wendy-Restaurant.
(Bitte Name und Adresse auf der Rückseite vermerken.)

H. *Noch mehr Wünsche*

1. Ich bin neugierig *(curious).*

   a. Was würden Sie gern lernen?
   b. Wo würden Sie gern leben?
   c. Würden Sie lieber in einem Haus oder in einer Wohnung wohnen?
   d. Welchen Film würden Sie sich gern ansehen?
   e. Was für ein Auto würden Sie sich am liebsten kaufen?
   f. Was würden Sie jetzt am liebsten essen? trinken?

2. Was wäre, wenn . . .? *(Chain reaction. Ask each other what you would do or be if . . . Follow up with* **Und dann***?)*

   BEISPIEL: Wenn heute Freitag wäre, **wäre morgen Samstag.**
   Und dann?   **Dann würde ich nicht zur Uni gehen.**
   Und dann?   **Dann würde ich lange schlafen.**

   a. Wenn das Wetter heute schön wäre, . . .
   b. Wenn ich Professor (Präsident . . .) wäre, . . .
   c. Wenn ich eine Million gewonnen hätte, . . .

3. Wie geht's weiter?

   BEISPIEL: Ich wäre stolz, wenn . . .
   Ich wäre stolz, wenn ich gut Deutsch sprechen könnte.

   a. Ich wäre froh, wenn . . .
   b. Ich fände es prima, wenn . . .
   c. Es wäre furchtbar, wenn . . .
   d. Ich würde mich ärgern, wenn . . .
   e. Ich würde sparen, wenn . . .

I. *Auf deutsch, bitte!*

1. Would you like to come on Saturday?
2. It would be nice.
3. We could swim in the lake.
4. We wish we had time.
5. If Walter didn't have to work, we would come.
6. Could you come on Sunday?
7. Yes, I believe we can come.

III. *The Past-Time General Subjunctive*

You already know that a simple-past form in English can express the present-time subjunctive (referring to *now* or *later*).

If I had time, I would come along.

The past-perfect form, or *would have* + past participle, expresses the same thought in the PAST-TIME SUBJUNCTIVE (referring to *earlier*).

If I had had time, I would have come along.

1. Forms

a. In German the forms of the past-time subjunctive are based on the forms of the past perfect. The past-time subjunctive is very easy to learn because it simply consists of a form of **hätte** or **wäre** plus the past participle:

$$\left.\begin{array}{l} \text{hätte} \ldots \\ \\ \text{wäre} \ldots \end{array}\right\} + \text{ past participle}$$

Wenn ich das **gewußt hätte, wäre** ich froh **gewesen.**	*If I had known that, I would have been happy.*
Ich wünschte, du **hättest** mir das **gesagt!**	*I wish you had told me.*

b. All modals follow this pattern in the past-time subjunctive:

hätte ... + verb infinitive + modal infinitive

Ich **hätte** dich **anrufen sollen.**   *I should have called you.*

For now, avoid using these forms in dependent clauses.

2. Uses

The past-time subjunctive is used for the same purposes as the present-time subjunctive, except that there are no polite requests in the past.

a. Hypothetical Statements and Questions

Ich wäre zu Hause geblieben.	*I would have stayed home.*
Was hättet ihr gemacht?	*What would you have done?*
Hättet ihr mitkommen wollen?	*Would you have wanted to come along?*

b. Wishes

Wenn ich das nur gewußt hätte!	*If only I had known that.*
Ich wünschte, du wärest da gewesen.	*I wish you had been there.*

c. Unreal Conditions

Wenn du mich gefragt hättest, hätte ich es dir gesagt.	*If you had asked me, I would have told you.*
Wenn du da gewesen wärest, hättest du alles gehört.	*If you had been there, you would have heard everything.*

ÜBUNGEN

J. Wechseln Sie von der Gegenwart zur Vergangenheit! *(Change from the present to the past, using the past-time subjunctive.)*

1. BEISPIEL: Sie würde das tun. **Sie hätte das getan.**

    a. Sie würde euch anrufen.   *c.* Ihr würdet sofort kommen.
    b. Ihr würdet ihr helfen.   *d.* Du würdest alles für sie tun.

2. BEISPIEL: Er sollte nicht so viel Schokolade essen.
          Er hätte nicht so viel Schokolade essen sollen.

    a. Wir dürften ihm keine   *c.* Er könnte auch Obst essen.
        Schokolade geben.   *d.* Wir müßten besser aufpassen.
    b. Das sollten wir wissen.

K. Was wäre gewesen, wenn?

1. *Wechseln Sie von der Gegenwart zur Vergangenheit!*

    BEISPIEL: Wenn ich es wüßte, würde ich nicht fragen.
          Wenn ich es gewußt hätte, hätte ich nicht gefragt.

    a. Wenn wir eine Theatergruppe hätten, würde ich mitmachen.
    b. Wenn das Radio billiger wäre, würden wir es kaufen.
    c. Wenn ich Hunger hätte, würde ich mir etwas kochen.
    d. Wenn sie fleißiger arbeitete, würde es ihr besser gehen.

2. *Kettenreaktion. (Chain reaction. Ask each other what you would have done or what might have been if... Follow up with* **Und dann?***)*

    BEISPIEL: Ich hatte keinen Hunger. Wenn ich Hunger gehabt hätte, ...
                ... wäre ich in die Küche gegangen.
    Und dann?   **Dann hätte ich mir ein Wurstbrot gemacht.**
    Und dann?   **Dann hätte ich noch einen Apfel gegessen.**

    a. Gestern hat es geregnet. Wenn das Wetter schön gewesen wäre, ...
    b. Ich bin nicht lange auf der Party gewesen. Wenn ich zu lange gefeiert hätte, ...
    c. Natürlich hatten wir letzte Woche Vorlesungen. Wenn wir keine Vorlesungen gehabt hätten, ...

L. Auf deutsch, bitte!

1. We should have stayed at home.
2. If the weather had been better, we could have been swimming in the lake.
3. But it rained all day.
4. I wish they hadn't invited us.
5. If only we hadn't visited him.

ZUSAMMENFASSUNG

M. *Indikativ oder Konjunktiv? Analysieren Sie die Sätze! Was bedeutet das auf englisch?*

1. Wenn er uns besuchte, brachte er immer Blumen mit.
2. Können Sie mir Horsts Telefonnummer geben?
3. Wenn du früher ins Bett gegangen wärest, wärest du jetzt nicht so müde.
4. Gestern konnten sie nicht kommen, aber sie könnten uns morgen besuchen.
5. Er sollte gestern anrufen.
6. Ich möchte Architektur studieren.
7. Sie waren schon um 6 Uhr aufgestanden.
8. Ich wünschte, er ließe nicht immer alles auf dem Sofa liegen.
9. Er ließ seine Bücher zu Hause.
10. Wenn ich könnte, was du kannst, dann wäre ich glücklich.

N. *Auf deutsch, bitte!*

1. Would you *(sg. fam.)* like to go with us to Salzburg? *2.* We could go by train. *3.* It ought to be quieter now than in the summer. *4.* That would be nice. *5.* I'd come along, if I could find my passport. *6.* I wish you *(pl. fam.)* had thought of it earlier. *7.* Then I could have looked for it. *8.* If I only knew where it is. *9.* I'd like to see the churches, the Mozart house, and the castle (**die Burg**). *10.* The city is supposed to be wonderful. *11.* Without my passport I'd have to stay home.—Here it is! *12.* If you *(sg. fam.)* hadn't talked (**reden**) so much, you'd have found it faster.

The oldest German-speaking universities date back to the late Middle Ages: the university of Vienna was founded in 1365 and the university of Heidelberg in 1385. The **Freie Universität Berlin**, however, was founded in 1948 as a counterpart to

Heidelberg hat eine der ältesten deutschen Universitäten.

the **Humboldt Universität** (1810), which is located in East Berlin. Over the last twenty years, more than twenty new universities have been founded in the FRG, as well as a large number of technical colleges. Students are admitted to a university after they have passed the **Abitur**, a comprehensive exam given after thirteen years of schooling, which includes rigorous requirements in mathematics, science, and languages. In the FRG admission to certain fields of study, like medicine and pharmacy, is limited, and keen competition results. Practically all universities in both Germanys are state supported. There is no tradition of private universities, and tuition payments are very low.

EINBLICKE

WORTSCHATZ 2

das Problem, -e	*problem*
an deiner (seiner . . .) Stelle	*in your (his . . .) shoes, if I were you (he) . . .*
ausländisch	*foreign*
erst	*first of all; not before, not until*
gar nicht	*not at all*
jedenfalls	*in any case*
meinen	*to think, be of an opinion*
sowieso	*anyhow*
teil·nehmen (an + *dat.*)(nimmt teil), nahm teil, teilgenommen	*to participate (in), take part (in)*

WAS IST DAS? der Grammatikkurs, Intensivkurs, Lesesaal, Semesteranfang; das Archiv, Sommersemester, System, Wintersemester; die Sprachprüfung; teilmöbliert

---

(Gespräch an einer amerikanischen Universität)

Ein Jahr drüben wäre super!

TINA Hallo, Margaret!

MARGARET Tag, Tina! Kennst du Bernd? Er ist aus West-Berlin und studiert ein Jahr bei uns. 5

TINA Guten Tag! Wie gefällt es dir hier?

BERND Sehr gut. Meine Kurse und Professoren sind ausgezeichnet. Ich wünschte nur, es gäbe nicht so viele Prüfungen!

TINA Habt ihr keine Prüfungen?

instead

BERND Doch, aber weniger. Dafür° haben wir nach ungefähr vier Se- 10
mestern eine große Zwischenprüfung¹ und dann am Ende des Studiums das Staatsexamen.

TINA   Ich würde gern einmal in Europa studieren.

MARGARET   Das solltest du wirklich tun.

TINA   Es ist bestimmt sehr teuer.   15

MARGARET   So teuer ist es gar nicht! Mein Jahr in München hat auch nicht mehr gekostet als ein Jahr hier.

Viele Studenten essen in der Mensa, weil das Essen dort billig ist und auch nicht viel Zeit kostet.

TINA   Wirklich?

BERND   Ja, bestimmt. Unsere Studentenheime und die Mensa sind viel billiger als bei euch, und unsere Studiengebühren° sind viel 20 niedriger°. Ohne mein Stipendium könnte ich hier nicht studieren.

TINA   Ich muß noch mal mit meinen Eltern sprechen. Sie meinen, daß ich ein Jahr verlieren würde.

MARGARET   Wieso denn? Wenn du mit einem Auslandsprogramm° nach 25 Deutschland gingest, würde das genauso wie ein Jahr hier zählen.

TINA   Ich weiß nicht, ob ich genug Deutsch kann.

tuition

lower

foreign study . . .

In Deutschland studieren junge Leute aus der ganzen Welt, wie z.B. diese Studenten aus Afrika.

MARGARET Bestimmt! Viele Studenten können weniger Deutsch als du. Du lernst es ja schon seit vier Jahren. Außerdem haben die meisten 30 Programme vor Semesteranfang einen Intensivkurs für ausländische Studenten. Damit würdest du dich auch auf die Sprachprüfung am Anfang des Semesters vorbereiten°. Wenn du die Prüfung wirklich nicht bestehen solltest—was ich mir nicht vorstellen kann, denn dein Deutsch ist gut—, dann müßtest du 35 eben° einen Grammatikkurs belegen und sie am Ende des Semesters wiederholen.

TINA Das geht°. Vielleicht kann ich im Herbst ein Semester nach Deutschland.

MARGARET Nur im Herbst ginge nicht, weil das Wintersemester erst Ende 40 Februar aufhört.

TINA Im Februar? Und wann ist das Frühlingssemester?

BERND Bei uns gibt es ein Wintersemester und ein Sommersemester. Das Wintersemester läuft von November bis März, das Sommersemester von April bis Ende Juli². Du müßtest also° ein 45 ganzes Jahr bleiben oder nur für das Sommersemester kommen. Aber ein ganzes Jahr wäre sowieso besser, denn dann hättest du zwischen den Semestern Zeit zu reisen.

MARGARET Stimmt. Da bin ich auch viel gereist. Ich war in Italien, Griechenland und danach noch in der Tschechoslowakei und der 50 DDR.

TINA Wunderbar! Was für Kurse sind am Anfang nicht zu schwer?

BERND Im ersten Semester würde ich nur Vorlesungen³ belegen, keine Seminare. Da hört man nur zu und macht Notizen°. Im zweiten Semester könntest du dann auch ein Seminar belegen. Bis dann 55 ist dein Deutsch jedenfalls gut genug, daß du auch eine längere Seminararbeit schreiben oder ein Referat halten° könntest.

TINA Seminararbeiten und Referate auf deutsch?

MARGARET Am Anfang geht's langsam, aber man lernt.

BERND Ich tue's ja auch auf englisch. Übrigens, was bei euch viel besser 60 ist, sind die Bibliotheken. Wir müssen Bücher immer erst bestellen, was oft Tage dauert. Man kann nicht einfach in die Archive wie hier. Und die Fachbibliotheken⁴ leihen keine Bücher aus°, außer am Wochenende.

TINA Ich kann mir ja die Bücher kaufen. 65

BERND Das wäre furchtbar teuer! Dann würde ich schon lieber im Lesesaal sitzen.

TINA Und wie ist das mit Studentenheimen?

MARGARET Wenn du an einem Auslandsprogramm teilnimmst, hast du keine Probleme. 70

BERND An deiner Stelle würde ich versuchen, ein Zimmer im Studentenheim zu bekommen. Auf diese Weise würdest du leichter andere Studenten kennenlernen. Die Zimmer sind oft sehr schön, teilmöbliert und mit Bad. Dazu müßtest du auf deinem Flur die Küche mit fünf oder sechs anderen Studenten teilen. 75

TINA Da habe ich nichts dagegen. Meint ihr Berlin wäre besser als Heidelberg oder München?

BERND Ach, das ist schwer zu sagen.

MARGARET Wenn ich Berlin gekannt hätte, hätte ich vielleicht dort studiert. Mir hat es dort sehr gut gefallen. Aber erst mußt du wissen, ob 80 du wirklich nach Deutschland fahren willst. Wenn du das weißt, dann kann ich dir weiterhelfen°.

assist

TINA Danke!

MARGARET An deiner Stelle würde ich erst mal mit deinen Eltern sprechen! Denk mal, was du alles lernen und sehen würdest! 85

TINA Ja, das wäre super!

ZUM TEXT

A. *Was fehlt?*

Berlin, Europa, ein Jahr, eine Küche, München, Prüfungen, Sommersemester, Sprachprüfung, andere Studenten, Vorlesungen, West-Berlin, Wintersemester

1. Bernd ist aus _____ und studiert _____ in Amerika.
2. Ihm gefallen nur die vielen _____ nicht.
3. Tina möchte gern in _____ studieren.
4. Margarets Jahr in _____ hat nicht viel mehr gekostet als ein Jahr zu Hause.
5. Ausländische Studenten müssen vor Semesteranfang eine _____ schreiben.
6. Das _____ ist von November bis Ende Februar, das _____ von April bis Ende Juli.
7. Im ersten Semester sollte Tina nur _____ belegen.
8. In einem Studentenheim kann man leichter _____ kennenlernen.
9. In einem deutschen Studentenheim muß man _____ mit anderen Studenten teilen.
10. Margaret hätte auch gern in _____ studiert.

B. *Das Studium hier und dort.* (*In brief statements compare what Bernd says about studying in West Berlin with what you know about studying here.*)

1. Prüfungen
2. Studiengebühren
3. Semesterkalender
4. Kurse
5. Bibliotheken

C. Was fehlt?

1. Bernd _____ nur, es _____ nicht so viele Prüfungen. *(wishes, there were)*
2. Wenn Bernd kein Stipendium _____ , _____ er nicht hier studieren können. *(had gotten, could have)*
3. Wenn Tina mit einem Austauschprogramm in die BRD _____ , _____ das wie ein Jahr hier zählen. *(would go, would)*
4. Wenn sie die Sprachprüfung nicht _____ , _____ sie einen Grammatikkurs belegen. *(should pass, would have to)*
5. Tina _____ ein ganzes Jahr bleiben, oder sie _____ nur für das Sommersemester gehen. *(would have to, could)*
6. Ein ganzes Jahr drüben _____ besser. *(would be)*
7. Dann _____ Tina zwischen den Semestern Zeit zu reisen. *(would have)*
8. Im zweiten Semester _____ sie auch ein Seminar belegen, weil sie dann gut Deutsch _____ . *(could, speak)*
9. Es _____ zu teuer, alle Bücher zu kaufen. *(would be)*
10. In einem Studentenheim _____ Tina leichter deutsche Studenten kennenlernen. *(would)*
11. Wenn Margaret Berlin _____ , _____ sie dort studiert. *(had known, would have)*
12. Wenn sie nicht an einer deutschen Uni _____ , _____ sie nicht so gut Deutsch sprechen. *(had studied, could)*

> **Wir nutzen nur 10 % unseres geistigen Potentials**
> A. Einstein

D. Was wäre, wenn . . .?

1. Wenn ich könnte, würde ich einmal in . . . studieren.
2. Ich würde . . . bleiben.
3. Während der Semesterferien . . .
4. Am Anfang des Semesters . . .
5. Wenn ich die Prüfung nicht bestehen würde, . . .
6. Am liebsten würde ich in . . . wohnen, weil . . .

E. Wunschwelt

(insgesamt = *total*, Bio-Läden = *health-food stores*, Frauenbewegung = *women's movement*)

1. *Lesen Sie die Statistik, und sagen Sie, (a) was es am meisten und was am wenigsten gäbe, (b) wem was wichtiger wäre!*

2. *Was gäbe es in Ihrer Wunschwelt? Was nicht? Was wäre Ihnen egal? (Decide what would be the most important and what would be the least important to you in an ideal world. Then poll the class to see what others think.)*

Wunschwelt

»Was gäbe es in deiner idealen Welt, was nicht, und was wäre dir egal?«

	Das gäbe es			Das gäbe es nicht	Das wäre mir egal
	Jugendliche insgesamt	Jungen	Mädchen		
Blumen	89	84	95	1	7
Geld	78	79	78	9	10
Fernsehen	74	74	73	5	20
Rockmusik	73	72	74	6	18
Alte Leute	62	56	68	7	26
Kirche	54	48	60	12	31
Theater	52	40	64	10	35
Bio-Läden	37	30	44	8	48
Frauenbewegung	36	22	51	13	42
Die Grünen	27	27	26	22	44
Sexfilme	14	19	9	32	47

F. Schreiben Sie Ihren Eltern, was wäre, wenn Sie ein Jahr in Europa studieren würden. *(Write eight sentences in the subjunctive, telling them what you would do, could learn, etc.)*

ÜBRIGENS

1. Traditionally, German university students were not required to take exams in courses during their studies. However, to obtain their degree, students were expected to know their chosen field thoroughly and to be prepared for a very comprehensive and demanding exam (**Staatsexamen**) at the end of eight or ten semesters. There is now a tendency to require more papers and exams, most notably the **Zwischenprüfung** (midway exam) that students must pass after about four or five semesters.

2. The exact dates for the beginning and end of each semester vary in various parts of the FRG since each state (**Land**) is autonomous in regard to education.

3. The registration process at German universities permits students to attend lectures and seminars for three weeks before making a final decision to enroll. That allows them to select only those courses that are suited to their needs and likes.

4. Besides the large university library (**Universitätsbibliothek**), there is a separate library (**Fachbibliothek**) with a reading room for each of the major disciplines, normally located in the building housing these departments.

GESPRÄCH

Hier ist immer etwas los.

HEIKE Und das ist die Gedächtniskirche mit ihren drei Gebäuden. Wir nennen sie den „Hohlen Zahn", den „Lippenstift" und die „Puderdose[1]".

MARTIN Ihr Berliner habt doch für alles einen witzigen Namen!

HEIKE Der alte Turm der Gedächtniskirche soll kaputt bleiben als Erinnerung an den Krieg. Die neue Gedächtniskirche mit dem neuen Turm ist eben modern.

MARTIN Und sie sieht wirklich ein bißchen aus wie ein Lippenstift und eine Puderdose! Sag mal, wie ist das Leben hier?

HEIKE Phantastisch! Einmalig! Berlin hat sehr viel zu bieten, nicht nur historisch, sondern auch kulturell.

MARTIN Das stimmt schon. Hier ist immer etwas los. Außerdem habt ihr eine wunderschöne Umgebung.

HEIKE Ja, ohne die Seen und Wälder wäre es bestimmt nicht so schön! Und wenn du durch die Geschäfte bummelst, fühlst du die Luft der großen weiten Welt.

MARTIN Aber die Mauer[2] und der Stacheldraht! Ich meine, ihr habt doch rings um euch die Grenze. Ihr lebt doch wie auf einer Insel! Stört dich das nicht? Hast du nicht manchmal Angst?

HEIKE Angst, nein. Man gewöhnt sich daran.

MARTIN Glaubst du, daß es einmal wieder anders wird?

HEIKE Bestimmt nicht bald. Vielleicht wenn es mal ein Vereintes Europa gibt. Jedenfalls wird die deutsche Frage[3] so lange offen bleiben, wie das Brandenburger Tor[4] zu ist.

1. The Berliners are known for their humor (**Witz**) and "big mouth" (**freche Schnauze**), as seen in the amusing names they give to various places. Besides the nicknames mentioned above, there's the **Schwangere Auster** *(pregnant oyster)*, a cultural center in West Berlin; the **Palazzo Prozzo** (**protzen** = *to brag*, hence *Braggart's Palace*), the House of Parliament in East Berlin; and the **Hungerkralle** *(hunger claw)*, the monument to the Berlin airlift in 1948–1949.

2. The Berlin Wall, erected in 1961 by GDR authorities, was built to stop the growing exodus from the GDR. Since the founding of the GDR in 1949, over three million people had crossed the open border, which put a severe strain on the country's economy. Today the heavily guarded border has largely stopped any unauthorized crossing.

3. Germany still has no peace treaty, which means that legally the German question is still open. But few Germans in either Germany believe that a reunification is possible.

4. The **Brandenburger Tor**, once a symbol of a united Germany, now symbolizes the country's division. Located near the **Reichstagsgebäude** (the old House of Parliament), the Brandenburg Gate is on GDR territory.

Blick aufs Brandenburger Tor und die Mauer.

There's always something happening here

HEIKE And that's the Memorial Church with its three buildings. We call them the "Hollow Tooth," the "Lipstick," and the "Compact."

MARTIN You Berliners have a witty name for everything.

HEIKE The old tower of the Memorial Church is to stay in ruins as a reminder of the war. The new Memorial Church with the new tower is modern.

MARTIN And it does look a little like a lipstick and a compact. Tell me, what's life here like?

HEIKE Fantastic! Unique! Berlin has a lot to offer, not only historically but also culturally.

MARTIN That's true. There's always something happening here. Besides, you also have beautiful surroundings.

HEIKE Yes, without the lakes and forests it certainly wouldn't be as nice. And when you stroll through the stores, you feel the air of the whole wide world.

MARTIN But the wall and the barbed wire! I mean, you have the border all around you. You live as if on an island. Doesn't that bother you? Aren't you scared sometimes?

HEIKE Scared, no. You get used to it.

MARTIN Do you think it'll change someday?

HEIKE Not soon, for sure. Maybe someday when there's a United Europe. In any case, the German question remains open as long as the Brandenburg Gate remains closed.

Damals und jetzt

WORTSCHATZ I

DAMALS UND JETZT *then (in those days) and now*

der Frieden	*peace*	
Krieg, -e	*war*	
Turm, ¨e	*tower*	
das Gebäude, -	*building*	
die Erinnerung, -en	*reminder; memory*	

die Grenze, -n	*border*
Insel, -n	*island*
Luft	*air*
Mauer, -n	*wall*
Mitte	*middle*
Umgebung	*surroundings*

WEITERES

aus·sehen (sieht aus), sah aus, ausgesehen	to look, appear
aus·sehen wie (+ *nom.*)	to look like s.th. or s.o.
bieten, bot, geboten	to offer
erinnern (an + *acc.*)[1]	to remind (of)
sich erinnern an (+ *acc.*)[1]	to remember
nennen, nannte, genannt	to name, call
stören	to bother, disturb
teilen	to divide
eben	after all, just (gesture word)
einmalig	unique
historisch	historical(ly)
kulturell	cultural(ly)
mitten durch	right through (the middle of)
rings um (+ *acc.*)	all around
witzig	witty, funny
wunderschön	beautiful

1 **Erinnere mich** an die Karten! *(Remind me of the tickets.)* BUT: **Hast du dich** an die Karten **erinnert**? *(Did you remember the tickets?)*

PASSIVES VOKABULAR der Lippenstift, -e *(lipstick)*; der Stacheldraht *(barbed wire)*; das Tor, -e *(gate)*; die Puderdose, -n *(compact)*; hohl *(hollow)*; vereint *(united)*

ZUM THEMA

A. ***Wie geht's weiter?*** *(Use the phrases below in complete sentences. Use your imagination.)*

BEISPIEL: . . . sieht gut aus. **Heike sieht gut aus.**

1. . . . sieht . . . aus.
2. . . . sieht aus wie ein(e) . . .
3. . . . hat viel zu bieten.
4. Bitte erinnere mich nicht an . . . !
5. Ich kann mich schlecht an . . . erinnern.
6. . . . ist immer etwas los.
7. Meine Freunde nennen mich manchmal . . .
8. Es stört mich, wenn . . .
9. Rings um die Uni ist/sind . . .
10. Mitten durch . . .

B. ***Besuch in . . . Was sagen Sie?*** *(What would you say while you are taking a foreign visitor through your own or some other city?)*

X Und das ist _____ .
Y _____ .
X Ja, wir sind sehr stolz darauf.
Y Wie ist das Leben _____ ?
X _____ .
Y Ist hier kulturell viel los?
X _____ .
Y Die Umgebung ist _____ .
X Wie findest du/finden Sie _____ ?
Y _____ .

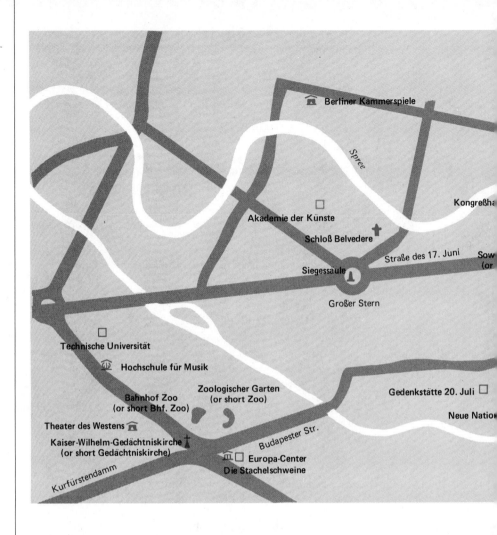

Berliner Kammerspiele

Spree

Akademie der Künste

Kongreßha

Schloß Belvedere

Straße des 17. Juni

Siegessäule

Sow
(or

Großer Stern

Technische Universität

Hochschule für Musik

Zoologischer Garten
(or short Zoo)

Gedenkstätte 20. Juli

Bahnhof Zoo
(or short Bhf. Zoo)

Neue Natio

Theater des Westens

Kaiser-Wilhelm-Gedächtniskirche
(or short Gedächtniskirche)

Budapester Str.

Europa-Center
Die Stachelschweine

Kurfürstendamm

C. ***Bilder aus der Geschichte*** *(Find the places mentioned below, and tell
where they are.)*

1. 1770 wurde eine breite Straße mit Lindenbäumen zur
Repräsentationsstraße Berlins. Heute ist sie das Gegenstück
(counterpart) zum Westberliner Kurfürstendamm. Wie heißt sie?
2. Früher hatte Berlin 18 Stadttore *(. . . gates),* heute nur noch eins. Wie
heißt es? *3.* 1805 besuchte Zar Alexander I. Berlin. Heute ist der Platz mit
seinem Namen das Zentrum von Ost–Berlin. Wie heißt er? *4.* 1809 bekam
Berlin seine eigene Universität (seit 1945 Humboldt–Universität). Warum
baute man 1948 die Freie Universität Berlin? *5.* Am 20. Juli 1944
versuchten deutsche Offiziere, Hitler zu töten *(assassinate).* Was erinnert
daran? *6.* 1945 war die Gedächtniskirche nur noch eine Ruine. Woran
soll sie erinnern? *7.* 1946 bauten die Russen ein Denkmal. Die Panzer

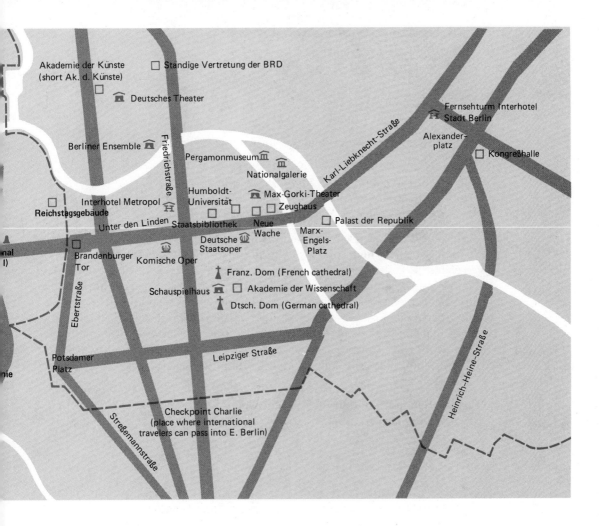

Akademie der Künste (short Ak. d. Künste)

Ständige Vertretung der BRD

Deutsches Theater

Fernsehturm Interhotel Stadt Berlin

Berliner Ensemble

Friedrichstraße

Karl-Liebknecht-Straße

Alexander-platz

Kongreßhalle

Pergamonmuseum

Nationalgalerie

Humboldt-Universität

Max-Gorki-Theater

Zeughaus

Interhotel Metropol

Reichstagsgebäude

Unter den Linden

Staatsbibliothek

Neue Wache

Palast der Republik

nal I)

Brandenburger Tor

Komische Oper

Deutsche Staatsoper

Marx-Engels-Platz

Ebertstraße

Franz. Dom (French cathedral)

Schauspielhaus

Akademie der Wissenschaft

Dtsch. Dom (German cathedral)

Heinrich-Heine-Straße

nie

Potsdamer Platz

Leipziger Straße

Streßemannstraße

Checkpoint Charlie (place where international travelers can pass into E. Berlin)

(tanks) daneben sollen 1945 als erste Berlin erreicht (reached) haben. Wie heißt es? *8.* Welche Theater, Opern, Konzerthallen und Akademien gibt es in Berlin? *9.* Am 17. Juni 1953 rebellierten die Ostberliner und die Deutschen in der DDR gegen die Sowjetunion. Was erinnert daran? *10.* Seit 1961 läuft eine Mauer mitten durch Berlin. Wie heißt der internationale Grenzübergang (. . . *crossing*)?

D. *Aussprache* *(See also III. 19, 21, and 22 in the pronunciation section of the Appendix.)*

1. [pf]   **Pf**arrer, **Pf**effer, **Pf**efferminz, **Pf**ennig, **Pf**und, A**pf**el, Ko**pf**, em**pf**ehlen

2. [ps]   **Ps**ychologe, **Ps**ychiater, **Ps**ychologie, **ps**ychologisch, **Ps**alm, **Ps**eudonym, Ka**ps**el

3. [kv]   **Qu**atsch, **Qu**alität, **Qu**antität, **Qu**artal, **Qu**ote, be**qu**em

STRUKTUR

I. *Relative Clauses*

RELATIVE CLAUSES supply additional information about a noun in a sentence.

There is the professor who teaches the course.
He taught the course (that) I enjoyed so much.
He teaches a subject in which I'm very interested (I'm very interested in).
He's the professor whose course I took last semester.

English relative clauses may be introduced by the relative pronouns *who, whom, whose, which,* or *that.* The noun to which the relative pronoun "relates" is called the ANTECEDENT. The choice of the relative pronoun depends on the antecedent (is it a person or a thing?) AND on its function in the relative clause. The relative pronoun may be the subject *(who, which, that)*, an object, or an object of a preposition *(whom, which, that)*, or it may indicate possession *(whose)*. German relative clauses work essentially the same way. However, while in English the relative pronouns are frequently omitted (especially in conversation), IN GERMAN THEY MUST ALWAYS BE USED.

Ist das der Roman, **den** ihr gelesen habt?
Is that the novel you read?

1. Forms

a. The German relative pronouns have the same forms as the definite article, EXCEPT FOR THE GENITIVES AND THE DATIVE PLURAL.

	masc.	neut.	fem.	pl.
nom.	der	das	die	die
acc.	den	das	die	die
dat.	dem	dem	der	den**en**
gen.	dessen	dessen	deren	deren

b. The form of the relative pronoun is determined by two factors:

- *its* ANTECEDENT
  Look back and determine whether the antecedent is singular or plural and whether it is masculine, neuter, or feminine.
- *its* FUNCTION *in the relative clause*
  Determine whether the relative pronoun is the subject, an accusative or dative object, or an object of a preposition, or whether it indicates possession.

```
. . . ANTECEDENT, (preposition) RP ─────────── V1, . . .
gender? number?                    function?
```

Das ist der Professor. Er lehrt an der Freien Universität.
Das ist **der Professor, der** an der Freien Universität lehrt.
*That's **the professor who** teaches at the Free University.*
antecedent: der Professor; sg./masc.
function: subject > nom.

Wie heißt der Kurs? Du findest ihn so interessant.
Wie heißt **der Kurs, den** du so interessant findest?
*What's the name of **the course (that)** you find so interesting?*
antecedent: der Kurs; sg./masc.
function: object of **finden** > acc.

Da ist der Student. Ich habe ihm mein Buch gegegeben.
Da ist **der Student, dem** ich mein Buch gegeben habe.
*There's **the student to whom** I gave my book (I gave my book to).*
antecedent: der Student; sg./masc.
function: object of **geben** > dat.

Kennst du den Professor? Erik hat sein Seminar belegt.
Kennst du **den Professor, dessen Seminar** Erik belegt hat?
*Do you know **the professor whose seminar** Erik is taking?*
antecedent: den Professor; sg./masc.
function: related possessively to **Seminar** > gen.

Das Buch ist von einem Autor. Ich interessiere mich sehr für ihn.
Das Buch ist von **einem Autor, für den** ich mich sehr interessiere.
*The book is by **an author in whom** I'm very interested.*
antecedent: von einem Autor; sg./masc.
function: object of **für** > acc.

Die Autoren sind aus der DDR. Der Professor hat von ihnen gesprochen.
Die Autoren, von denen der Professor gesprochen hat, sind aus der
  DDR.
The authors of whom the professor spoke are from the GDR.
antecedent: die Autoren; pl.
function: object of von > dat.

☞ *CAUTION:*

▶ *Don't use the interrogative pronoun in place of the relative pronoun!*

                    Wer hat das Seminar gegeben?
Das ist der Professor, **der** das Seminar gegeben hat.

                    Who gave the seminar?
That's the professor *who* gave the seminar.

2. Word order

a. Relative pronouns can be the objects of prepositions. If that is the case, the preposition will always precede the relative pronoun.

Das Buch ist von einem Autor, **für den** ich mich sehr interessiere.
The book is by an author in whom I'm very interested.

b. The word order in the RELATIVE CLAUSE is like that of all SUBORDINATE clauses: the inflected part of the verb (V1) comes last. Always separate the main clause from the relative clause by a COMMA.

$$\ldots,\ \text{RP} \underline{\hspace{3cm}} \text{V1}, \ldots$$

Das ist der Professor, **der** den Prosakurs **lehrt.**
                                                    V1

c. Relative clauses immediately follow the antecedent unless the antecedent is followed by a prepositional phrase that modifies it, a genitive, or a V2.

Das Buch von Dürrenmatt, **das wir lesen sollen**, ist leider ausverkauft.
Das Buch des Autors, **das wir lesen sollen**, ist teuer.
Ich kann **das Buch** nicht bekommen, **das wir lesen sollen**.

ÜBUNGEN

A. *Analysieren Sie die Sätze!* (Find the antecedent and state the function of the relative pronoun in each relative clause.)

> BEISPIEL: Renate Berger ist eine Arbeiterin, die für gleiche Arbeit gleiches Einkommen möchte.
> **antecedent: eine Arbeiterin, sg./fem.**
> **function: subject > nom.**

1. Der Mann, der neben ihr arbeitet, verdient pro Stunde 1,80 DM mehr.
2. Es gibt leider noch viele Frauen, deren Kollegen ein höheres Einkommen bekommen.
3. Und es gibt Frauen, denen schlecht bezahlte Arbeit lieber ist als keine Arbeit.
4. Was denken die Männer, deren Frauen weniger Geld bekommen als ihre Kollegen?
5. Der Mann, mit dem Renate Berger verheiratet ist, findet das nicht so schlecht.
6. Aber die Frauen, die bei der gleichen Firma arbeiten, ärgern sich sehr darüber.
7. Es ist ein Problem, das die meisten Firmen haben.
8. Es gibt Berufe, in denen Männer für gleiche Arbeit mehr verdienen.

9. Und die Berufe, in denen fast nur Frauen arbeiten, sind am schlechtesten bezahlt.

10. Wir leben in einer Welt, in der Gleichberechtigung noch nicht überall Realität *(reality)* ist.

B. *Rundfahrt in Ost-Berlin.* *(While Sepp shows slides from his visit to East Berlin, his Austrian friends ask questions. Answer according to the model, using relative pronouns.)*

1. BEISPIEL: Ist das der Alexanderplatz?
   Ja, das ist der Alexanderplatz, der so bekannt ist.

   a. Ist das der Dom?
   b. Ist das das Pergamonmuseum?
   c. Ist das die Akademie der Wissenschaft?
   d. Ist das der Fernsehturm?
   e. Sind das die Wissenschaftler?

2. BEISPIEL: Ist das der Dom?
   Ja, das ist der Dom, den du da siehst.

   a. Ist das das Hotel Metropol?
   b. Ist das die Staatsbibliothek?
   c. Ist das der Potsdamer Platz?
   d. Sind das die Volkspolizisten *(GDR policemen)*?

3. BEISPIEL: Ist das das Brandenburger Tor?
   Ja, das ist das Brandenburger Tor, zu dem wir jetzt kommen.

   a. Ist das die Friedrichstraße?
   b. Ist das (der) Checkpoint Charlie?
   c. Ist das die Humboldt Universität?
   d. Sind das die historischen Gebäude?

4. (Note the change in pattern. Combine the two sentences into one.)

   BEISPIEL: Wo ist der Student? Sein Vater lehrt an der Freien Universität.
   Da ist der Student, dessen Vater an der Freien Universität lehrt.

   a. Wo ist die Studentin? Ihre Eltern wohnten früher *(formerly)* in Berlin.
   b. Wo ist das Mädchen? Ihr Bruder war so witzig.
   c. Wo ist der Herr? Seine Frau sprach so gut Englisch.
   d. Wo sind die alten Leute? Ihre Kinder sind jetzt in Amerika.

C. Was gefällt Ihnen? Geben Sie Beispiele!

BEISPIEL: Stück
Ein Stück, das mir gefällt, ist Goethes *Faust*.

1. Buch
2. Film
3. Fernsehsendung
4. Zeitschrift
5. Schlagersänger(in) *(pop singer)*
6. Komponist(in)
7. Kurs
8. Restaurant
9. Auto
10. Stadt

D. Was fehlt?

1. Der junge Mann, _____ da steht, heißt David.
2. Das Mädchen, mit _____ er spricht, heißt Tina.
3. Das andere Mädchen, _____ daneben steht, heißt Margaret.
4. Sie sprechen über einen Film, _____ momentan im Kino läuft.
5. Der Film, über _____ sie sprechen, spielt in Berlin.
6. Die Geschichte spielt kurz vor dem Bau der Mauer, _____ seit 1961 Berlin teilt.
7. In den fünfziger Jahren, in _____ man noch mit der S-Bahn von Ost-Berlin nach West-Berlin fahren konnte, war die Flucht *(escape)* leichter.
8. Der junge Mann, _____ Freundin auch weg wollte, fuhr mit der S-Bahn nach West-Berlin und blieb.
9. Die Freundin, _____ Eltern in Weimar wohnten, wollte noch einmal ihre Eltern sehen.
10. Das war aber gerade an dem Tag, an _____ sie die Mauer bauten.
11. Das bedeutete, daß sie den Freund, _____ sie in West-Berlin zurückgelassen hatte und _____ dort auf sie wartete, nie wiedersehen würde.
12. Am Ende des Filmes, _____ sehr spannend war, blieb nur die Erinnerung an den Freund.

E. Bilden Sie aus zwei Sätzen einen Satz! Verbinden Sie sie mit einem Relativpronomen!

BEISPIEL: Der Ku(rfürsten)damm ist eine bekannte Straße. Die Straße ist in West-Berlin.
Der Ku'damm ist eine bekannte Straße, die in West-Berlin ist.

1. Die Gedächtniskirche gefällt mir. Ihr habt schon von der Gedächtniskirche gehört.
2. Der alte Turm soll kaputt bleiben. Die Berliner nennen ihn den „Hohlen Zahn".
3. Die Berliner nennen den neuen Turm „Lippenstift". Die Berliner haben für alles einen Namen.
4. Der Ku'damm beginnt bei der Gedächtniskirche. Am Ku'damm gibt es viele schöne Geschäfte.
5. Die Geschäfte sind nicht billig. Sie sind sehr elegant.
6. Da gibt es auch viele Cafés. Man kann in den Cafés gemütlich sitzen.
7. Das Café war prima. Ich habe seinen Namen vergessen.
8. Heike hat mir alles gezeigt. Ihre Eltern wohnen in Berlin.

9. Ihr Bruder war auch sehr nett. Ich bin mit ihm am Abend in einen Jazzkeller gegangen.
10. In dem Jazzkeller konnte man auch tanzen. Ich fand den Jazzkeller übrigens einmalig.
11. Berlin ist wirklich eine interessante Stadt. In dieser Stadt ist immer etwas los.

F. *Auf deutsch, bitte!*

1. Where's the lecture hall in which Professor Schulz is lecturing (reading)? 2. The course he teaches is modern German history. 3. The students who take his courses must work hard. 4. History is a subject that I find very interesting. 5. But I have a roommate who finds nothing interesting. 6. He's a person (**Mensch**) I don't understand. 7. He studies subjects he doesn't like. 8. The friends he goes out with (with whom he goes out) are boring. 9. He makes fun of his father, whose money he gets every month. 10. But the girl he's engaged to (to whom he is engaged) is very pleasant.

Informationen, die Ihr Geld wert sind

II. *Indirect Speech*

When reporting what someone else has said, you can use direct speech and quotation marks:

Heike said, "Berlin has a lot to offer."

or INDIRECT SPEECH without quotation marks:

Heike said (that) Berlin has a lot to offer.

Often, corresponding direct and indirect speech will require different personal pronouns and possessive adjectives, depending on who reports the conversation:

▪ *If Heike says to Martin, "I'll bring my map," and she reports the conversation, she will say:* I told him I would bring my map.
▪ *If Martin reported the conversation, he would say:* She told me she would bring her map.
▪ *If a third person reported, he or she would say:* She told him she would bring her map.

In spoken German such indirect reports are generally in the INDICATIVE when the opening verb is in the present (**Sie sagt, . . .**). However, when the opening verb is in the past (**Sie sagte, . . .**), the SUBJUNCTIVE usually follows. We will focus on the latter.

„Ich bringe meinen Stadtplan mit."
  Sie sagt, sie bringt ihren Stadtplan mit.
  Sie sagte, sie **würde** ihren Stadtplan **mitbringen.**

NOTE: In German opening quotation marks are placed at the bottom of the line.

1. Statements

The tense of the indirect statement is determined by the tense of the direct statement.

a. Direct statements in the present or future are reported indirectly in the present-time subjunctive or the **würde**-form:

present tense	
future tense	$\longrightarrow$ present-time subjunctive or **würde**-form

„Ich komme später." Sie sagte, sie **käme** später.
  Sie sagte, sie **würde** später **kommen.**
„Ich kann dich anrufen." Sie sagte, sie **könnte** ihn **anrufen.**
„Ich werde dir Berlin zeigen." Sie sagte, sie **würde** ihm Berlin **zeigen.**

b. Direct statements in any past tense are reported indirectly in the past-time subjunctive:

present perfect	
simple past	$\longrightarrow$ past-time subjunctive
past perfect	

„Sie ist nicht gekommen." Er sagte, sie **wäre** nicht **gekommen.**
„Sie hatte keine Zeit." Er sagte, sie **hätte** keine Zeit **gehabt.**
„Sie hatte aber angerufen." Er sagte, sie **hätte** aber **angerufen.**

▪ *The conjunction* **daß** *may or may not be used. If it is not used, the sentence is in the original word order. If* **daß** *is used, the inflected part of the verb comes last.*

Sie sagte, sie käme morgen. ↓
Sie sagte, **daß** sie morgen **käme.**

Sie sagte, sie hätte andere Pläne gehabt. ↓
Sie sagte, **daß** sie andere Pläne gehabt **hätte.**

2. Questions

The tense of an indirect question is also determined by the tense of a direct question. Indirect YES/NO QUESTIONS are introduced by **ob**, and indirect INFORMATION QUESTIONS by the question word.

| Er fragte: „Hast du jetzt Zeit?" | He asked, "Do you have time now?" |
| Er fragte, **ob** sie jetzt Zeit hätte. | He asked if she had time now. |

| Er fragte: „Wo warst du?" | He asked, "Where were you?" |
| Er fragte, **wo** sie gewesen wäre. | He asked where she had been. |

3. Imperatives

Direct requests in the imperative are expressed indirectly with the auxiliary **sollen**.

| Sie sagte: „Frag(e) nicht so viel!" | She said, "Don't ask so much." |
| Sie sagte, er **sollte** nicht so viel **fragen**. | She said he shouldn't ask so much. |

ÜBUNGEN

G. *Schreiben Sie die indirekten Aussagen als Gespräch!* (Be sure to change the pronouns accordingly.)

BEISPIEL: Phillip sagte, er wäre im Theater gewesen.
Phillip sagte: „Ich bin im Theater gewesen."

1. Phillip sagte, er hätte das Stück sehr gut gefunden.
2. Stephan sagte, er wollte es sich auch ansehen.
3. Sonja sagte, sie würde mit Stephan ins Theater gehen.
4. Sonja sagte, sie würde heute nachmittag die Karten dafür kaufen.
5. Stephan sagte, er würde lieber Freitag abend ins Theater gehen.
6. Stephan sagte, er wollte das Stück erst lesen.

H. *Wiederholen Sie die Sätze als indirekte Aussagen* (statements)!

1. *Aussagen in der Gegenwart oder Zukunft (referring to now or later). Beginnen Sie die Sätze mit* Sie sagte, . . .! *(Trudi's friend reports what Trudi told her. Now report what the friend said.)*

BEISPIEL: „Trudi will Zahnärztin werden."
Sie sagte, Trudi wollte Zahnärztin werden.
(Sie sagte, daß Trudi Zahnärztin werden wollte.)

„Gute Zahnärzte braucht man immer. Sie kann leicht kürzere Stunden arbeiten, wenn sie mal kleine Kinder hat. Außerdem verdient man gut. Natürlich muß man lange studieren. Aber darauf freut sie sich schon."

2. *Aussagen in der Vergangenheit (referring to earlier). Beginnen Sie die Sätze mit* Er sagte, . . .! *(Margaret's friend reports what Margaret told him about her year abroad. Now write what the friend said.)*

BEISPIEL: „Margaret hat letztes Jahr in Deutschland studiert."
Er sagte, Margaret hätte letztes Jahr in Deutschland studiert.

„Es hat ihr gut gefallen. Sie hat die Sprachprüfung leicht bestanden. Während der Semesterferien ist sie in die Schweiz gefahren. Im Winter ist sie Ski laufen gegangen. Sie ist erst vor drei Wochen zurückgekommen."

I. *Martin und Heike im Gespräch. Wiederholen Sie die Fragen indirekt!* *(Watch out for changes in pronouns.)*

1. Ja/nein-*Fragen. Beginnen Sie mit* Er fragte, . . .! *(Martin asks.)*

   BEISPIEL: „Hast du nicht manchmal Angst?"
   Er fragte, ob sie nicht manchmal Angst hätte.

   „Hast du dich an die Mauer gewöhnt? Stört dich das nicht? Ist das nicht wie auf einer Insel? Glaubst du, daß das einmal anders wird? Bleibst du nach dem Studium in Berlin?"

2. *Informationsfragen. Beginnen Sie mit* Er fragte, . . .! *(Martin asks.)*

   BEISPIEL: „Wann haben sie die Mauer gebaut?"
   Er fragte, wann sie die Mauer gebaut hätten.

   „Wo ist das Brandenburger Tor? Wie kommt man dorthin? Wohin fährt die U-Bahn? Wie viele Menschen leben in West-Berlin? Wie alt ist Berlin?"

3. *Imperative. Beginnen Sie mit* Sie sagte ihm, . . .! *(Heike suggests.)*

   BEISPIEL: „Fahr auch in die DDR!"
   Sie sagte ihm, er sollte auch in die DDR fahren.

   „Bummel durch Ost-Berlin! Sieh dir die Museen an! Geh auch ins Potsdamer Schloß! Hör dir ein Konzert an! Besuch die Westberliner Filmfestspiele!"

J. *Was hat er/sie gesagt? (Ask your neighbor five questions about himself or herself and then report to the class, using indirect speech.)*

   BEISPIEL: **Er hat mir erzählt, er wäre aus Chicago, er hätte zwei Brüder . . .**

ZUSAMMENFASSUNG

K. *Schreiben Sie Relativsätze! (Make up a relative clause for each of the nouns below.)*

   BEISPIEL: die Universität   **die Universität, an der er studiert, . . .**

   1. der Kurs
   2. die Professorin
   3. das Austauschprogramm
   4. die Studenten
   5. das Stipendium
   6. der Hörsaal
   7. der Beruf
   8. die Leute

L. *Margaret erzählt Tina über Martin. (Margaret tells Tina about Martin. Write what Margaret said or asked.)*

   „Martin wohnt jetzt in Berlin. Er ist dort Student. Es gefällt ihm gut. Er studiert deutsche Geschichte. Er hat einen Sommerkurs in der DDR mitgemacht. Er ist auch in der Tschechoslowakei gewesen. Besuch

Martin in Berlin, wenn du drüben *(over there)* studierst! Reise mit ihm durch die DDR!"

BEISPIEL: **Margaret hat gesagt, Martin wohnte jetzt in Berlin.**

M. *Auf deutsch, bitte!*

1. Brecht, who was from Augsburg, studied medicine (**Medizin**) at first. *2.* But it was the theater in which he was really interested. *3.* Kurt Weill was a composer with whom Brecht often worked. *4. Die Dreigroschenoper* is a play that Brecht and Weill wrote together. *5. Mutter Courage* and *Der kaukasische Kreidekreis* are two plays he wrote in 1938. *6.* The theater that Brecht directed (**leiten**) after 1948 is in East Berlin. *7.* Berlin is also the city in which he died (**starb**) in 1956. *8. Der Augsburger Kreidekreis* is a story by Brecht that many students read.

Berlin became the seat of the electors of Brandenburg in 1486 and later, after 1701, of the Prussian kings. After 1871 it gained political, economic, and cultural prominence as the capital of the German nation. At the beginning of World War II, Berlin was the sixth-largest city in the world, with over four million inhabitants. More than a third did not survive the war. East Berlin is now the capital of the GDR, while West Berlin is an industrial and cultural center surrounded by 154 kilometers of wall and barbed wire. The city's rich cultural fare attracts numerous visitors. West Berlin alone has more than twenty-eight museums, not to mention concert halls, theaters, and an opera house. With over one hundred educational institutions, Berlin is also an important center of learning. West Berlin's isolation is mitigated to some extent by its forests, lakes, parks, meadows, and even farms, which make up one-third of its area.

Der Weltkugelbrunnen (globe fountain) *auf dem Brandscheidtplatz in West-Berlin in der Nähe der Gedächtniskirche. Dieser Platz ist ein beliebter Treffpunkt* (meeting place), *besonders für Studenten.*

der Gedanke, -ns, -n	*thought*
Schutz	*protection*
das Denkmal, ¨er	*monument*
die Bevölkerung	*population*
Heimat	*homeland, home*
Jugend	*youth*
Macht, ¨e	*power*
berühmt	*famous*
bunt	*colorful*
froh	*glad, happy*
kaum	*hardly*
nun	*well; now*
aus·tauschen	*to exchange*
erkennen, erkannte, erkannt	*to recognize*
scheinen, schien, geschienen	*to seem, appear like*
verlassen, verließ, verlassen	*to leave (a place)*
zerstören	*to destroy*

750 Jahre Berlin 1987

WAS IST DAS? der Besuch, Bomber, Einmarsch, Esprit, Fernsehturm, Jeep, Sonderstatus, Wiederaufbau; das Kabarett, Transportflugzeug, Turmcafé, Wunder; die Akademie, Blockade, Industriestadt, Luftbrücke, Metropole, Paßkontrolle, Restaurierung, Rote Armee, Stadtrundfahrt, Teilung, Viereinhalbmillionenstadt; *(pl.)* die Besucher, Filmfestspiele, Kaffeehäuser, Medikamente, Schutzmächte, Westmächte; fliehen, hinterlassen, reagieren, verschönern, wiedererkennen; blockiert, enorm, kapitalistisch, kommunistisch, restauriert, repräsentativ, sowjetisch, ummauert, (un)freiwillig, vital

„**I**ch bin ein Berliner.“

Da saßen wir nun, Vater und Tochter, im Flugzeug auf dem Weg zu der Stadt, die er eigentlich nie vergessen konnte: Berlin. „Ich bin schon lange° in Amerika, aber Berlin . . . Nun, Berlin ist eben meine Heimat.“ Und jetzt wanderten seine Gedanken zurück zu den zwanziger bis vierziger Jahren, als er dort gelebt hatte. Die Viereinhalbmillionenstadt, von deren Charme und Esprit er heute noch schwärmt°, hatte seine Jugend geprägt°. Und er erzählte mir von dem, was er dort so geliebt hatte: von den Wäldern und Seen in der Umgebung und von der berühmten Berliner Luft; von den Museen, der Oper und den Theatern, deren Angebot° damals einmalig war; vom Kabarett[1] mit seiner „frechen Schnauze“° und den Kaffeehäusern, in denen immer etwas los war. „In Berlin kamen eben alle Fäden zusammen, nicht nur kulturell, sondern auch politisch und wirtschaftlich°. Es war damals die größte Industriestadt Europas. Die zentrale Verwaltung° aller deutschen Industriefirmen war in Berlin. Und man kannte sich, tauschte Gedanken aus, auch mit der Hochschule°. Einfach phantastisch! . . .“ 5

„Und dann kam 1933[2]. Viele verließen Berlin, teils freiwillig, teils unfreiwillig. Die Nazis herrschten° und beherrschten° das Straßenbild°. Bei der Olympiade 1936 sah die ganze Welt nicht nur Berlins moderne S-Bahn und schöne Straßen, sondern auch Hitler. Ja, und drei Jahre später war Krieg!“ Nun sprach er von den schweren Luftangriffen° und den Trümmern°, die diese hinterließen, vom Einmarsch der Roten Armee, der Teilung Deutschlands unter den vier Siegermächten° (1945) und auch von der Luftbrücke[3], mit der die Westmächte auf die sowjetische Blockade reagierten. „Plötzlich waren wir total blockiert, eine Insel. Es gab nichts zu essen, keine Kleidung, kein Heizmaterial°, keine Medikamente, kaum Wasser und Elektrizität. An guten Tagen landeten in den nächsten zehn Monaten alle paar Minuten britische und amerikanische Transportflugzeuge—wir nann- 10 15 20 25

405

raisin . . ./ provided

made

wide-open space/ unlim-
ited

all across

exhibitions/ conferences

GDR police (i.e., = Volks-
polizei)

was put up

Braggart's Palace
house of representatives
turns

patrolled
come together
display windows/ opposite

agree

ten sie die „Rosinenbomber°"—und versorgten° uns mit dem, was wir   30
brauchten. Ohne die Westmächte, die nun unsere Schutzmächte wurden,
hätten wir es nie geschafft°!"

Dann kamen wir in West-Berlin an. Erst machten wir eine Stadtrundfahrt. Wir fuhren auch an dem Haus vorbei, in dem wir damals gewohnt
hatten und das, wie durch ein Wunder, nicht zerstört war. „Es ist wieder   35
schön hier, und doch, die Weite° ist weg. Berlin schien früher grenzenlos°,
und jetzt . . . überall diese Grenze. Der Anhalter Bahnhof, von dem man
früher überall hinreisen konnte, liegt noch in Trümmern." Und immer
wieder steht man vor der Mauer, die seit 1961 quer durch° Berlin läuft. Und
doch gefiel mir diese ummauerte Insel mit ihren fast zwei Millionen   40
Menschen, von denen fast eine Viertel Million Ausländer sind. Berlin ist
wieder eine vitale westliche Metropole, die enorm viel zu bieten hat. Immer
wieder gibt es Messen°, Kongresse° und Festspiele. Wenn man möchte,
kann man abends auch leicht ins Theater oder die Oper nach Ost-Berlin
fahren. West-Berlin ist heute die größte Universitätsstadt der BRD; allein an   45
der Freien Universität studieren etwa 30 000 Studenten. Die Seen und
Wälder sind heute so schön wie damals.

Der Besuch in Ost-Berlin, der Hauptstadt der DDR, war wie eine Reise
in eine andere Welt. Allein schon die Gesichter der Vopos° am Checkpoint
Charlie[4] und das komische Gefühl, das man bei der Paßkontrolle hatte!   50
Berlin-Mitte war für meinen Vater schwer wiederzuerkennen. Der Potsdamer Platz, der früher voller Leben war, war leer. Leichter zu erkennen waren
die historischen Gebäude entlang „Unter den Linden[5]": die Staatsbibliothek,
die Humboldt Universität, die Staatsoper und das Denkmal Friedrichs des
Großen, das erst vor ein paar Jahren wieder aufgestellt wurde°. Interessant   55
war auch das Pergamonmuseum, der Dom und gegenüber der Palast der
Republik, den die Berliner „Palazzo Prozzo°" nennen und in dem die Volks-
kammer° sitzt. Dann natürlich überall der Fernsehturm, dessen Turmcafé
sich dreht°. Am Wiederaufbau und der Restaurierung historischer Gebäude
sieht man, wie sehr die DDR ihre Hauptstadt repräsentativ machen will,   60
nicht nur für die ausländischen Besucher, sondern auch für die eigene
Bevölkerung. Ost-Berlin ist ja die größte Stadt in der DDR, größer als Leipzig
und Dresden! Wir sahen auch einen britischen Jeep, der „Unter den Linden"
Streife fuhr°, was uns an den Sonderstatus Berlins erinnerte. Hier treffen
die kapitalistische und die sozialistische Welt aufeinander°, und für beide   65
Welten sind Ost- und West-Berlin Schaufenster° zweier gegensätzlicher°
Systeme.

Ich war froh, Berlin endlich mal kennenzulernen. „Es WAR eine schöne
Stadt, und es ist WIEDER eine schöne Stadt", sagte mein Vater als wir
gemütlich am Ku'damm entlang bummelten. Meine Gedanken gingen zu-   70
rück zu Präsident Kennedys Worten 1963 an der Mauer: „Alle freien
Menschen sind Bürger Berlins . . . Ich bin ein Berliner[6]!" Und ich mußte ihm
zustimmen°.

ZUM TEXT

A. *Richtig oder falsch?*

___ 1. Der Vater und die Tochter fliegen nach Amerika.

___ 2. Der Vater hatte 40 Jahre in Berlin gelebt.

___ 3. Er hatte Berlin sehr geliebt.

___ 4. In Berlin war damals nicht viel los gewesen.

___ 5. 1939 hatte der Krieg begonnen.

___ 6. 1945 teilten die Siegermächte Deutschland und Berlin.

___ 7. Die Luftbrücke brachte den Berlinern nur Rosinen.

An vielen Stellen haben junge
Leute die Mauer mit bunten
Bildern bemalt (painted).

___ 8. Seit 1961 teilt die Mauer Berlin.

___ 9. Man kann abends leider nicht ins Theater nach Ost-Berlin.

___ 10. 3000 studieren an der Freien Universität.

___ 11. „Unter den Linden" ist eine große Straße in Ost-Berlin.

___ 12. In Ost-Berlin hat man viele historische Gebäude restauriert.

___ 13. Ost-Berlin ist ein Schaufenster des Kapitalismus.

___ 14. Präsident Nixon sagte 1963: „Ich bin ein Berliner!"

B. *Suchen Sie die Relativpronomen im Text!* (*Working in groups of two to four students, underline all the relative pronouns and their antecedents that you can find in the text. Which group can find the greatest number?*)

C. *Bilden Sie Relativsätze!* (*Make up two relative clauses for each pronoun, then compare results with the rest of the class.*)

1. Berlin ist eine Stadt, die . . .
2. Berlin ist eine Stadt, in der . . .
3. Berlin ist eine Stadt, deren . . .
4. Berlin ist eine Stadt, von der . . .
5. Berlin ist eine Stadt, um die . . .

D. *Was fehlt?*

1. Mir gefällt diese Stadt, in _____ fast zwei Millionen Menschen wohnen. *2.* Es ist ein Kulturzentrum (*n.*), _____ enorm viel zu bieten hat. *3.* Die Filmfestspiele, _____ Filme wirklich einmalig sind, muß man einmal gesehen haben. *4.* Der letzte Film, _____ ich mir angesehen habe, war sehr witzig. *5.* Ein anderer Film, an _____ Titel (*m.*) ich mich nicht erinnern kann, war etwas traurig. *6.* Es war ein Film, in _____ mehrere berühmte Schauspieler mitspielten. *7.* Der Hauptschauspieler, _____ am Ende seine Heimat verläßt, hieß Humphrey Bogart. *8.* Morgen abend gehe ich mit Heike, _____ Vater Extrakarten hat, ins Kabarett. *9.* Das Kabarett, _____ Name nicht nur in Berlin bekannt ist, heißt „Die Stachelschweine" (*The Porcupines*). *10.* Die Leute, über _____ sie sich lustig machen, sind meistens Politiker oder andere berühmte Persönlichkeiten (*pl.*), _____ jeder kennt.

E. *Lesen Sie das Gespräch zwischen Vater und Tochter, und erzählen Sie dann indirekt, was sie gesagt (oder gefragt) haben!*

TOCHTER Wie lange hast du dort gewohnt?
    VATER Ungefähr 25 Jahre.
TOCHTER Waren deine Eltern auch aus Berlin?
    VATER Nein, aber sie sind später nachgekommen.
TOCHTER Hast du dort studiert?
    VATER Ja, an der Humboldt Universität.
TOCHTER Hast du dort Mutti kennengelernt?
    VATER Ja, das waren schöne Jahre!
TOCHTER Und wann seid ihr von dort weggegangen?
    VATER 1949.

TOCHTER Erzähl mir davon!

    VATER Ach, das ist eine lange Geschichte. Setzen wir uns in ein Café! Dann werde ich dir davon erzählen.

F. ***Wenn Sie die Wahl*** *(choice)* ***hätten, würden Sie in Berlin leben wollen? Warum oder warum nicht?*** *(Write down five things that would appeal to you and five that wouldn't.)*

ÜBRIGENS

1. The term *cabaret* (**Kabarett**) describes both a form of theatrical entertainment and the dance halls and taverns in which it emerged at the turn of the century. Performers satirized contemporary culture and politics through skits, pantomime, poems, and songs *(chansons)*. This kind of variety show was forbidden during the last years of the Nazi regime because of its political criticism, but since the end of World War II the cabaret has resurfaced as a popular form of entertainment. Its atmosphere has been depicted in such films as *Der blaue Engel*, with Marlene Dietrich, and *Cabaret*, with Liza Minnelli. Some famous cabarets are „**Lach- und Schießgesellschaft**" (Munich), „**Floh de Cologne**" (Cologne), „**Mausefalle**" (Hamburg), and „**Die Stachelschweine**" (West-Berlin).

2. In 1933 Adolf Hitler became chancellor of Germany. This began a twelve-year dictatorship that ended in the total defeat and division of Germany in 1945, and the loss of millions of lives.

3. On June 24, 1948, at the height of the cold war, Soviet troops tried to force the integration of West Berlin into the GDR by blocking all vital supply lines—roads, railroads, and canals leading into the city. The West then sustained the more than two million West Berliners through the famous airlift. The Russians finally ended their blockade on May 12, 1949.

4. Since all of Berlin is still officially governed by the four World War II allies, the British, French, Russians, and Americans have access to and patrol all of Berlin regularly. The one East-West crossing reserved exclusively for non-German visitors is "Checkpoint Charlie."

5. **Unter den Linden** was one of Berlin's busiest, most famous, and elegant boulevards. Now in East Berlin, it is still beautiful but is in sharp contrast to busy streets in West Berlin like the **Kurfürstendamm**, which is full of people late at night, while **Unter den Linden** is empty after 9:30 P.M.

6. He should have said „**Ich bin Berliner**"; **ein Berliner** is a jelly-filled donut!

GESPRÄCHE

Bürger-initiative

ROBERT Schön ist es hier! Wie alt sind denn die Häuser da drüben?

NICOLE Über 500 Jahre! Man hat sie alle in den letzten paar Jahren renoviert[1].

ROBERT Da habt ihr aber Glück gehabt!

NICOLE Was heißt hier Glück? Was meinst du, wie wir kämpfen mußten! Man wollte sie abreißen, aber durch eine Bürgerinitiative haben wir sie gerettet.

ROBERT Allerhand! Ich finde es auch prima, daß hier keine Autos fahren.

NICOLE Das war auch so ein Kampf. Aber die Abgase zerstören einfach zuviel.

ROBERT Ja, man sieht's. Die Fassade des Domes hat ziemlich gelitten[2].

NICOLE Den restaurieren wir jetzt auch, und die Luft ist schon viel besser geworden.

ROBERT Das glaube ich gern. Da sieht man's mal wieder: Wo ein Wille ist, ist auch ein Weg.

ÜBRIGENS

1. In recent years the initiative for fighting pollution and promoting conservation has frequently come from concerned citizens who have pressured slow-moving officials by collecting signatures, printing pamphlets, and organizing rallies. These **Bürgerinitiativen** have been especially effective in preventing the inner cities from becoming exclusively commercial.

2. Many of the original façades of old buildings, especially those of soft sandstone dating from the Middle Ages, are deteriorating because of air pollution and have to be replaced with new ones made of concrete. Old stained-glass windows in churches are now protected by ordinary glass on the outside. Special crews maintain these magnificent structures.

Citizens' Initiative

ROBERT It's lovely here. How old are those houses over there?

NICOLE Over 500 years old. They were all renovated during the last few years.

ROBERT You were lucky.

NICOLE What do you mean by lucky? You can't imagine how we had to fight. First they wanted to tear them down, but through a special citizens' initiative we saved them.

ROBERT How about that! I think it's great, too, that there are no cars here.

NICOLE That was also quite a fight. But the exhaust fumes destroy too much.

ROBERT Yes, you can see it. The façade of the cathedral has suffered quite a bit.

NICOLE We're restoring that now, too, and the air has improved already.

ROBERT I believe it. That just goes to show you: where there's a will, there's a way.

Die Umwelt

WORTSCHATZ 1

DIE UMWELT *environment, surroundings*

abreißen, riß ab, abgerissen	*to tear down*	reden (mit)	*to talk (to)*
gebrauchen[1]	*to use, utilize*	renovieren	*to renovate*
erklären	*to explain*	restaurieren	*to restore*
finanzieren	*to finance*	retten	*to save, rescue*
kämpfen	*to fight*	verändern	*to change*
parken	*to park*	verbieten, verbot, verboten	*to forbid, prohibit*
planen	*to plan*		

WEITERES

Das glaube ich gern.	*I believe it.*
Da sieht man's mal wieder.	*That just goes to show you.*
Wo ein Wille ist, ist auch ein Weg[2].	*Where there's a will, there's a way.*

1 Don't confuse **brauchen** *(to need)* with **gebrauchen** *(to use)*: Ich **brauche** einen Kuli. BUT Ich kann diesen Kuli nicht **gebrauchen**, weil er kaputt ist.

2 For other proverbs, see "Zum Thema," exercise C.

PASSIVES VOKABULAR der Kampf, ⁻e *(fight, struggle)*; die Abgase *(pl., exhaust fumes)*; die Bürgerinitiative, -n *(citizens' initiative)*; die Fassade, -n *(façade)*; leiden, litt, gelitten *(to suffer)*; Allerhand! *(How about that!)*

ZUM THEMA

A. **Reporter im Rathaus.** *(You're a radio reporter attending a meeting of the city-planning commission. Read what one man says, then report to YOUR listeners.)*

BEISPIEL: **Er hat gesagt, wir sollten nicht auf die Bürger hören, die immer . . .**

„Hören Sie nicht auf die Bürger, die immer wieder alles, ja die ganze Altstadt retten wollen. Viele alte Innenhöfe *(inner courts)* sind dunkel und häßlich. Abreißen ist viel billiger und einfacher als renovieren! Wenn man die alten Gebäude abreißt und die Innenstadt schön modern aufbaut, dann kommt bestimmt wieder Leben in unser Zentrum. Auf diese Weise kann man auch die Straßen verbreitern *(widen)* und alles besser planen. Fußgängerzonen sind schön und gut, aber nicht im Zentrum, denn alle wollen ihr Auto in der Nähe haben. Das ist doch klar, weil's viel bequemer und sicherer ist! Ich kann Ihnen garantieren, wenn Sie aus dem Zentrum eine Einkaufszone machen, zu deren Geschäften man nur zu Fuß hinkommt *(gets to)*, dann verlieren Sie alle, meine Damen und Herren, viel Geld!"

B. ***Wo würden Sie lieber wohnen, in einem Altbau oder Neubau? Was spricht dafür und was dagegen? Stellen Sie eine Liste auf!*** *(Afterward take a poll.)*

C. ***Sprichwörter*** *(proverbs)*

   1. Was bedeuten diese Sprichwörter? Was ist die englische Version?

     a. Eine Hand wäscht die andere.

     b. Wer nicht wagt°, der nicht gewinnt.   *dares*

     c. Ohne Fleiß kein Preis.

     d. Probieren° geht über Studieren.   *trying*

     e. Aller Anfang ist schwer.

     f. Übung macht den Meister°.   *master*

     g. Es ist noch kein Meister vom Himmel°   *sky*
        gefallen.

     h. Rom ist nicht an einem Tag gebaut worden.

     i. Morgen, morgen, nur nicht heute, sagen alle
        faulen Leute.

     j. Was Hänschen nicht lernt, lernt Hans
        nimmermehr°.   *nevermore*

     k. Viele Köche° verderben° den Brei°.   *cooks/ spoil/ porridge*

     l. Hunger ist der beste Koch.

     m. Lügen° haben kurze Beine.   *lies*

     n. Morgenstund' hat Gold im Mund.

     o. Jeder ist seines Glückes Schmied°.   *blacksmith*

     p. Ende gut, alles gut.

Viele Köche verderben den Brei.

2. Schreiben Sie einen kleinen Aufsatz *(essay)*! (Tell an anecdote or describe a situation demonstrating one of the proverbs. Write about eight to ten sentences.)

D. *Aussprache: Glottal Stops* (See also II. 42 in the pronunciation section of the Appendix.)

1. +Erich +arbeitet +am +alten Dom.
2. Die +Abgase der +Autos machen +einfach +überall +alles kaputt.
3. +Ulf +erinnert sich +an +ein +einmaliges +Abendkonzert +im +Ulmer Dom.
4. +Otto sieht +aus wie +ein +alter +Opa.
5. +Anneliese +ist +attraktiv +und +elegant.

STRUKTUR

1. *The Passive Voice*

English and German sentences are in one of two voices: the active or the passive. In the ACTIVE VOICE the subject of the sentence is doing something; it's "active."

The students ask the professor.

In the PASSIVE VOICE the subject is not doing anything, rather, something is being done to it; it's "passive."

The professor is asked by the students.

Note what happens when a sentence in the active voice is changed into the passive voice. The direct object of the active becomes the subject of the passive:

subj.   obj.
The students ask the professor.

The professor is asked by the students.
subj.   obj. of prep.

In both languages the active voice is used much more frequently than the passive voice, especially in everyday speech. The passive voice is used when the focus is on the person or thing at whom the action is directed, rather than on the agent who is acting.

1. Forms

a. In English the passive is formed with the auxiliary *to be* and the past participle of the verb. In German it is formed with the auxiliary **werden** and the past participle of the verb.

werden . . . + past participle

Der Professor **wird** von den Studenten **gefragt**.

ich	**werde** . . . gefragt	*I am (being)*	
du	**wirst** . . . gefragt	*you are (being)*	
er	**wird** . . . gefragt	*he is (being)*	
wir	**werden** . . . gefragt	*we are (being)*	*asked*
ihr	**werdet** . . . gefragt	*you are (being)*	
sie	**werden** . . . gefragt	*they are (being)*	

b. The passive voice has the same tenses as the active voice. They are formed with the various tenses of **werden** + the past participle of the verb.

PRESENT	Er **wird** . . . gefragt.	*He is being asked . . .*
SIMPLE PAST	Er **wurde** . . . gefragt.	*He was asked . . .*
FUTURE	Er **wird** . . . gefragt **werden**.	*He'll be asked . . .*
PRES. PERF.	Er **ist** . . . gefragt **worden**.	*He has been asked . . .*
PAST PERF.	Er **war** . . . gefragt **worden**.	*He had been asked . . .*

NOTE: In the perfect tenses of the passive voice, the past participle of **werden** *is* **worden**. *When you see or hear* **worden**, *you know immediately that you are dealing with a sentence in the passive.*

Die Altstadt wird renoviert.	*The old part of town is being renovated.*
Die Pläne wurden letztes Jahr gemacht.	*The plans were made last year.*
Alles wird finanziert werden.	*Everything will be financed.*
Alles ist entschieden worden.	*Everything has been decided.*
Manche Gebäude waren im Krieg zerstört worden.	*Some buildings had been destroyed during the war.*

c. Modals themselves are not put into the passive voice. Rather, they follow this pattern:

modal . . . + past participle + **werden**

In this book only the present and simple-past tense of the modals will be used.

PRESENT	Er **muß** . . . gefragt **werden**.	*He must be asked . . .*
SIMPLE PAST	Er **mußte** . . . gefragt **werden**.	*He had to be asked . . .*

Das Gebäude muß renoviert werden.	*The building must be renovated.*
Die Pläne sollten letztes Jahr gemacht werden.	*The plans were supposed to be made last year.*

2. Expression of the Agent

If the AGENT who performs the act is expressed, the preposition **von** is used.

Alles wird **vom Staat** finanziert.   *Everything is financed by the state.*

3. Impersonal Use

In German the passive voice is frequently used without a subject or with **es** functioning as the subject.

Hier darf nicht gebaut werden.   *You can't build here.*
Es darf hier nicht gebaut werden.   *Building is not permitted here.*

4. Alternative to the Passive Voice

One common substitute for the passive voice is a sentence in the active voice with **man** as the subject.

Hier darf nicht gebaut werden.
⎫
⎬ ⟶ **Man** darf hier nicht bauen.
Es darf hier nicht gebaut werden.
⎭

ÜBUNGEN

A. *Etwas Geschichte. Aktiv oder Passiv? (Decide which statements are in the active voice and which are in the passive.)*

1. The city of Trier on the Moselle River recently celebrated its 2000th anniversary.
2. Trier was founded by the Romans in 15 B.C.
3. Its original name was *Augusta Treverorum*.
4. Under Roman occupation, *Germania* along the Rhine and Danube had been transformed into a series of Roman provinces.
5. The names of many towns go back to Latin.
6. Remnants from Roman times can still be seen today.
7. New discoveries are made from time to time.
8. Beautiful Roman museums have been built.
9. One of them is located in the former *Colonia Agrippina* (= **Köln**).

Die Porta Nigra in Trier

B. Was bedeutet das auf englisch?

1. *a.* Köln wurde während des Krieges schwer zerstört.
   b. 80 Prozent *(percent)* der Innenstadt war zerbombt *(destroyed by bombs)* worden.
   c. Heute wird Köln wieder von vielen Touristen besucht.
   d. Vieles ist wieder aufgebaut und restauriert worden.
   e. Und vieles wird noch renoviert werden.

2. *a.* Erst sollten natürlich neue Wohnungen gebaut werden.
   b. Manche alten Gebäude konnten gerettet werden.
   c. Der Dom mußte restauriert werden.
   d. Aber die alten Kirchen aus dem zwölften Jahrhundert dürfen auch nicht vergessen werden.
   e. Das kann natürlich nicht ohne Geld gemacht werden.
   f. Durch Bürgerinitiativen soll genug Geld für die Restaurierung gesammelt werden.

3. *a.* In der Altstadt wird in Parkgaragen geparkt.
   b. Es wird viel mit dem Bus gefahren.
   c. In der Fußgängerzone wird nicht Auto gefahren.
   d. Dort wird zu Fuß gegangen.
   e. Dort wird gern eingekauft.

C. Sagen Sie die Sätze im Aktiv! *(Say each sentence in the active voice, but retain the tense of the original sentence.)*

1. **BEISPIEL:** Nicht alle Gebäude waren vom Krieg zerstört worden.
   Der Krieg hatte nicht alle Gebäude zerstört.

   a. Viele Gebäude sind von Baggern *(bulldozers)* zerstört worden.
   b. Dieses Haus wurde von den Bürgern gerettet.
   c. Viele Unterschriften *(signatures)* wurden von Studenten gesammelt.
   d. Das Haus ist von der Uni gekauft worden.
   e. Die Fassade wird von Spezialisten renoviert werden.
   f. Die Hauspläne werden von Architekten gemacht.

2. **BEISPIEL:** Der Hausplan darf von den Architekten nicht sehr verändert werden.
   Die Architekten dürfen den Hausplan nicht sehr verändern.

   a. Ein Teil soll von der Stadt finanziert werden.
   b. Der Rest muß von der Uni bezahlt werden.
   c. Das Haus konnte von der Universität als Gästehaus ausgebaut werden.
   d. Das Parterre darf von den Studenten als Café gebraucht werden.

3. **BEISPIEL:** Das Gästehaus wird viel besucht.
   Man besucht das Gästehaus viel.

   a. Dort werden Gedanken ausgetauscht.
   b. Es wird auch Englisch und Französisch gesprochen.
   c. Heute abend wird ein Jazzkonzert gegeben.
   d. Letzte Woche wurde ein Film gezeigt.
   e. Hier werden auch Seminare gehalten werden.

Schild (sign) *an einem Hotel*

Dieses Haus
wird vom ADAC
empfohlen

Allgemeiner Deutscher Automobil-Club

UMWELTSCHUTZ
viel ist noch zu tun

D. Wiederholen Sie die Sätze im Passiv, aber in einer anderen Zeit! *(Use the suggested tense.)*

BEISPIEL: Ein alter Film wird gespielt. *(simple past)*
Ein alter Film wurde gespielt.

1. Er wird von den Studenten sehr empfohlen. *(pres. perf.)*
2. Während des Krieges wird er nicht gezeigt. *(simple past)*
3. Er wird verboten. *(past perfect)*
4. Es wird viel darüber geredet. *(future)*
5. Daraus kann viel gelernt werden. *(simple past)*
6. Er soll übrigens wiederholt werden. *(simple past)*

E. Wiederholen Sie die Sätze im Passiv, aber mit einem Modalverb! Was heißt das auf englisch? *(Use the suggested modal.)*

BEISPIEL: Das Paket wird zur Post gebracht. (sollen)
Das Paket soll zur Post gebracht werden.

1. Die Postkarte wird noch ausgefüllt. (müssen)
2. Dann wird es am ersten Schalter abgegeben. (können)
3. Auf der Post werden auch Telefongespräche gemacht. (dürfen)
4. Dollar werden auf der Bank umgewechselt. (sollen)
5. Nicht überall wird mit Reiseschecks bezahlt. (können)
6. Taxifahrer werden mit Bargeld bezahlt. (wollen)

F. Sagen Sie die Sätze im Passiv! *(Do not express the agent.)*

BEISPIEL: Hier spricht man Deutsch.
Hier wird Deutsch gesprochen.

1. Am anderen Tisch spricht man Französisch.
2. Mittags ißt man warm.
3. Dabei redet man gemütlich.
4. Natürlich redet man nicht mit vollem Mund.
5. Übrigens hält man die Gabel in der linken Hand.
6. Und vor dem Essen sagt man „Guten Appetit!"

G. Wir geben eine Party.

1. Was wird auf der Party gemacht?

BEISPIEL: Man tanzt.   **Es wird getanzt.**

a. Man spielt Spiele.
b. Man ißt Pizza.
c. Man trinkt etwas dazu.
d. Man erzählt Witze *(jokes)*.

e. Man lacht viel.
f. Man hört Platten an.
g. Man redet über Politik oder das Wetter.

2. Was muß noch gemacht werden? *(Answer by saying that things have already been done.)*

BEISPIEL: Fritz und Frieda müssen noch angerufen werden.
Fritz und Frieda sind schon angerufen worden!

a. Die Wohnung muß noch geputzt werden.
b. Der Tisch muß noch in die Ecke gestellt werden.
c. Die Gläser müssen noch gewaschen werden.
d. Das Bier muß noch kalt gestellt werden.
e. Die Kartoffelchips müssen noch in die Schüssel *(bowl)* getan werden.
f. Die Pizza muß noch bestellt werden.
g. Die Kassetten müssen noch gesucht werden.

II. *Review of the Uses of* werden

Distinguish carefully between the various uses of **werden**.

1. werden + predicate noun / adjective = a FULL VERB

Er wird Arzt.   *He's going to be a doctor.*
Es wird dunkel.   *It's getting dark.*

2. werden + infinitive = auxiliary of the FUTURE TENSE

Ich werde ihn fragen.   *I'll ask him.*

3. würde + infinitive = auxiliary in the PRESENT-TIME SUBJUNCTIVE

Ich würde ihn fragen.   *I would ask him.*

4. werden + past participle = auxiliary in the PASSIVE VOICE

Er wird von uns gefragt.   *He's (being) asked by us.*

ÜBUNG

H. *Analysieren Sie, wie* werden *gebraucht wird! Was bedeutet das auf englisch?*

BEISPIEL: Jutta ist nach Amerika eingeladen worden.
      werden + past participle = passive voice
      Jutta was invited (to go) to America.

1. Jutta möchte Lehrerin werden.
2. Das Studium dort mußte von ihr bezahlt werden.
3. Es ist teuerer geworden als sie dachte.
4. Das wurde ihr nie gesagt.
5. Was würdest du an ihrer Stelle tun?
6. Ich würde ein Semester arbeiten.
7. Das wird nicht erlaubt werden.
8. Übrigens wird ihr Englisch schon viel besser.

III. *The Special Subjunctive*

German has another subjunctive, often called the SPECIAL SUBJUNCTIVE (or SUBJUNCTIVE I). English only has a few remnants of this subjunctive.

So be it. Long live the Queen. Be that as it may.

In German, too, the special subjunctive is rarely used, and then primarily in formal writing and indirect speech. It is most frequently encountered in critical literary or scientific essays, in news reports, and in literature.

In general, the forms of the third person singular are the ones used most often because they clearly differ from those of the indicative. When the forms of the special subjunctive are identical with those of the indicative, the general subjunctive is used. At this point, you only need to be able to recognize the forms of the special subjunctive and know why they are used.

1. Here are the PRESENT-TIME forms of the special subjunctive for the most common verbs as well as examples of all the verb types you have learned. They have the same endings as the general subjunctive, **-e, -est, -e, -en, -et, -en,** and are added to the stem of the INFINITIVE.

ich	könne	habe	sei	werde	lerne	bringe	komme
du	könnest	habest	seiest	werdest	lernest	bringest	kommest
er	könne	habe	sei	werde	lerne	bringe	komme
wir	können	haben	seien	werden	lernen	bringen	kommen
ihr	könnet	habet	seiet	werdet	lernet	bringet	kommet
sie	können	haben	seien	werden	lernen	bringen	kommen

Er sagte, er **habe** keine Zeit.   *He said he had no time.*
Er sagte, sie **sei** nicht zu Hause.   *He said she wasn't home.*

■ *If referring to the future* (to later), *the special subjunctive of* **werden** *is combined with an infinitive.*

werde . . . + infinitive

Er sagte, er **werde** bald fertig **sein.**   *He said he'd be finished soon.*

2. The PAST-TIME special subjunctive is formed by using the special subjunctive of **haben** or **sein** with a past participle.

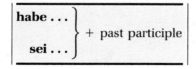

habe . . .
sei . . .   } + past participle

| Er sagt, er **habe** keine Zeit **gehabt**. | *He says he didn't have time.* |
| Er sagte, sie **sei** nicht zu Hause **gewesen**. | *He said she hadn't been home.* |

ÜBUNGEN

I. *Finden Sie den Konjunktiv!* (Indicate the forms of the special subjunctive.)

Tom schrieb, München liege etwa *(about)* 50 km nördlich der Alpen. Es sei die drittgrößte Stadt der Bundesrepublik, wachse schneller als alle anderen deutschen Städte und habe etwa 1,5 Millionen Einwohner *(inhabitants)*. Die Geschichte Münchens sei etwa 1200 Jahre alt. Die Stadt habe eine Oper, mehr als zwanzig Theater, einen schönen Zoo und viele bekannte Museen. Er sei jeden Tag von morgens bis abends unterwegs und habe schon viel gesehen, werde aber noch wenigstens zwei Wochen bleiben.

J. *Lesen Sie!* (Indicate all subjunctive forms and state whether they are in the general or special subjunctive.)

1. In dem Artikel stand *(it said)*, zwischen Weihnachten und der Fastenzeit *(Lent)* feiere man den Fasching oder Karneval. Die Feiern in München, Mainz und Köln seien besonders bekannt. In den drei Tagen vor Aschermittwoch *(Wednesday)* gebe es viele Umzüge, und manche Leute schliefen drei Tage und Nächte fast gar nicht.

2. Er schrieb, er habe gefunden, daß man auch in Deutschland viel Shakespeare zitiere *(quote)*. Aber viele der Leute wüßten nicht, woher die Zitate *(quotes)* kämen. Zum Beispiel höre man oft, daß „etwas faul im Staate Dänemark" sei. Diese Zitate finde man in der ausgezeichneten Übersetzung der Werke Shakespeares von August Wilhelm Schlegel. Ein weiteres Zitat, das viele kennen würden, auch wenn sie nicht wüßten, woher es komme, sei: „Was ist ein Name? Was uns Rose heißt, wie es auch hieße, würde lieblich duften *(smell lovely)*."

3. Der Professor erzählte von dem Archäologen Heinrich Schliemann. Schliemann habe sich als achtjähriges Kind für die Geschichte von dem Trojanischen Krieg interessiert und habe gesagt, er wolle später Troja *(Troy)* finden. Er sei als junger Mann sehr arm gewesen, aber er habe in Rußland und Amerika viel Geld verdient. Erst mit vierzig Jahren habe er angefangen, Archäologie zu studieren und er habe später auch Troja gefunden. Besonders interessant sei, daß Schliemann etwa zwölf bis vierzehn Sprachen gelernt habe. Er habe eine besondere Methode entwickelt *(developed)*: z.B. habe er jeden Tag zwanzig Seiten von *Vikar of Wakefield* und *Ivanhoe* gelernt und habe nach sechs Monaten gut Englisch gesprochen. Später habe er Sprachen in etwa sechs Wochen gelernt!

ZUSAMMENFASSUNG

K. ***Bilden Sie ganze Sätze im Passiv!*** *(Use the tenses suggested.)*

> BEISPIEL: Köln / besucht / von / Touristen aus aller Welt *(present)*
> **Köln wird von Touristen aus aller Welt besucht.**

1. während / Krieg / zerstört / die meisten Häuser *(simple past)*
2. heute / alles / wieder / aufgebaut / schön *(pres. perf.)*
3. nächste Woche / gefeiert / Fasching *(future)*
4. da / sollen / viel / gesungen und getanzt *(present)*
5. das / müssen / einmal / mitgemacht *(present)*

L. ***Auf deutsch, bitte!***

1. Yesterday was a bad day. *2.* First I lost my passport. *3.* Then my handbag and my money were stolen (**gestohlen**). *4.* I tried to pay with traveler's checks. *5.* But without my passport, my checks weren't accepted (**angenommen**). *6.* It was good that Anne was there. *7.* Anne paid the bill (The bill was paid by Anne). *8.* This morning I was called by the police (**die Polizei**). *9.* They had found my handbag. *10.* But my passport hasn't been found yet. *11.* I wish I knew what I did with my passport. *12.* I hope it'll be found soon.

EINBLICKE

WORTSCHATZ 2

der Gastarbeiter, -	*foreign worker*
das Gebiet, -e	*area, region*
Jahrhundert, -e	*century*
Volk, ¨-er	*people, nation*
die Landschaft, -en	*landscape, scenery*
anders	*different(ly)*
inzwischen	*in the meantime*
typisch	*typical(ly)*
unter (+ *dat./acc.*)	*among*
betonen	*to stress, emphasize*

Volkszählung '87 **Zehn Minuten, die allen helfen.**

WAS IST DAS? der Chauvinismus, Dialekt, Extremist, Flohmarkt, Intellektuelle, Nationalismus, Weltkrieg, Wunschtraum; das Ausländische, Gärtchen, Geburtsland, Straßencafé; die Chance, Ferne, Partei, Region, Umweltzerstörung; Partei; demonstrieren, existieren, organisieren; bergig, charakteristisch, informiert, kritisch, nämlich, regional, reiselustig, sogenannt

424 KAPITEL 15

Typisch deutsch?

viewpoint/ FRG citizen — (Aus der Sicht° eines Bundesbürgers°)

Typisch deutsch? Was ist das eigentlich?
Die 60 Millionen Menschen, die hier in der
Bundesrepublik wohnen, sind ziemlich zusammengewürfelt° worden.
thrown together
Nicht jeder, der hier lebt, wurde auch hier geboren. Es gibt viele, die Ende 5
des Krieges als Flüchtlinge° aus den ehemaligen° Ostgebieten[1] gekommen
refugees/ former
waren, es gibt Flüchtlinge aus der DDR und natürlich auch Gastarbeiter[2],

In Berlin gibt es besonders viele Gastarbeiter aus der Türkei.

themselves — die manchmal selbst° nicht wissen, ob sie schon hier oder noch in ihrem
each/ come from — Geburtsland zu Hause sind. Von je° zehn Einwohnern unter uns stammen°
rest — mehr als drei aus anderen Regionen, und die übrigen° wissen auch, daß 10
provisional state/ founded — unsere Republik vor 40 Jahren eigentlich nur als Provisorium° gegründet°
worden ist, als ein Staat, in dem nicht alle Deutschen leben. Damals glaub-
temporary — ten wir natürlich noch, daß die Teilung Deutschlands nur vorübergehend°
reunification/ rather — wäre. Heute aber ist die Wiedervereinigung° Deutschlands eher° ein
Wunschtraum, der in weiter Ferne liegt. Hinter der Elbe ist die Welt in- 15
in many ways — zwischen ganz anders geworden, wenn auch die Menschen in vieler Weise°
die gleichen geblieben sind. Auch sie sind Deutsche.
can be found — Wir sind doch alle sehr verschieden. Es läßt sich nur wenig finden°,
social — was charakteristisch wäre für uns alle: Vielleicht sind wir gesellig°, sitzen
tavern — gern in Straßencafés, in der Kneipe° oder im Restaurant, organisieren uns 20
clubs — in Vereinen°, lieben Fußball und besuchen Flohmärkte. Vielleicht sind wir

425

auch ein reiselustiges Volk. Wir sind internationaler geworden. Nach all dem Nationalismus im 19. Jahrhundert und besonders in der ersten Hälfte° dieses Jahrhunderts hatten wir genug von Chauvinismus und Sendungs-bewußtsein°. Die Familie und die Freizeit bedeuten uns meistens mehr als der Staat; und das gilt° für Ost und West. 25

Aber wir lieben unsere Heimat: die Landschaft, in der wir aufgewachsen° sind, die Großstadt, das Dorf oder die Siedlung° mit ihren Schrebergärten[3]. Viele sind wieder stolz auf ihren Volksstamm; regionale Dialekte werden wieder mehr gesprochen und auch im Radio und Theater betont. Das ist verständlich°, denn unsere Bevölkerung bestand° schon immer aus ver-schiedenen Volksstämmen°, und wir waren eben nur kurze Zeit EIN Staat, nämlich nur von Bismarcks Reichsgründung° 1871[4] bis zum Ende des Zweiten Weltkrieges 1945. 30

Wenn es schon schwer ist zu sagen, wie wir, DIE Deutschen, sind, so kann man doch sehen, daß wir uns verändert haben: Wir sind weltoffener°, europäischer, informierter, vielleicht auch kritischer geworden und nicht mehr so autoritätsgläubig° wie am Anfang dieses Jahrhunderts. Das soge-nannte Typisch-Deutsche ist nicht mehr so wichtig; das Ausländische ist interessanter geworden. Es werden Jeans statt Lederhosen° getragen und viele englische Wörter gebraucht. Man ißt besonders gern chinesisch oder italienisch, und französischer Wein wird genauso gern getrunken wie deutsches Bier. Und man engagiert sich° wieder. Jung und alt, Arbeiter und Intellektuelle demonstrieren gemeinsam° für den Frieden oder kämpfen für die Umwelt. Luft- und Wasserverschmutzung° und saurer° Regen, der die Wälder zerstört, sind so wichtig geworden, daß es sogar eine neue Partei (die Grünen[5]) gibt. Viele Altstädte sind durch Bürgerinitiativen gerettet und restauriert worden. Es wird gemeinsam geplant, weil Lebensqualität sehr wichtig geworden ist. Ja, und der Staat? Nun, er wird im Osten kritisch gesehen, und im Westen wird ihm mehr auf die Finger geschaut° als je zuvor°. Und das ist gut so. 35 40 45 50

ZUM TEXT

A. Was paßt? *(Indicate the correct answer.)*

1. Die Menschen, die in der Bundesrepublik wohnen, sind . . .
   a. alle typisch deutsch
   b. aus allen Teilen des früheren Deutschlands
   c. alle in der Bundesrepublik geboren

2. Die Gastarbeiter kommen . . .
   a. aus den ehemaligen Ostgebieten Deutschlands
   b. aus der DDR
   c. aus südeuropäischen Ländern

3. Die Bundesrepublik wurde vor 40 Jahren als . . ., gegründet.
   a. der Staat, in dem alle Deutschen leben
   b. ein Staat, in dem nicht alle Deutschen leben
   c. ein Staat, in dem Deutsche und Gastarbeiter gemütlich zusammenleben

4. Die Wiedervereinigung Deutschlands ist . . .
   a. ein Wunschtraum
   b. ein schlechter Traum
   c. nur vorübergehend

5. Vielleicht kann man von den Bundesbürgern sagen, daß sie . . .
   a. internationaler als andere Völker sind
   b. genug Chauvinismus und Sendungsbewußtsein haben
   c. ziemlich reiselustig sind

6. Den Bundesbürgern bedeutet . . .
   a. die Familie und die Freizeit mehr als der Staat
   b. der Staat mehr als Familie und Freizeit
   c. das Ausländische nichts

7. Deutschland war . . .
   a. vor kurzer Zeit EIN Staat
   b. EIN Staat von Bismarcks Reichsgründung bis zum Anfang des 2. Weltkrieges
   c. nicht lange EIN Staat

8. Die Deutschen sind . . .
   a. auch heute noch so autoritätsgläubig wie am Anfang des Jahrhunderts
   b. interessante Ausländer
   c. heute weltoffener, informierter und kritischer

9. Heute engagiert man sich wieder: Man kämpft für . . .
   a. Luft- und Wasserverschmutzung
   b. sauren Regen
   c. die Umwelt

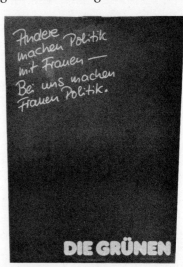

10. Der Kommentar wurde von einem ... geschrieben.
    a. DDR-Bürger
    b. BRD-Bürger
    c. US-Bürger

B. Was fehlt?

1. Nicht alle, die hier leben, _____ hier _____ . *(were born)*
2. Hinter der Elbe _____ die Welt ganz anders _____ . *(has become)*
3. Regionale Dialekte _____ wieder mehr _____ . *(are spoken)*
4. Wir _____ weltoffener, informiert, vielleicht kritischer _____ . *(have become)*
5. Jetzt _____ Jeans statt Lederhosen _____ . *(are worn)*
6. Viele englische Wörter _____ . *(are being used)*
7. Heute _____ auch gern französischer Wein _____ . *(is drunk)*
8. Viele Altstädte _____ durch Bürgerinitiativen _____ . *(have been restored)*
9. Auch im Osten _____ der Staat kritisch _____ . *(is seen)*
10. Aber es _____ nicht ganz so offen gegen ihn _____ . *(may be spoken)*

C. Typisch deutsch! *(Find eight points the author makes about citizens of the FRG. How do they compare to your picture of "the Germans"?)*

D. Typisch amerikanisch / kanadisch! *(Write eight to ten sentences about what you consider typical of people here. You may use the questions below as points of departure.)*

1. Woher kommen viele in unserer zusammengewürfelten Gesellschaft *(society)*? Warum kamen sie?
2. Ist Nationalismus wichtig? Lieben die meisten Amerikaner (Kanadier) ihren Staat? Woran sieht man das?
3. Wo engagieren sich die Menschen hier?
4. Gibt es hier auch regionale Dialekte? Wo?
5. Stellen Sie sich vor, Sie hätten in ein anderes Land geheiratet. Was würde Ihnen als typisch amerikanisch / kanadisch dort fehlen? Oder glauben Sie, daß Sie überall gleich *(equally)* zu Hause wären?

ÜBRIGENS

1. According to the Potsdam Agreement of 1945, the area east of the Oder and Neiße rivers, about one-fourth of the former German Reich, was put under Polish and Soviet administration. The twelve million Germans who lived there were forced to leave for what is now the GDR and the FRG.

2. During the economic boom of the FRG, especially during the 1960s after the Berlin Wall had halted the flow of people from the east, German industry needed additional workers. These "guest workers" (**Gastarbeiter**) came from countries

Was sich die Deutschen wünschen

Umfragen in der Bundesrepublik Deutschland brachten es an den Tag:

1 Gesundheit

2 Umweltschutz

3 Flexible Altersgrenze

like Spain, Italy, Yugoslavia, and Turkey. With automation and the economic slow-down, the need for such workers has diminished. But there are still over four million foreign workers in the FRG. Although they have equal rights before the law, many have not been integrated into society because of language and cultural differences.

3. Usually leased from the city over a long period of time, **Schrebergärten** are small gardens, often located at the outskirts of a city at some distance from the gardeners' living quarters. Named for Dr. Schreber, a nineteenth-century physician who created the first playgrounds for children, the gardens not only supplement the family menu with fresh fruit and vegetables, but they also provide outdoor recreation for apartment dwellers.

4. **Otto Graf von Bismarck** was instrumental in the founding of the Second German Empire in 1871, when the Prussian king was made emperor (**Kaiser Wilhelm I**). Bismarck served as chancellor until 1890, when he was dismissed by the young **Kaiser Wilhelm II**.

5. One of the most interesting phenomena in the postwar political scene in the FRG is the emergence of the **Partei der Grünen**. Somewhat resented by the traditional parties, the Greens represent an alliance of dissenting forces, such as radical peace and antinuclear groups, as well as people of all ages and walks of life who are deeply concerned about the mounting ecological problems of densely populated Central Europe.

I. *Comparison*

1. The COMPARATIVE is formed by adding **-er** to an adjective; and the SUPER-LATIVE, by adding -**(e)st**. Many one-syllable adjectives and adverbs with the stem vowels **a, o,** or **u** have an umlaut.

schnell	schneller	schnellst-
lang	länger	längst-
bunt	bunter	buntest-

A few adjectives and adverbs have irregular forms in the comparative and superlative.

gern	**lieber**	**liebst-**	hoch	**höher**	**höchst-**
groß	**größer**	**größt-**	nah	**näher**	**nächst-**
gut	**besser**	**best-**	viel	**mehr**	**meist-**

2. With predicate adjectives and adverbs, the comparative ends in **-er**. The superlative is preceded by **am** and ends in **-sten**.

Ich esse schnell. Du ißt schneller. Er ißt **am** schnell**sten**.

3. In the comparative and superlative, adjectives preceding nouns have the same endings under the same conditions as adjectives in the positive form.

der gute Wein	der bessere Wein	der beste Wein
Ihr guter Wein	Ihr besserer Wein	Ihr bester Wein
guter Wein	besserer Wein	bester Wein

4. Here are four important phrases used in comparisons:

Gestern war es nicht **so heiß wie** heute.	*Yesterday it wasn't as hot as today.*
Heute ist es **heißer als** gestern.	*Today it's hotter than yesterday.*
Es wird **immer heißer.**	*It's getting hotter and hotter.*
Je länger du wartest, **desto heißer** wird es.	*The longer you wait, the hotter it gets.*
Je heißer, desto besser.	*The hotter, the better.*

II. *Relative Clauses*

1. Relative clauses are introduced by RELATIVE PRONOUNS.

	singular			plural
	masc.	**neut.**	**fem.**	
nom.	der	das	die	die
acc.	den			
dat.	dem	dem	der	denen
gen.	dessen	dessen	deren	deren

The form of the relative pronoun depends on the NUMBER AND GENDER OF THE ANTECEDENT and on the FUNCTION of the relative pronoun WITHIN THE RELATIVE CLAUSE.

> . . . antecedent, (preposition) RP _____ V1, . . .
> gender? number?   function?

2. The word order in the relative clause is like that of all subordinate clauses: the inflected part of the verb (V1) comes last.

> . . ., RP _____ V1, . . .

Der junge Mann, der gerade hier war, studiert Theologie.
Die Universität, an der er studiert, ist schon sehr alt.

III. *The Future*

1. The future consists of a present-tense form of

> **werden** . . . + infinitive

> ich werde . . . gehen   wir werden . . . gehen
> du wirst . . . gehen   ihr werdet . . . gehen
> er wird . . . gehen   sie werden . . . gehen

Er wird es dir erklären.

2. The future of a sentence with a modal consists of

> **werden** . . . + verb infinitive + modal infinitive

Er wird es dir erklären können.

431

IV. *The Subjunctive*

English and German follow very similar patterns in the subjunctive, as for instance:

If he came...	Wenn er käme, ...
If he would come...	Wenn er kommen würde, ...
If he had come...	Wenn er gekommen wäre, ...

German, however, has two subjunctives, the GENERAL SUBJUNCTIVE (SUBJUNCTIVE II) and the SPECIAL SUBJUNCTIVE (SUBJUNCTIVE I), of which the latter is primarily used in writing. The endings of both subjunctives are the same.

ich	**-e**	wir	**-en**
du	**-est**	ihr	**-et**
er	**-e**	sie	**-en**

1. Forms

a. GENERAL SUBJUNCTIVE (II)

present time or future time		**past time**
Based on the forms of the simple past; refers to *now*	Based on the forms of werden + inf.; refers to *later*	Based on the forms of the past perf.; refers to *earlier*

er **lernte**	er **würde lernen**	er **hätte gelernt**
brächte	würde bringen	hätte gebracht
hätte	würde haben	hätte gehabt
wäre	würde sein	wäre gewesen
nähme	würde nehmen	hätte genommen
käme	würde kommen	wäre gekommen

▪ *In conversation the* **würde**-*form is commonly used when referring to present time. However, avoid using the* **würde**-*form with* **haben, sein, wissen,** *and the modals. When referring to past time, the* **würde**-*form is hardly ever used.*

Er würde es dir erklären.

▪ *Modals in the past-time subjunctive follow this pattern:*

hätte ... + verb infinitive + modal infinitive

Er hätte es dir erklären können.

b. The SPECIAL SUBJUNCTIVE (I)

present time	future time	past time
Based on the forms of the infinitive; refers to *now*	Based on the forms of the future; refers to *later*	Based on the forms of the pres. perf.; refers to *earlier*

er **lerne**	er **werde lernen**	er **habe gelernt**
bringe	werde bringen	habe gebracht
habe	werde haben	habe gehabt
sei	werde sein	sei gewesen
nehme	werde nehmen	habe genommen
komme	werde kommen	sei gekommen

2. Use

a. The GENERAL SUBJUNCTIVE is quite common in everyday speech and is used in:

■ *Polite Requests or Questions*

Könnten Sie mir sagen, wo die Universität ist?   *Could you tell me where the university is?*

■ *Hypothetical Statements or Questions*

Er sollte bald hier sein.   *He should be here soon.*
Was würdest du tun?   *What would you do?*
Was hättest du getan?   *What would you have done?*

■ *Wishes*

Wenn ich das nur wüßte!   *If only I knew that!*
Wenn ich das nur gewußt hätte!   *If only I had known that!*
Hätte ich das nur gewußt!
Ich wünschte, ich hätte das gewußt!   *I wish I had known that!*

■ *Unreal Conditions*

Wenn wir Geld hätten, würden wir fliegen.   *If we had the money, we'd fly.*
Wenn wir Geld gehabt hätten, wären wir geflogen.   *If we had had the money, we would have flown.*

■ *Indirect Speech* (see p. 434)

b. The SPECIAL SUBJUNCTIVE is used primarily in formal WRITING and in indirect speech, unless the form of the indicative is the same as the subjunctive, in which case the general subjunctive is used (ich komme = **ich komme > ich käme;** ich frage = **ich frage > ich würde fragen**).

V. *Indirect Speech*

The tense of the indirect statement is determined by the tense of the direct statement.

direct statement   indirect statement

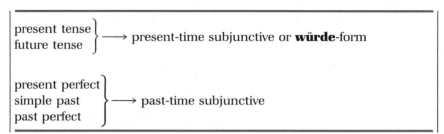

present tense	
future tense	→ present-time subjunctive or **würde**-form

present perfect	
simple past	→ past-time subjunctive
past perfect	

| „Ich komme nicht." | Sie sagte, sie käme (komme) nicht. |
| „Ich werde nicht kommen." | Sie sagte, sie würde (werde) nicht kommen. |

| „Ich bin nicht gegangen." | Sie sagte, sie wäre (sei) nicht gegangen. |
| „Ich hatte keine Lust." | Sie sagte, sie hätte (habe) keine Lust gehabt. |

This is also true of questions. Remember to use **ob** when the question begins with the verb.

„Kommst du mit?"	Er fragte, ob ich mitkäme (mitkomme).
„Wirst du mitkommen?"	Er fragte, ob ich mitkommen würde (werde).
„Wann seid ihr zurück gekommen?"	Sie fragte, wann wir zurück gekommen wären (seien).

Indirect requests require the use of **sollen**.

„Frag nicht so viel!"   Er sagte, sie sollte (solle) nicht so viel fragen.

VI. *The Passive Voice*

In the active voice the subject of the sentence is doing something. In the passive voice the subject is not doing anything; rather, something is being done to it.

1. Forms

werden ... + past participle

ich werde ... gefragt	wir werden ... gefragt
du wirst ... gefragt	ihr werdet ... gefragt
er wird ... gefragt	sie werden ... gefragt

2. The tenses in the passive are formed with the various tenses of **werden** + past participle.

er **wird** . . . gefragt	er **ist** . . . gefragt **worden**
er **wurde** . . . gefragt	er **war** . . . gefragt **worden**
er **wird** . . . gefragt **werden**	

Das ist uns erklärt worden.

3. Modals follow this pattern:

modal . . . + past participle + infinitive of **werden**

Das muß noch einmal erklärt werden.

4. In German the passive is often used without a subject or with **es** functioning as the subject.

Hier wird renoviert.
Es wird hier renoviert.

5. Instead of using the passive voice, the same idea may be expressed in the active voice with the subject **man**.

Man hat alles noch einmal erklärt.

VII. *Review of the uses of* werden

1. FULL VERB	: Er **wird** Arzt.	*He's going to be a doctor.*
2. FUTURE	: Ich **werde** danach **fragen.**	*I'll ask about it.*
3. SUBJUNCTIVE	: Ich **würde** danach **fragen.**	*I'd ask about it.*
4. PASSIVE	: Er **wird** danach **gefragt.**	*He's (being) asked about it.*

WORTSCHATZWIEDERHOLUNG

A. *Fragen*

1. Wie viele Berufe kennen Sie auf deutsch? Sie haben eine Minute.
2. Woran denken Sie dabei?
   Zahnarzt, Hausfrau, Note, finanzieren, sich fühlen, parken, bunt
3. Was muß der Artikel dieser Wörter sein, und was bedeuten sie auf englisch?
   Haushaltsgeld, Chemielabor, Weltkrieg, Zwischenprüfungsnote, Rechtsanwaltsfirma, Universitätsparkplatz, Liebesgeschichte, Berglandschaft, Hals-Nasen-Ohrenarzt

B. Was paßt?

1. *Nennen Sie das passende Verb!*

der Gedanke, Kampf, Plan, Schutz, Traum, Verkäufer, Versuch, Wunsch; das Gebäude; die Erklärung

2. *Nennen Sie das passende Hauptwort!*

beruflich, frei, sportlich, verlobt; arbeiten, sich erinnern, leben, lehren, studieren, teilen

C. *Geben Sie das Gegenteil davon!*

arm, dick, faul, furchtbar, häßlich, hell, langweilig, leicht, schmutzig; damals, nie; rennen, suchen, vergessen, verlieren; der Krieg, das Nebenfach, die Vergangenheit

STRUKTURWIEDERHOLUNG

D. *Komparativ und Superlativ*

1. *Geben Sie den Komparativ und den Superlativ!*

BEISPIEL: lang   **länger, am längsten**

berühmt, bunt, dumm, faul, gern, groß, gut, heiß, hoch, hübsch, kalt, kurz, sauber, typisch, viel, warm

2. *Ersetzen Sie das Adjektiv!*
   a. Rolf ist nicht so alt wie Karl-Heinz.
      charmant, freundlich, bekannt, witzig
   b. Karl-Heinz ist älter als Rolf.
      sympathisch, nett, talentiert, ruhig
   c. Die Stadt wird immer schöner.
      groß, reich, interessant, international

3. *Was fehlt?*
   a. Wir wohnen jetzt in _____ Stadt. *(a prettier)*
   b. Die Umgebung ist noch _____ als vorher. *(more beautiful)*
   c. Es gibt keine _____ Umgebung. *(more interesting)*
   d. Peter hat _____ Arbeit. *(the most strenuous)*
   e. Aber er hat _____ Einkommen. *(the highest)*
   f. Er hat immer _____ Ideen. *(the most and the best)*
   g. Es gibt keine _____ Kollegen *(pl.)*. *(nicer)*
   h. Sie geben ihm _____ Freiheit *(freedom)*. *(the greatest)*
   i. _____ er hier ist, _____ gefällt es ihm. *(the longer, the better)*
   j. Die Lebensmittel kosten _____ bei euch. *(just as much as)*
   k. Aber die Häuser kosten _____ bei euch. *(less than)*

E. Relativsätze. Bilden Sie Relativsätze!

BEISPIEL: die Dame, _____ , ... Sie wohnt im dritten Stock.
die Dame, die im dritten Stock wohnt, ...

1. der Freund, _____ , ...
Er war gerade hier. / Du hast ihn kennengelernt. / Ihm gehört das Büchergeschäft in der Goethestraße. / Seine Firma ist in West-Berlin.
2. die Ärztin, _____ , ...
Ihre Sekretärin hat uns angerufen. / Sie ist hier neu. / Wir haben durch sie von dem Programm gehört.
3. das Gebäude, _____ , ...
Ihr werdet es bald sehen. / Du bist an dem Gebäude vorbeigefahren. / Es steht auf der Insel. / Man hat von dem Gebäude so einen wunderschönen Blick *(view, m.)*.
4. die Leute, _____ , ...
Sie sehen aus wie Amerikaner. / Dort steht ihr Bus. / Die Landschaft gefällt ihnen so gut. / Du hast dich für sie interessiert. / Du hast mit ihnen geredet.

F. Zukunft. Sagen Sie die Sätze in der Zukunft!

1. Ich nehme an einer Gruppenreise teil.
2. Das ist billiger.
3. Du mußt ihnen bald das Geld schicken.
4. Meine Tante versucht, uns in Basel zu sehen.
5. Wie kann sie uns finden?
6. Das erklärst du ihr bestimmt.

G. Konjunktiv (Subjunctive)

1. Bilden sie ganze Sätze im Konjunktiv der Gegenwart oder mit der würde-*Form!*

a. ich / mich / fühlen / besser // wenn / die / Arbeit / sein / fertig
b. das / sein / wunderschön
c. ihr / können / uns / dann / besuchen
d. ich wünschte // Rolf / haben / mehr Zeit
e. wenn / ich / nur / können / sich gewöhnen / daran!
f. erklären / du / mir / das?
g. ich wünschte // er / nicht / reden / so viel am Telefon
h. was / du / tun?

2. Bilden Sie ganze Sätze im Konjunktiv der Vergangenheit!

a. wir / nicht / sollen / in / Berge / fahren
b. ich wünschte // sie *(sg.)* / zu Hause / bleiben
c. das / sein / einfacher
d. wenn / wir / nur / nicht / wandern / so viel!
e. wenn / du / mitnehmen / bessere Schuhe // die Füße / wehtun / dir / nicht
f. du / sollen / mich / erinnern / daran
g. ich / es / finden / schöner // bleiben / zu Hause

3. *Variieren Sie den Satz!*
Ich studiere dort.

- *a.* I'll study there.
- *b.* I'd study there.
- *c.* Would you *(sg. fam.)* like to study there?
- *d.* I wish I could study there.
- *e.* She could have studied there.
- *f.* If I study there, my German will get better.
- *g.* If I were to study there, I could visit you *(pl. fam.)*.
- *h.* I should have studied there.

Bad Wimpfen am Neçkar

H. *Indirekte Rede* (indirect speech). **Lesen Sie erst, was David aus Amerika geschrieben hat, und erzählen Sie es indirekt!**

„Ich habe eine nette Wohnung. Mein Zimmerkollege ist aus New York. Ich lerne viel von ihm. Ich spreche nur Englisch. Manchmal gehe ich auch zu Partys. Ich kenne schon viele Studenten. Viele wohnen im Studentenheim. Aber das ist mir zu teuer. Die Kurse und Professoren sind ausgezeichnet. Aber ich muß viel lesen. Eigentlich habe ich keine Probleme. Nur gibt es zu viele Prüfungen. Ich kann mehr Geld gebrauchen. Ich muß etwas nebenher *(on the side)* verdienen. Ich will mir eine Stelle als Ober suchen."

1. *Erzählen Sie, was David geschrieben hat!*

BEISPIEL: **David schrieb, er hätte eine nette Wohnung. Sein Zimmerkollege wäre aus New York. . . .**

2. *Was schrieb David damals über seine Zeit in Amerika?*

BEISPIEL: **David schrieb, er hätte eine nette Wohnung gehabt. Sein Zimmerkollege wäre aus New York gewesen . . .**

I. *Passiv* (Passive voice). **Sagen Sie die Sätze im Passiv!** *(Do not express pronoun agents.)*

1. Viele Studenten besuchen diese Universität.
2. Man renoviert dieses Gebäude.
3. In den Hörsälen gibt man Vorlesungen.
4. Wir müssen viel für die Kurse lesen.
5. Am Wochenende zeigte man hier einen Film.
6. Man hat Marlene Dietrich oft photographiert.
7. Diesen Film soll man wiederholen.
8. Man muß den Hörsaal noch einmal reservieren.

AUFGABE

J. *Was fehlt? Sehen Sie auf das Bild!*

1. Die Straße, _____ man hier sieht, heißt die Drosselgasse.
2. Die Stadt, in _____ sie liegt, heißt Rüdesheim.
3. Die Leute, _____ durch diese Gasse *(narrow street)* bummeln, müssen Zeit haben.

Die Drosselgasse in Rüdesheim

4. Die Busse, mit _____ sie gekommen sind, kommen von überall her.

5. In den Hotels, _____ Namen man auf den Schildern *(signs)* lesen kann, kann man gut essen und Wein trinken.

6. Der Wein, _____ Ernte *(harvest)* im September groß gefeiert wird, kommt aus der Umgebung von Rüdesheim.

7. Er ist auf den Weinbergen *(vineyards, pl.)* gewachsen, _____ man links und rechts des Rheins sieht.

8. Die Gasthöfe, _____ Sie auf dem Bild sehen, sind alt.

9. Der Gasthof, in _____ wir übernachtet haben, heißt „Linderwirt".

10. Es ist das Hotel, _____ Sie auf der linken Seite sehen.

11. Unser Zimmer, _____ Fenster offen ist, war sehr bequem.

12. Der Wein, _____ wir dort getrunken haben, war phantastisch.

13. Die Musik, zu _____ wir getanzt haben, war auch prima.

K. *Auf deutsch, bitte!*

1. Now I have finished (**fertig werden mit**) my first year of German. *2.* I've really learned a lot. *3.* I never would have thought that it could be so much fun. *4.* Not everything has been easy. *5.* I had to learn many words. *6.* Many exercises had to be done. *7.* Soon we'll have our last exam. *8.* Because I've always prepared (myself) well, I don't have to work so much now. *9.* On the day after the exam there'll be celebrating. *10.* I've been invited to a party by a couple of friends. *11.* If I had the money, I'd fly to Europe now. *12.* Then I could see many of the cities we read about, and I could use my German.

1. *Predicting the Gender of Some Nouns*

As a general rule, nouns must be memorized with their articles because their genders are not readily predictable. However, here are a few hints to help you determine the gender of some nouns in order to eliminate unnecessary memorizing.

a. Most nouns referring to males are MASCULINE.

der Vater, **der** Bruder, **der** Junge

- *Days, months, and seasons are masculine, too.*

der Montag, **der** Juni, **der** Winter

b. Most nouns referring to females are FEMININE:

die Mutter, **die** Schwester, **die** Frau

- *Many feminine nouns can be derived from masculine nouns. Their plurals always end in* **-nen:**

der Schweizer > die Schweizer**in**
der Österreicher > die Österreicher**in**

die Schweizerin**nen**, Österreicherin**nen**

- *All nouns ending in* **-heit, -keit, -ie, -ik, -ion, -schaft, -tät,** *and* **ung** *are feminine. Their plurals end in* **-en.**

die Schön**heit**, Richtig**keit**, Geograph**ie**, Mus**ik**, Relig**ion**, Nachbar**schaft**, Quali**tät**, Rech**nung**

die Qualität**en**, Rechnung**en** usw.

- *Most nouns ending in* **-e** *are feminine. Their plurals end in* **-n.**

die Sprach**e**, Woch**e**, Hos**e**, Kreid**e**, Farb**e**, Seit**e**

die Sprache**n**, Woche**n** usw.

c. All nouns ending in **-chen** or **-lein** are NEUTER. These two suffixes make diminutives of nouns, i.e., they make them smaller:

der Bruder > das Brüder**chen** *(little brother)*
die Schwester > das Schwester**lein** *(little sister)*

- *Because of these suffixes, two nouns referring to females are neuter:*

das Mäd**chen**, Fräu**lein**

- *Most cities and countries are neuter, too.*

    (das) Berlin, **(das)** Deutschland
  BUT die Schweiz, die Tschechoslowakei

2. Summary Chart of the Four Cases

	use	follows . . .	singular masc.	neut.	fem.	plural	personal pronouns and interrogative pronouns				
nom.	Subject, Predicate noun	**heißen** **sein** **werden**	der dieser[1] ein mein[2]	das dieses ein	die diese eine	die diese keine	ich wir	du ihr wer?	er sie	es was?	sie sie	Sie Sie
acc.	Direct object	**durch, für, gegen, ohne, um**	den diesen einen meinen	mein	meine	meine	mich uns	dich euch wen?	ihn sie	es was?	sie sie	Sie Sie
		an, auf, hinter, in, neben, über, unter, vor, zwischen										
dat.	Indirect object	**aus, bei, mit, nach, seit, von, zu**	dem diesem einem meinem	dem diesem einem meinem	der dieser einer meiner	den diesen keinen meinen	mir uns	dir euch wem?	ihm ihnen	ihm —	ihr ihnen	Ihnen Ihnen
		antworten, danken, fehlen, gefallen, gehören, glauben,[3] gratulieren, helfen, schmecken usw.										
gen.	Possessive	**statt, trotz, während, wegen**	des dieses eines meines	des dieses eines meines	der dieser keiner meiner	der dieser keiner meiner		wessen?		—		

NOTE: 1. The *der*-words are *dieser, jeder, welcher, alle, manche, solche.*
2. The *ein*-words are *kein, mein, dein, sein, ihr, unser, euer, Ihr.*
3. *Ich glaube **ihm.*** BUT *Ich glaube **es.***

3. Verbs with Prepositional Objects

acc.: **sich ärgern über, denken an, (sich) erinnern an, sich freuen auf, glauben an, sich gewöhnen an, sich interessieren für, sich lustig machen über, schreiben an, sprechen über, warten auf**
dat.: **Angst haben vor, halten von, erzählen von, reden mit, teilnehmen an, träumen von**

4. *Reflexive Pronouns*

	nom.	acc.	dat.
sg.	ich	mich	mir
	du	dich	dir
	er		
	es	**sich**	
	sie		
pl.	wir	uns	
	ihr	euch	
	sie	**sich**	
sg./pl.	Sie	**sich**	

5. *Relative Pronouns*

	singular			plural
	masc.	neut.	fem.	
nom.	der	das	die	die
acc.	den			
dat.	dem	dem	der	den**en**
gen.	de**ssen**	de**ssen**	de**ren**	de**ren**

6. *Adjective Endings*

a. Preceded Adjectives

	singular			plural
	masc.	neut.	fem.	
nom.	**-e/-er**	**-e/-es**	**-e**	
acc.				-en
dat.		-en		
gen.				

COMPARE:

nom.	der gute Saft ein guter Saft	das gute Brot ein gutes Brot	die gute Wurst eine gute Wurst
acc.	den guten Saft einen guten Saft	das gute Brot ein gutes Brot	die gute Wurst eine gute Wurst
dat.	dem guten Saft einem guten Saft	dem guten Brot einem guten Brot	der guten Wurst einer guten Wurst
gen.	des guten Saftes eines guten Saftes	des guten Brotes eines guten Brotes	der guten Wurst einer guten Wurst

b. Unpreceded adjectives have the endings that the definite article would have if it were used.

Der Wein und das Bier schmecken bei dem Wetter prima.
Guter Wein und kaltes Bier schmecken bei heißem Wetter prima.

7. *n-Nouns*

	singular	plural
nom.	der Student	die Studenten
acc.	den Studenten	die Studenten
dat.	dem Studenten	den Studenten
gen.	des Studenten	der Studenten

Other nouns are:

Herr (-n, -en), Franzose, Gedanke (-ns, -n), Journalist, Junge, Komponist, Mensch, Nachbar, Name (-ns, -n), Polizist, Tourist, Zimmerkollege usw.

8. *Adjectival Nouns*

	singular		plural
	masc.	fem.	
nom.	der Deutsche ein Deutscher	die Deutsche eine Deutsche	die Deutschen keine Deutschen
acc.	den Deutschen einen Deutschen		
dat.	dem Deutschen einem Deutschen	der Deutschen einer Deutschen	den Deutschen keinen Deutschen
gen.	des Deutschen eines Deutschen	der Deutschen einer Deutschen	der Deutschen keiner Deutschen

Other adjectival nouns are:

der Beamte (BUT **die Beamtin!**) and **der Angestellte**

9. *Comparison of Irregular Adjectives and Adverbs*

gern	lieber	liebst-
groß	größer	größt
gut	besser	best-
hoch	höher	höchst-
nah	näher	nächst-
viel	mehr	meist-

10. *Verb Forms in Different Tenses*

INDICATIVE *(INDIKATIV)*

PRESENT *(GEGENWART)*

I ask, I am asking, I do ask

I drive, I am driving, I do drive

ich	frage	ich	fahre
du	fragst	du	fährst
er	fragt	er	fährt
wir	fragen	wir	fahren
ihr	fragt	ihr	fahrt
sie	fragen	sie	fahren

SIMPLE PAST *(VERGANGENHEIT)*

I asked, I was asking, I did ask

I drove, I was driving, I did drive

ich	fragte	ich	fuhr
du	fragtest	du	fuhrst
er	fragte	er	fuhr
wir	fragten	wir	fuhren
ihr	fragtet	ihr	fuhrt
sie	fragten	sie	fuhren

FUTURE *(ZUKUNFT)*

I will ask

I will drive

ich	werde		ich	werde	
du	wirst		du	wirst	
er	wird	} fragen	er	wird	} fahren
wir	werden		wir	werden	
ihr	werdet		ihr	werdet	
sie	werden		sie	werden	

PRESENT PERFECT (PERFEKT)

I have asked, I ask

ich	habe	
du	hast	
er	hat	gefragt
wir	haben	
ihr	habt	
sie	haben	

I have driven, I drove

ich	bin	
du	bist	
er	ist	gefahren
wir	sind	
ihr	seid	
sie	sind	

PAST PERFECT (PLUSQUAMPERFEKT)

I had asked

ich	hatte	
du	hattest	
er	hatte	gefragt
wir	hatten	
ihr	hattet	
sie	hatten	

I had driven

ich	war	
du	warst	
er	war	gefahren
wir	waren	
ihr	wart	
sie	waren	

SUBJUNCTIVE (KONJUNKTIV)

PRESENT-TIME (GENERAL AND SPECIAL)

I asked, I would ask

ich	fragte	= ich	würde	
du	fragtest	= du	würdest	
er	fragte	= er	würde	fragen
wir	fragten	= wir	würden	
ihr	fragtet	= ihr	würdet	
sie	fragten	= sie	würden	

ich	frage
du	fragest
er	frage
wir	fragen
ihr	fraget
sie	fragen

I drove, I would drive

ich	führe	= ich	würde	
du	führest	= du	würdest	
er	führe	= er	würde	fahren
wir	führen	= wir	würden	
ihr	führet	= ihr	würdet	
sie	führen	= sie	würden	

ich	fahre
du	fahrest
er	fahre
wir	fahren
ihr	fahret
sie	fahren

PAST-TIME (GENERAL AND SPECIAL)

I would have asked

ich	hätte	
du	hättest	
er	hätte	gefragt
wir	hätten	
ihr	hättet	
sie	hätten	

I would have driven

ich	wäre	
du	wärest	
er	wäre	gefahren
wir	wären	
ihr	wäret	
sie	wären	

ich	habe	
du	habest	
er	habe	} gefragt
wir	haben	
ihr	habet	
sie	haben	

ich	sei	
du	sei(e)st	
er	sei	
wir	seien	} gefahren
ihr	seiet	
sie	seien	

PASSIVE VOICE *(PASSIV)*

PRESENT *(GEGENWART)*

I am (being) asked

ich	werde	
du	wirst	
er	wird	} gefragt
wir	werden	
ihr	werdet	
sie	werden	

SIMPLE PAST *(VERGANGENHEIT)*

I was (being) asked

ich	wurde	
du	wurdest	
er	wurde	} gefragt
wir	wurden	
ihr	wurdet	
sie	wurden	

FUTURE *(ZUKUNFT)*

I will be asked

ich	werde	
du	wirst	
er	wird	} gefragt werden
wir	werden	
ihr	werdet	
sie	werden	

PRESENT PERFECT *(PERFEKT)*

I have been asked

ich	bin	
du	bist	
er	ist	} gefragt worden
wir	sind	
ihr	seid	
sie	sind	

PAST PERFECT *(PLUSQUAMPERFEKT)*
I had been asked

ich	war	
du	warst	
er	war	gefragt worden
wir	waren	
ihr	wart	
sie	waren	

11. *Principal Parts of* N-VERBS *("strong verbs")* and IRREGULAR T-VERBS *("irregular weak verbs")* *Listed Alphabetically*

This list is limited to the active n-verbs and irregular t-verbs used in this text. Compound verbs like **ankommen** or **abfliegen** are not included, since their principal parts are the same as those of the basic verbs **kommen** and **fliegen.**

infinitive	present	simple past	past participle	meaning
anfangen	fängt an	fing an	angefangen	*to begin*
backen	bäckt	buk (backte)	gebacken	*to bake*
beginnen		begann	begonnen	*to begin*
bekommen		bekam	bekommen	*to receive*
bleiben		blieb	ist geblieben	*to remain*
bringen		brachte	gebracht	*to bring*
denken		dachte	gedacht	*to think*
einladen	lädt ein	lud ein	eingeladen	*to invite*
empfehlen	empfiehlt	empfahl	empfohlen	*to recommend*
essen	ißt	aß	gegessen	*to eat*
fahren	fährt	fuhr	ist gefahren	*to drive, go*
fallen	fällt	fiel	ist gefallen	*to fall*
finden		fand	gefunden	*to find*
fliegen		flog	ist geflogen	*to fly*
geben	gibt	gab	gegeben	*to give*
gefallen	gefällt	gefiel	gefallen	*to please*
gehen		ging	ist gegangen	*to go*
geschehen	geschieht	geschah	ist geschehen	*to happen*
gewinnen		gewann	gewonnen	*to win*
haben	hat	hatte	gehabt	*to have*
halten	hält	hielt	gehalten	*to hold; stop*
hängen		hing	gehangen	*to be hanging*
heißen		hieß	geheißen	*to be called, named*
helfen	hilft	half	geholfen	*to help*
kennen		kannte	gekannt	*to know*
klingen		klang	geklungen	*to sound*
kommen		kam	ist gekommen	*to come*
lassen	läßt	ließ	gelassen	*to let; leave (behind)*

infinitive	present	simple past	past participle	meaning
laufen	läuft	lief	ist gelaufen	to run; walk
lesen	liest	las	gelesen	to read
liegen		lag	gelegen	to lie
nehmen	nimmt	nahm	genommen	to take
nennen		nannte	genannt	to name, call
rennen		rannte	ist gerannt	to run
rufen		rief	gerufen	to call
scheinen		schien	geschienen	to shine; seem
schlafen	schläft	schlief	geschlafen	to sleep
schreiben		schrieb	geschrieben	to write
schwimmen		schwamm	geschwommen	to swim
sehen	sieht	sah	gesehen	to see
sein	ist	war	ist gewesen	to be
singen		sang	gesungen	to sing
sitzen		saß	gesessen	to sit
sprechen	spricht	sprach	gesprochen	to speak
stehen		stand	gestanden	to stand
steigen		stieg	ist gestiegen	to climb
tragen	trägt	trug	getragen	to carry; wear
trinken		trank	getrunken	to drink
tun	tut	tat	getan	to do
verlieren		verlor	verloren	to lose
wachsen	wächst	wuchs	ist gewachsen	to grow
waschen	wäscht	wusch	gewaschen	to wash
werden	wird	wurde	ist geworden	to become; get
wissen	weiß	wußte	gewußt	to know
ziehen		zog	gezogen	to pull

12. *Principal Parts Listed in Groups*

This is the same list as above, but this time it is divided in groups with the same stem changes.

I.	essen	(ißt)	aß	gegessen
	geben	(gibt)	gab	gegeben
	geschehen	(geschieht)	geschah	ist geschehen
	sehen	(sieht)	sah	gesehen
	lesen	(liest)	las	gelesen
	liegen		lag	gelegen
	sitzen		saß	gesessen
II.	empfehlen	(empfiehlt)	empfahl	empfohlen
	helfen	(hilft)	half	geholfen
	nehmen	(nimmt)	nahm	genommen
	sprechen	(spricht)	sprach	gesprochen
	beginnen		begann	begonnen

gewinnen		gewann	gewonnen
schwimmen		schwamm	geschwommen
bekommen		bekam	bekommen
kommen		kam	ist gekommen
III. finden		fand	gefunden
klingen		klang	geklungen
singen		sang	gesungen
trinken		trank	getrunken
IV. bleiben		blieb	ist geblieben
scheinen		schien	geschienen
schreiben		schrieb	geschrieben
steigen		stieg	ist gestiegen
V. fliegen		flog	ist geflogen
verlieren		verlor	verloren
ziehen		zog	gezogen
VI. einladen	(lädt ein)	lud ein	eingeladen
fahren	(fährt)	fuhr	ist gefahren
tragen	(trägt)	trug	getragen
wachsen	(wächst)	wuchs	ist gewachsen
waschen	(wäscht)	wusch	gewaschen
VII. fallen	(fällt)	fiel	ist gefallen
gefallen	(gefällt)	gefiel	gefallen
halten	(hält)	hielt	gehalten
lassen	(läßt)	ließ	gelassen
schlafen	(schläft)	schlief	geschlafen
laufen	(läuft)	lief	ist gelaufen
heißen		hieß	geheißen
rufen		rief	gerufen

VIII. *n-verbs that do not belong to any of the groups above:*

anfangen	(fängt an)	fing an	angefangen
backen	(bäckt)	buk (backte)	gebacken
gehen		ging	ist gegangen
hängen		hing	gehangen
sein	(ist)	war	ist gewesen
stehen		stand	gestanden
tun	(tut)	tat	getan
werden	(wird)	wurde	ist geworden

IX. *irregular t-verbs*

bringen		brachte	gebracht
denken		dachte	gedacht
haben		hatte	gehabt
kennen		kannte	gekannt
nennen		nannte	genannt
rennen		rannte	gerannt
wissen	(weiß)	wußte	gewußt

13. *Proverbs*

Eine Hand wäscht die andere.	*One hand washes the other.*
Wer nicht wagt, der nicht gewinnt.	*Nothing ventured, nothing gained.*
Ohne Fleiß kein Preis.	*No pain, no gain.*
Probieren geht über Studieren.	*Practice is better than theory.*
Aller Anfang ist schwer.	*All beginnings are hard.*
Übung macht den Meister.	*Practice makes perfect.*
Es ist noch kein Meister vom Himmel gefallen.	*No man is born a master of his craft.*
Rom ist nicht an einem Tag gebaut worden.	*Rome wasn't built in a day.*
Morgen, morgen, nur nicht heute, sagen alle faulen Leute.	*Tomorrow, tomorrow, not today, all the lazy people say.*
Was Hänschen nicht lernt, lernt Hans nimmer mehr.	*If you don't learn it when you're young, you'll never learn it.*
Viele Köche verderben den Brei.	*Too many cooks spoil the broth.*
Hunger ist der beste Koch.	*Hunger is the best sauce.*
Lügen haben kurze Beine.	*Lies have short legs.*
Morgenstund hat Gold im Mund.	*The early bird catches the worm.*
Jeder ist seines Glückes Schmied.	*Everyone is the architect of his own future.*
Ende gut, alles gut.	*All's well that ends well.*

SUMMARY OF PRONUNCIATION

Pronunciation is a matter of learning not just to hear and pronounce isolated sounds or words, but to understand entire phrases and sentences, and to say them in such a way that a native speaker of German can understand you. You will need to practice this continuously as you study German.

This section summarizes and reviews the production of individual sounds. We have tried to keep it simple and nontechnical, and to provide ample practice of those German sounds that are distinctly different from American English. Often we have used symbols of pronunciation in a simplified phonetic spelling. Upon completing this section, you should hear the difference between somewhat similar English and German words (*builder* / **Bilder**), and between somewhat similar German words (**schon** / **schön**).

To develop a good German pronunciation—or at least one without a heavy American accent—you will have to bear three things in mind. First, you must resist the temptation of responding to German letters with American sounds. Second, at the outset you will probably feel a bit odd when speaking German with a truly German accent; however, nothing could give you a better start in your endeavor. (Imposing a German accent on your English may be hilarious, but it also is very good practice!) Third, you will have to develop new muscular skills: Germans move their jaws and lips more vigorously and articulate more precisely than Americans. After a good practice session your face should feel the strain of making unaccustomed sounds.

We will point out those cases where English sounds are close enough to German to cause no distortion. However, we purposely avoid trying to derive German sounds from English, because such derivations often do more harm than good. Listen carefully to your instructor or the tape. If you can tape your own voice in the language lab, do so and compare how you sound with the voice on the master track. With patience and practice you should be able to develop new speech habits quite rapidly. You will also find that German spelling reflects pronunciation very well.

I. *WORD STRESS*

In both English and German, one syllable of a word receives more stress than others. In English, stress can even signal the difference between two words (*ob'ject* / *object'*). In native German words, the accent is on the stem of the word, which is usually the first syllable (**Hei'rat, hei'raten**) or the syllable following an unstressed prefix (**verhei'ratet**). Words borrowed from other languages are less predictable; frequently the stress falls on the last or next-to-last syllable (**Universität'**, **Muse'um**). You will find such words marked for stress in the German-English end vocabulary.

II. *VOWELS*

One of the most important differences between English and German is the fact that in English most vowels are to some degree glides—that is, while they are being pronounced there occurs a shift from one vowel sound to another (*so, say*). German vowel sounds do not glide, they do not change quality. The jaw does not shift while a German vowel is being produced (**so, See**).

Three German vowels occur with two dots over them (**ä, ö, ü**). These vowels are called *umlauts*. Short and long ä sounds like short and long **e**, but **ö** and **ü** represent distinct sounds.

Certain vowels appear in combinations (**ei, ey, ai, ay; au; äu, eu**). These combinations are called *diphthongs*. While diphthongs in American English may be drawn out or drawled, the German diphthongs are short.

Pay special attention to the length of a vowel. In many words the length of the stressed vowel is the only clue to their meaning. When spoken, **Rate!** with a long **a** [a:] means *Guess!* whereas **Ratte** with a short **a** [a] means *rat*.

A. *Short Vowels* [i, e, a, u, o, ə, ʌ]

Keep these vowels really short!

1. [i]   in, immer, Zimmer, Kind, Winter, Finger, bitte, dick

2. [e]   es, essen, Fenster, schnell, März, Länder, Sätze

3. [a]   alt, kalt, Klasse, Tasse, Tante, Wand, wann, man

4. [u]   um, und, Mund, Mutter, Butter, Stunde, Sekunde

5. [o]   oft, Onkel, Sonne, Sommer, Sonntag, morgen, kommen, kosten

6. [a] and [o]   Be sure to distinguish clearly between these sounds.

Kamm / Komm! *comb / Come!*	Fall / voll	*fall / full*
Bann / Bonn *ban / Bonn*	Baß / Boss	*bass / boss*

7. [e]   Don't forget that ä doesn't sound like [a], but like [e].

Kamm / Kämme / Semmel	*comb / combs / roll*
Schwamm / Schwämme / Schwemme	*sponge / sponges / watering place*
Fall / Fälle / Felle	*fall / falls / furs*
Mann / Männer / Messer	*man / men / knife*

8. Unstressed short e [ə]   In unstressed syllables [a], [i], [o], and [u] retain their basic quality in German, whereas in English they become rather neutral (**Amerika′ner** / *Amer′ican;* **Aro′ma** / *aro′ma*). The German unstressed short **e** [ə], however, becomes neutral, too.

heute, Leute, fragen, sagen, beginnen, Gesicht, Geschenk, Geburtstag

9. Final **er** [ʌ]   When **r** occurs after a vowel at the end of a syllable or word, and especially in the ending **-er**, it sounds like a weak **a** [ʌ]. It requires a good deal of attention and practice for speakers of American English not to pronounce the **r**. The German sound resembles the final vowel in the word *comma*.

Vater, Mutter, Kinder, der, wir, vier, Uhr, Ohr, schwer, Donnerstag, wunderbar, erzählen, verstehen

10. [ə] and [ʌ] Listen carefully to the difference between these two sounds.

bitte / bitter	*please / bitter*
esse / Esser	*I eat / eater*
leide / leider	*I suffer / unfortunately*
zeige / Zeiger	*I show / watch hand*
diese / dieser	*these / this*

B. *Long Vowels* [i:, a:, u:, e:, o:]

Be sure to stretch these vowels until they are really long.

11. [i:] Draw your lips far back.

prima, minus, Musik, **ihn, ihm, ihnen, die, wie, wieder, sieben,** studieren, Papier, Biologie

12. [a:] **Haare, Saal, Jahr, Zahl, Zahn,** sagen, fragen, **Name, Nase**

13. [u:] Round your lips well.

du, gut, Kuli, Juli, Minute, **Bluse, Schuh, Stuhl, Uhr, Tour**

14. [e:] and [o:] These two vowels need particular attention. First listen carefully for the differences between English and German.

say / **See**	*boat* / **Boot**
bait / **Beet**	*pole* / **Pol**
vain / **wen**	*tone* / **Ton**

15. [e:] Draw your lips back and hold the sound steady.

See, Tee, Idee, zehn, nehmen, gehen, sehen, Zähne, Mädchen, **Käse,** lesen, spät, Universität, Qualität

16. [o:] Purse your lips and don't let the sound glide off.

Zoo, Boot, Ohr, ohne, Bohne, wohnen, so, rot, oben, Hose, holen

C. *Contrasting Short and Long Vowels*

As you were practicing the short and long vowels, you probably discovered that spelling provides some clues to the length of the stressed vowel. Here are the most reliable signals. Some apply only to the dictionary forms of words, not to the inflected forms.

The stressed vowel is **short**

- *when followed by a double consonant.*

immer, essen, alle, Butter, Tennis, Lippe, Mütter

- *usually when followed by two or more consonants, including* **ch** *and* **sch.**

Winter, Fenster, kalt, unten, Kopf, Hände, Wünsche, Gesicht, Tisch

- *in many common one-syllable words before a single consonant.*

mit, es, an, um, von

The stressed vowel is **long**

- *when doubled.*

Idee, Haare, Zoo

i *and* **u** *cannot be doubled, but* **i** *followed by* **e** *is always long.*

die, sie, wieviel, vier, Phantasie

- *when followed by* **h. h** *is silent; after a vowel it is strictly a spelling device to signal length.*

ihn, ihm, sehen, nehmen, Zahn, Zahl, Uhr, Schuh

- *usually, when followed by a single consonant.*

Kino, lesen, Tafel, Bluse, Hose, Väter, Türen, hören

17. [i] and [i:]

innen / **ih**nen	*inside / to them*	still / Stil	*quiet / style*
im / **ih**m	*in / him*		

18. [e] and [e:]

denn / den	*for / the*	Wellen / wählen	*waves / to dial*
Betten / beten	*beds / to pray*		

19. [a] and [a:]

Stadt / Staat	*city / state*	nasse / Nase	*wet / nose*
Kamm / kam	*comb / came*		

20. [u] and [u:]

muß / Mus	*must / mush*	Sucht / sucht	*mania / looks for*
Busse / Buße	*busses / repentance*		

21. [o] and [o:]

offen / Ofen	*open / oven*	Motte / Mode	*moth / fashion*
Wonne / wohne	*delight / I live*		

D. *Umlauts*

There are also a long and short ü and ö.

22. [i:] and [ü:] To make the [ü:], say [i:], keep your tongue and jaw in this position, and round your lips firmly.

diene / Düne	*I serve / dune*	liegen / lügen	*to lie / to (tell a) lie*

Biene / Bühne   *bee / stage*   diese / Düse   *these / nozzle*

23. [ü:]   Note that the German letter **y** is pronounced like **ü.**

über, übrigens, müde, Füße, kühl, Frühling, grün, natürlich, Typ, typisch

24. [u:] and [ü]:   Observe the change in tongue position as you shift from one sound to the other.

Fuß / Füße   *foot / feet*   Kuh / Kühe   *cow / cows*
Stuhl / Stühle   *chair / chairs*   Hut / Hüte   *hat / hats*

25. [i] and [ü]   To make the [ü], begin by saying [i], then round your lips.

Kissen / küssen   *pillow / to kiss*
missen / müssen   *to miss / must*
Kiste / Küste   *box / shore*
sticke / Stücke   *I embroider / pieces*

26. [ü]   dünn, fünf, hübsch, Glück, zurück, Flüsse, München, Nymphe

27. [u] and [ü]   Observe the tongue again as you shift from one sound to the other.

Busch / Büsche   *bush / bushes*   Kuß / Küsse   *kiss / kisses*
Fluß / Flüsse   *river / rivers*   Kunst / Künste   *art / arts*

28. [ü:] and [ü]

Hüte / Hütte   *hats / hut*   fühle / fülle   *I feel / I fill*
Wüste / wüßte   *desert / would know*   Düne / dünne   *dune / thin*

29. [e:] and [ö:]   To make the [ö:], begin by saying [e:]. Keep your tongue in this position, then round your lips firmly for [ö:].

Hefe / Höfe   *yeast / courts*   Sehne / Söhne   *tendon / sons*
lesen / lösen   *to read / to solve*   Besen / bösen   *broom / bad*

30. [ö:]   schön, Möbel, hören, möglich, Brötchen, französisch, Österreich

31. [o:] and [ö:]   Observe the tongue position as you shift from one sound to the other.

Ofen / Öfen   *oven / ovens*   Sohn / Söhne   *son / sons*
Ton / Töne   *tone / tones*   Hof / Höfe   *court / courts*

32. [e] and [ö]   Begin by saying [e], then round your lips.

kennen / können   *to know / can*   fällig / völlig   *due / total*
Helle / Hölle   *light / hell*   Zelle / Zölle   *cell / tolls*

33. [ö]   öffnen, östlich, zwölf, Wörter, Töchter

34. [o] and [ö]   Observe the tongue position as you shift from one sound to the other.

Kopf / Köpfe   *head / heads*   Stock / Stöcke   *stick / sticks*
Rock / Röcke   *skirt / skirts*   konnte / könnte   *was able to / could*

35. [ö:] and [ö]

Höhle / Hölle	*cave / hell*
Schöße / schösse	*laps / I'd shoot*
Röslein / Rößlein	*little rose / little horse*

36. [ü:] vs. [ö:] and [ü] vs. [ö]

Sühne / Söhne	*repentance / sons*	Hülle / Hölle	*cover / hell*
Güte / Goethe	*grace / Goethe*	Stücke / Stöcke	*pieces / sticks*
blüht / blöd	*blooms / stupid*	rücke / Röcke	*move / skirts*

E. *Diphthongs*

German diphthongs are short. They are not drawled.

37. [ai]   eins, zwei, drei, mein, dein, kein, Seite, Kreide, Meyer, Mai, Bayern, Haydn

38. [oi]   neu, neun, heute, Leute, teuer, deutsch, träumen, Häuser; toi, toi, toi!

39. [au]   auf, Auge, Haus, Frau, grau, faul, auch, Bauch, brauchen

40. Remember that ie [i:] is not a diphthong.

Wien / Wein	*Vienna / wine*	Biene / Beine	*bee / legs*
Lied / Leid	*song / suffering*	Lieder / leider	*songs / unfortunately*

41. Can you pronounce these words correctly without hesitation?

schreiben, schrieb, hieß, heiß, wieder, weiter, sei, Sie, wie, wieso, weiß, Beispiel, wieviel

F. *Glottal Stop*

Both English and German use a glottal stop (+) to avoid running words together. German uses it much more frequently than English, where the last consonant of one word is often linked with the first vowel of the next (mit +einem +Eis, *with an ice cream*). A good way to become aware of the glottal stop is to say *Oh oh!* as if in dismay.

42. Use the glottal stop where indicated:

+Am +Abend +essen wir +in +einem Restaurant.
Wir sitzen +in +einer kleinen +Ecke.
Der +Ober bringt +uns +ein +Eis.
Wir +erzählen von der +Uni.
Hans be+obachtet +andere Leute.

III. *CONSONANTS*

A. *Single Letters*

1. f, h, k, m, n, p, t, x: These are pronounced alike in both languages.

fünf, haben, kaufen, müde, nein, Park, Tag, extra

2. j: It is prounounced like the English *y*.

ja, Jahr, Januar, Juni, Juli, jung, jetzt

3. b, d, g: They usually sound like their English counterparts (**g** as in *garden*).

bitte, danke, gut

However, when they occur at the end of a word or syllable, or before **s** or **t**, they sound like [p], [t], [k], respectively.

[p] ob, gelb, halb, abhängig, gibst, [k] Tag, täglich, weg, genug,
    gebt   liegst, liegt

[t] und, Mund, Bild, abends, Stadt

[p] vs. [b]	[t] vs. [d]	[k] vs. [g]
habt / haben	Kind / Kinder	sagt / sagen
gibst / geben	Wand / Wände	fragst / fragen
siebzig / sieben	abends / Abende	Zug / Züge

4. v: It usually sounds like [f], but in words of foreign origin it is pronounced [v] unless it is at the end of the word.

[f] vier, von, verstehen, Vater, Volkswagen
[v] Vokabeln, Vase, Vision, Variation, November, Revolution

5. w: It is pronounced [v] in German.

was, wo, wer, wie, warum, welche, womit, wunderbar

6. s, ss, ß: The pronunciation of the letter **s** depends on its position in the word. If it is in front of a vowel, it is pronounced [z] as in the English *fuzz*. Otherwise it is pronounced [s] as in the English *fuss*.

[z] sehen, Sofa, Salat, Gemüse, Nase, lesen
[s] was, das, aus, Bus, Eis, Glas, Hals, als

ss and **ß** are also pronounced [s]. **ß** [ɛstsɛt] is used after long vowels (**Füße**), before **t** (**mußt**), and at the end of a word (**muß**).

[s] Tasse, Wasser, besser, wissen, Professor, Gruß, Grüße, heiß, heißen, groß, Größe, läßt, weißt

7. z: It is pronounced [ts] as in English *rats*.

[ts] zu, Zoo, Zahn, Zeit, zwischen, Dezember, Medizin, duzen, März, schwarz, Tanz, Toleranz, zick zack

8. s and z: Watch the contrast between these two letters.

so / Zoo	*so / zoo*	siegen / Ziegen	*to win / goats*
sauber / Zauber	*clean / magic*	sagen / zagen	*to say / to hesitate*

9. l: There is an important difference between English and German in the pronunciation of the letter **l**. When an American pronounces [l], his tongue forms a hump toward the back of the mouth, which makes the [l] sound "dark." For the German [l], the tongue is flat and touches just behind the front teeth; it is a very "light" sound. Listen for the difference between American and German [l]:

feel / viel   *felt* / fällt   *built* / Bild

[l]   laut, lernen, logisch, Limo, Klasse, kalt, Film, hell, Hotel, April, will, kühl

10. r: To avoid a noticeable American accent in German, avoid using the American [r]. In German you can either us a tongue-tip trill or a uvular trill. (The uvula is the little skin flap in the back of your mouth which vibrates when you gargle.) Listen for the difference between American and German [r]:

rest / Rest   *fry* / frei   *ring* / Ring   *wrote* / rot

[r]   rot, Rose, Radio, Rathaus, Reis, Rhein, fahren, hören, orange, Büro, Frage, Kreide, braun, grau, grün

Remember that **r** after a vowel at the end of a syllable or word, especially in the ending **-er**, is usually pronounced [ʌ].

[ʌ]   Bilder, Kinder, aber, Zimmer, Körper, Lehrer, schwer, Papier, dir, ihr

B. *Letter Combinations*

11. sch: This sound [š] resembles the English *sh*, but in German the lips protrude more.

Scheck, Schach, Schiff, Schule, Schokolade, schreiben, schwer, waschen, Tisch, Fisch

12. st, sp: At the beginning of a word or word stem, they are pronounced [št] and [šp].

[š]   **Stock, Stein, still, Stadt, Statistik, Frühstück, verstehen**
[šp]   **Sport, spät, spielen, Sprache, versprechen, Gespräch**

Otherwise they sound the same as in English.

[st]   **ist, bist, Osten, Westen, Fenster, Gast, Post, Prost**
[sp]   **Wespe, Kaspar, lispeln**

13. ch: There are no English equivalents for the two German sounds [x] and [ç].

■ *[x]—the "ach-sound"—is produced in the same place as [k]. However, for [k] the breath stops, whereas for [x] it continues to flow through a narrow opening in the back of the throat.* **ch** *is pronounced [x] after* **a, o, u,** *and* **au.**

ach, Bach, acht, Nacht, machen, lachen, noch, doch, Woche, suchen, Kuchen, Bauch, auch

Be sure to distinguish clearly between [k] and [x].

akt / acht	*act / eight*	Dock / doch	*dock / indeed*
nackt / Nacht	*naked / night*	buk / Buch	*baked / book*

- [ç]—the "**ich**-*sound*"—*is produced much farther forward in the mouth.* **ch** *is pronounced* [ç] *after the vowels* **e, i, ä, ö, ü,** *the diphthongs* **ei** (**ai**) *and* **eu** (**äu**), *and the consonants* **l, n,** *and* **r.** *The diminutive suffix* **-chen** *is also pronounced* [çən]. *The ending* **-ig** *is always pronounced* [iç]. *You can learn to make this sound by whispering loudly* you *or* Hugh.

ich, mich, nicht, schlecht, sprechen, lächeln, möchten, Bücher, Zeichnung, Bäuche, Milch, München, furchtbar, Mädchen, richtig, ruhig, brummig

Be sure not to substitute [š] *for* [ç].

mich / **misch**	*me* / *to mix*
ficht / **fischt**	*fights* / *fishes*
Männchen / **Menschen**	*dwarf* / *people*

Often [x] *and* [ç] *alternate automatically in different forms of the same word.*

Buch / **Bücher**	*book* / *books*	**Bauch** / **Bäuche**	*belly* / *bellies*
Nacht / **Nächte**	*night* / *nights*		

14. chs: It is pronounced [ks].

sechs, Wachs

15. ck: It sounds like [k].

dick, Picknick, Rock, Jacke, packen, Scheck

16. ph: It sounds like [f].

Philosophie, Physik, photographieren, physisch, Phantasie

17. th: It sounds like [t].

Thema, Theater, Theologie, Theorie, Mathematik, Bibliothek

18. tz: It sounds like [ts].

Satz, Platz, setzen, trotz, Hitze
also: **Nation, Information, Portion, Variation**

19. qu: It must be pronounced [kv].

Quatsch, Quäker, Qualität, Quantität, Quartier, Quote

20. ng: It always is [ŋ] as in English *sing,* not [ŋg] as in *finger.*

lang, englisch, singen, Finger, Hunger, Übung, Prüfung

21. pf: Both letters are pronounced: [pf].

pfui, Pfeffer, Pfennig, Pfefferminz, pflanzen, Kopf, Dummkopf

22. ps: Both letters are pronounced: [ps]

Psychologie, Psychologe, psychologisch, Psychiater, Psalm, Pseudonym

23. kn, gn: They sound just as they are spelled: [kn, gn].

Knie, Knoten, Knackwurst, Knirps
Gnu, Gneis, Vergnügen

GERMAN-ENGLISH

The vocabulary includes all the ACTIVE AND PASSIVE vocabulary used in *Wie geht's?* The English definitions of the words are limited to their use in the text. Each active vocabulary item is followed by a number and a letter indicating the chapter and section where it first occurs.

NOUNS Nouns are followed by their plural endings unless the plural is rare or nonexistent. In the case of n-nouns the singular genitive ending is also given: **der Herr, -n, -en.** Nouns that require adjective endings appear with two endings: **der Angestellte (ein Angestellter).** Female forms of masculine nouns are not listed if only **-in** needs to be added: **der Apotheker.**

VERBS For regular t-verbs ("weak verbs"), only the infinitive is listed. All irregular t-verbs ("irregular weak verbs") and basic n-verbs ("strong verbs") are given with their principal parts: **bringen, brachte, gebracht; schreiben, schrieb, geschrieben.** Separable-prefix verbs are identified by a dot between the prefix and the verb: **mit·bringen.** Compound mixed and n-verbs are asterisked to indicate that the principal parts can be found under the listing of the basic verb: **mit·bringen*, beschreiben*.** When **sein** is used as the auxiliary of the perfect tenses, the form **ist** is given: **wandern (ist); kommen, kam, ist gekommen.**

ADJECTIVES and ADVERBS Adjectives and adverbs that have an umlaut in the comparative and superlative are identified by an umlauted vowel in parentheses: **arm (ä) = arm, ärmer, am ärmsten.**

ACCENTUATION Stress marks are provided for all words that do not follow the typical stress pattern. The accent follows the stressed syllable: **Balkon', Amerika'ner, wiederho'len.** The stress is not indicated when the word begins with an unstressed prefix, such as **be-, er-, ge-.**

ABBREVIATIONS

~	repetition of the key word	*nom.*	nominative
abbrev.	abbreviation	*o.s.*	oneself
acc.	accusative	*pl.*	plural
adj.	adjective	*refl. pron.*	reflexive pronoun
adv.	adverb	*rel. pron.*	relative pronoun
comp.	comparative	*S*	Schritt
conj.	subordinate conjunction	*sg.*	singular
dat.	dative	*s.th.*	something
fam.	familiar	*W*	Wortschatz 1
gen.	genitive	*G*	Grammatik
inf.	infinitive	*E*	Einblicke
lit.	literally		(Wortschatz 2)

ab- away, off

der **Abend, -e** evening; **am ~** in the evening (6E); **Guten ~!** Good evening. (S1)

— abend evening (8G); **gestern ~** yesterday evening (8G); **heute ~** this evening (8G)

das **Abendessen, -** supper, evening meal (3W); **zum ~** for supper (3W)

abends in the evening, every evening (S6)

aber but, however (S3,2G,5G); *gesture word expressing admiration* (7G)

ab·fahren* (von) to depart, leave (from) (8W)

die **Abfahrt, -en** departure (8W)

ab·fliegen* (von) to take off, fly (from) (8W)

die **Abgase** *(pl.)* exhaust fumes

ab·geben* to give up, hand over

abhängig (von) dependent (on)

die **Abhängigkeit** dependence

das **Abitur, -e** final comprehensive exam (at the end of the Gymnasium)

ab·nehmen* to take s.th. from, take off

abonnieren to subscribe

ab·reißen* to tear down (15W)

der **Absender, -** return address (8W)

absolut' absolute(ly)

die **Abwechslung, -en** distraction, variety

ach oh; **~ so!** Oh, I see.

das **Adjektiv, -e** adjective

der **Adler, -** eagle

der **Adlige (ein Adliger)** aristocrat

die **Adres'se, -n** address (8W)

der **Advents'kranz, -e** Advent wreath

die **Advent'szeit** Advent season

das **Adverb', -ien** adverb

die **Abwechslung, -en** variety, distraction

(das) **Ägy'pten** Egypt

der **Ägy'pter, -** the Egyptian **ägy'ptisch** Egyptian **Aha'!** There, you see. Oh, I see.

die **Ahnung: Keine ~!** I've no idea.

die **Akademie', -n** academy

der **Akade'miker, -** (university) graduate; professional

akade'misch academic

der **Akkusativ, -e** accusative

der **Akt, -e** act (play)

das **Aktiv** active voice

aktiv' active

aktuell' up to date, current

der **Akzent', -e** accent

all - all (7G); **vor ~em** above all, mainly (10E); **~e drei Jahre** every three years

allein' alone

Allerhand! How about that!

alles everything (2E); **Das ist ~.** That's all.

allgemein general; **im allgemeinen** in general

der **Alltag** everyday life

die **Alpen** *(pl.)* Alps

die **Alpenblume, -n** Alpine flower

das **Alphabet'** alphabet

als as; *(conj.) (at the time) when* (11G); *(after comp.) than* (12G)

also therefore, thus, so; well

alt (ä) old (S3); **ur~** ancient

das **Alter** age

die **Altstadt, -e** old part of town

der **Amateur', -e** amateur

(das) **Ame'rika** America (1W)

der **Amerika'ner, -** the American (1W)

amerika'nisch American (10W)

die **Ampel, -n** traffic light

an- to, up to

an (+ *acc.* / *dat.*) to, at (the side of), on (vertical surface) (6G)

analysie'ren to analyze

an·bieten to offer

ander- other (10W)

andererseits on the other hand

anders different(ly) (15E); **etwas anderes** something else, something different

anerkannt recognized, credited

die **Anerkennung, -en** recognition

der **Anfang, -e** beginning, start (10W): **am ~** in the beginning (10W)

an·fangen* to begin, start (10W)

das **Angebot, -e** offering

angeln to fish; **~ gehen*** to go fishing

angepaßt geared to

angeschlagen posted

der **Angestellte (ein Angestellter)** employee, clerk

die **Angestellte (eine Angestellte)** employee, clerk

die **Angli'stik** study of English

der **Angriff, -e** attack

die **Angst, -e** fear, anxiety; **~ haben* (vor** + *dat.*) to fear, be afraid (of) (12E)

sich **an·hören** to listen to (9G); **Hör dir das an!** Listen to that.

an·kommen* (in + *dat.*) to arrive (in) (7E); **Das kommt darauf an.** That depends.

die **Ankunft** arrival (8W)

an·machen to turn on (a radio etc.) (10W)

die **Anmeldung** reception desk

die **Annahme, -n** hypothetical statement *or* question

an·nehmen* to accept

an·reden to address

an·richten to do (usually s.th. wrong)

der **Anruf, -e** call

an·rufen* to call up, phone (7G)

an·schlagen* to post

der **Anschluß, -sse** connection

die **Anschrift, -en** address

(sich) **an·sehen*** to look at (9G)

an·sprechen* to address, speak to

anstrengend strenuous (12W)

der **Antrag, -e** application

die **Antwort, -en** answer **antworten** to answer (S2)

die **Anzeige, -n** ad

(sich) **an·ziehen*** to put on (clothing), get dressed (9G)

an·zünden to light

der **Apfel, -** apple (2W)

der **Apfelstrudel, -** apple strudel

die **Apothe'ke, -n** pharmacy (2E)

der **Apothe'ker, -** pharmacist
der **Appetit'** appetite; **Guten ~!** Enjoy your meal (food). (3W)
der **April'** April (S5); **im ~** in April (S5)
der **Äqua'tor** equator
das **Äquivalent'** equivalent
der **A'raber, -** the Arab
ara'bisch Arabian
die **Arbeit, -en** work (12W); **~** (term) paper (13W); **bei der ~** at work
arbeiten to work (4E)
der **Arbeiter, -** (blue-collar) worker (12W)
die **Arbeitserlaubnis** work permit
arbeitslos unemployed
die **Arbeitslosigkeit** unemployment
die **Archäologie'** archeology
der **Architekt', -en, -en** architect
die **Architektur'** architecture
das **Archiv', -e** archive
sich **ärgern über** (+ *acc.*) to get annoyed (upset) about (10G)
die **Arka'de, -n** arcade
arm (ä) poor (11W)
der **Arm, -e** arm (9W)
die **Armbanduhr, -en** wristwatch
die **Armee', -n** army
die **Armut** poverty
arrogant' arrogant
die **Arroganz'** arrogance
das **Arsenal', -e** arsenal
die **Art, -en** kind, type
der **Arti'kel, - (von)** article (of)
der **Arzt, ⸚e** physician (12W)
die **Ärztin, -nen** physician (12W)
ästhe'tisch aesthetic
der **Astronaut', -en, -en** astronaut
die **Atmosphä're** atmosphere
die **Atom'kraft** atomic power
der **Atom'müll** atomic waste
die **Atom'waffe, -n** atomic weapon
die **Attraktion', -en** attraction
attraktiv' attractive (11W)
auch also, too (S1)
auf (+ *acc. / dat.*) on (top of) (6G); open (7W)
auf- up, open
auf·bauen to build up
aufeinan'der·treffen* to come together

der **Aufenthalt, -e** stay, stopover (8W)
die **Aufenthaltserlaubnis** residence permit
auf·essen* to eat up
die **Aufgabe, -n** assignment; task, challenge
auf·geben* to give up
auf·halten* to hold open
auf·hören (zu + *inf.*) to stop (doing s.th.) (11E)
auf·machen to open (7G)
auf·nehmen* to take (a picture)
auf·passen to pay attention, watch out (7G); **Passen Sie auf!** Pay attention.
auf·stellen to put up
der **Aufsatz, ⸚e** essay, composition
auf·schreiben* to write down (7G)
auf·stehen* to get up (7G)
auf·stellen to put up
auf·wachsen* to grow up
der **Aufzug, ⸚e** elevator
das **Auge, -n** eye (9W)
der **August'** August (S5); **im ~** in August (S5)
aus (+ *dat.*) out of, from (a place of origin) (3G); **Ich bin ~ . . .** I'm from (a native of) . . . (1W)
aus- out, out of
aus·arbeiten to work out
aus·(be)zahlen to pay out
die **Ausbildung** training, education (12W)
aus·füllen to fill out (8W)
der **Ausgang, ⸚e** exit (7W)
aus·geben* to spend (money)
aus·gehen* to go out (7G)
ausgezeichnet excellent (6E)
aus·helfen* to help out
das **Ausland** foreign country; **im ~** abroad
der **Ausländer, -** foreigner
ausländisch foreign (13E)
das **Auslandsprogramm, -e** foreign-study program
aus·leihen* to loan, lend out
aus·machen to turn off (a radio etc.) (10W)
aus·packen to unpack
aus·reiben* to rub out
die **Aussage, -n** statement

aus·sehen* (wie + *nom.*) to look (like) (14W)
außer (+ *dat.*) besides, except for (3G)
äußer- outer
außerdem (*adv.*) besides (6E)
außerhalb outside (of)
die **Aussprache** pronunciation
aus·steigen* to get off (8W)
der **Austausch** exchange; **das ~programm, -e** exchange program
aus·tauschen to exchange (14E)
die **Auster, -n** oyster
(das) **Austra'lien** Australia
der **Austra'lier, -** the Australian
austra'lisch Australian
ausverkauft sold out
die **Auswahl** choice, selection
der **Ausweis, -e** ID, identification (7W)
aus·zahlen to pay out
(sich) **aus·ziehen*** to take off (clothing), get undressed (9G)
authen'tisch authentic
das **Auto, -s** car (5W)
die **Autobahn, -en** freeway
autofrei free of cars
automatisiert' automated
der **Autor, -en** author (10W)
autoritäts'gläubig believing in authority

B

backen (bäckt), buk (backte), gebacken to bake
das **Backblech, -e** cookie sheet
der **Bäcker, -** baker
die **Bäckerei', -en** bakery (2W)
das **Bad, ⸚er** bath (6W)
der **Badeanzug, ⸚e** swimsuit
die **Badehose, -n** swimming trunks
baden to take a bath, swim (6W)
die **Badewanne, -n** bathtub
die **Bahn, -en** railway, train (8W); **~übergang, ⸚e** railroad crossing
der **Bahnhof, ⸚e** train station (5W)
der **Bahnsteig, -e** platform (8W)
bald soon (11E)
der **Balkon', -s** balcony (6W)
der **Ball, ⸚e** ball
die **Bana'ne, -n** banana (2W)
die **Bank, -en** bank (7W)

die **Bank, -̈e** bench

der **Bann** ban

der **Bär, -en** bear; **Du bist ein Brumm~.** You're a grouch.

barfuß barefoot

das **Bargeld** cash (7W)

der **Bart, -̈e** beard

basteln to do crafts

der **Bau, -ten** building, construction

der **Bauch, -̈e** stomach, belly (9W)

bauen to build (6E)

der **Bauer, -n** farmer

der **Bauernhof, -̈e** farm

das **Baugesetz, -e** building code

das **Bauland** building lots

der **Baum, -̈e** tree (6W)

der **Bayer, -n, -n** the Bavarian

(das) **Bayern** Bavaria (in southeast Germany)

bayrisch Bavarian

der **Beamte (ein Beamter)** civil servant (12W)

die **Beamtin, -nen** civil servant, clerk (12W)

beantworten to answer

bedeuten to mean, signify (7E)

die **Bedeutung, -en** meaning, significance

beherrschen to dominate

sich **beeilen** to hurry (9G)

beeindrucken to impress

beeinflussen to influence

beenden to finish

der **Befehl, -e** instruction, request

beginnen, begann, begonnen to begin (S6)

die **Begrenzung, -en** limitation, limit

begrüßen to greet, welcome

die **Begrüßung, -en** greeting; **zur ~** as greeting

die **Behandlung, -en** treatment

bei (+ *dat.*) at, near, at the home of (3G); **Hier ~ __.** This is __'s office, residence

beid- both (11W)

das **Bein, -e** leg (9W); **auf den Beinen** on the go

das **Beispiel, -e** example; **zum ~ (z.B.)** for example (e.g.)

bekannt well known (5E)

der **Bekannte (ein Bekannter)** acquaintance

die **Bekannte (eine Bekannte)** acquaintance

bekommen* (hat) to get, receive (4W)

belegen to sign up for, take (a course) (13W)

beliebt popular

die **Belohnung, -en** reward

benutzen to use

das **Benzin'** gas(oline)

beobachten to watch, observe

die **Beobachtung, -en** observation

bequem' comfortable, convenient (6W)

der **Berater, -** counselor

berauben to rob

der **Berg, -e** mountain (1W)

die **Bergbahn, -en** mountain train

der **Bergbau** mining

bergig hilly, mountainous

bergsteigen gehen* to go mountain climbing

der **Bericht, -e** report

berichten to report

berieseln to irrigate, water, spray

der **Beruf, -e** profession (12W)

beruflich professional(ly)

der **Berufstätige (ein Berufstätiger)** someone who has a job

berühmt famous (14E)

beschreiben* to describe

beschriftet labeled

besichtigen to visit (an attraction)

der **Besitz** property

besitzen* to own

besonders especially (3E); **nichts Besonderes** nothing special (9W)

besser better (12G)

die **Besserung** improvement; **Gute ~!** Get well soon.

best- best (12G); **am besten** it's best (12G)

bestätigen to verify

bestehen* to pass (an exam) (13W); **~ aus** (+ *dat.*) to consist of

bestellen to order (3W)

die **Bestellung, -en** order

bestimmt surely, for sure, certain(ly) (11W)

der **Besuch, -e** visit

besuchen to visit (8W); attend

der **Besucher, -** visitor

beten to pray

der **Beton'** concrete

betonen to stress, emphasize (15E)

betreten* to enter, step on

die **Betriebswirtschaft** business administration

betrunken drunk

das **Bett, -en** bed (6W); **ins ~** to bed

betteln to beg

der **Bettler, -** beggar

die **Bevölkerung** population (14E)

bevor (*conj.*) before (4G)

bezahlen to pay (for) (3W)

die **Bezahlung** pay

der **Bezirk, -e** district

die **Bibel, -n** Bible

die **Bibliothek', -en** library (5W)

die **Biene, -n** bee

das **Bier, -e** beer (2W)

bieten, bot, geboten to offer (14W)

der **Biki'ni, -s** bikini

das **Bild, -er** picture (S2)

bilden to form; **~ Sie einen Satz!** Make a sentence.

die **Bildung** education

billig cheap, inexpensive (2E)

die **Biochemie'** biochemistry

der **Bioche'miker, -** biochemist

der **Bio-Laden, -̈** health-food store

die **Biologie'** biology

bis to, until (S4); **~ später!** See you later! So long!

bißchen: ein ~ some, a little bit (4E); **Ach du liebes ~!** Good grief!, My goodness!, Oh dear!

bitte please (S1); **~ schön!** You're welcome. (S6); **Hier ~!** Here you are.; **~ schön?** May I help you?; **Wie ~?** What did you say? Could you say that again? (S3)

die **Bitte, -n** request

das **Blatt, -̈er** leaf; sheet

blau blue (S2)

das **Blei** lead

bleiben, blieb, ist geblieben to stay, remain (4E)

der **Bleistift, -e** pencil (S2)

der **Blick (auf** + *acc.*) view (of)

der **Blickpunkt, -e** focus

blind blind

blitzen to sparkle

der **Block, -̈e** block

die **Blocka′de, -n** blockade

blockiert blocked

blond blond

blühen to flourish

die **Blume, -n** flower (2E)

die **Bluse, -n** blouse (S3)

die **Blütezeit** golden age, heyday

der **Boden** ground, floor

die **Bohne, -n** bean (2W)

der **Bomber, -** bomber

der **Bonus, -se** bonus

das **Boot, -e** boat

böse angry, mad, upset (11E)

die **Bouti′que, -n** boutique

boxen to box

die **Bowle, -n** alcoholic punch

der **Braten, -** roast

die **Bratwurst, -̈e** fried sausage

der **Brauch, -̈e** custom

brauchen to need (S4)

braun brown (S2)

die **Braut, -̈e** bride

das **Brautkleid, -er** wedding dress

die **BRD (Bundesrepublik Deutschland)** FRG (Federal Republic of Germany) (1E)

brechen (bricht), brach, gebrochen to break

der **Brei, -e** porridge

breit broad, wide (12E)

das **Brett, -er** board; **Schwarze ~** bulletin board

die **Brezel, -n** pretzel

der **Brief, -e** letter (8W)

der **Briefkasten, -̈** mailbox (8W)

brieflich by letter

die **Briefmarke, -n** stamp (8W)

der **Briefträger, -** mailman

die **Brille, -n** glasses

bringen, brachte, gebracht to bring (3W)

das **Brot, -e** bread (2W)

das **Brötchen, -** roll (2W); **belegte ~** sandwich

der **Brotwürfel, -** small piece of bread, cube

die **Brücke, -n** bridge (5W)

der **Bruder, -̈** brother (1W)

das **Brüderchen, -** little brother

brummig grouchy

der **Brunnen, -** fountain

das **Buch, -̈er** book (S2)

der **Bücherwurm, -̈er** bookworm

die **Buchführung** bookkeeping

das **Büchlein, -** booklet, little book

buchstabie′ren to spell

sich **bücken** to stoop

der **Buddha, -s** Buddha

die **Bude, -n** booth, stand; **Schieß~** shooting gallery

die **Bühne, -n** stage; **auf der ~** onstage

bummeln (ist) to stroll (5E)

der **Bund, -̈e** confederacy

der **Bundesbürger, -** citizen of the FRG

die **Bundesfeier, -n** Swiss national holiday

die **Bundespost** federal postal service of the FRG

die **Bundesrepublik (BRD)** Federal Republic of Germany (FRG) (1E)

bunt colorful (14E)

die **Burg, -en** castle

der **Bürger, -** citizen (9E)

der **Bürgerkrieg, -e** civil war

der **Bürgersteig, -e** sidewalk

das **Bürgertum** citizenry

das **Büro′, -s** office (12W)

die **Bürokratie′** bureaucracy

der **Bus, -se** bus (5W); **mit dem ~ fahren*** to take the bus (5W)

der **Busbahnhof, -̈e** bus depot

der **Busch, -̈e** bush

die **Butter** butter (2W)

C

das **Café′, -s** café (3W)

campen gehen* to go camping

der **Campingplatz, -̈e** campground

das **Cello, -s** cello

charakteri′stisch characteristic

charmant′ charming (11W)

der **Charme** charm

der **Chauffeur′, -e** chauffeur

der **Chauvinis′mus** chauvinism

der **Chef, -s** boss

die **Chemie′** chemistry

(das) **China** China

der **Chine′se, -n, -n** the Chinese

chine′sisch Chinese

der **Chor, -̈e** choir (10W)

der **Christkindlmarkt** Christmas fair

der **Clown, -s** clown

der **Club, -s** club

die **Cola** coke (2W)

das **College, -s** college

die **Combo, -s** (musical) band

der **Compu′ter, -** computer

computerisiert′ computerized

cremig creamy, smooth

D

da there (S2); **~ drüben** over there (5W)

dabei with / on you (me . . .)

das **Dach, -̈er** roof

der **Dackdecker, -** roofer

dafür instead

die **Dahlie, -n** dahlia

damals then, in those days (14W)

die **Dame, -n** lady (5W)

der **Däne, -n, -n** the Dane

(das) **Dänemark** Denmark

dänisch Danish

der **Dank: Vielen ~!** Thank you very much. (5W)

dankbar grateful

danke thank you (S1); **~ schön!** Thank you very much. (S6); **~ gleichfalls!** Thanks, the same to you. (3W)

danken (+ *dat.*) to thank (3G); **Nichts zu ~!** You're welcome.

dann then (3E)

dar·stellen to portray

darum therefore (12E)

das that (S2)

daß (*conj.*) that (4G); **so ~** (*conj.*) so that (12E)

der **Dativ, -e** dative

das **Datum, Daten** date (calendar) (4W)

dauern to last (duration) (4W); **Wie lange dauert das?** How long does that take? (4W)

die **DDR (Deutsche Demokratische Republik)** German Democratic Republic (GDR) (1E)

dein (*sg. fam.*) your (7G)

die **Dekoration′, -en** decoration

dekorie′ren to decorate

delikat′ delicate

der **Demokrat'**, -en, -en demo-crat

die **Demokratie'** democracy

demokra'tisch democratic

demonstrie'ren to demon-strate

denken, dachte, gedacht to think (4W); **~ an** (+ *acc.*) to think of (10G)

der **Denker,** - thinker

das **Denkmal,** ⁻er monument (14E)

denn because, for (2G); *gesture word expressing curiosity, interest* (7G)

die **Depression'**, -en (mental) depression

deutsch: auf ~ in German (S2)

(das) **Deutsch: Sprechen Sie ~?** Do you speak German? (1W)

der **Deutsche (ein Deutscher)** the German (1W,12G)

die **Deutsche (eine Deutsche)** the German (1W)

die **Deutsche Demokratische Republik (DDR)** German Democratic Republic (GDR)

(das) **Deutschland** Germany (1W)

deutschsprachig German-speaking

der **Dezem'ber** December (S5); **im ~** in December (S5)

d.h. (das heißt) that is (i.e.)

der **Dialekt'**, -e dialect

der **Dialog'**, -e dialogue

dick thick, fat (S3); **~ machen** to be fattening

dienen to serve

der **Diener,** - servant

der **Dienst,** -e service

der **Dienstag** Tuesday (S5); **am ~** on Tuesday

dienstags on Tuesdays (2E)

dies- this, these (7G)

das **Diktat'**, -e dictation

die **Dimension'**, -en dimension

direkt' direct(ly)

der **Dirigent'**, -en, -en (music) conductor

das **Dirndl,** - peasant dress *(in southern Germany)*, dirndl

die **Diskothek'**, -en disco-theque

die **Diskussion'**, -en discussion

diskutie'ren to discuss

sich **distanzie'ren** to keep apart

die **Disziplin'** discipline

die **DM (Deutsche Mark)** Ger-man mark

doch yes (I do), indeed, sure (2W); yet, however, but; *gesture word expressing concern, impatience, assur-ance* (7G)

der **Dokumentar'film,** -e docu-mentary

der **Dollar,** - dollar (7W)

der **Dolmetscher,** - interpreter

der **Dom,** -e cathedral (5W)

dominie'ren to dominate

der **Donnerstag** Thursday (S5); **am ~** on Thursday

donnerstags on Thursdays (2E)

das **Doppelzimmer,** - double room (7W)

das **Dorf,** ⁻er village (8E)

dort there (4E)

draußen outside; **hier ~** out here; **weit ~** far out

drehen to turn

die **Droge,** -n drug

die **Drogerie'**, -n drugstore (2E)

die **Drossel,** -n thrush (bird)

duften to smell good

dumm (ü) stupid, silly (10W)

die **Dummheit,** -en stupidity

der **Dummkopf,** ⁻e dummy

dunkel dark (6W)

dünn thin, skinny (S3)

durch (+ *acc.*) through (2G); **mitten ~** right through; **quer ~** all across

durchbre'chen* to break through, penetrate

durcheinander mixed up, confused

durch·fallen* to flunk (an exam)

der **Durchschnitt** average; **im ~** on the average

dürfen (darf), durfte, ge-durft to be allowed to, may (5W); **Was darf's sein?** May I help you?

der **Durst** thirst (2E); **Ich habe ~.** I'm thirsty. (2E)

die **Dusche,** -n shower

der **Duschvorhang,** ⁻e shower curtain

(sich) **duschen** to take a shower (9G)

das **Dutzend,** -e dozen

E

eben after all, just *(gesture word)* (14W)

die **Ebene,** -n plain

echt real, genuine

die **Ecke,** -n corner (6W)

egal' the same; **es ist ~** it doesn't matter; **~ wie** no matter how

die **Ehe,** -n marriage

ehemalig former

das **Ehepaar,** -e married couple

eher rather

die **Ehre** honor

das **Ei,** -er egg (2W)

die **Eidgenossenschaft** Swiss Confederation

das **Eigelb** egg yolk

eigen- own (12W)

die **Eigenschaft,** -en character-istic (11W)

eigentlich actual(ly) (4E)

die **Eigentumswohnung,** -en condo(minium)

eilig hurried; **es ~ haben*** to be in a hurry

ein a, an (1G,7G); **die einen** the ones; **einer** one

ein- into

einan'der each other

die **Einbahnstraße,** -n one-way street

einbegriffen in (+ *dat.*) in-cluded in

der **Einblick,** -e insight

der **Eindruck,** ⁻e impression

einfach simple, simply (7E)

die **Einfahrt,** -en driveway; **Keine ~!** Don't enter.

der **Einfluß,** ⁻sse influence

der **Eingang,** ⁻e entrance (7W)

einig- *(pl. only)* some, a few (10G); **so einiges** all sorts of things

ein·kaufen to shop; **~ gehen*** to go shopping (2E,7G)

die **Einkaufsliste,** -n shopping list

das **Einkommen** income (12W)

ein·laden* (zu) to invite (to) (11W)

die **Einladung,** -en invitation

ein·lösen to cash (in) (7G); **einen Scheck ~** to cash a check (7W)

einmal once, (at) one time (5E); **auch ~** for once; **nicht ~** not even; **noch ~** once more, again (S3); **es war ~** once upon a time

einmalig unique (14W)

der **Einmarsch, -̈e** marching in

ein·packen to pack (in a suitcase)

sich **ein·schreiben*** to register

ein·steigen* to get on or in (8W)

der **Eintritt** entrance fee

der **Einwohner, -** inhabitant

das **Einwohnermeldeamt, -̈er** resident registration office

der **Einzelgänger, -** loner

das **Einzelzimmer, -** single room (7W)

einzig- only

das **Eis** ice, ice cream (3W)

eisern (made of) iron

eisig icy

eiskalt ice-cold

der **Elefant', -en, -en** elephant

elegant' elegant

der **Elek'triker, -** electrician

elek'trisch electric

die **Elektrizität'** electricity

der **Elek'tromecha'niker, -** electrical mechanic

die **Elek'trotech'nik** electrical engineering

das **Element', -e** element

die **Eltern** (pl.) parents (1W)

die **Emanzipation'** emancipation

emanzipiert' emancipated

emotional' emotional(ly)

empfangen* to receive

die **Empfangsdame, -n** receptionist

empfehlen (empfiehlt), empfahl, empfohlen to recommend (3W)

die **Empfehlung, -en** recommendation

das **Ende** end (10W); **am ~** in the end (10W); **zu ~ sein*** to be finished

enden to end

endlich finally (11E)

die **Energie'** energy

eng narrow

sich **engagie'ren** to get involved

der **Engel, -** angel

(das) **England** England (1W)

der **Engländer, -** the Englishman (1W)

englisch: auf ~ in English (S2)

(das) **Englisch: Sprechen Sie ~?** Do you speak English? (1W)

der **Engpaß, -̈sse** narrow street, bottleneck

enorm' enormous

die **Ente, -n** duck; **Lahme ~!** Poor baby!

enthalten* to contain

der **Enthusias'mus** enthusiasm

entlang along; **die Straße ~** along the street

sich **entscheiden, entschied, entschieden** to decide (13W)

entschuldigen to excuse; **~ Sie bitte!** Excuse me, please. (5W)

die **Entschuldigung, -en** excuse

entsprechen* to correspond to

entstehen* (ist) to develop

(sich) **entwickeln** to develop

die **Entwicklung, -en** development

die **Erbse, -n** pea (2W)

die **Erdbeere, -n** strawberry (2W)

die **Erde** earth (12E); **unter der ~** underground

die **Erfindung, -en** invention (12E)

der **Erfolg, -e** success

ergänzen to supply, complete

ergreifen, ergriff, ergriffen to grab

erhalten* to keep up, preserve

die **Erholung** recuperation, relaxation

erinnern (an + acc.) to remind (of) (14W)

sich **erinnern (an + acc.)** to remember (14W)

die **Erinnerung, -en (an + acc.)** reminder, memory of (14W)

sich **erkälten** to catch a cold (9G)

die **Erkältung, -en** cold

erkennen* to recognize (14E)

erklären to explain (15W)

die **Erklärung, -en** explanation

erlauben to permit

die **Erlaubnis** permit

das **Erlebnis, -se** experience

die **Ermäßigung, -en** discount

die **Ernährung** nutrition

die **Ernte, -n** harvest

erreichen to reach

erscheinen* (ist) to appear

erschrecken (erschrickt),

erschrak, ist erschrocken to be frightened

ersetzen to replace

erst- first (4W)

erst only, not before (time) (13E)

erstaunlich amazing

erwärmen to heat (up)

erzählen (von + dat.) to tell (about) (8E,10G)

die **Erziehung** education

der **Esel, -** donkey; **Du ~!** You dummy.

eßbar edible

essen (ißt), aß, gegessen to eat (S6)

das **Essen, -** food, meal (2W); **beim ~** while eating

das **Eßzimmer, -** dining room (5W)

etwa about, approximately

etwas something (3W); (sg.) a little, some (2W); **so ~ wie** s.th. like; **noch ~** one more thing, s.th. else; **sonst noch ~?** anything else?

euer (pl. fam.) your (7G)

(das) **Euro'pa** Europe

der **Europä'er, -** the European

europä'isch European

der **Evangelist', -en, -en** evangelist

exakt exact(ly)

das **Exa'men, -** exam

existie'ren to exist

extra extra

der **Extremist', -en, -en** extremist

F

das **Fach, -̈er** subject (13W); **Haupt~** major (field) (13W); **Neben~** minor (field) (13W)

der **Fachbereich, -e** field (of study)

die **Fachrichtung, -en** specialization

das **Fachwerkhaus, -̈er** half-timbered house

der **Faden, -̈** thread

die **Fähigkeit, -en** ability

fahren (fährt), fuhr, ist gefahren to drive, go (by car etc.) (3G)

die **Fahrkarte, -n** ticket (8W)

der **Fahrplan, -̈e** schedule (of trains etc.) (8W)

das **Fahrrad, -̈er** bicycle (6E);

mit dem ~ fahren* to bicycle

der **Fahrradweg, -e** bike path

die **Fahrt, -en** trip, drive (8W)

fair fair

der **Fall, ‑e** case; **auf jeden ~** in any case

fallen (fällt), fiel, ist gefallen to fall (4E); **~ lassen*** to drop; **ins Wasser ~** to get canceled

falsch wrong, false (S2)

die **Fami'lie, -en** family (1W)

fangen (fängt), fing, gefangen to catch

die **Farbe, -en** color (S2); **Welche ~ hat . . . ?** What's the color of . . . ? (S2)

der **Farbstoff, -e** dye, (artificial) color

der **Fasching** carnival; **zum ~** for carnival (Mardi gras)

die **Fassa'de, -n** façade

fast almost (7E)

die **Fastenzeit** Lent

die **Faszination'** fascination

faszinie'ren to fascinate

faul lazy (11W)

die **Faulheit** laziness

der **Februar** February (S5); **im ~** in February (S5)

fechten (ficht), focht, gefochten to fence

der **Federball, ‑e** badminton (ball)

fehlen to be missing, lacking

der **Fehler, -** mistake

feierlich festive

feiern to celebrate (4W)

der **Feiertag, -e** holiday (4W)

feige cowardly

der **Feind, -e** enemy

feindlich hostile

das **Feld, -er** field

das **Fenster, -** window (S2)

die **Ferien** (pl.) vacation (4W)

der **Ferienplatz, ‑e** vacation spot

fern far, distant

die **Ferne** distance

das **Ferngespräch, -e** long-distance call

fern·sehen* to watch TV (9W)

das **Fernsehen** TV (the medium) (10W); **im ~** on TV (10W)

der **Fernseher, -** TV set (6W)

fertig finished, done (S6)

fertig·machen to finish

das **Fest, -e** celebration (4W); **~spiel, -e** festival

festlich festive

fest·machen to fasten

das **Feuer, -** fire

das **Feuerwerk, -e** firework(s)

die **Feuerzangenbowle** flaming alcoholic punch

die **Figur', -en** figure

der **Film, -e** film (10W)

die **Finan'zen** (pl.) finances

finanziell' financial(ly)

finanzie'ren to finance (15W)

finden, fand, gefunden to find (S5); **Ich finde es . . .** I think it's . . . (S5)

der **Finder, -** finder

der **Finger, -** finger (9W)

der **Finne, -n, -n** the Finn

finnisch Finnish

die **Firma, Firmen** company, business (12W)

der **Fisch, -e** fish (2W); **ein kalter ~** a coldhearted person

fit: sich ~ halten* to keep in shape (9E)

die **Flamme, -n** flame

die **Flasche, -n** bottle (3E); **eine ~ Wein** a bottle of wine (3E)

flechten (flicht), flocht, geflochten to weave (baskets)

das **Fleisch** (sg.) meat (2W)

der **Fleischer, -** butcher

die **Fleischerei', -en** butcher shop

fleißig industrious(ly), hard-working (13W)

flexi'bel flexible

die **Flexibilität'** flexibility

fliegen, flog, ist geflogen to fly (8W); **mit dem Flugzeug ~** to go by plane (8W)

fliehen, floh, ist geflohen to flee, escape

fließen, floß, ist geflossen to flow

fließend fluent(ly)

der **Flohmarkt, ‑e** flea market

das **Floß, -e** raft

die **Flöte, -n** flute, recorder

der **Flüchtling, -e** refugee

der **Flug, ‑e** flight (8W)

der **Flügel, -** wing

der **Flughafen, ‑** airport (8W)

die **Flugkarte, -n** plane ticket

der **Flugsteig, -e** gate

das **Flugzeug, -e** airplane (8W)

der **Flur** hallway, entrance foyer (6W)

der **Fluß, ‑sse** river (1W)

folgen (ist) (+ *dat.*) to follow

das **Fondue', -s** fondue

fördern to encourage

die **Förderung** advancement, promotion, encouragement

die **Form, -en** form, shape

das **Formular', -e** form

formulie'ren to formulate

der **Förster, -** forest ranger

die **Forstwirtschaft** forestry

die **Frage, -n** question (1W); **eine ~ stellen** to ask a question

fragen to ask (S2); **sich ~** to wonder (9G)

fraglich questionable

(das) **Frankreich** France (1W)

der **Franzo'se, -n, -n** Frenchman (1W)

die **Franzö'sin, -nen** Frenchwoman (1W)

(das) **Franzö'sisch: Ich spreche ~.** I speak French. (1W)

die **Frau, -en** Mrs., Ms.; woman; wife (S1)

die **Frauenbewegung** women's movement

das **Fräulein, -** Miss, Ms.; young lady (S1); **~!** Miss! Waitress! (3W)

frech impudent, sassy, fresh

frei free, available (7W)

freigiebig generous

die **Freiheit** freedom

das **Freilichtspiel, -e** outdoor performance

frei·nehmen* to take time off

der **Freitag** Friday (S5); **am ~** on Friday (S5)

freitags on Fridays (2E)

freiwillig voluntary

die **Freizeit** leisure time (9W)

fremd foreign

die **Fremdsprache, -n** foreign language

die **Freude, -n** joy

sich **freuen auf** (+ *acc.*) to look forward to (10G); **Freut**

mich. I'm glad to meet you. (S1)

der **Freund, -e** (boy)friend (3E)

die **Freundin, -nen** (girl)friend (3E)

freundlich friendly (11W)

die **Freundlichkeit** friendliness

die **Freundschaft, -en** friendship

der **Frieden** peace (14W)

friedlich peaceful

frieren, fror, gefroren to freeze

frisch fresh (2W)

froh glad, happy (14E)

der **Frosch, -̈e** frog

früh early, morning (8G)

früher earlier, once, former(ly) (12E)

der **Frühling, -e** spring (S5)

das **Frühstück** breakfast (3W); **zum ~** for breakfast (3W)

der **Fuchs, -̈e** fox; **ein alter ~** a sly person

sich **fühlen** to feel (a certain way) (9W)

führen to lead

die **Führung, -en** guided tour

füllen to fill

funkeln to glitter

die **Funktion', -en** function

für (+ *acc.*) for (S2,2G); **was ~ ein?** what kind of a? (2W)

die **Furcht** fear, awe

furchtbar terrible, awful (S5)

sich **fürchten (vor)** to be afraid (of)

der **Fürst, -en, -en** sovereign, prince

der **Fuß, -̈e** foot (9W); **zu ~ gehen*** to walk (5W)

der **Fußball, -̈e** soccer (ball) (9W)

der **Fußgänger, -** pedestrian; **~überweg, -e** pedestrian crossing; **~weg, -e** pedestrian walkway; **~zone, -n** pedestrian area

G

die **Gabel, -n** fork (3W)

die **Gallerie', -n** gallery

die **Gans, -̈e** goose; **eine dumme ~** a silly person (*fem.*)

ganz whole, entire(ly) (10W); very

die **Gara'ge, -n** garage (6W)

gar nicht not at all (13E)

der **Garten, -̈** garden (6W)

die **Gasse, -n** narrow street

der **Gast, -̈e** guest (7W)

der **Gastarbeiter, -** foreign worker (15E)

das **Gästezimmer, -** guest room

das **Gasthaus, -̈er** restaurant, inn

der **Gasthof, -̈e** small hotel (7E)

die **Gaststätte, -n** restaurant, inn

das **Gebäck** pastry

das **Gebäude, -** building (14W)

geben (gibt), gab, gegeben to give (3G); **es gibt** there is, there are (2W); **Was gibt's?** What's up?; **Was gibt's Neues?** What's new? (9W); **Was gibt's im . . . ?** What's (playing) on . . . ? (10W)

das **Gebiet, -e** area, region (15E)

gebildet well educated (11W)

geboren: Ich bin . . . ~ I was born . . . (S5); **Wann sind Sie ~?** When were you born? (S5)

gebrauchen to use, utilize (15W)

die **Gebühr, -en** fee

der **Geburtstag, -e** birthday (4W); **Wann haben Sie ~?** When is your birthday? (4W); **Ich habe am . . . (s)ten ~.** My birthday is on the . . . (*date*) (4W); **Ich habe im . . . ~.** My birthday is in . . . (*month*) (4W); **Herzlichen Glückwunsch zum ~!** Happy birthday!; **zum ~** at the / for the birthday (4W)

der **Gedanke, -ns, -n** thought (14E)

die **Gefahr, -en** danger (12E)

gefährlich dangerous

das **Gefälle, -** decline

gefallen (gefällt), gefiel, gefallen (+ *dat.*) to like, be pleasing to (3G); **Es gefällt mir.** I like it. (3G)

gefettet greased

der **Gefrierschrank, -̈e** freezer

das **Gefühl, -e** feeling

gegen (+ *acc.*) against (2G); toward (time)

die **Gegend, -en** area, region (8E)

gegensätzlich opposite

das **Gegenteil, -e** opposite (S3); **im ~** on the contrary

gegenüber (von + *dat.*) across (from) (5W)

die **Gegenwart** present

das **Gehalt, -̈er** salary

gehen, ging, ist gegangen to go (S3): **Es geht mir . . .** I am (feeling) . . . (S1); **Das geht nicht.** That's impossible. That doesn't work. You can't.; **Es geht.** That's all right.; **So geht's.** That's the way it goes.; **Wie geht's? Wie geht es Ihnen?** How are you? (S1); **zu Fuß ~** to walk (5W)

gehören (+ *dat.*) to belong to (3G)

die **Geige, -n** violin

geistig mentally, intellectual(ly)

geizig stingy

gelb yellow (S2)

das **Geld** money (7W); **~ aus·geben*** to spend money (8E); **Bar~** cash (7W); **Klein~** change (7W)

die **Gelegenheit, -en** opportunity, chance

gelten (gilt), galt, gegolten to apply to, be valid for, be true

gemeinsam together, shared, (in) common

die **Gemeinschaft, -en** community

gemischt mixed

die **Gemse, -n** mountain goat

das **Gemüse, -** vegetable(s) (2W)

gemütlich cozy, pleasant, comfortable (5E)

die **Gemütlichkeit** nice atmosphere, coziness

genau exact(ly); **~so** the same; **~ wie** just like (9E)

die **Generation', -en** generation

generös' generous

genießen, genoß, genossen to enjoy

der **Genitiv, -e** genitive

genug enough (5E)

geöffnet open (7W)

die **Geographie'** geography

die **Geologie'** geology

das **Gepäck** baggage, luggage (7W)

gerade just, right now (4W); **~ als** just when

geradeaus' straight ahead (5W)

germa'nisch Germanic

die **Germani'stik** study of German language and literature

gern (lieber, liebst-) gladly (2W); **furchtbar ~** very much

das **Geschäft, -e** store (2W); business (12W)

geschäftlich concerning business

die **Geschäftsfrau, -en** businesswoman (12W)

der **Geschäftsmann, -leute** businessman (12W)

geschehen (geschieht), geschah, ist geschehen to happen (11E)

das **Geschenk, -e** present (4W)

die **Geschichte, -n** story (10W); history (10E)

geschickt clever(ly)

geschieden divorced

geschlossen closed (7W)

die **Geschwindigkeit, -en** speed

die **Geschwister** (pl.) brothers and sisters, siblings

gesellig social

die **Gesellschaft, -en** society

das **Gesetz, -e** law

gesetzlich legal(ly)

gesichert secure

das **Gesicht, -er** face (9W)

das **Gespräch, -e** conversation, dialogue

gestern yesterday (4W,8G)

gesucht wird wanted

gesund (ü) healthy (9W)

die **Gesundheit** health

das **Getränk, -e** beverage

getrennt separated

die **Gewalt** violence

gewinnen, gewann, gewonnen to win (9E)

sich **gewöhnen an** (+ dat.) to get used to (12W)

gewöhnlich usual(ly) (3E)

gießen, goß, gegossen to pour

die **Gitar're, -n** guitar (9W)

die **Gladio'le, -n** gladiola

das **Glas, ⸚er** glass (2E); **ein ~** a glass of (2E)

der **Glaser, -** glazier

glauben (an + acc.) to believe (in), think (12W); **Ich glaube es. Ich glaube ihm.** I believe it. I believe him. (12W); **Das glaube ich gern.** I believe it. (15W)

gleich equal, same (12W); right away

gleichberechtigt with equal rights

die **Gleichberechtigung** equality, equal rights

gleichfalls: Danke ~! Thank you, the same to you. (3W)

das **Gleis, -e** track (8W)

der **Gletscher, -** glacier

glorreich glorious

das **Glück** luck; **~ haben*** to be lucky (7E); **Viel ~!** Good luck.

glücklich happy (11W)

der **Glühwein** mulled wine

der **Gnom, -e** gnome, goblin

das **Gold** gold

golden golden

(das) **Golf** golf

der **Grad, -e** degree

die **Gramma'tik** grammar

gramma'tisch grammatical(ly)

das **Gras, ⸚er** grass

gratulie'ren (+ dat.) to congratulate (4W); **Wir ~!** Congratulations.

grau gray (S2)

die **Grenze, -n** border (14W)

grenzenlos unlimited

der **Grieche, -n, -n** the Greek

(das) **Griechenland** Greece

griechisch Greek

groß (größer, größt-) large, big (S3)

die **Größe, -n** size

die **Großeltern** (pl.) grandparents (1W); **Ur~** great-grandparents

die **Großmutter, ⸚** grandmother (1W); **Ur~** great-grandmother

der **Großvater, ⸚** grandfather (1W); **Ur~** great-grandfather

grün green (S2); **im Grünen** out in the country, in the midst of nature

der **Grund, ⸚e** reason

gründen to found

die **Gründung, -en** founding

die **Gruppe, -n** group

der **Gruß, ⸚e** greeting; **Viele Grüße (an + acc.) . . .!** Greetings (to . . .)!

grüßen to greet; **Grüß dich!** Hi!; **Grüß Gott!** Hello! Hi! (in southern Germany)

gurgeln to gargle

die **Gurke, -n** cucumber (2W); **saure ~** pickle

gut (besser, best -) good, fine (S1); **~aussehend** good-looking; **na ~** well, all right; **Mach's ~!** Take care.

das **Gute: Alles ~!** All the best.

die **Güte** goodness

das **Gymna'sium, Gymna'sien** academic high school

H

das **Haar, -e** hair (9W)

haben (hat), hatte, gehabt to have (S6,2G)

der **Hafen, ⸚** port

halb half (to the next hour) (S6); **~tags** half time; **in einer ~en Stunde** in half an hour (8W)

die **Hälfte, -n** half

die **Halle, -n** hall

Hallo! Hello! Hi!

der **Hals, ⸚e** neck (9W)

halten (hält), hielt, gehalten to stop (a vehicle) (5W); **~ von** to think of, be of an opinion (10G)

die **Haltestelle, -n** (bus etc.) stop (5W)

das **Halteverbot, -e** no stopping or parking

die **Hand, ⸚e** hand (3E,9W)

die **Handarbeit, -en** needlework

der **Handball, ⸚e** handball

der **Handel** trade

der **Handwerker, -** craftsman

hängen to hang (up) (6G)

hängen, hing, gehangen to hang, be hanging (6G)

harmo'nisch harmonious

hart (ä) hard

hassen to hate

häßlich ugly (11W)

die **Häßlichkeit** ugliness

das **Hauptfach, ⸚er** major (field of study) (13W)

die **Hauptsaison** (main) season

die **Hauptstadt, ⁼e** capital (1W)
die **Hauptstraße, -n** main street
das **Hauptwort, ⁼er** noun
das **Haus, ⁼er** house (6W); **nach ~e** (toward) home (3W); **zu~e** at home (3W)
das **Häuschen, -** little house
die **Hausfrau, -en** housewife (12W)
der **Haushalt** household (12W)
die **Hauswirtschaft** home economics
hauswirtschaftlich domestic
das **Heft, -e** notebook (S2)
der **Heiligabend** Christmas Eve; **am ~** on Christmas Eve
der **Heimcomputer, -** home computer
die **Heimat** homeland, home (14E)
heiraten to marry, get married (11W)
heiratslustig eager to marry
heiß hot (S5)
heißen, hieß, geheißen to be called; **Ich heiße . . .** My name is . . . (S1); **Wie ~ Sie?** What's your name? (S1)
die **Heizung** heating
das **Heiz'material'** heating material, fuel
helfen (hilft), half, geholfen (+ dat.) to help (3G)
hell light, bright (6W)
das **Hemd, -en** shirt (S3)
die **Henne, -n** hen
heran'- up to
der **Herbst, -e** fall, autumn (S5)
der **Herd, -e** range
herein'- in(to)
herein'·kommen* to come in, enter (11E)
herein'·lassen* to let in
der **Herr, -n, -en** Mr., gentleman (S1); lord
herum'- around
herum'·laufen* to run around
herum'·reisen (ist) to travel around
das **Herz, -ens, -en** heart
der **Heurige, -n** (sg.) new wine
die **Heurigenschenke, -n** Viennese wine-tasting inn
heute today (S4); **für ~** for

today (S2); **~ morgen** this morning (8G)
heutig- of today
hier here (S2)
die **Hilfe, -n** help
der **Himmel** sky
hin und her back and forth
hinauf'·fahren* to go or drive up (to)
hinein'·gehen* to go in(to), enter
hin·legen to lay or put down; **sich hin·legen** to lie down (9G)
sich **hin·setzen** to sit down (9G)
hinter (+ acc. / dat.) behind (6G)
hinterlassen* to leave behind
hinun'ter down
histo'risch historical(ly) (14W)
das **Hobby, -s** hobby (9W)
hoch (hoh-) (höher, höchst-) high(ly) (12W)
das **Hochhaus, ⁼er** high-rise building
die **Hochschule, -n** university
die **Hochzeit, -en** wedding (11W)
(das) **Hockey** hockey
der **Hof, ⁼e** court, courtyard
hoffen to hope (12E)
die **Hoffnung, -en** hope
höflich polite
die **Höhe, -n** height
der **Höhepunkt, -e** climax
hohl hollow
die **Höhle, -n** cave
holen to (go and) get, pick up, fetch (13W)
der **Holländer, -** the Dutchman
holländisch Dutch
die **Hölle** hell
hörbar audible
hören to hear (S2)
der **Hörer, -** listener; receiver
der **Hörsaal, -säle** lecture hall (13W)
das **Hörspiel, -e** radio play
die **Hose, -n** slacks, pants (S3)
das **Hotel', -s** hotel (5W,7W)
hübsch pretty (11W)
der **Hügel, -** hill
das **Hühnchen, -** chicken
der **Hund, -e** dog
der **Hunger** hunger (2E); **Ich habe ~.** I'm hungry. (2E)

die **Hungersnot** famine
hungrig hungry
der **Husar', -en** cavalryman
die **Hütte, -n** hut, cottage

I

ideal' ideal
das **Ideal', -e** ideal
der **Idealis'mus** idealism
die **Idee', -n** idea (9W)
idyl'lisch idyllic
ihr her, its, their (7G)
Ihr (formal) your (1W,7G)
die **Imbißstube, -n** snack bar, fast-food stand
die **Immatrikulation'** enrollment (at university)
immer always (4E); **~ geradeaus** always straight ahead (5W); **~ länger** longer and longer (12G); **~ noch** still; **~ wieder** again and again (12G)
der **Imperativ, -e** imperative
das **Imperfekt** imperfect, simple past
in (+ acc. / dat.) in, into, inside of (6G)
der **Inder, -** the Indian
(das) **Indien** India
der **India'ner, -** the Native American
der **In'dikativ** indicative
in'direkt indirect(ly)
die **Individualität'** individuality
individuell' individual(ly)
die **Industrie', -n** industry
industriell' industrial
die **Informa'tik** computer science
die **Information', -en** information
informativ' informative
(sich) **informie'ren** to inform, get informed
der **Ingenieur', -e** engineer (12W)
die **Initiati've, -n** initiative
innen inside
die **Innenstadt, ⁼e** inner city, center (of town)
inner- inner
innerhalb within
die **Insel, -n** island (14W)
das **Institut', -e** institute
das **Instrument', -e** instrument
integrie'ren to integrate
intellektuell' intellectual(ly)

der **Intellektuel'le (ein Intellektuel'ler)** intellectual
intelligent' intelligent (11W)
die **Intelligenz'** intelligence
intensiv' intensive
interessant' interesting
(5E); **etwas Interessantes**
s.th. interesting
das **Interes'se, -n an** (+ *dat.*)
interest in
sich **interessie'ren für** to be interested in (10G)
international' interna-
tional(ly)
interpretie'ren to interpret
das **Interview, -s** interview
intervie'wen to interview
in'tolerant intolerant
inzwi'schen in the mean-
time (15E)
irgendwo somewhere
(das) **Ita'lien** Italy (1W)
der **Italie'ner, -** the Italian (1W)
italie'nisch Italian (1W)

J

ja yes (S1); *gesture word expressing emphasis* (7G)
die **Jacke, -n** jacket, cardigan
(S3)
das **Jahr, -e** year (S5)
die **Jahreszeit, -en** season
das **Jahrhun'dert, -e** century
(15E)
-jährig years old; years long
der **Januar** January (S5); **im ~**
in January (S5)
(das) **Ja'pan** Japan
der **Japa'ner, -** the Japanese
japa'nisch Japanese
je (+ *comp.*) **. . . desto** (+
comp.) **. . .** the . . . the . . .
(12G)
die **Jeans** (*pl.*) jeans
jed- (*sg.*) each, every (7G)
jedenfalls in any case (13E)
jeder everyone, everybody
jederzeit any time
der **Jeep, -s** jeep
jemand someone, some-
body (11W)
jetzt now (S6)
joggen gehen* to go jog-
ging
das **Joghurt** yogurt
(das) **Judo: ~ kämpfen** to do
judo
der **Journalist', -en, -en** journalist (12W)
die **Jugend** youth (14E)

die **Jugendherberge, -n** youth
hostel (7E)
der **Jugosla'we, -n, -n** the Yu-
goslav
der **Juli** July (S5); **im ~** in July
(S5)
jung (ü) young (11W)
der **Junge, -n, -n** boy (1W)
der **Junggeselle, -n, -n** bache-
lor
der **Juni** June (S5); **im ~** in
June (S5)
die **Jurisprudenz, Jura: Er studiert ~.** He's studying law.
der / das **Juwel', -en** jewel

K

das **Kabarett', -e** *or* **-s** cabaret
das **Kabelfernsehen** cable TV
der **Kaffee** coffee (2W)
der **Kaffeeklatsch** chatting over
a cup of coffee (and cake)
der **Kaiser, -** emperor
das **Kalb, -̈er** calf; **Kalbsleber**
calf's liver
der **Kalen'der, -** calendar
kalt (ä) cold (S5)
die **Kälte** cold(ness)
die **Kamera, -s** camera
der **Kamm, -̈e** comb
(sich) **kämmen** to comb (o.s.) (9G)
die **Kammer, -n** chamber;
~frau, -en chambermaid
der **Kampf, -̈e** fight, struggle
kämpfen to fight, struggle
(15W)
(das) **Kanada** Canada (1W)
der **Kana'dier, -** the Canadian
(1W)
kana'disch Canadian
der **Kanal', -̈e** channel
die **Kano'ne, -n** canon
die **Kanti'ne, -n** cafeteria (at a
workplace)
das **Kanu', -s** canoe
die **Kapel'le, -n** chapel
kapitalis'tisch capitalist
das **Kapi'tel, -** chapter
die **Kapsel, -n** capsule
kaputt' broken
kaputt'·gehen* to get broken, break (11E)
der **Karneval** carnival
die **Karot'te, -n** carrot (2W)
die **Karte, -n** ticket (8W); card
(9W); **~n spielen** to play
cards (9W)
die **Kartof'fel, -n** potato (3W);
~brei (*sg.*) mashed potatoes; **~mehl** cornstarch;

~salat potato salad
der **Käse** cheese (2W); **Das ist
(doch) ~!** That's nonsense.
die **Kasse, -n** cash register,
cashier's window (7W)
die **Kasset'te, -n** cassette (9W)
die **Katze, -n** cat; **ein
~nsprung zu** a stone's
throw from
kaufen to buy (2W)
das **Kaufhaus, -̈er** department
store (2W)
der **Kaufmann, -leute** merchant
kaum hardly (14E)
die **Kegelbahn, -en** bowling al-
ley
kein no, not a, not any (1G)
der **Keller, -** basement
kennen, kannte, gekannt
to know, be acquainted with
(6G)
kennen·lernen to get to
know, meet (7E)
der **Kenner, -** connoisseur
die **Kenntnis, -se** knowledge,
skill
der **Kerl, -e** guy
der **Kern, -e** core
die **Kerze, -n** candle (4E)
die **Kette, -n** chain; necklace
die **Kettenreaktion, -en** chain
reaction
das **Kilo, -s (kg)** kilogram
der **Kilome'ter, - (km)** kilometer
das **Kind, -er** child (1W)
der **Kindergarten, -̈** kindergarten
kinderlieb fond of children
das **Kinn, -e** chin
das **Kino, -s** movie theater (5W)
die **Kirche, -n** church (5W)
die **Kirsche, -n** cherry
klappen to work out
klar clear; **~!** Sure!
die **Klasse, -n** class
das **Klassenzimmer, -** classroom
klassisch classical
klatschen to clap (10W)
das **Klavier', -e** piano (9W)
das **Kleid, -er** dress (S3)
die **Kleidung** clothing (S3)
klein small, little (S3)
das **Kleingeld** change (7W)
das **Klima, -s** climate
die **Klimaanlage, -n** air condi-
tioning
klingeln to ring a bell
klingen, klang, geklungen

to sound; **Das klingt gut.**
That sounds good.

klopfen to knock

der **Kloß, ⸚e** dumpling

das **Kloster, ⸚** monastery

die **Knappheit** shortage

die **Kneipe, -n** tavern, pub

das **Knie, -** knee (9W)

der **Knirps, -e** little fellow, dwarf

der **Knoblauch** garlic

der **Knöd(e)l, -** dumpling (*in southern Germany*)

der **Knopf, ⸚e** button

der **Knoten, -** knot

der **Koch, ⸚e** cook

kochen to cook (6W)

die **Köchin, -nen** cook

der **Koffer, -** suitcase (7W)

der **Kolle´ge, -n, -n** colleague; **Zimmer~** roommate (13W)

die **Kolle´gin, -nen** colleague

die **Kolonisation´** colonization

kombinie´ren to combine

der **Komfort´** comfort

ko´misch funny (strange, comical) (10W)

kommen, kam, ist gekommen to come (1W); **Komm ´rüber!** Come on over!

der **Kommentar´, -e** commentary

kommerziell´ commercial

die **Kommo´de, -n** dresser (6W)

kommunis´tisch communist

der **Kom´parativ, -e** comparative

der **Komponist´, -en, -en** composer (10W)

die **Konditorei´, -en** pastry shop

der **Kongreß, -sse** conference

der **König, -e** king (11E)

die **Königin, -nen** queen

der **Kon´junktiv** subjunctive

können (kann), konnte, gekonnt to be able to, can (5G)

das **Konservie´rungsmittel, -** preservative

das **Konsulat´, -e** consulate

die **Kontakt´linse, -n** contact lense

das **Konto, -s** *or* **Konten** account

kontrollie´ren to control, check

die **Konversation´, -en** conversation

konzentriert´ concentrated

das **Konzert´, -e** concert (10W)

der **Kopf, ⸚e** head (9W)

kopf·stehen* to stand on one's head

der **Korb, ⸚e** basket

der **Korbball, ⸚e** basketball

der **Körper, -** body (9W)

körperlich physical(ly)

korrigie´ren to correct

kosten to cost; **Was ~ . . .?** How much are . . .? (S4); **Das kostet (zusammen) . . .** That comes to . . . (S4)

die **Kosten** (*pl.*) costs

das **Kostüm´, -e** costume

die **Kraft, ⸚e** strength, power

die **Kralle, -n** claw

krank (ä) sick, ill (9W)

das **Krankenhaus, ⸚er** hospital

die **Krankenkasse, -n** health insurance

die **Krankenpflege** nursing

die **Krankenschwester, -n** nurse (12W)

die **Krankheit, -en** sickness

der **Kranz, ⸚e** wreath

die **Krawatte, -n** tie

kreativ´ creative

die **Kreativität´** creativity

die **Kredit´karte, -n** credit card

die **Kreide** chalk (S2)

die **Kreismeisterschaft, -en** county championship

die **Kreuzung, -en** crossing

das **Kreuzworträtsel, -** crossword puzzle

der **Krieg, -e** war (14W)

der **Kri´tiker, -** critic

der **Krimi, -s** detective story (10W)

kritisch critical(ly)

kritisie´ren to criticize

die **Krone, -n** crown

krönen to crown

krumm (ü) crooked

die **Küche, -n** kitchen (6W)

der **Kuchen, -** cake (2W)

die **Kugel, -n** ball

kühl cool (S5)

der **Kühlschrank, ⸚e** refrigerator (6W)

der **Kuli, -s** pen (S2)

die **Kultur´, -en** culture

kulturell´ cultural(ly) (14W)

die **Kunst, ⸚e** art (9E)

der **Künstler, -** artist

der **Kurfürst, -en, -en** elector

der **Kurort, -e** health resort, spa

der **Kurs, -e** course (13W)

die **Kurve, -n** curve

kurz (ü) short (S3); **~ vor** shortly before; **vor ~em** recently

die **Kürze** shortness, brevity

die **Kusi´ne, -n** (female) cousin

küssen to kiss

die **Kutsche, -n** carriage, coach

L

das **Labor´, -s** *or* **-e** lab (13W)

lachen to laugh (10W)

laden (lädt), lud, geladen to load

die **Lage, -n** location

lahm lame

das **Lamm, ⸚er** lamb

die **Lampe, -n** lamp (6W)

das **Land, ⸚er** country, state (1W); **auf dem ~** in the country (6E); **aufs ~** in(to) the country(side) (6E)

landen (ist) to land (8W)

die **Landkarte, -n** map (1W)

die **Landschaft, -en** landscape, scenery (15E)

die **Landung, -en** landing

der **Landwirt, -e** farmer

die **Landwirtschaft** agriculture

landwirtschaftlich agricultural

lang (ä) (*adj.*) long (S3)

lange (*adv.*) long; **schon ~** for a long time; **wie ~?** how long? (4W)

langsam slow(ly) (S3)

langweilig boring, dull (10W)

der **Lärm** noise

lassen (läßt), ließ, gelassen to leave (behind) (7W)

(das) **Latein´** Latin

laufen (läuft), lief, ist gelaufen to run, walk (3G)

laut loud(ly), noisy (4E); **Sprechen Sie ~!** Speak up. (S3)

der **Lautsprecher, -** loudspeaker

leben to live (6E)

das **Leben** life (12E)

die **Lebensfreude** joy of living

die **Lebensmittel** (*pl.*) groceries (2W)

die **Leber, -n** liver

der **Lebkuchen, -** gingerbread
die **Lederhose, -n** leather
    pants
    ledig single
    leer empty
    legen to lay, put (flat) (6G);
    sich ~ to lie down (9G)
die **Lehre, -n** apprenticeship
    lehren to teach (13W)
der **Lehrer, -** teacher (12W)
    leicht light, easy (10E)
    leid: Es tut mir ~. I'm
    sorry. (5E)
    leiden, litt, gelitten to suffer
    leider unfortunately (5E)
    leihen, lieh, geliehen to
    lend
    leise quiet(ly), soft(ly)
    lernen to learn (S2)
    lesbar legible
    lesen (liest), las, gelesen to
    read (S2)
der **Leser, -** reader
die **Leseratte, -n** bookworm
der **Lesesaal, -säle** reading
    room
    letzt- last (10W)
die **Leute** *(pl.)* people (1W)
das **Licht, -er** light
    lieb- dear (5E)
die **Liebe** love (11W)
    lieben to love (6E)
    lieber rather (12G)
der **Liebling, -e** darling, favorite;
    ~sdichter favorite poet;
    ~sfach favorite subject
    liebst-: am liebsten best of
    all (12G)
das **Lied, -er** song (4E); **Volks~**
    folk song
    liegen, lag, gelegen to lie,
    be (located) (1W); be lying
    (flat) (6G)
der **Liegestuhl, -e** lounge chair
die **Lilie, -n** lily, iris
die **Limona'de, -n** soft drink,
    lemonade (2W)
die **Lingui'stik** linguistics
    link- left; **auf der ~en Seite**
    on the left
    links left (5W); **erste Straße**
    ~ first street to the left
    (5W)
die **Lippe, -n** lip
der **Lippenstift, -e** lipstick
der **Liter, -** liter
das **Loch, -er** hole
der **Löffel, -** spoon (3W)
    logisch logical

    lokal' local(ly)
    los: ~ werden* to get rid
    of; **etwas ~ sein*** to be
    happening, going on; **Was**
    ist ~? What's the matter?
    (9W)
    lösen to solve
die **Lösung, -en** solution
der **Löwe, -n, -n** lion
die **Luft** air (14W); **mit ~post**
    by airmail; **~brücke, -n**
    airlift
die **Lüge, -n** lie
die **Lust** inclination, desire; **Ich**
    habe (keine) Lust (zu) . . .
    I (don't) feel like (doing
    s.th.) . . . (9W)
    lustig funny (4E); **sich ~**
    machen über (+ *acc.*) to
    make fun of (11E); **reise~**
    eager to travel
    luxuriös' luxurious
der **Luxus** luxury

M

    machen to make, do (2W);
    Spaß~ to be fun (4E);
    Mach's gut! Take care!;
    Was machst du Schönes?
    What are you doing?; **Das**
    macht nichts. That
    doesn't matter. (5E); **Das**
    macht zusammen . . .
    That comes to . . .
die **Macht, -e** power (14E)
das **Mädchen, -** girl (1W)
die **Magd, -e** maid
der **Mai** May (S5); **im ~** in May
    (S5)
der **Mais** corn
der **Makler, -** real-estate agent
    mal times
das **Mal, -e: das erste ~** the
    first time; **zum ersten ~**
    for the first time
    malen to paint
der **Maler, -** painter
    man one (they, people) (3E)
das **Management, -s** manage-
    ment
    manch- many a, several,
    some (7G)
    manchmal sometimes (3E)
    manipuliert' manipulated
der **Mann, -er** man, husband
    (5W)
    männlich masculine, male
der **Mantel, -** coat (S3)
das **Manuskript', -e** manuscript
das **Märchen, -** fairy tale

die **Margari'ne, -n** margarine
die **Mark (DM)** mark (S4); **zwei**
    Mark two marks (S4)
der **Markt, -e** market (2W)
die **Marmela'de, -n** marmalade,
    jam (2W)
der **März** March (S5); **im ~** in
    March (S5)
die **Maschi'ne, -n** machine
der **Maschi'nenbau** mechanical
    engineering
die **Maske, -n** mask
die **Massa'ge, -n** massage
die **Masse, -n** mass
die **Mathematik'** mathematics
die **Mauer, -n** wall (14W)
der **Maurer, -** bricklayer
die **Maus, -e** mouse; **~efalle, -n**
    mousetrap
der **Mecha'niker, -** mechanic
die **Medail'le, -n** medal
die **Medien** *(pl.)* media
das **Medikament', -e** medicine,
    prescription
die **Medizin'** medicine
das **Mehl** flour
    mehr more (12G); **immer ~**
    more and more (12G)
    mehrer- *(pl.)* several (10G)
    meiden, mied, gemieden
    to avoid
    mein my (1W,7G)
    meinen to mean, think (be
    of an opinion) (13E)
die **Meinung, -en** opinion; **mei-**
    ner ~ nach in my opinion
    meist-: am meisten most
    (12G)
    meistens mostly (7E)
der **Meister, -** master
die **Mensa** student cafeteria
    (3W)
der **Mensch, -en, -en** human
    being, person; people *(pl.)*
    (1E); **~!** Man! Boy! Hey!;
    Mit~ fellow man
die **Menschheit** mankind
das **Menü', -s** dinner, daily spe-
    cial
    merken to notice
die **Messe, -n** (trade) fair
das **Messer, -** knife (3E)
der **Meter, -** meter
die **Metropo'le, -n** metropolis
die **Metzgerei', -en** butcher
    shop
    mies miserable
    mieten to rent (6W)
die **Miete, -n** rent

der **Mieter, -** renter, tenant

die **Mietwohnung, -en** apartment

der **Mikrowellenherd, -e** microwave oven

die **Milch** milk (2W)

milita′risch military

die **Million′, -en** million

der **Millionär′, -e** millionaire

die **Mineralogie′** mineralogy

das **Mineral′wasser** mineral water

minus minus (S4)

die **Minu′te, -n** minute (S6)

mischen to mix; **darunter ~** to blend in

die **Mischung, -en** mixture

misera′bel miserable

die **Mission′** mission

mit (+ *dat*.) with (3G); along

mit·bringen* to bring along (7G)

mit·fahren* to drive along

mit·feiern to join in the celebration

mit·gehen* to go along (7G)

mit·kommen* to come along (7G)

mit·machen to participate (9E)

der **Mitmensch, -en, -en** fellow man

mit·nehmen* to take along (7G)

mit·schicken to send along

mit·singen* to sing along

mit·spielen to participate

der **Mittag, -e** noon

— **mittag** noon (8G); **heute ~** today at noon (8G)

das **Mittagessen, -** lunch, noontime meal (3W); **beim ~** at lunch; **zum ~** for lunch (3W)

mittags at noon (S6)

die **Mitte** middle, center (14W)

das **Mittel, -** means (of)

das **Mittelalter** Middle Ages; **im ~** in the Middle Ages (14W)

mittelalterlich medieval

(das) **Mitteleuropa** Central Europe

mittelgroß average size

mitten: ~ durch right through (14W); **~ in** in the middle of (6E)

die **Mitternacht: um ~** at midnight

der **Mittwoch** Wednesday (S5); **am ~** on Wednesday; **Ascher~** Ash Wednesday **mittwochs** on Wednesdays (2E)

die **Möbel** (*pl.*) furniture (6W)

die **Mobilität′** mobility

möbliert′ furnished

möchten *or* **möchte** (*see* **mögen**)

das **Modal′verb, -en** modal auxiliary

die **Mode** fashion; **~puppe, -n** fashion doll

modern′ modern

mögen (mag), mochte, gemocht to like (5G); **Ich möchte . . .** I would like (to have) . . . (2W)

möglich possible (7W)

die **Möglichkeit, -en** possibility

der **Moment′, -e** moment; **~!** One Moment. Just a minute.

momentan′ at the moment, right now

der **Monat, -e** month (S5); **im ~** a month, per month (6W)

monatelang for months

-monatig months long

monatlich monthly (10E)

der **Mond, -e** moon

der **Montag** Monday (S5); **am ~** on Monday

montags on Mondays (2E)

die **Moral′** moral

der **Mörder, -** murderer

morgen tomorrow (S4,4W); **Bis ~!** See you tomorrow; **für ~** for tomorrow (S2)

der **Morgen** morning: **Guten ~!** Good morning. (S1)

— **morgen** early morning (8G); **heute ~** this morning (8G)

morgens in the morning (S6), every morning

das **Motto, -s** motto

müde tired (S1); **tod~** dead tired

die **Müdigkeit** fatigue

der **Müll** garbage

der **Müller, -** miller

der **Müllschlucker, -** garbage disposal

der **Mund, ⁻er** mouth (9W)

die **Mundharmonika, -s** harmonica

mündlich oral(ly)

das **Muse′um, Muse′en** museum (5W)

die **Musik′** music (9E)

musika′lisch musical (11W)

die **Musik′wissenschaft** study of music

(der) **Muskat′** nutmeg

der **Muskelkater** charley horse; **Ich habe ~.** I'm sore.

müssen (muß), mußte, gemußt to have to, must (5G)

das **Muster, -** sample

die **Mutter, ⁻** mother (1W); **Groß~** grandmother; **Urgroß~** great-grandmother

mütterlich motherly

N

na well; **~ gut** well, all right; **~ ja** well; **~ und!** so what?

nach (+ *dat*.) after (time), to (cities, countries, continents) (3G)

der **Nachbar, -n, -n** neighbor (1E)

die **Nachbarschaft, -en** neighborhood; neighborly relations

nachdem′ (*conj.*) after (11G)

nacherzählt retold, adapted

nach·kommen* to follow

nach·laufen* to run after

nach·machen to imitate

der **Nachmittag, -e** afternoon; **am ~** in the afternoon

— **nachmittag** afternoon (8G); **heute ~** this afternoon (8G)

nachmittags in the afternoon (S6), every afternoon

der **Nachname, -ns, -n** last name

die **Nachricht, -en** news (10E)

nächst- next (12G)

die **Nacht, ⁻e** night (7W); **Gute ~!** Good night!

— **nacht** night (8G); **heute ~** tonight (8G)

der **Nachteil, -e** disadvantage

die **Nachteule, -n** night owl

der **Nachtisch** dessert (3W); **zum ~** for dessert (3W)

nachts during the night, every night (8G)

nah (näher, nächst-) near (5W,12G)

die **Nähe** nearness, vicinity; **in der ~** nearby; **in der ~ von** (+ *dat*.) near (5W)

nähen to sew

der **Name, -ns, -n** name (7E,8G); **Mein ~ ist ...** My name is ... (S1); **Vor~** first name; **Nach~** last name; **Spitz~** nickname

nämlich namely

die **Nase, -n** nose (9W); **pro ~** per person

naß (nässer, nässest-) wet

national' national

der **Nationalis'mus** nationalism

die **Nationalität', -en** nationality

die **Natur'** nature

natür'lich natural(ly), of course (2W)

natur'verbunden nature-loving

die **Natur'wissenschaft, -en** natural science

natur'wissenschaftlich scientific

neben (+ acc. / dat.) beside, next to (6G)

nebeneinander next to each other

das **Nebenfach, ⸚er** minor (field of study) (14W)

der **Nebensatz, ⸚e** subordinate clause

negativ negative(ly)

nehmen (nimmt), nahm, genommen to take (S4); to have (food) (3G)

nein no (S1)

nennen, nannte, genannt to name, call (14W); **Ich nenne das ...** That's what I call ...

nett nice (11W)

neu new (S3); **Was gibt's Neues ...?** What's new? (9W)

neugierig curious

der **Neujahrstag** New Year's Day

nicht not (S1); **gar ~** not at all (13E); **~ nur ... sondern auch ...** not only ... but also ... (3E); **~ wahr?** isn't it? (S5)

nichts nothing (3W); **~ Besonderes** nothing special (9W)

nie never (4E); **noch ~** never before, not ever (4E)

niemand nobody, no one (11E)

nimmermehr never again

nobel noble

noch still (4W); **~ ein** another (3W); **~ einmal** once more, again (S2); **~ nicht** not yet (6E); **~ nie** never before, not ever (4E); **sonst ~ etwas?** anything else?; **was ~?** what else?; **weder ... ~** neither ... nor (10E)

der **Nominativ, -e** nominative

der **Norden: im ~** in the north (1W)

nördlich (von) to the north, north (of) (1W)

normal' normal; by regular mail

(das) **Nor'wegen** Norway

der **Nor'weger, -** the Norwegian

nor'wegisch Norwegian

die **Note, -n** grade (13W)

nötig necessary, needed

die **Notiz', -en** note; **~en machen** to take notes

der **Novem'ber** November (S5); **im ~** in November (S5)

nüchtern sober

die **Nudel, -n** noodle (3W)

null zero (S4)

die **Nummer, -n** number (7W)

nun well (14E); now (14E)

nur only (S4)

O

ob (conj.) if, whether (4G)

oben upstairs (6W); up

der **Ober, -** waiter (3W); **Herr ~!** Waiter! (3W)

die **Oberin, -nen** mother superior

das **Objekt', -e** object

das **Obst** (sg.) fruit (2W)

obwohl (conj.) although (4G)

oder or (S3,2G)

der **Ofen, ⸚** oven

offen open (2E)

öffnen to open (S4)

öffentlich public

oft often (2E)

ohne (+ acc.) without (2G)

das **Ohr, -en** ear (9W)

der **Okto'ber** October (S5); **im ~** in October (S5)

das **Öl, -e** oil, lotion

die **Olympia'de, -n** Olympics

die **Oma, -s** grandma

das **Omelett', -s** omelet

der **Onkel, -** uncle (1W)

die **Oper, -n** opera (10W)

oran'ge orange (S2)

die **Oran'ge, -n** orange (2W)

das **Orche'ster, -** orchestra (10W)

die **Ordungszahl, -en** ordinal number

die **Organisation', -en** organization

organisie'ren to organize

das **Original', -e** original

der **Ort, -e** place, town

der **Osten: im ~** in the east (1W)

(das) **Ostern: zu ~** at / for Easter (4W); **Frohe ~!** Happy Easter.

(das) **Österreich** Austria (1W)

der **Österreicher, -** the Austrian (1W)

österreichisch Austrian

östlich (von) east (of), to the east (of) (1W)

der **Ozean, -e** ocean

P

paar: ein ~ a couple of, some (2E)

das **Paar, -e** couple, pair

packen to pack (7E)

die **Pädago'gik** education

das **Paddelboot, -e** canoe

paddeln to paddle

das **Paket', -e** package, parcel (8W)

die **Paket'karte, -n** parcel form

die **Palatschinken** (pl.) dessert crêpes

das **Panora'ma** panorama

das **Papier', -e** paper (S2)

der **Papierkrieg** paper work

der **Park, -s** park (5W)

parken to park (15W)

das **Parkett': im ~** in the orchestra

der **Parkplatz, ⸚e** parking lot

die **Partei', -en** (political) party

das **Parter're: im ~** on the first floor (ground level) (6W)

das **Partizip', -ien** participle

der **Partner, -** partner (11W)

die **Party, Parties** party (4W)

der **Paß, ⸚sse** passport (7W)

passen to fit

passend appropriate, suitable

das **Passiv** passive voice

die **Pause, -n** intermission, break (10W); **eine ~ machen** to take a break

das **Pech** tough luck; **~ haben*** to be unlucky (7E)

pendeln to commute

die **Pension'**, **-en** boarding house; hotel (7E)

das **Perfekt** present perfect

permanent' permanent

persön'lich personal(ly)

die **Persön'lichkeit**, **-en** personality

der **Pfarrer**, **-** minister

der **Pfeffer** pepper (3W)

die **Pfefferminze** peppermint

der **Pfennig**, **-e** German penny, pfennig (S4); **zwei ~** two pennies (S4)

das **Pferd**, **-e** horse

das **Pflichtfach**, **⁻er** required subject

das **Pfund**, **-e** pound (2W); **zwei ~** two pounds (of) (2W)

die **Phantasie'**, **-n** fantasy, imagination

phantas'tisch fantastic (9W)

die **Pharmazie'** pharmaceutics

die **Philologie'** philology

der **Philosoph'**, **-en**, **-en** philosopher

die **Philosophie'** philosophy

die **Photographie'** photography

photographie'ren to take pictures (9W)

die **Physik'** physics

der **Physiker**, **-** physicist

physisch physical(ly)

das **Picknick**, **-s** picnic

picknicken gehen* to go picnicking

der **Pilot'**, **-en**, **-en** pilot

der **Plan**, **⁻e** plan (12W)

planen to plan (15W)

die **Platte**, **-n** record (9W); platter

der **Plattenspieler**, **-** record player (10W)

der **Platz**, **⁻e** square, place (5W); seat

die **Platzanweiserin**, **-nen** usher

das **Plätzchen**, **-** cookie (2W)

plötzlich suddenly (11E)

der **Plural**, **-e** **(von)** plural of (S2)

plus plus (S4)

das **Plusquamperfekt** past perfect

die **Politik'(wissenschaft)** political science, politics

poli'tisch political(ly)

die **Polizei'** *(sg.)* police

der **Polizist'**, **-en**, **-en** policeman (12W)

der **Pole**, **-n**, **-n** the Pole

(das) **Polen** Poland

polnisch Polish

die **Pommes frites** *(pl.)* French fries

der **Pool**, **-s** pool

populär' popular

der **Portier'**, **-s** desk clerk

das **Porto** postage

(das) **Portugal** Portugal

der **Portugie'se**, **-n**, **-n** the Portuguese

portugie'sisch Portuguese

die **Post** post office (5W); mail (8W)

das **Postfach**, **⁻er** P.O. box

das **Posthorn**, **⁻er** bugle

die **Postkarte**, **-n** postcard (8W)

prägen to shape

praktisch practical(ly) (6W)

die **Präposition'**, **-en** preposition

der **Präsident'**, **-en**, **-en** president

die **Praxis** practical experience

der **Preis**, **-e** price; prize

die **Presse** press

das **Presti'ge** prestige

prima great, wonderful (S5)

der **Prinz**, **-en**, **-en** prince

die **Prinzes'sin**, **-nen** princess

privat' private

das **Privat'gefühl**, **-e** feeling for privacy

pro per

die **Probezeit** probation

probie'ren to try

das **Problem'**, **-e** problem (13E)

problema'tisch problematic

das **Produkt'**, **-e** product

die **Produktion'** production

produzie'ren to produce

der **Profes'sor**, **-en** professor (13W)

das **Programm'**, **-e** program, channel (10W)

der **Programmie'rer**, **-** programmer

das **Prono'men**, **-** pronoun

proportional' proportional(ly)

Prost! Cheers!

protestie'ren to protest

protzen to brag

das **Proviso'rium** provisional state

die **Prüfung**, **-en** test, exam (9E); **eine ~ schreiben*** to take an exam (13W)

der **Psalm**, **-e** psalm

das **Pseudonym'**, **-e** pseudonym

der **Psychia'ter**, **-** psychiatrist

die **Psy'choanaly'se** psychoanalysis

der **Psycholo'ge**, **-n**, **-n** psychologist

die **Psychologie'** psychology

psycholo'gisch psychological(ly)

das **Publikum** audience

die **Puderdose**, **-n** compact

der **Pudding**, **-s** pudding (3W)

der **Pullo'ver**, **-** pullover, sweater (S3)

pünktlich on time

die **Puppe**, **-n** doll

putzen to clean; **sich die Zähne ~** to brush one's teeth (9G)

Q

die **Qualifikation'**, **-en** qualification

die **Qualität'** quality

die **Quantität'** quantity

das **Quartal'**, **-e** quarter (university)

das **Quartett'**, **-e** quartet

das **Quartier'**, **-s** lodging

der **Quatsch** nonsense

die **Quelle**, **-n** source

quer durch all across

das **Quintett'**, **-s** quintet

die **Quote**, **-n** quota

R

rad·fahren (fährt Rad), fuhr Rad, ist radgefahren to bicycle

das **Radio**, **-s** radio (6W)

der **Rand**, **⁻er** edge

der **Rang**, **⁻e** theater balcony; **im ersten ~** in the first balcony

der **Rasen**, **-** lawn

sich **rasie'ren** to shave o.s. (9G)

der **Rat** advice, counsel

raten (rät), riet, geraten to advise; guess

das **Rathaus**, **⁻er** city hall (5W)

die **Ratte**, **-n** rat

der **Raum** space

reagie'ren to react

die **Reaktion'**, **-en** reaction

rechnen to calculate

die **Rechnung**, **-en** check, bill (3W)

recht: Du hast ~. You're right. (11W)

recht-: auf der ~en Seite on the right side

das **Recht, -e** right

rechts right (5W); **erste Straße ~** first street to the right (5W)

der **Rechtsanwalt, ̈-e** lawyer (12W)

die **Rechtsanwältin, -nen** lawyer (12W)

die **Rechtswissenschaft** study of law

die **Rede, -n** speech

reden (mit / über) to talk (to / about), chat (15W)

die **Redewendung, -en** idiom, saying

das **Referat, -e** report; **ein ~ halten*** to give a report

reflexiv' reflexive

das **Regal, -e** shelf (6E)

der **Regen** rain

der **Regenschirm, -e** umbrella

die **Region', -en** region

regional' regional(ly)

der **Regisseur', -e** director (film)

registrie'ren to register s.th.

regnen to rain; **Es regnet.** It's raining. (S5)

regulie'ren to regulate

reiben, rieb, gerieben to rub

reich rich (11W)

das **Reich, -e** empire, kingdom

der **Reichtum, ̈-er** wealth

reif ripe; mature

die **Reihe, -n** row

der **Reis** rice (3W)

die **Reise, -n** trip (7E,8W); **eine ~ machen** to take a trip, travel

das **Reisebüro, -s** travel agency

reiselustig fond of traveling

reisen (ist) to travel (7E)

reißen, riß, ist gerissen to tear

der **Reisescheck, -s** traveler's check

reiten, ritt, ist geritten to ride (on horseback)

die **Reitschule, -n** riding academy

die **Rekla'me, -n** advertisement, advertising (10W)

relativ' relative(ly)

das **Relativ'pronomen, -** relative pronoun

der **Relativ'satz, ̈-e** relative clause

die **Religion', -en** religion

rennen, rannte, ist gerannt to run (11E)

renovie'ren to renovate (15W)

repräsentativ' representative

reservie'ren to reserve (7E)

die **Residenz', -en** residence

resignie'ren to resign, give up

der **Rest, -e** rest

das **Restaurant', -s** restaurant (3E)

restaurie'ren to restore (15W)

die **Restaurie'rung** restoration

retten to save, rescue (15W)

die **Rezeption', -en** reception (desk)

das **R-Gespräch, -e** collect call

richtig right, correct (S2)

die **Richtigkeit** correctness

die **Richtung, -en** direction; **in ~** in the direction of

riechen, roch, gerochen to smell

riesig huge

die **Rindsroulade, -n** stuffed beef roll

der **Ring, -e** ring

rings um (+ *acc.*) all around (14W)

das **Risiko, Risiken** risk

der **Ritter, -** knight

der **Roboter, -** robot

der **Rock, ̈-e** skirt (S3)

die **Rolle, -n** role

der **Roman', -e** novel (10W)

die **Romani'stik** study of Romance languages

die **Roman'tik** romanticism

der **Roman'tiker, -** romantic

roman'tisch romantic

rosa pink (S2)

die **Rose, -n** rose

die **Rosi'ne, -n** raisin

rot (ö) red (S2)

das **Rotkraut** red cabbage

rötlich reddish

die **Roula'de, -n** stuffed beef roll

der **Rückblick, -e** review

die **Rückfahrkarte, -n** round-trip ticket (8W)

der **Rückgang** decline

der **Rucksack, ̈-e** knapsack, rucksack

das **Ruderboot, -e** rowboat

rudern to row

rufen, rief, gerufen to call

die **Ruhe** peace and quiet

der **Ruhetag, -e** holiday, day off

ruhig quiet (7W)

der **Ruhm** fame

die **Rundfahrt, -en** round trip

rühren to stir

der **Rum** rum

der **Rundfunk** radio, broadcasting

der **Russe, -n, -n** the Russian

russisch Russian

(das) **Rußland** Russia

S

der **Saal, Säle** large room, hall

die **Sache, -n** thing, matter

der **Saft, ̈-e** juice (2W)

sagen to say, tell (S3); **Sag mal!** Say. Tell me (us etc.).; **wie gesagt** as I (you etc.) said

die **Saison', -s** season

der **Salat', -e** salad, lettuce (2W)

das **Salz** salt (3W)

die **Salzstange, -n** pretzel stick

sammeln to collect (9W)

der **Sammler, -** collector

der **Samstag** Saturday (S5); **am ~** on Saturday (S5)

samstags on Saturdays (2E)

der **Samt** velvet

der **Sand** sand

der **Sängerknabe, -n** choir boy

der **Satellit', -en** satellite

der **Satz, ̈-e** sentence (1W); **Bilden Sie einen ~!** Make a sentence.

sauber clean, neat (S3)

die **Sauberkeit** cleanliness

sauber·machen to clean

sauer sour; acid

der **Sauerbraten** marinated pot roast

das **Sauerkraut** sauerkraut

die **S-Bahn, -en** commuter train

das **Schach: ~ spielen** to play chess (9W)

schade too bad (5W)

das **Schaf, -e** sheep

schaffen to work hard

schaffen, schuf, geschaffen to create

der **Schaffner, -** conductor

die **Schale, -n** shell, peel
die **(Schall)platte, -n** record (9W)
der **Schalter, -** ticket window, counter (7W)
der **Schaschlik, -s** shish kebab
die **Schatzkammer, -n** treasury
schauen to look, see; **auf die Finger ~** to hold in check
das **Schaufenster, -** display window
der **Schauspieler, -** actor (10W)
der **Scheck, -s** check (7W)
scheinen, schien, geschienen to shine (S5); to seem (like), appear (to be) (14E)
schenken to give (as a present) (4W)
schick chic, neat (11W)
schicken to send (8W)
die **Schießbude, -n** shooting gallery
das **Schiff, -e** ship, boat; **mit dem ~ fahren*** to go by boat
das **Schild, -er** sign
der **Schinken, -** ham
schlafen (schläft), schlief, geschlafen to sleep (3E)
das **Schlafzimmer, -** bedroom (6W)
schlagen (schlägt), schlug, geschlagen to hit
der **Schlager, -** popular song, hit
die **Schlagsahne** whipped cream
die **Schlange, -n** snake
schlank slim, slender (11W)
schlecht bad(ly) (S1)
schließen, schloß, geschlossen to lock; close
schlimm bad, awful
das **Schloß, ¨sser** palace (5W)
der **Schlüssel, -** key (7W)
schmecken to taste; **Das schmeckt gut.** That tastes good. (3W)
schmelzen (schmilzt), schmolz, geschmolzen to melt
der **Schmerz, -en** pain, ache; **Ich habe (Kopf)schmerzen.** I have a (head)ache. (9W)
der **Schmied, -e** blacksmith
der **Schmutz** dirt
schmutzig dirty (S3)

der **Schnee** snow
schneiden, schnitt, geschnitten to cut
schneien; es schneit it's snowing (S5)
schnell quick(ly), fast (S3)
die **Schnellimbißstube, -n** fast-food stand
der **Schnellweg, -e** express route
das **Schnitzel, -** veal cutlet
die **Schokola'de** chocolate
schon already (5E)
schön fine, nice, beautiful (S5)
die **Schönheit** beauty
der **Schrank, ¨e** closet, cupboard (6W)
der **Schrebergarten, ¨** leased garden
schreiben, schrieb, geschrieben to write (S3); **~ an** (+ acc.) to write to (10G); **eine Prüfung ~** to take an exam (13W)
der **Schreibtisch, -e** desk (6W)
schriftlich written; in writing
der **Schriftsteller, -** writer
der **Schritt, -e** step
der **Schuh, -e** shoe (S3); **Sport~** gym shoe
die **Schule, -n** school (5W)
der **Schüler, -** pupil, student
der **Schutz** protection (14E)
schützen to protect
der **Schwabe, -n, -n** the Swabian
(das) **Schwaben(land)** Swabia
schwäbisch Swabian
die **Schwäche, -n** weakness
schwanger pregnant
schwärmen to rave
schwarz (ä) black (S2)
das **Schwarzbrot, -e** rye bread
der **Schwede, -n, -n** the Swede
(das) **Schweden** Sweden
schwedisch Swedish
das **Schwein, -e** pig, pork; scoundrel; **~ haben*** to be lucky
die **Schweinshaxe, -n** pigs' knuckles
die **Schweiz** Switzerland (1W)
der **Schweizer, -** the Swiss (1W)
Schweizer or **schweizerisch** Swiss
schwer heavy; difficult, hard (10E)

die **Schwester, -n** sister (1W)
das **Schwesterchen, -** little sister
schwimmen, schwamm, geschwommen to swim (9W); **~ gehen*** to go swimming (9W)
der **Schwimmer, -** swimmer
der **See, -n** lake (1W)
die **See** sea, ocean
das **Segelboot, -e** sailboat
segelfliegen gehen* to go gliding
segeln to sail; **~ gehen*** to go sailing
sehen (sieht), sah, gesehen to see, look (3G); **Mal ~!** Let's see!
die **Sehenswürdigkeit, -en** attraction
sehr very (S5)
die **Seide, -n** silk
die **Seife, -n** soap
die **Seilbahn, -en** cable car
sein his, its (7G)
sein (ist), war, ist gewesen to be (S1,S2,2G); **Wie wär's mit . . . ?** How about . . . ?; **Ich bin's.** It's me.
seit (+ dat.) since, for (time) (3G)
die **Seite, -n** page; **auf ~** on page, to page (S4)
die **Sekretä'rin, -nen** secretary (12W)
der **Sekt** champagne (4W)
die **Sekun'de, -n** second (S6)
selbst -self; **~ wenn** even if
selbständig self-employed, independent (12W)
die **Selbständigkeit** independence
selten seldom
das **Seme'ster, -** semester (13W)
das **Seminar', -e** seminar (13W)
die **Seminar'arbeit, -en** term paper
die **Sendung, -en** (part of) TV or radio program (10E)
das **Sendungsbewußtsein** sense of mission
der **Septem'ber** September (S5); **im ~** in September (S5)
die **Serie, -n** series
servie'ren to serve (food)
die **Sesamstraße** Sesame Street
der **Sessel, -** armchair (6W)
der **Sessellift, -e** chairlift

setzen to set (down), put (11W); **sich ~** to sit down (9G)

das **Shampoo′, -s** shampoo

die **Show, -s** show

sicher sure, certain (4W); safe, secure (12W)

die **Sicherheit** safety, security

sicherlich surely, certainly, undoubtedly

sichern to secure

die **Siedlung, -en** settlement, subdivision

der **Sieger, -** victor

das **Silber** silver

(das) **Silve′ster: zu ~** at / for New Year's Eve (4W)

singen, sang, gesungen to sing (4W)

der **Sinn, -e** mind, sense

die **Situation′, -en** situation

sitzen, saß, gesessen to sit, be sitting (6G)

die **Sitzecke, -n** corner bench

Ski laufen gehen* to go skiing (9W); **Wasserski laufen gehen*** to go waterskiing

der **Skiläufer, -** skier

die **Slawi′stik** study of Slavic language and literature

so so, like that; **~ daß** (conj.) so that (12E); **~ ein** such a (7G); **~ so** fair; **~ . . . wie** as . . . as (12G)

das **Sofa, -s** sofa, couch (6W)

sofort′ immediately, right away (8E)

sogar′ even (6W)

sogenannt so-called

der **Sohn, -̈e** son (1W)

solch - such (7G)

der **Soldat′, -en, -en** soldier

sollen (soll), sollte, gesollt to be supposed to (5G)

der **Sommer, -** summer (S5); **im ~** in the summer (S5)

das **Sonderangebot, -e: im ~** on sale, special

sondern but (on the contrary) (5W,5G); **nicht nur . . . ~ auch** not only . . . but also (3E)

der **Sonderstatus** special status

die **Sonne** sun; **Die ~ scheint.** The sun is shining. (S5)

das **Sonnenöl** suntan lotion

der **Sonnenuntergang, -̈e** sunset

der **Sonntag** Sunday (S5); **am ~** on Sunday (S5)

sonntags on Sundays (2E)

sonst otherwise; **~ noch etwas?** anything else?

die **Soße, -n** sauce, gravy

sowieso′ anyway, anyhow (13E)

sowje′tisch Soviet

sowohl . . . als auch as well as

die **Sozial′kunde** social studies

die **Soziologie′** sociology

(das) **Spanien** Spain (1W)

der **Spanier, -** the Spaniard (1W)

spanisch Spanish (1W)

spannend exciting, suspenseful (10W)

sparen to save (money) (6E)

die **Spartakia′de, -n** major sports competition in the GDR

sparta′nisch Spartan, frugal

der **Spaß, -̈e** fun; **~ machen** to be fun (4E)

spät late; **Wie ~ ist es?** How late is it? (S6)

später later; **Bis ~!** See you later! (4W)

spazie′ren·gehen* to go for a walk (9W)

der **Spazier′gang, -̈e** walk

die **Speise, -n** food, dish

die **Speisekarte, -n** menu (3W)

die **Spekulation′, -en** speculation

das **Spezial′geschäft, -e** specialty shop

die **Spezialisie′rung** specialization

der **Spezialist′, -en, -en** specialist

die **Spezialität′, -en** specialty

der **Spiegel, -** mirror

das **Spiel, -e** game, play (9W)

spielen to play; **Tennis ~** to play tennis (S6)

der **Spielplan, -̈e** program, schedule

der **Spielplatz, -̈e** playground

der **Spieß, -e** spit; spear

spinnen, spann, gesponnen to spin (yarn); **Er (sie) spinnt.** He (she) is crazy.

der **Spitzname, -ns, -n** nickname

spontan′ spontaneous

der **Sport** sport(s) (9E); **~ treiben*** to be active in sports

die **Sportartikel** (pl.) sports equipment

der **Sportler, -** athlete

sportlich athletic, sporty (11W)

die **Sprache, -n** language (1W)

-sprachig -speaking

sprechen (spricht), sprach, gesprochen to speak (S3); **~ Sie laut!** Speak up. (S3); **Man spricht . . .** They (people) speak . . . ; **~ über** (+ acc.) to speak about (10G)

der **Sprecher, -** speaker

das **Sprichwort, -̈er** saying, proverb

springen, sprang, ist gesprungen to jump

das **Spritzgebäck** cookies shaped with a cookie press

der **Spruch, -̈e** saying

die **Spülmaschine, -n** dishwasher

der **Staat, -en** state (9E)

staatlich public

die **Staatsangehörigkeit** citizenship

der **Staatsbürger, -** citizen

der **Stacheldraht, -̈e** barbed wire

die **Stadt, -̈e** city, town (1W)

das **Stadtbild, -er** character of a town

das **Städtchen, -** small town

der **Stadtplan, -̈e** city map (5W)

der **Stahl** steel

der **Stamm, -̈e** tribe, clan

stammen (aus + dat.) to stem (from), originate

der **Standard, -s** standard

das **Standesamt, -̈er** marriage registrar

stark (ä) strong

die **Station′, -en** station (bus stop)

statt instead of (8G)

stehen, stand, gestanden to be standing (6G); **Wie steht der Dollar?** What's the exchange rate of the dollar? (7W)

stehen·bleiben* to come to a stop, remain standing

stehlen, stahl, gestohlen to steal

steif stiff

steigen, stieg, ist gestiegen to go up, rise, climb

steigern to increase

steil steep

der **Stein, -e** stone

die **Stelle, -n** job, position, place (12W); **an deiner ~** in your shoes; if I were you (13E)

stellen to stand (upright), put (6G)

sterben (stirbt), starb, ist gestorben to die

der **Stern, -e** star

die **Stereoanlage, -n** stereo set

die **Steuer, -n** tax

der **Stier, -e** bull

der **Stil, -e** style

still quiet

stimmen: Das stimmt. That's true. That's right.

das **Stipen'dium, Stipen'dien** scholarship (13W)

der **Stock, -werke: im ersten ~** on the second floor (6W)

stolz proud (11E)

der **Stolz** pride

das **Stopschild, -er** stop sign

stören to bother, disturb (14W)

die **Straße, -n** street (5W)

die **Straßenbahn, -en** streetcar (5W)

strate'gisch strategic

der **Stre'ber, -** grind

streng strict

das **Stroh** straw

die **Struktur', -en** structure, grammar

das **Stück, -e** piece; **ein ~** a piece of (2W); **zwei ~** two pieces of (2W); (theater) play (10W)

der **Student', -en, -en** student (2G)

die **Studen'tin, -nen** student (2E)

das **Studen'tenheim, -e** dormitory (6W)

die **Studiengebühr, -en** tuition

studie'ren (an + dat.) to study a particular field, be a student at a university (4E)

das **Studium, Studien** study (13W)

der **Stuhl, ¨e** chair (S2)

die **Stunde, -n** hour, class (S6); **in einer halben ~** in half an hour (8W); **in einer Viertel~** in 15 minutes (8W); **in einer Dreiviertel~** in 45 minutes (8W)

stundenlang for hours (5E)

der **Stundenplan, ¨e** schedule (of classes)

das **Subjekt', -e** subject

die **Suche** search

suchen to seek, look for (11W)

der **Süden: im ~** in the south (1W)

südlich (von) south (of), to the south (of) (1W)

der **Su'perlativ, -e** superlative

der **Supermarkt, ¨e** supermarket (2W)

su'permodern' very modern

die **Suppe, -n** soup (3W)

das **Symbol', -e** symbol

sympa'thisch congenial, likable (11W)

die **Symphonie', -en** symphony

synchronisiert' dubbed

das **System', -e** system

die **Szene, -n** scene

T

die **Tafel, -n** (black)board (S2); **Gehen Sie an die ~!** Go to the (black)board. (S3)

der **Tag, -e** day (S5); **am ~** during the day (6E); **eines Tages** (gen.) one day (8G); **Guten ~!** Hello. (S1); **jeden Tag** every day (8G)

tagelang for days

-tägig days long

täglich daily (10E)

das **Tal, ¨er** valley

das **Talent', -e** talent

talentiert' talented (11W)

die **Tante, -n** aunt (1W)

der **Tanz, ¨e** dance

tanzen to dance (4W)

die **Tasche, -n** bag, pocket (7W)

die **Tasse, -n** cup (2E); **eine ~** a cup of (2E)

die **Tatsache, -n** fact

tauchen (in + acc.) to dip (into)

tauschen to trade

das **Taxi, -s** taxi (5W)

der **Techniker, -** technician

technisch technical

der **Tee, -s** tea (2W)

der **Teenager, -** teenager

der **Teil, -e** part (1E)

teilen to divide (14W)

teilmöbliert partly furnished

die **Teilnahme** participation

teil·nehmen* (an + dat.) to participate (in), take part (in) (13E)

die **Teilung, -en** division

das **Telefon', -e** telephone (6W)

telefonie'ren to call up, phone (8W)

der **Teller, -** plate (3W)

temperament'voll dynamic (11W)

die **Temperatur', -en** temperature

das **Tennis: ~ spielen** to play tennis (S6)

der **Teppich, -e** carpet (6W)

die **Terras'se, -n** terrace

teuer expensive (2E)

der **Text, -e** text

das **Thea'ter, -** theater (5W)

das **Thema, Themen** topic

der **Theolo'ge, -n, -n** theologian

die **Theologie'** theology

die **Theorie', -n** theory

das **Thermome'ter, -** thermometer

der **Tiefbau** civil engineering

das **Tier, -e** animal

tierlieb fond of animals

der **Tip, -s** hint

der **Tisch, -e** table (S2)

der **Tischler, -** carpenter

das **Tischtennis: ~ spielen** to play Ping-Pong

der **Titel, -** title

die **Tochter, ¨** daughter (1W)

der **Tod** death

Toi, toi, toi! Good luck!

die **Toilet'te, -n** toilet (6W)

tolerant' tolerant

toll great, terrific (5E)

die **Toma'te, -n** tomato (2W)

der **Ton, ¨e** tone

der **Topf, ¨e** pot

das **Tor, -e** gate

die **Torte, -n** (fancy) cake

total' total

die **Tour, -en** tour

der **Tourist', -en, -en** tourist (5W)

das **Tournier', -e** tournament

traditionell' traditional(ly)

tragen (trägt), trug, getragen to carry (3G); to wear (3G)

die **Tragetasche, -n** carrying case

der **Trainer, -** coach

trainie'ren to train, practice

das **Training** training
das **Transport'flugzeug, -e** transport plane
der **Traum, ⸚e** dream **träumen (von)** to dream (of) (11W)
der **Träumer, -** dreamer **traurig** sad (10W)
die **Traurigkeit** sadness **treffen (trifft), traf, getroffen** to meet
treiben, trieb, getrieben to push
die **Treppe, -n** stairs, stairway **treten (tritt), trat, ist getreten** to step
treu faithful
der **Trimm-dich-Pfad, -e** exercise trail
trinken, trank, getrunken to drink (2W)
das **Trinkgeld, -er** tip
der **Trockner, -** dryer
die **Trommel, -n** drum
die **Trompe'te, -n** trumpet **trotz** (+ *gen.*) in spite of (8G)
trotzdem nevertheless, in spite of that (6E)
der **Tschechoslowa'ke, -n, -n** the Czech
die **Tschechoslowakei'** Czechoslovakia
tschechisch Czech
Tschüß! So long; Goodbye. (4W)
tun (tut), tat, getan to do (4W)
die **Tür, -en** door (S2)
der **Türke, -n, -n** the Turk
die **Türkei'** Turkey
der **Turm, ⸚e** tower (14W); steeple
turnen to do sports *or* gymnastics
typisch typical(ly) (15E)

U

die **U-Bahn, -en** subway (5W)
über (+ *acc. / dat.*) over, above (6G); about (10G)
überall' everywhere (3E)
überein'·stimmen to agree
das **Überhol'verbot, -e** no passing
übermorgen the day after tomorrow (4W)
übernach'ten to spend the night (7E)

überra'schen to surprise (4W)
die **Überra'schung, -en** surprise (4W)
die **Überreste** *(pl.)* leftovers
überset'zen to translate
die **Überset'zung, -en** translation
üblich usual, customary
übrigens by the way; **die übrigen** the rest
die **Übung, -en** exercise, practice
das **Ufer, -** riverbank
die **Uhr, -en** watch, clock; o'clock (S6); **Wieviel ~ ist es?** What time is it? (S6); **~zeit** time of the day (7W)
um (+ *acc.*) around (the circumference) (2G); at ... o'clock (S6); **~ ... zu** in order to (11E)
umge'ben surrounded
die **Umge'bung** *(sg.)* surroundings (14W)
umgekehrt vice versa
ummau'ert surrounded by a wall
um·steigen* (ist) to change (trains etc.) (8W)
um·wechseln to exchange (7G)
die **Umwelt** environment, surroundings (15W)
der **Umzug, ⸚e** parade
unabhängig (von) independent (of)
unattraktiv unattractive
unbedingt definitely, necessarily
unbegrenzt unlimited
unbequem uncomfortable, inconvenient (6W)
und and (S1,2G)
unfreundlich unfriendly (11W)
der **Ungar, -n, -n** the Hungarian
(das) **Ungarn** Hungary
ungebildet uneducated
ungeduldig impatient
ungefähr about, approximately (1E)
ungemütlich unpleasant, uncomfortable
ungestört unhindered
das **Unglück** bad luck
unglücklich unhappy (11W)
die **Uni, -s** *(abbrev.)* university (13W)

die **Universität', -en** university (5W)
unmöbliert unfurnished
unmöglich impossible
unmusikalisch unmusical (11W)
das **Unrecht** wrong
unrecht haben* to be wrong (11W)
uns us, to us (5G); **bei ~** at our place (3G)
unser our (7G)
unsportlich unathletic (11W)
unsympathisch uncongenial, unlikable (11W)
untalentiert untalented (11W)
unten downstairs (6W)
unter (+ *acc. / dat.*) under, below (6G); among (15E)
der **Untergang** fall, downfall
die **Unterhal'tung** entertainment (10W)
unterneh'mungslustig enterprising (11W)
der **Unterricht** instruction, lesson, class
der **Unterschied, -e** difference
unterschrei'ben* to sign (7W)
die **Unterschrift, -en** signature
unterstüt'zen to support
unterwegs' under way, on the way, on the go
untreu unfaithful
unverheiratet unmarried, single (11W)
die **Unwahrscheinlichkeit** unreal condition
unzerstört intact
unzufrieden discontent
der **Urlaub, -e** paid vacation
ursprünglich original(ly)
u.s.w. (und so weiter) etc. (and so on)

V

die **Vanil'le** vanilla
die **Variation', -en** variation
variie'ren to vary
die **Vase, -n** vase
der **Vater, ⸚** father (1W); **Groß~** grandfather (1W); **Urgroß~** great-grandfather
verallgemei'nern to generalize
verändern to change (15W)
verantwortlich responsible

die **Verantwortung, -en** responsibility
verantwortungsvoll responsible
das **Verb, -en** verb
verbannen to ban
verbessern to improve
verbieten, verbot, verboten
to forbid, prohibit (15W)
verbinden, verband, ver-
bunden to link, connect,
combine, tie together
das **Verbot, -e** restriction
verboten forbidden (15W)
der **Verbraucher, -** consumer
verbreiten to distribute,
spread
die **Verbreitung, -en** distribu-
tion
verbrennen, verbrannte,
verbrannt to burn
verbunden in touch, close
die **Verbundenheit** closeness
verdammen to curse
verderben (verdirbt), ver-
darb, verdorben to spoil
verdienen to deserve; earn,
make money (12W)
der **Verein, -e** club; **Turn~**
athletic club
die **Vereinigten Staaten (U.S.A.)**
(pl.) United States (U.S.)
vereint united
Verflixt! Darn it.
die **Vergangenheit** past; simple
past
vergehen* (ist) to pass
(time)
vergessen (vergißt), vergaß,
vergessen to forget
(11W)
vergleichen, verglich, ver-
glichen to compare
das **Verhältnis, -se** relationship
verheiratet married (11W)
verhungern to starve
die **Verkabelung** connecting
everything by cable
verkaufen to sell (2W)
der **Verkäufer, -** salesman, sales
clerk (12W)
der **Verkehr** traffic
das **Verkehrsmittel, -** means of
transportation
verlassen (verläßt), verließ,
verlassen to leave (behind)
(14E)
sich **verlieben (in** + *acc.*) to fall
in love (with)

verliebt (in + *acc.*) in love
(with) (11W)
verlieren, verlor, verloren
to lose (11W)
sich **verloben (mit)** to get engaged (to)
verlobt (mit) engaged (to)
(11W)
die **Verlobung, -en** engagement
verlockend tempting
vermieten to rent out (6W)
der **Vermieter, -** landlord
verneinen to negate
(sich) **vernichten** to (self-)destruct
die **Vernichtung** destruction
verrückt crazy (4E)
verschenken to give away
verschieden various, different (9E)
verschlechtern to deterio-
rate
die **Verschmutzung** pollution
verschönern to beautify
die **Version', -en** version
die **Verspätung, -en** delay; **Der**
Zug hat ~. The train is
late.
versprechen* to promise
verständlich understand-
able
die **Verständigten Staaten** understanding (11W)
verstecken to hide
verstehen* (hat) to understand (S3)
versuchen to try (11W)
die **Verteidigung** defense
der **Vertrag, -e** contract
die **Verwaltung, -en** administration
der **Verwandte (ein Verwand-**
ter) relative
verwitwet widowed
verwöhnen to spoil
das **Verzeichnis, -se** index,
catalog
der **Vetter, -n** cousin
viel- (mehr, meist-) much,
many (3W,10G,12G)
vielleicht' perhaps (3E)
das **Viertel, -: (um) ~ nach** (at)
a quarter past (S6); **(um) ~**
vor (at) a quarter to (S6); **in**
einer ~stunde in a
quarter of an hour (8W); **in**
einer Dreiviertelstunde
in three quarters of an hour
(8W)
die **Vision', -en** vision

vital' vital
der **Vogel, :-** bird
die **Voka'bel, -n** (vocabulary)
word
das **Vokabular'** vocabulary
das **Volk, -er** folk; people, nation (15E)
das **Volkslied, -er** folk song
der **Volkswagen, -** VW
die **Volkswirtschaft** economics
voll full
der **Volleyball, -e** volleyball
von (+ *dat.*) of, from, by
(3G); **~ ... bis ...** from ...
until ... (S4); **vom ... bis**
zum ... from the ... to
the ... (4W)
vor (+ *acc. / dat.*) in front
of, before (6G); **~ einer**
Woche a week ago (4W); **~**
allem mainly (10E)
voran'·kommen* to advance
vorbei'·bringen* to bring
over
vorbei'·fahren* to drive by,
pass
vorbei'·gehen* (bei + *dat.*)
to pass by (7G)
vorbei·kommen* to come
by, pass by
vorbei sein* to be over, finished
(sich) **vor·bereiten (auf** + *acc.*)
to prepare (for)
die **Vorbereitung, -en** preparation
die **Vorbeugung, -en** preven-
tion
die **Vorfahrt** right of way
vorgestern the day before
yesterday (4W)
der **Vorhang, -e** curtain (6W)
vorher ahead (of time), in
advance, before
vor·kommen* (in) to appear (in)
die **Vorlesung, -en** lecture,
class (university) (S6)
— vormittag midmorning
(8G); **heute ~** this
(mid)morning (8G)
der **Vorname, -ns, -n** first name
die **Vorsicht: ~!** Careful!
vor·stellen: Darf ich ~?
May I introduce?
sich **vor·stellen** to imagine (12E)
die **Vorstellung, -en** performance (10W)

der **Vorteil, -e** advantage
der **Vortrag, ̈-e** talk, speech
vor'übergehend temporary
vor·wärmen to preheat
vor·ziehen* (hat) to prefer

W

das **Wachs** wax
wachsen (wächst), wuchs, ist gewachsen to grow (12E)
die **Waffe, -n** weapon
wagen to dare
der **Wagen, -** car (8W); railroad car (8W)
die **Wahl** choice, selection
wählen to chose; elect
das **Wahlfach, ̈-er** elective (subject)
wahnsinnig crazy
während (+ *gen.*) during (8G); while (*conj.*)
wahr true; **nicht ~?** isn't it? (S5)
der **Wald, ̈-er** forest, woods (6E)
der **Walzer, -** waltz
die **Wand, ̈-e** wall (S2)
der **Wanderer, -** hiker
wandern (ist) to hike (9W)
der **Wanderweg, -e** hiking trail
wann? when?, at what time? (S5,11G)
die **Ware, -n** goods, wares, merchandise
warm (ä) warm (S5)
warten to wait; **~ auf** (+ *acc.*) to wait for (10G)
warum? why? (2E)
was? what? (S2,2G); **~ für (ein)?** what kind of (a)? (2W)
das **Waschbecken, -** washbasin, sink
die **Wäsche** laundry
die **Waschecke, -n** corner reserved for washing
(sich) **waschen (wäscht), wusch, gewaschen** to wash (o.s.) (9G)
die **Waschmaschi'ne, -n** washing machine
das **Wasser** water (2W); **ins ~ fallen*** to get canceled
Wasserski laufen* to water-ski
der **Wasserstoff** hydrogen
der **Wechsel** change
der **Wechselkurs, -e** exchange rate
wechseln to change (7W)

weder . . . noch . . . neither . . . nor . . . (10E)
weg away
der **Weg, -e** way, path, trail (5W); route; **nach dem ~ fragen** to ask for directions
wegen (+ *gen.*) because of (8G)
weh tun* to hurt; **Mir tut (der Hals) weh.** My (throat) hurts. (9W)
die **Weide, -n** willow
(das) **Weihnachten: zu ~** at / for Christmas (4W); **Fröhliche ~!** Merry Christmas!
der **Weihnachtsbaum, ̈-e** Christmas tree
das **Weihnachtslied, -er** Christmas carol
der **Weihnachtsmann, ̈-er** Santa Claus
weil (*conj.*) because (4G)
die **Weile: eine ~** for a while
der **Wein, -e** wine (2W)
der **Weinberg, -e** vineyard
weinen to cry (10W)
die **Weinstube, -n** inn
weise wise
die **Weise: auf diese ~** (in) this way (11W); **in vieler ~** in many ways
weiß white (S2)
weit far (5W)
die **Weite** distance; wide-open feeling
weiter: und so ~ (usw.) and so on (etc.); **~ draußen** farther out; **Wie geht's ~?** How does it go on?
Weiteres additional words and phrases
weiter·fahren* (ist) to drive on (8E); continue the trip
weiter·geben* to pass on
weiter·gehen* (ist) to continue, go on
welch- which (7G); **Welche Farbe hat . . . ?** What's the color of . . . ? (S2)
die **Welle, -n** wave
die **Welt, -en** world (12E)
weltoffen cosmopolitan
wem? (to) whom? (3G)
wen? whom? (2G)
wenig- little (not much), few (10G)
wenigstens at least
wenn (*conj.*) if, (when)ever (4G,11G); **selbst ~** even if

wer? who? (1G); who(so)ever
werden (wird), wurde, ist geworden to become, get (3G); **Was willst du ~?** What do you want to be? (12W); **Ich will . . . ~.** I want to be a . . . (12W)
werfen, (wirft), warf, geworfen to throw
wert worth
wertvoll valuable
wessen? (*gen.*) whose? (8G)
der **Westen: im ~** in the west (1W)
westlich von west of
der **Wettbewerb, -e** contest
das **Wetter** weather (S5)
das **Wettrüsten** arms race
wichtig important (1E)
widersteh'en* (+ *dat.*) to withstand
wie? how? (S1); like, as; **~ bitte?** What did you say? Could you say that again? (S3); **so . . . ~** as . . . as (1E); **~ lange?** how long? (4W); **~ gesagt** as I (you etc.) said
wieder again (S5); **immer ~** again and again, time and again (12G); **Da sieht man's mal ~!** That just goes to show you. (15W)
der **Wiederaufbau** rebuilding
wieder·erkennen* to recognize again
wiederho'len to repeat (S2)
die **Wiederho'lung, -en** repetition, review
wieder·hören: Auf Wiederhören! Goodbye. (on the phone)
wieder·sehen*: Auf Wiedersehen! Goodbye. (S1)
die **Wiedervereinigung** reunification
der **Wiener, -** the Viennese
wieso' (denn)? how come? why? (13W)
wieviel? how much? (3W); **Der wievielte ist . . . ?** What is the date . . . ? (4W)
wie viele? how many? (3W)
wild wild
die **Wildwest'-Serie, -n** Western series
der **Wille, -ns, -n** will; **Wo ein ~ ist, ist auch ein Weg.**

Where there's a will, there's a way. (15W)

der **Wind, -e** wind

der **Winter, -** winter (S5); **im ~** in (the) winter (S5)

das **Winzerfest, -e** vintage festival

wirken to appear

wirklich really, indeed (S5)

die **Wirklichkeit** reality

die **Wirtschaft** economy

wirtschaftlich economical(ly)

wissen (weiß), wußte, gewußt to know (a fact) (6G); **Ich weiß nicht.** I don't know. (S3)

die **Wissenschaft, -en** science, academic discipline (13W)

der **Wissenschaftler, -** scientist (12W)

der **Witz, -e** joke

witzig witty, funny (14W)

wo? where? (S2,6G)

die **Woche, -n** week (S5)

das **Wochenende** weekend; **am ~** on the weekend (4W)

wochenlang for weeks

wöchentlich weekly (10E)

-wöchig weeks long

woher'? where from? (1W)

wohin'? where to? (6G)

die **Wohngemeinschaft, -en** group sharing a place

wohnen to live, reside (1E)

das **Wohnsilo, -s** high-rise apartment cluster

die **Wohnung, -en** apartment (6W)

der **Wohnwagen, -** camper

das **Wohnzimmer, -** living room (6W)

der **Wohnsitz, -e** place of residence

die **Wolke, -n** cloud

wollen (will), wollte, gewollt to want to (5G)

das **Wort, -e** (connected) word; **in anderen Worten** in other words

das **Wort, ¨er** (individual) word

das **Wörtchen, -** little word

das **Wörterbuch, ¨er** dictionary

der **Wortschatz** vocabulary

das **Wunder, -** wonder, miracle

wunderbar wonderful(ly) (S1)

sich **wundern: ~ Sie sich nicht!** Don't be surprised.

wunderschön beautiful (14W)

der **Wunsch, ¨e** wish (11W); **~traum, ¨e** ideal dream

(sich) **wünschen** to wish (9W)

die **Wunschwelt** ideal world

der **Würfel, -** small piece of, cube

die **Wurst, ¨e** sausage (2W); **Das ist doch ~!** That doesn't matter.

würzen to season

Z

die **Zahl, -en** number (S4)

zählen to count (S4)

der **Zahn, ¨e** tooth (9W); **sich die Zähne putzen** to brush one's teeth (9G)

der **Zahnarzt, ¨e** dentist (12W)

die **Zahnärztin, -nen** dentist (12W)

die **Zahnmedizin'** dentistry

zart tender

zärtlich affectionate

z.B. (zum Beispiel) i.e. (for example)

das **Zeichen, -** signal, sign

der **Zeichentrickfilm, -e** cartoon, animated film

die **Zeichnung, -en** drawing

zeigen to show (5W); **Zeig mal!** Show me (us etc.)!

die **Zeit, -en** time (S6); tense; **die gute alte ~** the good old days

die **Zeitschrift, -en** magazine (10W)

die **Zeitung, -en** newspaper (10W); **Wochen~** weekly newspaper

die **Zelle, -n** cell, booth

das **Zelt, -e** tent

zentral' central(ly)

das **Zentrum, Zentren** center; **im ~** downtown

zerstören to destroy (14E)

die **Zerstörung** destruction

ziehen, zog, gezogen to pull (11E)

ziemlich quite, fairly (6W)

die **Zigeu'nerin, -nen** gypsy

das **Zimmer, -** room (S2)

der **Zim'merkolle'ge, -n, -n** roommate (13W)

die **Zim'merkolle'gin, -nen** roommate (13W)

der **Zimmernachweis, -e** room-referral service

der **Zirkel, -** club, circle

das **Zitat', -e** quote

die **Zitro'ne, -n** lemon (2W)

der **Zoll** customs; toll

die **Zone, -n** zone, area

der **Zoo, -s** zoo

zu (+ dat.) to, in the direction of, at, for (purpose) (3G); too (S3); closed (2); (+ inf.) to (9G)

zu·bleiben* (ist) to stay closed

der **Zucker** sugar (3W)

zuerst' first (of all)

zufrie'den satisfied, content

der **Zug, ¨e** train (8W); **mit dem ~ fahren*** to go by train (8W)

zu·halten* to hold closed

zu·hören to listen (7G); **Hören Sie gut zu!** Listen well.

die **Zukunft** future (12W)

zu·machen to close (7G)

zurück'- back

zurück'·bekommen* to get back

zurück'·bleiben (ist) to stay behind

zurück'·bringen* to bring back

zurück'·fliegen* (ist) to fly back

zurück'·geben* to give back, return

zurück'·halten* to hold back

zurück'·kommen* (ist) to come back, return (7G)

zurück'·nehmen* to take back

zurück'·sehen* to look back

sich **zurück'·ziehen* (hat)** to withdraw

zusam'men together; **alle ~** all together; **~gewürfelt** thrown together

die **Zusam'menfassung, -en** summary

die **Zusam'mengehörigkeit** solidarity

zwischen (+ acc. / dat.) between (6G); **~durch** in between

die **Zwischenlandung, -en** stopover

ENGLISH-GERMAN

Except for numbers, pronouns, **da-** and **wo-**compounds, this vocabulary includes all active words used in this book. If you are looking for certain idioms, feminine equivalents, or other closely related words, look at the key word given and then check it in the German-English vocabulary. Irregular t-verbs ("irregular weak verbs") and n-verbs ("strong verbs") are indicated by an asterisk (*); check their forms and auxiliaries in the list of principal parts (pp. 448–449).

A

able: to be ~ können*

about (approximately) ungefähr

above über (+ *dat. / acc.*)

academic discipline die Wissenschaft, -en

ache: I have a (head)~. Ich habe (Kopf)schmerzen.

across (from) gegenüber (von + *dat.*)

actor der Schauspieler, -

actual(ly) eigentlich

address die Adresse, -n; **return** der Absender, -

advertising die Reklame, -n

afraid: to be ~ (of) Angst haben* (vor + *dat.*)

after (time) nach (+ *dat.*); **~** (+ *past perf.*) nachdem; **~ all** (*gesture word*) eben

afternoon der Nachmittag, nachmittag; **in the ~** nachmittags

afterward danach

again wieder, noch einmal; **Could you say that ~?** Wie bitte? **~ and ~** immer wieder

against gegen (+ *acc.*)

ago vor (+ *dat.*); **a week ~** vor einer Woche

ahead: straight ~ geradeaus

air die Luft; **by ~mail** mit Luftpost

airplane das Flugzeug, -e

airport der Flughafen, ̈

all all-, alles (*sg.*); **after ~** (*gesture word*) eben

allowed: to be ~ to dürfen*

almost fast

already schon

also auch

although (*conj.*) obwohl

always immer

America (das) Amerika

American (*adj.*) amerikanisch; **(person)** der Amerikaner, -

among unter (+ *dat. / acc.*)

and und

angry böse; **to get ~ about** sich ärgern über (+ *acc.*)

another ander-; noch ein

to **answer** antworten

answer die Antwort, -en

anyhow sowieso

anyway sowieso

apartment die Wohnung, -en

to **appear (to be)** scheinen*

to **applaud** klatschen

apple der Apfel, ̈

approximately ungefähr

April der April; **in ~** im April

area die Gegend, -en, das Gebiet, -e

arm der Arm, -e

armchair der Sessel, -

around um (+ *acc.*); **all ~** rings um (+ *acc.*)

arrival die Ankunft

to **arrive (in)** an·kommen* (in + *dat.*)

art die Kunst, ̈e

as wie; **~ . . . ~** so . . . wie

to **ask** fragen

at an (+ *dat.*); **(o'clock)** um . . . (Uhr); **(the place of)** bei (+ *dat.*)

athletic sportlich; **un~** unsportlich

attention: to pay ~ auf·passen

attractive attraktiv, hübsch

August der August; **in ~** im August

aunt die Tante, -n

Austria (das) Österreich

Austrian (person) der Österreicher, -

author der Autor, -en

available frei

B

bad(ly) schlecht; schlimm; **too ~** schade

bag die Tasche, -n

baggage das Gepäck

bakery die Bäckerei, -en

balcony der Balkon, -e *or* -s

banana die Banane, -n

bank die Bank, -en

bath das Bad, ̈er; **to take a ~** baden

to **be** sein*; **(become)** werden*; **Be . . . !** Sei (Seid, Seien Sie) . . . !

bean die Bohne, -n

beautiful (wunder)schön

because (*conj.*) weil, denn; **~ of** wegen (+ *gen.*)

to **become** werden*

bed das Bett, -en; **~room** das Schlafzimmer, -

beer das Bier

before vor (+ *acc. / dat.*); (*conj.*) bevor; **not ~** (*time*) erst; (*adv.*) vorher

to **begin** beginnen*, an·fangen*

beginning der Anfang, ̈e; **in the ~** am Anfang

behind hinter (+ *acc. / dat.*)

to **believe (in)** glauben (an + *acc.*); **(things)** Ich glaube es; **(persons)** Ich glaube ihm

belly der Bauch, ̈e

to **belong to** gehören (+ *dat.*)

below unter (+ *acc. / dat.*)

beside neben (+ *acc. / dat.*)

besides (*adv.*) außerdem

best best-, am besten

better besser

between zwischen (+ *acc.* / *dat.*)

bicycle das Fahrrad, ⸚er

to **bicycle** mit dem Fahrrad fahren*

big groß (ö)

bill die Rechnung, -en

birthday der Geburtstag, -e; **on the / for ~** zum Geburtstag

bit: a little ~ ein bißchen

black schwarz (ä)

blackboard die Tafel, -n

blouse die Bluse, -n

blue blau

boarding house die Pension, -en

body der Körper, -

book das Buch, ⸚er

border die Grenze, -n

boring langweilig

born geboren (ist); **I was ~ May 3, 1968, in Munich.** Ich bin am 3.5.68 in München geboren.

both (things, *sg.***)** beides; *(pl.)* beide

to **bother** stören

bottle die Flasche, -n; **a ~ of** eine Flasche

boy der Junge, -n, -n

bread das Brot, -e

break (intermission) die Pause, -n

to **break** kaputt·gehen*

breakfast das Frühstück; **for ~** zum Frühstück

bridge die Brücke, -n

bright (light) hell

to **bring** bringen*; **to ~ along** mit·bringen*

broad weit

broken: to get ~ kaputt·gehen*

brother der Bruder, ⸚

brown braun

to **brush (one's teeth)** sich (die Zähne) putzen

to **build** bauen

building das Gebäude, -

bus der Bus, -se

business das Geschäft, -e

businessman der Geschäftsmann, -leute

businesswoman die Geschäftsfrau, -en

but aber; doch; **not only . . . ~ also** nicht nur . . . sondern auch

butter die Butter

to **buy** kaufen

by von (+ *dat.*)

C

café das Café, -s

cafeteria (student) die Mensa

cake der Kuchen, -

to **call** rufen*; **to ~ (up)** an·rufen*, telefonieren; **to ~ (name)** nennen*; **to be called** heißen*

campground der Campingplatz, ⸚e

can können*

Canada (das) Kanada

Canadian *(adj.)* kanadisch; **(person)** der Kanadier, -

candle die Kerze, -n

capital die Hauptstadt, ⸚e

car das Auto, -s; der Wagen, -; **(railroad)** der Wagen, -

card die Karte, -n; **post~** die Postkarte, -n

cardigan die Jacke, -n

carpet der Teppich, -e

carrot die Karotte, -n

to **carry** tragen*

case: in any ~ jedenfalls

cash das Bargeld; **~ register** die Kasse, -n

to **cash (in) (a check)** ein·lösen

cassette die Kassette, -n

cathedral der Dom, -e

to **celebrate** feiern

celebration das Fest, -e

center die Mitte

century das Jahrhundert, -e

certain(ly) bestimmt

chair der Stuhl, ⸚e; **arm~** der Sessel, -

chalk die Kreide

champagne der Sekt

change das Kleingeld

to **change (trains)** um·steigen*; **(money)** wechseln

channel das Programm, -e

charming charmant

cheap billig

check der Scheck, -s; **traveler's ~** der Reisescheck, -s

cheese der Käse

chic schick

child das Kind, -er

choir der Chor, ⸚e

Christmas (das) Weihnachten; **at / for ~** zu Weihnachten

church die Kirche, -n

citizen der Bürger, -

city die Stadt, ⸚e; **~ map** der Stadtplan, ⸚e; **~ hall** das Rathaus, ⸚er

to **clap** klatschen

class (group) die Klasse, -n; **(time)** die Stunde, -n; **(instruction, school)** der Unterricht; **(instruction, university)** die Vorlesung, -en

clean sauber

to **clean** putzen

clerk: (civil servant) der Beamte (ein Beamter); **(salesman)** der Verkäufer, -

clock die Uhr, -en; **o'clock** Uhr

to **close** zu·machen

closed zu, geschlossen

closet der Schrank, ⸚e

clothing die Kleidung

coat der Mantel, ⸚

coffee der Kaffee

coke die Cola

cold kalt (ä)

cold: to catch a ~ sich erkälten

to **collect** sammeln

color die Farbe, -n; **What's the ~ of . . . ?** Welche Farbe hat . . . ?

colorful bunt

to **comb** (sich) kämmen

to **come** kommen*; **to ~ along** mit·kommen*; **to ~ back** zurück·kommen*; **to ~ in** herein·kommen*; **That comes to . . . (altogether).** Das kostet (zusammen) . . .

comfortable bequem

comical komisch

company die Firma, Firmen

composer der Komponist, -en, -en

concert das Konzert, -e

congenial sympathisch: **un~** unsympathisch

to **congratulate** gratulieren

to **continue** weiter·gehen*, weiter·machen

convenient bequem

to **cook** kochen

cookie das Plätzchen, -

cool kühl

corner die Ecke, -n

correct richtig

to **cost** kosten

to **count** zählen

counter der Schalter, -

country das Land, ⸚er; **in(to) the ~(side)** aufs Land

couple: a ~ of ein paar
course der Kurs, -e; **of ~** natürlich
cozy gemütlich
crazy verrückt
to **cry** weinen
cucumber die Gurke, -n
cup die Tasse, -n; **a ~ of . . .** ein Tasse . . .
cupboard der Schrank, ⁼e
cultural(ly) kulturell
curtain der Vorhang, ⁼e

D

daily täglich
to **dance** tanzen
danger die Gefahr, -en
dark dunkel
date das Datum, Daten; **What's the ~ today?** Der wievielte ist heute?
daughter die Tochter, ⁼
day der Tag, -e; **during the ~** am Tag; **one ~** eines Tages; **all ~ long, the whole ~** den ganzen Tag; **each ~** jeden Tag; **in those days** damals
dear lieb-
December der Dezember; **in ~** im Dezember
to **decide** sich entscheiden*
desk der Schreibtisch, -e
dessert der Nachtisch
to **destroy** zerstören
difference der Unterschied, -e
different(ly) verschieden, anders
difficult schwer
dining room das Eßzimmer, -
dinner das Mittagessen; das Abendessen
dirty schmutzig
to **disturb** stören
to **divide** teilen
to **do** tun*, machen
doctor der Arzt, ⁼e, die Ärztin, -nen
dollar der Dollar, -
door die Tür, -en
dorm das Studentenheim, -e
downstairs unten
to **dream (of)** träumen (von)
dress das Kleid, -er
dressed: to get ~ (sich) an·ziehen*; **to get un~** (sich) aus·ziehen*
dresser die Kommode, -n
to **drink** trinken*
to **drive** fahren*; **to ~ on (keep on driving)** weiter·fahren*; **to ~ up** hinauf·fahren*
drugstore die Drogerie, -n
dull langweilig
during während (+ *gen.*)
dynamic temperamentvoll

E

each jed-
ear das Ohr, -en
earlier früher
early früh
to **earn** verdienen
earth die Erde
east der Osten; **~ of** östlich von
Easter Ostern; **at / for ~** zu Ostern
easy leicht
to **eat** essen*
egg das Ei, -er
to **emphasize** betonen
end das Ende; **in the ~** am Ende
engaged verlobt
engineer der Ingenieur, -e
England (das) England
English (*adj.*) englisch; **in ~** auf englisch; **(language)** Englisch; **Do you speak ~?** Sprechen Sie Englisch?; **(person)** der Engländer, -
enough genug
to **enter** herein·kommen*
entertainment die Unterhaltung
entire(ly) ganz
entrance der Eingang, ⁼e
environment die Umwelt
equal gleich
especially besonders
etc. usw., und so weiter
even sogar
evening der Abend, -e, abend; **Good ~.** Guten Abend!; **in the ~** abends, am Abend
every jed-
everything alles
everywhere überall
exact(ly) genau
exam die Prüfung, -en; **to take an ~** eine Prüfung schreiben*
excellent ausgezeichnet
to **exchange** aus·tauschen; **(money)** um·wechseln; **What's the ~ rate of the dollar?** Wie steht der Dollar?
exciting spannend
to **excuse** sich entschuldigen; **~ me!** Entschuldigen Sie!
exit der Ausgang, ⁼e
expensive teuer
to **explain** erklären
eye das Auge, -n

F

face das Gesicht, -er
fairly ziemlich
to **fall** fallen*
fall der Herbst, -e; **in (the) ~** im Herbst
false falsch
family die Familie, -n
famous berühmt
fantastic phantastisch, toll
far weit
fast schnell
fat dick
father der Vater, ⁼
February der Februar; **in ~** im Februar
to **feel (a certain way)** sich fühlen; **How are you (feeling)?** Wie geht es Ihnen? Wie geht's?; **I'm (feeling) . . .** Es geht mir . . .; **to ~ like (doing something)** Lust haben* zu (+ *inf.*)
few wenig-; **ein paar**
to **fight** kämpfen
to **fill out** aus·füllen
film der Film, -e
finally endlich
to **finance** finanzieren
to **find** finden*
fine gut (besser, best-), schön
finger der Finger, -
finished fertig
firm die Firma, Firmen
first erst-; **~ of all** erst
fish der Fisch
flight (plane) der Flug, ⁼e
to **fly** fliegen*
floor: on the first ~ im Parterre; **on the second ~** im ersten Stock
flower die Blume, -n
to **follow** folgen (ist) (+ *dat.*)
food das Essen; **Enjoy your ~.** Guten Appetit!
foot der Fuß, ⁼e
for für (+ *acc.*); **(since)** seit (+ *dat.*)
to **forbid** verbieten*
forbidden verboten
foreign ausländisch
foreign worker der Gastarbeiter, -
forest der Wald, ⁼er
to **forget** vergessen*

fork die Gabel, -n
foyer der Flur
France (das) Frankreich
free frei
French *(adj.)* französisch; **in ~** auf französisch; **(language)** Französisch; **Do you speak ~?** Sprechen Sie Französisch?; **(person)** der Franzose, -n, die Französin, -nen
fresh frisch
Friday (der) Freitag; **on Fridays** freitags
friend der Freund, -e
friendly freundlich; **un~** unfreundlich
from von (+ *dat.*); **(a native of)** aus (+ *dat.*); **I'm ~ . . .** Ich bin aus . . . , Ich komme aus . . .; **(numbers) ~ . . . to** von . . . bis . . .; **(place) ~ . . . to** von . . . nach . . .
front: in ~ of vor (+ *acc. / dat.*)
fruit das Obst
fun der Spaß; **to be ~** Spaß machen; **to make ~ of** sich lustig machen über (+ *acc.*)
funny lustig, witzig; komisch
furniture die Möbel *(pl.)*
future die Zukunft

G

game das Spiel, -e
garage die Garage, -n
garden der Garten, ̈
gentleman (Mr.) der Herr, -n, -en
German *(adj.)* deutsch; **in ~** auf deutsch; **(language)** Deutsch; **Do you speak ~?** Sprechen Sie Deutsch?; **(person)** der Deutsche, -n (ein Deutscher)
Germany (das) Deutschland; **West ~** Westdeutschland, die Bundesrepublik (BRD); **East ~** Ostdeutschland, die Deutsche Demokratische Republik (DDR)
to **get (become)** werden*; **(fetch)** holen; **(receive)** bekommen* (hat); **to ~ off** aus·steigen*; **to ~ on** *or* **in** ein·steigen*; **to ~ up** auf·stehen*; **to ~ to know** kennen·lernen; **to ~ used to** sich gewöhnen, an -
girl das Mädchen, -
to **give** geben*; **(as a present)** schenken
glad froh

gladly gern (lieber, liebst-)
Glad to meet you. Freut mich.
glass das Glas, ̈er; **a ~ of . . .** ein Glas . . .
to **go** gehen*; **to ~ by (bus)** fahren* mit; **to ~ by plane** fliegen*; **to ~ out** aus·gehen*; **to ~ up** hinauf·fahren*
good gut (besser, best-)
goodbye Auf Wiedersehen! Tschüß!
grade die Note, -n
grandfather der Großvater, ̈
grandmother die Großmutter, ̈
grandparents die Großeltern *(pl.)*
gray grau
great (size) groß; **(terrific)** prima, toll
green grün
greeting der Gruß, ̈e
groceries die Lebensmittel *(pl.)*
to **grow** wachsen*
guest der Gast, ̈e
guitar die Gitarre, -n

H

hair das Haar, -e
half halb; **in ~ an hour** in einer halben Stunde
hallway der Flur
hand die Hand, ̈e
to **hang (up)** hängen
to **hang, be hanging** hängen*
to **happen** geschehen*
happy glücklich, froh
hard (difficult) schwer
hardly kaum
to **have** haben*; **to ~ to** müssen*
head der Kopf, ̈e
healthy gesund (ü)
to **hear** hören
heavy schwer
Hello. Guten Tag!
to **help** helfen* (+ *dat.*)
her ihr
here hier
Hi! Guten Tag! Hallo!
high hoch (hoh-) (höher, höchst)
to **hike** wandern (ist)
his sein
historical(ly) historisch
history die Geschichte
hobby das Hobby, -s
holiday der Feiertag, -e
home: at ~ zu Hause; **(toward) ~** nach Hause; **at the ~**

of bei (+ *dat.*); **(homeland)** die Heimat
to **hope** hoffen
hot heiß
hotel das Hotel, -s, der Gasthof, ̈e, die Pension, -en
hour die Stunde, -n; **for hours** stundenlang
house das Haus, ̈er
household der Haushalt
housewife die Hausfrau, -en
how wie; **~ much?** wieviel?; **~ many?** wie viele?; **~ much is . . . ?** Was kostet . . . ?; **~ much are . . . ?** Was kosten . . . ? **~ are you?** Wie geht's? Wie geht es Ihnen?; **~ come?** wieso?
however aber; doch
human being der Mensch, -en, -en
hunger der Hunger
hungry: I'm ~ Ich habe Hunger.
to **hurry** sich beeilen
to **hurt** weh tun*; **My (throat) hurts.** Mir tut (der Hals) weh.
husband der Mann, ̈er

I

ice, ice cream das Eis
idea die Idee, -n
identification der Ausweis, -e
if *(conj.)* wenn; ob
ill krank (ä)
to **imagine** sich vor·stellen
immediately sofort
important wichtig
in in (+ *dat. / dat.*)
income das Einkommen
independent selbständig
inexpensive billig
indeed wirklich, doch
industrious(ly) fleißig
inn der Gasthof, ̈e
inside in (+ *dat. / acc.*)
in spite of trotz (+ *gen.*)
instead of statt (+ *gen.*)
intelligent intelligent
interest (in) das Interesse (an + *dat.*)
interested: to be ~ in sich interessieren für
interesting interessant
intermission die Pause, -n
invention die Erfindung, -en
to **invite (to)** ein·laden* (zu)
island die Insel, -n
isn't it? nicht wahr?
Italian *(adj)* italienisch; **in ~**

auf italienisch; **(language)** Italienisch; **Do you speak ~?** Sprechen Sie Italienisch?; **(person)** der Italiener, -

Italy (das) Italien

its sein, ihr

J

jacket die Jacke, -n

jam die Marmelade, -n

January der Januar; **in ~** im Januar

job die Arbeit; **(position)** die Stelle, -n

juice der Saft, ̈-e

July der Juli; **in ~** im Juli

June der Juni; **in ~** im Juni

just gerade; **~ like** genau(so) wie; **~ when** gerade als

K

keep: to ~ in shape sich fit halten*

key der Schlüssel, -

kind nett; **what ~ of (a)?** was für (ein)?

king der König, -e

kitchen die Küche, -n

knee das Knie, -

knife das Messer, -

to **know (be acquainted with)** kennen*; **(a fact)** wissen*; **(a skill)** können*

known bekannt

L

lab das Labor, -s

lady die Dame, -n; **young ~ (Miss, Ms.)** das Fräulein, -

lake der See, -n

lamp die Lampe, -n

to **land** landen (ist)

landscape die Landschaft

language die Sprache, -n

large groß (ö)

last letzt-

late spät; **How ~ is it?** Wie spät ist es? Wieviel Uhr ist es?

later später; **See you ~.** Bis später!

to **laugh** lachen

lawyer der Rechtsanwalt, ̈-e, die Rechtsanwältin, -nen

lazy faul

to **learn** lernen

to **leave (behind)** lassen*; **(~ from)** ab·fahren* von, ab·fliegen* von; **(~ a place)** verlassen*

lecture die Vorlesung, -en; **~ hall** der Hörsaal, -säle

left links; link-

leg das Bein, -e

leisure time die Freizeit

lemonade die Limonade, -n

to **let** lassen*

letter der Brief, -e

lettuce der Salat

library die Bibliothek, -en

to **lie (to be located)** liegen*; **(to be lying flat)** liegen*; **to ~ down** sich (hin·)legen

life das Leben

light leicht; **(bright)** hell

likable sympathisch; **un~** unsympathisch

like wie; **just ~** genau(so) wie; **s.th. ~** so etwas wie

to **like** gefallen*; **I would ~ (to have)** ... Ich möchte ...; mögen*

to **listen** zu·hören (+ *dat.*); **to ~ to** sich an·hören

little klein; **(amount)** wenig, ein bißchen; **(some)** etwas

to **live** leben; **(reside)** wohnen

living room das Wohnzimmer, -

long *(adj.)* lang (ä); *(adv.)* lange; **how ~?** wie lange?; **So ~!** Tschüß!

to **look** sehen*; **to ~ (like)** aus·sehen* (wie + *nom.*); **to ~ at** sich an·sehen*; **to ~ for** suchen; **to ~ forward to** sich freuen auf (+ *acc.*)

to **lose** verlieren*

loud(ly) laut

love die Liebe; ; **to be in ~ (with)** verliebt sein (in + *acc.*)

to **love** lieben

luck das Glück; **to be lucky** Glück haben*; **to be unlucky** Pech haben*

luggage das Gepäck

lunch das Mittagessen, -; **for ~** zum Mittagessen

M

mad böse

magazine die Zeitschrift, -en

mail die Post; **~box** der Briefkasten, ̈-; **by air~** mit Luftpost

mainly vor allem

major (field of study) das Hauptfach, ̈-er

to **make** machen

man der Mann, ̈-er; **(human being)** der Mensch, -en, -en; **gentle~** der Herr, -n, -en

many viele; **how ~?** wie viele?; **~ a** manch-

map die Landkarte, -n; **city ~** der Stadtplan, ̈-e

March der März; **in ~** im März

mark (German) die Mark (DM)

market der Markt, ̈-e

marmalade die Marmelade, -n

married verheiratet

to **marry, get married** heiraten

matter: What's the ~? Was ist los?

may dürfen*

May der Mai; **in ~** im Mai

meal das Essen, -; **Enjoy your ~.** Guten Appetit!

to **mean (signify)** bedeuten; **(think)** meinen

meanwhile inzwischen

meat das Fleisch

meet (get to know) kennen·lernen; **Glad to ~ you.** Freut mich (sehr, Sie kennenzulernen).

memory die Erinnerung, -en

menu die Speisekarte, -n

middle die Mitte; **in the ~ of** mitten in / auf (+ *dat.*)

milk die Milch

minor (field of study) das Nebenfach, ̈-er

minute die Minute, -n

Miss Fräulein

Monday (der) Montag; **on Mondays** montags

money das Geld; **to earn ~** Geld verdienen; **to spend ~** Geld aus·geben*

month der Monat, -e; **per ~** im Monat, pro Monat; **for one ~** einen Monat

monthly monatlich

monument das Denkmal, ̈-er

more mehr; **once ~** noch einmal

morning der Morgen; **Good ~.** Guten Morgen!; **in the ~** morgens; **early ~** früh, morgen; **mid~** der Vormittag, vormittag

most meist-; am meisten

mostly meistens

mother die Mutter, ̈-

mountain der Berg, -e

mouth der Mund, ̈-er

movie (film) der Film, -e; **(theater)** das Kino, -s

Mr. Herr

Mrs. Frau

Ms. Frau
much viel (mehr, meist-); **how ~?** wieviel?
museum das Museum, Museen
music die Musik
musical musikalisch; **un~** unmusikalisch
must müssen*
my mein

N

name der Name, -ns, -n; **What's your ~?** Wie heißen Sie?; **My ~ is . . .** Ich heiße . . . , Mein Name ist . . .
to **name** nennen*
nation das Volk, ¨-er
near (distance) nah (näher, nächst-); **(vicinity)** bei (+ dat.), in der Nähe von (+ dat.)
neat prima; schick
neck der Hals, ¨-e
to **need** brauchen
neighbor der Nachbar, -n, -n
neither . . . nor . . . weder . . . noch . . .
never nie
nevertheless trotzdem
new neu; **s.th. ~** etwas Neues; **nothing ~** nichts Neues; **What's ~?** Was gibt's Neues?
New Year's Eve Silvester; **at / for ~** zu Silvester
news die Nachricht, -en
newspaper die Zeitung, -en
next nächst-; **~ to** neben (+ dat. / acc.)
nice schön, nett
night die Nacht, ¨-e, nacht; **at ~** nachts; **to spend the ~** übernachten
no nein
nobody niemand
noisy laut
no one niemand
noodle die Nudel, -n
noon der Mittag, -e, mittag; **~** mittags; **after~** der Nachmittag, nachmittag
north der Norden; **in the ~** im Norden; **~ of** nördlich von
nose die Nase, -n
not nicht; **~ any** kein; **~ only . . . but also** nicht nur . . . sondern auch; **~ yet** noch nicht; **~ at all** gar nicht
notebook das Heft, -e

nothing nichts; **~ special** nichts Besonderes
novel der Roman, -e
November der November; **in ~** im November
now jetzt, nun; **just ~** gerade
number die Nummer, -n; die Zahl, -en
nurse die Krankenschwester, -n

O

o'clock Uhr
October der Oktober; **in ~** im Oktober
of course natürlich; doch
to **offer** bieten*
office das Büro, -s
often oft
old alt (ä)
on auf (+ acc. / dat.); **~ the first of July** am ersten Juli
once einmal; **~ more** noch einmal; **~ in a while** manchmal; **(formerly)** früher
one (people, they) man
only nur; **(not before)** erst; **not ~ . . . but also** nicht nur . . . sondern auch
open auf, offen, geöffnet
to **open** öffnen, auf·machen
opposite das Gegenteil, -e
or oder
orange die Orange, -n; **(color)** orange
orchestra das Orchester, -
order: in ~ to um . . . zu (+ inf.)
to **order** bestellen
other ander-
our unser
out of aus (+ dat.)
over (location) über (+ acc. / dat.); **(finished)** vorbei; **~ there** da drüben
own (adj.) eigen-

P

to **pack** packen
package das Paket, -e
page die Seite, -n; **on / to ~** auf Seite
to **paint** malen
palace das Schloß, ¨-sser
pants die Hose, -n
paper das Papier, -e; **(term paper)** die Arbeit, -en
parcel das Paket, -e
parents die Eltern (pl.)

park der Park, -s
to **park** parken
part der Teil, -e; **to take ~ (in)** teil·nehmen* (an + dat.)
to **participate (in)** teil·nehmen* (an + dat.); mit·machen
party die Party, -s
to **pass (an exam)** bestehen*; **to ~ by** vorbei·gehen*, vorbei·kommen*, vorbei·fahren*
passport der Paß, ¨-sse
past: in the ~ früher
to **pay** bezahlen
pea die Erbse, -n
peace der Frieden
pen der Kuli, -s
pencil der Bleistift, -e
penny der Pfennig, -e; **two pennies** zwei Pfennig
people die Leute (pl.); **(human beings)** der Mensch, -en, -en; **(nation)** das Volk, ¨-er
pepper der Pfeffer
per pro
performance die Vorstellung, -en
perhaps vielleicht
person der Mensch, -en, -en
pharmacy die Apotheke, -n
to **phone** an·rufen*, telefonieren
piano das Klavier, -e; **to play the ~** Klavier spielen
picture das Bild, -er; **to take ~s** photographieren
piece das Stück, -e
pink rosa
place (location) der Platz, ¨-e; **at our ~** bei uns; **in your ~** an deiner Stelle
plan der Plan, ¨-e
to **plan** planen, vor·haben*
plane das Flugzeug, -e
plate der Teller, -
platform der Bahnsteig, -e
to **play** spielen
play (theater) das Stück, -e
pleasant gemütlich; **un~** ungemütlich
to **please** gefallen*
please bitte, bitte schön
pocket die Tasche, -n
policeman der Polizist, -en, -en
policewoman die Polizistin, -nen
poor arm (ä)
population die Bevölkerung
position die Stelle, -n

possible möglich; **im~** un-möglich

(post)card die Postkarte, -n

post office die Post

potato die Kartoffel, -n

pound das Pfund, -e

power die Macht, ¨e

praktisch practical(ly)

to **prefer** lieber tun*

present (gift) das Geschenk, -e

pretty hübsch

problem das Problem, -e

profession der Beruf, -e

professor der Professor, -en

program das Programm, -e; die Sendung, -en

protection der Schutz

proud stolz

pudding der Pudding, -s

to **pull** ziehen*

pullover der Pullover, -

purple lila

to **put (set down)** setzen; **(stand upright)** (hin·)stellen; **(lay down)** (hin·)legen; **(hang up)** (hin·)hängen; **to ~ on (clothing)** (sich) an·ziehen*

Q

quarter das Viertel; **a ~ to** Viertel vor; **a ~ past** Viertel nach; **in a ~ of an hour** in einer Viertelstunde

question die Frage, -n

quick(ly) schnell

quite ziemlich

R

radio das Radio, -s

railway die Bahn, -en

to **rain** regnen; **It's raining.** Es regnet.

rather lieber

to **read** lesen*

ready fertig

really wirklich

to **receive** bekommen*

to **recognize** erkennen*

to **recommend** empfehlen*

record die Platte, -n; **~ player** der Plattenspieler, -

red rot (ö)

refrigerator der Kühlschrank, ¨e

region die Gegend, -en; das Gebiet, -e

regular normal

to **remain** bleiben*

to **remember** sich erinnern (an + acc.)

to **remind (of)** erinnern (an + acc.)

reminder die Erinnerung, -en

to **renovate** renovieren

to **rent** mieten; **to ~ out** vermieten

to **repeat** wiederholen

reporter der Journalist, -en, -en

to **rescue** retten

to **reserve** reservieren

to **reside** wohnen

responsible verantwortungs-voll

restaurant das Restaurant, -s

to **restore** restaurieren

return address der Absen-der, -

to **return** zurück·kommen*

rice der Reis

rich reich

right rechts, recht-

right: (correct) richtig; **You're ~.** Du hast recht.; **isn't it (right)?** nicht wahr?; **~ away** sofort

river der Fluß, ¨sse

roll das Brötchen, -

room das Zimmer, -; **bed~** das Schlafzimmer, -; **bath~** das Badezimmer, -; **dining~** das Eßzimmer, -; **living ~** das Wohnzimmer, -; **guest ~** das Gästezimmer, -; **single ~** das Einzelzimmer, -; **double ~** das Doppelzimmer, -; **roommate** der Zimmerkollege, -n, -n, die Zimmerkollegin, -nen

to **run** laufen*; rennen*

S

sad traurig

safe sicher

salad der Salat, -e

salt das Salz

same gleich; **the ~ to you** gleichfalls

Saturday (der) Samstag; **on Saturdays** samstags

sausage die Wurst, ¨e

to **save (money)** sparen; **(rescue)** retten

to **say** sagen; **What did you ~?** Wie bitte?

scenery die Landschaft

schedule der Fahrplan, ¨e

scholarship das Stipendium, Stipendien

school die Schule, -n

science die Wissenschaft, -en

scientist der Wissenschaft-ler, -

second die Sekunde, -n

secretary die Sekretärin, -nen

secure sicher

to **see** sehen*

to **seek** suchen

to **seem** scheinen*

self-employed selbständig

to **sell** verkaufen

semester das Semester, -

seminar das Seminar, -e

to **send** schicken

sentence der Satz, ¨e

September der September; **in ~** im September

several mehrer- (pl.)

to **shave** sich rasieren

shelf das Regal, -e

to **shine** scheinen*

shirt das Hemd, -en

shoe der Schuh, -e

shop das Geschäft, -e

to **shop** ein·kaufen; **to go ~ing** einkaufen gehen*

short kurz (ü)

to **show** zeigen

shower die Dusche, -n; **to take a ~** (sich) duschen

sick krank (ä)

to **sign up for** belegen

silly dumm (ü)

simple, simply einfach

since (time) seit (+ dat.)

to **sing** singen*

single (unmarried) unverhei-ratet

sister die Schwester, -n

to **sit (be sitting)** sitzen*; **to ~ down** sich (hin·)setzen

to **ski** Ski laufen*; **to go ~ing** Ski laufen gehen*

skinny dünn

skirt der Rock, ¨e

slacks die Hose, -n

slender schlank

to **sleep** schlafen*

slim schlank

slow(ly) langsam

small klein

to **snow** schneien

soccer: to play ~ Fußball spielen

sofa das Sofa, -s

some etwas (sg.); einig- (pl.); **(many a)** manch-; **(a couple of)** ein paar

somebody jemand

something etwas

sometimes manchmal

son der Sohn, -̈e

song das Lied, -er

soon bald

sorry: I'm ~. Es tut mir leid.

so that *(conj.)* so daß

soup die Suppe, -n

south der Süden; **in the ~** im Süden; **~ of** südlich von

Spain (das) Spanien

Spanish *(adj.)* spanisch; **in ~** auf spanisch; **(language)** Spanisch; **Do you speak ~?** Sprechen Sie Spanisch?; **(person)** der Spanier, -

to **speak** sprechen*; **~ up!** Sprechen Sie laut!

special: something ~ etwas Besonderes; **nothing ~** nichts Besonderes

spectator der Zuschauer, -

spoon der Löffel, -

sport(s) der Sport

spring der Frühling, -e; **in (the) ~** im Frühling

square der Platz, -̈e

stamp die Briefmarke, -n

to **stand, be standing** stehen*

start der Anfang, -̈e

state der Staat, -en

to **stay** bleiben*

still noch

stomach der Bauch, -̈e

stop (for buses etc.) die Haltestelle, -n

stopover der Aufenthalt, -e

to **stop (in a vehicle)** halten*; **(doing, s.th.)** auf·hören (zu + *inf.*)

store das Geschäft, -e; **department ~** das Kaufhaus, -̈er

story die Geschichte, -n; **detective ~** der Krimi, -s

straight gerade; **~ ahead** geradeaus

strange komisch

strawberry die Erdbeere, -n

street die Straße, -n; **main ~** die Hauptstraße, -n

streetcar die Straßenbahn, -en

strenuous anstrengend

to **stress** betonen

to **stroll** bummeln (ist)

student der Student, -en, -en, die Studentin, -nen

study das Studium, Studien

to **study** lernen; **(a particular field, be a student at a university)** studieren (an + *dat.*)

stupid dumm (ü)

subject das Fach, -̈er

subway die U-Bahn

such so ein *(sg.)*; solch- *(pl.)*

sudden(ly) plötzlich

sugar der Zucker

suitcase der Koffer, -

summer der Sommer, -; **in (the) ~** im Sommer

sun die Sonne; **The ~ is shining.** Die Sonne scheint.

Sunday (der) Sonntag; **on Sundays** sonntags

supermarket der Supermarkt, -̈e

supper das Abendessen; **for ~** zum Abendessen

supposed: to be ~ to sollen*

sure sicher; doch; **for ~** bestimmt

surely bestimmt, sicher

surprise die Überraschung, -en

to **surprise** überraschen

surroundings die Umgebung; **(ecology)** die Umwelt

suspenseful spannend

sweater der Pullover, -

to **swim** schwimmen*; baden

Swiss (person) der Schweizer, -; *(adj.)* Schweizer

Switzerland die Schweiz

T

table der Tisch, -e

to **take** nehmen*; **to ~ along** mit·nehmen*; **to ~ off (clothing)** (sich) aus·ziehen*; **to ~ off (plane)** ab·fliegen*; **(last)** dauern; **to ~ a course** belegen; **to ~ an exam** eine Prüfung schreiben

talented talentiert; **un~** untalentiert

to **talk** reden, sprechen*; **to ~ to** reden mit, sprechen* mit; **to ~ about** reden über (+ *acc.*), sprechen* über (+ *acc.*)

to **taste** schmecken; **That tastes good.** Das schmeckt gut.

taxi das Taxi, -s

tea der Tee, -s

to **teach** lehren

teacher der Lehrer, -

to **tear down** ab·reißen*

telephone das Telefon, -e

tell sagen; erzählen (von + *dat.*)

tennis Tennis

terrible, terribly furchtbar

terrific toll

test die Prüfung, -en; **to take a ~** eine Prüfung schreiben*

than *(after comp.)* als

to **thank** danken (+ *dat.*)

Thank you. Danke!; **~ very much.** Danke schön! Vielen Dank!

that das; *(conj.)* daß; **so ~** *(conj.)* so daß

the ... the ... je (+ *comp.*) ... desto (+ *comp.*) ...

theater das Theater, -; **movie ~** das Kino, -s

their ihr

then dann; **(in those days)** damals

there da, dort; **over ~** da drüben; **~ is (are)** es gibt

therefore darum

thick dick

thin dünn

things: all sorts of ~ so einiges

to **think (of)** denken* (an + *acc.*); **(be of an opinion)** meinen; **I ~ it's ...** Ich finde es ...

thinker der Denker, -

thirst der Durst

thirsty: I'm ~. Ich habe Durst.

this dies-

thought der Gedanke, -ns, -n

throat der Hals, -̈e

through durch (+ *acc.*)

Thursday (der) Donnerstag; **on Thursdays** donnerstags

ticket die Karte, -n; **(bus)** die Fahrkarte, -n; **(return ticket)** die Rückfahrkarte, -n; **~ window** der Schalter, -

time die Zeit, -en; **What ~ is it?** Wie spät ist es? Wieviel Uhr ist es?; **at what ~?** wann?; **in the mean~** inzwischen; **one ~** einmal

tired müde

to **to** zu (+ *dat.*); an (+ *acc.*); **(a country etc.)** nach

today heute

together zusammen; **~ with** mit (+ *dat.*)

toilet die Toilette, -n

tomato die Tomate, -n

tomorrow morgen; **the day after ~** übermorgen

too (also) auch; **(too much)** zu viel

tooth der Zahn, ⸚e

tourist der Tourist, -en, -en

tower der Turm, ⸚e

town die Stadt, ⸚e

track das Gleis, -e

traffic der Verkehr

trail der Weg, -e

train der Zug, ⸚e, die Bahn, -en; **~ station** der Bahnhof, ⸚e

training die Ausbildung

to **travel** reisen (ist)

tree der Baum, ⸚e

trip die Reise, -n, die Fahrt, -en; **to take a ~** eine Reise machen

true richtig, wahr

to **try** versuchen

Tuesday (der) Dienstag; **on Tuesdays** dienstags

to **turn: to ~ off (radio etc.)** aus·machen; **to ~ on (radio etc.)** an·machen

TV (medium) das Fernsehen; **(set)** der Fernseher, -; **to watch ~** fern·sehen*

typical(ly) typisch

U

ugly häßlich

unathletic unsportlich

uncle der Onkel, -

under unter (+ acc. / dat.)

to **understand** verstehen*

understanding verständnisvoll

unfortunately leider

unfriendly unfreundlich

United States (U.S.) die Vereinigten Staaten (U.S.A) *(pl.)*

university die Universität, -en (die Uni, -s)

unlucky: to be ~ Pech haben*

unmarried unverheiratet

unmusical unmusikalisch

unique einmalig

untalented untalentiert

until bis; **not ~** erst

upset: to get ~ about sich ärgern über (+ acc.)

upstairs oben

usual(ly) gewöhnlich

to **use** gebrauchen

to **utilize** gebrauchen

V

vacation die Ferien *(pl.)*

various verschieden-

vegetable(s) das Gemüse, -

very sehr; ganz

viewer der Zuschauer, -

village das Dorf, ⸚er

to **visit** besuchen

W

to **wait (for)** warten (auf + acc.)

waiter der Ober, -; ~! Herr Ober!

waitress das Fräulein, -; ~! Fräulein!

to **walk** zu Fuß gehen*, laufen*; **to go for a ~** spazieren·gehen*

wall die Wand, ⸚e; **(thick)** die Mauer, -n

to **want to** wollen*, möchten*

war der Krieg, -e

warm warm (ä)

to **wash (o.s.)** (sich) waschen*

watch (clock) die Uhr, -en

to **watch: (TV)** fern·sehen*; **(pay attention)** auf·passen; **~ out!** Passen Sie auf!

water das Wasser

way der Weg, -e; **this ~** auf diese Weise

to **wear** tragen*

weather das Wetter

wedding die Hochzeit, -en

Wednesday (der) Mittwoch; **on Wednesdays** mittwochs

week die Woche, -n; **all ~ long** die ganze Woche; **this ~** diese Woche

weekend das Wochenende; **on the ~** am Wochenende

weekly wöchentlich

welcome: You're ~. Bitte schön! Nichts zu danken!

well *(adv.)* gut; *(gesture word)* nun

west der Westen; **in the ~** im Westen; **~ of** westlich von

what? was?; **~ did you say?** Wie bitte?; **~'s new?** Was gibt's (denn)?; **~'s on . . . ?** Was gibt's im . . . ?; **So ~!** Na und!; **~ kind of (a)?** was für (ein)?

when (at what time) wann?; **(whenever)** *(conj.)* wenn; *(single action in past)* *(conj.)* als; **just ~** *(conj.)* gerade als

where? wo?; **~ from?** woher?; **~ to?** wohin?

whether *(conj.)* ob

which? welch-?

wide weit

while *(conj.)* während

white weiß

who? wer?

whole ganz

whom? wen?, wem?

whose? wessen?

why? warum?, wieso?

wife die Frau, -en

wild wild

to **win** gewinnen*

window das Fenster, -; **ticket ~** der Schalter, -

wine der Wein, -e

winter der Winter, -; **in (the) ~** im Winter

to **wish** (sich) wünschen (+ dat.)

with mit (+ dat.); **(at the home of)** bei (+ dat.); **~ me (us . . .)** bei mir (uns . . .)

without ohne (+ acc.)

witty witzig

woman (Mrs., Ms.) die Frau, -en

wonderful(ly) wunderbar, prima

woods der Wald, ⸚er

work die Arbeit

to **work** arbeiten

worker der Arbeiter, -

world die Welt, -en

to **write** schreiben*; **to ~ to** schreiben an (+ acc.); **to ~ about** schreiben über (+ acc.); **to ~ down** auf·schreiben*

wrong falsch; **You are ~.** Du hast unrecht.

Y

year das Jahr, -e; **all ~ long** das ganze Jahr; **next ~** das nächste Jahr

yellow gelb

yes ja; doch

yesterday gestern; **the day before ~** vorgestern

yet doch; **not ~** noch nicht

young jung (ü)

your dein, euer, Ihr

youth die Jugend

youth hostel die Jugendherberge, -n

This index is limited to grammatical entries. Topical vocabulary (days of the week, food, hobbies, etc.) can be found in the table of contents. Entries appearing in the "Rückblicke" (Reviews) are indicated by parentheses.